THE LIFE AND DEATH OF

PETER SELLERS

THE LIFE AND DEATH OF
PETER SELLERS

Roger Lewis

APPLAUSE
NEW YORK • LONDON

Applause Books

THE LIFE AND DEATH OF PETER SELLERS
Roger Lewis

Library of Congress Cataloging-in-Publication Data

Library of Congress Catalog Card Number: 96-78574

ISBN: 1-55783-248-X

Permission to reprint copyrighted material from the following sources is gratefully acknowledged: BBC Written Archives Centre; the Mary Emett Collection (for the drawing reproduced on page 168); Faber and Faber Ltd. (for extracts from *The ABC of Reading* by Ezra Pound and *The Dyer's Hand and Collected Poems* by W.H. Auden); Victor Gollancz Ltd. (for extracts from *That Uncertain Feeling* by Kingsley Amis); Lord Grade of Elstree (for surviving material from the Lew & Leslie Grade talent agency); *Playboy* Magazine (for quotations from 'Playboy Interview: Julie Andrews and Blake Edwards', from *Playboy* Magazine December 1982, and also for extracts from the Peter Sellers interview by Robert Miller of October 1962); Elwood Rickless (Executor of the Peter Sellers Estate); Straight Arrow Publishers, Inc. (for 'The Strange World of Peter Sellers' by Mitchell Glazer, from *Rolling Stone*, April 17th 1980. Straight Arrow Publishers, Inc. 1980. All Rights Reserved. Reprinted by permission); Times Newspapers Ltd. (for quotations from 'Peter Sellers: A Monologue' by Dilys Powell, first published in the *Sunday Times Magazine* on January 14th and 21st 1962 Times Newspapers Ltd. 1962); *TV Times* and IPC Magazines Ltd. (for the reproduction of 'Star Turn-Table' by Peter Sellers, from the *TV Times* of July 20th 1956).

The author and publishers have made all reasonable efforts to contact copyright holders for permission, and any omissions or errors in the form of credit given will be corrected in future printings.

First Applause Printing 1997

APPLAUSE BOOKS

211 West 71st Street
New York, NY 1002
Phone (212) 496-7511   Fax: (212) 721-2856
Trade Orders: 1-800-798-7787

10   9   8   7   6   5   4   3   2   1

CONTENTS

To
Barry Humphries

*The author wishes to express special thanks
to the editor of the Applause American edition, Bruce G. Bradley.*

... being is the reverse of subtle. It is simple, though the principle of analogy shows it to be paradoxically complicated as well. A locomotive is both simple in essence and complicated in detail; one would scarcely call a locomotive subtle. And one should beware of trying to describe a locomotive to the uninitiated by rationalistically describing its workings, beginning with the vaporization of heated water, lest its puffing power come to seem very subtle indeed. One does better to call it an iron horse.

—Hugh Kenner, *Paradox in Chesterton*

Introduction

"Tis in ourselves, that we are thus, or thus.' *Othello*.

My first movie love was Norman Wisdom. His films were telecast in the early evening, and the horizontally streaky flicker from the screen—we had a peeling, teak-veneer, Coronation-era television set with a wonky contrast control which plunged everything into a zig-zag of green shadow—is of a piece in my mind with the rain-lashed industrial South Wales beyond the window panes and my mother snarling in the kitchen, out of sight, creating a meal from pastry speckled with soot and heated-up potato water. Norman's hysteria and gormlessness, in the face of impossible odds, were my own.

I enjoyed his films as a child because, in always being told to behave, pull himself together, and quiet down, Norman *was* a child—a child stuck in a man's body, obstreperous and defiantly retarded.* He seemed to be an innocent always placed in dangerous or unpleasant circumstances—that is, he was pitched into adult scrapes and he dealt with them by donning multiple disguises, by pratfalls, and by pumping up the volume on being a fool or a funny foreigner. In *The Square Peg* he for some reason finds himself the identical twin of a Nazi General. In *On the Beat* he doubles the parts of a constable and a gang-leader. Norman was all over the place. A milkroundsman, a window cleaner, a newspaper reporter, a jockey. Somewhere along the line I recall his ghastly croon dubbing an opera singer. But despite the costumes and showing off, his weeping and wailing, he was always Norman, a happy-go-lucky brat; if the innocence was mock innocence, or if there was any malice in his violent revenge on grown-up nonchalance (exemplified by Jerry Desmonde in impeccable evening dress with a boutonnière), it didn't register with me or spoil my fun. Norman had energy—unlike that other man-child, Jimmy Clitheroe, or Wee George Wood, whose mummified features scared me then and terrify me now, as I remember them. Jimmy and Georgie, genuine dwarves, were freaks. Mother Nature had played a trick on them, and their having to wear blazers and carry satchels well into old age—when there was still a strong chance that they'd be spanked and forced to sing a comic ballad with an unbroken voice—was a sign of this. They aged without growing. Norman's nature, by contrast, seemed natural and, to me, the very spirit of *my* age. He was an escapee from all that school uniforms, organised team games and parental persecutions try to curb. He was displaced from my heart one Saturday afternoon by Peter Sellers.

I was making the most of having a cold and had been left at home alone, everybody else in Wales being intent on running about in the damp playing rugby.

---

* I refer, of course, to his rôles. Off-screen Mr Wisdom may very well be a Nobel Laureate in science, medicine, literature, and the promotion of peace.

Wrapped in my mother's Glenurquart tartan travelling rug, eating Custard Creams, and drinking Ribena through a straw, I settled down, in a bored sort of way, to watch a double bill on the only channel not killing time with sports commentaries. The films were *Two Way Stretch* and *Wrong Arm of the Law*. As cops-and-robbers capers, with police cars having bells instead of sirens, they looked set fair to amuse me in the Norman Wisdom manner—the villains were folk heroes, with whom we at once sided in their battles against manic authority, personified by Lionel Jeffries, whose Nosey Parker and Sidney Crout are, I now see, comic variations on his hissing and spitting Marquess of Queensberry, the maddened upholder of all things Victorian in *The Trials of Oscar Wilde*. And there, amidst the slapstick, the explosions, the melodrama of characters getting themselves smuggled in and out of prison; there, at the centre of each film, was a self-absorbed, diffident, yet powerful presence, around whom the action and the rest of the cast whirred and whirled—Sellers.

In *Two Way Stretch*, when they are in the cramped jail cell at the start, David Lodge and Bernard Cribbins do all the talking and complicated bits of business with a breakfast fry-up. A big fat warder further fills the room and carries off a cat. Sellers' Dodger Lane, however, is the focus of the scene. Sitting in bed, doing nothing except peer over the top of *The Investors' Chronicle*, he could be the greatest straight man who ever lived. His reactions to the pseudo-domesticity about him, his exasperation and world-weariness, are full of irony and resignation. Such texture, such reserve. I'd personally never noticed before that stopping still could be funny—where were Norman's cock-a-doodle-doo line readings and the dashing about I thought synonymous with humour? Even Sellers' weight was funny. Thickset and ponderous (from all that prison stodge), he was miles away from Norman's springy physicality. Here was a comedy of reactions—of the way everybody was knocking themselves out to amuse and attract the star. Sellers was solemn and hilarious, simultaneously. (In fact, Sellers often played these extremes off against each other. His art had little to do with the suddenness of jokes, except in the live-cartoon conventions of the *Pink Panther* series; his genius was for creating an atmosphere, vibrating and fluttering between gaiety and sorrow. Even Inspector Clouseau, as Sellers said, 'is a sad and serious man.')

In *Wrong Arm of the Law*, Sellers played not, like Norman, a criminal mastermind and a copper, but an underworld chieftain, Pearly Gates, and his double, or public persona, Monsieur Jules, the couturier. Pearly is all Cockney wit and bottle; M. Jules, foppish, charming, and camp. I'll never forget the moment when I first saw Sellers as the one go through a bead curtain and emerge as the other. It was a total transformation—voice, demeanour, temper. It was more than just dextrous; it involved no change of make-up or clothes. It went beyond acting. It was a reconstitution. This book originates in my desire to know more about the magician who could accomplish feats like that. Sellers, in that split second on the screen when I was on my own in Wales, and when my great curiosity was born, enacted one of my deepest desires—the ability to disappear and return as someone else.

◆ ◆ ◆

Soon after I'd watched that double bill and had my rapturous encounter, there was a general uprush of interest in Sellers. I'd not known about the Goons before, yet here they were reuniting for *The Last Goon Show of All*, broadcast on Boxing Day, December 26, 1972. (What on earth was Harry Secombe doing in the trio? He was known to me then only as a pop-eyed concert tenor whose brother, the Rev. Fred Secombe, had married my parents in Machen church.) Though a performance for radio, it was shown on television, and the variety of accents and impersonations coming out of Sellers—a tall, thin, grey man now, having once been squatter and brown—was definitely eerie. He stood there at the lectern and voices and ideas bubbled up from inside him, whisked and eddied over the airwaves, to richly amuse the Royal Family. Princess Anne clopped the coconuts for a horse noise, Prince Philip grinned, Prince Charles sent apologies for his absence ('my knees dropped off with envy at the thought of my father and sister attending the show'), and Princess Margaret left the Camden Theatre on Sellers' arm. 'Excuse me, sir, how do you think the evening went?' asked a young reporter, who'd nipped to the stage door to meet the couple. Sellers pushed past regally without a word. As he was climbing into the limousine, the hack tried again: 'Excuse me, sir, just one last thing—how are you spelling your name?'—'It's Sellers Schmellers, now fuck off,' boomed the star.

His was evidently a free-floating, fizzy intelligence. In action, it was like witnessing a man being possessed by demons. Bloodnok's gastro-enteric groans, Grytpype-Thynne's caddish murmur, Henry Crun's senile mutterings, Bluebottle's epiglottal squawk, etc. poured out with a restless, propulsive force. He was a Niagara. I remember going on from listening to Goon records to being interested in the masks and special effects of *Alice's Adventures in Wonderland*—and there was Sellers, nutty and natty, as the March Hare. (Spike Milligan was the Gryphon and my old enemy, Sir Robert Helpmann, the Child Catcher in *Chitty Chitty Bang Bang*, was the Mad Hatter.) I recall not having the courage to join an expedition of cronies trying to bluff their way into the AA-rated ($\approx$ R-rating) *There's a Girl in My Soup*, in which Sellers, if the stills outside the nickelodeon were any clue, was impersonating the Earl of Lichfield. I started to familiarise myself with the Boultings' output and colourful trash like *Casino Royale*—then, as now, often on the telly as midweek matinées.

From Fred Kite, in his one ill-fitting demobilization suit, to Evelyn Tremble, in a vast wardrobe tailored by Dougie Hayward, what became clear to me very quickly was that in Sellers I was watching an artist who could take a rôle to a lot of highs. I could see him, as Clare Quilty in *Lolita*, compulsively enlarging his character, improvising through his scenes with James Mason, spreading across the movie like a damp stain coming through a ceiling; he sent himself further and further into his character's narcissism. I could see Sellers taking over—becoming an egocentric before my eyes—and acting was clearly an ideal home for his excesses, as it was for mine. Sellers, having aroused hidden feelings in me, became the hero of my adolescence, as Norman Wisdom had represented and idealised my childhood. I used to want to *be* Peter Sellers. I went about in tinted spectacles (rare then), a French fireman's helmet, and a fake leather lady's raincoat, which was the nearest I could find to an ankle-length Nazi great-coat—the intention being to ape the Sellers who'd appeared on Michael Parkinson's talk show, when he'd astounded me with his floor-show of stories, anecdotes, and exhibitionism. Sellers, of course, was reproducing Kenneth Mars from *The Producers*. (Mars reproduced Sellers' Dr Strangelove in *Young Frankenstein*.) I copied Sellers imitating everybody else. I used to goose-step up and down my bedroom, ranting that 'Churchill voss a rotten painter, *rotten*. Hitler, now zere voss a painter for you. Could paint an entire apartment, two coats, one afternoon!' My friend Harries used to record the stuff on a portable Sony tape recorder.

It didn't end there. After seeing *What's New, Pussycat?* I decided I wanted to be a psychiatrist. Not because I was in the least bit interested in rehabilitating people who'd gone bonkers, but because (a) it was a license to snoop and pry around people's fantasy levels and (b) I fancied myself in a Richard III wig and a red velvet smoking jacket living in a Parisian folly. (Psychiatry was out when I realised you'd need medical qualifications and I, surprising nobody, was in the Arts stream from the word go.) What I think I was doing, beyond all the teenage tomfoolery, was conducting experiments with personality. Adolescence, so threatening and fateful, is a time for assembling and assuming what will become the adult identity—a repertoire of mannerisms and inklings, a gathering of experiences, desires, anxieties, and feelings, which are one way or another brought to order: our sense of self, which we will labour at keeping constant. We grow an armoury of attitudes, develop a style; what John le Carré's spies would refer to as our handwriting. What drew me to Sellers once, and once again as I approached thirty, was that he plainly had no such organising principle. His virtuosity implied that new and different selves, odd voices and elaborations, distracted him from moment to moment. And if he renewed himself for each film, why not for each day? Or for each person he was with who'd give him what he wanted?

◆ ◆ ◆

It was this, the motor of his genius as an actor, his insistence on being discontinuous, which, I was to learn, constituted his madness. In his films, he was concealing his neurosis, making a virtue out of the insomnia of his impersonations, parrotings, oddness. But in reality, to adopt a conclusion Sir Kingsley Amis came to about women, Sellers was off his head in more than a manner of speaking. When, at precisely double the age I was when running around the Rhymney Valley in a blue plasticine nose, I began my research into his life, it was primarily to explain why, having once loved the funny voices and carryings-on, I was now seeing in Sellers' transfigurations something sad and lost. The solution involves the fact that, as a schoolboy, I was responding to the delinquency in Sellers' masquerades and acts of flight. Now, studying a man who was fully alive only when acting, who could unknot himself only through mimicry, I am alert to the psychotic manoeuvrings, the emotional incontinencies, in a grown-up's always wanting to be a juvenile—in wanting 'always to be a little boy and to have fun.' Peter Sellers was the man in Peter Pan.

In interview after interview, Sellers explained his strangeness by claiming: 'I have no personality of my own, you see. I could never be a star because of this. I'm a character actor. I couldn't play Peter Sellers the way Cary Grant plays Cary Grant, say—because I have no concrete image of myself. I look in the mirror and what I see is someone who has never grown up—a crashing sentimentalist who alternates between great heights and black depths. You know, it's a funny thing, but when I'm doing a rôle I feel it's the *rôle* doing the rôle, if you know what I mean. When someone tells me "You were great as so-and-so", I feel they should be telling this to so-and-so, and when I finish a picture I feel a horrible sudden loss of identity.'

The suggestion that when he was not employed as an actor he was an empty space, disembodied like a ghost (he told Kermit the Frog on 'The Muppet Show' that 'There used to be a me, but I had it surgically removed'), was a convenient and complicated fiction. Convenient because he could detach himself from the consequences of his bad behaviour. (He was a moral amnesiac.) Cruelty to wives and family, tantrums in front of directors and colleagues, could be wiped from his mind, consigned to a trackless wilderness which is actually where the secrets of this deeply enigmatic man are to be found. When the camera wasn't turning he was often recessive and withdrawn, and it satisfied a need to pretend he didn't exist. As a first and obvious point, when he stated again and again that he had no personality or self, by fending us off with a blankness, the actor as zero, he meant to be inscrutable, magically invisible—like Shakespeare, say, a king of shadows. And second, whilst ostensibly searching for a personality of his own, he could give himself thousands of faces—and, though this was dismaying (he was befuddled by all the available possibilities), it provided him a glorious freedom. 'I try to hop into a new personality as often as I can,' he admitted, not denying that his transformations went beyond the confines of the studio. (Theo Cowan said to me, 'He was happier making himself up and slipping into characters. If he was sitting here now he'd be doing somebody.')

Indeed, Sellers felt confined by anything which looked like stability or repetition. Thus the written-off marriages, the frequent changes of address, the fecklessness of his relationships. Domestic duties, for example, were incompatible with his wandering nature. As fame and money denatured him and he became emotionally dead, he could go so far as abandoning his children, cutting them from his will. He wanted to be unconstrained, with no living connections. Milligan thinks it indicative that he never saw Sellers enjoy a hearth or home. He never put a kettle on and made a cup of tea; he'd never 'sit round a fireplace—all those primitive tribal things that give each of us a sense of ordinariness and order. They seemed to be denied to him. He *had* no fireplace.'

He hated rehearsal; he hated the live theatre ('because it means doing the same thing over and over again'). He thrived on whims and spontaneity. To this extent, at least, for all the mimicry, his characters are not artificial creations. Sellers was drawing on himself in some way. As his daughter, Sarah, concedes, 'I don't think Dad modelled himself on other people; it all came from inside. He was very psychic—in tune with what people were feeling. He didn't study people—it was more a feeling he got about people—intuitive. That's what he was like in his films and his life. That's the way he was. More than impersonation—because his own personality would change a lot. One day you saw him he'd be one way, another time he'd have picked up other moods. Very sensitive to things going on around people—quite often negative states...'

How did his twisted greatness come to the surface of his art? How did the surface, the faces and funny noises, connect with the subterranean talent—which eventually became a lunatic's mind, a harbour for insult and rejection, certain only that compliments and admiration were hypocrisy and conspiracy? What were the pressures shaping him? If the source of his originality and power as an actor lay in the problems he had with personal identity, was the price too high? Sellers, who in his demented wizard's way could work up a tiff into a declaration of war and a slight into a bloody feud, was capable of giving shadows substance, of subdividing into multiple selves, and a peculiar facet of researching this book was that in interviewing over three hundred of his relicts and dependents, colleagues and collaborators, enemies and advocates, I met about three hundred different versions and facets of Peter Sellers. ('See them all', orders the editor after the newsreel sequence in *Citizen Kane*. 'Get in touch with everybody that ever worked for him—whoever loved him—whoever...hated his guts.')

Like Charlie Kane, Sellers won't lie still in anybody's mind. On the whole he is remembered, a decade plus after his death, with a mixture of incredulity and horror, whilst at the same time there is a consensus that, regarding his films, he gave the public a huge amount of pleasure. In several pictures, of course, he played half the cast and showed how he could *be* three hundred people, if he wanted: the President, the Group Captain, the Nazi boffin in *Doctor Strangelove*; the citizenry of the Duchy of Grand Fenwick, in *The Mouse that Roared*; the brothel-creepers in *Soft Beds, Hard Battles*; the yellow peril and his nemesis, Nayland Smith, in *The Fiendish Plot of Dr Fu Manchu*, which was released after Sellers' death and seemed to have been made by his ghostly remains. (Sellers also does assorted voices on the soundtrack which adds to the disembodied, spectral effect.) 'We are kindred spirits,' says Nayland affectionately of Fu, 'He is evil to my good, ying to my yang...' Sellers could dart across contraries on the screen—conciliatory Muffley, maniacal Strangelove, for instance, holding a conversation—and in real life he could veer, in the space of a minute, between heartless egotism and a suffocating generosity, the charm of the devil and invisibility. People remember him variously as stout or slim, frail or fleshy with hair sprouting out of his shirt, werewolf fashion. The man of the people, the chum known to wartime colleagues and the stuntman contingent, somehow coexisted with the toffee-nosed invitee to Kensington Palace, the treacherous business partner, the defaulter, saboteur, shit, and genius. The various women in his life were unable to agree on whether or not, as a Jew, he was circumcised. Sellers, membrum virile and all, evidently shrank and grew, as if he existed in a hall of distorting mirrors.

No single person ever knew him. (He recoiled from genuine intimacy: husband, father, patron, client, etc. were so many rôles and moods.) Nor was he open or certain about what might have been his own normal voice. For all their make-up and many-sidedness, there's never any mistaking Alec Guinness' purr or Orson Welles' rumble, which was like thunder across the bay. Sellers was not regionally bound by accent, and in Britain, especially, the grain of your voice is a signal of class and provenance, region and attitudes. The whole of your history and background is in the noise you make. (Where would Michael Caine be without Old Kent Road, Sean Connery without Scotland?) Sellers' facility with dialect meant he could escape these constraints (another aspect of his curious freedom), with the delimiting factor that he was thereby rootless, placeless, with no point of origin. Sir Guy Grand, in *The Magic Christian*, has unassailably Mayfair tones, but when Sellers spoke to journalists on the set, such was the effect of Ringo, who played Sir Guy's adopted son, Youngman, that Sellers became a native of Liverpool. On other occasions he'd lapse into Cockney or a Yorkshire lilt. Then again he'd try to be flat, featureless, as if in a drug-like stupor. (Oscar Moore, in *A Matter of Life and Sex*, says that Sellers' character in *Being There*, Chance the gardener, a Mr Nobody, speaks 'like a man with a needle hanging out of his arm.') Challenged, towards the end of his life, about how he *really* spoke, so ventilated was his conversation with take-offs and goonery, he said: 'I think it's something like what you're hearing now ... Well, maybe I'm trying to sound a bit more posh. This voice is not made up, because I cannot relax and talk openly in someone else's voice. I've heard myself on recordings in background conversation, and I think I talk like this ... I hear myself at other times, though, and I'm talking like this ...'— and he modulated into South London. 'It depends on whom I'm with. Sometimes I start out in my own voice and no matter who I'm with, I take on their thing.'

It is an unnerving facet of Sellers that, as his own face faded, he created his own world by feeding off his companions. When he started copying people, he didn't recreate them—he took them over. He was like a real-life Leonard Zelig, the human chameleon in Woody Allen's film, who takes on the colour of his surroundings. (The young Allen worked with Sellers in *What's New, Pussycat?* and *Casino Royale*, and a Columbia executive, Leo Jaffe, once mistook Sellers for Allen at the Dorchester Hotel, precipitating a major Sellers tantrum.) But where Zelig's imitation game is benign and ingratiating, Sellers' was sinister and satirical. He'd throw you back at yourself, making self-expression an extreme of self-mockery. As Milligan said, 'Peter feasts off people—he finds himself so totally boring that he's got to escape from himself and find refuge and security in another personality—that's the only form of communication left open to him.'

♦ ♦ ♦

If ever there was an actor hollowed out and dissolved by the mysterious processes of his art, it was Sellers. There have been plenty of casualties, of course: the humiliations and bruisings endured by Marilyn Monroe; the pill popping of Montgomery Clift; Rachel Roberts' and Richard Burton's Celtic boozing; Charles Laughton's wheedling masochism ... And the melancholy clown is nothing new, from Pagliacci's smeary Pierrot's face to Tony Hancock's exasperation and suicide. What picks Sellers out is the comprehensiveness of his conflicts. He lived in reverse. Insubstantial off camera, coming alive through the lens; goading people into leaving him, or disagreeing with him, so that he could then feel forsaken; profoundly homesick, he yet never had a home; a solitary, he relied on being a public figure—nothing enraged him more than passport officials asking to see his documents. He once stormed past the customs and excise man at Heathrow and slapped a sticker on the fellow's forehead. He wanted the flattery of being waved through—to waft in and out of countries unfettered by visas and the ordinary rules of wayfaring. Also, a passport is a proof of identity. For all his obsessions with the puzzle of who he was ('Having no genuine personality of my own gives me such a complex, you know...'), this actually was the last thing he wanted. Sellers wished to cross frontiers at will, not by queuing up with the mob, even if he was waiting to board the Concorde and the next seat was occupied by Dustin Hoffman. During the last few years of his life he travelled by private jet or chartered luxury yacht. He was constantly in and out of hospitals and hotels. New York, London, Copenhagen, Rome, Geneva, Majorca... 'This constant journeying of his', said Milligan. 'He's like a panther in a cage, pacing backwards and forwards for eternity... He daren't stand still because he'd sink and drown in his own tears, so he has to keep going though he knows he has nowhere to go.'

Translated into practical terms, Sellers' restlessness, his running, jumping, and standing still, meant a compulsion to keep on making films and recordings, one after the other, regardless of whether they were any good or not. In 1960 alone, to give but one example, he released *The Running, Jumping, Standing Still Film*; *Two Way Stretch*; *Battle of the Sexes*; *Never Let Go*; and *The Millionairess*. He travelled out of himself to become an jailbird, an Edinburgh weaver's clerk, a hoodlum flashing a gold tooth, a medicine man from the Sub-Continent... From 1948, when he was first employed by the BBC, to his death in 1980, when *The Romance of the Pink Panther* was in pre-production, Sellers was never out of work. (Indeed, from his early twenties onwards, Sellers, his complaining and feeling very sorry for himself notwithstanding, was able to live exactly as he pleased, if financial wherewithal is any indicator.)

He claimed to be searching for perfection. 'I just cannot take mediocrity. I just cannot take it on any level.' It is thus paradoxical that in a lifetime of films he made so few masterpieces (if the significance of Sellers was limited to his non-flops, you could count up the number of important pictures on the fingers of a two-toed sloth). And if he was such a perfectionist—'I'm just a guy who tries to do things right. I'm a guy in search of the perfect "something". I've got a real psycho thing about it.'—why did he more often than not behave so destructively and sulkily? He early on learned the despot's trick of surrounding himself with weaklings in a bid to enhance the look of his own power, and the collapse of *Casino Royale*, *Ghost in the Noonday Sun*, and *The Prisoner of Zenda* were all due to Sellers' caprice. He tried to have John Cleese sacked from *The Magic Christian* because Cleese's performance was funnier than his own. (He had to be satisfied with the reshooting of Cleese's scenes so that Cleese wasn't so favoured by the camera angles.) He had Piers Haggard sacked from *The Fiendish Plot of Dr Fu Manchu* because, shooting in Paris, he was jealous of the director for being able to speak French with the French crew.

He decided to direct the picture from the top himself. Sellers' method of inspiring confidence and telling the company what to do was remarkably unfussy: he'd act out a scene, doing all the parts and voices, and he'd then expect everybody to copy him exactly. (He didn't want actors, he wanted automata.) Clive Dunn went over to Paris to play a Beefeater: 'Peter would perform it; then I would do my version of Peter Sellers playing my part.' One of the few people to receive a note, as the theatrical profession calls a bit of formal instruction, was David Lodge. He played a police sergeant in charge of an identification parade. 'What I want you to do after you've delivered your lines,' said Sellers, 'is to be like Gene Hackman.' 'And what does Gene Hackman do?' inquired Lodge. 'Fuck all,' said Sellers.

Most of Dunn's scene and all of Lodge's were cut. Sellers then insisted that his own name be removed from the mess he'd proceeded to make from the extraneous footage,* thus crediting Haggard with a movie Haggard had long left and which to this day he cannot bear going to see.

Sellers courted people and exploited them. Hypersensitive to his own needs and treatment, claiming that a stray criticism or nuance could undo him ('A person can destroy me with two words. It can just be the way they say them, the inflection'), he was brutal to others, totally inconsiderate. Charles Feldman, producer of *Casino Royale*, had his health so undermined by Sellers' antics that he died soon after the film's premiere. Richard Quine's suicide went back to *The Prisoner of Zenda*. 'Was I really awful today?' Sellers asked Lionel Jeffries, 'Well...' he started to reply, expecting Sellers to apologise for his misbehaviour. Instead, Sellers gave a satisfied laugh and hung up. Blake Edwards faced a nervous breakdown after dealing with Sellers on *Revenge of the Pink Panther*. 'I had so much pent-up rage and frustration within me,' he claimed. Peter Medak couldn't work for five years after the calamities of *Ghost in the Noonday Sun*. 'Nobody could control him,' he disclosed to me about his star. 'He'd create situations where he'd stop the production, which fell behind schedule on Day One. Little by little, systematically, he'd turn up later and later on the set. He should be in make up at seven, he'd be there at nine. Stuff like that. Every day there would be something else. He wouldn't film, supposedly sick— and then he'd be seen water-skiing in the harbour. Or he wanted to come back from the Cyprus location for a ball given by Princess Margaret. He simply got on a plane and left for London. He sent back a certificate from a crooked doctor friend of his. So the film lost another two or three days... After it was all finished, I got all the blame—for going over budget, for turning in a picture which wasn't box office. Yet the producers left me high and dry to cope with Peter Sellers. Nobody from Columbia would put their foot down with him. I was the only person trying to say no, no, no. Everybody else was willing to give him his head. By the end of the movie I wasn't talking to him. I couldn't talk to him. I hated him so much.'

---

* Sellers sent this telex to Elwood Rickless on May 12, 1980: 'I hereby authorise you as my lawyer to inform Orion [the production company] immediately that my name must be deleted from every screen credit other than that of actor, i.e. no writing and/or directing credits whatsoever. This applies to both screen and all paid advertising. This, my decision, is irrevocable and leaves no room for any further discussion. Please deal with this as quickly as possible.'

So it went on. Sellers would discuss yoga and mysticism and relaxation methods, and then he'd slap his women around, smash up the furniture, pulverise jewellery and Cartier watches and toss the debris into the toilet bowl. People and possessions went, pell-mell, onto the Peter Sellers Scrap Heap. Which is why, I think, he was happy only when keeping company with his gadgets. His Leicaflex and Summicron-R f/2 50mm, Elmarit-R f/2.8 35mm and 90mm cameras, for example, which shielded him from the world: he could take pictures instead of participating. His succession of expensive motor cars took him from whim to whim. He collected toy railways, hi-fi hardware, anything clockwork or robotic. Covetous and acquisitive, he could always then give his playthings away or abandon them the moment they started to bore him. Bit players often tended to inherit his bits. Vacuum cleaners, obsolete tape recorders, lenses, a mechanical elephant, archery targets, a trampoline. During the filming of *Doctor Strangelove* he decided to have a Rolls Royce engine transplanted into a Mini Minor. George C. Scott looked at the freakish conveyance outside Shepperton Studios and asked, 'Who on earth will buy the thing when you get tired of it?' 'I'm already looking for a rich midget,' Sellers replied.

What was no joke at all was the way Sellers regarded his family as discardable, his wives as trinkets through whom he could arouse the envy of others. Part of his intolerance over his children was linked to the fact that he had made them, and this undermined his comforting fantasy that he was a nothing, a nobody, a trick of the light. Children, much more than wives (who could without too much difficulty be traded in when they'd lost their freshness)* represented a responsibility he wanted to shirk—and yet, though neglectful, he'd instantly become the rod-brandishing patriarch if he suspected them of independence or if they broke a rule he'd just silently made up. Children belonged with a world of sun and solid things, as Chesterton would put it; Sellers was more for shades and chimeras. When he cut the children from his will, he was literally and conclusively dispossessing them—like the disposal of an unwanted fleet of vehicles; or perhaps it was more that wives and children were like films of his that could be disowned and he himself removed from the credits.

◆ ◆ ◆

Sellers was heartless, hence the fittingness of all those heart attacks. He virtually died in 1964 and spent his remaining sixteen years in the shadow of a cardiac arrest. Perhaps the main aspect of his topsy-turviness was the interchangeability of life and death. He went in for spiritualism and table-rapping in a big way. (He was the biggest sucker for soothsayers since the Roman emperors.) If you died, your relationship with Sellers wasn't necessarily impeded. Larry Stephens, a co-writer on 'The Goon Show', continued to watch over his career. When his beloved

---

* 'I married Sellers at twenty-one,' writes Britt Ekland in her book *Sensual Beauty and How to Achieve It* (London, 1984), '[and] I will never forget the horror of finding myself for the first time in close proximity to a man on a twenty-four hour basis. How on earth could I deal with going to the bathroom? It wasn't enough to close the door: there was the odd odour to contend with, not to mention ...' (pp. 18–19).

mother died, he could at last have her to himself. He conducted transworld telephone calls with her by filtering the conversation through his medium, Maurice Woodruff. According to another of his psychic surgeons, Doris Collins, there was a fair old gathering of ghosts at his Memorial Service; and Lynne Frederick, his last widow, got Sellers' sanction, through Doris, to marry David Frost. A séance was held at Michael Bentine's house. 'It was a very moving experience, but I didn't cry,' Lynne said. 'In fact, Peter was a very happy man and he certainly hasn't lost his sense of humour.'

Sellers' morbidity helped him to explain his style of acting. If the characters he played were to have emerged from the dumb-show of his subconscious, how was the material placed there in the first instance? He decided he was a reincarnationist: 'When I am searching for a character', he said in 1974, 'I leave myself open, as does a medium. And I think that sometimes you can be inhabited by the spirit of someone who lived at sometime, or who was a bit like the person you are doing. And maybe they come in and use you as a chance to relive again.'

For The *Optimists of Nine Elms*, he reckoned he was invaded by Dan Leno— perhaps unaware that Leno, 1860–1904, whose real name was George Galvin, and who started out as 'Little George, the Infant Wonder, Contortionist, and Posturer,' ended his days with General Paralysis of the Insane in a Balham bedlam.

That death was playing an active part in his life was further confirmed by a conversation he had on the set of *Being There* with Shirley MacLaine, herself a former Priestess of Isis, dairymaid at the court of Catherine the Great, or some such. He was feeling uneasy because the limo mock-up they were sitting in was situated on the same sound stage in the Goldwyn Studios as the one where *Kiss Me, Stupid* was attempted before being scrapped (and started again with Ray Walston) owing to his heart attack; Sellers began gasping and clutching at his chest. 'This is the sound stage where I died,' he explained, before going on to tell MacLaine of his coma and the sense he had had of being pulled back from the next world by the doctors at the Cedars of Lebanon Hospital. When Dr Kennamer massaged his heart to get it beating again, 'I felt myself floating back into my body... I know I have lived many times before, and that experience confirmed it to me, because in *this* lifetime I felt what it was for my soul to actually be *out* of my body. But ever since I came back, I don't know why, I don't know what it is I'm supposed to do, or what I came back for.'

This is a variation on his multiple-entry visa and passport conundrums. MacLaine encouraged him to have confidence in his past-life incarnations. 'That's probably why you are so good at acting. You just have better past-life recall on a creative level than most people... You feel you are drawing on those experiences and feelings that you actually remember living in other lifetimes...'

'I don't go into this with many people, you know,' said Sellers, having warmed to his audience, 'Or they'll think I'm bonkers.'

That he thought he was a man who could cheat death and recur, because he was without end, throughout human history, is another example of his solipsism (shall we call it?), to be sure. Sellers was angry at being mortal. Though he might have considered himself invulnerable on one plane, he worried constantly about the future because he didn't want to see his death there. The prospect of oblivion always before him, he spent much of his time looking back. He'd revisit the boarding houses of his childhood; he'd reminisce. One of his last utterances (to Auberon Waugh, who tells me 'I had a premonition that he would die within the week, although he was up and about and apparently quite healthy') was 'I am proud to have been a Goon. I would like to be remembered for that'—despite the fact that, when 'The Goon Show' was in full swing, during the fifties, he was always threatening to walk out and demanding more money. (It was against his nature to be satisfied with being one of three, with Milligan and Secombe.) He hated growing old and time passing, so he coloured his hair and had his eyelids lifted and his neck tucked. Paradoxically, it was always little old men that he played when he was young (Percy Quill in *The Smallest Show on Earth*, Mr Martin in *Battle of the Sexes*, Morganhall in *The Dock Brief*, his many generals and geezers), but he never did live to be elderly himself, dead at fifty-four, having long looked wheezy and frail, like his image of the 160-year-old Fu Manchu, his final rôle.

Sellers' problems of self-representation and the mystery of his moods, explained by the spirits of the dead taking possession of him, is so much gobbledygook—except that deathliness is apparent in his work and knowing this adds to our understanding of it: the explosions and dismemberments in 'The Goon Show'; the revenants in *The Smallest Show on Earth* watching silent movies; the murder sprees of *The Ladykillers* and *The Naked Truth* and the annihilation of the world in *Doctor Strangelove*; the vampiral theme of *Hoffman*, in which Sellers plays a woebegone widower who imprisons a beautiful virgin; the death of the music hall in *The Optimists of Nine Elms*; the living death of the entombment in *The Blockhouse*. We might even add to the list Inspector Clouseau's misreported deaths and resurrections, premature funerals and orations. The death-register peaks with *Trail of the Pink Panther*, which Sellers seemed to have managed to make *after* his own extinction—and was explained by Blake Edwards' ingenious use of doubles and outtakes from previous pictures. But still ... And, of course, the sepulchral *Being There*, which takes place in a winter garden and is full of the feeling that death was closing in on its star, who putters off across the surface of a misty lake at the end. 'He lived for his work', Anne Levy, his first wife, said to me. 'He couldn't relax; he couldn't go on holiday, couldn't really just be himself. He was only happy when he was playing a part. And I don't think he ever got anything out of life eventually. I find it difficult to watch *Being There*, because it is too near the truth ...'

◆ ◆ ◆

Like Chance the gardener, Sellers was an erasure. On leaving La Haute Grange, his chalet in Gstaad, for the last time, he organised a bonfire of photographs and memorabilia—an immolation of his past. And he had no future. He felt he kept seeing omens (birds behaving oddly, etc.), and when he flew to London, he insisted on paying a visit to Golders Green Crematorium, wanting to see the ovens—where five days later he himself would be torched, enkindled to the tune of Glenn Miller's 'In the Mood'. It adds up to a macabre story. Sellers' life, a fever chart, is a combination of cautionary tale and case history. To put it bluntly, he was more seriously fucked up than a chameleon crossing a kilt. As the flappers sing in *Zelig*:

If you hold your breath till you turn blue
You'll be changing colors like they do,
And you're doin' the Chameleon!
Vo—do—do—de—o …

A friend recently reckoned that I must have had a scream, a ball, a lark, re-searching Sellers, the artful dodger. After all, there are the vocal marvels of the Goons, the Panavision pratfalls of Clouseau; there is the loony sieg-heiling of Dr Strangelove's arm and the innocent ingenuity of Chance, silencing muggers with his television's remote control … There is much there, and in fifty-odd other pic-tures, to generate laughter. But laughter, I soon discovered, was less than the half of it with Sellers—even when you left his emotional self-questioning and private life scandals to one side. Hunched before my video, watching those old Boulting efforts yet again, or locked in a bunker at the British Film Institute, discovering lost classics, like *Mister Topaze*, I was struck by the pervasive melancholia in Sellers' work. Has nobody ever *looked* at it before? Fred Kite, far from being the Napo-leonic shop steward critics always describe, is a tremendously touching portrait of a clumsy idealist; Mr Martin, far from being the meek Scottish accountant whom we are told Sellers plays in *Battle of the Sexes*, has eyes which glint with awakening anarchy and love; John Lewis, the librarian of *Only Two Can Play*, and General Fitzjohn, from *Waltz of the Toreadors*, aren't, as the reference books have it, lechers at all. Lewis is a thirty-ish family man with a college degree whose quite normal demands are dampened by a low income; he lives in a squalid flat where his wife is exhausted by two energetic toddlers and the milk goes bad because they don't have access to a fridge. Sellers expresses the man's ironic self-awareness of his plight—as he does Dodger Lane's in the prison cell. And as for General Fitzjohn, he is a sort of sombre Bloodnok, angry at growing old and impotent, and fantasising about the escapades of his youth, which probably never happened. The films were made together early in 1962, and in each Sellers is exploring the problems of age-ing and loneliness—problems confronting him personally as his first marriage was drawing to a messy close. 'I never want to marry again,' he said, 'I feel it would be better to remain a bachelor and die a bachelor. I wasted twelve years of life with the wrong woman.' The General's resentment of his wife (Margaret Leighton) might be seen as Sellers' for Anne; Lewis' desire for Elizabeth Gruffydd-Williams (Mai Zetterling) is Sellers' for the white goddess who became Britt.

Even Clouseau, 'a fool who was shrewd around fools' and who never smiles, was hilarious in a low-key way. Blake Edwards may immerse the character in ex-plosions, firework factories, collapsing walls, and the rest of it, but Sellers decides to be imperturbable—Clouseau walks away as dazed and withdrawn as Keaton be-neath a falling house. The actor took this almost supernatural immunity to an ex-treme in *Being There*, and to a further extreme as the immobilised, god-like Fu in *The Fiendish Plot*. The opposite of the tranquillised part is the manic Fritz Fassbender in *What's New, Pussycat?*, which really is a portrayal of lechery (Sellers was satirising the voyeuristic whimperings of sex-obsessed psychoanalysts); and Fritz grew out of Dr Strangelove himself, looking forward to the post-apocalypse breeding boom—looking forward to his rôle in personally re-populating the world.

If his famous portrayals have been misrepresented, Sellers' best performances have often been plain ignored—badly distributed, or unreleased, or accepted as fiscal losses by the Inland Revenue (which means they can never be shown for gain), or else the companies which made the films are long defunct and the prints lost. I'm thinking particularly of the depressive barrister in *The Dock Brief*, a work I had to hire on 16mm and project in my kitchen; the essay in corruption, *Mister Topaze*, which took me two years to locate—all prints, save one, were melted down and the celluloid sent to Nigeria to be re-cycled into combs. ('You mean,' said Milligan, aghast, 'that there are women in Africa combing their hair with Peter Sellers?') Why isn't the busker in *The Optimists of Nine Elms*, a part written for Buster Keaton, better known? Or the saturnine jailer in *Hoffman*, the suicide in *The Blockhouse*, the psychopath in *Never Let Go* (where we understand why Bernard Miles wanted Sellers to play Richard III)? On anybody's reckoning, this is all the work of a great actor.

The sadness of Sellers is manifold. First, there is the unexpected grace and gravitas of the performances themselves (the rat-a-tat-tat Chief Petty Officer in *Up the Creek*; the laconic lawyer in *I Love You, Alice B. Toklas*) which he was never encouraged to build upon; second, there is the regret that so much of his work was stupidly received when it came out, by producers, reviewers, and audiences who seemed to want only goonery and superficial slapstick. It was tantamount to a cover-up. What chance had his career when *Never Let Go* was advertised thus:

You roared at—'The Ladykillers'
You laughed at—'The Mouse that Roared'
You howled at—'The Naked Truth'
Now thrill and chill with Peter Sellers in his first completely straight rôle—as a cold, heartless gang leader—*showing at this theatre soon…*

The publicists went on to suggest that cinema managers invite the local police, probation officers, JPs, and crime prevention officers to a charity premiere. Marginally worse than this klunky wholesomeness was the bogus titillation heralding *Mister Topaze*: LEARN THE FACTS OF LIFE IN TEN EASY LESSONS, prompted no doubt by somebody noticing that Marcel Pagnol's hero was a schoolmaster.

Sellers was marketed as a laughter machine and he gradually allowed himself less depth. The biggest joke in *Being There* is that the protagonist, his responsiveness clouded and denied, is an ambling allegory of what had happened to the actor playing him. 'He *was* Chauncey Gardiner,' Shirley MacLaine said to me. In *The Bobo* his disconsolate singing matador is simply dopey, his Evelyn Tremble in *Casino Royale* is off-hand, dissociated, and the Clouseau of the late period *Pink Panthers* is flattened into a cartoon—he's far less animated than Richard Williams' credit sequence animation.

Sellers was gradually ruined by success; he was disabled by the very talents and susceptibilities which had made his name. Which is to say his gnawing professional insecurities grew into, and grew out of, deep personal insecurity—the way he found his sense of self dissolving and disintegrating, his mind a phantasmagoria of changing impressions, imaginings and affinities. He was constant only in his pathetic rage at being Peter Sellers. Everything he started to do was born out of this torment. People who met him, in the seventies, found him either maudlin or hysterical. People who knew him found him either generous or vindictive. ('One day he gives us diamonds, next day stones,' as one of Timon of Athens' sycophants complained.) He was difficult to live with because he found it difficult to live with himself. He was terrified of falling short of other people's estimation; he flew immediately into a temper if he encountered what he took to be incompetence in anybody else. He was afraid that what was funny today wouldn't work on the set tomorrow. His personal and professional insecurity was at such a pitch that success was as much a terror for him as failure.

The more he was paid (he was given Rolls Royces as inducements to read a script), the more he loathed himself, and the cars, women, alpine chalets, Mediterranean yachts, etc. only served to remind him that he wasn't happy. 'I'd like to be happy very much,' he said, so often it was his mantram, 'I'd very much like to be happy.' The patina of a high-living star covered up his real inner-life of suspicion and disease and he managed to make elaborate spending an expression of the despair: he'd organise parties he'd refuse to attend, refurbish houses he wouldn't live in, return from holidays because he'd taken against the people he'd chosen to invite. Timon again:

> He's but a mad lord, and nought but humours sways him.
> He gave me a jewel th' other day, and now he has beat it out o' my hat.

Sellers hid behind his money—what he called his FUCK YOU money, the large amounts of money which bought him the power to hire and fire and to walk out if he felt like it. To those members of his private circus (his train in the Shakespearean sense of the word) his partiality became oppressive—phoning them all through the night, demanding their presence (and then absenting himself). But he had no real chums. 'I don't have any friends. I suspect everybody. I have the feeling that because of my success and fame they want to use me...'

An edict unto himself, he played up on the set, abused the powers with which he was contractually invested; he was a chaos of uncertainty and bad judgement. He took rôles he should not have done (in endless cops and robbers junkets); he rejected rôles he should have embraced, rôles with which his inward, gloomy, and secretive nature would have found sympathy. Great men great losses should endure, but even so it is hard to forgive Sellers for depriving himself of *When I Grow Rich*: he was to have been an impoverished professor of philology, visiting Istanbul to study medieval Islamic documents, who earns a little extra cash by reading American newspapers out loud for an old lady, a former burlesque queen who'd been a concubine in the Sultan's harem. She now lives in one of the decrepit royal villas on the banks of the Bosporus and despatches drugs around the world in boxes of Turkish Delight. Sellers' co-star, in this exotic variation on *Sunset Boulevard*, would have been Marlene Dietrich.

A similar-sounding plot unfolds in Michael Frayn's *The Russian Interpreter*. Proctor Gould is an exchange student at the University of Moscow. He imports secondhand text books from England—and some of the volumes are receptacles for, yes, contraband and foreign currency. His smuggling is being spied on by the authorities, and one of the ardent Communists, Raisa, becomes the hero's girl... The film rights to the literary property were acquired by Michael Powell, and in February 1967 he and Frayn went to visit Sellers, by appointment, at Elstead.* Though he had declared an interest in the project ('I like it very much... I want to do it... It should be done') Sellers, showing full command of his petulance and pretensions, saw Powell off in fine style. He'd recognized at once that, like him, here was a man very horribly full of himself.

Powell had arrived at Sellers' Surrey mansion in an open-top Rolls Bentley, poop-pooping loudly; he wore motoring goggles and scarves; and he had had the cheek to drive straight over the flagstones and into the master's personal garage. 'Is this Sellers'?' he'd then demanded of a blonde ten-year-old child, who turned out to be Britt Ekland.

There's only space for one Toad at Toad Hall. Sellers, loathing Powell as soon as he saw the vintage car enthusiast get-up, decided to be the very opposite of his ebullient guest. He shrivelled and became grey, cold, affectless—playing the wraith. His taciturnity was compensated for by the gang of wild-eyed agents and lawyers he'd invited to be present—fellows eager for their percentage of the seven hundred and fifty thousand dollars, which was Sellers' going rate at that time. (He liked seeing them try to contain their avidity.) Members of the household, dressed in their livery, came in and out with tea and, after a very long while, a cut-glass decanter of whisky. 'Glenfiddich,' said Powell. 'Michael is a connoisseur of the best,' said David Begelman (a talent agent, later a convicted embezzler, later still the president of MGM). 'Of course,' quipped Powell, 'that's why I'm here.' Sellers inclined forwards and bowed gently, working it all over in his mind.

The more excited everyone grew, heaping praise on Frayn's book, the less likely it looked that the material subject of contracts would be broached. Finally, Powell tried to come out with it. 'Peter... are you in?' 'Oh, I see... yes,' murmured Sellers, as if he didn't quite know for certain what a contract was. 'You want a piece of paper?' 'I want a piece of paper, yes,' said Powell brightly, as it slowly dawned on him just what degree of deliberate objectionableness he might be up against.

On March 4 they all met again in a suite at the Dorchester, where Sellers had installed his own piped music system, which he refused to switch off. Ministering to the master was an augmented turn-out of lawyers and agents. Britt, bolstered by members of her family babbling in Swedish, reclined on a couch. Monja Danischewsky, who had written the screenplay for *Battle of the Sexes*, and now Sellers' choice for the Frayn screenplay, was another added voice. Was a food-taster there,

---

* Powell's account of the episode is in the second (posthumous) volume of his memoirs, *Million-Dollar Movie* (London, 1992), pp. 525–532; Frayn has had his say in 'Remembering Michael Powell,' *Sight and Sound*, Vol. 2, no. 6 (October 1992), p. 24.

too, to check Sellers' grub for poison? Nubians waving ostrich plume fans? Dwarves in motley? People practising Elizabethan dance steps to a *viol da gamba*?

Powell announced that *The Russian Interpreter* should be approached as 'out of Chekhov by Billy Wilder.' After giving ear to a bit of this, Sellers said: 'How about John Schlesinger to direct? Clive Donner?' People fell silent. Powell was startled. Wasn't the famous director of *The Red Shoes* and *A Matter of Life and Death* there before his eyes? 'Rather than bringing in a new voice at this stage,' said Powell, trying to pretend Sellers was making light, 'I propose to direct the film myself.'

'No, no, Michael, I wouldn't agree to that … I wouldn't approve that. It's not your subject.'

Powell went home and recorded the word 'Peterloo' in his diary—he had been massacred, in full public view. At what point did Sellers start to scheme and decide to take his malice to such lengths? When he was indoors and heard the poop-poop? When Powell barked 'Is this Sellers'?' at Britt? (Sellers wouldn't have been wrong in detecting a sneer at stockbroker mock-Tudor ostentation in Powell's tone.) When people began to chatter as if his involvement was a foregone conclusion? When Powell's own expectations and assumptions about being in charge had seemed such an easy target? He may have scuppered the project there and then, on the spur of the moment—he couldn't resist the mischief of it. Surely Sellers' motive for revenge didn't go back to 1957, when he'd auditioned for the rôle of a Greek partisan in Powell's *Ill Met by Moonlight* (in which Dirk Bogarde helps to kidnap a German General on the island of Crete*). Powell had rejected the young actor and radio Goon, calling him 'an india rubber owl.'

So Sellers had a bit of luck ten years later, looking out of his window on that February afternoon to see a rival Mr Toad down in the forecourt. To his mind, his encounter with Powell wasn't about film-making; it was a struggle for domination. Perhaps, at some level, he did believe in the possibility of the film. He'd held prolonged discussions with his managers; he'd talked about the script. But, under the surface, in the violent surges of his semi-conscious, he was setting a trap.

The story doesn't quite end there. I wrote to Michael Frayn, asking him what else he could recall of the episode, and he said: 'Powell's option on *The Russian Interpreter* eventually lapsed, and it was then picked up by Sellers himself. My only contact with him, however, was a letter from Los Angeles in which he said he had "two of the finest minds in Hollywood working on the project." That was the last I heard.'

Which is further evidence that it was Powell-as-Powell whom Sellers was wanting to punish, and that he did recognize Proctor Gould's surreptitiousness as being up his street.

♦ ♦ ♦

---

* The film was the subject of surrealist revision on 'The Goon Show'. 'Ill Met by Goonlight' was the title of the programme broadcast on March 14, 1957.

Sellers was to have been Rex Harrison's Caesar in *Cleopatra*, Ron Moody's Fagin in the musical *Oliver!* He was to have done a film about the interior visions of a cross-eyed man, another about an interplanetary alien for Satyajit Ray. He was to have been Captain Hook capturing Hayley Mills' Wendy and duelling with Audrey Hepburn's Peter Pan; he was offered the tramp in Pinter's *The Caretaker*, Vladimir or Estragon in *Waiting for Godot*, Henry VIII in *Anne of a Thousand Days*. Billy Wilder wanted him as Watson alongside Peter O'Toole's Baker Street 'tec in *The Private Life of Sherlock Holmes* (parts which went to Colin Blakely and Robert Stephens). He was to have been Leopold Bloom, with O'Toole as Daedalus and Diane Cilento as Molly, in a Wolf Mankowitz adaptation of *Ulysses*. He was to have starred in a biopic of Chaplin ... and not only did Lord Miles want Sellers to play in Shakespeare at The Mermaid, but 'Olivier wanted me to do *Lear* down at this Chichester Festival place of his ... Larry said, "Do it, you'd be good." He said the best Lears were nearly always those new to Shakespearean tragedy.'

The catalogue goes on and on and adds up to a resplendent career which Sellers, because of his cocktail of cussedness and his pathological lack of confidence, never had. That he always had a hankering to play Hitler, and did so fleetingly in *Casino Royale* and *Soft Beds, Hard Battles*, speaks volumes: 'I had no personality of my own, at least I felt I hadn't, and I remember at one stage wanting to be Hitler—so that in a great patriotic gesture I could commit suicide and save the world...'*

♦ ♦ ♦

In writing about Sellers—and in this book I want to see him as he really was, 'for I profess to write not his panegyrick, which must be all praise, but his Life' (James Boswell on Samuel Johnson)—I have had to become accustomed to inversions and irreconcilabilities. The great actor who was seldom in anything good; the materialist who liked to dematerialise; the star who created the problems he suffered from and whose bizarre behaviour grew in proportion to his fame, which unleashed his dormant lawlessness... Though the subject of profiles galore when he was alive, and of a highly professional and polished authorised (by whom?†) bi-

---

* The origin of the idea that Hitler was a baggy-pants comic goes back to Chaplin, who recalls his first view of the Führer in a series of picture postcards: 'The face was obscenely comic—a bad imitation of me, with its absurd moustache... and disgusting, thin, little mouth. I could not take Hitler seriously. Each postcard showed a different posture of him: one with his hands claw-like haranguing the crowds, another with one arm up and another down, like a cricketer about to bowl, and another with hands clenched in front of him as though lifting an imaginary dumb-bell. The salute with the hand thrown back over the shoulder, the palm upwards, made me want to put a tray of dirty dishes on it. "This is a nut," I thought...'
  My Autobiography, by Charles Chaplin, (London, 1964), p. 316.

† I ask the question because Sellers' family did not co-operate with him—they collaborated on their own book, *P.S. I Love You*; and in an article in the *Standard*, on August 14, 1981, Walker made the comment 'Lynne Frederick does not mince words. I learned this when I approached her a year ago, on starting to write the authorised life of Peter Sellers...' The construction of that sentence does not seem to suggest to me that the widow instigated the project—so who was authorising whom?

ography (by Alexander Walker) the moment he was dead, Sellers' private life and public career have completely eluded his commentators. And, a dozen years and more since his death, this fantastically interesting and complex figure, who continues to be known and loved by millions all over the world, still gets to us in a special way. I feel that, like T. E. Lawrence and Andy Warhol, other of our century's Peter Pans, Sellers is one of those who stands in a symbolic relation to their age. As Milligan said of his fitful colleague: 'Peter's nightmares are our nightmares, too; his ghosts, our ghosts. He's Mr I Don't Know of the twentieth-century, he *is* Mr Twentieth-Century.'

If, on the one hand, I wish to explore the agony and the ecstacy of Sellers' creativity, I am also aware of the more pragmatic need to remind people that there was rather more to him than Inspector Clouseau. My purpose, when accounting for Sellers' career and explaining the considerable mythology which has accrued around his name, has been to find out what struck him day by day. I attempt to interweave the artist and the man. This has involved tracking down dozens of those lost or forgotten films I talked about earlier, hunting for recordings, screenplays, unreleased material, and even unreleased whole features. I have examined written archives at the BBC and in the basements of Sellers' various agents and lawyers' offices. Directors, producers, and authors have given me files of correspondence, notes, draft scripts, and unpublished photographs. (I particularly treasure Satyajit Ray's reports—the brownish ink on the thick mauve paper resembles dried blood.) I have collected copies of Sellers' eccentric telegrams and telexes and bootleg cassette tapes of his private conversation—all the memorabilia, the spots and dots, that remain of a life. And after all the inquiries, the legwork, the letters, telephone calls, tapes, the exhumations I have made, I find it impossible not to see something tragic in Sellers, sick at heart and alone, in those sunless hotel rooms right at the end.

Part One

♦♦♦

The Man Who Never Was

It doesn't, in our contemporary world, so much matter where you begin the examination of a subject, so long as you keep on till you get round again to your starting point. As it were, you start on a sphere, or a cube: you must keep on till you have seen it from all sides.

Ezra Pound, *The ABC of Reading.*

Chapter One

♦♦♦

Variety Lights

Peter Sellers' origins were in open-air concert parties, tatterdemalion music halls, and worse. In February 1911, his maternal grandmother, Welcome Mendoza, a relic of the Sephardic Jewish Community which had been given permission by Oliver Cromwell to settle in London and to establish a burial ground, used the money left to her by her husband, Solomon Marks, about whom nothing is known, to form a touring variety company. Having seen Seymour Hicks' *Under the Clock* at the Court Theatre, back in 1893, she'd become particularly interested in revue, which differed from traditional vaudeville in that emphasis was given to parades, costume display, and dancing, rather than to individual novelty acts. Albert de Courville had introduced the form to England, having been impressed by Florenz Ziegfeld's *Follies* in New York. Revues, when they weren't being flesh-shows, belonged more with circus and spectacle than the theatre; they harked back to a world of misfits and wandering Pierrots. Also, the tableaux and disguises, the blackouts and special effects, prophesy the cinema—the very development which would put an end to the revue's cheap magic.

Welcome, who adopted the stage name of Miss Belle Ray (Sellers was to have WELCOME WITHIN engraved on a brass plate outside his offices in Panton Street in punning homage), along with Andre Charlot and Austen Hurgon, devised an entertainment for the provinces, using a seaside theme as an excuse to get the audience to take leave of its senses. The chorines would fondle their ankles and comb their long green hair in the glow of the footlights; they would then pretend to appear startled and dive into a large tank, which had been constructed to look like a rock pool. Once submerged, the mermaids would peel and fellate bananas, and frolic with any other bits of fruit or greengroceries lying about. 'Very daring...' as Sellers once said. 'Of course the tank used to overflow; every time the girls dived in there was a great splash, and the musicians were always getting soaked.* And naturally the management was always getting complaints from Watch Committees [local censorship organizations] and so on about the girls appearing in nothing but bathing dresses.'

Miss Ray moved from Hackney, her ancestral beat, to Highbury Grove with her daughter Agnes, who, as Peg, was to become Sellers' mother. For professional

---

* He improved on this remembrance when he was on the 'Parkinson Show' (BBC TV, November 9, 1974): The 'enormous water tank which filled the stage ... eventually drowned the band because it broke,' claimed Sellers, miming the trombonists struggling for air, using their instruments as snorkels. 'At Huddersfield I think it was. Several were drowned. Seriously drowned.'

purposes, however, Miss Ray was to be contacted c/o the 'Letter Box' of *The Era*, a trade paper. Sometimes she billed herself as Madame Belle Ray, the suggestion of being a continental artiste adding a touch of the exotic, but soon she was known as Ma, and had many an aquatic extravaganza on the road. By the twenties *Lido Follies* was in Dover, *Splashes* in Bradford, *Fun Showers* in Southport, *Mermaids* in Bath, and *Ripples* in Newport.

In my attempts to recover these performances, leafing through disintegrating call sheets day after day, and sending myself home whimpering with migraine, I was beaten hollow with a sense of sadness—all this long-lost fun and tat, the come-and-gone laughter and applause; the gags, the little shows meant to delight, the suitcases of tricks and pantaloons being toted down gaslit lanes to railway stations on windy nights. The artistes and the audiences are now no longer there, yet Sellers' childhood, and the grief he carried within him, are to be found in this vanished world of terminus hotels, professional apartments (as digs were called) and morbidity.

◆ ◆ ◆

Peg met her future husband, Will Sellars [*sic*] in 1921. She was appearing in *More Splashes* at the Kings Theatre, Portsmouth. She played a charlady and an unfaithful housewife who flirts with the milkman. She sang 'Roses of Picardy' and introduced the band's scene-change music, 'There's a Long, Long Trail Awinding'. Between performances she went with her mother to the Corner House Café where, because she was twenty-four* and getting on, she was encouraged to flirt with the resident pianist, who said he'd been the organist at Bradford Cathedral. Will amused everybody by tinkling 'I'm Forever Blowing Bubbles' in the style of a hymn; he then did hymns in the style of a cakewalk. He joined the Ray Company at the end of the week and he played in a Cossack sketch with a violinist, a Negro drummer, and a refugee from Moscow who owned an authentic balalaika. Sellers, incidentally, reproduced a remnant of the act in *The Optimists of Nine Elms*: lots of hey-hey, hey-hey shouts and gurgles, which begin slow and get faster and faster (the song begins as a dirge and ends as preposterous).

That he and Peg were only eventually married in 1923, at the Bloomsbury Registrar's Office, i.e. over two years later, suggests neither a need to hasten nor love at first sight. What might be their wedding photograph, with the men in best collars and ties, shows Ma Ray, huge and draped in fox stoles, dominating her group of good companions. With her languid, droopy eyelids, hatpins, clutching a crocodile handbag, she's the Grand Duchess Gloriana from *The Mouse that Roared* combined with Crystal Jollibottom from 'Ray's A Laugh'—a stately slagheap of a woman. Peg is on her left, neat, dimpled, and prim—a governess, except for the slight actressy curve of her wide-brimmed hat. She is as alert as a bird, sharp featured and ready to flutter and peck—one which would perch on the hippopotamus flanks of Ma, nipping at ticks. Behind her, hands defiantly in pockets,

* Yet if she was seventy-two when she died in 1967, as Walker states categorically, then she'd have been twenty-six in 1921—i.e., born in 1895, not 1897.

is Bill (as the Rays called him). His eyes are dark and the mouth sullen and pouting, the lower lip in an accentuated droop because of the cigarette lodged there. This is no put-upon chap—unless the marriage itself was something he'd rather not be going through, in which case he is acting. His stance, the sharpness of the waistcoat and the cut of the jacket, is that of a blade. He outstares the camera, whereas the others are on edge, guarded, or (in Peg's case) demurely flirtatious or coy. The brim of his Homburg is angrily horizontal. The photograph could have been posed for by the cast of a Peter Sellers film.

The newlyweds had no honeymoon. Though ostensibly residing at Aylmer Court, Aylmer Road, on the borders of Highgate and East Finchley, they went straight back to the theatre, to perform in *The Vanity Box*, which was across town in Willesden. By now, Miss Belle Ray had dispensed with being Madame Belle Ray and had settled for the maturity of plain Mrs. Ray. She'd relinquished control of her company to her sons, and Harry Ray applied to the London County Council for accreditation as Ray Bros. Productions Ltd., under the Theatrical Employers' Registration Act, in December 1925. More than this, the tours were to be brought under the aegis of The London Syndicate Companies, managed by Walter Payne at Cranbourn Mansions, Cranbourn Street. This was also the head office of Moss Empires Ltd., which owned the chain of theatres where the revues were actually housed, week by week, across the country. All might have been prosperous and efficient had not a personal disaster struck. A baby born to Peg and Bill had died while they were on tour with *The Vanity Box* in Dublin.

The baby's name was Peter.

◆ ◆ ◆

John Updike, in his purple-passage-y memoir, *Self-Consciousness*, says that it was seeing Sellers in *Being There* which made him want to look over his own life and search for lost time; the film (like an autobiography) is an analysis of origins and ancestry. Who is Chance? Where has he come from? The reason Chance will make a good President of the United States is that he has no family background; there is no hidden past to be revealed which might ruin him. (His is like a virgin birth—and he walks on water in the last scene.) Sellers himself could see that ancestors—'relations which grow on family trees,' as Old Sam puts it in *The Optimists of Nine Elms*—need to come and go if you are going to get born. His own illustrious forbear was Daniel Mendoza, the eighteenth-century prize fighter—Welcome/Belle/Ma's grandfather.

An engraving by J. Grozer from a painting by C. R. Ryley, produced to commemorate Mendoza's match against Humphreys at Doncaster on September 29, 1790, shows a rather pretty young man, stripped to the waist, his fists up in pugilistic pose. The picture was to have been the logo for the company Sellers was forming with Wolf Mankowitz; if you are sharp-eyed and look at what is hanging on the walls of Nayland Smith's cottage in *The Fiendish Plot of Dr Fu Manchu*, there is the framed print once again.

Mendoza was much more than a boxer. He was a ruin. His life, accounted for in periodicals like *Egan's Boxiana*, *The Fancy*, and *Bell's Life in London*, consisted of little but pummellings and exhausting pitched battles, sessions in debtors' prisons and grab-anything jobs to make ends meet. Mendoza, it was said, 'never was truly himself unless he carried on more than one activity.'

What he really was, his chronic unemployability aside, was a fledgeling actor. If the newspapers of the day described him as an exotic—'the youthful Jew', 'the star of the East,' and so on—he himself, in his many letters to the press, said he had appeared 'before the public in the character of a fighter on the stage.' His matches, against Richard Humphreys (1789), John Jackson (1795) or Harry Lee (1806), which went to fifty-three rounds, were in the nature of brutal theatrical performances, with the combatants, gloves off, disfiguring each other's faces. Having been victorious against Humphreys in a rematch, Mendoza toured the music halls, a showman, giving exhibition bouts—and it was Mendoza's idea to put the bouts on a roped and raised dais, and that nobody be allowed on the stage during a fight except the principals and their seconds.

◆ ◆ ◆

In *Memoirs of the Life of Daniel Mendoza*,* the boxer presents himself as a Regency buck, an innocent hero always being dragged against his will into scrapes and duels of honour. He could be an invention of Henry Fielding. Fisticuffs were never his fault. It is comical, his high-minded detection of insolence. When some butcher's boys shouted and frightened his horse, 'I immediately dismounted and having singled out the instigator of the disturbance and insisting on his fighting me on the spot, I convinced him in half an hour that he had much better have let me alone.'

Mendoza thinks of himself as reserved ('I forbore to take many advantages which were in my power'), but the reader quickly has him marked as a particularly nasty delinquent who ages into somebody violent and mad. After his career had peaked—when he'd met George III at Windsor ('No Jew had ever spoken with the King before')—he declined and fell, entering the Debtors' Prison in Carlisle, an archetypal rake's progression. Freed on that occasion by the Masons, he was hounded by creditors wherever his posters went up. He toured England and Wales, gradually slipping down the bill. From having been a character who had held his own exhibitions, a name that relegated news of the French Revolution to the inside pages of journals and magazines, he became part of a troupe, going on to display his scars between the jugglers and the comic songs.

Mendoza finally met his match as a stooge sparring partner for Lord Camelford, who was even more of a psychopath than he was himself. 'I found his Lordship a better proficient than myself; he struck with great force as well as skill, and I received a violent blow over the ear, which caused great pain at the time.'

---

* *Memoirs of the Life of Daniel Mendoza*, edited by Paul Magriel (London, 1951).

His Lordship then took a rapier to Mendoza, which luckily broke, and when he went to look for a dagger, Mendoza saw his chance to run out of the house and 'as may readily be imagined, never felt the least inclination to re-enter it.'

◆ ◆ ◆

Mendoza died in Horseshoe Alley, Petticoat Lane, on September 3, 1836, leaving no money and eleven children, of which only ten are in the synagogue register at the Bevis Marks Hall (the Spanish and Portuguese Jews' Congregation, founded in 1657). These are Sarah (1788), Abraham (1790), Sophia (1792), Isabella (1796), Daniel (1797), Jesse (1801), Louisa (1803), Aron (1807), Isaac (1808), and Matilda (1810). The last but one of these grew up to be Welcome's father and, after marrying a lady surnamed Lesser, helped to transfuse whatever we are to make of Daniel Mendoza into Sellers' bloodstream, where the circus and street-fighting lived and waited.

On one level, Mendoza's life was farce—the way, even when he goes with his wife to Vauxhall Gardens, he is 'assailed by sticks in all directions' and makes 'desperate resistance.' This is Clouseau and Cato two hundred years ago, flying through the air aiming kicks and punches. Or the scene with Lord Camelford and the hecklers at the music hall—that is Sellers' and Milligan's portrayal of the penurious, stupefied, and eternally optimistic William McGonagall, forever flattened under weights, slapped full in the face by cabbages, and humiliated generally. In *The Great McGonagall*, the itinerant versifier with his cardboard suitcase of poetic gems, like the wandering boxer, visits his Sovereign: not eccentric George III, but Sellers as Queen Victoria: 'This day I have given audience to a man who was a Scottish artistic genius. He read me some of the most exquisite poetry I have ever heard in my life with the rich and powerful tones of his voice which rose and fell like the sea. Both Prince Albert and I were deeply moved by him. But then he left and in came William McGonagall.'

On another level, however, what placed Mendoza out of the ordinary, the mock heroic idiom of his own *Memoirs* aside, and reverting to contemporary sources, was the way he attempted to capitalise on his violent streak ('the reward of money was high in his mind all his long life') by converting brawls into a recognised sport. His efforts to circumscribe his unruliness with rules—to use Richard Ellmann's phrase for boxing's other brute, the Marquess of Queensberry—was received in a variety of ways. To the readers of *Pugilistica*, Mendoza was a 'scientific professor in the art of self-defense.' *Boxiana*, however, viewed him as the noble savage which lurks inside each of us; that spirit of courage and gusto which we tend to deny with compromises, failure of nerve, old age. The pugilist exemplified a purified masculinity; 'he might be termed a complete artist.'

The embodiment of a divine right to be selfish and repulsive in the guise of an independent spirit—this is the Mendoza of use to Sellers, the Sellers who justified his pitched battles with directors, producers, or any authority figure by referring to his artistic integrity and his private and proprietary rights. The adult Sellers was still the boy who 'to protect his top or marbles ... puts himself in a posture of defense and dares his oppressor to the hostile combat'—the words of *Box-iana*, when its correspondent tried to get to the bottom of Mendoza's youth.

Sellers, who took to an extreme Mendoza's asseveration that 'a man ought not to be harassed with unnecessary and vexatious restrictions', may be given the boxing ring as a symbol of his modus operandi. The hard flashes of Mendoza's eighteenth-century life and times almost pre-incarnate the modern star's behaviour and rant. He used to retell with approval a conversation he'd overheard in Wales, when he was making *Only Two Can Play*: 'I remember Richard Burton was down there and one of Kenneth Griffith's Welsh cronies went up to him and said, "Do you know this Marly Brandon then?" When Burton said, "Yes—he's a fine actor," the man said: "That's as may be, boyo—but can you *beat* him?" And he put up his fists. What he meant of course, was "can you beat him *up*?" That's what counted in his world.'

If there was an extra dimension to Sellers' destructiveness, something that went well beyond the immediate provocation or catalyst, it might go back all the way to the primal test of manhood. For the Mendoza who defined boxing as a means 'to enable men to stand in their own defense against the assaults they are daily exposed to' is the knockout idolised by the Jewish community. As was said at the time, 'Royalty besought him. Even the King! Who else among the schoolfellows of his boyhood could have risen to such an experience! It was almost in the realm of fantasy!'—the very same realm Sellers would be in when he was romancing Princess Margaret and Roman goddesses like Sophia Loren.

◆ ◆ ◆

Mendoza, the primitive, the poet, the ruffian, the conqueror and man of destiny—the 'intelligent and communicative man', in the opinion of *Boxiana*—was evidently as multiform as his great-great grandson. Sellers played him once. When he was regaining consciousness after his first big heart attack, the first programme he saw and enjoyed on the television was 'Not Only... But Also'. 'He'd seen Peter Cook and Dudley Moore,' says Joe McGrath, 'and asked if he could do a guest spot on the show. We wrote a sketch about a boxer, called Danny, who had become an abstract painter and who'd gone back to boxing again.'

As a punch drunk old pug with finer feelings, Sellers' Danny is a nice little caricature and very distant homage. Further linking the historical Mendoza to the modern actor's temperament was their shared attitude to money. Mendoza earned large fees and spent it 'like a drunken sailor' ('All he knew of economics was that his money had been easy to come by'). Sellers, equally heedless and improvident, frittered away fortunes on cars and electronic toys. Yet where Sellers died a multimillionaire, the receipts from Inspector Clouseau rolling in, Mendoza's last years were 'piteous, lamentable, and ruinous'—words apt for Sellers in every sense *except* the financial.

Mendoza's widow lived on until 1855, running a pub called The Royal Oak in Whitechapel Road. Welcome (and later Peg) grew up amid a landscape of prize fights and music rooms and girls singing in four-ale bars. Whatever effect her marriage to Solomon Marks may have had (sources differ as to whether she was wedded or widowed at the age of forty-four), that the touring revue company was established at all implies a need, late on in life, to revert to her grandfather's round of nomadic entertaining. There was a wanderer in her soul (as there was to be a restlessness in her grandson's).

Provincial music hall and revue, however, was not a healthy existence, especially at the lower levels, where Peg and Bill operated. People were over-worked by the non-stop shows, and there was a good deal of boozing. Suppers were served in the orchestra stalls and audiences and cast alike could swig on fizz at seven shillings a bottle or take concoctions such as sherry and egg or rum and honey for sixpence a glass. Peg became a soak in her final phase—gin concealed in Optrex eye-drops bottles, all that. And there was almost a tradition of either dying young or lingering on degraded by poverty and disability—a fate common amongst the trampolinists and trapezists, the people who'd come up from the circus.

It was no place for raising babies—one-night cheap hotels, damp, unaired rooming-houses smelling of drains and mouse; diphtheria, whooping cough, bow-legs, leg-braces, and meningitis. No wonder its adherents took to the bottle and broke their health. They never saw the sun. They lived by the artificial lights flickering off the dressing room mirrors or float-guards (footlight shades). Peter Sellars (note the spelling) was a casualty. So was the child's mother. So was his younger brother, raised in his place.

Peg, highly strung anyway, and dependent on Ma for stability, was demented with grief; she'd take the layette kit out of its drawer and, as if it were a boy's collection of blown birds' eggs, weep on the tissue paper. When you keep faith with the dead like this, your dead child is idealised; he never needs to fall short or be humbled by life's confusion and contingency. He'd be an angel. He'd be a boy forever.

Sellers' very existence, therefore, owed itself to anguish. Come to replace a lost boy, conceived as a double, he was literally born to be a great impersonator, the child who'd get silently measured against somebody who was no longer there. And it was he, *Richard Henry Sellars*, born a year after Peter, on Tuesday, September 8, 1925, who had to fulfill Peg's super-normal expectations. He'd never be allowed to grow up, he'd never fail or be less than perfect—an attitude which doomed him instantly. ('I knew, you see, that his destiny was exceptional'.) It was never going to be feasible for Sellers to be at home in this world. He'd always be afraid he was not quite real.

◆ ◆ ◆

Flash forward half a century, to Sellers' last outflinging, when he was making *The Prisoner of Zenda, Being There*, and *The Fiendish Plot of Dr Fu Manchu*. What attracted him to the old-fashioned, Victorian atmosphere of these tales? It is not that they are simply romances about disguise, sundered twins, counterfeiting, and the illusion of order. They are also, each of them, stories about the problems of identity and who people really are. *The Prisoner of Zenda*, for example, is a campy cousin of Stevenson's *Dr Jekyll and Mr Hyde*: doubles who are opposites, and yet interlinked. In the Sellers film, the division is between a regal buffoon and decadent, Prince Rudi, and the honourable commoner, Sidney Frewin of Bethnal Green. (Their mother was a music hall actress, Tessy Frewin, and the two boys join in a chorus of her famous song: 'She was a sweet little dickie bird, tweet-tweet-tweet she went'—i.e., Sellers sings a duet with himself on screen.)

The two sides of Sellers' own nature are there: the night-clubbing and womanising versus the reclusiveness. And Sellers, indeed, could be both at once. When, to many witnesses, he was moping in his hotel in Paris during the winter before he died, full of sorrow because his last marriage seemed to have failed, he was also, on the evidence of his chauffeur's log book, 'out on the town eating and drinking very late many nights … and the jet trips every weekend are very debilitating.'*

Sellers plays Rudi as a caricature of twittishness; he is perfectly brainless and nobody has ever talked with a lisp like that. But Frewin, the hackney-carriage driver, has a solidity, a decency, and he talks like Michael Caine. (Sellers coined Caine's 'not many people know that' catchphrase.) A forlornness comes over Sellers whenever he does an East-Ender or a Northerner, as though he is suddenly in touch with the sort of fellow he could have been, had stardom not made him run riot. *The Optimists of Nine Elms*, *The Dock Brief*, *Mister Topaze*—in such films as these Sellers played the un-famous, men who have not managed to come adrift from their origins; yet it is Frewin's fate, as Rudi's double, to be accelerated to celebrity and the public gaze, going from the stables to a new life in a Mittel-Europa operetta. His prize is Lynne Frederick's girlish Princess Flavia. She has a knowing innocence to match his quiet depths. She is quite aware that he is an imposter and when, during the Coronation scene, she declares her fealty to the new King—'I, Flavia, do become thy vassal, swearing to serve thee in truth, with love, life, and limb'—it is impossible not to detect a private joke going on between the husband and wife team. The young or non-notorious Sellers, scruffy, a little greasy, puffy, bespectacled, fat, would not have been looked at twice by any Princess Flavias.

◆ ◆ ◆

The fun of *The Prisoner of Zenda* is in seeing one actor appear on screen with himself—serving himself drinks, talking to himself. He overcomes his singularity. It is an obvious bit of cinematic illusion. When the camera allows Sellers to proliferate, however, what we see, and become conscious of, is his multiple personality. Which is the natural man? Which the spirit? Who deciphers them? Such questions loomed large in my mind as I travelled to Harborne, in the Midlands, to meet John Taylor, Sellers' stand-in and double from *The Fiendish Plot of Dr Fu Manchu*. When I rang the bell and the frosted glass door was immediately opened, I received the shock of my life: there stood Peter Sellers. Or, I should say, Sellers as he would be now, had he hidden himself away and survived into his mid-sixties.

Taylor, his voice actorishly velvet, though marred now and then by the Birmingham diphthongs which chimed in when he dropped his guard, told me that he had been a salesman with a hankering for amateur dramatics. Taylor struck me

---

* From a memo sent to Sellers' lawyer on December 12, 1979.

as a rather woebegone man, his face thin and pinched. Though he did his best to appear genial and courteous, I sensed he was apprehensive; he'd quite recently been through the adversity of a divorce and he didn't mind admitting that, in contrast to the experience of the last year, his adventure with Sellers stood out all the more as the big unexpected highlight in his life.

My children's friends always thought I looked like Sellers, but I never made anything of the comparison, not until I went to meet a theatrical agent in London in May 1979. The girl in the agency suddenly said: 'My God, I've never seen anything like it. Stand up again. There's Peter Sellers standing there.' That was the first time anybody had remarked on any serious similarity. In June...my agent, Joyce, phoned me to say...would I like to go for a proper audition, preferably on Monday...On the Wednesday I had another call—would I meet Sellers on the Friday. He was staying at the Inn on the Park. I went in with Tom Smith, the make-up man. Sellers was with Michael Jeffery. We had tea and biscuits. Sellers suddenly said, 'See you over there in Paris. We'll have some bloody fun.' He gave me a list of addresses. His car took me to the wig makers, his tailors, his shirt makers, his shoe shop, and then back to Euston. Michael Jeffery had designed the Fu gear, and Sellers had said, 'Whatever I'm having, duplicate it for John.' We were identical in weight, height, our shoe size...

Things started to get quite eerie during the test shots. I started on a Monday. Sellers arrived the following Friday afternoon. We went to a viewing theatre to see all the test film. It sent shivers up and down my spine, the likeness was so remarkable. You wouldn't know which one of us you were looking at. At the end of it, Sellers stood up, picked up his bag, walked to the doors at the top of the stairs and said, 'Right, I'm off home. That bugger can do it.' It really was remarkable. And it fooled Roman Polanski. He was at the Studios de Boulogne finishing *Tess*. He took hold of my hand, when I was Fu, and we did a waltz—he thought it was Peter.

Ever afterwards, Sellers kept squinting and staring at me...'I've never seen anything like it,' he said. 'Where have we been at relative times in our lives? What did you look like when you were younger?'

Well, I used to be quite chubby, you see, in my twenties and thirties; and I looked out a number of old photographs and the likeness was *there*. Most mornings I had to go and see him for a briefing and to collect the costumes. He'd always say, 'You give me the creeps, mate, you really do.' He'd phone me up at all hours of the night—at three A.M. for instance—and he'd say he wasn't ever happy unless he was involved in a film. 'When I'm not in front of a fucking camera it's not worth being here.' He had no other interest—he was bored even by his still photography. I never saw him with one of his cameras in his hand, not even in the Alps. He didn't read. He didn't listen to music. He phoned me once in quite a state...'John,' he said, 'I'm wondering if I'll ever make another film.'

Well, he booked me to be in his next one, *The Romance of the Pink Panther*. I was going to be his double again. It turned out to be a hectic day or two. I arrived in London, went to my hotel, and called Sue Evans, his secretary, who said he'd been taken to hospital. Michael Jeffery phoned me late in the evening, from the Dorchester, having come back briefly from the hospital, and he said he'd be in touch the next day. The next morning I read in the Stop Press that he'd died. Ever since, I have been accosted so many times by strangers—long after his death, people would stop me in the street...'Eh mate, you're Peter Sellers aren't you?'

In the folklore of the *doppelgänger* (German for 'double-goer'; defined by the *OED* as 'wraith of living person') to meet your duplicate is a premonition of death. Sellers, who had visited Roger Moore on the set of *The Man Who Haunted Himself*, must have felt as if he'd toppled headlong into a similarly horrific plot*. As *The Fiendish Plot of Dr Fu Manchu*, on Sellers' orders, was being re-re-re-written through the night, every night, by just about anybody who could stay awake and hold a pen, this element was worked in at the last moment (though it was lost again when the film was edited after Sellers' passing). As Sellers intended it, the rejuvenated Fu, and Taylor as Nayland, were to walk off into the sunset together, the opposites reconciled, the doubles united. 'You are the only worthy adversary I ever had, Nayland. They were the good old days. We can recapture them and start all over again.'

Do the emotions, under the surface, reach back to the lost boy of Peg's? *The Fiendish Plot of Dr Fu Manchu* is crammed with old Goon gags and music hall allusions. Sellers was reliving things he'd already done, and by going backwards, Sellers' nostalgic cycle turned full circle.

◆ ◆ ◆

'From the very beginning—why I don't know—I was called Peter,' he said in 1976. Alterations of nomenclature were not uncommon in his family. As we have seen, Welcome Mendoza became Mrs Solomon Marks, Belle Ray, and Ma; Agnes Marks became Peg; Will Sellars turned into Bill Sellers—Sellars into Sellers having taken no more thought than everybody deciding to acquiesce to a printer's error on a flier. Richard Henry's instant alteration into Peter, however, was a signal that here was the little changeling boy to be Peg's henchman, and her control over him was both total and scant. The obnoxious everyday presence was the one she could goad, organise, and bully. 'My son doesn't need to think,' she'd say proudly, 'I do all his thinking for him.' Sellers was pale, pampered, and protected. He had a beehive of hair which was smeared with vaseline to give it a healthy and glossy appearance. This repellent tangle on the top of his head almost symbolises the sticky, blobby, inchoate mass, with no personality of its own, which Sellers liked to project in interviews: 'Now I'm probably one of *the* most unfunny people there is in private life. I'm dull ...'

Where Peg could not follow, however, was into that part of his brain where he carried out his transformations. He got away from her through the conjurings and aliases of the theatre. 'I find,' he was to say, 'that I operate much better if I'm behind a voice or a moustache where my own personality is disguised. I get a freedom that I don't normally have.' If Peg had lunch with him at the studio, and was asked afterwards how her son was, she used to say, 'I don't know. I didn't see him.' Sellers set himself loose by being other people, imitating and experimenting all the live long day. 'He used to go off on these flights of fancy,' says Joe McGrath.

---

* *The Man Who Haunted Himself* (1970), in which Moore is trailed by his double in the aftermath of a car accident, was directed by Basil Dearden who, back in 1957, had directed Sellers in *The Smallest Show on Earth*. Spookily, Dearden was to die in 1971—in a car crash.

'Sellers liked working in that semi-improvised way, when art and life mingle. He liked to feel he wasn't being constricted. A lot of the Quilty and Dr Strangelove stuff—he got into the character and was allowed to *go*. This is what Sellers was best at doing.'

◆ ◆ ◆

'A man of genius,' said Ezra Pound 'cannot help where he is born.' Sellers was born less into a place than a condition. If it wasn't bad enough being ungrounded by his mother's interdependence of love and death, the vagrancy of the vaudevillians ensured a placeless childhood. 'I didn't always mean to be an actor,' he complained, 'I was carried onto the stage when I was two days old, but I never acted as a child. My parents were stage people. I was an only child and I was taken round with them on tour, living in theatrical digs. It was Mum and Dad's life and it had to be like that.'

Sellers, whom many might assume had been beamed down from the Never-Never Land, was officially born in Southsea, near Portsmouth, at 20 Southsea Terrace. His family had taken a flat above a shop selling sweets and postcards of the naval dockyards. Sellers, revisiting the premises forty years on, claimed that 'I knew where my cot was, the shape of the ceilings. It was uncanny, really uncanny...it all looked much smaller and older and sadder.'

He was delivered by Dr Robert J. Lytle, who was unhappy about Peg's desire to continue working, but she was insistent that she revert as soon as possible to the make-believe of the revue. *The Vanity Box* left the King's Theatre, in Albert Road, Southsea, on Saturday, September 11, 1925. Peg and Bill remained above Postcard Corner to join up with *The Side Show* company, which had visited South Shields, Salford, Crewe, York, and Darlington, and was at present in Southampton. The local attraction, meantime, was Dickie Henderson Snr., the father of the more recent Dickie Henderson, that little drunkard with a small amount of charm who is now dead. Henderson, it is alleged, is the one who carried Sellers in his swaddling bands onto the King's Theatre stage and led the audience in a chorus of 'For He's A Jolly Good Fellow'. ('I didn't know anything about it,' Sellers later claimed, with some justification.)

The audience could well have been singing for Henderson himself. He had recently returned to Britain after an American tour. On August 17 he had begun a circuit of the provincial music halls that would last for three solid years. Henderson was something of a luminary, looked at from the vantage point of Peg and Bill, and Ray Brothers Productions Ltd. were glad to have an association with him, now that he was 'at liberty', in the theatre world's euphemistic phrase. Because he weighed over 220 pounds, he had been tested by Hal Roach as the potential fat man in a duo with Stan Laurel, but although he did make a few films, his growling presence, as he chewed on a cigar, didn't adapt well to either silent movies or to the early talkies. He did not possess that loony aura which W.C. Fields and Oliver Hardy—and Sellers—had, which makes you want to keep on watching them on the screen.

Born in 1891 (nine years Bill's senior, four or six years Peg's), by 1925 Henderson was already at the start of his decline. He dipped and splashed in and out of a lot of the Ray water shows, going away to make a new career for himself, returning when he'd failed; and his fate is of significance because it hints at the increasing fragility of the business Sellers' parents were in. The idea of the wandering revue company itself, as Ma Ray defined it, was set to be extinguished within a few years. This only added to the twilight mood of Sellers' childhood. From every direction he met with things dying.

During one engagement, the baby fell ill with bronchial pneumonia. 'A coloured doctor saved his life,' said Peg, for whom the experience—the coughing baby in a Moses basket at the back of the stage amongst the props, and the black man emerging out of the fog—had the quality of an hallucination.

'I really didn't like that period of my life, as a kid,' recalled Sellers. 'I didn't like the touring. I didn't like the smell of greasepaint which hit you when you went into any stage door. The smell of size—that's the stuff they paint on scenery—and baritones with beer on their breath and make-up on the collar—all big voices, like "Hello, little sonny, how are you? Dear little boy. Who is he?" And I used to spend my time sitting in dressing rooms ... so I didn't like that.' Yet he was to grow fond of at least impersonating these grandiose actor types. Sitting in his hotel, during location work for *The Return of the Pink Panther*, Sellers spent his time leafing through the London *A-Z Street Atlas*, gathering names for a whole platoon of thespians: Theydon Bois, Turnham Green, Montagu Mews West (his favourite). Aside from being a gift to the caricaturist, these Victorian tragedians were, from the start, Sellers' way of demonstrating just how subtle his own humour could be. Anybody can ape an old ham making a fool of himself with quasi-Shakespearean diction, playing King Lear on stage and off. What Sellers could touch on was the desperation—the crumpled, ordinary, and vainglorious flop lurking underneath the mannerisms.

His masterpiece in this regard is Dr Pratt in *The Wrong Box*. Though an unkempt, shuffling dotard, whose consulting room is awash with mangy cats and (we surmise) the unspeakable detritus of botched abortions, Pratt, in his frock coat and wing collar, is like a Henry Irving who has fallen from grace—the pathos he gets into his line 'I was not always as you see me now' is so gentle and expressive, we picture him in a private coach, paying professional calls on the aristocracy, or hobnobbing with Lord Lister at the Royal College of Surgeons. Or rather, we don't. When these sorts of characters dream about their better days—Morganhall in *The Dock Brief*, General Fitzjohn in *Waltz of the Toreadors*—what Sellers suggests more than anything is their gullibility. His ripe and ancient magicians can respond only to things that never were; they are incurable romantics—and what makes the comedy deep-toned is the suggestion that, hovering not very far away at all, is the more tragic observation that here we have people who have had wasted lives.

◆ ◆ ◆

The brief notices on *The Side Show* which appeared in provincial newspapers, now yellowed and crumbling in forgotten archives, the leaves about to disintegrate, seem to be the only references to Sellers' parents' career in existence. For example, when they were at the Pavilion, Liverpool: 'The Ray Brothers Productions are presenting "The Side Show," an entertaining revue, in which appear Willie Cave, Arthur Lewis, Harry Ray's Syncopators, Will Sellers [*sic*] and Monty Golding.'

Peg's own act was called 'Fire and the Woman'. It was devised around the character of Sir Henry Rider Haggard's *She*, the jungle priestess who'd bathed in the Flame of Eternal Youth five centuries ago, and the idea was that Peg, portraying a princess who was immortal, had recurred throughout time as all its queens and heroines. 'My mother wore white tights,' said Sellers, 'and stood in front of a plain white screen. Behind the audience a magic lantern cast slides of different costumes on to the screen. The result was that my mother would appear as all kinds of women in history or mythology, from Britannia to Joan of Arc, and yet never really change.'

The concept of being a consistent blank whilst exotic other lives flickered across your face appealed to Sellers: 'My mother's act moved me in a way I still can't explain.' Her performance was a version of Sellers' own procedure as an actor. A click, a fast fade, another slide. 'The colour and warmth and the applause and the feeling of being part of something that could give so much happiness to other people, made me want to be up there with her taking a more positive part than just watching from the wings.'

Watching and waiting, however, whilst his mother came and went phantasmagorically, was all there was to do. He was anonymous amongst the entourage—and they were always on the move. Sellers' youth lacked youthfulness and everywhere looked the same: 'The bedrooms were all alike, with marble washstands and brass beds. I'd look up at the ceiling and say to myself "Oh God, I do wish we had a home."'

Whether he did voice that sentiment then, it was not one he did much about later, when he had ample chance. He had a definite liking for hotels and hospitals, places designed for transients who'd leave no trace. Just as he could be lots of people—each new lantern slide taking its place—so he never seemed to mean to live in a single place. The Manor House at Chipperfield was exchanged for a suite at the Carlton Tower Hotel, which became a penthouse flat in Frognal Lane, then a room at the Dorchester. All this upheaval went on with a total disregard for wife and children. Physically, as well as mentally, Sellers would be scattered and dissipated. Rimbaud, in *The Season in Hell*, says that 'I was forced to travel to ward off the apparitions assembled in my brain', and there's something of this anxiety to Sellers. 'He thinks "Wherever I am, it's boring,"' says Milligan. 'Can you imagine the agony of that? If he hadn't made it financially I think he would have killed himself.'

Part of his problem was that, as a nomadic child, he never encountered other children, who might have knocked the edges off him and given him some perspective. He was surrounded only by busy adults and spent forces. He called his mother and father by their first names, and he was like a miniature grown-up, but with a child's inner rage and loneliness. Indeed, children in the music hall world were represented by dwarves. Sellers never forgot being nightmarishly engulfed by a pack of munchkins called Fred Roper's Midgets, who jumped through hoops like dogs: 'I could never figure out why I couldn't make contact with them. They were the same height as me, but all had deep voices and smoked cigars and pipes.' Old men in infants' bodies—the reverse of Sellers.

With no people of his own age available, and with those of his own size being freaks, Sellers had no opportunity to make a pal; he had no contemporaries, and he never would, in all of his life, be capable of forming a secure friendship, with the give-and-take that such a relationship demands. He was closed. He never developed the emotions that go with being able to share; he never overcame a maximum reluctance not to be selfish. The best he'd feel he could hope for from other people was loyalty, which he tried to buy by giving away presents of cameras and shockproof wrist watches and hi-fi equipment (symbols of his own detachment: listening and looking devices, etc.). He very early on gave up hoping to attract affection.

It was a mournful existence, Sellers' progress around Britain, enough to drive anybody in on himself. The most affecting scene he ever played is in *The Optimists of Nine Elms*: Old Sam, who is wearing a dress-suit with a huge paper bloom in the button hole, so that he looks like Lear and the Fool in one, is sitting on a gilded prop throne, amusing the children by reciting his tired little Dan Leno rhymes. Gradually a melancholy creeps in to what he is saying—especially when he tells what is no longer a bit of patter about coming home from school one day and finding that his folks had moved, without leaving any new address. Why hadn't he taken the hint? For the past week they'd been wrapping his sandwiches in a road map...

As a parable of abandonment it hangs in the air. Sellers sits there, like a deposed king, and under his calm many memories are stirring. It is one of those moments, on the screen, which seem beautifully finished.

◆ ◆ ◆

It was easier, as he shed his yesterdays, to be thought of as somebody new. There is nothing more humiliating than spending time with somebody and then, when you see them again, and you are a blank to them, you realise you have been erased; you registered *that* much. You haven't imprinted at all. It is as if you were dressed in white and positioned before a white screen, but there is nobody to work the magic lantern's coloured filters. At receptions, as a successful man, unless he was holding the floor and working the room with his voices, people would always take a couple of seconds to realise who he was. (Harry Secombe said that Sellers, in horn-rims and dour suits, had the charisma of a tax inspector.) Even in company he was isolated, loathing the way 'people expect you to be funny...I go to parties and people lurch over and say "Do us one of those funny things you do on the films". Eventually you go to a party, in the hope it will quench all the thirst of all the people that want to see you*—because that's what your agent says. You arrive there—all the photographers in the world, all the press agents in the world: "This is your town, baby, you can buy it." An odd thing happens: they shake hands with you, look at you closely in the eyes for a few seconds—and then their eyes wander over your shoulder, to see who else is coming into the room.'

Nobody likes not to be memorable and one of Sellers' methods of defying his loneliness was to behave badly. His first action, as a toddler, was to push a woman, who was bending over the grate, into the fire, where she burnt her hands. He spat on people's heads and in their hats. He squashed a cat in a sofa-bed. He'd show his parents up in cafes, eat the last cake without asking permission, and dismember toys he had been bought. If ever he saw a march band he wanted to conduct it; and when he was taken to see *Peter Pan* at the Shaftesbury Theatre he tried to jump off the balcony and join the Darling children on their flight to the Never-Never Land.

Nothing here is out of the ordinary to anybody with frequent exposure to the under-fives. Most parents could cap that catalogue. What was abnormal was Peg's absolute refusal to reprimand her son. Whatever Sellers did was fine by her. It was like Papal Infallibility. Between Ma Ray, Aunt Cissie, and all the chorines, he was spoiled rotten. Being cheeky, being flip, was how he conversed. 'You didn't wash today,' his mother would say. 'I did, Peg, but I had my knees crossed, so one's still dirty,' he'd respond, to general glee. It doesn't take a nanosecond for children to learn how much they can get away with, and Sellers was no exception. 'There were too many adoring, worshipping women round that baby,' remembered Herbert Ray. 'If Peg went out of the room for a moment he just lay down on the floor and kicked and screamed. He was a horror, a monster; we would have gladly cut his throat.'

I can believe it. The tantrum was to continue as his way of expressing himself. Having been taught to wail at authority figures, starting with his own father, Sellers had no compunction about throwing a fit in front of a director, producer, writer, fellow actor. Or anybody. If a shop didn't have what he wanted, instantly he'd be in a rage. Jimmy Grafton, who helped him to first get work on the radio and who scripted that earliest of films, *Penny Points to Paradise*, was once witness to a revealing scene. They were in Victoria Street when Sellers saw a complete outfit in cavalry twill he decided he wanted. Sellers started to get annoyed when the tailors didn't have one in exactly his size; or perhaps it was one in solid gold which he was insisting on. 'How dare you put something in the window you can't supply,' he raged. The manager offered to track down the requisite fitting from another branch. 'When?' snapped Sellers. By tomorrow, he was informed. 'I don't want it tomorrow. *I want it now.*' The manager offered personally to find the right suit by later on that very afternoon. 'No thank you. You've already wasted enough

---

* In the 1970s, Sellers would expect to be paid—many thousands of pounds—to turn up at receptions: 'I was in his penthouse flat in Victoria,' said Peter Eton in 1976. 'He wasn't there, but I was talking to his secretary and a call came through asking him to appear for half an hour at a party—for an enormous sum of money. I said to Sue Evans "Is he going to do this?" and she said "He might." All that money just so the host could say "I've got Peter Sellers coming along…"!'

of my time.' And he stormed out, not pacified, noted Grafton (who doesn't say whether or not he should have hit his companion very hard), until he'd purchased a hat in Dunn's—for only then was 'the acquisitive urge satisfied.'

As he had been instilled with a contempt for the forces of law and order, his conduct never curbed, Sellers became accustomed to a star's mischievousness when he was still a child. His behaviour later on was an enlargement of the liberty hall he had lived in with Peg. In a curious sort of way, because his outrages were applauded, they became part of his desire to please—his way of keeping in with Peg, Ma, et al. This is the satirical moral distortion Sellers brought out in the 'Auntie Rotter' sketch in the fifties. Sellers gurgles gleefully as the old lady encourages the moppets to chop up their families with a hatchet. The sketch colludes with, and respects, the demon inside every child. ('Here is your stabbing music... Come along! No lazing!')

♦ ♦ ♦

Sellers further thrilled his personal pack of Auntie Rotters by giving what Bill called 'a perfect rendering' of Albert Chevalier's 'My Old Dutch' and 'It Gits Me Talked Abaht': 'Even as a child of two,' Bill said resignedly, 'he had talent. We had a little evening dress specially made for him with top hat and silver-headed walking stick.' The performing monkey also appeared, c. 1930, in an advertisement for Mazda, the electric lightbulb manufacturers.

A lot of children were used for the advertisements, which continued to appear until November 1936. There was a bimonthly competition for models, and Sellers' portrait must have been ideal: the boy, unsmiling and stubborn, stares hard at the camera. These eyes aren't dim! Sellers resembles, in fact, Freddie Bartholomew or Dean Stockwell, one of those hateful Hollywood lambkins. His rich hair manages to be both tousled and combed, and it receives a bit of a nimbus from the light source, off to the left. The monochrome gives his face a creamy, dreamy texture, which adds to the alien hardness of those eyes, those lips. (It is a portrait of Peter Pan.)

How the picture contrasts with a snap of Sellers taken when he was twelve. There, in cricketing whites outside St Aloysius', his school, he looks like Billy Bunter.* His fulsome hair is unsuccessfully greased down—it looks like a lap dog has taken up position on his scalp and dropped dead. The outdoor light, instead of softening the face, as the lamp does in the studio photograph, fattens it. We see the shadow-accentuated crevices and the contours formed by pudgy cheeks and chins. Those plates of eclairs have taken a toll. Sellers blinks at the light (his eyes disappear into two dark holes) and he slightly tilts himself back, his mouth, a sharp black line, set in a sneer. But by leaning back he also pushes out his belly, and his trouser belt, into which his thumbs are thrust, is pulled up high over the blubber. The last thing he looks is sporty. Over one arm he has the red-with-green-trim regulation school blazer, which perhaps he has just collected before he

---

* Bunter was a popular schoolboy character who resembled a bespectacled, pubescent Fatty Arbuckle.

betakes himself and his spotless kit home. The wall he is against, splotched with shadow, is ornate. Medieval? Victorian? Sellers, anyway, looks like a gargoyle which has recently dropped off it.

◆ ◆ ◆

Sellers' first non-family environment was Miss Whitney's School of Dancing, King's Road, Southsea; he later went to Madame Vacani's Dancing Classes, when the family moved up to London. 'I longed for him to carry on where I left off,' said Peg. Underlying all the spoiling and the fussing and the petting, which to some degree over-compensated for the times when he was left on his own whilst the rest of them were on stage, there was, with regard to Peg's attitude towards her son, a conviction that he was other-worldly and miraculous. Her clinging form of love trained him not to be ordinary. She expected him to have the successful career she and her ancestors had been denied: Sellers would appease the penurious legacy of Daniel Mendoza. Here they all were, a hundred years later, still at but one remove from trestle table stages in pubs, gin palaces, and the circus. Peg's boy, her Peter, her fair son, her food, her all-the-world, would change all that. He'd be a brilliant duplication of herself. He'd *be* her; she'd *be* him.

Just about every single one of his problems was to stem from this. Roy Boulting believes that the smothering caused Sellers to resent his mother: 'I am absolutely certain that this woman he should have loved, professed to love, his mother, he genuinely hated.' She was certainly the only person for whom he had strong feelings of any complexion, and she drove out his capacity for affection towards anybody else. His wives, for example, were versions of his mother he could hit back at.

Mother and son were so interwoven that parapsychologists might like to investigate whether it is possible to be a reincarnation of a living person. Though Peg's passion created both Sellers' feinting and dodging and his bloody-mindedness, the effect in the short-term was the exclusion of Bill. 'Peg was overwhelming. She overwhelmed Peter,' Milligan said to me. 'When they kissed, mother and son, it wasn't pleasant. It was more like they were lovers—not that anything of *that* kind happened, I'm sure. He didn't become Oedipus Rex. But it was an unhealthy relationship, though a very deep and loving one. Though I don't know what stamp you put on that quality of love or on that kind of life. Bill was relegated to second place in the male hierarchy. Peg lived for, and top place was for, Peter and Peter alone. She doted on him and he doted on her.'

◆ ◆ ◆

By 1929 Bill had started to have enough. The last time the family worked together, in one of Ma's divertissements, was when Herbert Ray opened his new revue, *Ha! Ha!! Ha!!!*, at the Bedford Music Hall, Camden Town, on February 13. The show then toured, and when Bill left with the troupe to tinkle daydreams for his audiences, Peg stayed behind in the quarters they were renting upstairs at the Bedford. She now had her son in her heart and in her arms. At root rootless, the pair began several years of flitting across London, as Peg became absorbed into the Mendoza house-agency side of the family. They occupied a succession of lit-tle flats on end-leases. Sellers, on whom nothing was lost (the low-grade music hall entertainers would come together as Old Sam; 'Fire and the Woman' would be adapted for Chance the blank, who is given a personality by the television screen), never forgot the litany of addresses. He thought he'd come to rest in London, but it was like traipsing the outback all over again. When he wrote an article in *Vogue*, in the last year of his life, he was specific about having lived 'in a flat at 43b Park Street (now Parkway), Camden Town, opposite the pet shop and above Heals the builders.'

The excuse Peg had for remaining behind whilst the others went off on tour was that Sellers needed to start his compulsory education. She dreaded this sepa-ration and did her best to cushion him against the depredations of the masses, who could not be relied upon to be as dainty as the pupils at Miss Whitney's or Madame Vacani's, by patrolling the school gates and telling the teachers what to do.

Sellers, knowing his mother didn't really approve of schools (she herself had left before the age of ten), saw immediately that this could work to his advantage. He would get her to bribe him to get up and go out each morning. Along the street was a toy shop and confectionery store, where he would feast on licorice and sodas. In the window was a scale model of Sir Malcolm Campbell's Bluebird. 'I gazed longingly at this vision for days and eventually persuaded my mother that there was no hope in the world for me unless I could become the owner of this splendid, shining blue car...Finally she gave in.' Sellers took the object to school—St Mark's Private Kindergarten on the Gloucester Road ('now Glouces-ter Avenue')—and he excited the admiration and envy of the class. It wasn't Christmas or his birthday or anything. One of the children in Miss Helen Penn's charge came too near for Sellers' comfort and 'I resolved to hit him if he came any closer'. The boy's ingenious reaction to the threat of violence was to nominate himself as the chap who'd thump everybody else out of range: 'Can I be the man,' he asked Sellers, 'who sees that no one touches it for you?'* Sellers tells this story as the beginnings of his warped worship for cars ('a forerunner of things to come'). What it mostly prefigures, I think, is his tolerance of the hoodlums and bodyguards, the men friends, from the outright effeminate homosexual to the burly stunt double, whom he would get to protect and mother him.

His way of coping with Miss Penn, who had the cheek to try and impart crappy knowledge and rudiments like reading and writing, was to go into a trance—to teletransport himself elsewhere. Often, after one of Peg's heavy kosher lunches, the snooze was authentic. This retreat into a dream kingdom of his own Peg called 'The Imagines.' For reasons best known to himself, Sellers started to show signs of compulsive ritualistic behaviour. He'd switch lights on and off six times; he'd lift the lavatory seat up and down six times; he'd flush the cistern six times before quitting the john. If there was a superstitious motive behind the drill,

---

* Sellers remembered and 'improvised' the line in *What's New, Pussycat?*: O'Toole is having girl-friend trouble, and Sellers' psychiatrist suggests that 'I could be the man that sees no one touches her for you.'

akin to not stepping on the pavement cracks or spilling salt (Michael Sellers re-members a ban on open umbrellas inside the house nor were bunches of keys to be left on the hall table because 'that was apparently a very unlucky thing to do'), then a Catholic convent, dedicated to the dogmas of death and judgement and heaven and hell, was going to be perfect for such a one of Sellers' susceptibilities.

♦ ♦ ♦

The Schoolboy Sellers[†]

Readers may be interested to learn the probable origins of Peter's inner rage.

In 1936 I was at St Aloysius' College, Highgate. Some weeks after a term had started, a new entrant arrived—Sellers. He was being placed with us much younger children because his previous schooling had been repeatedly disrupted due to his parents being in a touring theatre business.

Peter was very quiet, and must have deeply resented his being made to appear a dunce. In his later life he was brilliant in portraying characters who were out-wardly fools but inwardly really very clever. This, I believe, was the driving force of his career—to demonstrate that he was NOT a dunce and that he brilliantly out-shone the rest...

> *Gerald Meteau*
> Worthing
> Sussex

♦ ♦ ♦

I don't think anybody thought Sellers was stupid. He was simply lazy and lacked application, as he well knew: 'I was never a good scholar. Perhaps I never really settled down to it,' he confessed in 1962. 'Perhaps that's what was wrong with my education. But I didn't dislike it at St Aloysius'. I've sometimes been back to see the people there...'

I never managed to locate Mr Meteau, but with the help of some long con-versations I had with Bryan Connon, another of Sellers' classmates, a picture of some of the best (note that qualifying double negative: 'I didn't dislike it...') years of my man's life emerges.

The Founding Religious Order of St Aloysius' College, in 1879, was the Brothers of Our Lady of Mercy, from Malines in Belgium. The Belgians had been invited to the Archdiocese of Westminster by Cardinals Wiseman and Manning, and the intention was to create an establishment for 'respectable boys of the mid-dle class'—i.e. grocers' sons, in Connon's father's view. The school would be less exclusive than Ampleforth or Stoneyhurst, and science and commercial subjects would be taught, not just the classics.

By Sellers' time, St Aloysius' Boarding and Day School for Boys had two hun-dred 'day dogs' and one hundred and sixty 'boarder bugs'. They were accommo-dated in a building, completed in 1911, which looks from the photographs like Castle Dracula or an insane asylum—a charcoal pink edifice, an example of mu-

---

[†] This letter was printed in *The Guardian*, July 15, 1990.

nicipal Edwardian gothic. There was an ornate chapel, where Mass was said every morning and where hymns were sung every night, and Sellers enjoyed the high-camp of the incense-impregnated ceremonies, the lace-trimmed scarlet vestments, and the theatrics. Brother Cornelius, Sellers' and Connon's master, 'was a convert to Catholicism and as such was more avid about it all than those born in the faith. He took his class to the chapel a lot.'

The services, their colour, light, and precision, the singing and the recitatives, were like sophisticated revues. (The object, uplift, was the same.) Here was the world of the stage without the underlying pennilessness and misery. There was no need to strike the set and trudge to the midnight tram. Religion was a secure theatre. The antiquity of the words and routines, the decorum: it implied a branch of fakery you could come to believe in. The dead walked, had lives *after* death. Water became wine. Virgins gave birth. How was it all done? By magic?

◆ ◆ ◆

Catholicism intrigued Sellers because he had just discovered he was a Jew—he was someone on the outside of the mysteries of faith. He was referred to as 'The Jew' in front of the other boys, and as he said in later life: 'My father was solid Church of England but my mother was Jewish—Portuguese Jewish—and Jews take the faith of their mother.'

What did being a Jew mean to him? The photograph of the sombre-looking fellow in a yarmulka (one of those little skull caps) which accompanied his obituary in the *Jewish Chronicle*,* is not actually of Sellers, as such. It is a still of Harold Fine, the Jewish lawyer in *I Love You, Alice B. Toklas*. He was not barmitzvah'd, did not belong to a synagogue, and his four marriages were to non-Jewish ladies. Sir Evelyn de Rothschild, however, who knew him for over twenty years, sees Sellers as quite archetypically Jewish: 'He was a wanderer. He could never have roots, if you look at the way he lived and how he lived. He was...afraid people only befriended him for favours. I think he felt comfortable with me. He could say anything he liked and I wasn't going to take advantage of him. He would sit and talk to me about his problems most of the time—he always had problems of one sort or another, personal to him: worries about what he should do, where he had to live, his relationships with people. We used to go over that. Maybe because I represented something he couldn't be—here was I, outside the acting world and his professional career, and yet we were both Jewish. He was...very cognizant of his Jewishness. It was part of his background, and maybe because of my name and position I represented another side of life which he hadn't thought about, and he had the opportunity now to express himself.'

Sellers' Jewish heritage came up regularly when he talked to Wolf Mankowitz, too. But where the descendant of Meyer Amschel Rothschild, the legendary Austro-Hungarian money-lender, was sympathetic to the botherations besetting the scion of Daniel Mendoza, the son of a tradesman from East Ham remains much more sceptical: 'He didn't understand anything at an intellectual level. He

---

* Sellers shared the page with the Shah of Iran, who had died the same week.

became at one time fascinated with Jewish things because of his mother and Mendoza. That famous engraving of Mendoza looks awfully like him. He got interested in Jewish things and I spent a lot of time answering questions on Jewish subjects. He became a heavy would-be student of the Torah. He never got very far. He did this with Indian religions as well, and dropped those. The thing is, he was tremendously superstitious...'

Sellers had spent his childhood observing and absorbing the little backstage rituals, the signs and magic symbols a nervous actor makes to give himself confidence and courage before he steps into the spotlight. He took it all to extremes, of course. The aversions to various colours; the obsession with omens and oracles; the way he treated astrologers as learned men: Sellers was out of *I, Claudius*. And yet what was to happen with him and the occult is implied, also, by his attitude to Jewishness. It was a way to justify feeling different, feeling a refugee from normal life. If the spirit medium/witchcraft side of the question made him superior (he'd been told early on he'd be a household name and live to be seventy-four—a prediction which became half right), Jewishness, like a stammer for Philip Larkin, was 'a built-in handicap to put him one down'—or, more accurately, if he wanted to pretend to be one down. It was a pretext for grudges.

Sometimes his touchiness came and went in a flash. On a breakfast television talk show in America, in 1964, he was asked by the host if he'd care for some juice. 'I am Jewish myself,' snapped Sellers. 'No, juice *de l'orange*,' the host explained, gesturing to a jug. 'I'd love a little of that, too,' conceded the star. On other occasions, rooting for trouble, he'd allow his sensitiveness to take hold for weeks. *The Prisoner of Zenda* was made in Vienna, and Sellers attributed the cause of his anxieties to the fact that Austria was an anti-Semitic country. He banished six people from the film whom he believed had looked at him disparagingly, i.e. less than worshipfully. He took each individual aside and said 'We don't have the right chemistry together.' One of his victims, the veteran unit publicist Al Hix, told me that he'd so looked forward to working for Sellers, being an admirer of his talent—'but then I met the man, and it was such a shock. He was really dangerous. It wasn't as if you could call him childish; he was bitter and paranoid.' When Hix was sacked, Sellers made the production manager, Peter McGregor Scott, order Hix to move out of the Wien Hilton, where the bulk of the company was billeted.

As Sellers himself was residing at the Hotel Bristol, his attempted persecution of people he was unlikely to meet in the elevator or dining room is pathetic and spiteful. But he enjoyed the idea of riding people out of town. It had once nearly happened to him. Early in his career, when he'd bought his first Rolls, he thought he'd take it for a spin on the Continent. 'I was going to Calais,' he explained to Terry-Thomas' sister, Mary Hoar Stevens, 'but my new car wouldn't fit on the ferry, so I've decided to spend my holiday in Brighton.' (A typical Sellers reaction—a deckhand had probably asked him to reverse or manoeuvre into a tight space, and he could never cope with requests like that.) Mary said gaily, 'What a good idea! You'll like this hotel, Peter. It's very quiet—and there are no Jews here.' 'Well, Mary,' said Sellers, equally gaily, 'There are now!'

Milligan told me that 'Peg had disregarded her religion—a lost Jewess—when she married Bill, and Peter was haunted by the uncertainty of his religion, and who he was, and he never did find out.' The Jews which Sellers played on 'The Goon Show' were oy-vay caricatures, with names like Geraldo or Izzy; and concurrent with his death he was to be seen on television as a Jewish con-man, Monty Casino, urging viewers to invest their money in Barclays Bank. (His fee for the ad, shot in Dublin, was £80,000.) A bit further up the scale, he turned down the Alan Bates part in Bernard Malamud's *The Fixer* and Fagin in the Dickens musical *Oliver!* because 'I couldn't finally see any way of playing either rôle outside the usual interpretation.' Yet his reticent Los Angeles legal eagle in *I Love You, Alice B. Toklas* (which he made in 1968 instead of appearing in *Oliver!*) shows that there was a way to avoid the Yiddish weeping, wailing, smiting, and the rending of garments. Harold Fine is filial, obedient, ambitious, successful—and full of tension. He has asthma; his jaw and shoulder tendons are firm-set. As a specialist in settling insurance claims, he is as cramped and confined as his clients, who sit in his office exhibiting their neck braces. 'I'm going crazy,' he admits.

As Sellers saw the film: 'It is a very interesting part. Probably the most interesting part I've played in my career to date. The part of a Jewish lawyer who eventually decides that the pressures in his life are so great he can't bear them; he can't face up to what he's doing anymore. He earns forty thousand dollars a year and has a nice big shiny car; he has an apartment and a forthcoming marriage. But he eventually drops out, as they say. He decides to become a hippy—he decides to try a new way of life and samples their philosophy. And likes it.'

Harold wants to find a way of being taken out of himself; he wants to disappear, and so did Sellers. As can be readily seen, his understanding of the character amounted to self-identification, and he gave a nuance-filled performance which is several million cuts above the surrounding film. Sellers didn't need Harold to smoke pot and pop pills to remain high and liberated; nor is he, as the low-key gloomy businessman freaking out in a flower-power smock, the object of derision which the script wants to make him. Sellers, without having to spell it out, conveys the melancholy of a man intuitive enough to know that, like his black suits and yarmulka, the blue and pink hippy shawls are another form of disguise. He has exchanged one kind of convention for another; a worse one, perhaps, because though marijuana makes the depression of ordinary life lift, its effects are illusionary. In the context of the film, it is no more than a gag when Harold keeps jilting his Jewish princess bride at the altar. Sellers, however, was attuned to deeper fears: 'At the end he runs off, because he doesn't know *where* he's going. He's a desperate man. Any man who would run out of a marriage ceremony in full swing has got to be a pretty desperate man. It's funny; it's tragic; it's all about today...'

Sellers conveys the man's humiliations well enough; but there is also a paradox at the heart of the character. For Harold to be able to claim 'for the first time in my life I feel free' he also needs to be 'just being, that's all'. Not thinking, doing, choosing, judging: nothing. He is in a state of suspended animation, ghostly and blurred. He is thrilled to shout out 'Harold Fine no longer exists!' This makes me uneasy because it seems all too similar to the anaesthesia of Chance, in *Being There*, who is of course a nullity, and I wonder how much can be read into the very last words Sellers spoke on the screen? In the final scene of *The Fiendish Plot of Dr Fu Manchu*, in the Himalayan palace, the Oriental mastermind promises that everybody is to be 'wiped out'—by an Elvis impersonation, as it happens, but that's not what people expected him to have in mind.

These descriptions, or depictions, of bliss are vapourous—like death. Is this how Sellers thought life should be? Happiness as a state of oblivion? 'He was incapable of radiant happiness,' says Milligan. 'Even with his children he could only get a sad happiness from them—no warm glow, as towards something positive that's happened in your life. For Peter, life is just a terrible journey.'

◆ ◆ ◆

I Love You, Alice B. Toklas not only has the farcical weddings, it also has its knock-about funeral sequence, with the hippy contingent attired as Hopi Indians. The deceased is Mr Foley, the kosher butcher, and because of an L.A. hearse strike, he is taken to the cemetery in a multi-coloured van. Sellers himself, when he was about to be laid under, was transported to Golders Green, and the rites of the Church of England, by a more conventional conveyance. But on July 26, 1980—a Saturday—there was darkness at noon. Black clouds and a downpour, lightning and thunderclaps, raged and foamed. It was as if someone in the world, a modern Caesar, too saucy with the gods, had incensed them to send destruction. The only wonder is that fire didn't fall from the sky. And before these strange stage effects began, the phone had been ringing non-stop at the Dorchester. It was a terrified Cockney Jewish taxi driver, well known to Sellers. The switchboard eventually put him through to Michael Jeffery. 'I've taken Mr Sellers in my cab many a time,' the voice said, 'He spoke of his mum. He's Jewish and you *cannot* bury him on the Sabbath. You *must not*...' Although gentiles often don't realise, the seventh day of the week is observed by the Jews as a day of abstention from all work and is regarded as sacred to the Lord, in commemoration of his rest from the work of Creation. So what was all this about? A blasphemous note to end on? Some final rebellion? (Mendoza, it was regretted in contemporary reports, had no compunctions about fighting on a Saturday.)

◆ ◆ ◆

St Aloysius' was unusual in taking non-Catholics on to its roll. Bryan Connon (son of an Episcopalian and a Presbyterian) recalls a strange mix of 'creeds and nationalities' at the school. It was this cosmopolitan aspect which appealed to Peg, who was suddenly nervous of how people would treat Sellers' semi-gypsy background and history. There were plenty of foreign accents for Sellers to absorb, in what was virtually (his short stay at St Mark's aside) his first foray into a world beyond the variety house. 'My ears were a sound radar that picked up every noise blip,' he later said of these years.

It was a school for refugees. Sellers later tried to laugh off being labelled as the class Jew—and one word-perfect in the Catholic liturgy at that—but the fact was,

Peter Evans & Bryan Connon

Gulliver in Lilliput: Sellers (standing behind Bro. Cornelius)
at St. Aloysius' College, Highgate (c. 1937)

he *was* different. From the class photograph of the academic year 1936/37, Sellers stares across the years, gormless and huge. He has been made to stand directly behind Brother Cornelius, whilst all the other boys either sit or are given extra height by a bench—though even with this expedient he is out of scale. This is Gulliver in Lilliput,* the highly-embarrassed-relegated-Sellers of Gerald Meteau's letter in the *Guardian*. There is something quite sinister about his enormity. It is as if all the boudoir fingers, treacle tarts, onion flans, brioche sausages, and waffles which Peg, Ma, and Cissie stuffed down him have inflated him cartoonishly. He looks like Daniel Mendoza.

Regardless of who he became later on, Sellers would have been memorable to his classmates because of his sheer size alone. 'He was extraordinarily large for his age—well over five and a half feet, and broad and chubby with it. A massive figure,' says Connon. His method of coping with the massiveness was to contrive to vanish into air. He wanted to be as anonymous as possible—and achieved this aim: 'It is difficult to remember Sellers making any impression whatsoever. He merged into the woodwork. He had little in common with any of us, and his educational

---

* In later life, if there was a lull in the conversation at a dinner party, Sellers would mystify those present by reciting a passage he had memorised from *Gulliver's Travels*: 'The Most Mighty Emperor, Delight and Terror of the Universe, Monarch of all Monarchs, Taller than the Sons of Men, at whose nod the Princes of the Earth shaked their knees, pleasant as the spring, comfortable as summer, fruitful as autumn, dreadful as winter.' Sellers would then helpfully add: 'You know, that Emperor was no more than six inches tall.'

standard was very low. He sat at the back of the class and kept to himself in the playground.'

It is as a nondescript that Sellers was recalled by Brother Cornelius in 1960*: 'He was just...average, not a memorable scholar, not a memorable athlete, no, nothing very outstanding at all'—except that Sellers was such a big boy: 'Although only ten years old when at the college he looked more like fourteen.' Because of his lack of educational attainments he was given special treatment: on Peg's instructions, he was not allowed to be caned—and the Brothers, out of the Lord He Knoweth what repressed sexual need, were enthusiastic beaters. ('Today those masters would be had up for assault,' says Connon. 'They were physically violent.') Sellers, instead, was given the meaninglessness of lines—page upon page of copperplate. 'The next trouble,' said Peg, 'was that he got so many lines that he couldn't have done them all if he stayed at school forever.' Some of the gobbledygook which he'd been made to copy out over and over again (like the passage from Swift) resurfaced when he was filming *The Blockhouse*, forty years later. As a teacher imprisoned underground, Sellers' character, Rouquet, kills time chalking quotations over the walls:

> Now I am ten and growing tall
> My mother said to me
> Soon you will be strong enough
> To dive into the sea.

The little poem? Where did that come from? inquired a journalist who visited the set, a genuine dark and damp blockhouse deep under Guernsey. 'Oh, something I remembered from school,' shrugged Sellers, not willing to be drawn.

◆ ◆ ◆

The deep sea Sellers was diving into was that of his own imagination. He was stocking it with material which would be a bit more useful than his toilet flushing spells and household superstitions. At the same time as he was forestalling humiliation by hiding at the back of the class and praying for invisibility, he was also, as when in the wings, eavesdropping: 'I didn't talk much, I listened, and people thought I was shy.' The Rev. John Smallwood, in *Heavens Above*, is the obvious outcome of Sellers' attention to the details of this period. Sellers' priest, with his serene (and maddening) assurance and convictions, was inspired by the blessedly pure-hearted Brothers at St Aloysius'. Radiating a grin, which is often a smirk, Smallwood is too bloody smug for this world, and so he is shot skyward in a space rocket at the end. He orbits the planet as a star—a heavenly body.

Smallwood is not only a bachelor, he is sexless. It must be the only Sellers performance that is totally free from any bodily appetite—lust, greed, thirst, hunger, and so on. (Even Chance has to totter out of his garden and into the streets because his meals, which he is accustomed to receiving on the dot from Louise the maid, have stopped arriving.) With his thick-lensed oblong spectacles and his severely

---

* And again in 1980. Brother Cornelius, aged seventy-eight, attended Sellers' funeral and described his old pupil for the press as 'a quiet boy.'

brushed gleaming hair, Smallwood was an impersonation of Brother Cornelius. But Sellers' need for his teacher went beyond an actor's raw research. He kept up with the priest for the rest of his life, wanting, in some way, to acquire the man's certainties and composure. He treated Brother Cornelius as a guru, and Brother Hilary Cluderay, who was the Headmaster from 1960 to 1970, confirms that Sellers was 'often a private visitor,' usually bringing a gift or a cheque for the school funds.

It became his habit to revisit in times of personal anxiety and chaos. A St Aloysius' secretary from round about the time the marriage to Anne was disintegrating, recalls: 'He was here in a state. Very tearful. I think he saw Brother Cornelius as a sort of sanctuary. He had come back to seek comfort. He invested a spiritual value in the school.' He turned up again after his mother had died, when 'I'll See You Again' had been played at her cremation. This time he discussed receiving religious instruction and just stopped short of committing himself to becoming a Catholic. He was looking (in the absence of his first wife and his mother) for a way of life that did without women.

Sellers also made the acquaintance of an Anglican priest, Canon John Hester, now of Chichester Cathedral. He officiated at Sellers' funeral and had flown out to anoint the actor in California after the heart attack in 1964 ('we had a day of National Prayer for his recovery' says Wolf Mankowitz). Sellers was into Yoga. He was into the occult. He told the *Jewish Chronicle* 'I am fully Jewish ... a sentimental Jew ...' His son Michael puts it best: 'Dad could be Jewish, Moslem, Hindu, or any other religious faith on a given day. If someone offered a cut-price, special-offer-gift-wrapped religion that guaranteed miracles and a personal audience with the Maker, then Dad would apply for instant enrollment.'

Sellers wanted a direct line of communication with God—like the telephone wire between President Muffley, in the war room, and the (unseen) Russian premier, Dmitri Kissoff. (The end of the world is nigh and all they can do is bicker: 'I'm sorry too, Dmitri. I'm very sorry. All right, you're sorrier than I am, but I am sorry as well ...', etc.) Though Sellers' doctrinal loyalties were fickle, his search for infallibilities and order; his need to explain why, despite being successful in his career, he felt uncomfortable and morose; and why, since he was a comedian, his life yet felt stark and tragic—all these were constant concerns. More than anything, he wanted to know if there was any purpose, or calling, beneath his artistic skills. As his first wife said to me: 'When he started making those ghastly little films with the Goons, he'd ring me up and say "I don't know what to do with my hands." Later on he'd still be panicking: "I can't do this—I can't feel the man at all." Looking for the voice, and then it would fall into place. He'd hear a voice, which suggested a picture to him and his imagination would do the rest. Totally intuitive. No plan, structure, formula. It would either happen or it wouldn't.'

◆ ◆ ◆

Sellers wanted what he did to be, not corny, like revue, but full of texture and richness, like the presentation of the Latin Mass. He was thrilled when a real priest, the Rev. Ironmonger, watched him shoot the church service scene in

Heavens Above at Shepperton: '"Very convincing, very moving," he told me afterwards. It made me feel like taking the cloth.' Sellers always needed faith that his creativity was not a charade—that his performances had weight and strength. (This is what his search for perfection originally entailed.) The break-up of his marriages; the death of his mother; the dust and ashes of material success: traumas like these could trigger his insecurity and make him feel again the weakness of being the defenseless boy at the back of the Hornsey Lane classroom—who, knowing nothing, when asked to name one of the Seven Seas said 'the BBC'.

Emotionally a boy, he'd re-traverse his boyhood sites ('to see and discover and taste the places that kicked me off'); and the places represented moods which refused to drop away. This is why, when he talked about his neuroticism or this or that crisis ('I don't think there is such a thing, you see, as idyllic happiness' etc.) his tone always had a whining edge. He was petulant, and the very melodrama of his spiritual searchings, so to call them, suggests something trivial and shallow. No matter how patient his inquiries with Brother Cornelius or Canon Hester or Wolf Mankowitz, his desire, really, was for *gratification*—of a kind not procurable in the normal way. Spiritual well-being was the one thing he could not send his handyman, Bert Mortimer, over to Harrods to buy; the one thing nobody could give him in part exchange for a red Lamborghini Miura. There is farce, here, in the notion of this wildly impatient creature trying with all his might to discover what makes holy men tick. Sometimes he'd be hysterical at the lack of an answer (he led Canon Hester a dance); at other times he'd be plaintive. 'I'm just a real right twit,' he told an audience at the National Film Theatre. 'I am only a little thing,' he'd wheedle to Lynne Frederick, in the aftermath of some outrage, 'I am really Bluebottle and nothing else. All this acting is brown paper and string.' He'd disarm people, keep himself at a distance, by pretending to be a tattered Boy Scout, concerned with nothing much more than dolly mixtures (candy) and train spotting. He would become at will a manipulative child.

Hence the coyness of the telegram he sent to his school from America, when he was filming *Being There*, his essay on infantilism. He had promised to contribute a whole article to the Centenary Brochure, but in the end cabled:

> TO THE BOYS OF ST ALOYSIUS' COLLEGE. PETER SELLERS WAS EDUCATED HERE, BUT TO NO AVAIL STOP HE TURNED OUT A RIGHT TWIT STOP SEE THAT YOU DON'T DO THE SAME STOP EXCELSIOR! PETER SELLERS.

♦ ♦ ♦

Of course it was by no means all unavailing. He didn't get topped up with solemn things and academic knowledge, but school was no less character-forming for that. The combination of crafty naivety, genuine ignorance, and saving shafts of quick-wittedness—all features of the Sellers known to Bryan Connon and Gerald Meteau—underprop many of Sellers' characters, starting with Inspector Clouseau. And if the St Aloysius' era gave him a taste of mockery and a fear of being thought worthless, it did nothing to alter his loneliness. His chief company, apart from his mother, was to be found on the screen and out of the radio. 'Early on in life,' he once said, 'I found that *sounds* fascinated me. I became a listener.' Connon was a witness to this. When walking home from school, Sellers would imitate the goings-on of the school day: 'We were two boys,' says Connon, 'playing the fool. Him inventing the plots, me doing some of the dialogue. We'd use characters from... radio shows... what's interesting is not the wealth of his impersonations—boys of that age are always doing characters and noises... The point is more that he suddenly came so *alive*, on that twenty-five minute walk home. He changed completely, when talking about the radio or films. He was mad about the radio—he could do all the voices. Then we'd arrive at Peg's, on Muswell Hill Road, and Sellers would change again. An extrovert away from the school gates, and then he'd go back into his shell just as we reached his front door. I didn't live far away at all and it is a curious facet of my having known Sellers that there was absolutely none of the interplay between the two homes that you might normally expect. I think I'd been keen to go into his house one day, but his mother was *not* encouraging about the idea. There was no encouragement for any people of his own age to become part of his life. No contact.'

◆ ◆ ◆

If Peg wanted to keep Sellers to herself, she could not prevent the conversations he might conduct in his head, or behind closed doors, with radio stars like Robb Wilton or Tommy Handley, when he felt the need to challenge his sequestration. Nor could she stop him from peopling his imagination with the cinema. Asked once who he would like to have been, who was his main movie love, he said 'Just about everybody really.' The throng on the sound stage and screen made up for the solitariness of his life at home. The first film he saw, *The Gold Diggers of 1933*, had impressed him for just that reason: 'There were a lot of people moving on the screen. Big dance routines going on...' Busby Berkeley's geometric choreography, the girls forming and re-forming as shapes and grand pianos, or tip-tapping on aeroplane propellers and such, was a Ray Bros. revue with knobs on. Noisy, blowsy, absurd. As regards individuals, Sellers first fell for Loretta Young, and his first impersonation, around the house, was of Don Ameche, amongst the whoo-whoo of an angelic choir, making his folksy farewells in the Western *Ramona*. The trouble was, there was nobody at St Aloysius' who looked like Loretta Young—'so I went around wearing this Apache band around my hair, with a terrible headache, and when it slipped I nearly garrotted myself. However, such is life.'

Sellers also said he lost his heart to Hedy Lamarr, whom he saw in a Czech film called *Extase*: 'Her husband tried later to buy up all the copies—he considered it a naughty film [*Bluebottle voice*] not suitable for young men to see because they could come to harm, see. [*Normal voice*] I don't care if I do come to harm. I went with a friend of mine to see it at the Electric Palace on Highgate Hill. He said "During a certain place in this film what is on there, she runs across the screen, and you can see *it* as she goes past." That was enough for me. We rushed in there. I was wearing a heavy leather overcoat and was muffled up to the eyebrows, trying to do an impersonation of an eighty-year-old man, and actually we sat next to an eighty-year-old man, heavily perspiring, who said "Do you come here often?" "Only during the Lamarr season, you know." Anyway, we waited for this moment—and she ran across the screen so quickly that I couldn't see anything at all. I said "When is it going to happen?" And the old man said, "It went there—it's gone now."

'Later, when I was at the Windmill, when things didn't go by *quite* so quickly, one was reminded of that. By that time I'd got over the aches and pains of the Electric Palace, Highgate Hill.'

♦ ♦ ♦

Sellers' first erections coincided with his grandmother's death and his father's decision to walk out. Through Ma's family connections with the Mendoza Estate Agency, of Sidmouth Parade, Willesden, they had all had hutches to inhabit; through Ma, again, and Ray Bros. Productions Ltd., there had been employment. And they knew they were expected to be grateful. Homage had to be accorded Crystal Jollibottom-cum-Grand Duchess Gloriana. 'I remember her quite well,' said Sellers in 1962. 'I remember whenever one of my uncles gave me a toy or anything, she always used to say to me: "Your grandma gave you that…'

If Peg overbore Sellers, Ma manipulated Peg. Part of Peg's grief over the death of the first Peter lay in her failure to produce a grandchild—and she was approaching thirty when the lost boy was replaced. The Mendozas had always had huge families (today there are over seven hundred names on the ten generation pedigree which goes back to the eighteenth-century prize fighter), but Peg settled for Sellers. He was the focus for her attention, gave Ma somebody else to think about, and he easily eclipsed her already feeble feelings for Bill. Bill, indeed, was not simply the pit pianist. When he was approached in that Portsmouth café, his offer of a new job depended on whether he could drive a motor car. There was thus, from the start, an element of the underling in his rôle. He was primarily Ma's chauffeur, steering her scarlet Ford whilst she sat in the back, amidships, waving at people out shopping on the Edgeware Road—a scene even more out of *The Mouse That Roared*.

When Peg and Ma stayed at the Bedford after the premiere of *Ha! Ha!! Ha!!!*, the mahout duties lapsed and Bill was gone; and when Ma died, sometime before 1933, Bill was even less needed or welcome around the premises. When the revue organisation went out of business, having finally been obliterated by the cinema, he went off on his own, with his friend Arthur Lewis, to play the piano at dances and bars. It was now that Peg moved to Muswell Hill and took over the lease of a junk shop. The shop dealt in broken furniture, chipped china and glass, and utensils made out of copper. Peg was an outlet for the rubbish left behind in the Mendoza property by departing tenants. She augmented the stock by knocking on people's doors and asking them for their old clothes, spoutless tea pots, non-legal tender coins. These trips she called 'totting' or 'golding' and Peg would hope to charm her customers into giving away at least some decent trinkets with their dross. Sellers was impressed by his mother's patter as she exhorted and connived. As a set routine it was as impressive as the Brothers of Our Lady of Mercy chanting psalms: 'Good-morning-madam-I'm-from-the-London-Gold-Refining-Company-and-we-are-very-interested-in-purchasing...

Some excursions were made with an 'Uncle Joe Barnet', who had a car. A spurious relative, hailing from the district of Friern Barnet in north London, not far from Muswell Hill at all, Uncle Joe kept Peg amused and ferried her about. 'Oi, oi, fat arse,' he'd shout at lady cyclists. But, said Sellers, 'he did have a smashing car... I vowed then that one day I would own a car of my own, a great car, the best there was.' (A machine, as it were, with which, like Uncle Joe, he could whisk his mother away.)

◆ ◆ ◆

'Ever since I was a kid I knew one thing. That if I ever had enough money I would buy cars, cars, cars...' And he did: literally hundreds of them, from the humble (a Mini Cooper) to the grandiose (a Daimler Conquest); from the mundane (a Volkswagen) to the exotic (a Lotus Elan); from the sublime (a Rolls-Royce) to the ridiculous (an ambulance, kitted out with a stretcher, which would whizz the busy and momentarily prostrate actor between appointments).

The shortest time he ever owned a car was two hours: 'An AC. Took it out in the morning. Didn't like it. Took it back in the afternoon. Traded it in for an early one-and-a-half-litre Jag, which had a very tiny motor and very heavy coachwork—it was all you could do to keep the car going. Silver with red upholstery. That was the main thing—you could use it as a home, really. "Come and visit me in my car."'

Milligan regarded Sellers' private motor show with not quite amusement, as he explained to me: 'Always changing his cars, Peter. I used to call it Metal Underwear because he used to change them so regularly. But he played an appalling trick on me. In the early days of our relationship he bought an Austin 12 Soft-Top Tourer, 1929. My wife bought it off him. This car went backwards and forwards between us about four times. Finally, not long before his death, I was about to go to Australia, and he turned up at the door with the car, all restored, and with a bottle of Dom Perignon: "I want to give you this car as a present. It belongs to you. You've spent more time in it with your family than me." When I was in Australia, he decided to have it taken away and sold. That's one of the things he did—I don't know whether because of his illness, or what. Whenever he gave people things, there was always lurking in the back of his mind the thought that he wanted the gifts back. He gave Alan Clare a piano—that was taken away...'

I told Milligan that during my delvings I'd found a yellowing, closely typed list, pages and pages long, of all the license plate numbers of all the cars that Sellers had once possessed. 'It's like his testament...' Milligan didn't speak for a while. He sat stock-still and pale-eyed.

'Very sad,' he said at last, in a cracked and feathery monotone. 'A sad ending. That's sad. He left great pools of sadness...'

◆ ◆ ◆

The absence of Bill ensured that, between mother and son, there were no serious rivals for affection. And if Bill was an absent presence in Sellers' life, he has been a lacuna in my research. Other writers have turned him into a cliché: 'a quietly graceful grey-haired man with sadly amused eyes' (Evans); 'the shy, quietly spoken Yorkshireman who came from dour but solid farming folk' (Draper); 'Bill Sellers came of the sort of country stock that always lent a hand to the neighbours in season. He had the look of a farmer's son, he was good natured and he also did as he was bid' (Walker); 'Bill originated from Yorkshire ... He came from a working-class home in which family discipline was strong ... Unlike the more dominant and animated Peg, he was modest, quiet and shy, prepared to play a supporting rôle which he uncomplainingly fulfilled throughout his lifetime' (Michael Sellers); 'He seemed to exist in a private world of peace at any price, particularly where Peg was concerned, and it's some indication of their relationship that you never thought of them as husband and wife, only as Bill and Peg' (Stark).

Bill has been turned into Chance the gardener from *Being There*, vapid, tossing hay, doing his best to deflect the stings and irritabilities of his wife, who could be a part for Agnes Moorehead at her most vampish. The fact is, far from being the weak man Peg wanted (like her father, Solomon Marks, another faceless male in this story: 'Nobody ever said whether he was successful or not, so I expect he wasn't,' said Sellers), Bill had had considerable resource: (a) to leave tenant farming for show business; (b) to endure Peg for as long as he did; and (c) to have generated the following curriculum vitae: Sellers claimed that his father was in the Royal Navy in the First World War and the Merchant Navy in the Second. He was a ship's cook on the SS. *Riveaulx Abbey* and sang 'There'll Be Plenty Of Boys In Khaki By The Sea' in the mess. He had been an organist and choirmaster at Bradford Cathedral and had become estranged from his family after appearing— so sinfully—at the Alhambra Theatre. He was Talbot O'Farrell's accompanist and Tallulah Bankhead's when she was in cabaret. He was a cricketer for Yorkshire. And (lastly) 'legend has it that he taught George Formby the ukulele—I don't know whether he ever did actually, but he used to boast about it. Anyway he probably did, because he was quite good on guitar.'

Bill is the Apocryphal Man. Did he spin all these yarns himself, or did Sellers invent a background for his parent, augmenting and elaborating upon the fantasies he'd been handed? Mrs Barbara L. Craven, Administrator of Bradford Cathedral, responded to my query by saying 'I have made several enquiries about Mr Bill Sellers, but regret to say I have not been successful.' He nowhere appeared in the muniments as organist or chorist. The department of the Head of Navy Pay, Pensions and Conditions of Service, based in the Old Admiralty Buildings, London, could not help; neither could the Departmental Record Offices of the Ministry of Defense (Navy Search Division). The Registrar General of the General Register and Record Office of Shipping and Seamen also made a thorough search of the files but failed to find any trace of Sellers' father.

It is one thing not to have been a war hero; not to have played county class cricket. It is quite another to have left such little evidence of your passing that you

may as well have been disembodied, a revenant, all along. Hence the poignancy
of *The Side Show* write-ups—proofs that Bill did put in an appearance. But though
Bill has faded into insignificance (archivally) and stereotype (biographically), what
may reasonably be hypothesised about the father of Peter Sellers?

That he had the determination (or fecklessness) to leave the farm outside
Bingley and to descend into the theatrical world (perhaps indeed first learning
some musical skills in the manse) suggests that a creative need took him there. He
was worlds away from the entertainment tradition of the Mendozas, and he enjoyed being affiliated with it—it was like a boy's dream of running away to join a
circus. 'Our Willie' had become Bill and, unlike Peg, who tagged along with Ma,
he had chosen his career—and, again unlike her, the protectiveness of family feeling was not something he took for granted. If the Jews felt generically ostracised,
Bill knew cold shouldering from personal experience. By going into the music hall
he had put himself, as far as his kin were concerned, outside the clan. Despite the
attempt to appease the Sellars' side by calling a son Richard Henry, when Bill took
the boy to meet the grandparents in Yorkshire he was met off the three o'clock
Express with the words 'There's a good train goes back at five.'

If all that Tallulah Bankhead/playing cricket stuff is invention, as it has to be,
then Bill, like his son (when playing Dr Pratt et, no doubt, al.), was a dreamer and
romantic. And it is Bill, I think, not Peg, who is Sellers' precursor as an actor.
Peg's function was to provide the fire of ambition—but it was Bill's career, as a
musician, which Sellers was first to follow. He was an ironist, too. When Sellers
was swankily taking his parents over the Harlequin Suite at the Dorchester, Bill
said, with a view to defusing the playboy pretensions, 'Yes, Peter, nice, but nothing that a good joanna [piano] wouldn't improve.'

It has obviously been all too easy to mistake the nature of Bill's meekness and
quiet, which I think points away from compliance. The busker's voice in *The Optimists of Nine Elms*, and that film's Formby and Formby-esque songs, acknowledge
the timbre and repertoire of Sellers' father. Old Sam's loneliness, too, is Bill's—and
his peppery temper. Bill is less Chance in *Being There* than Sellers' many rebels and
reactionaries—characters like Mr Martin in *The Battle of the Sexes*, who would like
nothing more than to kill the chirpy, interfering Mrs Barrows; or the lawyer in *I
Love You, Alice B. Toklas*, who exchanges his suit for a hippy's motley; or the embattled Fred Kite… Sellers' muted, deeper characters (as opposed to his outright caricatures). From Bill, Sellers learned the art of stillness and observation; and where
Peg tried to interfuse herself with him, Sellers saw his father as someone separate
and individual. Bill was independent, and as such, in his interplay with other people, he could be subtle and variegated—and this was misread as anonymousness.
Bill silently putting up with Peg is Sellers at St Aloysius', seeing the virtues of being inconspicuous—but let no man say that inwardly you cannot seethe.*

◆ ◆ ◆

At the end of the summer term, in 1939, it was announced that St Aloysius'

---

* When this book is made into a film the actor to play Bill is Sir Anthony Hopkins.

would close and that its pupils must prepare to evacuate to Stainsby Hall, Smalley, near Derby, for the following October. Sellers, who would not be fourteen (when mandatory education ceased) until the September, by rights should have been schooled for a further term. But Peg, her nerves abraded by the German bomb which had totalled her junk shop, wasn't having that—and Sellers never in his life caught up. She decided to gather her family—i.e., find Bill—and retreat to the country, taking with her an antique copper kettle belonging to a Mrs Clarke. Bill was needed, quite simply, because without him Peg would never get a job—the quasi-divorced Jewess with an overweight son to support. Bill could find work piano-playing or something and Peg herself could tear tickets and take people's coats.

They went to Ilfracombe—where the Rays, or Wreys as it was spelled in Devon, were meant to have a connection with the Victoria Pavilion Theatre, though I have found no evidence that one of Peg's brothers owned the place, as Sellers maintained. ('The Pavilion Theatre was burned down afterwards. I think that killed my uncle—the loss of his theatre,' said Sellers airily in 1962, of a building still standing today.) The manager was a Mr A. Humphrey, and when in 1921 the theatre was enlarged, to accommodate an extra eight hundred people, the improvements were planned and paid for by the District Council.

The rendezvous with Bill took place in St Martin's Lane, near Long Acre. Seeing his father again was an important enough event for Sellers to want to stop and stare at the spot over forty years later. 'It's just over there,' he said to his male companion, Michael Jeffery, the two of them standing and looking. 'Me and me mum came to meet Bill.'

They had got together again. It was still going through his mind.

Chapter Two

♦ ♦ ♦

Wartime

'You see … I was evacuated to Ilfracombe during the war,' Sellers told Freddy Clayton, a trumpeter in 'The Goon Show' orchestra, 'and it was there that I got my first professional job … I joined one of the leading bands of the day …' 'Which one?' asked Clayton eagerly, thinking of Geraldo or Victor Silvester. 'Waldini,' said Sellers. 'Who?' asked Clayton, mystified. 'Waldini,' said Sellers again, rather flatly, his expression growing pained, 'Surely you remember him?'

Waldini was really Wally Bishop (b. 1895), who'd graduated from accompanying silent movies at the Olympia, Queen Street, Cardiff, to playing a cello in Roath Park and Sophia Gardens. Along with Bill Morgan, Benny Lodwick, George Cromer, and Cliff Thomas, clarinettists and guitarists, he dressed up in colourful bandanas, made a gimmick out of Romany accoutrements, demoted himself from a Bishop to a Dean, took the Y off Wally, and Waldini and his Gypsy Band were born.

'Peter Sellers started with us,' confirmed Elaine Parsons, the accordionist in Waldini's Gypsy Band, when I spoke to her in Wales. 'He started with us in Ilfracombe. His father used to play the piano and his mother worked in the box office at the Victoria Pavilion Theatre. Peter, who was a jolly boy, dabbled in the drums, and I used to play along with him, to help his rhythm, in the empty hall. He used to enjoy keeping time. There used to be tea-dances in the town, another band on the pier, another on the bandstand itself, by Capstone Parade—Waldini had three bands going and Peter was generally in one of them … This was just before the war. The beaches were coiled with barbed wire and a lot of the amusements were shuttered up.'

By chance, a recording of one of Waldini's Ilfracombe performances, in which Sellers participates, has survived. The seaside show is full of communal singing, operetta, clapping along and full-throated emotional stuff. When the accordion dominates, it's like a circus band; when the violin takes over, with the piano in support, it's colourful and jaunty, but with an undertone of melancholy. ('There are tears on the string of a gypsy's violin,' sang Sellers in a Waldini-inspired sketch on 'The Muppet Show'.) The ballads are songs about loss, and it is spooky, hearing these voices and artistes coming through the crackle, holding nothing back, promising that we'll gather lilacs in the Spring again and walk together down an English lane. Now aged and retired (or dead) there is a forlorn atmosphere about these stout coryphées and limelit tenors—an atmosphere that is to do with the whole rough magic of show business. Deepening it, too, is the

knowledge that, under the cover of music such as this, Sellers' parents were reuniting after up to a decade of being apart. They were returning to the sort of
low-level theatrics where they'd met, courted, and begun married life, and they
were getting together as a couple, for the very first time without Ma and the extended family. But now there was Peter, and the trouble was, as Peg used to crow,
'Peg never left Peter and Peter never left Peg. Did we, Bill?' 'You never did,' he
had to concede.

Ilfracombe, where Sellers was to spend the only three years of his life that was
in a single place, was the last word in seaside genteelisms. It is Henry Crun's back-
drop in 'The Goon Show', Mrs Wilberforce's in *The Ladykillers*. In the cafés and
hotels, guests drank Chelspa Natural Aperient Water (for functional disorders of
the digestive tract), and if they ventured up Capstone Hill or Lantern Hill to view
Lundy Island or the South Wales coast across the waves and foam, there were
plenty of benches and cast-iron shelters, 'so that visitors can remain in the open
air even on rough days without inconvenience, a matter of no slight importance
to invalids.'

Bill had joined the troupe and went on their incursions into Bideford and
Barnstaple on Sundays and Thursday nights for hunt balls, with Blodwen, Singer
Superb (Welsh Eisteddfod Winner), Elaine and her Accordion, and Jeanne
Humphries, posthorn. Peg tried to make herself useful looking after the tinker
costumes, but Sellers had much more mundane tasks than even being a launderer
and darner. 'My mother used to say that you should never ask anybody in the
theatre to do another job you couldn't do yourself. So I was an apprentice,
sweeping out after the performance. That was the first job—I got ten bob a
week. And then after that I used to take tickets on the door; then I did front of
house which, as most people know, is box office, and then from box office I went
to assistant stage manager'—and he operated the limelights and, when companies arrived with a play, trying it out before going up to the West End, he was
co-opted as a dresser.

Sellers saw Paul Scofield and Mary Clare, pupils from the London Mask
Theatre School, now evacuated to nearby Bideford, who brought Emlyn
Williams' *Night Must Fall* to the town. ('Not long ago I met Scofield,' said Sellers
in 1962. 'I said, "I bet you don't remember where we met first time"—and of
course he didn't'.) When Joe Mitchenson arrived, Sellers was asked to go out and
get cream fancies from J.H. Hasking, the baker and confectioner, 105 High
Street.

'He got us all to sign his autograph book,' recalled Mitchenson for me. 'He
was the cleaner—and very proud of the theatre, *very* proud of it. He was very kind,
and we all treated him well…I often wonder about the boy at Ilfracombe, who
was always being around. Peter Sellers! And he went out and bought us cakes…'

◆ ◆ ◆

The opportunity to rise from general factotum to performer had come on
Friday, October 11, 1940:

PARTY NIGHT
Waldini requests the pleasure
A Really Jolly Night.
Can you Sing, Dance or Act?
Prices of Admission 2/-, 1/- and 6d.
Members of H.M. Forces (in uniform) Half Price

Coaxed by Peg and coached by Elaine, Sellers decided to have a crack. He teamed himself with a local barber's boy called Derek Altman, with whom, as Selman Investigations Inc., he'd hunted for people's lost cats (when he should have been at large distributing posters). They strummed a ukulele and told a goonish story about a mad Greek oboist who was threatening the lives of the band. Their opening chorus went thus:

We're Altman and Sellers,
The younger generation,
We always sing in the best syncopation,
And we hope we make a big sensation
With you-ooh-ooh!

'I suppose people knew us from seeing us give out tickets and so on,' said Sellers later, 'and probably they were well disposed towards us. Anyhow, we won.' The prize was a fiver, or about ten dollars.

Bill was sufficiently impressed to arrange music lessons for his son. Sellers was hopeless on the piano, having no patience, and he refused even to go and meet a replacement teacher when the first one had been sent packing (the first known instance of the future actor's highhandedness). What Elaine knew he wanted to concentrate on, however, was the drums. If ever she asked him 'How are you today, Peter?' or 'Where are you off?' or 'What's for dinner?' he'd answer, regardless, 'I want to be a drummer!' When a band called Joe Daniels and his Hotshots had come to Ilfracombe on an engagement, and Sellers was allowed to have a bash on the drum kit once he'd removed the fruit rinds and dirty beer glasses off the stage, Sellers told his mother: 'Now I know what I want. I want to be a drummer.' Bill made arrangements with Harold Leeding, Waldini's percussionist, to have Sellers tutored properly. 'In the empty theatre, lit only by a working light, I would take over his drums...'

◆ ◆ ◆

'...it was the drums that I was really keen on in the early days,' Sellers said a quarter of a century later. 'I suddenly went mad about the drums. I spent months learning from a professional drummer; and I was pretty good.' Good enough to appear twice in Waldini's *Symphony in Colour*, in August 1941.

Waldini was eased out of Ilfracombe by, of all things, Lydia Kyasht and the Imperial ballet from St. Petersburg (Book Early to Avoid Disappointment), so Sellers and his father had to traipse the West Country, playing in pubs for two or three pounds a night. If the discipline of reading music and the precision of most instruments was beyond the boy, the ability to absorb himself in the beat and thump, the rolls and riffs of snares and timps, was evidence of a perhaps deeper and more instinctive talent. Jazz drumming, as Sellers knew it, was both forceful, brutal—physical—and nostalgic. The music of slavery and migration, there was drama in it—and Sellers abandoned playing professionally when, after the war, he was unable to play expressively. Having to do what he was told at sedate ballroom dance evenings was not for him; the point about being a drummer was the freedom—being able to 'let loose and enjoy myself.'

There is a link to be made between Sellers' style of solo drumming and his eventual method of acting. Both must appear to be spontaneous, and both have a buoyancy, a weightlessness, which for all its skill and charm must, at its best, remain subversive, even belligerent. I'm thinking of Clare Quilty in *Lolita*, pinioning Humbert Humbert with gags and a rapidity of disguises; and Fred Kite, wearily treading across his carpet, wistful and defeated, his silent thoughts about his wife and erring daughter set to music by the sad, echoey trumpet and drum tattoo on the soundtrack. When he was making *The Magic Christian* with Ringo, 'I don't think we spoke about anything else other than drums and drummers.' Learning to play the drums, Sellers learned all about tempo.

With the drums he also discovered sex. The rush of excitement he felt when making music coincided with the hormonal thrum. This was different from Hedy Lamarr's puzzling gallop across the screen in *Exstase*. His sensibilities were newly stirred, like the 'boom-tiddy-boom' pulse Dr Kabir arouses in Sophia Loren in *The Millionairess*, or the tom-toms knocking and gyrating in Richard Rodney Bennett's score when the librarian is turned on in *Only Two Can Play*. Feeling very masculine, because he was an employed, professional musician, in demand at fifteen because anybody any older would be in the services, Sellers put his coat across his shoulders and took girls along the cliff paths to Bull Point Lighthouse, there to see the white beam giving three flashes in quick succession every thirty seconds, and to watch the secret signals giving warning to mariners, now that Ilfracombe had its naval defenses against German submarines lurking off the Bristol Channel. Or he took the ladies to the pier, claiming that he was related to its benefactors, the Wreys. But what he didn't do was take any girls out as Peter Sellers. Knowing himself to be plain and stout, he did his best to effect a transformation into Robert Donat—a winsome, bittersweet sort of an actor who had impressed Sellers in *Knight Without Armour*, which he'd seen at the Odeon, Swiss Cottage, when he was twelve.

'I was crazy about Robert Donat,' he said, 'and the girls I was with, they were pretty mad about him too, and I thought to myself—well, here is a chance to do an impersonation of him. You see, I could be, in a way, a bit like Robert Donat, but a girl's other crush, Errol Flynn—I hadn't a chance, you see. But at least I could *sound* slightly like Robert Donat—which I did. I remember I could say the word "because" like Robert Donat—the only word I could say, so I fiddled the others so that "because" came right in the middle. I relied on the "because" very strongly. She was very impressed, and she said "*More!*" and I said "*Because!*" again! I remember I was kissing her goodnight. I said "Well, I have to go now, dear, *because...*" [*breaking into Bluebottle*], "Because my mother says I have to go home."'

Prepubertal Bluebottle's balls eventually fell into place in Taunton. Sellers was with his father, who was beginning to associate himself with ENSA (Entertainments National Service Association) units and to drift apart again from Peg. They stayed the night at a hostel—rooms above an undertakers, Sellers claimed— and Sellers was invited to take advantage of the black-out by coming in to comfort one of the women instrumentalists, who found the dwelling a bit macabre. Sellers developed this into quite an anecdotal set-piece in later life, where his de-virgin-ification involved falling over a coffin and virtually having the corpse on the floor into the bargain.

If sex and death were entwined from the first, more to the point might have been Peg's unique absence from Sellers' side. She was stuck back in Ilfracombe, helping the ballerinas get their tutus on. She normally slept with her Peter (Bill took a separate room or the couch), so it was a wrench when Sellers announced he was going to Lytham St Anne's with his father, who was taking a job as concert party pianist for the 1942 summer season. Didn't this mean, at the very least, that he was leaving the Victoria Pavilion's set of drums behind? He'd take up the ukulele instead—hadn't he won the talent contest with a banjo when he was more or less just messing about? What about Waldini? He was going to Drury Lane, the ENSA Headquarters, to receive instructions for taking the Gypsy Band around RAF camps and hospitals...

As a bid for independence it was short-lived. Peg hadn't thought to follow her husband north, but she'd follow her son.

◆ ◆ ◆

Waldini and his vagabonds were eventually pressed into service overseas, and Elaine wore out fourteen accordions under enemy fire. They toured through Italy, North Africa, India, Ceylon, and Burma, where they met Sellers again. And such was Waldini's enjoyment of these adventures (his son, Ron Bishop, told me it was the only era of guaranteed employment, income, and gratitude) that the postwar end-of-the-pier shows continued to have an ENSA structure and theme. Whether you were at Llandudno or Ilfracombe, it made no difference: 'You are not at the seaside,' Waldini told the holidaymakers, 'You are under the blazing sun of North Africa'—and his gypsies would pretend to make their entrance on camels. Waldini would then give an illustrated lecture on 'the little people of the stage, the unknowns' (such as himself), who'd rig up a rostrum in an engine shed and have car lamps for footlights and upturned petrol cans for seats. During the war, Waldini was at long last like a gypsy baron, his caravan rocking and rolling across the desert.

◆ ◆ ◆

The little people of the stage included Sellers himself until he became indispensible to radio producers, clamoured after, just prior to 'The Goon Show'. The unknowns certainly numbered Bill and any of the survivors of Ray Bros. Productions Ltd. The reason I have belaboured the music hall background and heaped up the detail is that Sellers, who emotionally lived in the past, lived in *this* past. Milligan described Sellers to me as 'Little Boy Lost—Forever'; and what he was adrift from were these experiences of his childhood and early youth, when he'd been implanted with a sensation of acting's magical properties, and had perceived, too, its sorrow and dejections. The grief which he carried within him had its origins at the end-of-the-pier and in third-rate variety houses, where he saw, yes, the shoddiness of glamour ('I don't like the smell of grease paint... It used to waft out from the stage. I hated it...') but, more importantly, he became aware of people's need for fantasy and delusion; he saw that a demand for romance was not the audience's, or even his own (though it was that also), so much as a matter of life and death for the misfit actors and performers themselves. Sellers could see the deficiencies between the aspirations and the achievements, and no artist has ever been so expert as he in expressing the tragedy of that gap between people's feelings and their skill.

This is most easily instanced by referring to Sellers' comic songs. Time and again he becomes the wheezy, rheumy old Cockney, proudly giving a concert in what turns out to be the bathroom. Or he puts his grandiloquent Shakespeareans through the humiliation of an audition ('Oh, will somebody *please* get him out of here...' murmurs the shit of a director). A salty rendition of 'Thank Heavens, you know, for little girls,' the voice Chevalier's mingled with the March Hare's from *Alice's Adventures in Wonderland,* is accompanied by a lusty military brass band— but then it fades away to be replaced with traffic noises. The glorious number was the daydream of a French cop directing traffic.

Sellers' characters never let go of their dignity. Even when they are drunks, he gets their mock-gravity across. 'In A Free State' has a violent Irishman (Brendan Behan) smashing glasses and fighting his way to the gents lavatory, throwing a punch at the interviewer along the way. The joke is that the rascal thinks he's in the right, whereas really he's simply in a world of his own (like the bath-tub crooners, whose imaginations supply the orchestral strings). 'Suddenly It's a Folk Song' wonderfully sends up a bucolic idyll. The singers in the Somerset pub are drunk, the Irish jig is a drunken brawl, and the Scottish tenor weaves in and out of the Sauchiehall Street rush hour, staggering on and off the pavement, waving a bottle.

When they sing, Sellers' creations are either inebriates, buskers, or flops. His Palm Court artiste, attempting to trill 'Only A Rose' against an out-of-tune piano and a jeering audience, which make him start to forget the lyrics and fail to keep time, is funny because it is superbly executed, but also sad. Very often, his troubadours are out in the road, a drum and cymbal strapped to their backs, giving their all for throw money. 'Unchained Melody,' for example, a number by Bluebottle and Eccles, is packed with the shrieks, crashes, and thumps of a one-man-band.

There are dozens of such numbers, thirty years' worth. Many end with destruction and noise—with some form of outright physical violence or personal decrepitude. This was the fate, week upon week, of the characters in 'The Goon Show'. Major Denis Bloodnok is always ambushed and caught thieving, his impeccable Zulu War-era credentials exposed as cowardice and disloyalty, but by some miracle Sellers makes him lovable. Bluebottle, the epitome of acne-daubed adolescence ('dressed in brown paper, cardboard and string'), is consistently mangled, but sustains himself with his heroic dreams—he thinks he is reincarnating

Errol Flynn in *Dawn Patrol*. Henry Crun, misplaced in the 1950s, keeps himself alive by thinking it is still only the 1850s (so he is therefore not as ancient as he sounds); and Grytpype Thynne, an unsuccessful confidence trickster, who had to think up a new scam for Neddie Seagoon every week for over ten years, overlooks the farce his life has become by studious rôle-play: he's George Sanders or Basil Rathbone really, his ragged familiar, Moriarty, an aristocrat from France—Comte Toulouse-Moriarty of the House of Roland. ('Under Grytpype's careful management he is now bald, daft, deaf, and worthless.')

In Sellers' menagerie, nothing is what it seems. Fools triumph; the self-confident collapse under the pressure of their pretensions. And, if you look for recurrences of theme and fetish in his work, across the whole span of his life, it is (a) the threat of failure versus the melancholia of what-might-have-been which gives his characters heart and (b) his best characters, like Clouseau, are the ones who don't know they are funny. Beyond the hopeless serenaders and the classical actors muffing their lines on the record sketches and tapes, the dark theme of the blundering and fatigued music hall entertainer is at the core of Sellers' ability to be (say) Percy Quill, in *The Smallest Show On Earth*, gazing in rapture at the unreachable idyll on the silent movie screen; General Fitzjohn in *Waltz of the Toreadors*, realising he married the wrong woman and that life has lost its savour; the useless matador in *The Bobo* ('Don't you cry for the bulls that die/Save your tears for the men'); the useless pianist in *The World of Henry Orient*, pursued by two girls who have overvalued his talent; the useless doctor in *The Wrong Box*, thinking his stethoscope tube is part of his own entrails... A large part of Sellers' personality and imagination remained stranded in his early years, and we can account for his anxieties, his inability to settle at a single address, his obsession with identity, by realising that, when he looked back to the embankments and castellated hotels of Ilfracombe, touring revue, etc. with disgust, it was because it was as frightening as a fairy story.

◆ ◆ ◆

What was crucial were his surroundings, the forces at work before his own birth (which lay traps for him), what he absorbed and saw. It all lay in his mind, like shadows and fog that wouldn't lift. The dilapidations of the barrister in *The Dock Brief* (who semi-minces like a failed matinée idol); Fred Kite's defeats; the loneliness of Mr Topaze when he makes his corrupt million; the disappointments of John Lewis in *Only Two Can Play* ('Don't stand there giving me that little-boy face, you're getting too old for it'); the imbecility of the pirates in *Ghost in the Noonday Sun*, who got lost in the Aegean and stumble upon Ireland... The innermost purpose of Sellers' acting was to reproduce people making fools of themselves—when they fall in love (*Only Two Can Play*, *Hoffman*), or want to blow up the world (*Doctor Strangelove*), or have lots of sex (*Lolita*; *Soft Beds, Hard Battles*), or think they are irresistible (*There's a Girl In My Soup*), etc.—and to build on them extravagantly, robustly. Sellers catches his characters coping with fresh or strong emotions (jealousy, temptation, libido, fear). The return of a girlfriend from the past, the suggestiveness of something better, the chance to change—all this makes his tribe of major-generals and flâneurs suddenly stand out against their backgrounds. They become people, like those on a stage, who know we are looking at them. And if the source of Sellers' art was in recalling the sufferings and gaudy exposures of music hall, which were also never far below the surface of his own personal craving to escape from drabness (and thus linked all too closely with his follies and instincts), he also feared he'd return to the end of the pier one day and be like the character in *The Optimists of Nine Elms*, living off alms, or McGonagall (whom Sellers played on television long before appearing as Queen Victoria in Milligan's film), writing those poems nobody wants. As his career self-destructed in the seventies, with unfinished and unreleased whole movies, it was almost as if he was willing, engineering, a decline and fall back to basics.

In one respect, at least, he *did* go back to the open-air concert party. In July 1976, John Wells invited him to make a guest appearance in a programme called 'The End Of The Pier Show', which John Bird describes as 'a non-budget thing shot in the BBC's smallest studio—smaller than the one they do the weather from.' Wells himself says: 'I was so amazed to be working with my childhood hero, I still find it hard to be objective. He was really surprisingly kind. I once rang him on a Friday night to ask him if he'd be in a Saturday recording as Adolf Hitler with Percy Edwards, the bird impersonator, as Hercule Poirot...and he turned up and did it for virtually nothing.'

That Sellers, who was a versatile mimic amongst many other things, had to share the billing with a comedian who came across as a noisy simpleton and who made his living by squawking, whistling, and screeching, is a joke in itself. Wells' entertainment began with a seaside cinema organ and silent movie piano tinkles, and Sellers provided eager BBC announcer voices, Churchill's slack-jawed growl, and then came on as Hitler, giving a rendering of Noël Coward's 'Past Forgetting'. It all takes place in a railway carriage—*Murder on the 9.36 from Didcot*—and Sellers tries to impale commuters on an ivory tusk hatrack, prompting John Fortune to say 'I'll find the swine who started this grim dance of death, I'll find the swine who kidnapped Crispin.' Hitler, whom Sellers plays as Fritz Fassbender from *What's New, Pussycat?*, eventually strips off his disguise—and he's Grytpype Thynne, an Old Etonian fresh from an afternoon of passion with the engine driver.

No doubt everybody involved thought of it as 'goonish'. Sellers, whom John Bird says 'didn't seem to be doing anything, but was incredibly funny', acts everybody else off the screen. Where they mug and prance, Sellers goes beyond parody. Where the others are simply silly and exhibitionistic, Sellers is concentrated and his performances tingle. Wells and company send up tatty vaudeville, but have nothing to give, except their edge of condescension; Sellers' vocal quick-changes, the dexterity with which he moves, his lightness, are in the vaudeville tradition to begin with. 'The Goon Show' itself, which so influenced the humour of Wells' generation, was structured as music hall: the melodramatic playlets, the double acts (Hen and Min, Bluebottle and Eccles, Grytpype and Moriarty, etc.), the musical interludes by Max Geldray and Ray Ellington.

We may go further. Dr Strangelove is a pantomime devil, and his tiffs with his false arm are numbers, routines. Quilty's sequence of disguises, in *Lolita*, is a series of skits. Clouseau and Cato are slapstick tumblers. Chance, in *Being There*, has a voice derived from Stan Laurel, who stepped westwards from the British music hall with Fred Karno. The scenes Sellers devised and shot for *The Fiendish Plot of Dr. Fu Manchu*, after he'd sacked the original director, are perhaps the most revealing—for, when Fu takes time off from his villainy to play 'Daddy Wouldn't Buy Me A Bow-Wow' on the piano with Helen Mirren, and to talk about his nostalgia for the music hall, his tastes are Sellers'. Fu's embroidered satin robes are out of *Aladdin*, and his palace bedroom is littered with props and costumes, the bric-a-brac of theatre.

◆ ◆ ◆

The attitudes inherent in Sellers' style were from the music hall, and his aristocracy of eccentrics was born back stage. He was fond of grotesques, the heightened effect, and he liked, also, the plaintiveness of tramps who sing sad little numbers such as 'Sometimes', a track from *The Optimists of Nine Elms*, written by Lionel Bart:

> Sometimes, it wasn't half as bad as all that, sometimes;
> Don't know exactly what we had, but there were fun times.

Sellers was strangely happy when, for a sketch called 'Old Comrades on Hard Times,' he got into a hobo disguise and busked in Oxford Street with Secombe, carrying the hat, and Spike, tooting on a trumpet. He himself banged a drum, and they collected the grand total of £4.75 [less than ten dollars]. The result was broadcast on *Sing A Song of Secombe*, at Christmas 1974. It was a comfort to know that, if this were for real, there'd be no lower he could sink than the open air.

He was banging a drum for money, too, three decades earlier, up in Lancashire. His father settled at Lytham St Anne's, and Sellers found a job at a dance hall in Blackpool for £8 a week. He also learned the ukulele properly. 'He was a wizard with it,' said Bill. Perhaps this was the time when, one way or another, the Sellers family had a brush with the Formbys? Bill joined an ENSA unit which included, amongst its other three members, George Formby's sister, Ethel, and Sellers himself played Formby ditties at factory concerts. 'Each time he did this he stopped the show,' said Peg.

George Formby was to remain a Sellers favourite. On the 'Parkinson Show' in November 1974, after singing the Bart 'Sometimes,' and remembering with affection that 'Dad taught me to play the banjo,' he accompanied himself on the ukulele for 'When I'm Cleaning Windows' and 'I Haven't Told Her, She Hasn't Told Me.' The Harry Stoneham Trio have a tricky time matching the pace, and the bass rather unnecessarily clumps in the background—ready to come in and drown Sellers out, perhaps, if his fingerwork faltered. But Sellers is nifty. He captures Formby's glee, but alters it slightly, ages it and makes it wistful. 'He was one of my idols,' Sellers told Judith Simons in 1980, 'I saw all his films.'

The harum-scarum little-boy-lost persona of George's is one Sellers could recognise and use, and all those shoddy films of the thirties and forties prefigure the *Panthers*. George, the fool who could play the ukulele with assurance, is like scatterbrained Harpo or Chico when they take up their instruments for the serious interludes, careful not to let us take all the gormlessness too literally. There's a quick manipulator under the goofiness; the awkward innocent is also shrewd. George's imbecility is what protects him from harm (he's always encountering master criminals). Inspector Clouseau isn't far away from any of these descriptions: he, like George, is an innocent abroad; George, like Clouseau, tangles with bikes, horses, gym equipment, naturist clubs, and ladders; and, like Clouseau, George, who was by no means any oil painting to look at, co-starred with desirable women. Yet, where Clouseau is full of tension because he can't consummate a relationship, George's great fear is that he will be successfully seduced. All women are spider women, imperilling his chastity—hence his primal cry of 'MOTHER!' He can't cope with sex (that's why *he* is wound up like a top), and has kept himself a man-child out of fear. His arms and legs fly in all directions at once as he yells and blushes.

Of course, as with his skill with the uke, he's not such a dope. His songs are all saucy—the voyeuristic 'When I'm Cleaning Windows', the virtually priapic 'My Little Ukelele in My Hand'—and there's a knowingness in his chuckle, which is perhaps what audiences enjoyed. (It's certainly what Sellers responded to across his entire life.) George's immaturity and adventures are Peter Pan's, and in the formidable former clog-dancer Beryl Ingham he had his Wendy. Beryl masterminded the public's perception of his awkwardness—she could see that audiences would love him if he didn't come across as a fake. The appeal was in the simplicity—but the appeal was not universal. Michael Balcon thought Formby mentally retarded, and wanted the songs cut from the films. One of the directors felt that Formby could 'switch his simplicity on and off according to need', and Pat Kirkwood, from *Come On, George*, thought him 'in many ways … cretinous.'

In a broad sense this is also the paradox of Sellers, whom Milligan has called 'the most complex simpleton in the entire world … He had a level of immaturity that didn't fit in with his age at all.' And where Sellers had Peg, Formby had Beryl. Beryl forbade her husband the same leading lady, organised and protected his image, drove him to the top and negotiated his £100,000 contracts. She invested his money and got him accorded star status (all this during the years the Sellers family were living in diminished affluence in Ilfracombe). The result was that she kept him cut-off and childless and disabled him emotionally. The perfect show business marriage was a complete illusion. They'd given up sexual intimacy fifteen years before Beryl died, and Formby diverted his energy and interest to machines. He liked disassembling watches and clocks and he was always changing his motor car—he'd had over two hundred by 1949. He bought and sold houses and could never settle. He tried an Irish mansion (like Sellers) and had a manor house (like Sellers' Chipperfield).

The trouble with Beryl's keeping Formby a little-boy-who-always-wants-to-have-fun was that he became a lonely man who needed the affection of an anonymous public. (Amongst whom, slightly less than anonymous, was Princess Margaret.) He was safe, but repressed. And the entrepreneurial aspects aside, Peg's treatment of Sellers resembles, and had similar effects as, Beryl's treatment of her husband. 'He knew what he wanted,' it was said, 'but he let Beryl get it for him.' As much as Sellers would say he resented Peg's fuss and control, she was his motor and in his marriages he was looking for a dominatrix—an agent of his heart, a Beryl.

◆ ◆ ◆

The first thing Peg did in Lancashire was to insist on Sellers' having a better ukulele and his own drumkit—the better for him to be acceptable to ENSA. 'You see, he was so fussy about things,' said Peg of his instruments. 'A thing had to be perfect, or not at all. Peter had a *thing* about it.' In the autumn of 1942 they all moved southward again, Sellers side by side with his father's unit on tour. But something happened, because Bill and his unit went off alone, and Peg and Sellers turned up, early in 1943, in Brighton, looking for accommodation.

'Peter and his mother came to the door of the digs and the landlady was about to turn them away,' recalls Jack Salt, Waldini's saxophonist, who was then in Brighton working for Alan Green's dance band at the Dome. 'I said I knew them and so she took them in. They stayed together for a few weeks, and Peter was then playing the drums at the Regent Dance Hall. Peggy said it would be better if we looked for a flat, so we went to Ross' Mansions, 10 Middle Street—the flat was on the first floor.'

Salt went with Sellers and Peg, and for a few months he experienced their ménage. Peg reactivated her old sideline. She went around the big houses of Hove, knocking on the doors, trying to buy antiques and rocks, which she'd resell in Hatton Garden, the jewellery quarter. Sellers, who only worked between seven and eleven at night, spent the day idling and listening to the radio. 'He was very skilled in his mimicry,' says Salt. 'He knew the whole of the 'ITMA'* show. He would be in one room, and you'd be in the next, and you'd think the radio was on. He didn't make anything of this, though. Drumming was his interest. I'd reckon he was as good as any other dance-band drummer of that period.'

Sellers boasted to Salt that he'd 'slept with every girl in his band.' (He'd later boast to his son Michael that he'd slept with every one of his leading ladies. Irene Handl? Margaret Rutherford?) Other liaisons were apparently with a coalman's daughter and the cashier in a cake shop. Peg, says Salt, was very strict, and much of Sellers' romancing was invented and designed to shock her. 'His mother was very much his companion. She ran the home. She did all the cooking—huge, excellent meals concocted from our rations.' There was no mention of Bill, though, until Peg suddenly said at the end of June: 'I'd like to get Bill together with us again. ENSA is wanting their units to go overseas. I've some experience as a

---

* 'It's That Man Again': an influential radio comedy series, a welter of catch-phrases and puns, which starred Tommy Handley and Dorothy Summers. In 1942 the cast had been invited to Windsor Castle for Princess Elizabeth's birthday party, and 'the late King and his family fell about with laughter.' It commenced on July 12, 1939, and lasted (for three hundred and twelve episodes) until Handley's death ten years later. Characters included Mrs Mopp, Colonel Chinstrap, Ali Oop, and Claude and Cecil. They said things like 'Splash my spats!', 'Butter my Bath bun!', and 'Can I do you now, Sir?' It projected an England where everybody, from the lower-orders up, was a smart-aleck and far too quick-witted ever to get morose, hence its morale-boosting popularity. 'The Goon Show' would take off from it.

wardrobe mistress. If we could form a unit for ourselves, ENSA will accept us for the Home Circuit.'

Salt went with them up to London on July 1, 1943 (they'd been living together since the New Year). They went to Drury Lane. Peg went ahead to talk business, Salt and Sellers waited in a café. 'I've got good news and bad news,' she said, returning. 'Peter has been turned down—he's too near to being called-up [for military service, i.e. drafted]. So we can't do what we set out to do. If you wish, you can still go, though,' Salt was told. 'Waldini's new saxophone player has failed his medical, so you can go along.' Which he arranged to do, there and then. He returned with Peg and Sellers to Brighton, worked out his month's notice at the Dome and went off to be part of the front-line theatre.

Sellers, the authorities apprised of his whereabouts, was conscripted into the Royal Air Force the moment he passed his eighteenth birthday in September. He was now ACH(GD)2223033, a faceless service number assigned to aircraft-hand ground duties.

◆◆◆

It took Hitler and the Third Reich to sunder Sellers and Peg; the Nazis also liberated Milligan from his mother. After the call to arms ('the sense of emancipation!' remembers Milligan, 'the feeling of freedom!'), no longer did these young men need to fear the spectre of a parent at the top of the stairs, calling them a 'dirty stop-out'. Almost in gratitude, therefore, Sellers and Milligan made Hitler into a comic figure; and because, in the years to come, they dressed themselves up as Hitler at every professional opportunity, it is clear that their part in his downfall is counterbalanced by his rôle in their growing-up. Curiouser, perhaps, were the off-screen pranks. Sellers liked to don an SS officer's uniform, with Milligan dressed as Hitler, and drive his black Mercedes around London. When he was making *The Revenge of the Pink Panther* in Hong Kong, Sellers, knowing that his hotel was expecting a coach load of Jewish tourists, strutted up and down the waterfront as Hitler.

'He'd got this *thing* about Hitler,' says Michael Jeffrey, who was Sellers' companion in his last years. 'Peter really hated the concierge at the Plaza-Athenée in Paris, really hated him, and so he would go in and sing "Deutschland, Deutschland über alles" at the top of his voice in the lobby...'

Jeffrey also witnessed another of these vendettas. 'When Peter was in hospital in Geneva, in Christmas 1979, there was one nurse he didn't like because she switched the lights on early in the morning. So he put a chair on a table, climbed up, dismantled the fluorescent strip, and locked it in a cupboard. He then made me draw a swastika on his forehead, a Hitler moustache, and he just lay there, all night, waiting.'

To Milligan, I think, Hitler was an ogre whom you could defuse, or cope with, through humour. Sellers' Hitler(s), though caricatures, had an edge of cruelty, as Milligan himself detected: 'There has to be a reality to his impersonations—if he played Hitler, he'd end up in the bunker and commit suicide. He'd have no other choice. That's what makes him mad, you know.'

◆ ◆ ◆

Peg, as can readily be anticipated, didn't want her son leaving home to fight Adolf or anybody else. Taking the cue from the saxophonist who'd failed his medical examination, Peg did her best to convince the Royal Air Force that Sellers was a wreck. 'She tried everything,' said Milligan. 'She must have gone through the entire medical dictionary to find a disease that would get Peter back into civvy street, back to her loving care and protection: "He's got flat feet, he's got a flat head, flat ears, he's even got flat teeth..."'

I have come across no evidence that suggests, however, that Sellers himself objected to conscription, as his Hitler nostalgia helps to indicate. He was well used to the itinerant life and its discomforts, and 'the only grim memory', he said on the British Forces Broadcasting Service (in 1980), 'was the usual grim memory for everyone, the training period... once you are out of that, you know, it's one big black market.'

Sellers treated the wartime as playtime—it would literally be for him a few years of laughter and song. Encouraged by Peg, and seeing for himself the pointlessness of being an armer-assistant in Cardington, Bedfordshire, he applied to join the RAF Entertainments Division. 'The trouble was that the men I was working with were technicians, fitters and so on, by profession; the work interested them. I wasn't in the least interested in pushing bullets into the wings of planes. It seemed more sensible for me to be doing something I was good at. Anyhow, I managed to get myself re-mustered and attached to the Ralph Reader Gang Show. In fact, I became an official RAF concert entertainer.'

Peg did her best to petition Pilot Officer John Cracknell, Squadron Leader Ralph Reader's Administration Officer, to prevent Sellers from being drafted overseas—all much to everybody's embarrassment. She went to the extent of planting a weeping willow in Cracknell's garden, at Sarratt, Hertfordshire (which was known ever afterwards as 'Peggy's Tree'), in the hopes of propitiating him. The tree would be the object of a strange veneration years later. 'Peter, as we all know, was very close to his mother,' explained Cracknell, a week after Sellers had died, 'and he believed he was in spiritual touch with her. To be close to her he would come here and pay homage to her by hugging the tree. It was a very moving scene. He was very sentimental and used to say, "I feel my mother here." He was quite sincere and not a bit theatrical. Last October [1979] he said he would love some cuttings from the willow to plant in the garden of his house in Switzerland. I gave him three beautiful cuttings and I hear they have grown beautifully. He told me the day he planted them was a Friday, which meant a double celebration, because every Friday he would light a candle to his mother. His last visit to me was strange. I thought he looked ill. As I walked out with him to his car on leaving, Peter suddenly came up and kissed me on the cheek. It felt strange. I had never been kissed before by a man. But it was a very warm gesture. I did wonder about him. I think he did have a premonition about the end.'

His premonitions, indeed, were connected with that tree—which did not quite flourish in Switzerland, despite what Cracknell believed. Sellers had to receive permission from the customs and excise department before he could export the saplings. It was quite a bureaucratic palaver. On the day he was to make his last flight to England, he called Jeffery into the kitchen at the Gstaad chalet. Two big crows were pecking at the cuttings, and one of the birds flew at the window and flapped against it. Sellers took this as an omen of death. He had the willow pulled up and burnt.

◆ ◆ ◆

Peg needn't have fretted. Sellers was able to cope with military discipline by rising above it. In fact, rules and regulations brought out his rebelliousness and stubbornness, and the adult Sellers now starts to emerge. The grown-up society of his childhood had made him very direct, as far as dealing with other people went. Peg had given him no doubts about his superiority. As Jack Salt says: 'He would tell you to your face what he thought of you. He'd criticise your music, for example, whereas most people wouldn't do that.' And so, though molly-coddled and demeaned by Peg's presence, he was by no means a cat's paw. Actually, he felt inviolate, and he knew that the war would never be any more dangerous than being in the Wolfcubs [the junior branch of the Boy Scouts]—a view shared by Ralph Reader.

Reader never forgot their first encounter. He was on a RAF station where the notices had been posted inviting anyone interested in joining the Gang Shows to make contact, and Sellers did. Reader was only allowed to recruit from the ACH (GD) rank, and of this group he was not permitted to approach engineers, tradespersons, or people with a useful skill of any description. 'What do you do?' he asked Sellers, who was classed amongst these lowest of the low. 'Play the drums a bit,' he replied. 'Anything else?' 'Well, I can do some bits of "ITMA".' Reader said to come to the NAAFI (the Navy, Army and Air Force Institutes canteen) the next morning for an audition.

'The next day, as I walked in, I heard myself singing "Riding Along on the Crest of a Wave," even worse than I do sing it. I walked up the steps on to the stage and there was Peter Sellers entertaining six airmen, who were meant to be cleaning out the hall, by giving an impression of me! As soon as I stepped on the stage, the airmen, naturally, stood to attention. Sellers hadn't seen me and carried on until he realised something was up. He stopped and turned round: "Well," he said, "Do you want a drink or do I get jankers?*"'

They had a cup of tea and Sellers was hired.

◆ ◆ ◆

Reader was Sellers' second impresario, after Waldini. The difference between them was that where Waldini had given employment and security at Ilfracombe,

---

* *Jankers: n.obs.* British services term for punishment of defaulters. Origin uncertain, possibly echoic for jangles or janglers, the sound made by a provost sergeant's keys. See *Ross*, Rattigan's play about T.E. Lawrence: 'None of your lip, Parsons now—unless you want a dose of jankers.'

Reader was the one responsible for helping Sellers to run away from home. He was put into the RAF Gang Show Unit Number 10, and he toured the Hebrides and the Orkneys before leaving for the East—and he was always to be more like Ralph Reader than Ralph Reader. When Sellers went on a television show in the fifties called 'Alfred Marks Time', it was to appear in a sketch as the great Gang Show showman: 'an uncanny impersonation,' says Dick Vosbrugh, who wrote the script. 'The orchestra and the audience were hysterical. Later we had the real Ralph Reader himself on the series—we were told "He was funnier last time." People thought Sellers had been the real one.'

RAF Gang Shows had grown out of Reader's devotion to the self-sufficiencies of scouting. His account of his childhood seems like the tale of a cheerful boy from a Dickens musical. He would perhaps have been a reprobate, had he not, first, decided to structure his life according to the precepts in Baden-Powell's manly handbooks and, second, found a purpose in life through show business. He'd appeared in village concerts in Ireland; in America he met Al Jolson and Jack Oakie, with whom he toured. He even understudied Jolson (in a musical called *Big Boy*), who was to remain his idea of the perfectionist entertainer. Reader appeared in and choreographed Flo Ziegfeld revues for Broadway and though he returned to England to work for Sir Charles Cochran and devise shows with titles you'd never get away with today—*Gay Deceivers*; *Yes, Madam*; and *Please, Teacher*—he became much more American than British in his accent, dress, and disdain for the London sloth and cold. He produced Ivor Novello spectaculars at Drury Lane and directed the dance sequences in various plays by Noël Coward.

Meantime, bolstering all this moonlight and filigree was the wholesomeness of the Scouts. Reader was a Patrol Leader and made the observation that 'the healthiest smell of a Scout uniform should be smoke from a camp fire', though he had the lads on stage, not running about the woods and glades. He organised concerts with increasing hundreds of participants, and in October 1932, when people realised the performances were getting to be annual events, the Gang Shows were officially born. They were a mixture of sketches and songs—'Steer for the Open Sea', 'Birds of a Feather', 'These Are The Times', and, of course, the ritualistic 'We're Riding Along on the Crest of a Wave'. By order, this was sung at the start and end of every RAF Gang Show performance.

During the war, Reader produced patriotic masques and mystery plays at the Albert Hall, with Olivier in his Naval uniform, declaiming from Shakespeare; Churchill, the image of Sir John Falstaff, also put in a personal appearance. At the suggestion of Air Commodore Archie Boyle, the Deputy Director of Intelligence in the RAF, Reader went to France, with ten ex-Gang Show artistes, to give concerts under the ENSA banner. The previews at RAF stations outside London went well, so the first RAF Gang Show Unit soon became officially established, with routings arranged by the Air Ministry (i.e. Cracknell). Reader avoided paperwork if he could and appeared as a guest star in all his Units—there were ultimately twenty-five. Above Reader was a Wing Commander, who reported to a Group Captain, who was answerable to an Air Commodore. All these figures in the chain of command, none of them with a theatrical background, wanted to impose their stamp on the Gang Show. But Reader, who had total faith in his formula of apple-cheeked optimism and sentiment, by-passed the mandarins of Houghton House and met Tedder, Air Chief Marshal and top cheese. Reader, who by now had units in Normandy, wanted further men to tour India and Burma, hence his subsequent search for such as Sellers—chaps on the lowest pay scale in the Air Force, who would not be permitted (unlike official bandsmen) to augment their income with extracurricular concerts.

The huge and benumbing Scala Theatre and Albert Hall rallies were not to Sellers' taste. Men, in the manner of chorines in the Busby Berkeley films he'd seen as a child, were merged into a mass. It was crowd art—which did, however, appeal to Ribbentrop, who'd met Reader at the Holborn Restaurant and had offered him work in the Hitler Youth Movement. (Reader later conducted six Wagnerian gods around London, and they dined at his home. He was still 'closely in touch by mail with various members of the Hitler Youth Movement' in 1939. The information was divulged regularly to Archie Boyle.) What Sellers enjoyed, once he'd finished the briefings in London, were the Gang Show splinter groups, the ring of a dozen or so on the road. It was a continuation of his ordinary life (without his parents). And it released a recklessness in him, quiescent perhaps since Ma died and he'd lacked a round-the-clock admiring audience if he'd felt like pushing people into the fireplace. Now, in a bunch of boys he could charm and amuse with his mimicry, bound for Bombay, he could freak out.

Sellers played the drums in the five-piece band and took part in comedy sketches. He also began, as he travelled the sub-continent by truck and train, to pay attention to alien sounds and sights. The bearded holy musketeers and people who pissed in the street; the cripples, cows, monkeys, and rats; the colour, dust, and mobs clinging to the sleeping cars. With Ben Novak, Sellers developed a way of keeping back the natives, with their live chickens and tea things, when they threatened to swarm over the airmen's space—they'd start to quarrel in what sounded like Hindi, but which was, Jones explains, 'absolute codswallop [nonsense]. Neither of them spoke a word of it. But the four million Indians stood and gazed in wonder and no one ever tried to get into our carriage.'

As Sellers told Peter McDonagh in his British Forces Broadcasting Service interview: 'We became the remnants of the last of the British Raj. India was rampant with majors and colonels—types...we subsequently used in some of the [Goon] shows, before the Asians started coming over here...I must be attracted in some way to them, whether it's to a certain tic or idiosyncrasy, or the warmth of their personality, or their character. At the time, I didn't realise I was picking up their sounds, their styles, and their thinking. I was too young to realise the general sort of feeling of Indian philosophy; but, in later life, of course I have.'

By the end of 1944, they were in Calcutta: 'Laughs! Laughs!! and more Laughs!!!' the audience was promised by the poster. Performances were daily at ten-thirty, from Friday, December 1 to Thursday, December 7, at the New Empire (though they stayed over until the New Year). The advance publicity, for 'A

Ralph Reader Prodn.,' claimed that 'There are only ten of them, every one of them with a reputation on the Music Hall stage at home, and some who, I feel sure, will fill a big place in the entertainment world of the post war years.' They were indeed a hit. 'Two hours of laughter,' continued the local reviewer. 'The best of its kind in the last twenty years. Not a minute of boredom, not a second when we were not filled with admiration for the all-round talent of this happy group.'

The New Empire was in fact a cinema, built originally to house the touring theatre companies out from Edwardian England, but electrified with the arrival of the talkies. The General Manager of the Humayan Associated Theatres, in Calcutta, was Frank Wildish, who recalls that 'Peter Sellers was in the show and gave an outstanding performance as the drummer in the all-cast musical finale at the end of the first half. The show played to a packed house every morning...and in fact I went into the theatre each morning just to see and hear that fantastic finale to the end... and to watch this talented young man really give a resounding performance.'

Mr Wildish confirms the critic's comment in the Bombay *Sunday Standard*: 'The "baby" of the show is Peter Sellers, aged 19, the boy-drummer and impressionist. A big future lies before him.'

♦♦♦

A big future nearly lay behind him, for Sellers, if he is to be believed, was not content to confine his performances to the stage. As he said in 1962: 'I think it must have been while I was in India in the war that I found out I could do impersonations. I used to get up to all sorts of larks...We had skips [baskets] full of costumes and uniforms for the performances...Once...I dressed up as an Air Commodore. I must have been the youngest Air Commodore in the service—I was only about twenty-three. I put a bit of grey on the sides of my hair, it must have been too obvious for words—but, it was Christmas Eve, everybody was blind drunk, otherwise I should never have got away with it. I actually got talking to an Air Vice-Marshal, sitting at the bar, arm round my shoulders [*matey gesture, confidential tone*]: "I shaid to Tedder..."'

I have found no witnesses for the Far East pranks. When his tours took him back to Europe, however, and the Gang Show visited France and Germany, ('the Riviera, Cannes, and Bandol, marvellous luck...') people did start to notice a proliferation of anonymous flying officers and wing commanders—Sellers. The character actor David Lodge says Sellers once went into the Sergeants' mess as a Flight Lieutenant and led a rousing toast: 'Gentlemen, it has been delightful being with you this evening, but I am afraid I must drag myself away. My lad here [the towering and stocky Lodge] informs me that we have a long journey ahead of us...' And off they'd depart, the theatre troupe. 'I found it more agreeable,' Sellers later reasoned, 'spending my time in the Officers' Mess than in the crowded other-ranks canteen. In good time I would withdraw from the bar and duly make my appearance with the Gang Show. In the early morning we would be off again to the next stop. No one knew or cared who the young officer in the bar was or where he had gone.'

The Sikh Flying Officer, organising rations of fresh food; the South African

Group Captain, at large in Burma; the Indian fighter pilot, with medal ribbons and a white turban with the RAF badge, getting people to salute him in Dieppe; a Maharajah received with full honours... Even if Sellers was only some of these (a famous man's past engenders apocryhpha), there was more passing through his mind than a simple desire to dress up and get away with it. At one level, of course, it was indeed straightforward roistering—a love of the danger of exposure and discovery, tricks to get a lot of people admiring him. (That's how the behaviour has always been passed off by those who knew him: 'Peter was within an ace of being court-martialed dozens of times,' Lodge said delightedly in 1964.) But I rather think there was something unbalanced about the escapades. They were vanishing tricks. Sellers would leave behind, for a while, the muddle of touring and the pressure to be cheerful—Bluebottle's imbecile cub-scouting, etc. Now he could forage, amuse himself with the ease of his masquerades. It would be another ten years before he'd start to worry about disguise having closed him off from his real self ('What is me? I just don't know,' he'd sigh in *Picturegoer*). He removed himself from the world by treating it as theatre (or music hall).

◆ ◆ ◆

As Sellers' confidence in his ability to be taken for other people grew, his acting genius germinated at the expense of a capacity (or desire) to differentiate fantasy from reality—and in the long term his divorce from reality would be complete. (When he was demobilised he strutted around England believing he was an earl.) This was no sudden derangement. The chopping and changing of childhood addresses, a mercurial mother, an affectless father, and the nature of the flickering and giddy profession they were in: all this was recipe enough to create a flighty, floating temperament, which wouldn't be disoriented by war, which could *use* the disruptions to advantage. 'Good night to you all, and God bless you,' he liked to believe he'd once said, with feeling, when quitting a Sergeants' mess— where he'd graciously accepted a vote of thanks: 'I would like to thank you very much, sir, and say 'ow much we appreciate your coming into our mess. All the compliments of the season to you, sir.'

Sellers wished to be taken for a Lord of Misrule. 'Deceptions like these gave Dad a great kick,' said his son, Michael. *Deceptions*, note, not histrionics. When he was in France and Germany, travelling around the airfields, entertaining the victorious RAF and staying in what were until recently Luftwaffe messes (with their marble pissoirs and cubicles specially reserved for the Führer), Sellers became a dealer on the black market. He was a con-man, a spieler, and he enjoyed being one step ahead of the Military Police. On his way from the Place Vendôme, through Lyons, Avignon, the villages and towns of the Languedoc, and thence to the Pyrénées, he racketeered in shoes, soap, and blankets. 'A glorious orgy of free enterprise!' in the words of David Lodge. In Cannes, he arranged to sell a large tin of petrol for two thousand francs to the owner of the Toupée Nightclub—and this was an offense punishable by a long jail sentence there, Cannes being in an American zone. Sellers used his profits to buy champagne. Back in Paris, he took a private box at the Opéra Comique and watched *La Bohème*, sipping endlessly at fizz.

Lodge found Sellers' behaviour ulcer-inducing at the time. He'd first met the harum-scarum drummer at a camp in Gloucester. He was another of Ralph Reader's recruits and Sellers had the next bed along in the hut. Sellers was arguing heatedly with a singer called Freddie Brent, and Lodge, getting fed up, handed Sellers a poker: 'Listen, son, if he keeps on, wrap this across his bloody head!' Amazingly, Sellers took him at his word. Lodge intervened, Brent went off in disgust, and Sellers could see Lodge would be valuable from that moment. Not only Sellers. Lodge met Peg and Bill before the RAF Gang Show set forth for France, and was told: 'David, I want you to promise you will keep an eye on Peter while you are over there on the Continent.' So Lodge became another figure to disobey and run rings round. When they took the boat train to Paris and reported to the Dufayel Barracks, a transit camp, Sellers, outraged that the Americans had taken the best billets—and then, as later, not liking to be told where he'd be dossing down—made his group pool their cash and find an hotel, which they did: a brothel in the Pigalle district. Lodge had to rescue Sellers from the arms of two whores and push a wardrobe in front of the bedroom door to stop his charge from getting out and back at them.

◆ ◆ ◆

Sellers was in his early twenties. Why the chaperonage?

It was because carelessness and indifference to others had already encompassed his becoming a cold and absent father. As he said in 1980, reality slipping away: 'I've got an illegitimate daughter running around somewhere… She doesn't know I'm her Dad. Her mother decided to put her into a home… I just don't know where to begin to find her and I've made several attempts…' Explaining how he met her mother in India, Sellers added: 'I was a young twit and didn't realise what was going on around me. I was there because of the Second World War and we were the last remnants of the British Raj.' (A phrase he took to mean we were the conquerors and could do as we liked.)

How much of *this* is fantasy? Peter Evans, who wrote a book on Sellers in 1968, and interrogated him intensively on his past, recording hours of conversation and reminiscence, thinks we have to tread warily. 'Peter Sellers,' Evans said to me, 'was created by Peter Sellers. He was liable to invent any new history and background for himself—for example, the lost love-child and the early romance, which he decided had haunted him for years… Now, he never gave any hint of this to me, and we'd been all over his early life.'

Just as dressing up as Air Commodores and Lord Tedder were improvements on what really happened, so too may the adopted-away daughter have a number of ramifications. First, when the news was broken by Sellers, he was near death and the tackle of his heart, like King John's, was cracked and burned.[*] He felt he could only survive through the destruction of others, and was re-drafting his will, leaving people out and just as vindictively putting alternative names in. The principal non-beneficiaries were his three children. How it would have appealed to him, therefore, the vision of a lost child, who could take on, in his imagination,

---

[*] *King John*, Act V, Sc. 7: 'The tackle of my heart is crack'd and burn'd.'

George Brown Collection

'Sellers: Where is His Love Child?'—Looking into the past
from a balcony of the Dorchester Hotel (1980)

all the ideal qualities of absolute devotion and success, loving him more than words can wield the matter. He was duplicating Peg's feelings over his still-born elder brother: a lost child is a perfect child, immune from the depredations and lacks of those who live out their lives in the real world; real children might not feel like heaving their hearts into their mouths every five minutes.

Sellers' announcement of a hidden daughter, his preference for dream over flesh and blood, could be convincingly explained away, therefore, as a symptom of his solitariness and infirmity. He could cope best with those who didn't have a working pulse. If he *did* father an illegitimate child, then the futility of his quest wasn't missed by Lynne Frederick, his fourth and, as it happened, last wife: 'I know that Peter did try very hard several years ago to find her, but the adoption societies are very strict and would not open their books... You see, she doesn't know that she is Peter's daughter, because no one will have told her.'

It is possible that this 'several years ago' may have been connected with an Act Parliament passed in 1975 allowing adopted people over the age of eighteen the right to apply for information on their natural parents—a change in the law, incidentally, which inspired P. D. James' thriller about proofs of identity and forgotten crimes, *Innocent Blood*. ('I am the same person as I was yesterday,' one of the characters says, 'But who was I yesterday?' And of another character it is observed: 'None of us can bear too much reality. No one. We all create for ourselves a world in which it's tolerable for us to live. You've probably created yours with more imagination than most...') But that law is for the child, not the mother and father—though the publicity it received may have tipped Sellers off, encouraging him to unlock a secret. I'm guessing.

◆ ◆ ◆

Whether or not there was an actual child, rather than an apparition which filled a psychological need, it is possible to specify Sellers' candidate for the mother: Nora Barnacle,* whom he fell for way back at St Mark's Kindergarten, Regent's Park. His first love. (Was she re-discovered in India?)† When he met Anne Howe, whom he was to marry, Sellers insisted on taking her around the streets and favourite places he'd come to know with Nora. 'He was already living in the past,' Anne said to me. 'And the strange thing about this was, we'd been married a while and I was in hospital having a miscarriage and Peg... decided to get hold of Nora Barnacle, and invited her up to the flat and invited Peter, knowing of his sentimentality over old times. She wanted to get them together again. Of course he told me about it. He did see her, and maybe they went out. I don't know.' Anne also added, 'You see... it's because he'd had a child by her when he was quite young, when he went into the RAF.'

---

* With the author's apologies to James Joyce.
† Alexander Walker's 'Authorised Biography' mentions the episode only in the vaguest terms. The woman's identity is concealed behind the nickname 'Sky Blue' and she worked 'for a Government department in Whitehall.' The baby happened because Sellers 'got her drunk and deliberately made her pregnant.' Though I often think my subject was a very shabby human being indeed, statutory date-rape is not something I'd want to direct against him on this occasion.

Michael Sellers continues the story: 'This other woman, the one Peg wanted him to marry—they had a daughter. My father claimed it was with her anyway. He brought her round to meet me once—years and years ago. I was sick in bed, aged about twenty, with glandular fever, and he brought this woman to see me... Someone I know knows where she is—the child. She must be forty now at least, and married. She doesn't know who she is as far as being the daughter of Peter Sellers is concerned.'

A final sliver of evidence comes from Milligan, who said to me, 'You know he had an illegitimate child? Once, when we were in his car, he stopped outside a house in Highgate and told me to "go over to that house and ask them how my daughter is." Of course, I wouldn't go. His secret baby. *That* night he knew where she was.' The most likely explanation is that this was Nora's or her family's home. By sending Spike over with such a message, Sellers, with malice in his swelling heart, was calculating on causing maximum hurt.

There are connections to be made here with Sellers' own condition, of course, as Peg's changeling boy; and we might add in, too, his endless inquisitions about who he really was. 'I long ago gave up the search for my own personality,' he said in 1959, wishfully thinking himself a ghost. 'I sometimes feel I'm not really here as a person—only as a rôle in a play or a film or radio series.' But it would take a fabulist in the Edgar Allan Poe class to depict all the subterranean cross-currents which are at work. Richard Henry's becoming Peter; John Taylor eating his solitary meals; Anne's miscarriage; the dispossession of Sellers' known issue; the inquiries he said he made to the Registrar General for access to the original records of his lost child's birth—a lost daughter who was also an invisible step-sister... Also relevant to the psychodrama is his fondness for younger women as he got older—women who were his children's contemporaries. He said once to Dorothy Squires, 'Dot, love, I can't help it,' and she said 'You are your own worst enemy, going round with all these starlets.' 'But I just can't help it.' Sellers was a man divided against himself. Doubles, deaths; births, bereavements; disappearances, wronged suitors, and people discovering who they are. It is all one.

◆ ◆ ◆

Sellers looked back at the wartime as his Robin Hood days. When Lodge, who grew up to become a man much dedicated to charitable work asked him to read the manuscript of his memoirs, *Up The Ladder of Obscurity*, Sellers commented: 'It was a very nostalgic and enjoyable trip down memory lane and it brought back many thoughts of the wild times we had together. It is a barrel-load of laughs for us, but they don't make 'em like us anymore. You can't get the wood, you know.'

What comes through in Lodge's book, however, is that there was a fair amount of rage within the sapling Sellers' recklessness. He strutted about at night pretending his banjo case was a machine gun, and Lodge had his work cut out preventing Sellers from slinking off to find a woman. He did escape in Toulon—Lodge was nervous later lest his ward had copped a dose of clap (which presumably, in the absence of any hints about Sellers-being-a-father, Lodge must have assumed was the peril worrying Peg).

But there was another side to the hot-headedness, a sullenness—a maudlin streak which was the obverse of the impishness. Two years after having known Jack Salt in Brighton, Sellers phoned him in Poona from Ceylon. He was feeling lonely. (This was 1945.) He was delighted to rendezvous with Waldini, the gypsy band now plying their Hungarian airs in Rangoon. He was ready to reminisce. One girl he met amongst the paddy fields and coconuts, and who was exposed to his serious side, was Marjorie Smith, a member of the WRAF stationed in Colombo. She herself was involved with a concert party, in between less colourful duties, and was enchanted by *The No. 10 Gang Show*. 'It was a very slick revue, with female impersonations, sketches, and a band that brought the place alive...The drummer was a gawky young man with dark wavy hair called Peter Sellers, and to this day I've never heard anyone play the drums with the same skill...This particular young man obviously had a bit extra. His female impersonations were hilarious and his self-assurance and style...were nothing short of pure professionalism.'

There is a danger, when people look back at an early brush with somebody who went on to be a star (in any field), that their recollections are honed, somehow, to fit. The past organises itself to prophesy the future that came about. So with Sellers in the RAF Gang Show. Competent, lively, full of himself—but if he hadn't become Peter Sellers, he'd have faded along with other members of the travelling units, each group consisting of a dozen men under the leadership of a Flight Sergeant. Twenty-five Gang Show units at a complement of twelve is three hundred souls under Ralph Reader alone.

Where Marjorie Smith's account has value, however, when we are assessing and rejecting evidence, is in the glimpse we suddenly get of Sellers in repose. He was encountered on the beach, where my eye-witness shared a fresh pineapple with him, and he moaned about the fact he couldn't sing. 'I really do wish I could sing, Marjorie. It would be marvellous to have a voice like Sinatra.' She asked him why he simply couldn't go ahead and get himself trained. 'Because I'm no good at it,' he replied categorically. 'There is one thing though that I'd like to be able to do even more—act. I don't just mean run of the mill stuff. I mean proper acting, something that will gain respect.'

We may make of that last emphatic assertion what we will, but the fragment about Sellers lamenting he'd not develop into a straight romantic player, that for all his own energy and twinkle he'd never be like the lead in *Anchors Aweigh*, is worth attention. Never has a performer been more indignant about having to be a character actor than Sellers. He was envious of handsome men, and did his best to convert himself into one.* The wafer-thin Sellers of *Casino Royale* and the long-faced cockerel, Robert Danvers, in *There's a Girl in My Soup*, are nearly seventy pounds lighter than the burly figure photographed at radio microphones, doing

---

* And he tried to destroy at least one. His otherwise unfounded hatred of Anthony Franciosa, the co-star of *Ghost in the Noonday Sun*, is an example.

the Goons. Paradoxically, the slimmer he became, the less funny his films—the lustre of stardom waned as he did. This is because—Evelyn Tremble in *Casino Royale* is the prime example—he'd decided he wanted to stroll across the lens and be taken for himself, elegant and sophisticated. But the vanity would kill him. Losing weight very fast in 1964, the better to consort with Britt Ekland, he disrupted his metabolism and triggered the heart disease which haunted him always. (Taking off the pounds he'd gained for *Being There*, he arrived on the set of *The Fiendish Plot of Dr Fu Manchu* haggard, virus-prone, and inlaid with bedsores.) Sellers never forgave the world for not having made him automatically irresistible to women, so he'd always seduce them with a combination of his fame and the little-boy-lost act. Michael Sellers said to me: 'He knew he could have charisma... He said... "In *my* position, I can have any woman I want." ... He liked to identify with a lot of his womanising characters, especially Robert Danvers: "My God, but you're lovely!"'—though the joke *there* is that Sellers was giving, vocally, a sly impersonation of Roy Boulting, who'd recently married Hayley Mills.

It was as if he regretted having to be a comic actor. That way, it was harder to be adored. Asked once about his early heroes, he said it was mostly good-looking people he admired: 'Mostly the very handsome types—I used to envy them very much. Bob Wagner I did a film with once [*The Pink Panther*, 1963]. I remember sitting talking to him, and he said: "You know—I must say I've got great admiration for your acting ability. My problem is, I'm only good-looking." I thought, God Almighty—staving off all those birds!... If you really are particularly handsome—you've really got it made. You don't have to do anything else.'

Sellers seems not only to have confused womanizing with pheasant shooting, but to have also confused modelling with acting. (Robert Wagner is bearable in *The Pink Panther*, and elsewhere, not because of his grin and dimples, but *despite* these attributes: he mocks the stereotype of the college jock.) Sellers was always to complain that his own was the only brand of performance demanding work—as if instinct and intelligence weren't necessary if you are a fellow girls look at twice. And note how he talks of women! Birds literally as waterfowl to be gunned down. Sellers longed to be able to make an impression simply by being there, without having to exert himself. (His off-camera rages were efforts to do just that: to leave the impression of keen whips on crew and colleagues.) If he didn't play up, he'd vanish, like hailstones. Thus the rascality of the disguises and messing about—and thus, too, underneath, the wish that he didn't have to do any of it. (How he'd like to have lain back, a Sultan, dipping his fingers into bowls of hot cherry sauce. It would be like infancy all over again—in your bassinet, gazed upon with adoration by the houris waiting to take the stage.) Such were the lessons of his wartime experiences, and by 1964, in the wake of the blitzkrieging *Doctor Strangelove* success, he'd be saying: 'I mean I realise that certain actors project their own image on to the screen—those who are the same on as they are off. But I've never had the necessary statistics to be able to do that sort of thing, and so, anyway, I always wanted to be a character actor.' (As his father Bill would say, you never did.)

In November 1978, Sellers was to co-star with Lynne Frederick, who was nearly thirty years his junior, in *The Prisoner of Zenda*. (His remuneration: $32,142 per week; hers: $4,166.67, plus $2,500 joint living expenses.) Before flying to Vienna to begin the film, the ageing rakehell underwent plastic surgery. Yards of flapping, sagging skin were trimmed from his jawline and chins. (That's why, in *The Prisoner of Zenda*, he wears high collars—to hide the needlepoint in his neck.) He also had the bags under his eyes picked up and carried off. 'I went in the morning and was out in the afternoon,' he said of his trip to the clinic. 'I was recommended a plastic surgeon in Los Angeles who turned out to be an incredibly handsome young man. I went to see him and he said to me "What is it you want done, Mr Sellers?" I looked up at him and said, "Why, I'd like to look like you."'

◆ ◆ ◆

As a store of feelings to draw on and transmute, Sellers' war was, as they say, formative. It was by now clear that he had no moral sense, no judgement, and that he was never sure quite how to behave or gauge appropriate courses of action—or else he knew all too well and, as David Lodge told Peter Evans, 'All the time it was as if he was seeing how far he could go, what he could get away with next.' The anarchic glee found its way (artistically) into Sellers' taste for cops-and-robbers pictures—*Two Way Stretch*, *Never Let Go*, and *The Wrong Arm of the Law* amongst them—films in which Lodge, amusingly enough, is often cast in a supporting rôle which parodies his original real-life job as guardian and chum in the RAF Gang Show. Lodge's Jelly Knight, Dodger Lane's cell-mate in *Two Way Stretch*, for example, is a genial giant, crop-headed and unflurried by prison routine, who works away at his embroidery hoop, and the beauty of the scenes is that he is never less than Little John. The sewing is done casually, and seems a perfectly normal occupation. (The prison governor, Maurice Denham's Cmdr. Horatio Bennet, is an advocate of basket weaving, etc.) Watching the film today, seeing the easy relationship between Jelly and Dodger—Dodger full of wild plans which Jelly either talks him out of or, if he senses their genius, backs him up over—knowing of the two actors' background in the services enriches the flow of the performances they give. Jelly can never stop being amused by Dodger, even when Dodger is infuriating. And the pair of them play off against the third man in the cell, Bernard Cribbins' Lennie Price—the stooge who goes down the sewers or on to the roof of the moving train. (Lennie is a nervy equivalent of the rôle Sellers had in *The Ladykillers*.)

Sellers' craving for disguise, and its crisscross with crookedness, is the chassis of his vehicle with Britt Ekland, *After the Fox*, shot on the island of Ischia. Sellers is a jail-breaking quick-change artiste who is by turns a doctor, an Italian policeman (in full-feathered head-dress, like a Colonial Governor) and a gesticulatory movie-maker. Here we have the revue style of costumes and funny voices. Sellers has no need to sustain each impersonation for very long. The plot is convoluted, like the director's (Vittorio di Sica) orotund, drawn-out delivery of an English word, and the film is worthy of note at this point because of Sellers' evident relish at being, as in *Two Way Stretch* and *Wrong Arm of the Law*, at the centre of a gang, where he has a built-in audience, and none of its constituents can be certain of what the boss will do next. Dodger Lane, Pearly Gates, and Aldo Vanucci are

Aldo Vanucci in *After the Fox*: Sellers as a crooked film director (1966)

not just criminals: they are touched with majesty (and with the intemperance and caprice that can traditionally go with being a king).

Interestingly, when Sellers himself was rich, he bought a court of his own—first Chipperfield Manor, near Kings Langley, Herts., and later Elstead, near Guildford (Surrey). He fitted the seats out with actors, film folk, critics, would-be bit-players, astrologers, sycophants, and real royals, and he could imagine himself monarchical. He'd spend his time at his garden parties recording the gambols of his train with a cine camera—turning life into a newsreel, like the flickering, famous faces at Kane's Xanadu in the 'Time on the March' sequence. David Lodge, before he married, was a frequent guest at Chipperfield: 'Peter kept a razor, toothbrush and pyjamas for me in one of the many spare rooms and I just used it as my own.' Lodge was the one Anne knew who could calm Sellers down when he started to get violent and threaten her and the children. 'He'd keep the peace,' she said to me. 'Solid and dependable.' As Lodge said, 'I don't condone everything he did; he was apt to act like a child, a spoilt boy.'

Though he does not deny Sellers' ugly side, he would prefer people not to refer to it and vex Sellers' ghost. (It is as if everybody is still answerable to Peg.) After Michael Sellers' portrait of a demon daddy dearest, *P.S. I Love You*, was serialised in the *Daily Mail*, Lodge wrote in to the editor to complain:

> Peter, of course, made mistakes and was sometimes hurtful, especially to those he loved dearly. His biggest failing was finding it almost impossible to say he was sorry

when full of remorse. To paint the life of any man, warts and all, is one thing. To ignore totally the fair skin, beneath and between the blemishes is to commit a sin of hurtful insensitivity much more heinous than that levelled against the silenced victim.

The scaly, dermatological metaphor is apt. Time and again Lodge had to come between the dragon and his wrath. But if ever there was anybody hurtfully insensitive in the life of others, it wasn't Michael (and all the family collaborated on *P.S. I Love You*, the title of which isn't totally ironic), as Roy and John Boulting were quick to point out, replying to Lodge's letter c/o the editor of the *Daily Mail* on October 1, 1981:

> Throughout, *P.S. I Love You* is a cry of pain which David Lodge, apparently, has not recognised. For those of us who also knew Peter Sellers, Michael Sellers' story is only, and too sadly, too true.

Anne put the problem succinctly: 'Suddenly, after he died, Peter was canonized.'

◆ ◆ ◆

Lodge is correct to try and argue for a sense of proportion where Sellers' devilish practices are concerned—for Sellers himself tried to suppress his greed and bumptiousness, by dispersing into impersonations of docile Indians. Dr Ahmed el Kabir in *The Millionairess* is his most famous example. Sellers, his face stained the colour of Mocha coffee, has to resist the blandishments of Sophia Loren's Epifania Parerga—she's a temptress in Pierre Balmain pantyhose. He, however, is too committed a GP, in his slum-district practice, to bother about lust, love, and other human distractions. Kabir is selfless, saintly. He lives to relieve the sufferings of others—sufferings brought about by tycoonery and sweated labour, the very forces behind the Loren character's wealth. How paradoxical, and Shavian, then, that here she is, offering to fund the construction and running of a huge hyper-modern hospital.

Spoilt, rude, and insufferable, Epifania is much more like the off-screen Sellers himself, temperamentally, than Sellers was like the Doctor; and during the making of *The Millionairess*, it was he who capered nimbly around Loren, trying to be the seducer. Their rôles were reversed. He was avid for Loren *and* for Kabir's spirituality. As with the holy men of St Aloysius', Sellers envied his character's calm, which he describes in the film as a state he attains through yoga exercises: 'I try to forget who I am,' says Kabir, 'I sink down deep into my soul—an intermediary stage between being and non-being.'

Sellers was indeed trying to forget who he was—but through acting, not religion. And when he came across equanimity and poise, as in India, and found that other people's placidity nagged him, his way of buying into it was to mimic it. Acting *was* his religion because, to him, his performances were a sort of trance: 'You must keep the flow' he said in 1962. 'When I'm working in the studio I always eat in my room. I don't eat with other people. That way I keep the flow. When I was playing the Indian in *The Millionairess* I found myself living the part in the strangest way; I almost *became* the Indian. I grew so much like an Indian that off the set real Indians would take me for one of themselves.'

He certainly impressed the great film director Satyajit Ray, who wrote a screenplay for Sellers, called *The Alien*—all about a leafy, lush rural community which has its life transformed by an encounter with an extra-terrestrial.* (After infinite permutations and re-writes, the property, quasi-commissioned by Columbia, emerged years later as Spielberg's *E.T.*) Something extraordinary could have come of that project; it would have been hallucinatory, lyric. When Ray went to see Sellers, on the set of *The Party*, however, a coarsening was in evidence: the detail and imponderability of Kabir had gone, to be replaced with a brittle slapstick charm. The Indian sensibility was now an opportunity for gags.

♦ ♦ ♦

Did Sellers think that Ray was a relative—somebody to whom he could be pissy with impunity? Ray, a kind and generous, uncoercive man, six foot four inches tall and with a basso profundo voice, died on April 23, 1992. Though Sellers betrayed Ray, he did not quite abandon *The Alien*—or the idea of Ray-the-absent-guru. At least three years after *The Party*, when *The Magic Christian* was released, and Sellers was appearing on talk shows to try and drum up publicity for it, he was coming out with this sort of comment: 'The *Pather Panchali* trilogy,' he said, 'none of those films made money, but they are great films. Kubrick, whom I consider one of the five great directors in the world, reckons that Satyajit Ray is number two or number one, and I think so too... He operates the camera himself incidentally. But for some reason he can't get distribution. Nobody's interested, so he has an art house showing, unfortunately.'

There we have a strong motive for Sellers' obduracy and insensitivity: Ray was not much better than a home-movie maker; his stuff, however artistic and well-regarded by connoisseurs, was not going to beguile a vain international star. (What did Sellers make instead of *The Alien*? The narcissistic *There's a Girl in My Soup*.) There is more to it than this, though. The coincidence of his mentioning Ray's work when *The Magic Christian* had recently been completed is of considerable interest.

The Magic Christian, according to Joe McGrath, was very much Sellers's project. (It was his home-movie.) 'He found the money. He really believed in the movie. That last sequence, with the businessmen going into the shit to grab the free cash—we went to America on the QEII, and had an agreement to shoot the scene at the foot of the Statue of Liberty. The shit vat had already been constructed. But Commonwealth United, our financiers, Bernie Confeldt, Henry Unger, people like that, suddenly took grave offense and cut off all our money—so Sellers... raised the extra money himself, so that we could finish the film.'

City gents doing the breast stroke and dodging turds is a long way indeed from the dream-times of Satyajit Ray. I don't think he'd have had much to say about shit vats, unless it was to point out the circular ironies inherent in Sellers, on the one hand wanting to satirise businessmen, and on the other, needing them, and becoming one himself, in order to make a film satirising money and its misuse. But whatever else we might want to say about *The Magic Christian*, nobody is going to dispute

---

* The script is published in Ray's *The Chess Players and Other Screenplays* (London, 1989).

its misanthropy. 'The whole thing shows you that every man has his price,' said Milligan, who claimed that Sellers loved it (especially the men-diving-in-tank scene) and 'I loved every inch of it, too. You've really got to hate people to love this film.'

Now whatever else we might say about Ray, he was *not* a misanthrope. His temperament, which imbues his films, is the exact opposite of the narrow and wretched vision found in *The Magic Christian*. His films are about possibility, not restriction; they are poetic. (He is an Imagist—to alter a phrase of Ezra Pound's, Ray's shots and scenes are cinematic language charged with meaning to the utmost degree.) His themes are both personal and political: the effects of the Second World War on remote villages, who don't even know who is fighting whom; the status of women and their liege lords; the feudal caste system; the country versus the town; modern education versus thousands of years of peasant ignorance (but is it ignorance, as such?). Ray's films are about confrontations and awakenings.

The Alien was not only to have matched a spaceman and his magical powers with the hectic fever of rural India; it would also have set up Ray's big-hearted-ness against Sellers' malignancy and condescension. The rôle Ray wrote for him, Bajoria the businessman (the only rich man in a poor country—another collision) is an amazingly perceptive portrait of the actor. His avidity, his opportunism, his superstitiousness. The alien, having landed his ship in a pond, emerges from the water and begins a series of pranks and miracles. Bajoria thinks that the prongs of the spaceship, emerging through the petals and lotus blossom, are the minarets of a lost mosque. If he pumps away the pond water, reveals the temple, and restores it, he'll make himself into a hero. 'I'm giving religion a new lease of life,' he crows.

As we read the script we can see how Sellers' Bajoria was taking shape in Ray's mind. The character is super-subtle—obviously Indian, but full of Western habits and affectations. There's something slightly sinister and corrupt about him; he taints whatever he touches, especially the spaceship/temple, his involvement with which 'helps the country, helps his soul, helps his image.' It is Bajoria, perhaps, who is the alien. Whilst, obviously, not British or American, he is not totally in-tegrated locally, either. Who else but Sellers could have portrayed somebody who wasn't quite one thing, wasn't quite another? Who was over-ambitious and always shifting and melting? With the jewelled rings on his fleshy fingers, talkative, ner-vous and wholly selfish, Bajoria reminds me of Quilty. The line 'Fish are clean! Ever caught a dirty fish?' is pure Quilty.

Though Ray was simply drawing on his knowledge of the kinds of Mephisto-phelean rôles Sellers could best play, Sellers, who by the late sixties wanted to be considered a playboy in the Cary Grant tradition, was far from flattered by the portrait of Bajoria. He didn't want texture or mystery any longer. He wanted to be kissable. He didn't want to acknowledge his unprepossessing aspects (moral, mental, physical). Hence, instead, the debonair Danvers of *There's a Girl in My Soup* and the pretty-ish women co-stars in every single one of his later films, from Sinead Cusack, in *Hoffman*, to Lesley-Anne Down, in *The Pink Panther Strikes Again*, to Helen Mirren, Fu's girlfriend: 'Oh, I could really go for you, Fu,' she simpers. Irene Handl and Margaret Rutherford were a *very* long time ago.

As when he physically attacked his daughter Victoria, who'd said of his performance in *Being There*, 'It's really good. You look like a fat old man,' Sellers could not dissociate himself from the person he'd become on the screen. His vanity was all-encompassing. But *The Alien* was also the film he most regretted never having made. I know this because he'd memorised, or expropriated, some of the script.

When Bajoria has a drink with Devlin, the engineer, and tells him about the pond and its temple, he starts to hum and sing:

DEVLIN: You sing?

BAJORIA: Only when I'm very happy. Or very sad. This is a *bhajan*—a devotional song. You keep time by clapping when you sing. [BAJORIA *demonstrates, singing and clapping*.]
Raghupati Raghava Raja Ram
Patiatapavana Sita Ram
...like this!*

Three months before he died, when Sellers was granting interviews to the world's press in Gstaad (to publicise *Being There*), he suddenly and with much reverence, came out with the above chant, attributing it to Gandhi. It was a lunatic, unexpected little exhibition, whomever he'd decided to pin it on. But it came from *The Alien*. As the dusk deepened across the mountains, did Sellers agonise over the lost chances? 'I was in India because of the Second World War,' he then said, adding (as always) 'we were the last remnants of the British Raj. It must have been a terrible set-up in the old days.' Well, marginally less terrible for the master race; and yet it is startling that Ray was running through his head, *thirteen years* after they had last communicated. Was Sellers trying to recall what it was like, his life (and art) before he decided to mistrust his own sense of wonder?

◆ ◆ ◆

The Party, to this day, is playing somewhere in the sub-continent. As Sellers himself said in the year of his death: 'In India it's still running,...anywhere you go...in the East, *The Party* is one of the favourite films.' (Hrundi V. Bakshi is a Hindu Inspector Clouseau.) The transition from giving a performance, in *The Millionairess*, to a series of skits, in *The Party*, is Sellers' guest appearance in *The Road To Hong Kong*, where he goodness-gracious-me's himself silly. In the scene, Bob Hope is being examined by the Indian doctor because he has lost his memory—and without being able to croon 'Thanks for the Memory,' Bob is a blank. Sellers uses Dr Kabir's voice and Clouseau's stupidity—the gurgling noise in the stethoscope doesn't come from Bob, the quack is accidentally listening to his own innards: 'Too much curry in the cornflakes.' All Bing says, every other line, is 'Let's get out of here', and Bob, too, looks apprehensive. They are not very brilliant straight men for a Peter Sellers vaudeville sketch. He totally upstages them.

Sellers, once he'd broken on to the international market after *The Millionair-*

---

* Translation: 'You are the purifier; You grant understanding; Your name is Allah, Krishna, Rama, Rahim; You grant right understanding to all men.'

ess, would always settle for caricature, cartoonery. What was the Chinaman outfit in *Murder By Death* other than a New Year's Eve party disguise? Sellers' Sidney Wang had simply stepped out of Charles Addams' credit sequence cartoon. And after the Oscar-worthy rôle in *Being There*, when he was again one of the cinema's hottest properties, what did he choose? To be bedeviled by the comic-book orientalism of Fu Manchu—an astonishing retrogression, explicable only by understanding how important nostalgia was to Sellers in his final months. As a child he'd listened to Harry Agar Lyons portray Fu on the radio, in a fifteen part serial; and he'd seen Boris Karloff in *The Mask of Fu Manchu*, with Myrna Loy. ('Next to Fu Manchu, Dr. No was a yes-man' said Sellers.) Sellers, mixing goonery with music hall and corny old classical movies, was trying to re-live his past—and the advantage of the past over the future is that you know exactly what it contains.

Sellers' Fu is as wispy as cartoonist Al Hirschfeld's poster design; the original Clouseau of the very first *Pink Panther*, however, was not wholly the trench-coated blob in the DePatie-Freleng cartoons. Along with the clumsiness and solemnity, which are habitual to him, he tries to cope with the knowledge that he is a cuckold; his sexual frustrations add facets to the farce. Sellers plays it slow and he plays it straight. By *A Shot in the Dark*, however, Clouseau had started to fall off buildings and into lakes; when the series was revived, in the seventies, it was for Sellers to disguise himself as Toulouse-Lautrec, Laughton's Quasimodo, and so on endlessly. Clouseau had become a third-rate variety artiste, muffing not his lines (though he cannot speak intelligibly) but his cases. He is a buffoon, in a way the Clouseau of the 1963 film was not.

Sellers seemed to want to deny his gifts, which were for subtle and observant comedy. He flattened himself out—exasperated, perhaps, that he couldn't explain or get his private life to benefit from his perceptions and sensitivity, his depth. His error, I think, was to believe that intuition and stimulus should have been soft and sweet—should somehow have kept him alive. Instead of which, the mean-spiritedness he felt (instead of the spirituality he yearned for) shrivelled him.

'As you can see,' he once said to a visitor, gesturing to the throng of wig makers and costume fitters filling his house, 'life at the moment is fraught. If it weren't for my yoga I wouldn't be able to cope at all. I'd go berserk.' Yoga exercises, however, to Sellers, were not ways of coping but, far from it, another strategy for evading and avoiding his responsibilities. If he was needed, or if he just felt bored and/or mischievous, he'd stand on his head. He'd pretend he wasn't present—he was astrally meditating. Sir Evelyn de Rothschild's main memories of Sellers are 'his enjoyment of Indian foods. The last meal I ever had with him was in an Indian restaurant. And he used to run around my house and stand on his head. He was always standing on his head—for hours.'

His yoga was a clown's act. When Peter Medak went to see him, for example, he put on quite a show: '[Talking to him] one Saturday, a few months before we went off to Cyprus to shoot *Ghost in the Noonday Sun* ... I realised, is it possible he's never actually *read* the bloody script? I was to see him at eleven in the morning ... I waited twenty minutes ... I went upstairs and opened the door of the bedroom and a pair of feet greeted me. He was standing on his head doing a yoga pose. "Peter, it's half past eleven." He came downstairs. We started reading through the script, when the phone rang. It was Liza Minnelli phoning from New York. He babbled to her for ages and he put the phone down and burst into tears—started crying and crying. And that was the end of reading the script. We went for a walk. I realised we were in deep shit.'

◆ ◆ ◆

The nature of his intransigence would have surfaced in another part he never played—Orde Wingate, a surprising legacy from Sellers' Burmese days. In 1962 he described it as 'the film part I should like to play most of all.' He went to Israel to talk to many ex-Haganah people about him and 'I've done a good deal of research; and there's a script I'm trying to get hold of. The trouble is, if I were to play Wingate I should have to lose a stone [fourteen pounds]. One couldn't play Wingate and not look lean. I'm not sure I could lose as much and stay healthy.'

A dietary motive is one thing—but what else appealed to Sellers? What did he *see*?

Orde Charles Wingate (b.1903) boxed for Charterhouse and rode to the Sudan on a bicycle. He spent, like T. E. Lawrence, much time in the desert, on foot and with camels. He was sympathetic with the Jewish cause in Palestine (he was a friend of Chaim Weizmann's). He had adventures with Emperor Haile Selassie, in Addis Ababa, routing the Italians, and Sellers would first have heard of him when Wavell, the Commander-in-Chief in India, instructed Wingate to conquer the Japanese in Burma. Wingate penetrated the enemy front, dropping soldiers behind the lines from the air, and was himself killed when his plane went down in a tropical storm, in March 1944. Wavell said of him: 'Wingate...had a genius for novel and unorthodox methods of warfare and the opportunity and energy to put them into practice. Such men are seldom very tractable subordinates, nor are they always easy to serve...'

Wavell could be describing Sellers for me. The enigma of Wingate, and the anger and questing which inspired him, make explicit the two strands of Sellers I've been drawing out: the reflectiveness (which was moody and mystical) and the rashness—Wingate had an impetuosity which must have seemed almost crazy. Sellers responded to the drama of a heroic career (chasing around desert and jungle after dark—episodes for Dan Mendoza!), and felt an affinity, too, with Wingate's maverick nature. Both actor and soldier were loners who liked to spark off fear and wonder. When Wavell says that 'Wingate's dynamic personality won acceptance for his ideas,' we can imagine all kinds of persuasiveness and charisma being applied when he wanted to have things his way—again, like Sellers. Perhaps what both men shared was an ability to feign. To succeed at guerrilla warfare, to melt into the vegetation and the sand, you need, beyond the daredevilry, the actor's skill of invisibility. You have to deceive the enemy. Wingate's effrontery and intelligence call for ironic treatment—not the conventional historic pageant generals and adventurers normally receive from the cinema. Sellers, at his best when reserved or close, could have conveyed what his character was thinking because Wingate's shrewdness and head-strong aloofness were qualities he himself shared, and which sent him mad.

♦ ♦ ♦

Sellers was liberated from the RAF, with his Burma Star decoration, in 1946, after the Gang Show, under the ENSA Entertainments for Allied Forces banner, had presented *Jack and the Beanstalk* as '100 Minutes of High-Speed Variety' at the Théâtre Marigny, Paris. Sellers put his drums on the back of an open truck and played 'When the Saints Come Marching In' all the way up the Champs Élysées at dawn. 'The above-named,' said his Wing Commander on his release certificate, 'is strongly recommended for any work with entertainment.'

Back in Britain, life was not so amusing. 'After I came home I tried to get work as a drummer. I went to the agents. But it seemed that every drummer in London was out of a job. So I hung about in Archer Street with all the others. Sometimes I'd get an evening playing for some dance or other, but that was all.' Playing for Don Costa, he got the sack: 'I fell off the stand during "El Relicario". Mind you, the stand was a bit narrow, and the tempo was a bit fast.'

One person who saw the forlorn sight of Sellers hustling for work was Wally Stott, the conductor and composer who did all the orchestrations for 'The Goon Show': 'Archer Street used to be choc-a-bloc with musicians standing around hoping to get a gig for that night, or catching up with friends. Peter was in a RAF uniform, standing in a doorway, on the fringe of this activity, and with a side-drum under his arm, trying to get a job...'

For a while he recoursed to a desk job at the WAAF (Women's Auxiliary Air Force) headquarters in Cadogan Square, helping to organise the itinerary for the all-girl Gang Shows which Ralph Reader had newly set up. Sellers also helped them to rehearse three times a week, and there he met Paddy Black (now Mrs Margaretta Neilly, of Belfast). One day he rang her and asked if she'd go to the movies. She did so, and until her Gang Show left for a tour of Europe, they spent every available moment together. They danced at the Nuffield Centre and listened to music and the radio at the flat Sellers was sharing with his parents, 211B, High Road, Finchley, N2. 'He was generous and fun-loving', recalls Mrs Neilly, 'A mimic, who loved to perform.'

They went to see a film which was then showing in London and drawing vast crowds. Ignoring the long queue, Sellers said to his girlfriend, 'Watch this!' and guided her into the foyer. 'I wish to see the manager,' he announced. The manager arrived and Sellers, in a stage Irish accent, explained that Paddy, his sister, was due to go back to Dublin the next day, and wouldn't it be a pity if she should leave London without seeing this wonderful fillum. The manager showed them the street.

On another occasion, Sellers approached four young Scottish soldiers, whom he thought might jostle him, as they were the worse for drink, and demanded their names, rank, etc., declaring himself to be a Captain. One of the squaddies, swaying from side to side, told the fucking Captain what he could fucking do and where he could fucking go. 'Peter was left looking foolish,' remembers his companion.

Sellers gave Paddy a fur-lined jacket when she left for the continent: '"You'll need it," he said, and I did.' He also gave her a brooch, or pin, in the shape of a large P, for Paddy. Paddy said that that was doubly apt because her real name, Margaretta, was often abbreviated to Peggy. Sellers was thrilled 'because that's my mother's name!' Peg, meantime, took to her bed. Paddy seldom saw her, only heard an anguished and insistent 'Pet*ar*, Peeet*arr*!' summoning him away from behind a closed door.

Sellers, having been away for the best part of three years, was no longer comfortable with his mother; he didn't feel secure with her, and this showed itself in his over-anxiety to please. He'd continually telephone her during the evening if he was out in London. She made him feel guilty, as if he shouldn't have a life or any interests except for her. This tended to put a dampener on romance. As Mrs Neilly recounts: 'His mother would invariably call from the bedroom, and Peter would immediately go to her, until, in the end, I was obliged to ask, "Is your mother an invalid?" "No," he assured me, "But she is poorly and will have to stay in bed for a while."' Peg generally treated him like a child, telling him what to wear, 'ordering him to put his cap on as it was raining outside. I looked at Peter and he was decidedly embarrassed.'

Sellers was easily intimidated by Peg; the boundless love and devotion he was expected to demonstrate became a ritual, an act. Bill, however, was more stalwart. Mrs Neilly remembers thinking that 'here was a charming and gracious man, perhaps a little shy, but quick to start an intelligent conversation, especially when he learned that I came from Northern Ireland. He was genuinely interested and we had a discussion about the complexity of this troubled land.' As a Protestant who'd married into a Jewish dynasty, Bill knew about loyalists and outcasts first hand. Whilst they were discussing the Ulster/Eire divisions, Sellers came in and started to reminisce about having been sent to a Catholic school and being congratulated by Brother Cornelius for knowing the Articles of Faith. 'You see,' he said, imitating the master, 'He knows the answer and he's a Jew.'

As she had seen Sellers humiliated by an Odeon manager, soldiers in a state of beery exaltation, his mother, and (retrospectively) his teacher, it is little wonder that Mrs Neilly 'did not see a potential genius,' only a fantasist. One afternoon he announced that they were going to see an earl, 'a relation who had a title of some kind.' He and Paddy took the bus to Cumberland House, Thakeham, Sussex, to meet Gerald Rufus Isaacs, the Marquess of Reading. 'It was an enjoyable afternoon. Relics, regalia, and the family history were discussed and admired. When we left, Peter explained that the title was hereditary and he was next in line...' This would mean, he went on, spelling it out, that if Paddy would consent to marry him, she would then become a Countess. What Sellers must have known was that the Rufus Isaacs', a family of distinguished lawyers and stockbrokers, were able to trace themselves back to Daniel Mendoza. So Sellers decided to interweave himself with his distant cousins.

Sellers' could not reasonably (or fantastically) have had any sort of a chance at the coronet. He was living in a dream world. ('Though he was definite the title was coming his way.') The second marquess already had a son, Michael Alfred Rufus Isaacs, and he himself had a family well underway. The present (fourth) marquess, Simon Charles Henry, had been born in 1942. Knowing of Sellers' obsession with Alec Guinness, one can't help but wonder whether he intended to bump them all off, as Dennis Price does the D'Ascoynes in *Kind Hearts and Coronets*. But Simon Reading's brother, Lord Anthony Rufus Isaacs, *was* the producer of both *The Blockhouse* and the advertisement Sellers made for Benson & Hedges tobacco in 1973. 'He used to tell me that we were related,' says Lord Anthony. So even if Sellers' ruling class antics in 1946 were elaborate ways of impressing women, his tenuous connection with the marquessate surfaced again nearly thirty years on. He liked to think himself different in blood from just about everybody. Lord Anthony, incidentally, and his sister Jacqui, were part of a circle which included Lord Snowdon, Princess Margaret, and Miranda Quarry, the daughter of Lord Mancroft, who became Sellers's third wife in 1970, until they divorced, four years later, Sellers' debonair period. (And his least relaxed. He came to despise being treated as the Kensington Palace clown. 'I say, Sellers, old chep, do something funny, there's a good chep!')

Paddy Black was more shocked at the back-handed proposal of marriage than she was at the revelation that her swain was an incognito prince. 'As much as I liked Peter, the idea of getting engaged never entered my head; and if it ever had, this bizarre incident would have convinced me that it was something not to be considered.'

She had no need to worry about any long-term exposure to a crank. Her European trip beckoned and Sellers asked if he might sign her autograph album— to reveal another surprise. 'He wrote a message and signed it Peter Ray. When I questioned the signature, he told me that he intended to make show business his career, and would change his name.'

She never saw him again. In the autumn of 1971, Sellers flew over to Belfast in a private plane with the yoga guru, Swami Vishna Devananor, and sprinkled ten thousand pro-peace leaflets upon the city. He later fell to earth and autographed many of them for fans, and he gave a bouquet of flowers to Mrs Irene Gallagher, whose daughter, Angela, had been murdered by IRA gunfire. Mrs Neilly's children wanted her to find and meet her old suitor, but she wouldn't be persuaded. Even if Sellers didn't after all become Peter Ray, the superstar was no longer 'this wonderful lad with a mass of waving hair and just a little overweight.' Outwardly, and with nine years yet to live, he had indeed become a magnifico, more famous than any earl. The attempted rendezvous could have flopped, like Jack Salt's. The last time he saw Sellers was in 1951. Sellers had gone as a variety act to South Parade Pier. He was with Peg, and Salt was in Wally Fry's Band. 'He came to see me,' said Salt, 'when I was working in the ballroom, but he wouldn't wait until the interval. That was the last time I saw him—when he disappeared. Then, when he had his big heart attack in 1964, I went up to Elstead, where he was now living and recuperating, but the butler wouldn't let me in and I was turned away at the gate.'

Chapter Three

♦ ♦ ♦

Peace Work

To take his mother's maiden name like that, and become Peter Ray? It was a blatant attempt to appease Peg—a pseudo-marriage, a proclamation that no other woman could eclipse her in his eyes. It was also a way of siding with her when it came to signalling displeasure at Bill's wartime disappearances with 'The Welsh Deanna Durbin'. 'Peg took him back,' recalls Anne Levy. 'Bill suffered for the rest of his life for going back. I think he always had to feel grateful he'd been taken into the fold again. A very close Jewish family and he was the outsider.' The flat at 211B, High Road, East Finchley was a Mendoza property.

Sellers/Ray also kept up the falsehood that he was of lofty lineage—perhaps necessary to his esteem at a time of diminishing success. 'I couldn't get a job' he recalled of 1947, 'I was just living on Mum and Dad' (and *they* were being propped up by the network of cousins). It wasn't Rufus Isaacs he aligned himself with now, but another illustrious nineteenth-century Jew, Benjamin Disraeli, the first (and only—except for Sellers) Earl of Beaconsfield, who died in 1881. If Sellers didn't have a Regency pugilist to go on, he did have George Arliss' Oscar-winning biopic—the cunning Prime Minister, with his lock of hair and stagey mannerisms.

It was as Lord Beaconsfield that Sellers upgraded himself in Norwich, whither he'd gone as a fairground barker, his ambitions as a drummer in abeyance. He'd grown bored with Syd Seymour and His Mad Hatters, 'because it was mostly a matter of hitting things every time Syd fell over', and he lost bookings for dance bands because he didn't have his own van to transport his timps and snares. So instead he strode around the carnival in a frock coat, twirling a cane, and inviting people to step inside the tents and see the Bearded Lady, the Death by a Thousand Cuts, the Siamese Twins. It was a circus side-show and Sellers, fooling himself into thinking he was a lost blue blood, was one of the freaks—a view which struck Milligan in 1969: 'Peter is a freak, not a genius, which makes him even more unique. His ability to reproduce another character is so startling, he himself must have some kind of misshapeness inside him. Once, when I was on stage with him, he came on every night as a different person. As I looked at him, he wasn't Peter at all ...' It was as if, when performing, he was in the grip of a terrible enchantment.

The fol-de-rol ringmaster he played at the fair—all swank and beringed gloved fingers, and as grandiose and foxy as any con-man—merged into the attitudinising Disraeli when Sellers returned to his hotel. According to his own account, given to Alfred Draper, author of *The Story of the Goons*, porters and chambermaids bowed and curtsied and the manager allowed Sellers to make a ceremony out of signing the visitors' register. When Lord Beaconsfield returned from his evening stint with the Two Headed Baby and The Living Torso, however, the hotel staff had had leisure to decipher the curlicues of scratchy copperplate. Wasn't East Finchley an odd place for an earl to hail from? And wouldn't a patrician puff on gold-tipped Balkan Sobranies rather than Woodbines?

'Two gentlemen are waiting to see you, my Lord,' said the manager coldly.

Plain-clothes officers from the RAF Special Investigation Branch, who had been apprised by the suspicious servantry, came forward out of the gloom of the lounge. They were looking for a deserter.

'Lord Beaconsfield?'

'What can I do for you?'

'Wouldn't it be more correct to say 2223033 Aircraftsman Sellers?'

'You have a point there, it would.'

Sellers produced his discharge papers (the one including the testament 'The above-named is strongly recommended ...'), was laughed at and left alone.* He slunk back to London the following day, put his brass-buttoned costume back in the skip, and the survivors of Ray Bros. Productions Ltd. put their heads together to see if another job could be found. It was. Relief Entertainments Manager for the tail-end of the summer season at a holiday camp in Jersey.

He was still Lord Beaconsfield, though. Local newspapers took an interest in why a peer should be so egalitarian as to run the bingo competitions and adjudicate on knobbly knees. The job had actually come about because of Dick Ray Jnr., who lived with his family in another part of the Mendoza parish, Rosslyn Hill, Hampstead. Dick's father, also called Dick Ray, was in the stage curtain business with his brother, Ray Ray, making curtains for theatres. With the demise of variety, after the war, there was little demand for the acres of levitating velvet, so Dick Jnr., when he came out of the RAF, instead of taking over his father's firm, went to Jersey to put on shows and operate as an agent. (He is there today, and owns the Jersey Opera House and Caesar's Palace.) Dick Jnr.'s mother and Sellers' Peg were sisters—so it was a close cousin for whom he went to work.

The Beaconsfield charade could no longer be anything except a hoot—and publicity, until he was sacked—and wasn't there perhaps, after all, a superfluity of bright people named Ray? Sellers was back to being Sellers when he went, next, to Peterborough, as the bottom-of-the-bill comic in a show starring Dorothy Squires, who, in sunglasses and white rabbit fur, was then starting out as a songbird with Billy Reid's Accordion Band. Sellers' George Formby impressions and uke playing were boring the audience in Peterborough to distraction. 'To stand on a stage and be the centre of such hostility is a frightening experience. I was literally shaking when I came off', he remembered. 'During the interval between

---

* Peter Evans, perhaps more realistically, says that Sellers pretended to be Lord Beaconsfield only on the telephone, when making his reservation, and that the military police met Sellers in the privacy of the manager's office.

houses the manager came to the dressing room I was sharing with six others, and handed me a cheque for £12. "You're no good here, Sellers boy. Here's your money. There's no need for you to appear again." I sat there miserably, determined not to give up, but not knowing what to do.' Miss Squires, realising that her own vampish act was affecting the audience's mood, un-preparing people for Sellers' whimsicalities, interceded on the young man's behalf.

'I hear you've fired the comic,' she said to the manager, 'I'd like you to keep him on. You know Monday's always a bad house.'

'Well,' came back the grudging assent, 'I think he must be the worst comic in the business.'

Disconsolately, the non-comic went back to the drums, at the Aldershot Hippodrome, commencing February 9, 1948. 'As a story of total and absolute disaster,' Graham Stark has said of Sellers' appearance there, 'it unfailingly reduced me to tears of laughter.

No doubt Sellers improved on the truth, making an anecdote of a low ebb into a misadventure to rival Clouseau, but at the time it was mortifying. The missed lighting cues and a pit band chewing sandwiches and lagging four bars behind… 'I had a crushing defeat in Variety in Aldershot—a terrible thing it was,' was how he put it in more reflective moments. It was another experience to fill Sellers' heart with hate. And what this period was doing was to provide, not a fund of chuckles galore, but an excuse for Sellers to be an avenger for the rest of his life. When he misbehaved later on, reckons Milligan, and acted the rôle of deranged genius to perfection, 'every official that got ignored by Peter was not only paying for his own idiocy, he's paying for all the idiots in all Peter's past life; idiot producers who ruined wonderful material; idiot managers who told him he couldn't act; idiot BBC officials who treated him like a naughty boy. They were the enemy and had to be destroyed, or Peter couldn't survive.'

In 1948, however, Sellers was still trying to cling on. Remembering Ilfracombe, Jersey and the seaside, he went to the Kilburn Empire to audition before Hedley Claxton, an impresario who was casting his summer season revue for the Lido Theatre, Cliftonville, Margate. He lost out to Benny Hill who worked on a couple of radio shows with Peter a few years later. Sellers' patter, pretending to be that of a Red Indian journalist sending home his opinions of London to *The Pawnee Graphic*, was a bit saucy. Benny Hill, who sang a calypso, accompanying himself on a guitar, stayed at the Lido Theatre for three years. After the audition, he bought Sellers coffee and cake at Velotti's Café, where they exchanged addresses and phone numbers and promised to pass on news of any jobs. In 1955, when Sellers was quite the radio star, but his face unknown, Hill told *Picturegoer* to 'Watch Peter Sellers. He's going to be the biggest funnyman in Britain.'

◆ ◆ ◆

Peg was also foretelling the future. She was trying to find an agent to represent her son and informing them, as Sellers sat there nervously fiddling with his gloves: 'My son is going to be worth a lot of money in this business. Listen to an old woman who knows'—words which make her sound like a wild-eyed gypsy in a Verdi opera. Sellers said that his decision to audition for the Windmill, however, was his own. 'I had the idea of trying the Windmill Theatre. I got an act together—stories, impersonations... Those audiences waiting all day to see the nudes—it seemed lunatic for me to try. But I got the job: £25 a week for a month.'

Six weeks, actually, starting on Monday, March 17, 1948. Sellers was in the 211th edition of *Revudeville*, 'entirely conceived and produced by Vivian Van Damm.' The Windmill shows involved lots of moon-faced girls (was there ever a less becoming era for hair-dos and cosmetics than the forties?) baring their breasts and body stockings in tasteful tableaux. To get the performance past the Lord Chamberlain, the censor, the girls were not allowed to move. They had to be as pieces of classical statuary in a museum—alabaster casts of the Venus de Milo, etc.—and they made the best of being permitted to waft themselves with large ostrich feather fans.

Sellers eventually turned up in a sketch called 'Third Degree,' alongside Johnny McGregor and Pat Raphael. Having endured that, the audience was rewarded with muffs a-plenty, when the stage curtains parted on 'Eskimo Blues'. On and on it went, 'Cocktail Time', 'News girl,' until Sellers had a solo spot. He did Flying Officer Kite and the 'ITMA' characters, and a song written by Bill called 'I'll Never Worry'. Six times a day this cycle of tits, fans, gags, and lullabies was repeated.

Van Damm's 'ideas man' was the composer and pianist, Ronnie Bridges:

> I played for Peter at his audition. He did a little story and a song, which he said he'd written himself with his father—this I doubted... Sellers was the most determined of the lot without any doubt. He had *business*. All the others wanted to get on, of course... but the *determination* of Peter... He was quite ruthless in everything he did.
>
> He used to lean on me quite a bit, getting me to play, without charge of course, for all his auditions with agents... he'd take them out for meals; he'd give them presents. The first radio series he did, to get himself in with the BBC, he gave presents to each person in the cast—and this was unheard of; and nobody had heard of him, either...
>
> The snag was, with Sellers in the early days, he was only interested in people who could help him, and if he met somebody who could help his career more, you were forgotten. When Peter Sellers became big, he didn't want to know me—he tended to forget what I'd done for him. Harry and Mike were far more genial, and remain friends. Sellers was never genial.

♦ ♦ ♦

It succeeded though, didn't it—choking his virtue with foul ambition. Stardom, however, was won only at a terrible cost—to himself and to those whom he professed to love. When Sellers was breaking through from character actor to leading man in *The Millionairess*, it was his family who had to suffer. 'By the time he was having his relationship, consummated or not, with Sophia Loren,' Michael continued, 'we had gone from being his home-life and inspiration to being a chain round his neck. He begrudged us for impeding his chasing after Loren. He had to pay our bills ... He had to look after *this* ... he had to do *that* ... He resented us. He wanted freedom from family and obligation.' His family's opinion on the matter of his womanising didn't count because, as individuals, they no longer held any existence for him: they were simply hurdles keeping him away from his new pleasures. (That his new pleasures were to reach such a degree of dementia that he imagined Loren loved him back is a topic for the men in white coats—and this biographer—to classify.)

Peg gave up her freedom to facilitate her son's; he expected everybody else to be as accommodating. Uncle Bert made the observation that 'those first years after the war, when Peter was having such a lean time of it, aged Peg twenty years.' In addition to her over-assertiveness with agents—driving them away rather than the reverse—she pampered Sellers as never before, fattening him up, cocooning him. Milligan says that, because of this, 'he was in training for a heart attack from the age of twenty onwards. He ate everything that was fat and his mother told him always to rest and never overwork himself. He never did any exercise and I think he'd be alive today if he had. Isn't that a real Irish one? He'd be alive today if it wasn't for the fact he's dead.' He became, within the physical flab, purified egotism.

Ambitious past all thinking, Sellers may have dropped his viscounties and the desire to be Peter Ray, but there was much mileage to be gained from being a Sellers. For a start, he was handing sub-editors their headlines on a plate: 'In A Sellers Market,' 'Best Sellers,' 'The Rest is Sellers,' etc. Then, he was going through a period of being close to his father—practising the uke, learning his routines (which he was to replicate to such effect in *The Optimists of Nine Elms*). And though Bill, his face as expressive as a standing pond, might look like the ghost of what he'd become if he didn't shift, Sellers knew his own greed and curiosity were of a different order—and besides there were other Sellers' to meet.

He decided, for example, he was a relative of the Rt. Hon. Sir Frederick A. Sellers, a judge on the Northern Circuit and a Lord Justice of Appeal (he died in 1979). He knocked on m'lud's door, at Highwood Lodge, Mill Hill, NW7, and asked 'my uncle Fred' for a loan of £100 to help him start his career. (He was seen off.) Nobody with a Sellers surname was safe, then or later. When he was making *Tom Thumb* at Elstree, he met a local divine, the Rev. Dr Robert Sellers, who lived in Cheshunt and was a professor of Biblical and Historical Theology at London University. He cavorted in priest's clothes, and introduced himself to the congregation as the vicar's cousin, Sexy Recsy (recsy=rector). A few years later, at the Dorchester, he discovered that there was another Mr Sellers staying as a guest in the hotel. He pretended to be leglessly drunk and had himself carried to the namesake's room at three A.M., where, after rousing the occupant, the porters were to ask: 'Do you know this man?' They received an angry NO! The next morning, Sellers saw the second Sellers and yelled 'You bastard!' across the Grill Room.

◆ ◆ ◆

Sellers, very proud, revengeful, and ambitious, used the Windmill as a proving ground. 'And I'll tell you this,' he informed trumpeter Freddy Clayton, 'if you can get by there, you can get by anywhere. It really was wonderful experience.' When his stint ended, on April 24, Van Damm decreed that the name 'Sellers' be added to the plaque in the foyer: STARS OF TODAY WHO STARTED THEIR CAREERS IN THIS THEATRE. But, as Sellers said in 1962, 'Of course, that seemed like heaven. Then when it was over nothing else came of it. I simply couldn't get work with the BBC. I knew I could do impressions, but nobody would give me a chance.'

It was at this point he went outside his range, and won some eternal enemies. (My sources have requested anonymity.) Sellers became a Freemason. 'Sellers joined the Freemasons,' I was informed, 'purely as a way of seeking advancement. He made a mockery of it. He bandied the phrases and signals about at the BBC, to impress producers and executives—but he only bought dishonour upon himself and humiliation to those masons who had sponsored him. A disgrace.'

That he'd automatically wanted to mock the brotherhood's theatricality and religiosity will come as no surprise. (He was unable to go through with the rituals for joining the Grand Order of the Water Rats because he kept laughing too much.) The craft was a Ray Bros. revue and High Mass at St Aloysius' in one go. But the purposes of freemasonry, its mysterious boy-scout ceremonies aside, are charitable and social—the Grand Masters of the Order, especially in recent years, have worked hard to dispel the aura of an exclusive, secret sect. And when you are initiated, you swear an oath that you will not use the privileges of the society for personal gain. Sellers, by being the very worst kind of mason, the sort that brings the assembly into public hatred, ridicule, and contempt—well, it shows the emergence of the sort of man he was.

◆ ◆ ◆

It is true that, for all his running and jumping, he was standing still. Since coming back from Jersey he'd been trying, without success, to get employed by that fledgling medium, television. He'd tried again and again to make himself heard. On January 28, 1948, for instance, he'd written to the Booking Manager at Alexandra Palace, Muswell Hill, 'in the hope that you can fix me an audition for television. I shall be in London for the next twelve days prior to variety at Aldershot...', and he added; 'my act... is that of a comedian.' He received an invitation to a preliminary audition at Star Sound Studios, Baker St., on February 2, 1948. He celebrated receipt of the good news with Paddy Black—she remembers that he'd tried so hard to get the BBC to acknowledge his existence. The report card for Sellers' first audition describes him as a 'pleasant & vivacious young man in dinner jacket' and that his performance, which lasted eight and a half minutes, consisted of 'comedy impressions arranged as Black Market sketch, impersonating different types bartering for tin of sardines, followed by comic sketch "The Piccolo," with vocal finish.' 'The Gang Show' (and 'awaiting audition for Windmill Theatre') is mentioned as his only experience, and the conclusion is: 'A refreshing and talented performer. Parts of this act should prove ideal Tele. Variety.'

Sellers was informed that the BBC would 'be glad if you will attend a Camera Test, under normal Television studio conditions, at Alexandra Palace, on Thursday, 19 February, 1948, at 4.30 P.M.' The camera test went well enough for Sellers to be booked to appear on 'New To You' on March 18 and 23, at a fee of 7 guineas, and again on May 3, for 8 guineas (about $15). After that, television faded out, but this hardly mattered: he'd broken through to radio. Again, however, the start was sluggish. Sellers wrote to Michael Standing, the Head of Radio Variety, late in 1947 ('I am sorry I have not written before as I have just returned from Jersey'), only to have a note back from C. F. Meehan (Assistant Director of Variety), suggesting that he try Mr Dennis Wilson, at the Aeolian Hall, 'who will arrange for an audition as soon as possible.' On blue notepaper, engraved with the heading—

PETER SELLERS
'Bang On'

—and in the neatest, most elegant script ever seen outside of Miss Helen Penn's class at St Mark's Kindergarten, the following was set down on January 15, 1948:

> Dear Sir,
>
> I received the enclosed letter from Mr. Meehan. I shall be in town for the next three weeks prior to variety at the Hippodrome, Aldershot. Shall be glad if you can arrange an audition during my stay in town.
>
> Yours Very Truly
Peter Sellers

As an example of Sellers the suppliant—a humble petitioner—it is unique. But even in this early letter, the schoolboy formality of the calligraphic layout does not quite manage to hide the arrogance ('I would be pleased if you would give it your personal consideration,' he says to Standing); nor does he downplay his assurance: 'Bang On' indeed. (Is the allusion to his drumming, or to being spot-on with his mimicry?) There is a raffishness, too, in the references to 'my stay in town', and the briskness of 'shall be glad if' is almost offhand. Sellers is only ostensibly polite. Wilson replied on January 26:

> I am sorry it will not be possible for us to hear you at an audition within the next two or three weeks, but this is to let you know that we have added your name to our waiting list and we hope to be able to send you an invitation in due course…
> In the meantime I should be glad if you would send me some details of your act, together with any useful information about your professional experience.

In response to Wilson's final paragraph, Sellers compiled an extensive list of his many voices, impressions, and musical abilities. Ironically, his final album, *Sellers' Market*, recorded in Paris during 1979, when *The Fiendish Plot of Dr Fu Manchu* was in pre-production, includes a track called 'The Compleat Guide to Accents of the British Isles', and on the record as a whole he mimics forty-eight different dialects. He was circling back to a time when he had reasoned: 'I had an aptitude for dialects, and I'd studied them. I figured that the more dialects I could do and the more precise they were, the more chance there was of getting a job on the BBC. That's what I was after—to be a BBC voice man like Jon Pertwee, Maurice Denham and Kenneth Connor.' In 1979, he'd recently completed his deadpan rôle in *Being There*; it was as if he needed to unloose his tongue, exercise his baroque facility for funny voices again.

It is possible to see many of his future characters in the sounds he could make in 1948. The Rev. Smallwood from *Heavens Above* (Birmingham), Dick Scratcher from *Ghost in the Noonday Sun* (Irish), John Lewis from *Only Two Can Play* (South Wales). Civil Service and colonel types would recur, overlain with Grytpype Thynne and Bloodnok; George Formby, of course, Sellers had absorbed and would redeploy. Here is Sellers in embryo; and when it came to *Sellers' Market*, there was Sellers, about to die, full of nostalgia for his beginnings. Another track 'Don't Cry for Me, Argentina, There' was sung by a Cockney unsure of the words, accompanied by a drummer who'd lost the beat. 'The drummer on the record is me,' Sellers told Judith Simons proudly. 'I started in show business as a drummer and pianist and the beat is the music of the NAAFI.' He was also able, in a song called 'Eaton Square Blues', composed by Alan Clare, to be revenged upon the toffs at the Devonshire and Somerset hunt balls he'd long ago played at with his father. 'At every hunt ball I can recall there was some aristocrat wanting to pour his heart out like a man from Mississippi. They never addressed me as the pianist. When they wanted me to accompany their singing they would simply shout "Piano!"'

After these words appeared, Judith Simons was startled to receive this response from Sellers: 'I do not play the piano. I did not tell you I did and wish I had not seen Monday's *Daily Express*,' he curtly cabled. Why, she'd only printed an easy-going puff for his new record. Her editor must have stuck up for the reporter, because Sellers attacked again on October 15, 1979:

> Dear Show Business Editor Victor Davis: Your telex to hand. I do not send borish [*sic*] telegrams undeservedly. Only when it is disheartening to read badly written things I did not say. Peter Sellers. Show Business Person, Peter Sellers. P.S. Once again, Up Yours.

Even allowing for the fact that he was ill and mad, weekending on his own at Gstaad, this was an extraordinary over-reaction; yet it is possible to work out what was on his mind. He wouldn't have wanted to go into the motives behind 'Eaton Square Blues' with a newspaper interviewer, of course, but he'd been remembering Bill's belittlement, rather than his own, with that cry of *piano!*, and for the sake of anecdote he had simplified it all. He was sensitive, you see, to his father's having been held cheap, and seeing the mention of the piano player in print like that, the shame and contempt of the early days coursed back, memories flapping about him like uncaged birds.

As he modestly put it in 1948, he could manage only a 'bit of piano'. Bill was the one who'd lashed the NAAFI keyboard to the back of the van when they toured the West Country and Lancashire during the war. And Judith Simons, in her innocence, was not to know that Sellers' career, which had made him, as he told her, a tax exile,* was closely interwoven with Bill's discomfiture and frustration. Sellers had relived the crestfallen old man a dozen times—Henry Orient, the pianist; Juan Bautista, the ex-matador guitarist; Sam Hall and his uke, doing a wonderful bal-

---

* 'Though I can't come to Britain I still know what is going on. I read all the newspapers and I have a friend who tapes the BBC programmes for me ... And I listen continually to the BBC Overseas Service.'

alaika; Clouseau scraping his violin; Hrundi Bakshi concentrating on the sitar; and let's add, too, Queen Victoria playing jazz piano and Fu Manchu's music hall organ. Sellers' characters have the urge to vamp, twang, and fiddle, but they are barely better than gifted amateurs. They are too dippy to be hardened pros. And, flopping as musicians, they fail at their official occupations. The much-gored bull-fighter; the film extra who knocks down the sets; Clouseau, unlucky in love and at solving crimes; Old Sam, reduced to busking; and by extension, there's Fred Kite, locked outside the factory gates. Such characters are not overreachers, trying to get more out of life than it can reasonably give (*that* was Sellers' dilemma), nor under-achievers (which was Peg's problem, so she added her unfulfilled ambitions to her son's); but they are the people who don't jump out at you, whose eccentricity seems to come from their naivety rather than any demonic razzle-dazzle. Sellers got under their skin. Part of his riddle is that his success was based on playing bunglers and the outclassed. He understood the burden of their dreams; he knew what urged them on. And in describing this sympathy, in acknowledging Sellers' ability to unpack their hearts and let us sense their aspirations, we come close to what made him a great actor, able to produce great effects. Sellers' involuntary gift was the power of his imagination. If an artist is a person who makes something out of nothing (the blank canvas, the empty page, the silent orchestra), Sellers made somebodies out of his variations on Mr Nobody. His mice can roar.

♦♦♦

Dennis Wilson, however, couldn't have been much impressed by Sellers' catholic list of voices and imitations because he made no response. Did he think it simple showing off? It wasn't until the end of March, with Sellers at the Windmill, that another overture was made to the BBC, this time through a more professional channel. Sellers had finally found an agent: Russ Carr of Barney Jacobs Ltd., Piccadilly Circus, SW1. Wilson had coincidentally just been to the Windmill to see Robert Moreton. He'd watched Sellers' act by accident and had at last been impressed. Sellers betook himself to the Aeolian Hall with equal speed. It was his make-or-break audition—on April Fool's Day, 1948, at that. 'I was shown into a room with a microphone. No one else was there and I did my piece.'

The concealed adjudicators scribbled these comments:

Peter Sellars [*sic*]
Singing not bad, though no great asset. Very good at dialects. Impressions good. Likeable personality. With better material he could be a real find...

On the upper left and bottom right hand corner of the card, the word YES was typed. A handwritten scribble, 'Passed for Broadcasting' runs across the top edge. An acceptance letter was sent to Russ Carr the next morning. Nothing happened for another two months. It must have been during this period that Sellers, believing himself to be getting nowhere fast, made his historic telephone call from a public booth in Soho. He recounted the caper many times, and did so with particular gusto on the 'Parkinson' talk show in 1974:

I noticed that Roy Speer was doing a radio show at that time called 'Show Time', and the compère was Dick Bentley, and there were lots of new acts, you see. And I'd written in I don't know how many times to try and get in on the show, with no reply. One of the big shows on the air was 'Much Binding in the Marsh', with Kenneth Horne and Dickie Murdoch. Well, you know, you do things at certain times. You feel *you've got to get ahead, you've got to get ahead*! So I phoned up and I thought, being a senior producer, Speer would probably know Horne and Murdoch, you see, who were very big then. And I thought, if I click with the secretary, I'll get put through, right? So I said, 'Oh, hello, I'm Ken Horne, is Roy there?' 'Oh' she said, 'Yes he is'—and I *knew* I was all right. So Roy got on and said, 'Hello, Ken. How are you?' I said 'Listen, Roy, I'm phoning up because I know that new show you've got on—what is it? 'Show Time', or something?—Dickie and I were at a cabaret the other night, saw an amazing young fellow called Peter, what was his name? Sellers. Peter Sellers. And he was very good. Probably have him on the show, you know. Just thought I'd give you a little tip—a little tip ...

He said, 'Well that's very nice of you.' And then it came to the crunch, and I said, 'It's me.' He said, 'What?' I said, 'It's me, Peter Sellers talking, and it was the only way I could get to you, and will you give me a date on your show?' And he said, 'Oh, you cheeky young sod. What do you do?' I said, 'Well obviously, impersonations ...'

Sellers went to see Speer at his office, who told him again he was a 'cheeky young bastard, this is highly irregular ...', but he had a booking at last: 'Show Time', on July 1, 1948, rehearsals three o'clock until six, and the programme itself was broadcast from half-past seven until a quarter past eight that same evening. Sellers was paid ten guineas (about $22) for his three and a half minutes. The programme was made at The People's Palace, Mile End Road, and a recording of Sellers' act has miraculously survived.

The band plays a few bars of 'Happy Days' as an opening fanfare, and Sellers is suddenly explaining to us, rather formally, that he is going to do a sketch about a foreigner who has learned English from a short-wave radio set. And then he unleashes himself, doing all the hoots, rasps, whines, and white noise, as well as an oriental voice trying to cut through the crackle, his sentences broken up by the interference. Sellers keeps a grip on the tale he's weaving—it isn't a mess. But he must have looked strange, standing on stage in his tuxedo, discharging such a commotion. There was no doubting the versatility, however, or his precision—or the rapidity of his vocal changes and delivery, which was like lightning. And, as he said in 1962 'I began getting work ...' Indeed he did. He was back on 'Show Time' on August 19 and became a regular. He began to appear on Dennis Wilson's 'It's Fine to be Young' (August 31; September 7, 14, and 21) and A. Scott Johnson's 'Tempo for Today'. He appeared on Speer's 'Starlight Hour' eleven times in two months. He went on Henry Hall's 'Guest Night', recorded at the Jubilee Theatre, Blackpool. And Sellers' new agent, Montague Lyon, of Eagle House, Jermyn Street, had to write and admonish his client's employers for prolonging the taint of amateurism:

We feel from the point of view of his future stage engagements it would be highly inadvisable to publicise the fact that he is extremely young or that he was associated with a service show during his R.A.F. career.

The pattern would become a familiar one. Sellers didn't like to be beholden to his immediate past, or to the people left behind there (e.g. Ronnie Bridges) whom he'd climbed clear of. As Ralph Reader's boy scout-ism was to be suppressed, so, later, he'd hate radio for holding him back from films, and he'd betray the people in any of those mediums who'd helped him to become who he was. Spike Milligan, Wolf Mankowitz, Blake Edwards, amongst others, were targets of Sellers' not being able to share a credit. (His wives and children received similar treatment.) But back in 1948, his professionalism and eagerness to please wasn't yet truculent; Sellers was starting to ascend and, hogging the air waves, he was like a one man chorus. His fee went from ten to twenty-five guineas for approximately six minutes work, and he was doing heaps of programmes every week.

◆ ◆ ◆

To listen to old radio shows is, literally, to wake the dead. The phonograph hiss beneath the voices and music is like the air escaping from opened graves, and the particular edition of 'Variety Bandbox' I have discovered, which was done on Jan. 15, 1950, at the Camberwell Palace Theatre, London, resurrects it all: a Queen Mary and George VI atmosphere, with fogs and trolley buses, the Euston Arch and tin advertisements for Bourneville chocolate and Veno's Cough Cure; a time of soot and snow, with the colour leaked out during the war put back in by the gaudy of the Crazy Gang and Dame Laura Knight's backstage gouaches. Despite the rationing of foodstuffs, people are too plump for their coats—buttons are put under strain from canteen cookery and sandwich suppers. In this pre-deodorant era, when folk only took baths once a week, and everybody smoked, think of the stink, overlain, as it would have been, by menthol lozenges.

The show begins with a brisk rooty-toot from the orchestra, drum rolls and fanfares. The compère, Philip Slessor, speaks most precisely. Everything is formal and courteous. The audience, rapt, provides polite bursts of applause. Slessor introduces the performances which are expert, contained, and we can *see* the ball gowns and dinner jackets. More than old-fashioned, this is a window on a vanished world. Nobody has a sardonic edge to their material. It sounds all so very innocent. The programme is Edwardian—its technology and outlook belongs with the hoots and puffs of steam trains.

And then, at last:

Here we have one of the really up and coming personalities that the past year or so's broadcasting has produced. With his amusing comedy impressions, I'm always very glad to reintroduce the rising star of 'Ray's a Laugh' and 'Petticoat Lane' and so forth—Peter Sellers!

After letting the acclaim die away, Sellers speaks with a dark voice: 'This is Peter Sellers taking you over to theatreland, to hear some excerpts from the new pantomime *Sellerinda*, with an all-star radio cast.' He then has his excuse to become Ted Ray, Crystal Jollibottom ('You startled me so, I've swallowed me upper set'), William Mate Cobblers (Buttons) and Soppy (the squeaky forerunner of Bluebottle). Most of the actual wireless mimicries he does I don't recognise and cannot judge (Robert Moreton, for example)—but it does sound like a crowd.

Sellers does the ugly sisters, the broker's men, hecklers in the audience. He fin-
ishes with Max Miller and Crystal Jollibottom singing alternate verses of the tes-
ticular 'I've Got a Lovely Bunch of Coconuts,' and then he leads the community
singing for 'Roll a Ball, a Penny a Pitch.' This merges into 'Variety Bandbox's'
closing theme, everybody belting out, in a hurdy-gurdy rhythm, 'Give us another
one, before you leave me'—the meaning of which I don't dare dwell upon.

♦ ♦ ♦

Inside a year, Sellers was at the Palladium, London's most prestigious music
hall, sharing the night with Gracie Fields—his first flesh and blood appearance since
becoming a busy radio feature. His two-week season started on October 3, 1949.
Sellers was ninth in the line-up (Our Gracie the tenth). 'Of course,' he said, 'being
on the BBC made it easier to get work in variety...the Palladium audiences were
always nice to me. I liked the Palladium. You could be rude to them and they did-
n't mind. I'd come on and say: "Heads up out of the trough!" And they didn't mind.'

Sellers' act involved impressions of the famous mingled with his own characters, Jollibottom, Soppy, etc. He then announced he was going to do an impersonation of Queen Victoria 'When she were a lad.' He went behind a screen and
emerged in a wig, an unlaced corset, army boots, and a large ginger beard. Some
people swear he carried a stuffed crocodile. He sashayed to the footlights and announced in grave tones: 'I'd like to be the first to admit that I do not know what
Queen Victoria looked like when she were a lad.' Our Gracie had her work cut
out topping that little exhibition. Wearing a black gown ('It's so tight I thought
I'd have to be wheeled on'), she sang 'You Made Me Love You', 'Alfonso, My Hot
Spanish Knight', and 'The Nun's Chorus'. But though the audience sang along
gaily and cheered her at the end, there was a feeling that, with Gracie they'd met
with things dying, with Sellers, a comedy that was new born.

And Gracie didn't forget, either. When Sellers was making *After the Fox*, seventeen years later, he went to see her, at her retirement villa. Gracie took Sellers
to tea, at a café she owned—and left him to pay the bill. 'That's for you, love.'

Sellers was already feeling the need to develop and change. The mimic is little better than a parasite feeding off the style and manners of the real achievers—
and Sellers knew himself to be more talented than the people he parroted: 'I hate
everything I do so much,' he said, 'that I always think I'm going to go one better
before I die. I mean, I always think there's something left in me. I know there is—
there's something sort of in there somehow that I want to get out.' That (apocryphal) stuffed crocodile is a clue to what would hasten Sellers on to a new and
more accomplished career. He had a power inside himself, kicking and fighting to
be let loose—intimated in the long ago by the drums—an iconoclastic streak; and
he'd recently met the only man on the planet who could help him to make any use
of it—Spike Milligan.

Part Two

♦♦♦

Radio Days

He pressed a key in the semi-darkness, and with a rending crackle there leaped between two brass knobs a spark, streams of sparks, and sparks again.

'Grand, isn't it? That's the Power—our unknown Power—kicking and fighting to be let loose,' said young Mr Cashell. 'There she goes—kick-kick-kick into space. I never get over the strangeness of it, ... waves going into space you know ...'

Rudyard Kipling, 'Wireless,' in *Traffics and Discoveries*

Chapter Four

◆ ◆ ◆

Old Comrades

There was always a great competitiveness between them—Sellers envious of Milligan's writing and inventiveness ('there's something about being left alone with that blank piece of paper...'), Milligan, in his turn, wishing he could break into films and make millions ('... he had the Midas Touch, chum. If ever that was passed on to somebody, it was Peter')—but the fact is, without the electrifying, jangly Irishman stinging him to the heart, Sellers would never have found his own unique style and method. I don't mean he'd have vanished. Sellers would have gone on to be like, say, Frankie Howerd, Dick Emery, or Benny Hill, a much-loved British comedian who also died of a heart attack—but he'd never have been an innovator, veering away from mimicry to 'beautifully observed vocal cartoons' (in the opinion of the Prince of Wales). Milligan released something in Sellers.

'We hit it off from the word go,' Sellers remembered. 'We were brimming over with ideas and we had sessions where we sat around and built mad, lightning sketches. The only way I can describe the form of humour we enjoyed is that we took any given situation and carried it to an illogical conclusion. That's where I find my comedy. You take a situation and think what would happen if you didn't do what you would normally do but something else. It's the runaway idea. You take an idea and just let your mind wander. I became saturated with it.'

Milligan, through the dream-like trappings of the Goons, made Sellers into Sellers. He never had the same effect on Harry Secombe, whose later career as a knighted doxologist denies his one-time feverishness. Nevertheless, Sir Harry, even if he has grown out of it all, is shrewd about Milligan's modus operandi: 'Spike had this crazy way of thinking, this illogically sane thing that goes beyond the gag. He's got a tremendous ability to evoke crazy mental pictures. He thinks visually, which is most unusual for a comic.'

The visions thus conjured gave Sellers a new reality—a home for his excesses. Goonery is a world without rules. Caddishness, cowardice and ignorance replace virtue and heroism, and become qualities to admire. The Rep. Company of characters—Eccles, Crun, Minnie Bannister, and Bloodnok amongst them—spend their time climbing Everest from the inside, searching for the piano Nappy played at Waterloo, or racing across the desert sands on a fifty-ton Wurlitzer organ. They encounter phantom batter pudding hurlers, head-shavers, and teeth-rustlers (who convert the gob crockery into castanets); and they travel gaily towards death and dismemberment by horse-drawn motor cars and atomic dustbins, transports which delightfully mutate: 'The ship was disguised as a train—to make the train sea-worthy it was done up to look like a boat and painted to appear like a tram...' Sound effects, advancing the action, included strangulations, boiling custard, exploding policemen, exploding fingers, exploding shirttails. One instruction in the script, for a solo Chinese lady singing a high-pitched wailing dirge, was to be speeded up to get an agonising vibrato—to be followed by the line, 'Gad—how Our Gracie has changed.'

As Milligan says, 'We *had* to create 'The Goon Show'—a fantasy world. You could make characters do what you wanted because you were writing the script. You always win. You can't get arrested in a fantasy world unless you wanted to. For anyone who found reality a bug, like Peter did, 'The Goon Show' was sheer therapy. Characters, like Neddy Seagoon, could be struck, beaten, burnt, boiled, drowned, clubbed, nailed to a cross—and Peter would love it. For him the characters were real, and they came alive.'

One of the first things Sellers had in common with Milligan, therefore, was misanthropy.

There was much else to intertwine them. Milligan's parents, like Sellers', had appeared in music hall—though only as a diversion from his father's real job, which was as a Quarter Master Sergeant in the Royal Artillery, out in Burma and India. Leo and Flo Milligan, as Leo Gann and Gwen Gorden, appeared at the Bombay Palace of Varieties, in an act called 'Fun Round the Sentry Box', and they sang in the Governor-General's band. Spike was born into the last five minutes of the Raj, and his childhood was cushioned by servants and ceremony—the regimental dances and the starlight, the quiet of the sub-continent's nights, the order of the society all made for a sense of proportion and measurement, which Milligan has striven to rediscover in his life ever since. For, in 1933, Leo was made redundant from the Indian Army. The family was ejected into a cold, unwelcoming England, which was to remain a foreign land, 'a damp, dead greyness that seemed to go on forever.' Milligan has lived the life of an exile.

His parents eventually emigrated to Australia. Towards the end of his days, Leo wrote his son a magnificent letter, which could be Bill talking to Sellers: 'I, too, had a creative mind, but was frustrated all the time...I suffered in silence, outwardly I was a happy and contented family man—I was a born actor.' Milligan himself is far from able to disguise his feelings. Periodically he suffers nervous collapses. He retreats to his bedroom and communicates with his wife and children by telegram, or else he checks himself into mental hospitals for injections of evipan and of sodium pentothal. He has had shock treatments and deep sleep narcosis, where he is generally anaesthetised for weeks on end. Such comas must be like dying and coming back—like Sellers' return visit to the underworld during his heart attacks. ('Of course, after his heart attacks Peter was never quite sure about which world he was living in...It became as if he was always wanting to die again so as to enjoy the moment and talk about it. Then he died once too often, didn't he?')

Milligan's psychiatrist commented in 1958: 'He really wants to hide himself from the world.' When he is not being ill, Milligan achieves this by escaping into his work—the goonish kingdom, where he can reduce behaviour to chaos and the ridiculous, for this is what he genuinely sees: 'We're a nasty bloody species... I'm very depressed about what's happening all over the world, when I see how ugliness has crept into our lives... You'd have to be a total idiot to be happy today.'

Thus, his archetypal hero is the tramp. In *The Bed Sitting Room*, he's Mate: 'Old cloth cap, ragged overcoat, zip-up boot slippers, large iron frame spectacles, old, about fifty-five, unshaven, long hair.' The joke is that, in a lawless environment, the tramp, a thick-witted outcast, is ridden with petty regulations—he's officious, a jobsworth.* Pettifoggery keeps him alive: you can't park there, put that cigarette out, keep off the grass, etc.

Such rules ruin the peace and quiet of Milligan's other hobo-figure, William McGonagall—the artist as extreme down-and-out. In *The Truth at Last*, illustrated by Sellers in 1976, the poet is imprisoned, starved, operated on for hemorrhoids, and infected with rabies, and when he returns home, 'his father split his head open with a loaded sock. Fourteen stitches later McGonagall repaired to his little room which his mother had carefully kept exactly how he had left it—filthy.' This would be a house fit for Eccles, the original stray:† 'Eccles was really the innocent creature that I was—the one that didn't want to cause any offense and loved simplicity, which I do. Yes, Eccles was the essential me.'

Milligan has played further variations on the shaggy tramp on stage in and on screen. In reality, Milligan is obsessively punctual and spotless; he is highly organised, and much enjoys the Victorian graces. Until he retired to Henry James' Rye, he lived in a large Gothic villa at Monken Hadley, Barnet, where gentlemen were expected to dress for dinner and fine wines were served. The Prince of Wales was a guest. In his house in Sussex, I noticed, on the walls above the waxed and polished antiques, a drawing by John Singer Sargent and watercolours by Hercules Brabazon-Brabazon; shelves contain neatly labelled geological specimens and arrow-heads. You expect the master to appear wearing a quilted crimson jacket, a fez, and pince-nez spectacles.

If Milligan is isolated not in poverty and muddle but by a sense of nineteenth-century scrupulosity, perhaps his problems began when he realised he was born in the wrong era. And the decorum he craves—the treasure island he's looking for—isn't cheap to maintain: 'I couldn't live in an ordinary community unless people were quiet and didn't smoke or have barking dogs. Most people are noisy, and it costs money to keep away from them.' He doesn't *mind* being a supertramp. He has no desire to rejoin the human race. He prizes his individuality, and even the

---

* A jobsworth is a derogatory term for a menial labourer whose ego is in inverse proportion to his position. Derives from the much-quoted phrase: 'I can't let you park there, chum. It's more than my job's worth.'

† Eccles, a relative of Disney's gormless Goofy, is also 'The Original Goon', according to *'The Goon Show' Scripts*: 'Educated at a Convent till age 7—end of education. Has had 18,312 interviews for jobs. Has never been employed. Spends his days walking around saying "Hello dere" to anyone who will listen...'

That Eccles Street, Dublin, was Leo and Molly Bloom's address in 1904 is no doubt one of those coincidences which will keep professors profitably amused for generations.

attacks of manic depression can be used in his work. 'The moods come on very suddenly, and I try to exploit them to my advantage ... It gives you a new spectrum of emotions that you didn't realise you had and you go to areas of emotional depth that are not accessible to other people ...'

His illness gives him an intensity. Whether his hypersensitivity was the product of his upbringing and experience, however, and whether his depressions are added extras or somehow traceable to his past, are vexed questions. Milligan's own descriptions of his disease, 'the black hopeless rose within me,' can be found in his poems, letters, and interviews. A memo he sent to his secretary is indicative:

A.   I'm not in.
B.   I'm very very ill.
C.   Don't let ANYBODY GO IN MY ROOM.
D.   I've had enough—Jesus had it easy.
E.   I'm at home.

That he could write the message at all suggests a degree of control; and if he is exhausted and prostrate, at least he can be grimly humourous (D) and he lets his staff know where he is (E)—which perhaps countermands (A). Is (B) self-pitying?

Milligan's mentality hasn't overthrown him; on the contrary, it made him as a writer. We are also expected to appreciate the sacrifice and cost. As he said just prior to *The Last Goon Show of All* in 1972, recalling its heyday: 'The pressure and the tension of keeping up the standard drove me mad. I dedicated my whole life to it, seven days a week. Christ, it was terrifying. I used to get up, get to the BBC before nine, work right through the day and evening and get the last tube [subway] home. Sometimes I'd miss it and Peter would come and take me home in his car. It cost blood to put that show on for me. Sheer agony. It wrecked my first marriage and it wrecked my health. My nervous breakdown happened while I was on the show.' More recently he has said, 'I had to write a new show every week for six months. If Hitler had done that to someone it would be called torture. I was in such a state of hypertension, I was unapproachable by human beings ...' He was taken, straitjacketed, to an asylum in Muswell Hill, whence he continued to write 'The Goon Show' from, presumably, a padded cell. 'I have to write a script every week to make a lot of idiot people laugh,' he told the doctors. 'How can they fucking laugh when I'm in such fucking pain? I'm desperate.' When he was indisposed, Eric Sykes and Larry Stephens assisted with the scripts. Sellers effortlessly took over Milligan's voices (Minnie Bannister, Eccles, Little Jim, Moriarty). Harry Secombe paid Milligan's medical bills. When he returned to the fray, his psychiatrist, Dr Joe Robson, as a precaution, sat in the audience (with a large butterfly net?).

◆ ◆ ◆

Like Sellers, Milligan had a highly-strung mother, who went one better than Peg and sent him to a girl's school, the Convent of Jesus and Mary, in Poona, 'to protect me from the realities of life'; and his father, Leo, like Bill, was often absent on tours of duty. Milligan attended many schools, including one in Rangoon run by the Christian Brothers de la Salle, similar to the Order at Sellers' St Aloysius'. It was all disruptive, itinerant, and Flo, matriarchal like Peg, was at her most gratified when her son was ill in bed and needing to be nursed. 'She had total control then, you see.' When they came to England for the penniless existence in Catford, Milligan never managed to mix with the British boys and formal education ended early. 'I sort of got lost and turned in on my self—into a world of fantasy.'

He had various dead-end factory or bum-type jobs in Deptford and Chislehurst, and his salvation was the trumpet. He sought escape, freedom, through jazz, as Sellers did with the drums; again like Sellers, he only began to find himself in the camaraderie of the Forces. The army game gave him security and brief happiness. Indeed, Milligan is the Siegfried Sassoon of World War II. After having experienced the fighting at first hand, he has relived it in slow motion ever since through those proliferating autobiographies, which commenced with *Adolf Hitler: My Part in His Downfall*. In compiling his books from journals, letters home, old comrades' diaries, contemporary newspaper clippings, and Regimental archives, Milligan makes a comic brew out of the horrors of combat—he makes it bearable by making it goonish (more on this later); and, in fact, his theories about comedy generally are militaristic. 'I try to go out into enemy territory,' he has said, 'where nothing has happened before.'

Once conscripted into the 19 Battery 56th Heavy Rgt. RA, he played in cabaret, *Boys in Battery D.*, and began to make up jokes and exploit his gift for the spontaneous gag. 'We were the only entertainment in Bexhill [the training camp] so we did some concerts there. We used to get dressed up in rags and tell jokes. People used to laugh at me, but I didn't think of myself as being particularly funny.' After experiencing heavy shell burst at Lauro, Italy, Milligan was sent to hospital at Afrigola and Portici, as a psycho-neurotic. He was eventually moved to the Central Pool of Artists and, through the director, Raymond Agoult, was cast in a variety show called *Over the Page*, where the star, in this Combined Services Entertainment, was Lance Bombadier Harry Secombe, 'a little myopic blubber of fat from Wales who had been pronounced a looney after a direct hit by an 88-mm gun in North Africa. He was asleep at the time and didn't know about it till he woke up. General Montgomery saw him and nearly surrendered. He spoke like a speeded-up record, no one understood him, he didn't even understand himself; in fact, forty years later he was knighted for not being understood.'

After demobilization, in the autumn of 1946, Milligan toured the continent with his band, the Bill Hall Trio, and tried to get established.* Back in Britain, and following disagreements with his mother, who was against the improvidence and temptations of show business ('... a lot of snobbery in that, you know, because it wasn't regarded as a proper job'—very *unlike* Peg), he shared a bed-sitting room at 13, Linden Gardens, Notting Hill Gate, with Secombe and Norman Vaughan. Secombe was already on his way. He'd had spots on 'Variety Bandbox' and, in October 1946, had done a stint at the Windmill. (He sang a duet with himself, al-

---

* His adventures are chronicled in *Where Have All The Bullets Gone?* (1985) and *Goodbye Soldier* (1986). That description of Secombe comes from p. 183 of the former.

ternating the swollen larynxes of Nelson Eddy and Jeanette MacDonald, whilst messily shaving. He concluded by drinking the soapy water and the nudes complained that they kept slipping in his lather.) Despite Secombe's advocacy, however, he failed to have Milligan hired after his own season was through. 'NEXT PLEASE!' Van Damm had shouted from the stalls, when Milligan turned up for his audition loudly apologising for being fully dressed.

Milligan failed, also, to interest Val Parnell in the Bill Hall Trio, when they were appearing at the Hackney Empire. 'I didn't work at all,' he has said of this period, 'just sort of wandered around.' Despite the mendicancy, he kept himself trim (something Sellers never did) at Ladywell Athletics Track, Bellingham Baths, and the outdoor lido at Brockwell Park. Occasionally he'd play at a dance with the Harlem Club Band or the Ritz Revels. One way or another he turned up behind the bar at Major Jimmy Grafton's pub in Strutton Ground, SW1, near the Houses of Parliament. Milligan pulled pints and slept in the attic under a pile of coats. Grafton, in addition to being a Mine Host off the pages of Chaucer, wrote material for a radio comedian called Derek Roy, another 'Variety Bandbox' stalwart (and his second cousin), and 'Jimmy... asked me if I would like to write with him. He gave me a quid [pound] or two. I used to graft like bloody mad.'

◆ ◆ ◆

It was at Grafton's, or points roundabout, where Sellers first encountered Milligan, Secombe, and that other founder Goon, Michael Bentine. As regards precisely who first introduced who to whom, where, and when, sources differ. Peter Evans states that Sellers met Milligan late in 1949 at the Bedford Music Hall, Camden Town (where Sellers, of course, had once lived): 'Secombe was self-consciously appearing in an all-male ex-service revue called *Soldiers in Skirts*. They met backstage together with another young comic called Michael Bentine.' Sellers' Authorised Biographer, Alexander Walker, repeats this information, except that now it is Milligan and Bentine who are 'doing a show called *Soldiers in Skirts* at the Bedford Theatre, Camden Town.'

None of them was ever in such a production. Secombe's drag revue was called *Forces Showboat*; he wasn't required to doll up; it was in 1948, not 1949; and it was rehearsed in Clapham and performed in Harrow, not Camden, and then toured.

The true sequence of events leading up to the convergence of such high-pitched talent seems to be:

a) Secombe met Bentine at the Windmill. 'There's a Goon if ever I saw one' he reported to Milligan, having found that they shared a fondness for animated cartoons by Max Fleisher. Bentine, with his partner, Tony Sherwood, had a piano and bongos act (called Sherwood & Forrest), where they dressed in undertakers' outfits and told, in wild Russian accents, some sort of fairy story. All very hectic, like Secombe's shaving—indeed, they took over from him at the end of his six-week sentence. 'We quickly sized each other up,' remembers Bentine of the meeting in 1946 with a Camay-covered Welshman, 'and liked what we saw.' Bentine went on (inevitably) 'Variety Bandbox', and when his partner left to study music at the Guildhall, he reverted to his real name (after ruling out Mike Pike, Mick Park, and Mack Tuck) and perfected a solo routine, a zany lecture about a metamorphosing chairback: the bit of broken furniture became a comb, a plough, pair of handcuffs, a guillotine, prison bars, etc. (You can see him performing it in Sellers's early film, *Down Among the Z Men*.*) Bentine was signed up by Monty Lyon, and Val Parnell hired him for *Starlight Roof* at the Hippodrome, Leicester Square, in 1947, with Vic Oliver and Julie Andrews. After that he toured in variety, appeared in cabaret at the Embassy night-club, Mayfair, and by August 1949 was booked for the Palladium as 'The Happy Imbecile,' alongside Borrah Minevitch's Harmonica Rascals and the Ink Spots.

b) Bentine and Secombe met Sellers (and Benny Hill), through Pat Dixon's 'Third Division', recorded at the end of 1948. 'This was the first time that Mike, Peter, and I had worked together and was a forerunner of "The Goon Show",' Sir Harry has remarked. No tape survives, though, interestingly, the show contained an early version of the mock travelogue Sellers was to make famous on one of his record albums, *Balham—Gateway to the South*, in which a crappy London borough is described as if it were Monte Carlo, say, or the Côte d'Azur. Frank Muir, its writer, said to me, 'Denis Norden and I employed Sellers first on radio in any meaningful way...He was a child. He was frightened, and the more successful he became, the more frightened be became...'

c) Bentine had begun to write some of Secombe's gags for 'Variety Bandbox'. They received a letter from Jimmy Grafton, complaining that Secombe's comedy was 'too bloody funny' and hence making life hard for Derek Roy, the principal pantaloon. Secombe and Bentine went to the pub in Victoria and (says Sir Harry), 'I was able to introduce Mike Bentine to the man I had been raving about—Spike Milligan.' Bentine remembers seeing a wraith sitting up in bed wearing army boots and long-johns: 'This seemed to be totally in keeping with his persona.'

d) 'The Goon Show' came about, says Bentine, 'as a direct result of the evening Harry and I spent with Jimmy Grafton at The Grafton Arms...We later introduced Mine Host to the youthful Peter Sellers.' In his autobiography, *Arias and Raspberries*, Sir Harry concurs: 'It was a most propitious day for me, because this was the place where 'The Goon Show' was born, and in due course Jimmy Grafton was to become my agent and manager...Naturally Mike and I took Peter along to Grafton's. He was so obviously one of us and his repertoire of impressions was formidable. Like the rest of us, he had been in the services and shared our lunatic sense of humour. Spike and Peter took to each other immediately and soon the four of us were meeting regularly.'

e) Secombe, on introducing Milligan, warned Sellers, 'The only trouble is, he is quite mad!'; Sellers, asked what had intrigued him most originally about Milligan, replied 'His name!'; when Bentine was questioned on what drew him

---

* The letter 'Z' is pronounced 'Zed' not 'Zee,' thus making the title a pun on the old sea shanty "Down among the dead men, let him lie."

to Sellers, he said 'Because he had talent!'; Milligan's response to the same query was 'His haircut!'

f) Milligan decamped from the Major's attic (accessible by ladder) to the spare room in 211B, High Road, East Finchley, and thence to a Mendoza property in Shepherd's Hill, Highgate. In these early days, he and Sellers still voyaged by public transport. 'Fares please,' said the conductor. 'Where are we going?' asked Sellers. Milligan produced a telephone from a cardboard box. 'Hello? is zat zer German Embassy? Vere are ve going?' He hung up and turned to Sellers, 'Düsseldorf.' When the conductor said he was only going as far as Wood Green, Sellers jumped to his feet: 'Quick—it's zer wrong bus. Hurry or we'll miss dinner ...'

g) When I asked Milligan for his favourite memory, he said: 'One of the funniest moments of my life was being woken up in my flat—I lived opposite him—at three o'clock in the morning, and Peter was standing there naked in a bowler hat and asked, "Do you know the name of a good tailor?"'

◆ ◆ ◆

The Grafton Arms was a playpen of competing egos. 'I used to tell jokes,' recalls Milligan, 'Harry Secombe was there and I'd play the piano a bit and Harry would sing and Peter would come in and do a few impressions of Kenneth Horne and others. Michael Bentine was there. We all used to laugh a lot. We had a strange sense of humour.' The atmosphere was clubby, private—freemasonic. When Sellers opened at the Palladium, he received a telegram which stated: 'I am instructed by the Goon Council to forward the following message of congratulation. Quote. Ooly-Dooly-Osh. Unquote. P.S. Ool. Signed KOGVOS.' *Osh* was a password; *ool* what grammarians call a roving noun, a word applicable in any connotation; *KOGVOS*, Keeper of Goons and Voice of Sanity, was Major Grafton.

Other people's secret codes can be very boring, but the success of 'The Goon Show' lay in the fact that millions learned to love its language—a language which went beyond words. Crun's *Mnk-grnk-mnk-mnk-grmp*; Bloodnok's *Bleiough-aeioughhh-bleioughhh*, or Bluebottle's *Ye-he-he! Heuheuheuheuheuhe*! 'Why talk? Why speak words?' Milligan told a journalist, sent round to the pub to witness the commotion in 1949. 'Everybody speaks words.' The actual word 'goon' itself came from America and was popularised, along with 'gawkery' (stupidity) and 'clerd' (a strong form of disparagement) by Fred Allen on his radio show, which Sellers, Milligan, Bentine, and Secombe had stayed up all night listening to upstairs at Graftons, using a short-wave apparatus and antenna supplied by guess-who.

In addition to his powerful wireless, Sellers also introduced his Sound Mirror to the proceedings, a primitive semi-portable tape recording machine, weighing forty-five pounds and housed in a mahogany box. (He owned the first one, which conceivably ran on steam.) Into this device the quartet poured their gobbledygook. *Picture Post* came to the tavern to do a spread on a lodge meeting and described goonery as comedy 'that doesn't despise your intelligence.' And, indeed, a paradox of the style is that, whilst eulogising idiots, you do need a certain mental agility to follow its flow. Your imagination is made to work. Eccles, so dopey he's in a state of grace; Bluebottle, 'a short thin shivering youth heavily wrapped up in rice paper and dental string'; Henry Crun and Minnie, clucking and twittering like startled chickens; Grytpype Thynne, for all his attempts to be a master fraudster, always down on his luck—they are the dispossessed, scroungers, swindlers, and alms-hunters (worlds away from the middle-class domesticity of 'Ray's A Laugh', 'ITMA', 'Men from the Ministry', etc.) Yet, as Sellers said, 'the public identified themselves with these characters and situations, because to many of them they were more than just funny voices. They were caricatures of real people.' This was certainly Sellers' own response. Strip down the surrealism and the characters represent characteristics: greed, hunger, jealousy, rage, innocence, ignorance; basic drives which we try and curb in ourselves, but which 'The Goon Show' let out of school.

Though the quartet was in place by 1949, it would be another two years before their in-jokes and gibberish would be ready for the public. As the Major explained, 'these four young men are planning to form a new "crazy gang" when they have made even bigger names for themselves as single acts.' Milligan, by the autumn of 1949, had become the writer for a show called 'Hip-Hip-Hoo-Roy' (starring Derek Roy, whom he now says was 'about as funny as a baby with cancer') and he was devising material for Alfred Marks, Bill Kerr, Dick Emery, and Secombe. Secombe was regularly on radio. Bentine had added a sink plunger to his chairback and was flummoxing the audience of *Folies-Bergère*, and Sellers—well, Sellers was on radio so often that even when he wasn't, people thought it was still he. He wasn't so much speaking for the stars as instead of them. After the pre-recording of the *Arthur Askey Christmas Show*, on October 21, for example, a nervous Variety Booking Manager named Pat Newman wrote to all Sellers' victims, explaining that they'll be hearing themselves on a programme for which they had no contract—they were warned that they'd literally be hearing things. Not all celebrities were amenable, however, to Sellers co-opting them and turning the BBC into a one-man operation. Gracie Fields, her shrieks in much need of satirical deconstruction, had notified the Corporation that no unauthorised impersonation could be broadcast.

◆ ◆ ◆

Before the Goons became 'The Goon Show', therefore, they were reaching for the highest ranks in entertainment as individuals, and Sellers was there first. In 1950, Monty Lyon was negotiating with Pat Newman for Sellers to be given a three-year contract. This was to guarantee him a minimum of twenty-six broadcasts (as distinct from repeats) in one or more series per annum, with the fees ranging from twenty-five to thirty-five guineas (about $55 to $75) for each appearance. The assurance that he'd not suffer from complete financial aridity, however, didn't satisfy Sellers. As a man who did not wish to be circumscribed, he found that the offer raised problems. Sellers felt that if he was beholden to the BBC, if they had first call on his services, it might jeopardise his availability for stage work. On the other hand, if he rose to eminence with the BBC, his popularity with the public at large would increase, and he could capitalise on this by appearing at distant Hippodromes and Empire Theatres. Then again, if he was away travelling, how could he arrange to be standing at a microphone in London? Sellers was fond of independence, but the BBC (in the pre-ITV era) was a monopoly; he wanted to progress from penury, but he didn't want to be sold into bondage. The solution was to drag out negotiations for as long as possible. There was a lot of correspondence, to and fro, about how much notice Sellers would have to give, should a more lucrative offer than 'Workers' Playtime' or 'Henry Hall's Guest Night' arise. A contract was finally signed on April 26, 1951, to come into force on July 27 for a period of two years. It did indeed prove a bind. Dennis Selinger, who took over when Monty Lyon retired to breed pigs in Ireland (as he himself remarked, an unusual occupation for a Jewish man), was frequently writing to seek permission for Sellers to be released so he could play the Hippodrome, Dudley, for a week, or diversify in a late-night Delfont revue, and such. But by not tying Sellers down to any specific programme, by leaving the contractual mention of a thirteen-week radio series very vague, the BBC, in their innocence, had left wide a gap through which a particular quartet of stumblebums would be thrusting.

◆ ◆ ◆

Milligan freely admits that 'Peter Sellers was instrumental in getting "The Goon Show" on the air. He was doing very well on radio and went to Pat Dixon, a BBC producer, and said that we four would like to be together in a show.' Sellers had known Dixon (something of an eccentric who kept his office filled with memorabilia of the American Civil War) since working with him on 'Third Division' in December 1948 and on seven episodes of 'Petticoat Lane' a year later. He came to Grafton's, laughed at the antics, and promised that if a script could be concocted, he'd recommend a series to the planning department. Dixon had no real hope, however, of being taken up on this. The semi-drunken streams of consciousness in the saloon bar were little more than after-hours rags by delayed adolescents. He underestimated the Major and the Sound-Mirror.

Whilst the others were petting the pub's marmoset, Johnny, shooting lighted cigarettes out of each other's mouths with an air pistol, or demonstrating sumo wrestling holds, Sellers was fiddling with his tape machine, getting his pals to make battlefield noises, or to conduct long conversations in an incomprehensible Scottish brogue. The Major then suggested that, instead of baffling people, why don't we fill up a spool for Dixon? With everybody contributing ideas, he wrote a script, shaped around Sellers, called 'Sellers' Castle'. The characters and nonsense they'd tossed about during the past eighteen months, were gathered into a decrepit stately home to form a sort of Addams family, with Milligan's Eccles as the servant, Bentine a mad inventor locked in the dungeons, Secombe as a wandering minstrel, and Sellers as Crun-cum-Bloodnok, the reigning Lord of Misrule. With the assistance of Barry Barron, who had a private recording studio in Bond Street fancifully called 'Gui-de-Buire' (the sprig of mistletoe), the Major made arrangements for the demo disc. To introduce the story, provide links, and to generally add an air of mock gravity, he got in touch with the newscaster Andrew Timothy, whom he had met in Iceland during the war. 'I was rung up one day by a chap called Jimmy Grafton,' Timothy says, '[and] he said, "We're doing a rather unusual show...and I wonder if you'd like to announce it and take part in it?" And I said, "Well all right, yes, fine." So we went to a sleazy recording studio in Bond Street, which was covered in dust, and we did this; I didn't think it was the least bit funny, very lame, and I thought it was ghastly.'

Grafton took the result and played it to Roy Speer sometime in 1950. Speer took the unusual step of inviting the cast round to read the script to him personally in his cubby-hole at Variety Headquarters—he wanted to be sure there *was* a script and that those concerned could repeat their performances since it had sounded so improvised. Jacques Brown was then given the task of making a pilot in the BBC's Piccadilly studio. Without an audience for the cast to giggle with, though, and repeating the material of 'Sellers' Castle' for the third time, the atmosphere was cold and forced. The planners chucked it out. Dixon, however, according to one of the later producers of 'The Goon Show', John Browell, 'was firmly convinced that no matter how terrible the Goons were, he was going to persuade the BBC to keep them on.' Dixon had also heard some of the bootleg Sound Mirror gibberish. He'd enjoyed it, and cunningly resurrected the idea of a series for Sellers just when his colleagues were trying to get that long-term contract signed in early 1951. The trial recording for 'The Junior Crazy Gang', on February 4, was what induced Sellers to at last come to terms.

Dixon did not wish to produce the curiosa himself. He handed the programme to Dennis Main Wilson, as Dennis Wilson was then known—though not to Sellers, who preferred to call him Dennis Main Drain (revenge for those unanswered BANG ON letters of the late forties)—and the pilot and early shows bear little comparison to what we'd recognise as authentic goonery. For a start, it was not called 'The Goon Show'. The billing opted for clumsiness—

CRAZY PEOPLE
featuring
Radio's Own Crazy Gang
'The Goons'

The allusion to those madcap uncles—Bud Flanagan, Chesney Allen, Eddie Gray, Jimmy Nervo, Teddy Knox, Charlie Naughton, and Jimmy Gold—was apt. At the Palladium during the war (and during actual air raids), and at the Victoria Palace in the late forties and throughout the fifties, they were Britain's premier practical jokers. They never had script writers and refused to go on the radio, finding it restrictive. Above all, they loved spontaneity, and in this as much as anything the Crazy Gang clearly pre-incarnated 'The Goon Show', the task of Sellers, Milligan, Secombe, and Bentine being to find a sonic equivalent for their precursors' slapstick and inspired lunacy, which Churchill had said reminded him of the House of Commons. They had to get around fixed time schedules, engineers twiddling knobs, and producers who had the power to edit what you'd achieved before it was broadcast. 'I've followed the Goons ever since they started on the air,' said Bud Flanagan, 'and I'm one of their biggest champions. They're brilliant—especially Sellers.'

◆ ◆ ◆

'So we started,' said Andrew Timothy, 'and we used to do the recordings in the Aeolian Hall in Bond Street, and I thought I really was entering a madhouse. We started…rehearsing on Sundays…at 9:30, when the script, if there was a complete script, was delivered, and the Goons pored over it, criticised the jokes that the other Goons had put in, and thought of something much funnier themselves—and this went on steadily without a break until 7 o'clock in the evening, when there was a mass exodus, and the departure to a little Edwardian pub called The Grosvenor, just round the corner…'

After that, they returned and made the actual recording. A witness in the studio audience during the very first of the 'Crazy People' series* (which is what 'The Junior Crazy Gang' had become after the pilot) would have mingled with a crowd of about fifty persons who were disappointed not to be getting free tickets for 'The Bernard Braden Show'. They grumbled and clattered down many steps to find a small underground bunker, a low platform (no proper stage or stage curtains) and microphones with L-plates.† Bentine appeared to applause, adjusted the microphone stand to ten feet above his head, and exited, stage left, fiddling with his trousers. A piano was wheeled on, and wheeled off. Bentine reappeared, stage right, and went into a routine with an inflated inner-tube—he encouraged the audience to believe it was a canoe, Jane Russell's tits, and a Mexican hat. Secombe entered and blew raspberries, Milligan tried to break people's concentration with ad libs, and Sellers did his fanciful impersonations of Queen Victoria. The audience was rather more bemused than amused, and weren't totally overjoyed to be told 'If this hasn't recorded properly we may have to go through it all again, folks, so fasten your seat belts or at least your raincoat.'

Despite the bonhomie, 'Crazy People' showed more caution than innovation. Sellers did little more than come out with his Dick Barton parodies; Secombe's character was called Jones, and he got up to horseplay at a health clinic, in Russia, and on holiday during the Yukon Gold Rush; Milligan's appearances were few; and Bentine's Professor Osric Pureheart, his inventor from 'Sellers' Castle', gave lectures on his jet engines or a solid lead violin for deaf musicians. But nothing happens—there were no pay-offs. The scenes were monologues, or spots, and were interspersed with soggy musical interludes from Max Geldray, Ray Ellington, and The Stargazers. (There was no orchestra.)

They kept up the rhythm until July 1952. Sellers had introduced Major Bloodnok the previous August, and titles were growing Goonish ('The Bentine Lurgi Driven Tank', 'The Quest for Cloot Wilmington'), but the format continued to be, literally, sketchy. Secombe even contributed opera arias—straight, without farts. 'Crazy People' was a concert evening. Except for a pastiche of Rider Haggard's *She*, on March 18, entitled *Her*, in which the flame for everlasting life was cut off by the gas company, this was the variety circuit all over again. ('Hand-

---

*   The series (of seventeen) was recorded during the summer of 1951, the first installment being on May 28. Another series began on January 22, 1952.

†   L-Plates are legally required in Britain to be displayed on any vehicle operated by a student driver, 'L' denoting 'Learner.'

some Harry Secombe' instead of Henry Hall.) Sellers, Milligan, etc. were introduced by their real names; characters and voices don't interact much; the sound effects were perfunctory. At the end of 1951, in between the first and second series, Main Wilson wrote a lengthy report on the programme, and the fact there had been so few novelties must have boded well for its future.

From a political angle, the comments about Bentine are intriguing and imply why he was prevailed upon to leave before the start of the third series in November 1952.* Main Wilson says that, first, Bentine's character's manic voice is too similar to Secombe's (as far as complaints from listeners were concerned), and secondly, the Osric Pureheart spot was getting cumbersome—ideally it should be 'more relaxed in pace ... with more movement and more *clever* plot and situation comedy'. Yet, achieving this would only be to give it the same style as the Bloodnok adventure, which was the show's climax: 'these two sketches keep coming dangerously close in style ... resulting in lack of contrast throughout the half hour ... I suggest that Michael should be built into Bloodnok's second-in-command as a subaltern, using his powerful and resonant "dwarling/Hyde Pork [*sic*]" voice—in other words a clot with a private income.'

Sellers interpreted all this as a duel, himself v Bentine. Not long before he died, at the age of seventy-eight, Andrew Timothy confessed that the atmosphere during the first read-throughs of the script could be distinctly unpleasant: 'When the Goons would settle down to see how big their own particular part was that week, there would be considerable annoyance if Peter seemed to have got a bigger part than Mike or vice versa ... In fact,' Timothy went on, 'there was a permanent sparring match between Bentine and Sellers ... Bentine eventually got fed up with this and left. Sellers was a difficult chap. The way he had of creeping into himself suggested impatience and anger. *He sort of crept into himself ...*' (It's where he went to meet his characters.)

Main Wilson's other suggestions, that they go all out to identify the Goon performers with the characters they play in the show, and that dialogue be kept down to an intelligible pace—ensuring funny voices aren't gabbled, but shared with the audience—start to intimate 'The Goon Show' proper, as (in a specific sense) does his concluding remark:

> We hope that Planners will agree to build the programme as 'The Goon Show' rather than 'Crazy People'. This is purely because everybody, both in and outside the business, refers to it as the Goon Show (or *that* Goon Show) but never as 'Crazy People' (which quite frankly could be applied to almost any comedy show).

Sellers used to enjoy melting into doddering Henry Crun to explain what happened next:

---

* There were already jealousies between Bentine and Milligan as to whom was the chief supplier of ideas. 'We would turn up for a session,' Sir Harry recalls, 'Spike and Mike would spark each other off, and at the end of the session both of them would go away thinking that most of the ideas were theirs. So there was a little bit of friction in that respect. Each one accusing the other of plagiarism, though not seriously. But that disappeared when Mike decided he wanted Sundays to the family. Which was fair enough, and he left.'

In the early days we had a very small listening figure, but it soon got up to huge proportions. There used to be weekly meetings of the programme planners, and one week, one of the old boys looked at the agenda and asked an executive, 'Tell me about this "Go On Show".

'No sir, it's not "go on", it's actually "goon".

'Coon?'

'No sir, that's "goon", not "coon".'

'Goon? What is a goon? White-faced coons?'

'I don't quite know sir, but they are having very big listening figures.'

'Well then, they must go on.'

◆ ◆ ◆

Up at Oxford there are dons working for maybe as much as forty-eight hours a year establishing Shakespeare's texts. They sift through the leaves of the First Folio and the Bad Quarto, examining the principles governing the use of various spellings; they study Elizabethan Grammar and stagecraft; they footnote, gloss, ponder, fret. They hunt for symbols and lecture on imagery. Doctoral gowns are awarded and careers made if you can argue that (say) in *Timon of Athens*, Act III, sc. iv, l. 58, Will meant to write 'If 'twill' rather than 'if 't twill'. But the academic industry buoying up the Swan of Avon is a dry sponge compared with the scholarship generated by 'The Goon Show'. There are entire books (and countless articles) devoted to it, chief amongst them being Roger Wilmut's authoritative gazetteer, *The Goon Show Companion* and Alfred Draper's biographical *The Story of the Goons*. Milligan, in collaboration with Sellers and Secombe, has published *The Goon Show Scripts, More Goon Show Scripts, The Book of the Goons*, and *The Lost Goon Shows*. There are symposia (often held at Grafton's), conferences, monthly meetings of fans, who communicate solely in old catchphrases ('What-what-what-what-what') and, most important of all, there is The Goon Show Preservation Society, which produces a learned journal once a quarter. *The Newsletter* is the place where you find out that 'The Tuscan Salami Scandal' is correctly 'The Great Tuscan Salami Scandal', and that 'ying-tong-iddle-i-po', another of the catchphrases and the lyric of a Goon song, is actually Mandarin Chinese for 'I must have sexual intercourse'.

By analysing draft scripts, phonograph rolls, variant recordings in the BBC archives, and badgering anyone left alive who toiled behind the scenes, researchers have plotted the show's development from a series of random light comedy sketches into classics like 'The Scarlet Capsule' and 'Tales of Old Dartmoor.' Rehearsal notes and jokes from one week would be worked into scripts designed for broadcast the next; stories were often recycled; characters gradually took on a life of their own, and spoke their own stage directions. ('Enter Bluebottle with a smile and a song. Stands waist deep in snow so that Neddy Seagoon will not laugh at my legs. Smiles grimly and jabs alpenstock in snow—ooooh my footy.')

For all this Goonology, however, it does rather seem to me that the gist of 'The Goon Show', and the source of its power for its performers, has been overlooked until now. I mean of course that it was a surreal response to the violence and behaviour of the war. Explosions, machine gun fire, mortar blasts, bombs, and shells: the noises of combat punctuate each episode. Poor old Major Bloodnok's stomach is a battle zone of mines and fizzing shrapnel; Moriarty makes the mistake of smoking 'a nice big long red cigar with a wick on the end'; and Bluebottle and Eccles, as archetypal cannon fodder, have to be scraped off the walls after the frequent detonations and bangs. Right up until the final show in 1960, it was still the Germans the characters were up against. When Hen and Min take a clifftop stroll, in 'The Batter Pudding Hurler,' they worry about the blackout and whether Hitler will invade Bexhill-on-Sea. A running gag is that whenever anybody strikes a match, a doodlebug (Hitler's dreaded rocket bomb, the V-1) is launched from across the Channel and scores a direct hit on Min and Hen's legs, which are blown off time and again. In 'Tales of Men's Shirts,' Britain's generals are busy typing their memoirs and aren't aware that their armies are clapped in a POW Camp, and in 'The Jet Propelled NAAFI,' a mighty aerial fleet is despatched to drink the surplus service tea. There are dozens of shows with army themes—in 'Dishonoured' it's the turn of the North West Frontier, and Eccles does the 'Dance of the Seven Army Surplus Blankets'; 'The Histories of Pliny the Elder,' has the Romans threatening the English much as the Nazis do, and everybody ends up inside an active volcano, which erupts apocalyptically...Men marching, men grunting like pigs when at ease, army boots, (especially army boots: a Ph.D. could be written on the references to army boots in 'The Goon Show'), bivouacs, tanks made of cardboard, pistol shots, spies, counterfeit uniforms, medals, court martials, top secret plans—all this forms the background of Goonery, a world of conscription and England in the forties, re-lived in the fifties.

◆ ◆ ◆

The artistic style of the Great War was elegy—Rupert Brooke blowing his golden bugle over the rich dead; the works left by those mutilated and annihilated Grail Knights, Wilfred Owen, Edward Thomas, and Henri Gaudier-Brzeska, writing about loss or sculpting angels. Death was spoken of as an aesthetic deed in itself—Peter Pan's awfully big adventure. Photographs falling out of albums from the period depict rather serious, beautiful young men, the sepia casting them in the shadows of a death-wish; these boys went off, full of nobility and stoicism, to be blasted to bits for the King's shilling.*

World War II, however, was less of an Arthurian pageant. People had fewer illusions about barbed wire and bullets, and no patience with rhetoric. Is it only a coincidence that snapshots of officers and other ranks look less posed, less like a theatrical company stuck in the corner of a studio? Pictures taken for *Time-Life*, for example, are of men boozing, smoking, muddy, exhausted, playing the piano or sleeping. Perhaps it was the first documentary war, as against the literary affairs of the past. Whatever, its artistic consequences were satire and humour—from Evelyn Waugh's ironically entitled *Sword of Honour* trilogy to Anthony Burgess'

---

* In olden days, a silver coin of the realm (equivalent in value to one-twentieth of a pound) bearing the portrait of the sovereign, which was given to each new recruit.

Little Wilson and Big God to Milligan's adventure stories (as mentioned earlier, he has worked all his life with what he took out of the war).

'The Goon Show' often parodied contemporary war films, such as 'The Fear of Wages' (for Yves Montand's *The Wages of Fear*), 'Wings Over Dagenham' (for any ace-aviator thriller starring John Mills), and 'Rommels's Treasure' (for James Mason's Field Marshal in *The Desert Fox*), amongst many others. *I Was Monty's Double* became 'I Was Monty's Treble', and they had a go at Ronald Neame's *The Man Who Never Was* three times—perhaps because Sellers himself had dubbed lots of voices onto its soundtrack. There is also something about kitting out a corpse with false identity papers, to mislead the enemy over the invasion of Italy, which was goonish all on its own. David Lean's *The Bridge on the River Kwai* was thus an ideal subject: Japs, jungles, questions of honour. Though the episode was called 'African Incident', the plot mocked and followed the portentousness of Lean's epic closely. The source was further identified when Sellers gave an impersonation of Sir Alec Guinness' Col. Nicholson, falling on the dynamite plunger. This particular story was revived in 1962 by Parlophone. Sellers and Milligan, without Secombe, were joined by Jonathan Miller and Peter Cook. Amongst the gruesome sound effects the surviving Goons now wanted was that of a man's head being chopped off. A cleaver taken to a fresh cabbage bought in Alma Square did the trick and was (says George Martin, the producer) 'totally blood curdling.' After having made the album, however, EMI were confronted with a writ for copyright infringement. Not only did people seem to think that Lean's film was sacrosanct and that Japanese atrocities against British prisoners of war, in the Changi Jail, Singapore, were no laughing matter; but Columbia was as proprietorial over the proper noun *Kwai* as Warner Bros. had been when the Marx Bros. lampooned *Casablanca*. The solution was ingenious. An editor went through the master-tape snipping out every 'K' to create *The Bridge on the River Wye*.

◆ ◆ ◆

Hilarity needn't only be a response to the war, a release mechanism. Farce co-exists within the service atmosphere already. The disorder people were subjected to, the immense confusions, had made a Goon show out of ordinary life. No railway station signs or road markings, for example; the shortages and queues—there's an entire episode devoted to 'The Lone Banana'; the blunders. Each of the Goons had this sort of material to draw on. Secombe's Seagoon relives comically many of the trials Sir Harry faced as a member of Operation Torch, the invasion of North Africa. Secombe saw heavy action and was in the thick of dive bombers and mortar fire for months on end. The mud, the lice-ridden clothing, sand-fly fever, and malaria took its toll. 'All the fighting had affected my nerves,' he has admitted. After the heat of Tunisia, he suffered exposure in the snows of Italy's mountains, and 'I found the bitter cold hard to bear.' He spent five weeks in hospital, lost almost thirty pounds in weight, and when he met Milligan, who had experienced many horrors and had just been discharged from a psychiatric hospital near Sorrento, Sir Harry says rather cryptically, 'there but for the grace of God I too might have gone.'

The mangling of bodies and buildings, the gassings, and the threat of atomic radiation—objects of laughter on 'The Goon Show'—were lived through by Bentine, also. When he joined up he was nearly killed by the serum in a routine innoculation. He lost a lot of weight and came out in abscesses. When he trained in the RAF Intelligence, he was issued with a Crimea era kit, attended lectures on field latrines, and dealt with the dropping of tin toilets over Berlin (the Germans accused the British of conducting bacteriological warfare). He tried to help officers escape from POW camps by secreting radio parts in jam and printing messages in invisible inks on grey blankets—'personal evasion kits,' they were called. Could 'The Goon Show' improve on any bit of it? Like Secombe, he collapsed from the strain. 'My kindly C.O.,' he says, 'had guessed how near I was to going over the edge.' He became emaciated, could not control his flow of tears, and reached, after years of training navigation crews, 'the limits of endurance'. He, too, was hospitalised for weeks.

Milligan has made no mystery of his invalid status. When he was caught in a bomb blast he 'started to cry and shake and shiver…They gave me some tablets…some tranquillisers, I think, which sent me to sleep, sent me out of the lines for seven days. Then they sent me up to the guns and as soon as I heard the guns go, I started to stammer.' It is a paradox that, hating noise as much as he does—a neighbour's lawnmower, for instance, or a surge of muzak, can to this day trigger manic depression attacks—'The Goon Show' should be so full of it.

Other key personnel were casualties of war. Max Geldray, the harmonica player, was also caught in a bomb blast and flung into a foxhole. He recovered consciousness in a field hospital, and was surprised to see so few bloodied bandages. Then he noticed that the men were shuffling, shivering, screaming, weeping. The commonest symptom of a mental scar was the inability to speak. 'This silence, and the way they stared out at the world,' he says, 'was the most frightening of all.' Geldray himself suffered nightmares, which left him feeling his body was being crushed and compressed.

Dennis Main Wilson, the producer, as an officer in the Royal Armoured Corps, had been Head of Light Entertainment (*Unterhaltungschef*) for the Nord-West-Deutscher-Rundfunk, in Hamburg, part of the Propaganda Service of the Central Commission. He saw the results of Nazi atrocities in German occupied towns and, back in England, according to a profile on him in the *Observer* (June 1988), 'a sort of delayed shell-shock took hold of him for a while'. Throughout his career, the tension of those times recurred: 'He has, on occasion, overwound himself, which he does admit, and was once ordered to bed for a whole month to cool off.'

◆◆◆

And Sellers? His war, as we have seen in an earlier chapter, was joyous. 'The Goon Show', quite simply, brought his lawlessness into focus—gave it expression. 'They really were my happiest days, those Sundays when we did "The Goon Show",' he said in 1971, and he'd repeat the sentiment over and over. 'I can really say that it was the happiest professional period of my life. I never had such fun, enjoyment, or fulfillment either before or since,' he told Ray Connolly in 1972; a few years earlier when making *There's a Girl in My Soup*, he insisted to Freddy

Clayton that 'all my prayers were answered when along came "The Goon Show". I think it all really started from there. Whatever the future holds for me, I'm sure of one thing, there will never be another era quite like that one.'

As he approached his end, his beginnings loomed large in his mind. In the last weeks of his life, he was saying, '"The Goon Shows" were the happiest days I have spent in this industry—the entertainment industry, whatever it be. Those Sundays at the Paris Cinema or the Aeolian Hall were the happiest times I have ever had.' Auberon Waugh, one of the last people outside of Sellers' train to see him alive, commented that, time and again, in a conversation which ranged over the wives, the wealth, the films, Sellers always returned to the nine years he spent doing 'The Goon Show'; his reminiscences then seemed 'the truest and most deeply felt.'

The problem we face when trying to see the development of Sellers' ideas and technique, especially with regard to 'The Goon Show', is to make adequate allowance for his sentimentality and nostalgia. Only when suffering from vertigo at the pinnacles of international success did he start to idealise his radio days. And whenever there was a chance of reviving the series, he was the one who'd hesitate and spoil the deal. After the success of *The Last Goon Show of All*, a one-off, twelve years after the programme had officially finished, Peter Eton discussed the possibilities of further specials with the stars. 'They were all terribly keen on this,' he said in 1976, 'but recently Peter started backing out, having been frightfully keen. The other two, Secombe and Milligan, are still keen, available and willing—but now Peter is the problem.' Eton claimed that Sellers was employing a 'cultural advisor,' an American, who was advising him: 'don't do any more "Goon Shows"— they're all passé!' Also, Sellers was about to re-encounter Inspector Clouseau, and had film after film lined up. 'So it's going to be very difficult,' said Eton. Totally impossible, as it turned out (and Eton has died now, too).

So as regards his pining for the good old days, what did he really mean? What he was looking back so fondly at was the way, with his voice alone, he could create a wonderland. This, the province of the radio actor, is not quite possible in cinema, where appearances, too, have to be deceptive. It is revealing that, when Sellers had the almightiness to get scripts re-written, directors hired and fired, and sets torn down, reconstructed, and then never used, it was because he was trying to achieve, through the cumbersomeness of film studios, the fleeting quick-change of ideas he'd once accomplished at the microphone with no trouble at all. Quite clearly the welter of Goon catchphrases, jokes, and even plot-lines in *The Fiendish Plot of Dr Fu Manchu* is demonstration enough that, to the last, Sellers wanted to transform radio into cinematic terms.* It was a conversion he never managed, one mutation he couldn't make.

◆ ◆ ◆

* *The Fiendish Plot of Dr Fu Manchu* (1980) borrows heavily from 'The Terrible Revenge of Fred Fumanchu,' [*sic*] transmitted on December 6, 1955. Neddie Seagoon was the Chief Commissioner of Scotland Yard (played in the film by David Tomlinson), hunting for the bamboo saxophone thief. (Saxophones are blown into by Helen Mirren in the film.)

Making 'The Goon Show', fair seed time had his soul. 'We'd get back together and think, God, how marvellous! That's why the show was, for *us*, such an enormous release; and we used to pack so much energy into the show; and...we were just so keen to let people hear...this crazy, strange fantasy that used to take place in our minds...I remember when we first met up. We, all of us—Bentine, Harry, Spike, and I, had this feeling that we *had* to do something...We wanted to express ourselves in a sort of surrealistic form. We thought in cartoons. We thought of...mad characters, we thought of...a situation, and instead of letting it end normally, [we'd] twist it around. This grew and grew and grew and grew.'

Whether or not the vortex meant as much to the others in the long term, Sellers is certainly doing his best here (the 'we' and 'us' are royal) to describe his own creative processes and exfoliations. As an actor (and as a husband, father, etc.) he relied on his instincts to an inordinate degree. This made him vulnerable and volatile, but taking him purely as a performer, for the moment, there was always going to be a sense of danger about somebody so versatile, and to this audiences responded. 'It was almost unholy,' remarks Milligan, 'this skill. It was as if he had no choice about the depth of his impersonations. That's what made it mad.' And it is the sheer quality of his gift of tongues which was now becoming apparent. The voices became characters and he distributed himself amongst them. Bluebottle, the child; Bloodnok, the reprobate; Crun, the fool; Grytpype, the cad... Sellers cherished their oddities because they gave outer form to his own.

Whilst Secombe yodels and yells, and Milligan mugs, Sellers' acting, forty years on, has resonance and resolution. And if the Goons were caricaturing, in the main, what they'd endured for real during the war (idiots with power; the lying and cheating of propaganda; the fiction of military heroism—Main Wilson said that 'For years we'd been sold the idea that the British Army never loses. Now, in the figure of Bloodnok, you had a Major who would take any bribe, tell any lie, to save his skin'), then Sellers wasn't reacting against trauma, like the rest, but expanding upon an intuitive spirit of rebellion and anarchy which was already within him. The war was a stimulus for Milligan. It was thrust upon Secombe and Bentine. For Sellers, however, the war intensified his delinquencies, and 'The Goon Show' was a channel for his streak of cruelty and sense of the ridiculous, which were now heightened. He could *use* everybody else's excitable state (impersonate it?); their nervous illnesses struck, more figuratively, a nerve in him.

◆ ◆ ◆

On Sellers' memorial plaque in Golders Green Crematorium there is the rubric 'Life is a state of mind'. This comes from *Being There*, and in the context of that film, and as a funerary ornament, it is vacuous, meaningless. If applied to the Sellers who was setting sail in the early fifties, though, it is convenient. The state of mind which was being filled, in readiness for adulthood and independence, was one susceptible to exhibitionism, contempt, and anything anti-social. His fortunate friendship with Milligan confirmed his cynical vision and aloofness. Sellers fed off Milligan's mental processes and leaps, identified with his knottedness and the intensity of his feelings. And when the once-assured Milligan broke down, over-worked by dreaming up 'The Goon Show', still he kept typing, even though he was in bed with boards strapped to its sides, because he was so violent: 'The scripts he wrote during that worrying time were better than before,' said Sellers delightedly. 'The fact is that everything Spike does is part of his war against the human race.' (Including becoming a patient in a mental hospital? When somebody asked him if he had any sympathy with the agonies Milligan went through to work out the show, Sellers simply snapped 'I don't know why he did it for so long in that case.')

Sellers knew that the words his beloved characters spoke belonged to Milligan, but Sellers became proprietorial. He'd not been raised to share a single thing in his life, starting with his mother (Peg had nothing left for Bill); so towards Milligan, to whom he owed so much, he'd react with spite and envy. In America, for instance, where Milligan is not known, he'd use his friend's psychiatric problems to get an easy laugh. On March 20, 1964, he appeared on a syndicated talk show in Los Angeles, and told the host, Steve Allen, (who'd described 'The Goon Show' to the audience as 'wilder than any comedy that's ever been done here') that:

> I worked with a very brilliant colleague called Spike Milligan, who wrote the show. Who unfortunately is in a mental home at the moment. [*Laughter.*] No. He gets a bit under the weather. [*Laughter.*] But anyway, you know, it was great fun.

The gods were tuning into Allen's programme; eighteen days later they made sure Sellers suffered a series of massive coronary attacks. (He was only able to survive because of the state-of-the-art cardiac unit at the Cedars of Lebanon Hospital.) Worse was to come. In April 1980, Sellers told the magazine *Rolling Stone* about the loneliness and cheerlessness of touring in variety—'and Spike used to get suicidal because someone would shout at him. [*Sadly*] You know, he eventually did commit suicide.'

Within three months of speaking those words Sellers was dead—but how can we explain a fabrication like that? To be so anxious to appear the sole architect of your success that you kill off a confrere—it's aberrant. But let's try and enter Sellers' sickness and explain the state of his mind. The first point is that by the spring of 1980, *The Fiendish Plot of Dr Fu Manchu* was behind him and he knew he'd failed to pull off the most expensive 'Goon Show' of all time; Milligan's tone and range didn't seem to have a look—Goonery remained all in the mind. Second, he was not living with his fourth wife and his romantic life was in ruins, again. Third, his heart problems were intensifying and coronary by-pass surgery was in prospect... So there were professional and personal reasons a-plenty for being morose; he was trying to find anybody to blame for his errors and wrecks except himself. But Milligan? Clearly, Sellers' identification with Milligan's emotional reserves ran very deep. He'd wanted to take possession of his friend's talents, but now, having heard the chimes at midnight, Sellers felt left out and afraid. It was a terrifying thought: perhaps he never had got inside Milligan's head—he'd only ever imitated him? Sellers, cornered by his own genius for mimicry, felt himself shrivelling. He was gasping and choking.

Milligan, an old man now, remains puzzled by Sellers' cruel remarks. When

I met him, he was so pale, still, and white-haired, he seemed translucent, a mandarin—a benign Fu Manchu:

> Peter would compete with people in peculiar ways. He hated it when I was doing something he couldn't do, such as restoring the Elfin Oak in Kensington Gardens. Despite his fame and his talent he was jealous of me. When I was with him he was very warm—then I'd hear that he'd asked somebody, 'Why does Spike hate me?' I never had that hatred. I miss him very much, especially on a comedy level, because we used to discuss ideas which were way outside the scope of Hollywood...
>
> I thought Peter was much funnier in 'The Goon Show', more laughs per minute there, than in the Clouseau films. More original, too. The Pink Panthers were based on classic silents—expensive Hal Roach. Peter kept a lot of things that were important to me—films in eight millimetre. Experiments in comedy. I asked Lynne Frederick after Peter had died—can you let me have access to them? She said, 'Spike, one day Peter destroyed everything that had anything to do with you—he didn't want to have any knowledge of you.'* He destroyed it all.

◆ ◆ ◆

If Sellers was consumed with rival-hating envy and crooked malice before he died, Milligan, in the long ago, had moments when he, too, was angered to the heart—and on one occasion he was actually intent on committing murder. He was up to his neck in scripts for 'The Goon Show'; he was having to cope with all the queries from BBC producers, sound effects engineers, etc.; his parents had just emigrated to Australia; and he was living in a small flat with his wife June, who was ill, and a new-born baby named Laura. Sellers, oblivious to these pressures, and expecting to be enthusiastically greeted whatever the hour, would swan in late at night to play a new gramophone record. The frustrations were over-burdening and Milligan went for him with a kitchen knife. 'I was so mad,' he has since said, 'I thought that if I killed Peter it would all come right.' Sellers was saved by June, who thoughtfully screamed and forewarned him (their flats were in the same block): 'Peter! Don't come out—Spike's going to kill you!' I wonder if the cutlery was embedded in Sellers' doorway afterwards?

On Sundays, it was often up to Harry Secombe to keep the peace. Peter Eton used to take him aside and say 'Look, there's been a bit of an argument. Get here early, so if there's any trouble you can be here to smooth things over.' There never was much trouble on the actual day of the programme, recalls Sir Harry, 'because if Peter had a touch of the sulks, and perhaps Spike would go to adopt the foetal position, really I'd think of some Army joke I'd heard and within a few minutes we'd all break out and all be laughing. And, of course, the brandy helped. By God, the brandy helped.'

---

* The actual letter from Lynne Frederick, glazed and framed, met my gaze in the downstairs cloaks, Chez Milligan: 'Dear Spike, I don't know how to tell you this, but one day Peter destroyed everything that reminded him of you. I am very sorry. What more can I say? Lynne.' The letter is typed, the signature bold. Milligan has appended this superscription: 'After writing six times to her, this is the emotional reply I got from Lynne Unger—late Mrs David Frost, late Mrs Peter Sellers, late human being.' Milligan has dealt with the tremendous hurt by treating it as an offensive joke—one which cuts both ways.

'The Goon Show', for Sellers, wasn't so much the finished twenty-eight minute product as the whole afternoon and evening out, which was indeed lubricated by a cocktail of cognac and milk. John Browell, who laboured to produce the sound effects and later took over the programme from Peter Eton, has said that 'I noticed from time to time that the bottles of brandy were getting larger and larger, and I used to have to send my staff down there to drink copious quantities, to try and keep the cast sober. I had a sober cast and a drunk staff.'

Owing to the complexities on the technical side, the BBC were wanting the scripts delivered earlier and earlier so that the experts in the electronic department etc. could experiment with the new noises. This meant additional strain for Milligan, but ideally the time-table for 'The Goon Show' was that the new script would arrive on the Monday morning. By Tuesday the sound-effects people and the producer would have knocked it into broadcast-able shape. As Browell says, of the scripts, 'although they were idiotic, they were like great fantasies and there was a lot of serious talk and work that went into them'. On Wednesday, the actual sound-effects were tried out and, if possible, pre-recorded. On Thursday, the script was re-typed, duplicated, and distributed. On Sunday, at two o'clock, everybody would assemble—Milligan worrying about the looming deadline for *next* week, Sellers and Secombe having driven from wherever they were in the British Isles, appearing in variety. There would then be a stumble-through on the stage, at the microphone, with the sound-effects. 'Jim, the atomic bomb's not loud enough,' Milligan might say. 'Louder, go on, until it gets to feedback point.' Wally Stott next arrived with the musical arrangements, to rehearse with the orchestra.

The Goons derived much mirth from hearing the 'Old Comrades March', a traditional military number with a distinct patriotic underthump—an evocation of Chelsea pensioners, jingling with medals, tottering in step along Whitehall on Armistice Day. What was so funny? Simply the doddery dignity of the superannuated soldier, doing his best to look heroic, when really he's bewhiskered and well past it—the Goons could sentimentally see themselves getting to be like that, years hence, the spirit of adventure stirring in the veteran's heart. With the show over, and the play-out in full tump-tump-tump tiddle-tiddle tump-tump-tump, the Goons used to fall into line and march in procession around the stage. They'd continue frolicking until the producer, up in his booth, flashed the ALL CLEAR sign.

Stott, who has since had a sex-rectifying operation to become Miss Angela Morley, told me that 'I arranged all the music and composed the links for all ten years of the Goons, and for the last seven years I conducted the band. Outside the Camden Theatre on a Sunday evening there'd always be Peter's latest car—a different one every week. We were always expecting him to turn up in a steam roller. Peter played the drums on "The Goon Show", during the afternoon and during the warm-up.'

They then had a final dress rehearsal, and eventually the audience, which had been queuing for up to four hours, was let in. Feeling antic by now, Sellers, Secombe, and Milligan goofed and clowned. They'd clutch on to the tabs and be hoisted up and down; they'd pretend the wheeled music stands were scooters.

'Braces [suspenders] were a favourite,' says Browell 'Peter would come along and do the old time music hall bit—"Ladies and gentlemen" etc.—and whip away Harry's braces, whereupon Peter's trousers would fall down. One terrible occasion when they did it, he wasn't wearing underpants.' Wallace Greenslade, the dirigible-sized announcer who succeeded the spare Andrew Timothy, was their main stooge. Sellers once interrupted the actual recording: 'Stop the show—it's time to auction Greenslade's bum.' In no time at all, remembers Milligan, bids were coming in, 'even from the audience.'

It was Greenslade's job to introduce any VIPs who might be sitting in the front row—they'd stand to applause, and the sound-effects team would blast them with a round of machine gun crackle. Every week, without fail, Greenslade pointed to the balcony and said 'Are you all right on the shelf up there? Good, because you can't get out, the doors are locked.' He'd then have to race about the platform, picking up the leaves of his script which he'd scattered about. It was obviously tricky calling everybody to order to start the performance proper—the messing about was so integral—and the audience was already chuckling when the green signal blinked on: 'Recording in ten seconds from now':

GREENSLADE: This is the BBC.

SELLERS: Hold it up to the light—not a brain in sight.

♦ ♦ ♦

We can derive a fair impression of what these live sessions were like from watching the videotape of *The Last Goon Show of All*, made in April 1972 as part of the Corporation's fiftieth anniversary celebrations. If you've only ever heard recordings (*The Best of the Goon Shows*, Vols. One and Two, was my first rummage) and have been used to filling the dark space of radio with your own mental picture of the characters and their deeds, it is a giddy, abstract experience finally to see the actors at it. Milligan, for example, looks embarrassed, ill at ease. He doesn't make eye-contact with anybody, or touch anybody, whereas Secombe, a pirouetting Toby Jug, is always nudging and jostling his way to the microphone. He's the one who generates the turbulence and keeps the show together.

As for Sellers, he waves to his friends in the audience, talks to the band, leans over the footlights to chat to his children and wives, and only by the narrowest squeeze does he come back in on cue. He does a lot of pointing and ironic music hall ham bowing—he looks utterly happy, and he does whatever he wants. It is clearly suiting his sense of the spontaneous, and his sense of discipline, to be able to fool about and draw attention to himself. He simply lets his vocal skills get on with performing the script, it would seem, automatically. His timing and switches of character—Crun to Bloodnok to Grytpype to Bluebottle—are fast and spookily good.

It is as if he can be both concentrated and fixed on what he's doing, and yet remain loose and indefatigable. Slim, at the microphone, he is snappy, hyper-responsive. His elbows, legs, and fingers (which clutch the foolscap script) are all long and angular, like his chin and thin nose. Sellers is a human whiplash. He is at his most pure here, posing amidst the clutter of the orchestra, recording personnel, cables, booms, and amplifiers. We almost don't notice that no actual Goon Show story takes shape. 'In my opinion,' (and he's right) 'the script was very, very poor, very poor indeed,' said Andrew Timothy, brought out of retirement for the day because Greenslade had died (on the toilet in a pub called 'The George' in Langham Place, as it happens) back in 1961. What keeps *The Last Goon Show of All* going is the audience's goodwill.

♦ ♦ ♦

That the script was a rattle-bag of catchphrases and hubbub, too slip-shod even to be mistaken for something the cast had improvised, is one thing. What was unorthodox was the smut. 'The Goon Show', apart from references to Hugh Jampton* and Singhiz Thingz, was innocent of sex, and this accounts for some of its charm. The 1972 swan song, however, contains laugh-lines about knee tremblers, knobs, Bloodnok's perversions, and 'Psst!' as 'pissed' i.e., drunk, which can best be labelled as childish—and the point about the original programmes is that they were childlike. For all the belligerence and insanity that went into it, the spirit of Goonery could often leap beyond pain and disaster. One way it achieved this was by going back in time, setting its plots in an indeterminate period of the Imperial nineteenth century, an era of pioneering steam railways, Rorke's Drift, expeditions up the Limpopo, nutty professors journeying to the centre of the earth or intent on other odd scientific missions, revolting tribesmen in the Punjab, discoveries in the pyramids, Sahara forts under siege, tiger hunts, and the search for diamond mines. In other words, 'The Goon Show' recycled its Second World War violence through *Boys' Own* adventure annuals; its forebears and heroes were Sax Rohmer, Edgar Rice Burroughs, and Allan Quartermaine.

London, too, is still Queen Victoria's capital, with its fogs, horses, and carts, its clubmen in swirling capes. (It could be Anthony Hope's Ruritania.) And what's particularly Englishy English, in addition, are the loving references to Christmas. Plum puddings and turkey besplatter many an episode. 'Tales of Men's Shirts' has a sea battle in which the cannon are loaded with roast turkeys—the enemy retaliates with Christmas puddings and custard. The armoury in 'The Dreaded Batter Pudding Hurler' consists of mince pies, exploding sausages and, yes, Christmas puddings. The Dickens parody, 'Christmas Carol,' has a pudding crammed with coins, which Grytpype and Moriarty want to steal; and in 'The International Christmas Pudding,' the farinaceous ingredients come alive, are tracked to the Congo (or some such spot), and behave like a stag at bay, flashing the holly sprigs as if they were antlers.

Nostalgia for Christmas, for all the childhood excitements which it evokes, is perhaps what soldiers of fortune, when it comes down to it, fight for: times gone by spent in places they might well never live to see again. They romanticise, idealise, their home life and the past. It will all be over by Christmas—wasn't that the

---

* "Hugh Jampton" is a pun on "Huge Hampton;" Hampton is Cockney rhyming slang for "dick," derived from the area of London called Hampton Wick.

refrain, of men whose hearts were full of grief and uneasiness? War, adventure, wolf-cub braggadocio, and the oxymoron of military intelligence, all come together in 'Operation Christmas Duff', in which Bloodnok organises a gigantic pudding for Her Majesty's Forces Overseas. Eccles and Bluebottle drive the pudding to the desert, misread the map, and end at the South Pole. Unknowingly, they've been going backwards—and one of the Goon songs, for which Sellers provided the ropey piano obligato, was called 'I'm Walking Backwards for Christmas'. To put the clock back, to become again carefree kids, their minds brimming with Keystone two-reelers and bright-hued comics from the newsagent, Rider Haggard's exotica, Fu Manchu's threats, and music hall conjurors—all this lay underneath the battle-scarred reality which was the programme's stimulant. 'The Goon Show' had a juvenile heart, which remained Sellers'. These are his tastes, right up until the end, with his remake of *The Prisoner of Zenda* and what have you.

Chapter Five

♦ ♦ ♦

Her Man's a Scream

I had just written the confident sentence, '"The Goon Show" was a world without women,' before remembering that I was forgetting:

> MARIAN: Oh, sobs of despair—sobs!—locked in this dark dungeon with nothing but an old straw television set—this is the chamber of torture—oh, woe!, oh, misery! oh, fie! oh, whatever shall I do...
>
> SELLERS: The part of Maid Marion is being played by Miss Charlotte Mitchell, and a ripe little ham she's proving.

> —from 'Ye Bandit of Sherwood Forest' (1954)

Charlotte Mitchell also appeared as a guest artiste in 'Tales of Montmartre', two years later. The proposition holds, nevertheless. (When 'Ye Bandit' was re-made in 1956 as 'Robin Hood and His Merry Men', Miss Mitchell's part was re-assigned to Bluebottle.) The brothers-in-arms involved in thinking up and performing the programme, over two hundred and thirty editions (and ten series) between May 1951 and January 1960 were too busy with their comic-strip heroics to be muddled by females. I suppose Henry and Minnie may have held themselves in a passionate clinch several hundred years ago, Bloodnok's consumption of curried eggs may be a sublimation of other, baser needs, and Bluebottle's acne implies a hormonal surge—but Goonery, incubated in a pub, inflamed by beer, full of sentiment about wars and derring-do, generally can do without any suggestion of wives, mothers, girl-friends (i.e., responsibilities). Though, as I said towards the end of the previous chapter, the sexlessness contributes a measure of innocence, the machismo does make matters, when you think about it, rather cruel and cold-hearted. 'There was no warmth in the writing,' said Peter Eton, 'It was all rather bitter—sardonic, perhaps. There is warmth in the characters—William Mate Cobblers, Bluebottle—but not in the writing. If you look at the scripts you will see this is true.'

'The Goon Show' was a fantasy of invincibility. Gunned down or minced up one week, the characters are back again the next. There is a love of speed (in the content—rockets, racing cars, jets, etc.), and of gangs (in the performance atmosphere—from Gang Show to Goon Show in this respect was no distance at all). And not only were women not registering in the plots and dramatis-personae, I don't think the programme appealed to them, either. They see through its cloak-and-dagger and extreme silliness, much in the way my own mother used to laugh herself half to death when she had to launder my father's masonic apron and polish his trowel. Perhaps this, too, is part of the comedy—a spoof on men's tough view of themselves?

'It was a masculine world,' Charlotte Mitchell agrees, 'and they laughed to keep themselves going. With me they'd decided they'd met a mad woman—I was very flattered. I'm not sure many women would have been. I was also eight months pregnant, though your shape is irrelevant on radio. It was hysteria really. Full of ad-libs and they put everything into the warm-up. I distinctly remember thinking, if I'm still alive by the end I'll be lucky. I was scared but I was able to cope with what they were doing because all I did was fall about laughing—and this is what they liked.'

Her testimony suggests that what the Goons enjoyed was an idolatrous audience, even if only of one. Charlotte Mitchell was put in the rôle of dizzy, dippy younger sister. She didn't reprove—she encouraged them to be more themselves than usual. (How would the chemistry have been altered if they'd found a Margaret Dumont character—a straight-man dowager type?) This, in general, was what Sellers personally wanted from any woman he encountered—total adoration. He'd woo them with his talent, which was passing strange, as his first wife confirms: 'I have to tell you he was wonderful. His act was just magic. I remember meeting him—Dennis Selinger introduced us. I thought "strange fellow" ... Then I saw him do his stand-up act at the Regal, Edmonton, one Sunday night, a popular variety venue, and I thought: "This is the most incredible talent that I've seen in years." I'm sure that's what attracted me to him, his talent. That's what the problem was eventually between us. I'm sure I was in love with his talent long after I wasn't in love with him.'

◆ ◆ ◆

Sellers met Anne Howe in 1949, at the BBC studios in Great Portland Place. She was nineteen and a student at the Royal Academy of Dramatic Art. She was *not*, however, as other books have suggested, the former child actress Sally Ann Howes, who'd recently appeared in Korda's *Anna Karenina*. Her professional name was Anne Hayes, though Sellers soon saw to it that she'd not need to be going on with any career where she could deploy it. She had been raised in Melbourne, but all trace of an Australian accent had long since been eradicated by secondary schooling at Hendon, whither her mother had moved after the death of her father (or perhaps he'd simply gone off somewhere to plant tea?). What her background gave her, instead of Down Under Diphthongs, was common sense, patience, and a sense of the ridiculous—a combination of unflappability and a delight in the bizarre which was ideal for Sellers. What was additionally unique to Anne was that she could be strong and imaginative without needing to be prickly or flamboyant: she gave Sellers the strong domestic underpinnings for his fantasies and career. If Peg had nagged Sellers into becoming famous, Anne gave him the support to sustain and develop that fame during the crucial years of the fifties. Of course, Sellers being Sellers, when he became an international success as an actor, out on the scrap-heap she and the children had to go. He felt it wasn't commensurate with being a sophisticated star and playboy to have an ordinary family home-life so he destroyed it all. Quite literally.

'I can remember his breaking up every bit of furniture in our living room.

Terrible tantrums. He'd lash out. He had this underlying violence. His mother never believed in attempting to teach him self-control. She always used to tell the story about how he'd pushed some aunt in the fire. She thought it was very funny and I'm sure... he always got away with murder all the time. Peter was allowed to do anything Peter wanted. But she... was crazy. More like a caricature of a Jewish mother, played by Peter Sellers. She ate him up. She ruled him.'

Talking about Sellers today, a dozen years since his death and over forty since they were married, Anne manages to be neither sentimentally forgiving nor, which is the more surprising, bitter. As she sifted over their life together, it is as if she was remembering the plot of a rather harrowing play she once saw, or a television bio-pic mini-series about other unfortunate people. Her detachment is the product of two supervening decades of happiness with the architect Ted Levy, who died of cancer in 1986.

'He [Peter] had sticky hair, over-stuffed suits, and was the kind of person who'd grab all the cream cakes for himself without offering them round. He wouldn't put his glasses on—and he was very near-sighted. He used to look at himself in the dressing room mirror, during variety, full of self-disgust, and say "A big, fat, jolly boy, that's how I'm meant to see myself."'

By concealing his spectacles, he didn't have to see himself. Like Clouseau, he overlooked his fumbling and clumsiness—it didn't exist for him. Harry Secombe, too, pocketed his face furniture, but to make the audience disappear and to conquer stage fright, not to make himself vanish into the air.

'A lot of us used to go to the Edgwarebury Country Club, Earl Street, on a Saturday—Dennis Selinger, Spike, June [Marlowe, the first Mrs Milligan]. Peter asked me out. I was working in Rep., but this didn't deter him. He'd follow me around... When I was away in Bedford, I did three months up there, he was at his worst. He'd arrive and say "I've just taken a hundred aspirins" as I was about to go on. He hated the fact... that I was in the theatre—which is what he wanted to do. At that time all he was doing was variety and he wanted to be a straight actor and go on stage. So he resented me for that. Anyway, he said he'd taken an overdose. I didn't know what to do. "I'm going on," I said, "You'd better get on with it." He was always... afraid of losing me. He couldn't bear it, you see... He would always accuse me of having affairs—nobody that he knew, with nobody specific... He was a very jealous and possessive person. When I was working at the Lyric, Hammersmith, he locked the door of my bedroom and wouldn't let me out...'

Was ever woman in this humour woo'd? Was ever woman in this humour won? Instead of running for her life from a lunatic, and perhaps fearing that he would do himself in and she'd be to blame, or as is more likely, seeing past the destructive antics to the lonely man beyond, Anne agreed to become engaged. Sellers' proposal was novel. On April 9, 1950, he asked her 'Will you be my first wife?' It had been necessary to pop the question quite loudly, too, because he'd locked Anne in a cupboard at the time. He'd let her out only on condition that she promised never to as much as look at another man again in her entire life. Nearly three weeks later, the press broke the news: 'Her man's a scream,' said one paper. 'Twenty-year-old Melbourne actress Anne Hayes...has become engaged to radio comedian Peter Sellers...Here they are at Mr Sellers' Finchley home...'* Peg and Bill's home, in that case, 211B. Anne soon discovered that she wasn't so much thought of as marrying Sellers—she was more the cause of his divorce from Peg. 'She was fine with me until we got engaged. She then telephoned my mother, saying "Will you keep your daughter away from my son because she is going to ruin his life." Actually her language was more colourful than that. My mother was shocked. Peter had a terrible row with his mother, left home and found a flat in Montagu Square, off Baker Street. His first decisive adult action.'

Like Milligan, Anne found Sellers' and Peg's closeness repulsive: 'He'd go to say goodbye to her, and...the way she kissed him—slobbery. Made me feel sick. She enveloped him in a mass of bangles and beads. I can't say that Peter was in love with his mother, but it was a classic love-hate relationship. He'd be cuddling her and caressing her, then he'd be pushing her away, telling her to go to hell, and then buying her something. Even though he was earning about £150 [$300] a week, which was a lot of money in 1951, equivalent to a few thousand a week now, he never had any money. He was always buying things. He'd buy you a gold watch and then see something else, for himself or for Peg, and he'd say "Listen, can I borrow that?" and he'd hock it—to buy a toy train set...I didn't find he showered me with gifts, not until the time of our split-up—and once he felt insecure, out came the diamonds and the fur coats. Until then he never even knew when my birthday was—not from the moment I met him until after the end.'

◆ ◆ ◆

'We got married the year they started making "The Goon Show"'—on September 15, 1951, at Caxton Hall Registry Office, the groom's parents being conspicuously absent. They lived first at Flat 10, 29 Hyde Park Gardens, W2, where the rent was £13 a week. Sellers was also paying by installments for a second-hand Rolls, which achieved eight miles to the gallon. All rather swanky, but their home lacked one essential: a telephone. Michael Standing, the BBC Head of Variety, had to write to the viziers of the Centre Telephone Area, Shaftesbury Avenue, spelling out the important part which a telephone plays in the lives of people in the entertainment world.

The residence must have been wired up pretty sharpish, because Graham Stark, who was often on the premises assisting his nibs with his photography, recalls that on one occasion, Sellers was excitedly waiting for some glamour shots he'd taken to materialise in the developing tray, when the phone rang. Stark heard Sellers put on a laryngetic croak to speak to Peter Eton and excuse himself from a 'Goon Show' rehearsal.

Sellers never, in all conscience, knew what the concepts of accountability and duty would have entailed. He seemed to be back to front on so many subjects; his own vision was that of a photographic negative—everything reversed. His attitude to colleagues and consorts simply depended on how long they remained conve-

---

* *The Star*, April 26, 1950.

nient. He'd had his Lady Anne. The conquest was over. On to gratifying the next whim, be it acquiring another motor car, zoom lens, or what have you. Boredom was vanquished by spending sprees. 'Everything came easily to him,' says Anne today, 'he was never short of work. The only times we'd be short of money was when he grossly overspent. Once his accountant, Bill Wills, put him on a strict allowance of £10 a week pocket money, with a bit kept back to tip the stage hands. We'd started a trust fund for the children—so Peter broke into that.'

Retrenchment of a kind did come about on June 16, 1952, when the Sellers' moved to 3 Highview, Shepherd's Hill, Highgate, N.6—scene of Milligan's murder attempt a few months later. Here the rent (subsidised by the Mendozas) was only £6 a week. Milligan actually lodged in their spare room until his own wedding took place, when he decamped across the hall to another apartment. He and Sellers amused themselves by overlaying recordings of Chopin nocturnes with the grunts of a man straining at stool. This they'd play to guests during dinner, nonchalantly commenting after a while, 'the new Concerto by Le Roté—the pianist, he'd got the shits.'

◆ ◆ ◆

Ardent to the point of frenzy before his marriage, Sellers was 'inattentive, preoccupied, and often thoughtless' immediately afterwards. 'He would go away and forget Anne existed. Then he would be remorseful, but only for a day.' These words expressed the opinion of Max Geldray, who provided the harmonica interludes on 'The Goon Show'. 'At this point in his life someone said of him,' says Geldray, '"Peter Sellers will give you anything, except five minutes of himself."' What you'd get instead would be minutes, maybe hours, of impersonation and dissembling. And why? Because Sellers, at that precise moment when you'd have thought everything was coming together right—i.e. with regard to home and career—that was just when he decided to be racked and tortured. 'You know, people hate a comic,' he said. 'They feel resentment against a comic. They sit there saying: "Go on, make me laugh." ... If you have a reputation they'll laugh before you've done anything. You can move your hand from one pocket to the other and they'll laugh. But if they don't know you ...'

It hasn't really got much to do with familiarity or good report, though, has it, the pleasure we instantly take in seeing performers who simply love what they are doing so much that the audiences sense this and relax? Secombe can exude that level of generosity. He's ready, you feel, to give audiences everything. This was never Sellers' way. He was too self-centred. 'Once in Coventry—we were doing a three months' season, Spike Milligan and Harry Secombe and I. It was a revue ... I had a turn on my own—told stories, did impersonations. One afternoon I simply took a gramophone on to the stage and I said: "Now I'm going to play a record for you." I put on a record and when it was over I applauded [*he claps gravely. The head is inclined as if in respect of a stage partner*]. And do you know, *they* applauded too! I went right through like that. I dispensed with the band altogether ... The record was one side of an LP—Wally Stott, I think it was, playing Christmas melodies, "Jingle Bells," carols, all that sort of thing.'

As Sellers told this story (and he told it often), the point was the imbecility of members of the audience and his own Herculean efforts to get through to them. 'You've got to do things like that or else you go absolutely crazy ... So I said, "On behalf of Wally Stott, thank you *so* much." They went crazy about "Jingle Bells" and started singing it. I said, "Oh, I think we can stand to hear that again—and all sing it together!" "Yes, that's right!" they roared ...'

Whether Sellers moodily outstared the audience or led the community in a chorus (accounts vary) there is no doubting the intensity of his contempt—and that's what the anecdote reveals to me. I don't think he really believed in the idea of an audience, except as a means of boosting his self-esteem. He cared about and was interested only in himself, not in the people paying to see him; he wanted not to have to do anything and still dazzle. 'Once at Wolverhampton or somewhere I was desperate. I went on in a plastic mackintosh and a wide-brim hat ... I tilted the hat forward so that the shadow came right over the microphone, and I did the whole turn like that: the audience ... saw nothing but the top of the hat. One reviewer gave me a splendid crit. [notice]—he thought my way of performing was the latest thing. But I found out afterwards he was the local avant-garde boy. He used to lose his job every week ...'

The ecstatic twerp-critic appears in *After the Fox*, when Aldo Vanucci's unintelligible black-and-white home-movie is unspooled in the courtroom—it's a series of jump cuts, camera jerks, and out of focus close-ups—and, clapping wildly at the screen, the fan is taken away in a butterfly net. Is that how Sellers saw himself? As a sacrificial victim surrounded by the uncomprehending? He wanted to be loved for who he was, and when only his petulance came across, he retreated into vituperation and self-pity. This is the source of his need, beginning to be expressed now in interviews and profiles, to convince people he had no actual personality to call his own—he tried to cover his lacks with mystique, make the absence of any nice attributes into a sort of supernaturally empty space.

'I am quite unaware of what I am,' he told *Playboy* at the beginning of the sixties. 'A politician can see himself, can see what sort of an impact he's making. I can't ... As for the face in the mirror—well, my appearance is fattish, sometimes happy, but always trying to achieve a peace of mind that doesn't seem possible in this business. This business breeds a tension that is difficult to live with ... It's a tension of thinking that unless you are number one it's no good.'

◆ ◆ ◆

When Milligan failed to get a response from the Coventry audience, he jumped up and down on his trumpet, made the mistake of asking the punters the rhetorical question 'You hate me, don't you?', scurried back to his dressing room and, feeling degraded, tried to hang himself. Sellers and Secombe pushed through the door and disentangled their colleague from his noose before he came to harm. It is unlikely that Sellers would ever have crumpled like that. He was too proud to allow an audience to get to him and stamp him out, as if an actor was himself that flattened bugle. Hostility merely inflated his sense of superiority.

The outright rejection of Milligan was what he'd dreamt would one day come his way, if he appeared without an armoury of other people's voices—which is what virtually happened at the Glasgow Empire, where he barely spoke half a dozen words. The Clydeside audiences were so notoriously ungracious that there was a net across the stage to protect the artists and orchestra from flying glass. Milligan had drawn the short straw and was booked to appear there on his own. A drunk yelled from the balcony. 'Are you Spike Milligan?' 'Yes.' 'Well y're a fucking idiot.' 'Right,' said Milligan, 'Outside!' So they met at the stage door and Milligan gave the critic from *The Glasgow Herald* a black eye. Soon it was Sellers' turn in the life-disenhancing North. 'Is there anybody in from the *Herald*?' he asked. 'Yes!' came the answer from the balcony. 'Right!' said Sellers, marching into the wings and returning with his useful wind-up gramophone. He put on a record of 'God Save the Queen,' walked off the stage, hailed a taxi outside the theatre, and returned to London. 'The first time an Englishman had left a Scottish audience standing,' he claimed.

Sellers' performances were getting increasingly idiosyncratic, as he attempted to work Goonish flights of fancy into a traditional vaudeville spot—or was it, more basically, that he didn't give a damn? Max Geldray recalls seeing him crawling around the stage on his hands and knees like a giant baby, for no reason at all. He'd come on carrying a carpet or a picture frame, or wearing a shawl, and refuse to refer to these items—incongruous props, like Queen Victoria's stuffed crocodile in the Palladium act. At the Hippodrome, Wolverhampton, he interrupted Geldray's solo with the words: 'Sorry, sir, but I have to tell you something important. There's no danger mind you, but there is a fire drill next door.' 'My God,' thought Geldray, 'He's going to clear the theatre with a fire drill.'

Because he was a radio star, few people knew what Sellers looked like, so he could trick the audiences into believing his little hoaxes. ('They didn't always know when we were gagging and when we were serious,' he said cheerfully.) Trailing a hose, he came back on clad as a Chief of the Fire Brigade, and pointed his nozzle at the stalls. 'I stood there on stage,' says Geldray, 'not knowing what to do.' Sellers, booted and belted, and wearing a huge silver helmet, proceeded to give a lecture on the pros and cons of his job and concluded by saying 'I would like to thank you all for your attention. It is such a pleasure to deliver the message of fire prevention in such a luxurious temple of the Arts.'

Shouting 'Fire' in a crowded theatre is a traditional anarchist's action; so is shooting a gun in a public place. Sellers did that, too. When he was appearing at the Chiswick Empire, he gave an impersonation of Peter Lorre. On a darkened stage, with a gradually diminishing green spotlight, he wheedled as Joel Cairo, from *The Maltese Falcon*, and he screamed out, as the persecuted child murderer in Fritz Lang's *M*: 'I cannot help myself! I cannot help myself!' Sellers shattered the inevitable silence which ensued by blazing off several rounds from a revolver. It must have been enough to have induced a mass loss of bladder control. 'I'd do anything,' he admitted.

Sellers continued with his Dada-esque experiments beyond the theatre—all the world was his stage, including the Hagley Road, Birmingham. Due to board with a Mrs Reeve, whilst he had a week's engagement in the vicinity, he arranged for her to take delivery of his prop basket. The doorbell rang, and there was the wicker hamper. Mrs Reeve couldn't budge it unaided, so she called her husband and son to come and help. The three of them, huffing and puffing, carried it upstairs. Sellers then unbuckled the lid from the inside, plucked himself from the linen, and stepped out: 'Thank you—it's my legs you know.'

One man who remained boot-faced by Sellers' cavortings was Val Parnell, the Booking Manager, and later Director, of the Variety Theatre Controlling Co., the General Theatre Corporation Ltd., and Moss Empires Ltd. 'Frankly, Sellers didn't make much impression on me... He always had a new twist for an act, something semi-zany. Off-stage he made the cast laugh...', he said off-handedly, though he nevertheless invited Sellers back to the Palladium for *Mother Goose*, 'Val Parnell's 7th Magnificent Pantomime,' in 1954. He was the Squire and played the part as Major Bloodnok. Eric Sykes wrote the script, Erté did the decor, and Shirley Eaton, who was Margery Daw, tells me: 'He was stormy—temperamental—always ready with a tantrum if things went wrong—and yet then he could be very affectionate and extremely vulnerable. He... was never an attractive person, Peter—and he knew it. But he had charm. Women respond to that in men, and to their vulnerability. Peter used all this as part of his appeal. We all had our photos taken on stage with our mothers. Max Bygraves, Peter, myself. After his mother died—and he was absolutely distraught when his mother died—he tracked me down and asked for a copy: "Shirley, darling, do you have a copy of it? I'll get another copy made for myself..." He never did return it.'

Max Bygraves remembers *Mother Goose* as a disaster for Sellers, who walked down the ramp at the finale day after day to no applause. Worse, Sellers had no rapport with Richard Hearne, whose Mr Pastry creature had been cross-dressed as the dame. Mother Goose, as rich as you please, had sold her soul to become beautiful. She took a dip in a magic fountain and came out transformed with a diamanté wig and a silver play-suit. Sellers' Squire was meant to exclaim 'What is this!' For one matinée he decided to do his part as Groucho Marx, complete with lope, painted moustache, and eyes shifting wantonly behind his specs. Instead of his usual 'What is this!' line, he said 'I've heard of Lady *Dicker*, but this is *ridoculous*...' The band appreciated the gag but Hearne, recalls Bygraves, 'would not utter the next line until Peter had given him the proper cue... Hearne was a rigidly trained legitimate actor who would stand there all afternoon... and almost demand the right line. It seemed like an eternity of silence on the stage—Peter couldn't understand—it was the first big laugh he'd had in the show.'

The following day, Bygraves found Sellers crying backstage. He'd received a letter, hand-delivered from the Moss Empires head office:

Dear Mr Sellers,

I was in the theatre yesterday when you decided to change the text of *Mother Goose*.

When I require you to make the members of my orchestra laugh I will ask you.

Until then, do the job you are being paid for, otherwise I will have you personally kicked out of the theatre.

Yours etc.

Val Parnell

♦ ♦ ♦

Sellers was not somebody to whom you could say DON'T! or STOP! or NO! The only saving grace about variety, as far as he was concerned, was the chance he had to improvise. Isolated in the spotlight, he did what he pleased. 'If you went backstage,' says Anne, 'you'd hear every tannoy [loudspeaker] turned up, because he always departed from his scripts; there'd always be something new in his act, and I think it took tremendous courage for him never to want to be the same.' When inspiration failed, however, or he was thwarted, the after-effects were ugly. 'He became very aggressive—and I mean Peter had a lot of violence in him. Not so much verbal tongue-lashings—he was *physically* violent. I remember when he was doing variety, he got very frustrated one day sitting in his dressing room and he pulled all these large hooks out of the wall. The whole lot, in anger ... He was emotionally retarded. His reactions to things were always childish—always hitting out, or hurting himself, or hurting somebody who was close to him. And then feeling terribly sorry afterwards. Living with him, I learned a tremendous capacity for blocking out things I didn't like. You only survived if you didn't think about it.'

Sellers treated his wife like he treated his audiences—in the final analysis, making due allowance for his posturing and detachment, there was little left in his attitude but disdain. The purpose of other people was to convince him he was marvellous. He used people up. Anne helped him to close the gap between music hall jesting and being a comic actor, Britt was a fashion accessory, Miranda his entry card into the ruling classes, and as for Lynne—he fed off her youth and ambition.

'He was destructive to anybody that was close to him, apart from Peg.' Anne found her mother-in-law an incubus. '"My son doesn't have to think for himself, I think for him" she was always saying—her refrain. One day she got on the phone about something ... and I eventually said, "Oh, fuck off" and put the phone down. In those days I did not use words like that, I have to tell you. We rarely spoke to each other after that—not until after the divorce, and I was well and truly out of his life, when she was almost a friend.'

After that debacle, and after Anne had had her miscarriage, when Peg, laying plots and inductions dangerous, had invited Nora Barnacle, Sellers' old flame, to tea, it was plain that, pregnant now a second time, Anne was going to need protecting. What this meant in practical terms was getting out of the peppercorn Mendoza flatlet and into a home of their own. With this scheme in view, Sellers, in January 1954, attempted to raise a mortgage with the General Accident Fire & Life Assurance Corporation Ltd., of Perth. When the building society started to deal with the proposal, however, and wrote to the BBC for confirmation of the applicant's gross wages and details of other emoluments arising out of his employment, the response was snotty:

> It is regretted that in view of the clerical work involved we are unable to provide you with the information for which you ask...
>   Yours faithfully,
>   *G. M. Turnell*
>   Assistant Head of Programme Contracts

Michael Peter Anthony was born on April 2, 1954, and Sellers would not own his own property until February 21 the following year when, flush with the *Mother Goose* earnings, he and his young family moved to 72, Tetherdown, Muswell Hill, N20. Why was Turnell so truculent? Perhaps because, only two weeks previously, Sellers and his agents had refused to sign one of the precious long term agreements:

> We feel that by signing this agreement Mr. Sellers would have to be on first call to the B.B.C. for the next three years, and as he has varied commitments in the entertainment field, especially with films, we obviously could not tie ourselves down as per the terms mentioned in your contract.

Here we have the first reference to Sellers' forthcoming career in the cinema. With only quasi-home movies, like *Penny Points to Paradise* and *Down Among the Z Men* to his credit, he was already looking confidently ahead. Milligan was giving Sellers the key to his buried thoughts, helping him to devise characters and noises which got to him in a unique way, but there was another mentor on hand, demonstrating the more fundamental arts and crafts—Ted Ray, his spurious relative. Timing, for example, 'is something you have to learn,' Sellers said in 1980, three months before he died, 'but someone can't teach it to you. I learned timing from watching a great comedian who is now dead, God rest his soul, named Ted Ray. I worked on his radio show for about eight years. I was a straight man, and I also worked in vaudeville with him. I could *hear* when he knew the ultimate moment. I mean, he'd sling a gag at the audience and they'd laugh. And then he'd know the precise *second* to speak again to keep them on that level.'

In fact, Sellers appeared in 'Ray's A Laugh' concurrently with 'The Goon Show' for twelve years, and far from being the straight man, he's the only funny element in it. Sellers joined the show at its outset, in 1949, when it had a variety format. Ted told a few disconnected jokes which were followed by the show's central section, the domestic scene between Ted and his wife, played by Kitty Bluett. Sellers was the various persons with whom their days were sprinkled. His most celebrated creation was Crystal Jollibottom, the crone from across the street—her exuberant gurgles are those of a contralto Bluebottle, she mutters and harrumphs like Bloodnok in drag, but otherwise she is a querulous, flirty, lush creation. We can *see* a fat old baggage hoisting up her petticoats. The audience come alive, too, when she arrives: 'I'll thank you to stop fiddling with me feather duster...'; 'Me unmentionables are caught round me scrubbing brush...' When she takes a ballet class, Ray is warned, 'I'll thank you to keep your big nose out of me dying swan.' Her catchphrase was 'you old saucebox!' The mixture of innuendo and outright desire in this 'last of the GI brides' is rich indeed—Crystal is a pantomime dame, impudent and vampish, all whoops and sags.

Sellers was also Soppy, the boy who smuggled a telescope into the *Folies Bergère* and tells everybody to 'shut up, big gob'; and he played millions of yokels, cockneys, and various ethnics. Luigi was a happy Italian, singing about 'my spaghetti, she is so be-autiful,' and Giuseppi was his taciturn twin: 'What you a-want supposing we a-got it?' he'd growl. Sellers played Wilberforce, an over-ingenious and dumb detective who prefigures Clouseau—'hist, never fear, Hugo's here,' he'd say, coming out of a disguise. (One week he was a tent pole and a mole on his neck was a knot in the wood.) And he was Cedric the scout-leader ('life gets humdrum if you don't dabble') who met his match in Wilf the Tough ('We are going to get the gentleman's money, *aren't* we, Sydney…?'), a sort of menacing Grytpype-Thynne.

Sellers' vocal eccentricities seem all the more extraterrestrial when set besides Ray's monotonous nasal delivery, which lay somewhere between a snarl, a drawl, and a bark. In the scenes with Kitty Bluett—an Australian, apparently, who lost her original accent and never quite succeeded in perfecting another one—Ted comes across either as a bad-tempered old shag, a tight-fisted grouch, or a tyrannical bore. These playlets, popular in their day, are vomiters now, the reason being that the battle of the sexes is unequal. Ted browbeats Kitty like Punch hitting Judy. It doesn't help that Kitty's range of whines and simpers, during the bickering, is such a rasp. They call each other 'darling' so frequently, the endearment flies back and forth like a dirty word.

As much as Ted Ray leaves me cold, I can acknowledge that he does deliver his lines with conviction. When Kitty muffs her material (in one episode she says 'run a wace' for 'won a race' and remains on the edge of tears for the rest of the show), it comes as a surprise to remember that there *is* a script. Ray's crossness has seemed so off-hand and the jokes so pathetic, who would dare admit to having written any of it down in advance? Until Sellers errupts, you'd think a tape recorder had been left running by accident in a suburban home. (I suppose the chauvinistic slant of husband and wife's sparring is authentically in period.) This was precisely why the populace tuned in. As Ray himself said, 'I like to feel when Kitty and I are doing one of our sketches that all over the country married couples are looking at each other and saying: "But, darling, that's exactly what happened to us the other day!"'

◆ ◆ ◆

If Ray taught Sellers how to pace a line—gave him his rhythms—he also, more tellingly, demonstrated that comic acting could be naturalistic. The two elements are connected, of course, and their impact on Sellers should not be underestimated. His artistry depended, no matter how nutbrain his given rôle, on the casualness of his inflections. Even when elaborately made up—bulbous nose, lank wig, a seedy nineteenth-century tragic actor's costume as, for instance, Dr Pratt, in *The Wrong Box*—the words spill out guilelessly. We are not aware of Sellers, the other side of the character, manufacturing the entertainment. ('Look at that, sir. Scarcely human,' he sighs, blotting the ink on a fake death certificate with a live kitten.) In this film, especially, we can see that great acting is a product not of *obvious* artistry, but is a success precisely because of its apparent artlessness. Wilfrid Lawson, so drunk he can barely walk or speak—he communicates in a strange, wheezy hooting—is totally affecting. And Ralph Richardson, as the boring old uncle, is blissfully trapped in a world of his own, foraging around the alleys and crannies of his mind for useless facts and figures, just as he rummages in the dozens of pockets and flaps in his raffish suits and coats. Sellers is in this class—he relaxes into his gifts, as Cocteau would say. He, Lawson, and Richardson stand out in the film that is full, ostensibly, of funny and talented people. Peter Cook and Dudley Moore repeat their supercilious master and sex-mad servant routine, Cecily Courtneidge and Tony Hancock mug embarrassingly, and the more John Mills (putting on a silly old sod's squeaky voice) throws himself around in his bed-shirt, the less interesting he becomes. You can see many members of the cast straining for laughs, clenching their jaws, the veins bulging in their necks.

Whilst I am not saying that Sellers' sorrowful Dr Pratt (who appeared in 1966) is all thanks to Ted Ray—where would my man have been without Alec Guinness?—I am putting forward the argument that Ray was an indispensible element in Sellers' conversion from music hall artiste to multi-textured actor, whose fol-de-rols have weight.

♦ ♦ ♦

'Ray's A Laugh' began in April 1949 and the first series ran for sixty-five episodes without pause. Sellers received nine guineas a time; this was soon increased to twenty-five guineas (the same as Kitty Bluett). Ted Ray himself received a hundred and five pounds each week. The cast rehearsed at the Paris Cinema and the show went out at half past eight on a Thursday night. Sellers eventually decided he wanted a vacation, and in March 1953 put his case to Pat Newman at the BBC:

> As I have not had a holiday for the past three years, I feel badly in need of one and would like to go to the South of France for fourteen days, commencing the 4th of May. This would entail my being released from 'Ray's A Laugh' for that period ... Right now my nerves are tuned up like an XK. 120 and I feel that if I do not get a holiday soon I shall have a nervous breakdown.

Sellers' agent wrote a formal letter making the same request and only to this did the BBC respond:

> My own view—at the risk of seeming rather harsh—is that we will not feel able to release him; after all most of us have these clashes to cope with at times and, generally speaking, holidays have got to fit in to one's work schedule and I don't think Peter can really have it both ways ...
>
> You shall have our considered reply in a day or two.
>
> Yours sincerely,
Patrick Newman
Variety Booking Manager

In fact, it was to be a fortnight before Newman wrote again, for reasons which are contained in his letter of March 25:

Dear Dennis Selinger,

Re: *PETER SELLERS*

I understand that since the request to us to release him so that he could have a holiday in May, he withdrew that request because he had anyhow cancelled his holiday for a Palladium commitment. Indeed, I believe the suggestion was that we should now pre-record four of the 'Ray's A Laugh' programmes—instead of three as we had agreed to do anyhow (to release him for his summer season). Unfortunately it is already sufficiently complicated for us to cope with the agreed three, and, with regret, we are unable to add on another one and make it four.

So the outcome of all this is that the position is what it was [at the beginning of March]. Incidentally, one cannot help but note that his urgent need of a holiday—so urgent that he seeks release from his BBC contract—seems to become less pronounced when there is a question of appearing at the Palladium.

At the foot of Newman's carbon there is a handwritten note, saying that Selinger had telephoned on March 27 and 'everything OK'. Not so with Sellers himself, however, for there are further anxious scribbles: 'Sellers now asking for more money *now*—in the middle of the series! Selinger said 'NO' [to his client] but thinks Peter S. may attack me—so be it!!' It is initialed 'P.N.'

◆ ◆ ◆

Newman, an impressive diplomat who could give his firmness a light touch, did well to stand his ground. Sellers' mind was always made up, his resolve fixed, until something better came along. And as for holidays—his family learned to dread them. 'I don't think I ever went on holiday without him saying "I want a divorce,"' remembers Anne. 'That was normal, saying things such as that. He was impossible on holidays—he'd get there and want to come back immediately... On holidays he'd have to be Peter Sellers relaxing, you see; and left to his own devices, there'd be nothing there. He had no cover. All his insecurities came out. He was aware he couldn't talk to anybody with any intellect, and he came across a lot of people who were bright—and he was lost... He blamed his lack of education, but that really shouldn't have made any difference in the end... *Life* should teach you... He left school very early—I can't imagine him sitting in a classroom, can you? If darling didn't want to go to school, darling didn't go...'

Sellers did spend at least one holiday with the edifying Ted Ray and his teenage children. Andrew Ray was already a veteran juvenile actor (*The Mudlark*, etc.) and Robin Ray would partially grow up to be the know-all alongside Joyce Grenfell on 'Face the Music', a programme famous for its quiz master, Joseph Cooper, playing a piano through its locked lid. Michael Sellers informed me that they all frolicked at Pevensey Bay, on the English south coast, his father filming everybody with a cine camera. Was he hoping to remind himself later that they were happy? Peg and Bill were there, too, renting a little chalet.

The summer leaves are all faded now. 'Only vague memories of Peter at that time,' writes Robin Ray, 'Nice man, bought too many cars, child at heart—*great* fun. Sorry I can't be specific...' Fortunately, Michael is able to be less diffuse: 'When you were with him, a wrong word could put him in a temper for the day.

"What do you mean by *that*?" he'd snap. You learned to be very peaceable and diplomatic. Going on holiday with him was a nightmare—keeping him happy for a whole fortnight or a month. Impossible. He'd invariably storm off home early.'

'He was like a child with another child,' says Anne, 'quite unreasonable. He was very inconsistent. I wouldn't say that he was a good father at all. He didn't know how to cope with our children, and, later on, he often didn't want to see them—though, when he did want to see them, they'd more than willingly go.'

Sarah Jane Sellers, born on October 16, 1957, remembers being summoned: 'When we were with Dad, it wouldn't be unusual for us to be looked after by a secretary; all through the years, often when I'd see him I'd spend more time chatting to Bert Mortimer [Sellers' chauffeur]. It was very strange when I was a teenager, because he really didn't know anything about me. He didn't know who my friends were, whether I had a boyfriend or not, how I was doing at school. Nothing ... In the early seventies, we'd spend school holidays with him, especially in Ireland. I recall regular rows with Miranda there. After that, I didn't see him much. We were constantly on the receiving end of his moods—big blow ups. You'd be talking about something, ... you'd realise that, somewhere along the line, you'd said something wrong, but you weren't too sure what it was—you'd get this sarcasm back.'

Her testimony chimes with Michael's: 'You could be happily, merrily going along—and one word would be enough ... He would just *go*! And once his temper was gone, he'd take delight in upsetting as many people as possible ... After a while I'm sure he was no longer in control—because he used to be sorry afterwards, perhaps if only owing to acute embarrassment. But then he never genuinely apologised for anything. He did once—I think—when he whipped me for painting his Bentley. In later years he did actually say he was sorry about that.'

What happened is that Sellers had been showing off his new maroon car to his mates, when he noticed some minuscule flecks in the coachwork, caused by gravel from the driveway. Ranting and raving, he was coaxed back inside the house and presumably sedated. Michael, aged six or seven, having overheard the commotion, thought he'd set about fixing matters. He found a pot of Dulux red paint in the garage and daubed at the chips. Sellers, discovering the DIY re-spray, went wild. 'A major low point in my childhood,' says Michael, 'accompanied by the withdrawal of all toys, all permissions and privileges. I was in my room and all the toys were gone—except for his trains, which were still stacked on top of my wardrobe.'

'He suddenly had this wrath,' says Anne, 'Mike had said, looking at the patched up scratches, "But I thought I was going to make it beautiful again." Peter went berserk. Nearly murdered him.' Milligan has claimed that he was on hand and intervened when the assault started to get out of all proportion. ('Peter got hold of the boy and shook him so violently ... I thought he was going to kill him'.)

I don't think Sellers much cared for the fate of the Bentley Continental in itself (so as to get rid of it quickly, he sold it on at a huge financial loss); the fact is, his was the over-scaled rage of the spoilt child who, unused to sharing, can't abide having his space invaded or playthings touched. Note Michael's reference to his father's out-of-reach train set. His mother remembers how they were acquired.

'When I was pregnant he went out and bought three hundred pound's worth of trains—for a child which hadn't been born yet. That sort of money would be a lot now on toy trains. I can't imagine what it would be equivalent to...'

Sellers was enraptured, watching the Hornby locomotives whizz purposelessly around the miniature tracks. 'I wasn't allowed to touch it,' recalls Michael, 'until he'd finished. Once he'd finished and was bored, then I could play. He came home with this toy house building set. Oblong metal plates full of holes; you'd stick these poles in and slide in these panels—and he stayed up all night making this house, playing with it. Then he threw it back in the box and gave it to me. I was six years old—I couldn't make head nor tail of it. Didn't know what the hell it was about. He never ever made allowance for our age...'

This went beyond inappropriate gifts. 'The rules were adult rules which we had to obey—although at that age, how could we understand his reasonings? Of course, this gave him the excuse for losing his temper. After a while, we'd learn the things he'd lay first claim on—what he reckoned he possessed. Including the homes. We never really had rooms of our own. "Mike's Room" was only mine for as long as it suited him. In my room at Elstead I had two chests of drawers. He'd taken on a new cook, who was to live upstairs in the barn; so he came into my room, threw my stuff on the floor, and said to this cook, "Right, you can use these chests of drawers." I had no say in the matter...'

◆ ◆ ◆

Sellers begrudged his children their childhoods. He did his best, by behaving badly, to be more puerile than they ever were; and it puzzled him that he should continue to be accountable for them. As he believed himself to be a one-man species, their biological connections with him were a nuisance—a reminder of his own mortality. When Sarah was late sending a birthday card, or if Michael telephoned instead of writing a formal letter to acknowledge a gift, Sellers would be swift to tell him 'I no longer wish to be thought of as your father' or 'my final suggestion is that you have your name changed by deed poll...'

The sole advantage of fatherhood, as he saw it, the only aspect he enjoyed, as Sarah says, 'was going out and buying toys that he'd then play with.' Actually, I find Sellers' immersion in toys the reverse of endearing. His little-boy-in-a-man's-body act was bound up with a lot of aggression and sourness. Bentine once revealingly said that he'd 'thought of the perfect Christmas gift for someone with Peter's attention span: a set of two thousand lead soldiers depicting the Battle of Waterloo, which Peter could play with for ten minutes, and then melt.' It wasn't so much Sellers' low threshold of boredom which was frightening, however, as his destructiveness and need for expressions of power. To lay waste both Napoleon and Wellington's battalions! He did once glue a miniature army together, out of a bag of coloured plastic pieces. He also went in for anything, as Max Geldray says, 'that moved and crawled and flew and sparked and fired and banged.' He hid himself within the impedimenta. Others could surround themselves with knick-knacks and it would suggest a whimsical, silly nature. Sellers, no. He over-did the high spirits. His behaviour was frantic and mean.

'Though you learned to weather him, as you got older, as a child he was bewildering,' says Sarah. 'I came to terms with that after I'd grown up. And I also accept that he was mad... He couldn't have been a normal person to have achieved what only he did as an actor—so I don't feel angry at him... I feel almost more sadness now than back then, when he'd just died. His films... are more of a reminder...'

Sellers induces melancholy in me, too—a complete outsider. By following his hunger for eminence and fame, as I am in these chapters, I can't help but see his death in the distance, the paranoia which preceded it, the corruption of his genius. There would come a time when the sight of other people's happiness filled him with irritation and pain, and the terrible thing is, this streak in his nature was becoming evident in the fifties, in his attitude to family life. 'My mother tells me she heard me on the telephone, aged seven or so, humouring him to keep the peace,' discloses Michael. 'And from then on it was a constant problem: how to deal with him? It was hard to explain. If he rang up and said "Hi, Mike", it was fine. If he said "Hello Michael," there was trouble in the wind, definitely... It went like that. It could be the stupidest of things—the way you were sitting, if it was that sort of day.'

We can see from all this the further appeal of 'The Goon Show', the dream-world in which Sellers acted out his impulses—all those characters, liquidated week in, week out, like lead battalions. If a variation on Goonish make-believe rules seeped into his home life, Sellers also used the recording session itself as an opportunity to misbehave. In marked contrast to later on, in these early days he was not allowed to get away with it. (Though his early days were running out.) During the making of 'Shangri-La Again,' in November 1955, Peter Eton actually sent him packing: 'We were recording at the Camden,' the producer said, 'he did something which put Harry off. In the Max Geldray number I went behind and told him to stick to the script. We went back for the middle spot and he started fooling about again, and I said "If you do that again, I'll fire you." He thought I wouldn't dare, so he did it again, so I had to fire him. Later he came back and apologised.'

Whatever misdemeanour he'd committed, news of his dismissal went right to the top—for on November 14, Dennis Selinger, his agent, had been contacted, and his advice was for Sellers to lay the matter before Patrick Hillyard, the Head of Variety.

Hillyard's response was a headmasterly salvo. Two days later, Sellers responded:

> I repeat I am very sorry that I refused to obey Peter Eton last Sunday, and I do assure you it won't happen again. However... I would also like to add, we had in the audience last Sunday a very well known Actor Producer who is an ardent Goon fan, and he happened to mention that he thought it was the best show in the present series.

So fuck you, chum. Sellers, in typical spoilt gosling style, has turned upon those who dared try to chasten him. He's put *them* in the wrong. The trick is to overreact, play the innocent, give an exaggerated howl, and expect an apology to follow for the misjustice you make out has been caused. The horror whom Uncle Bert could never control, screaming the house down if threatened with a smack, still comes in handy—Sellers, man and boy, calculated his tantrums shrewdly:

So far as I am concerned the incident is forgotten, and I hope that you too will forget it.

> With kindest regards,
> Sincerely yours,
> *Pat Hillyard*
> Head of Variety

♦ ♦ ♦

In truth, Sellers could afford to be cocky; he knew they'd pacify him eventually. Larry Stephens, Eric Sykes, or Maurice Wiltshire could manufacture the script if Milligan was wired up for electro-convulsive therapy; Kenneth Conner played Seagoon's Old Uncle Oscar if Secombe was indisposed. But Sellers, if ever he was absent, couldn't be replaced, not by a multitude. (Conner, Valentine Dyall, Jack Train, and Graham Stark were drafted in when he missed 'The Spy Or Who is Pink Oboe?' in January 1959.) The BBC grandees were more than aware of this. A year before the contretemps with Hillyard, the Head of the Light Programme, H. Rooney Pelletier, had had an idea for Sellers to introduce and discuss new gramophone releases. Sellers would pretend to be the proprietor of a record shop as well as all the customers popping in and out: 'Can HV [Head of Variety] see any objection to my giving the go-ahead?' HV certainly could:

From: Head of Variety.

...If anything we are inclined to over-use him, but as he is the best in his particular field this is inevitable. To further dissipate his talents in a Gramophone programme would, in my opinion, be extremely foolish, and such a move would be bound to dilute his popularity in other series.

The idea did not go away, however. On December 28, 1955, Sellers made a broadcast for the Light Programme called 'The Listening Room', produced by Michael Bell, a member of Pelletier's staff. Instead of a hi-fi shop, the characters were now forming a critics' forum: Grytpype Thynne, Bloodnok, Crun, and Bluebottle (for some reason renamed John Britanearly) passed judgement on, amongst other items, 'I'm Walking Backwards for Christmas' and 'Dance With Me, Henry'—a Hen and Min boogie-woogie.

♦ ♦ ♦

The scheme of rifling through items for purchase or sale goes back to March 1950, when Sellers made half a dozen shows called 'Sellers' Market' with Miriam Karlin, using material which had been originally incorporated in *Third Division*. They played a couple of East End stall-holders and Sellers, of course, was also the various patrons and hagglers. Ronnie Bridges remembers them, late in 1949:

'[Peter and Miriam] experimented with "Sellers' Market" and recorded the material on paper tape. We all went back to Peter's parents' flat in Finchley to continue the rehearsals. I went there once and...someone had done something to upset Peg. Peter was furious. He wanted to go and bash them at the time and his mother had to restrain him. I remember that very well. And his mother looked after him and monitored every single thing he did in those early days. Then he met Anne and got married—it was not acknowledged by his family, that first marriage...'

Miriam Karlin, owing to her own vocal mannerisms, was originally thought of, by Brian Seers, the producer of 'Variety Bandbox', as 'a female Peter Sellers.' She, too, recalls rehearsing at 211B. 'Peter would get into a terrible sulk if he didn't have enough of the funny lines, or if my lines were better than his. I mean, he'd be a real spoilt little boy—and I'd think, fuck, let him have my lines, if it'll keep him quiet. What do I care?...He had enormous vanity. He always wanted approval and to be loved. And ambitious! He was eaten up with ambition. You didn't mind, though, because he was also obviously one of the most talented creatures who ever lived. Anne was around a lot, but Peg was vile to all women who came near Peter—but, of the two of us, Peg might have preferred me because I was Jewish at least...'

I wonder what would have happened if, instead of marrying a gentile actress, Sellers *had* courted another Jewish entertainer? Or would that have created worse ructions than the ones Anne already faced? Miss Karlin appeared in two of his films, and dubbed Yul Brynner singing 'Mad About the Boy' in *The Magic Christian*. In *The Millionairess*, she's a Mrs Joe, toiling in the basement bakery alongside Vittorio di Sica and Sophia Loren. In *Heavens Above*, she's Winnie Smith, Eric Sykes' sister-in-law at the gypsy camp. With her turbanned head interrogatively and defensively tilted, a cigarette permanently in her tight lips like a protruding, flickering tongue, and with her arms akimbo, she really does resemble the Peg photographed at Sellers' wedding to Britt Ekland.

Perhaps Miss Karlin's voice, prowling around vowels and making ordinary sentences sound like an opera libretto, was just too eccentric to succeed in concert for long with Sellers, because when the 'Sellers' Market' format was revived, much altered, as a half hour show called 'Finkel's Café', in the summer of 1956, the writing team (Muir and Norden) was the same, but Sellers' foil was now Sid James. The formula was to elicit jokes both from the people running the bar and the famous folk who visit it. Sellers, inter alia, became Eddie, manager of the café. 'I shall play him Irish,' he vouchsafed. 'Something quite different from my normal style. No comic voices this time.'

That he was still considered nothing more than a versatile mimic was starting to rankle. 'To begin with,' he told a put-in-his-place reporter from the *Radio Times*, sent round to preview 'Finkel's Café', 'I am not essentially a funny man in the sense that Ted Ray is a funny man. My normal approach to comedy is the actor's approach. I started as an actor, I'm still one. By the time I'm forty I should like to be established in the theatre and in films—as a straight actor.' Sellers was due to be forty in 1965. By then he would have demonstrated, with the exception of isolated masterpieces like the *The Optimists of Nine Elms* (1974) or *Being There* (1979), and odd performances like Mr Hoffman or Rouquet in *The Blockhouse*, just about his entire range. After that, when he should have been in his prime, he made over two dozen execrable pictures. Why? Why did he make a chaos of his talent? One reason is put forward by Anne: 'He didn't have any taste. He didn't know what was good or bad. He was very undisciplined—again, that's why a lot of his films turned out badly. What he needed was someone to guide him in his career.' (Someone other than the spectre of Dan Leno and others in the far-beyond, I suggested.) 'He needed dictatorial treatment—like from Kubrick. He respected Kubrick, and there were very few people in his life whom he did respect. He respected the Boultings, mainly John. They saw something *there* and cast him as an actor ...'

The BBC were not willing to treat Sellers as anything other than a variety artiste until it was too late. 'He gets a million pounds for a film now,' commented Milligan in 1979. 'He's not going to come along to the BBC for £75 and "Could you please speak up, Mr Sellers".' Back in the fifties, during the protracted negotiations for the long term exclusive contracts, we can see that Sellers' very success as a provider of funny voices was keeping him from moving on. 'Sellers is quite brilliant in all he undertakes,' wrote Pat Hillyard in an internal memorandum, 'and is always a tower of strength.' But when Sellers 'made the point that so long as he is a supporting artist or a member of a team as in "The Goons", he can never receive a star fee, as might be the case if he had his own programme ... I pointed out to him ... that his particular talents were being exploited in the way most suited to our needs, and that he could continue to make a much more valuable contribution to our programmes in the way he is now doing than if we were to star him in his own programme.'

If the derivative 'Finkel's Café', totally forgotten today, even by its authors, was the best the mandarins could devise by way of furnishing Sellers with his own personal equivalent of a 'Ray's A Laugh', no wonder he couldn't allow the corporation to continue having first call on his services. Also, 'Mr Sellers is doing a considerable amount of film work, also variety, both of which are not booked too far ahead,' Dennis Selinger wrote. 'To ask him to sign a contract which only guarantees him £3,000 a year, and which could quite possibly preclude him either filming or playing in variety where he could make this amount in a very few weeks, is quite out of the question ...'

Selinger continues to lay stress on his client's career in films when, in truth, all Sellers had achieved in recent times was a bit part in *John and Julie*. (Regarding *The Ladykillers*, Michael Balcon was rather favouring Richard Attenborough for the rôle of the nervous Harry.) But there was no over-estimating Sellers' ambition, or mistaking where his eye was presuming to reach.

Chapter Six

◆ ◆ ◆

Sound and Vision

Sellers' creative frustrations culminated in his getting the Grades, his agents, officially to inform the BBC, in early January 1956, that 'this artist now doesn't wish to be associated with "The Goon Show" ever again.' Towards the end of the month, when the contracts for a new series were being drawn up, he was 'still dickering...and though', wrote Patrick Newman, 'Spike Milligan tells me he's sure Sellers wants to go on, Harry Secombe's agent assures me that only last week Peter Sellers said he'd never do any more...'

Well, as we all know, the Goons did go on, and as a result of his huff Sellers managed to get his fee up to fifty guineas a show (and soon to eighty), whilst Milligan, pacific before the money men, stayed on half-measures at twenty-five. To signify his boredom and general ill-temper, Sellers, in fact, put a lot into niggardly queries about loot. From the Winter Gardens, Eastbourne, he wrote complaining about a five quid underpayment. From the Star & Garter Hotel, Wolverhampton, he wrote to say that he no longer held 'any charitable feelings' towards the BBC, and therefore expected to be paid in full, all over again, for any repeats—to which Newman, countered, 'the basic fee is what counts and anything extra ought to be looked on as a manna from heaven...you begin to look on it rather as a right!' From the Castle Hotel, Norwich, he wrote:

What's Milligan going to do? Is he coming back as well?

Did he seriously expect 'The Goon Show' to be feasible without Milligan? That he could slip the question in suggests his waning loyalty and enthusiasm for the programme, and before long his insouciance got him into an embarrassing predicament:

Dear Dennis,

...[I]f Peter Sellers, or any other artist for that matter, wants to stand up in Piccadilly Circus and announce what we pay him I suppose it's his own affair. However, if he wants to take such action he must be jolly sure he quotes the right fee because if he doesn't that is certainly the moment when we will step in. In point of fact Peter Sellers quoted something slightly in excess of his present fee.

Yours sincerely,
Patrick Newman
Variety Booking Manager

Which was followed compunctiously by:

Dear Pat,

    I had heard about this before I received your letter and had already told Peter this was a silly thing to do as I am sure he quite appreciates. As you know, so far as the three boys are concerned they are so particularly friendly that they don't consider each other as business associates and, unfortunately, discuss lots of things with each other that they shouldn't! ...

Kindest regards

> Yours sincerely,
> for and on behalf of,
> LEW & LESLIE GRADE LTD.,
> *Dennis Selinger*

    Again, by manoeuvreing himself into a position where he'd be connived at as a kid, a pup, a dreamer, Sellers was excused his mischief. He was, of course, in reality, sharper than a serpent's tooth. Before the start of each series, he enjoyed being the one who lingered until last, being the one whose signature was sought before the work could proceed—a small and satisfying power game.

♦ ♦ ♦

    When I listen to 'The Goon Show' today, it is obvious that there was more to him than a facility for different voices. Sellers, going against the grain of the quick-change music hall gag format, gave his characters lopsided depths, moony aspirations. The great actor in him was stirring—and yet so far all he was was a noise, a sound, a package of sweet airs. Except for those who'd seen him in his bewildering variety sketches, or in the salutary failure of *Mother Goose*—when Sellers learned how hard it could be to imprint himself physically on a rôle—he was invisible. Not that this was true for studio audiences, of course. According to the reporter for *Sound and Vision*, in October 1950: 'Uncontrollable laughter you hear sometimes... during a not intrinsically funny moment in "Ray's A Laugh" is almost certainly due to their witnessing a plaintive girlish voice emanating from the broad and weighty Peter.'

    Broad and weighty is about right. In a quasi-documentary called *London Entertains*, made in 1951, Eamonn Andrews, conducting a tour party of Swiss school girls* about the capital's pleasure spots, visits Grafton's to see 'those crazy people'. From the two still photographs which exist, it looks as though everybody crowded into the Major's upstairs parlour, and Milligan, Sellers, Bentine, and Secombe, crammed into a brightly lit alcove, are obviously performing from a script. (Only Sellers and Secombe have copies, the other two peer over their companions' shoulders.) The smallness of the space and the intentness of the audience, the make-shiftness of the stage and the darkness of the rest of the room make for an atmosphere of clandestiny. Sellers, beefy and blazered, is to the fore. (If there is a police raid, he can come and speak in his authoritative Air Commodore tones.) Secombe and Bentine seem to be having a good time; Milligan looks a bit wary.

    But Sellers is the focus of the comedy. Not because of his enormity, or the wave upon wave of his woolly hair, but because of his earnestness, which is almost

---

* The Swiss misses were played by members of the Eastbourne Girls' Choir.

a glumness. Sellers, right from the start, knew that 'there is one rule which, in the lighter side of my work, I always try to observe. Never try to be funny in a situation which is itself absolutely and essentially funny. The more normal you are the funnier that situation becomes.' Sellers, robust and lugubrious, and ever so slightly parodying his despondency, is the only one who comes across as natural—*unnaturally* natural, thus the pleasing complexity of our response, and our apprehensiveness over whatever it is he might decide to do next.

He has wit, the others only their zaniness, which can seem rigged. He is apart, but the common absurdity of their appearance was what was going against him when he tried to break into films. 'All this time,' he said of the early fifties, 'I couldn't get into films. I felt I had more to give than I'd been giving, but I simply... couldn't get a part. People would just look at me and that would be that.' What he therefore decided to do was apply his radio skills to moving pictures. 'I could find work doing voices—actors who'd had to go back to America before the film was finished and so on. I did lots of voices. Dubbing, looping... I did an awful lot of dubbing.'

One assignment was *The Black Rose* with Tyrone Power as Walter of Gurnie and Jack Hawkins as Tristram the Bowman. Sellers dubbed a Mexican actor called Alfonso Bedoya, whom you may remember as the primitive bandit in *The Treasure of the Sierre Madre*. This time he'd been asked to play a primitive *Chinese* bandit, 'but with his own accent on top of it,' explained Sellers, 'you couldn't make out a thing the poor fellow said—so I did an impersonation of him...'

It could be argued that, slight though his association was, in *The Black Rose*, released in 1950, he worked for the first time with Herbert Lom and Orson Welles—if he was not quite alongside them, then he was at least underneath them, on the tape. (He had to say 'Two days from here with his army' when Welles rode up and asked Bedoya a question.) Welles had appeared in the film to put himself in funds for the completion of *Othello*, his under-budgeted Shakespearean project. Welles used *The Black Rose* to his advantage, borrowing, appropriating, pinching what he could. Sellers also went about his business subversively. Though nobody could have complained that he'd travestied the film, his delivery of Bedoya's part contains satirical resonance—just as Welles' performances of Tartar chieftains and Borgia princes always do. Welles, in historical costumes, is a wizard out of grand opera—you feel he really is capable of black magic. And Sellers was a magus, too. The actors instinctively add an ironic top-spin to what they have been hired to do—to show that they are larger talents, more exuberant, than anybody else alive. They are hungry to perform.

Mike Frankovich, who two decades hence would produce *There's a Girl in My Soup*, noticed this virtuosity when, as European head of Columbia, he was being driven to Heathrow to catch a plane to Rome. On the car radio was a play, at the end of which the announcer said 'All the characters were played by Peter Sellers.' As Frankovitch recalls, 'We were doing *Fire Over Africa* with Maureen O'Hara at the time, and we required seven actors to dub the dialogue. I needed English and American voices of all classes. When I returned to London, I called Peter and asked him to do the seven voices and paid him £250 ($500) for the lot.' Sellers also worked on Frankovitch's *Malaga*, which 'Mike had just made ... in Spain with his wife, Binnie Barnes, and Macdonald Carey ... There were a lot of extras, and most of them were Cockneys who had never seen Spain, except perhaps the Costa Brava. The others were Spaniards who couldn't speak English at all, so I ended up dubbing the whole seventeen characters. So if you have ever seen *Malaga* they were all me! ... In one scene there are eleven of these, all characters talking at the same time, all of them me ... I also did four voices [including Bogart's*] in *Beat the Devil* and I did Churchill's voice in *The Man Who Never Was* ...'

♦ ♦ ♦

There is an eerie appropriateness about Sellers, about whom Stanley Kubrick said categorically 'there is no such person,' getting himself involved in the film version of Nigel Balchin's true wartime story. Operation Mincemeat was a top secret wheeze. A dead body, kitted out with an unopened parachute and falsified secret documents, had been deposited off the coast of Spain—the documents would fool the Germans into expecting an Allied assault on Greece, not Sicily. As I mentioned in an earlier chapter, 'The Goon Show' was onto the macabre comedy of this imaginative scheme instantly, and there was barely need to exaggerate when sending it up. In *The Man Who Never Was*, a Goonish tone is set immediately when, over stock shots of Westminster, Sellers' Churchill is heard addressing the House of Commons. Far from giving the film a documentary realism, such a scene simply alerts us to the plummy play being made out of words like 'impedimenta' (to describe an army's equipment). Sellers can't help but to over-colour the famous slack-jawed mannerisms.

Churchill, whose actorish streak was vast (recordings of his hammy speeches belong with Charles Laughton's public readings from the Gettysburg Address rather than to archives of modern history), must have warmed to the bizarre elements in the tale. It wasn't any old body that was needed—they had to snatch a corpse that would fool the German pathologists. The whole business had to be thought through. The body, which actually expired of bronchial pneumonia, is packed in a canister of dry ice and given the name of Willy Martin. An entire identity is faked for him—rank, background, interests. What would Martin have in his briefcase? Personal items like photos, love letters, and theatre ticket stubs are counterfeited. Eventually, the uniquely cast cadaver is dumped in the Mediterranean by a submarine—Martin's directors and stage-hands having studied ocean currents and off-shore winds—and the remainder of the film concerns the enemy's attempts to double check all the apparent credentials. Are a dead man's messages to be believed?

Sellers, in fact, is not only the ghost of Churchill. He provides the film with

---

* Sellers was needed for *Beat The Devil*, in 1954, because Bogart, involved in an automobile accident on his way to the location near Naples, had knocked his teeth out and bitten through his tongue. Naturally he couldn't speak coherently after that. Sellers also dubbed the Italian actors, who'd known no English and hadn't understood a word of John Huston's direction or Truman Capote's script.

its babble. When some of the characters go to a cinema, his is the urgent voice of the newsreel announcer. When they are investigating parachutes and visit an air show, Sellers caws over the planes and reels off aviation statistics through a loud-speaker. He's a drunk singing in the street, old hags in the music hall audience (sitting near to Clifton Webb and Gloria Grahame who have gone out for the evening to collect the ticket stubs), and he's also heard carousing to a hurdy-gurdy through the swing doors of a saloon bar. When Webb goes to Savile Row, to see Richard Wallis as the haberdasher, Sellers is the taxi driver's grunt of thanks on taking his tip; and lastly, when Cyril Cusack, the Fifth Columnist, has quite failed to invalidate the ingenious trails, Sellers is a variety of German Generals shouting 'Martin genuine! Martin genuine!'

Like Martin himself, who exists yet never existed, whose biography came out of nowhere, Sellers too, in this film, is peculiarly absent yet present. His vocal changes and ubiquity are a mocking commentary on the concept of single, ascertainable identity. Sellers' disembodied dubbing was a chance for comic fantasy—and nowhere more successfully than in the Joan Collins vehicle, *Our Girl Friday* (a.k.a. *The Adventures of Sadie*). He plays the part of a splendid white cockatoo.

The idea is that Joan has been marooned on a tropical isle (actually Majorca) with George Cole, a pompous old fart called Robertson Hare (who once appeared in farces put on at the Garrick Theatre by the Ray Bros. Ltd.), and Kenneth More, who plays a chirpy Oirish 'character'. It must be one of the worst performances the latter ever gave. Joan, as the spoilt daughter of rich and vulgar parents (her mother is Hattie Jacques), has evidently modelled her speech on Julie Andrews. 'Oh! I do wish this rotten old ship was on the bottom of the rotten old ocean,' she says, stamping her little foot.

Throughout the film, she acts in the obligatory, stilted style of the Rank Studio starlet—it's as if she's permanently posing for a stills camera. (When she moves, she could be sleepwalking, and when she runs, she has that halting, sideways-on scampering of a ballet dancer in the grip of strong emotion.)

They wouldn't dare make the film today—'We are alone on a desert island. Three men and one woman'—except as pornography. That's where Sellers comes in. His parrot screech is the voice of lubricious thoughts. When Joan takes off her stockings, we cut to the bird, perched high in a palm tree, which lets out a long, filthy peal of laughter. Sellers has invented a multi-layered squawk, that's part whoop, part guffaw, part hysterical cackle. It is difficult to believe that a human's larynx could produce it, let alone a parrot's. It's an other-worldly noise, full of grossness and insult. The only (negligible) humour in the film is in the gentlemen trying to remain gentlemen, making their pact not to touch Joan, when Joan probably wouldn't mind somebody copping a feel. Sellers' almost sinister cock-a-doodle-doo derides everybody's libido and pretensions.

♦♦♦

As ingenious as he was, leaving his vocal fingerprints over other people's scenes, 'at that time I could never get into films as an actor. I always used to remind people, "Don't forget me if there is anything going in the acting line."' But they did, so he reverted to television. His first series was called 'And So to Bentley', and thirteen episodes were broadcast live from Alexandra Palace, beginning in October 1954. Sellers, along with Rosemary Miller, Peter Jones, Bill Fraser, and Jill Day, was in a comic team supporting Dick Bentley. Also in the cast was Charlotte Mitchell. 'Peter *cared* about these programmes. I remember seeing him bend all this cutlery in half in the canteen, because he was angry that things weren't being done swiftly enough. *"There's* one person who is going to be a big star," I remember saying, but the others disagreed, "He'll never be a star on his own, he has to be part of a group." But Peter had an instinct for what was funny and what wasn't—which wasn't true of the director, Brian Tesler. He could only tell if a scene was funny if he saw Peter and me laughing. "Keep that in, Charlotte laughed at it" became an in-joke. When I met Brian twenty years later, the first thing he said was "Still corpsing,* Charlotte?" But as for Peter—it was as if something was always worrying him. He was easily upset ...'

I asked Charlotte Mitchell about whether Sellers had been in love with her: 'It was all a long time ago ... Peter was vulnerable. You can't be that funny as an actor without, in some ways, being difficult. He seemed to have a skin missing, he was so hypersensitive. Drawing on himself, all the time, to be funny, it made him frail. Anne used to come to the studio with the children [*sic*] in their woolly hats. He talked about his children with great love and affection—he was very proud of them. I knew him when he was happy. I wonder when he was ever happy again? What *happened?* He was sad, by the end. I wrote to him in 1964, when I thought he was dying. I saw him once, in later years, at Pinewood—but he walked past. He *did* see me, but he didn't want to recognise me ...'

It was as a result of 'And So To Bentley' ('I laughed all the way through it') that she was invited to participate in 'The Goon Show', the Robin Hood panto which was broadcast on December 18, 1954. Sellers also took her photograph. Charlotte is bright and apple-cheeked—you can quite imagine an infectious laugh, energy, bags of personality. If Sellers was in love with her when he took this picture, it's her confident high spirits he'd have wanted to possess. (He'd snapped, as she said to me, a 'jolly' picture of her.) At the time, his son Michael would have been not much above six months old. Anne, newly a mother, was perhaps not giving Sellers every moment of her attention, and he'd have resented her for this. Charlotte Mitchell, in Sellers' view, would have been unencumbered. He would never have seen a tired, preoccupied side of her. And all that guff about being a proud parent? That sounds like Sellers playing the rôle of new paterfamilias. I have seen photographs of him taken at this period and he's gesticulating with a pipe. Did he, weak and vindictive, go home to Anne and wear a tasselled smoking cap?

◆ ◆ ◆

---

* Theatrical slang, meaning to be mystifyingly reduced to uncontrollable giggles on the slightest pretext, as if the sheer absurdity of being an actor is suddenly apparent. The illusion of performance dies—hence the idea of a corpse. Sellers was more prone to corpsing than any actor in history, except for the young Laurence Olivier.

To Sellers, except that he'd be seen across the whole country in one go, live television was no better than doing his act in music halls. He was still getting no experience in extending, or deepening, a rôle. On 'The Glen Campbell Show', for example, he was skittishly Scottish, making his appearance in a red beard and a long kilt ('to hide the curse I was born with—bad legs'), and he uprooted every Highland myth ever known: sheep stealing, porridge, meanness, heather ('the heather is as high/as an elephant's eye'), etc. All this Scotch mist is paraded, along with McGonagall doggerel, and Sellers seemed to act as a stimulant on the poor material, making its unfunniness part of why it's funny. He gets us to collude with him—his extravagance draws us in. He puts us on the side of the gifted entertainer trapped with trash. We help him make the best of it, as when he's a Southern preacher, yelping out 'cigarettes and whiskey and wild, wild women/They'll drive you crazy, they'll drive you insane ...'—a sketch he reproduced on 'The Muppet Show' a quarter of a century later. The very form of the Kermit and Miss Piggy programme was a send-up of musty music hall. Here, Sellers, and Sellers alone, is fast and frolicsome.

It's precisely because they are skits and sketches that Sellers is being cramped—he is forced to be, figuratively, sketchy. It was still mainly as a mimic that television wanted him. All that remains of his appearance on Eric Sykes' 'The Arthur Ploughshare Show', for example, are his vocalisations. Having been introduced by wonky piano music, he bounds on stage as a homosexual: 'Goodness,' he says to Sykes, 'I don't like your tailoring very much ... Oh, I say, *look*, just *look*! Aren't they a lovely audience? Look at the colours of grey and a dash of pink ... I'd love to paint them ... I want to get the aura of pale mauve laughter coming through.'

Sellers, I admit, is awfully adroit at camp squeals and over-articulation (he's back in his parrot range), but the target of the joke—the "gaiety" of artists—is disagreeable, and the army song he proceeds to sing ('Oh a man on the march may be lonely/Though there are ten thousand men by his side') is a dubious link with Major Bloodnok.

He kept with it for the money, which, compared with his radio fees, was vast. He was paid five hundred pounds for appearing on 'The Billy Cotton Band Show', two hundred pounds for going on the 'Six Five Special'.* He was on 'Don't Spare the Horses', a variety show broadcast from the Princess Theatre; similar Saturday night entertainments beamed from the Palladium; Harry Secombe's songfests, called 'Secombe Here!', broadcast live from Earl's Court; you'd have also glimpsed him on 'The Dickie Valentine Show', and as the co-host, along with Valentine and Margaret Lockwood, of the 'Salute to Show Business', convened on board a Thames steamer, the *MV Royal Sovereign*, and broadcast on September 20, 1957, to celebrate the second anniversary of Independent Television.†

---

* December 14, 1957, and January 11, 1958, respectively.

† ITV started broadcasting in London, in opposition to the BBC, on September 22, 1955, and within the following two years spread to the Midlands, the North of England, and Scotland, reaching about four million homes by 1957—a fact disputed by Milligan, who reckons 'there were only 350 TV sets in England at the time.'

Sellers pretended to be the *MV Royal Sovereign*'s skipper-cum-barman. He kept his hair in the thick black cowlick of Amphibulous, the prime minister in *Carlton Browne of the FO*, and added the Hitlerian moustache of Fred Kite. He was dishevelled and slobby, deflating the mood of self-congratulation and glitter which carried the rest of the programme. He was remunerated with six hundred pounds, which was about what he'd come to expect: 'ITV pay Spike and I fabulous money for "Fred"—more than we dreamed. They gave us co-directing status, too. If they hadn't, we wouldn't have done it. The money wasn't all that important…'

By 'Fred' Sellers meant 'The Idiot Weekly, Price 2d' (half a dozen programmes, made between February and April 1956), 'A Show Called Fred' (five programmes throughout May), 'Son of Fred' (eight programmes in the autumn), and 'Yes, It's The Cathode Ray Tube Show' (six programmes early the following year, when Milligan was replaced as script-writer by Michael Bentine). Why Fred? 'We all used this name Fred,' he once explained. 'We absolutely revered it… You can ruin anything with Fred. Suppose somebody shows you a painting. Oh… he says, isn't it beautiful: it's a Rembrandt. Beautiful, you say. Then you look a bit closer and you see it's signed Fred Rembrandt. It's no good, you can't take it seriously if it's by Fred Rembrandt from East Acton.'

Unlike the other TV spots and dots, the 'Freds' were concerted efforts to visualise 'The Goon Show'. Sellers and his colleagues had tried since the very beginning to effect the transformation, but the BBC was not interested: 'I have some very good ideas for short sketches which Spike Milligan and Larry Stephens have written for me, which I think would do well on television,' Sellers had informed Ronnie Waldman, on October 4, 1951, just after the end of the first series of 'Crazy People'. 'If these "clicked" I would like to try for a series. As you may know, Larry and Spike wrote "The Goon Show" and I think this material, presented visually, is a cert. Can you help me in this line? I should be very grateful for any suggestions or comments. I went to see R. Afton,* but was kept waiting forty-five minutes, so I packed it up.'

Waldman, like Afton, did not respond. The prevailing philosophy was that Sellers, a prodigy with sound, would be an embarrassment when brought into vision. 'Isn't it wonderful that there is such a thing as radio,' Roy Speer once said to Fredric Raphael, 'because otherwise people like Peter wouldn't have anywhere to work? He could never make a living as an actor with a face like that!' The BBC's loss was Associated-Rediffusion's gain. Yet though the 'Freds' were to become Sellers' chief contribution to television, very little of the material survives today. When Associated-Rediffusion merged with, or was supplanted by, Thames Television, in the sixties, all the old tapes, film stock, and concomitant paperwork, was sent to a rubbish dump in Wembley.

But, briefly, ITV had an amateurish, free-for-all zest, and Sellers' 'Freds' embodied this. As Bryn Siddall, who worked on the shows, remembers: 'It was hard for commercial television to attract technicians—nobody wanted to leave the se-

---

* Richard Afton was a TV comedy producer—see *Trial Gallop*.

curity of the BBC; nobody wanted to leave the lucrative world of films—so Associated-Rediffusion had to hire staff from a bankrupted ballet company. That's why the carpenters, designers, and props-buyers went in for elaborate, ornate sets and costumes, which Sellers loved ... Money was no object. No thought was given by anybody to a budget ... everything went out live and filming was very slap-happy. Extras would wander about at will, to be joined by members of the public. People would go in and out of shot. The programmes all over-ran. Material not used one week would be used at the start of the next. If they asked the props department for "sculls", and it was a spelling mistake, they got oars, and the *Hamlet* sketch would be, "Alas, poor Yorick, I rowed him well." Most weeks, no two people had the same script—and Milligan would re-write material on air ... They had a catchphrase, too, amongst themselves, which was "You can't get the wood, you know." Sellers was always saying that.'

The 'Freds', by making use of whatever fell into the developing tray by accident—or at least by giving that impression—could make ill-discipline and daredevilry the basis of the humour. The programmes had the freedoms of a home movie, and indeed culminated in the team's making the eleven minute black and white silent, *The Running, Jumping, Standing Still Film*—which, as the co-director Dick Lester said, 'was an outgrowth of the filmed inserts we had been doing for the live TV shows. I'd enjoyed those inserts, because they were so flexible to work with. So the film was two Sundays shooting in a field with friends and chauffeurs and wives.'

Sellers loved the simplicity and informality of all this. He'd cause trouble, later on, in *Casino Royale* especially, when he'd try and force these nonconformist and liberal techniques on a top-heavy full-dress Hollywood-financed production. (Indeed, that he chose Joe McGrath, who'd worked on the 'Freds', to direct *Casino Royale*, suggests how he'd hoped, with his own inventiveness and Columbia studio's money, to re-create the happy anarchy of his early days on TV. It was not to be.)

♦ ♦ ♦

'... the show is being written week to week,' Sellers confided in Herbert Kretzmer, the columnist of the *Daily Sketch*, 'so you probably realise the difficulties.' They were difficulties, however, which he (at first) enjoyed trying to surmount. If the actual script wasn't funny, he'd suggest they speak their lines against a back projection screen of riots in Belgium or a bedstead travelling through the sea in the wake of a motorboat. Though Lester says that 'there was no tape. There was a primitive form of telerecording, but that was too expensive for the likes of us to use,' and though Bryn Siddall was certain that 'nothing survives of the programmes now,' I have managed to find a fragment in the National Film Archive.

Transferred to TV, the Goonish imagination has less to do. The sketches aren't exactly inspired, and Sellers simply impersonates his own radio characters or mimics Richard Dimbleby or Laurence Olivier's Richard III as Columbus: 'I've endured their sly mockery,' he says, whilst the wind whistles and the sea crashes, 'as they hint at that which they've not the courage to speak plainly to my face.' The staccato delivery and the mangled grammar are a faultless lampoon of Shakespearean gibber-

ish, as well as encapsulating Olivier's own convoluted real-life speech rhythms ('illusion' is pronounced with four pecks, 'ill-ooze-y-on'). But though the material slips
fast from the memory, Sellers' Olivier-as-Richard is chilling—as mimicry it is *too*
good. He appears to embody both the King's amorality *and* Olivier's own ambitions
and serpentine charm. In this sense, it is a dual impersonation, and becoming a fussy
elvish'd-marked son of hell, seductive and repulsive, intersected with something
deep in his own nature, where he had a heart like flint. We can see all this operat-
ing in a superb photograph, taken by Graham Stark, of Sellers in the full costume
and make-up. (I have seen it written that Sellers wore Olivier's actual Richard III
wig, having found it in storage at the Aldwych Theatre.) He sits back, in profile and
in darkness, and what light there is picks out, like the glints off a silver hatchet, the
severe nose, evil eyes, and lascivious mouth. (It is hard to credit it *isn't* Olivier.)
Sellers climbed into the full rig again, a few years later, when he decided to perform
the Beatles' number 'A Hard Day's Night' as a Shakespearean soliloquy ('It has been
a hard day's night and I have/Been working like a dog...', he barked, very nearly imposing the requisite iambic pentameter).

Sellers, like Richard, could add colours to the chameleon, change shapes with
Proteus for advantages. Roy Speer's jibe about his featureless potato head aside, it
is Sellers, and only Sellers, who claims our attention in the 'Freds' and associated
stills. Whether he's dressed as a doctor about to amputate his own nose, or a rally
driver sitting in a car made out of chairs and coats, or if he's doing things with a
Viking helmet, or is a boxer, the Muswell Hill Mauler, in a leotard embroidered
with shamrocks, he is in character and funny—but he is also something more. As
with all the face-pulling photographs posed for during recordings of 'The Goon
Show', where he, Milligan, and Secombe would be requested to look zany and
whacky, Sellers' expression always manages to be silly and sombre at the same
time. He is strangely detached from what everybody else is about, and therefore
(you feel) cannot be blamed for their imbecilities; and yet then he'll come out with
ideas and disguises screwier than the lot. Puffing out his cheeks, to impersonate a
gilded caryatid, holding up a box in a theatre, or simply staring into space, he's unpredictable, absurd, and sympathetic.

But, being on TV, the fairy tale potential of Goonery seems rather retrograde
here—and it does not fulfill him. There is far too much of Milligan's squeaky
voice, in the fractions of the 'Freds' I saw; and far too much of Valentine Dyall altogether. Senile gabblings and upper-class drawls are thrown in for their own
sake, as if they are automatically funny and that nothing more need be done. Military bands, explosions, and honky-tonk piano music are imported from 'The
Goon Show' (the sheer noise is from 'The Goon Show'), along with rolling
drums, amplified birdsong, and lots of over-hearty laughter from the orchestra
and studio hangers-on.

The 'Freds' went from a refreshing misrule to a boring unruliness very quickly.
'It wasn't too bad at the start, said Sellers. 'I think 'Idiot's Weekly' and 'A Show
Called Fred' were the best of the series. But it was a strain for Spike, writing a new
show every week. And later on—you know, we got together a group of young

script-writers to contribute—well, they had some good ideas—but sometimes there would be a good beginning but no end. In script-writing that isn't enough; the jokes have to be organised. That was when the show began to go downhill'— aided and abetted, he should have emphasised, by his own irresponsibility. Once, out filming at a quarry near Harefield with Dick Lester, in the summer of 1956, he had to be taken home and work abandoned for the day because he'd literally pissed himself laughing. They were doing a dervish attack on a ridge. Because of the dryness of the sand, Sellers couldn't get a foothold on the slope, and kept sliding back. He just couldn't reach the top. On the third attempt at storming the dune, he began to corpse, scrabbled frantically, gave up, and a trickle of urine streamed from between his legs, on to the sand, as he giggled and giggled. The rivulet raced him back to ground level. Professional incontinence indeed.

◆◆◆

'Goonery can't be done properly on TV because of the expense,' complained Sellers, forgetting that *The Running, Jumping, and Standing Still Film* had cost next to nothing. 'We want a lot of films and cartoons, with humans appearing among the cartoon characters...' He might be prophesying the nonsense approach of 'Monty Python's Flying Circus', which would be so effectively made for television about fifteen years later, except that what actually concerned Sellers, who'd often recourse to diversionary ranting about 'expense,' e.g. on *Casino Royale* or *The Fiendish Plot of Dr Fu Manchu* if he felt personally insecure, was not method or technical innovation but how best to develop and sustain his quirky gifts, with all their overtones and undertones. 'I'm not a comedian,' he'd decided, 'just an actor-cum-what-have-you... As I see it, I'd have to change my style [from clown and mimic to comic actor] inside five years—I'll be 35 then—so why not start the process now?'

His first reaction to the disarray of the 'Freds' was to decide he was disillusioned with Milligan—though, in actuality, an upheaval between himself and his creative godfather was 'something which I believe happens at fairly regular intervals,' Pat Newman had commented in a BBC memo.

His second operation was a surprise (and a forewarning). He reverted to the beginnings of his career by sending for Bentine. 'Lovely to have you back, Mike,' said Sellers, as the man he'd helped to transport to Australia returned from his exiles. 'Can you write some television shows for me? I've still got six more to do to finish my contract with Rediffusion. Could you please start right away?'

Sellers' bright and cheery request is an early example of his unnerving forgetfulness, which was to reach an amnesiacal abyss on *Ghost in the Noonday Sun*. He'd quite put out of his mind the fact that, but a few years previously, he'd schemed to have Bentine removed from 'The Goon Show'—a campaign which was so successful that Bentine's forty-one programmes and 'Crazy People' episodes had been melted down and wiped out of existence. Even his photograph (he says) 'had been neatly excised from the earlier Goon pictures,' and only since Sellers' death has he been able to have himself 'replaced in the group pictures of the original Goons displayed in many BBC buildings.' Bentine had become an un-person. 'I thought you were dead' was the waggish sort of remark producers made now he was back.

Sellers' power, his ability to consign people to the wilderness and then recall them or be nice to them—in this early stage of his career because he was choked with ambition, later on because he was destructive and schizophrenic—is reminiscent of nothing so much as the Roman Emperors. 'He used to forget things from one day to another,' said Peter Medak of his star-crossed Mediterranean movie-making. 'I saw him years later when I was doing another film at Shepperton and he'd forgotten anything had gone wrong between himself and me.'

By regularly emptying out his conscience, Sellers could rid himself of such human weaknesses and moral guides as, say, guilt. If he looked back, it was only to sentimentalise, never to apologise. Bentine came back into his orbit because Bentine was useful to him. That chair frame routine was *visual*, and the idea of objects like sink plungers taking on a life of their own would inspire Sellers, one day, to vivify Dr Strangelove's false arm. Also, Australia and family life having knocked the Etonian edges off him, Bentine interested Sellers as an individual case-study.

Bentine had a real knowledge of rejection and of being on the outside. 'We can't have non-Europeans in the RAF,' he was told, but he persevered and, as we know, he became an officer and later expiated his wartime experiences with Goonery. In the broadest sense, his background may be compared with Sellers'. The wayfaring Jewish music hall artistes, belonging nowhere in particular; the South American immigrants, anxious to become English, adopting the local habits (bridge parties with the Edwardian gentlefolk), and yet being scorned as outlaws and virtually interned. Sellers' total lack of education; Bentine's enthusiastic auto-didacticisms. Sellers' vocal facility; Bentine's speech impediments—as a child, his voice box was damaged by a botched tonsilectomy. (His subsequent delight in din, clamour, and squawks began as mandatory, recuperative speech therapy.) Their mutual obsession with spiritualism...

I'm afraid that, like the line in Keats about the sound of an owl being a 'night-bird's hated screech,' I personally find Bentine's comedy too high-pitched—manic—for my taste. His sketches are exercises in noise non-abatement, and amidst the babble and prattle, the explosions in a firework factory, the contests between military brass bands, and the insects driving people mad with their incessant tck-tck, the wonder was that Sellers still managed to give depth to his characterisations. (At least he had characters to play now: the 'Freds', by contrast, were just so much running amok.) His favourite part was Mr Charles Crumpet, winner of the Film Extra of the Century Award. Suddenly, Sellers' sympathetic understanding of proud old failures, such as he'd known in Ilfracombe and points round about, came pouring out. Extras, or crowd artistes are, says Bentine 'dreamers, hiring out their fantasies with tolerance and enthusiasm.' It is this sad whimsicality which Sellers could convey. 'Then I struck a bad patch,' the grand old man confesses to his interviewer, 'I was out of work for fifteen years.'

◆ ◆ ◆

Actors, earnest and dispirited, elderly and decrepit, lie within Sellers' Dr Pratt, General Fitzjohn, Morganhall, and Old Sam. His characters are men who believe themselves to be masters of illusion—or who are suffering from self-deceptions, if you prefer. Sonny MacGregor, Clare Quilty, C.P.O. Dockerty, Henry Orient, and his many confidence tricksters and crooks are also play-actors, in the sense that they pretend to be what they are not. Would it be to get ahead of my story to try and see something ominous in Sellers' early and heartfelt appreciation of the actor's art—actors being, by their very natures, watchful, dissembling, and mercurial? Applied to himself, acting was to entail an increasing lack of contact with real life. It was the tragic aspect of his comic genius that Sellers had nothing to replace acting with; and that beyond the jollity of his public appearances there was only solitude and disintegration. (As I once said in another book 'Sellers filled his life with toys, instead of filling it with life.') And yet, portentously perhaps, he can imply even *this* in his fops and hams. At the end of the fifties, Kenneth Tynan invited him to appear on an arts magazine programme called 'Tempo', produced live from Teddington on Sundays. It was one week ballet, the next week opera. 'One Sunday we were all surprised to see Sellers turn up,' a technician informed me. 'He stood at a lectern and recited McGonagall, and he did not laugh or even grin. In fact, all the crew without exception were in hysterics all day, and not once did Sellers crack up. Off camera, Bruce Lacey, in a brass helmet, was doing daft things, and still Sellers didn't corpse or even *look* at him...' You can tell, by his dramatic stance, that the botched balladry was being delivered as if it were a lecture on the way life imitates art, or on the hidden truths revealed by masks.

◆ ◆ ◆

'I wonder if it is now possible for you to reconsider the Peter Sellers situation?' asked Ronald Waldman, in a confidential memo to the BBC TV Head of Light Entertainment, on April 25, 1957. Having once so peremptorily turned him down, it had been galling for the BBC to watch Sellers succeed on the screen; and now that they wanted to entice him back from ITV, to sign an exclusive contract which would give him a dozen comedy shows and six drama programmes a year, he'd become expensive. 'He would want at least £500 per appearance. However, it is difficult to decline... such an excellent television artist and I am most keen to try and achieve this contract.' The finances were never resolved; neither could Sellers quite decide on what material suited him. He'd go through cycles of enthusiasm and hesitation; he'd put people through hoops, and then he'd withdraw.

Michael Barry, the Head of Drama, attempted to interest him in 'a very special project over which considerable trouble is being taken. This is no less than a serial dramatisation of *Pepys' Diary* made by screen writer and historian Colonel Rawlinson. It is turning out extremely well as an amusing and human story and... would you like to play Pepys?' (It would have been for a fourteen week series, so Sellers declined.) Roy Speer, eating his words about Sellers' geekiness, asked him: 'Have you ever thought of doing a thirty minutes series *entirely on your own*?' (Dennis Selinger replied to the effect that Sellers was already 'very much overworked' and that therefore his client could not guarantee to give of his best.)

He refuses to appear in some S.J. Perelman playlets 'unless it is financially outstanding for him'—likewise: 'He feels that he is not the right person to read 'Brugglesmith' [from Kipling's *Many Inventions*] on Christmas Day.' The last thing they tried to tempt him with—ominously, in view of his future removal of Anne Howe, his serial polygamy, and misogyny—was Maxwell Anderson's *Anne of a Thousand Days*. 'Jean Simmons is pencilled in for Anne Boleyn and we would like to know if Peter Sellers would care to play the part of Henry VIII?' (Sellers said no because the production would have entailed three weeks of rehearsal beforehand.)

It is only fair to add that radio, too, was failing to hook Sellers. Sellers' promise to play Estragon in *Waiting for Godot*, Beckett's intellectual re-working of Laurel and Hardy (think of Didi and Gogo's bowler hats, etc.) was taken seriously enough for the *Radio Times* to have carried his photograph announcing his forthcoming appearance. The embarrassment of his cancellation ('ostensibly because of some film engagement, but my [Martin Esslin, then assistant head of radio drama at Broadcasting House] impression was that he simply felt too much stage-fright about stepping into high literary drama') 'seemed to me to necessitate a little chat with Dennis Selinger,' said Pat Newman. The outcome of the pow-wow was that Sellers had gone into a sulk because he had expected the same fees for straight plays as he'd received for the traditionally more lucrative light entertainment. The BBC did not give up, however. On February 16, 1962, they wrote to Sellers c/o The Carlton Tower Hotel (whither Sellers had moved, the better to incommode his wife and young children) to suggest he attempt *The Killer* by Ionesco, *Oblomoff* by Gontcharoff, and two plays by Gogol, *The Gamblers* and *The Marriage*.

There is something inadvertently funny (and piteous) about all these indomitable BBC eggheads sending Sellers classical plots and trying to make him beetle-browed and serious. In time, Sellers would grow accustomed to everybody wanting to treat him like the most distinguished guest in an opulent restaurant. Sycophancy would become the norm (he'd have a psychological urge to be on the receiving end of it); and he would be, in every department, literally catered to. It was an increase on the glutinous veneration he'd fed off under Peg—and if, somewhere in his twisted nerves, he resented her extravagant doting—his flatterers, by casting themselves in the same baby-sitting rôle, only awoke his petulance and egotism.

There remained one person, though, who was cautious and non-spellbound—Pat Newman. Various departmental chiefs 'might feel we ought not to pay Sellers less than Hancock, though as I see it,' he counselled, 'Sellers is rather a law unto himself these days...'

◆ ◆ ◆

The mention of Tony Hancock is suggestive—Sellers named him as 'my favourite comedian' in 1960—for he and Sellers had a great deal in common,* starting with both of their sets of parents being in the part-time entertainment business.

---

* John Mortimer, author of the celebrated *Rumpole* stories, has said that 'The two saddest men I ever met were Peter Sellers and Tony Hancock, and I give daily thanks to God, or destiny, that I never took up life as a comic.' Instead, he became a barrister and QC.

They'd worked together in the RAF Gang Shows (Hancock helped Sellers with the wardrobe) and they'd appeared together in *Orders are Orders* and *The Wrong Box*— Sellers' delivery of the line 'In the old days the sick and the groggy would come to me from miles around' made Hancock helpless with laughter.

Hancock had done his stint at the Windmill and had been auditioned for the BBC (as Anthony Hancock, the Confidential Comic) by Dennis Main Wilson. When Sellers was on 'Ray's A Laugh', Hancock was on 'Educating Archie'; and 'Hancock's Half Hour' was as popular as 'The Goon Show'. Radio proved that they were comic actors, not stand up comedians. The two men had a fondness for fancy cars and place names that evoked old actors (Bovey Tracey, Throwley Forstall); they feared the prospect of long theatrical runs and were superstitious about the colour green; and, not the least of it, they had a sort of beguiling, canny helplessness which could be switched on and off depending on whether there were pretty demoiselles present. Above all, they were neurotics, and Hancock killed himself in 1968, an alcoholic wreck, while Sellers spent most of his final decade out on the arctic edge of paranoid schizophrenia. (Milligan said to me: 'Hancock kept looking for something to do when he thought his star was waning; like Peter, he got rid of people systematically. They both destroyed themselves over and over.')

What interests me here is that, as with Sellers, Hancock the man overlapped in complex ways with the version of himself he played on the screen. Hancock's depressive, hectoring persona shares much with Sellers' gloomy fantasising. Both actors made being personally lost, bewildered, and unhappy into a comic style. But where Hancock, consciously and ruthlessly, wanted to close the gap between acting and reality, Sellers, by contrast, had a horror of his individual hollowness, as he deemed it, being exposed.

Hancock's moroseness was the very content of his humour—a humour based on the boredom and exasperation of a man who hated being ordinary. Sellers' characters are in hyper-manic flight from the mundane. His people tend to be surreal, whereas Hancock was simply Hancock, sighing, shrugging his flabby shoulders, 'the bullying loser, the little big man, the idiot dupe inside all of us,' said Bill Kerr, who'd met Hancock originally, in Sellers' and Milligan's company, at Grafton's. Hancock's was a comedy of disillusion. At the end of his 'Half Hour', his schemes always end in ruin and the hero's come-uppance. Sellers, on the other hand (no matter how anxiety-prone he may have been in private), convinces us that his characters have exotic centres, weird dreams, which nobody will assail.

Sellers' characters have a well-defined sense of the ridiculous—and I'd go so far as to say that Hancock's success lay in his TV self having absolutely no sense of humour to speak of. He blusters too much. His is the rage of the thwarted artist, and this was the very plot, incidentally, of Hancock's two main films, *The Punch and Judy Man* and *The Rebel*. And, if Hancock's characters yearn to be outlaws and outsiders, Sellers' cling to that little bit in their natures which makes them different already—it's to do with their self-confidence, the willingness to be laughed at, of the music hall turn. If Hancock had played Sam the busker in *The Optimists of Nine Elms*, for example, he'd have been an object of ridicule. That would have been the point of the story: Hancock, silly old sod, dressing up and making a fool of himself for throw money... He'd have been belittled. Sellers' Sam has tremendous intractability. When he's bedecked with flags and a variety of hats, he's a wizard in the West End streets. He's Merlin.

Sellers' most Hancock-like performance was as Harry, in *The Ladykillers*, the tubby Teddy Boy,* yearning for money. He is farcically undone, as Hancock would have been, had he found himself in Professor Marcus' gang. It's Sellers' only rôle, too, where he used his plumpness as part of the rôle. Elsewhere, being fat was not why he was funny. With Hancock, however, his puddingy features—bulging eyes, sagging jowls, thick hooter, and clownish eyebrows, a face over-scaled and mouldering—did all the work. (A slim, cute Hancock is inconceivable.)

The 'biggest battle I ever won,' Hancock said, 'was to do comedy in close-up.' But what made him a star on the box denied him popularity in the movies, just as the moodiness and ennui which was comic in his work was tragic when it seeped into his private life. (One of the last things he said, before returning to his flat in Sydney, Australia, was 'What's ahead of me, but work, work, work?') He was therefore made for TV in a way Sellers, infinitely more varied as a performer, was not.

♦♦♦

Sellers, if he wished it, could be as invisible as the razor's edge (he could be Godot); and though the BBC wanted him to play a more manifest Beckett character, it was Hancock who, stripping himself of supporting cast and writers who wrote too many gags, wanted to achieve a purity of plotlessness and inaction, which he found in death, or in a wet Sunday afternoon alone in a bedsitter.

Sellers, who originally wanted to play James Bond in *Casino Royale* as a slack-faced, slouching sloth, as 'somebody like Tony Hancock, but of course Fleming would never let anybody do it,' admired his fellow actor at least enough to want to try and use his original scribes, Ray Galton and Alan Simpson, for his own ends.† 'We formed a company called Associated London Scripts,' Simpson told me. 'Spike Milligan, Eric Sykes, Ray Galton, and myself. Sellers was going to come in originally, but his financial adviser said Peter would only come in if we all contributed the same amount of money, whereas we'd planned to work on a ten-percentage basis and take our chance. No, said the financial adviser, that means Peter will be parting with more actual money than anybody else because he's already making more... Ray and I knew Peter well in the early days, when we had this agency with offices in Kensington High Street. Around about 1955, Peter came into the office and announced "I need £400 or I'll be thrown out of my flat." He was married to Anne, had children, and hadn't paid the rent. Ray, Spike, Eric, and I, we all gave him £100 in cash. Off he went. Spike said, "You won't see that again—he'll spend it." Three weeks later, Peter Sellers comes into the office again

---

* Teddy Boy: For fifties youth affecting vaguely Edwardian style of dress–square cut blue velveteen frock coats and bootlace neckties, for example. One of Tony Hancock's abysmal impersonations was of Johnny Ray, thus attired.

† They wrote the screenplay for *Wrong Arm of the Law*.

in a new suit, with £400 which he dealt out note by note, like playing cards. He'd just got the job in *The Ladykillers*, was flush, and came to pay us out. The point of the story is that there was once a Peter Sellers who was broke, before he became a star in America.'

But he was always running down his exchequer. 'He did worry about money,' Milligan explained. 'He'd put the names of his creditors in a hat—if they gave him trouble, he'd tell them their name wouldn't even go in the hat. He was for ever writing letters stalling banks. His credit went on and on and on. He never owned any of those cars; he didn't own a car for over ten years—all "on approval" or HP [on installment]...'

Sarah Sellers concurs that 'he never curbed his spending. Birthdays or Christmas presents—it depended on how he felt. He'd either bother about you or he wouldn't. He never really went through a rough patch. He might have stopped buying boats for a while, but...'

♦ ♦ ♦

Sellers, who couldn't settle on a television vehicle—Johnny Speight invented Alf Garnett* for him, but he turned it down—and who believed they'd never pay him enough money in any event, grew to hate the medium. He went on variety shows and was paraded as a freak. People were always expecting him to be different, and he was plagued by his apparent plurality—in this was meant to be his excitement. He didn't like it that viewers didn't have to make the effort to go out and see him—TV stars were part of a traffic that included news bulletins, documentaries, weather reports, ads (the 'Freds' were full of spoof commercials)—and his reaction to the undiscriminating blitz was characteristic. He staged a tantrum during a live broadcast.

The programme was called *The April 8th Show* and went out a week earlier, on All Fool's Day (a fact nobody seemed to notice). Sellers had planned to give an impersonation of Harold Macmillan, and he was standing outside a set of 10 Downing Street, in readiness to be accurately pompous and insufferable. He was suddenly told, whilst on the air, that some high-up in the Corporation objected to the Prime Minister's being mocked. Sellers therefore marched up to the camera and, as the credits started to roll, angrily tore up the paper spool which had all the names of cast and crew carefully printed on it and began to create:

> Lies, I tell you, all lies, cheap, lousy, lies. They didn't tell you he was in the show did they—it's all Tom Sloan's fault I tell you—him and his lousy liniment. He's the cause of it—he's another foreigner—going to Ronnie Waldman's party tonight— they are all at it, him, Pat Hillyard, all of them—and him, he's in it. You didn't know about him. They are all gone. They are mad this lot.

It remains to this day the nearest thing to a nervous breakdown anybody has had on air. (It is reminiscent of Peter Finch going bonkers in *Network*.) What can

---

* Alf Garnett was the central character in a long-running series called 'Til Death Us Do Part.' This formed the foundation for the hit American sit-com 'All in the Family,' where Alf became Archie Bunker.

be made out of his rant? Sellers clearly felt there was a conspiracy going on, a se-cret sect of heads of department and producers, who were thwarting his ministe-rial mimicry. But as to the specific identity (which keeps switching?) of each and every 'he' and 'him' in his speech, it is the incoherence of paranoia. It was Tom Sloan, however, the Acting Head of Light Entertainment, on BBC Television, who dealt with the matter—and his gravity quite quickly turned the affair into farce, which it was teetering on the edge of anyway, 'Sloan's Liniment' being a popular embrocation for sprains, groin injuries, etc.

The first thing Sloan did was to send absolutely everybody he could think of a blistering memo followed by a severe letter of admonishment to the Grades, Sellers' agents. Sellers, on receipt of the reprimand, pulled his usual stunt, turn-ing himself into a yowling infant, wrongfully accused. He blabbed his case to as many newspaper columnists as would listen. 'I will never appear on BBC televi-sion again,' he said, 'I can only work where I am happy. I cannot work where there is such a childish outlook.' To Sloan himself he addressed a rambling, almost in-coherent missive to which Sloan replied at length and immediately, concluding, no doubt, that he was dealing with either a liar or a lunatic—and that therefore, of course, truth, reason, and remorse were not likely to be forthcoming. His only course of action was to give up, concede defeat, as is acknowledged in the weary tone of his letter to Bill Wills (Sellers' 'financial adviser' in Galton and Simpson's account) of April 14:

> I do not think that there is anything I can usefully add at this stage. Our attitude is that the subject is closed as far as the Press is concerned, and I do not see how any further statements could serve any useful purpose.

Sellers even outmanoeuvred poor old Sloan when an 'impartial enquiry' (which he'd said bluffingly that he wanted) was set up—he simply absented him-self and hid out of town, whence he spoke to the press:

> Mr Sloan has now written to say he understands I wasn't given permission to ad-lib. This is nonsense. They don't know what the word means. The BBC said my behaviour was unforgivable and inexcusable. So is theirs. I'm getting half a dozen witnesses to sign a testimony saying I was asked to fill in at the end of the show. There's Graham Stark, Patricia Hayes, Mario Fabrizi…I did think of taking legal action—my lawyer friends say I've got a good case…

Stark, in his risibility-tickling memoir, *Remembering Peter Sellers*, mentions the episode (with approval) as an example of the star's anti-authority stance. 'To use a lovely English phrase, he never gave a bugger.' But Stark does not try to give the impression that he was there at the time of the outburst; as he tells the story, Sellers' battle with Sloan was something he'd overheard a producer outlining ('with malicious relish') sometime later, during rehearsals of a play he was doing with Warren Mitchell. If Stark had been an actual witness (as Sellers says), then surely, in his very own book, he'd have testified first-hand, and at more length, about *The April 8th Show*, and would not have distanced himself with hearsay? Secondly, if he'd have been there, he'd have known the ugliness of the scene, and that it involved more than Sellers' 'not caring for power and social position' (i.e. other people's). So why did Sellers fabricate?

What the episode actually demonstrates is not a folkloristic Sellers—Sellers the champion of ordinary actors against the moguls, Sellers making a stand against the grim-visaged BBC generalissimos, etc.—but Sellers the inheritor of Dan Mendoza's skill and savagery; a Sellers quite capable of converting fantasy into the only reality he'll abide by. Warren Mitchell said ironically to Stark that all those brainstorms 'did Peter's career a lot of harm!' And yet they *did*. If Mitchell (who made Alf Garnett his own after Sellers declined the part) had thought about it, his words needed no exclamation mark—Sellers' behaviour, especially during the aftermath, when he became so certain of his version of the matter, ought to have been a worrying sign. It was a prophecy of his treatment of Peter Medak or Blake Edwards, or ultimately of just about everybody, when, overtaken by his genius as an actor, he started to dupe even himself. He'd dream something, and it was so. In this manner he became unanswerable. 'Everyone, who has had the misfortune to talk with people in the heart or on the edge of mental disorder,' wrote G. K. Chesterton, 'knows that... He is more logical for losing certain sane affections. Indeed... the madman is not the man who has lost his reason. The madman is the man who has lost everything except his reason.'

Part Three

♦♦♦

Hope and Glory

Was what attracted him the nature of the job itself, the idea of having a secret self, inaccessible even to his friends, his wives and their former husbands and, as the agent of one intelligence agency inside another, a doubly secret self?

Was it not so much the cause, the vision of a twenty-one-year-old, never re-examined during a busy spy's life, but the love of deceit and by extension, of spying itself that kept him at his dead-letter drops and secret inks all those lonely years?

Murray Sayle, quoted in *Philby: The Life and Views of the KGB Masterspy*, by Phillip Knightley

Chapter Seven

♦♦♦

First Photoplays

'I'm very happy away from BBC TV,' he said, and I think it is true to say that, apart from the odd chat show or variety spot, Sellers never did work on the box again. Perhaps we need to remember what a cumbersome medium it was in those days—the heavy valve-driven, out-of-focus cameras which couldn't pan or dolly; the sets constructed from cardboard and string (as if by Bluebottle); the uneditable magnetic strip or piano rolls (or whatever it was they used). Television's monochrome smudge was no place for actors, though it was an ideal home for a new strain of would-be actor: the anchor-man, the game show host, the TV personality. Sellers was in first with a portrait of the type—Wee Sonny MacGregor, in *The Naked Truth*. Sonny is repulsive, insincere, and slightly menacing. Sonny doesn't care that he's not quite human. Sellers, by demonstrating how TV presenters exaggerate their good cheer and rehearse their spontaneity, reveals that the likes of Sonny are really cold-hearted bullies, feeding off the adulation and power. TV, like nothing else, satisfies their need for victims—and an extreme example of *that* type is Chance, in *Being There*, the moron whose very existence has gone by like a self-erasing video tape.

It is a paradox that Sellers, who didn't much respect television, should not only make one of his best rôles a TV addict, but that he should also decide to personally identify with the character. 'I *knew* Chauncey Gardiner,' he said. Perhaps he meant that he could transform himself and that he had a tendency to copy things he saw and heard. He, like Chance, was malleable. But where Chance simply mimics handshakes and gestures, Sellers' impersonations, of course, could be comprehensive. (Chance is a doped Sellers.) What they actually had in common was a blankness, the emptiness inside. 'I'd often thought of him over the years,' said Sellers, 'but when I had to play Chance, I realised I didn't know what he looked like, or how he spoke', because what had absorbed him up until then was the more instinctive reaction of knowing how the character felt:

> One thing had escaped me. The computer had said Chance had no identifiable accent or dialect [when a thorough check is ordered on his background by the President of the United States]. So I messed around for a long time ... until I found the one I was happy with—very clear enunciation, slightly American, with perhaps a little Stan Laurel mixed in. There's an almost total absence of colour—of inflection or emotion—in the voice. That was the most difficult part to play.'

The concept of Chance as the idealised man-baby, ignorant of the ways of the world, is what Sellers found appealing. He has no past, therefore no responsibilities. All he needs is food and shelter. Sellers 'had to create a Chance that would be believable to the intelligentsia, and acceptable to the audience.' Is that how he came up with a benign version of Andy Warhol, who also threw people away like so many empty soup cans?

♦ ♦ ♦

Television is disposable: 'Television didn't really exist then. Radio I'd had enough of. Vaudeville I just hated because I died everywhere I went.' So it had to be films. But films were 'a sort of closed shop. I never really wanted to do much in the theatre, legit. theatre as it's known among some circles. You see, I'd been a great film fan all my life...And I wanted to be a movie actor, mainly because I knew that in the future I couldn't survive very well on repetition. Because if you're lucky, you get into a long run on stage and then you're dead. At least I would be...'

Sellers had an idea of the theatre as a treadmill, or as the equivalent of a loop of film in which he'd be trapped, constrained forever to repeat his actions and words. Cinema suited his quick temper. Scenes could be broken down into shots, which he'd do once or twice and then forget about. (He could subdivide his work into sketches.) It would be for others to edit, splice, weld, and wrench a coherent story out of his fragments. One of the reasons he fell out with Billy Wilder on the set of *Kiss Me Stupid* was that the director liked a lot of takes; Sellers felt that this drained his performance of its natural rhythms, or its inspiration. In a strange sort of way, he was not enough of an actor to keep reduplicating a performance, because there was no technique or method. He simply had to become the people he played, and to accomplish this he needed to be emotionally and physically fluid; unhinged, you might say; mad. (The very plausibility of his performances ought to give us pause.) He never troubled to acquire the pro's knack of disguising his boredom. If you asked him to do a scene again, he'd throw a tantrum and push off home. Perhaps he was afraid that, through repetition, he'd collapse and deteriorate like a crumbling, melting sci-fi-monster—he'd lose the trick of it.

'George C. Scott,' said Kubrick, 'could do his scenes equally well take after take, whereas Peter Sellers was always incredibly good on one take, which was never equalled.' That's why, in *Doctor Strangelove*, if you look beyond and behind Sellers, the Russian ambassador or one of the war room throng are often smirking inappropriately, ruining the take in fact, but because Sellers himself was so good, it had to be printed. (Peter Bull is quite a culprit—if he's in a shot but not speaking, he's often out of character.)

It was the same in the endless Pink Panther series. One of the reasons that the films have all the polish of home movies is that when Clouseau is being sombre, the rest of the cast are often on the edge of corpsing. Not infrequently, the editor has to cut away too soon, to save us the sight of one of Sellers' chums getting the giggles. At other times, we have reverse shots by stand-ins and sequences by stunt men, from when Sellers was absent altogether and Blake Edwards had to go about the day's shoot as best he could. If he was applauded afterwards for the hilarity of scenes in which he himself did not personally appear (e.g. the Kung Fu fights with

Cato), Sellers was again like Warhol, being paid for pictures ingeniously manufactured by doubles.

♦ ♦ ♦

Perhaps if live television, which consumes itself as it goes along, had been more technologically sophisticated and less lame-brained, Sellers would have given himself up to it—but then films meant glamour and lush romance, and Sellers wanted to mix his blood with its ghosts. 'I once got a fan letter supposedly from Jeanette McDonald, who as you know is now dead,' he said, looking back in 1967, 'and she asked for some photographs—giving as her address the name of MGM Studios, Culver City, and the number of her dressing room ... I looked up, in an early *Picturegoer* annual, a photograph of Jeanette McDonald—and this fan letter had the identical signature.

'... I always had a big crush on Myrna Loy, especially in *The Thin Man* series. This friend of mine, a public relations man, said he knew her and that she was a fan of mine. I thought, how marvellous, I'll take her out to dinner—which I did. But I was ... tongue-tied, looking at her—she was much older, but still a very beautiful woman ... All I was able to trot out was this, I said: "I hope you don't mind my asking, but did you use the same dog in every film ... Asta I think he was called?"'

And before Myrna could take another spoonful of scallops, Sellers had launched himself into an impersonation of Nick and Nora Charles, bantering on the Twentieth Century, after which to-do, the actress informed him: 'No, we used a different dog in almost every film. They'd get trodden on, you know.'

Sellers found America itself awash with celebrity, and he was unable, or unwilling, to discriminate between the rôles people had played and the actors as real people in their own right. When he met a star, he expected to be treated to a continuation of their performances. Sometimes the heat was indeed still being given off. 'I remember talking to Gary Cooper about his Deusenberg [motor car]. I met him once. We were doing some rough [bird] shooting out in the country. He'd been a fantastic idol for me, ever since I saw him in *The Plainsman* ... the fact that he was as good with a gun as he was on the screen meant an awful lot ... Effortlessly marvellous man. I really did imagine he was doing it with six-shooters at the time ...'

At the other extreme, Sellers was crestfallen to find Stan Laurel living modestly in a little flat in a modest L.A. suburb; he was so unregarded, the address (849 Ocean Avenue, Santa Monica) and telephone number were still listed in the city directory. Sellers didn't want to know him after that. (Did he expect to be asked to help lug a piano across an Alpine ravine, or what?) He needed stars to retain their auras. When Jacques Tati wrote to him after an encounter ('I was ready to lie down and die for Tati! But when I met Tati! I've never been so disappointed. He's not at all like Hulot'), he didn't even have the common courtesy to reply. Stars, after all, are heavenly bodies, and Sellers wished to zoom to such a supernatural height—to become a darling of the Gods, an *enfant du paradis*, in Marcel Carné and Jacques Prevert's phrase, his life encompassed by harlequinades, the acting and miracles never stopping.

But knocking on Laurel's door in Hollywood ('Laurel and Hardy—my two great favourites—very under-rated—the two funniest men who ever lived, probably'), or escorting Myrna Loy to Peter Duchin's opening at the Maisonette ('where he was rather shy and as full of wonder about my career as any fan. He even asked for an autographed photograph,' Miss Loy confirms), or scouting across the underbrush with Gary Cooper, pointing Purdeys at partridges at high noon—all that was a few years hence. For now he was in a makeshift studio, situated somewhere in the Maida Vale/Marylebone region of London, making his very first photoplay, a short called *Let's Go Crazy*.

♦ ♦ ♦

If the documentary style of *London Entertains* made it look like bootleg film smuggled out of a secret meeting, the atrocious quality of *Let's Go Crazy*, also shot and given extreme unction in 1951, makes it reminiscent of a lost German Expressionist classic. The nitrate stock bubbles and burns as you watch. The photography is not simply blurred, it is fogged. You expect the grandsires of Dr Strangelove, Dr Caligari, and Rotwang, the mad scientist in *Metropolis*, to materialise out of the smoke. The soundtrack music is atonal, and when we get a glimpse of the orchestra, we notice that somebody is cooking over a campfire stove.

Is the nightclub set purposely stylised, with its eerie lighting effects and the jutting, cut-off angles, or simply ineptly painted? For we are to be treated to a sort of abstract cabaret, with some of the performers and most of the guests being played by Sellers and Milligan.

Let's Go Crazy is so amateurishly done—it lasts thirty-two minutes and proba-

First Photoplay: 'Blimey, potato-worshipper 'ere!' Sellers and Milligan in *Let's Go Crazy* (1950)

George Brown Collection (Adelphi Films Ltd.)

Penny Points to Paradise: Sellers and Alfred Marks (1951)

bly took less time than that to create—that Sellers clean forgot about its existence. But as an experiment in visual and verbal non-sequiturs it is something of a curious success, and you have to squint very hard to tell it is Sellers behind the various disguises, he is so deliberative. (Sometimes he is in the orchestra, at other moments he's in a false nose and moustache as the maître d'.) It is close in spirit to the well-known *Running, Jumping and Standing Still Film*—i.e., an attempt to put on celluloid what they'd enjoyed doing in radio. The director, Alan Cullimore, went on to produce, later the same year, the film which Sellers considered his debut, his 'very first appearance in front of a camera, if you like to call it an appearance, [*Penny Points to Paradise*] ... Harry, Spike, and I were billed for it as the White Faced Coons—the word Goons hadn't registered yet: "Chocolate Coons or White Coons: Peter Sellers acts, Harry Secombe sings, and Spike Milligan plays the fool in *Penny Points to Paradise*." It was a pretty shocking movie and yet we thought—Hollywood here we come! We thought that, but we didn't come—neither did the film ...'

There's simply too much plot, and Sellers said of the retired military con-man he played, Major Arnold P. Fringe, 'it was a sort of character part—running around saying "Ah, there you are, Harry m'boy!"; I didn't know what to do with my hands. If you see the film, you'll find me waving and pointing. "Ah, there you are, Harry m'boy!" Every time he came in the room, whenever anything was happening—"Ah, there you are, Harry m'boy!"'

Bloodnok, of course, but also the nutty nostalgia of General Fitzjohn, in

Waltz of the Toreadors, whose persona is here and intact. 'I'm always playing old Colonels, actually,' Sellers commented, and he's at it again in *Down Among the Z Men*, made, as were all these little shorts and featurettes, for an impresario called E.J. Fancey. Sellers had scant respect for the minor mogul: '[W]e were working with crap. We thought, it didn't matter what you did, it's Hollywood! This is it! But this film fellow said, "They don't understand that Goon stuff... You've got to give it to them on the nail. And don't do none of them funny voices, because they don't understand 'em, either..."'

Hence, after the glancing Dada of *Let's Go Crazy*, the obviousness of the sequels. Perhaps the biggest surprise of *Down Among the Z Men* is the straight heroic rôle assigned to Harry Secombe, here portraying a grocer's assistant called Harry Jones. The point about the character 'Seagoon' is that he was a screechy take-off of the romantic lead. Here, however, his rôle suggests that within the roly-poly singer and good sport of 'The Goon Show' somebody very earnest and sympathetic is behind the imbecile's mask. We feel for him when he's ordered to 'get back behind the cheese where you belong,' because we've heard of Jones' private detective agency sideline, and it's amidst stirring adventures in that area where he wants to be at home. (It is as if Bluebottle's aspirations have been added to Seagoon's—and to Sellers' of the 'Selsman' Ilfracombe days.)

The early scenes, with Jones being fleeced of his savings by B-movie villains (one of whom is played by Andrew Timothy), and with Bentine's Osric Pureheart getting his grocery list mistaken for a secret formula, were shot on location in what might have been Britten's Aldeburgh. The streets are leafy and dappled, there is little motor traffic, and the shop fronts are quaint and Edwardian. Everybody does their utmost to be clottish, but Sellers' old colonel is on parade with remarkably little fuss. 'Sugar, daddy?' his orchidaceous step-daughter asks. 'By Jove, yes,' he says, by no means over-doing the double-entendre.

Sellers, as he would in his mainstream films, keeps still and leaves being frantic to the others. (He sits down for his scenes and, on the one occasion when he stands, gets a laugh for his extraordinary jodhpurs.) Bentine is wretched; Milligan is already reliving the war. But it is only Sellers, as the military head of Warwell Atomic Research Station ('Fearfully Secret. Spies Please Knock'), who is truly interested in giving a performance. He is suddenly acting properly. Reserved, slowly examining his food, or just posing at his desk, clutching at his heart in surprise, there are no eye-catching mannerisms—but it is exactly his large, sad eyes which we are forced to meet. Then, suddenly, we are yanked back into the nonsense about espionage and undercover weapons, which soon goes to pieces, and the remainder of the spool is given up to Bentine's chair-back routine, which I'll not mind never seeing again; and Sellers, casting off his old Col., does a routine about American soldiers discussing a plan to escape a Panzer division. Decades drop off him as, switching helmets, he impersonates a lieutenant and a private. He alters instantly—the uninterrupted mid close-up shot allows us to marvel at and grasp the detail and economy of his changes of expression. It is as fascinating as those stop-motion sequences in old horror movies, when Lon Chaney Jr. gets transformed into the wolfman, except that here there are no special effects, as such. It is possible to see just how Sellers could have accomplished his war-time officer duplicities.

♦ ♦ ♦

Sellers was morose. 'The essence of Goonery must be captured,' he argued, 'or we're liable to lose a lot of adherents. Which is just why the two attempts to date to make Goon films have, in the long run, done us a disservice, although they made a large amount of money. *Penny Points to Paradise*, which cost £9,000, has made, up to the present time [1955], £75,000. *Down Among the Z Men* has also amassed profits running into thousands. In neither film was the story ours, nor had we any say in the direction. Until a brilliant director with an acute sense of contemporary humour, who would be prepared to let us co-direct, comes along, 'The Goon Show' must remain purely radio entertainment; by allowing ourselves to be presented into unsuitable films, we end by pleasing no one...'

Television, as we know, offered only a limited solution ('Television is a muddle at the moment,' he said. 'It's where one goes to earn a quick pound'), and he had high hopes for their next outing, *The Case of the Mukkinese Battle Horn*, a twenty-nine minute hors d'oeuvre, made in November 1955. It was the better for not dragging its material out beyond the length of an episode of 'The Goon Show'—and also, it must be said, for the lack of Secombe and Bentine and their one-note performances. (Secombe was busy on his TV show and was in demand for concerts.) In their stead is Dick Emery, who fits in well with the absurdist style. Indeed, unlike Secombe and Bentine, he seems to know that *not* being too flamboyant is the key to comedy. He takes a number of rôles—Nodule, a museum curator; Mr Crimp, the janitor; etc.—and his jolly countenance, the obvious pleasure he's taking in dressing up, is, like Secombe's giggle, infectious. We don't mind him.

Emery went on to have a successful TV career. He devised a gallery of popular characters, and yet Sellers was still so much superior to this sort of artiste. Why? Because Emery never went further than caricature. You never needed to believe— it never crosses your mind—that his funny folk had lives and thoughts beyond the sketch in which they appear. Emery's acting had no intense depths. He didn't need to excavate anything except his enjoyment of drag and daffy costumes. His old codger, Lampwick, for example, looked the twin of Sellers' William Mate Cobblers; but where Sellers' infuriating senior citizen had recesses of frayed pride and melancholia, Lampwick was nothing more than an elderly lecher with a filthy cough.

Offstage, as it were, he was rather more like Sellers, at least in his appetites. He married five showgirls and said 'I need a woman who is prepared to put up with my miseries and my worries. I'm a pig to live with, completely selfish. It's been murder sometimes and I've paid in pain and money. I was looking for someone near perfection and I never found her, of course. I was looking for a mother replacement, with a sexual life as well.' Such words could have been taken right out of Sellers' mouth; yet the crucial difference between the two actors is that Sellers' personality and flaws seep into his work, whereas Emery's lies and guilt never did. Sellers' pent-up feelings gave the art of comic acting new dimensions;

Emery acted to get away from the obligations and ramifications of a messy private life. When he grew bored and refused another BBC series, in ridding himself of his characters he was ridding himself of his illusions. He immediately proceeded to drop dead from a heart attack—as Sellers did, when he, too, could no longer fool himself that he was ague-proof.

In 'The Goon Show', Milligan said that the starting point for their humour was 'one man shouting gibberish in the face of authority, and proving by fabricated insanity that nothing could be as mad as what passes for ordinary living.' In *The Case of the Mukkinese Battle Horn*, the target for satire is the police.

Sellers' main character is Detective Superintendent Quilt (Milligan is his assistant constable), who moves purposefully, is heavily moustached and Homberg-hatted, is serious, and is seriously dense. He is a Scotland Yard trial gallop for Inspector Clouseau. 'There's been a robbery,' he is told. 'Really? Anything stolen?' he inquires briskly. Sellers and Milligan were exerting themselves to incorporate accident and irrelevance. The opus was made at Merton Park Studios, and whenever anybody visited the set, John Penington, the producer, would tell them that the actors were 'exhilarating to work with—but terribly trying. They're changing the gags all the time.' Later he and the director, Joe Sterling, put it more succinctly: 'They're mad.'

He was not totally jesting; halfway through the shooting period Milligan had one of his mental breakdowns. Sellers never quite forgave him and lost faith in the film—going on record to call *The Case of the Mukkinese Battle Horn* 'a very unfortunate affair which I would like to explain. This was going to be a short film made ex-

Henry Crun in *The Case of the Mukkinese Battle Horn* (1956)

George Brown Collection

actly as we wanted it. We had a group of filmmakers who were interested in doing this with us; but at the time it went to the floor, my colleague Spike Milligan was taken ill and we were left with an uncompleted script. These people couldn't put off the shooting date as they had already booked the studios, so we had to go ahead and literally write from day to day on the floor, which spoilt it. We had about three ideas in the beginning of the film which were good, but the rest was made up as we went along. This is no way to make a picture...' (But at one time he'd think it was.)

To put the blame on Milligan for what was, on the set, his own frivolity, is another example of his essential need to displace blame. It was Sellers who, if asked a question, would peer through a large magnifying glass and say 'Follow that floor!'; Sellers who caused Pam Thomas, playing an ingénue rôle, to weep because 'Nobody tells you anything. I think that I'm in this scene now—but I don't know'; Sellers who goaded Barbara Cole, the continuity girl, into a shouting match: 'You've changed a line in that scene, haven't you?' she asked, despairing. ('You're privileged they've told you,' a props man said, trying to comfort her when Sellers snarled an acknowledgement.) Milligan, and no wonder, retreated behind his Eccles facade. 'Fine, fine, fine,' was all they could get out of him.

Despite Sellers' complaints, the film isn't a total dud. Sir Jervis Fruit, the Assistant Chief Commissioner, is an amusing portrait of Hercules Grytpype Thynne, from 'The Goon Show'. As he reclines on a chaise longue and speaks to Quilt on a white telephone, he is a send-up of other people's send-ups of homosexuals and Liberace. He rolls his eyes and wears a smoking jacket with braided cuffs. Fruit tells Quilt (Sellers talking to Sellers) to try looking for the battle horn in a pawn shop—an excuse for Sellers to convert himself into Henry Crun. The hunchbacked elder statesman, in tasselled night cap, pince-nez, and Santa Claus wig, creeps about his junk-strewn room (reminiscent of Peg and Bill's flat) and tells Quilt that 'you can't get the wood, you know,' for battle horns.

The ending, a duel using a rapier and a revolver ('Touché,' 'Three-ché'), is as random and frantic as the chase-in-a-wax-museum of *Penny Points* or the laughing-gas-making-everybody-collapse playout of *Z Men*. We are meant to be in Max's Club. Eccles does a Salome dance ('O fairest of the fair, O sublime siren' says Quilt) and, when the fight starts, musketeers and cavaliers come in from nowhere and join the fray, as they do during the pandemonium which concludes *Casino Royale*.

◆ ◆ ◆

We've seen little of what would make Sellers a revelation—his scope; his renewals; his audacity—but in fact there *is* something extra and significant about his appearances in these bits of piffle. Already he is attuned to the audience. This was not lost on a man called John Redway, the casting director at Associated British Pictures, a powerful conglomerate based at Elstree, which was partly owned by Warner Bros. and Pathé. It was he who could perceive, before anybody else, that Sellers was being limited by 'The Goon Show' and its spin-offs, and he suggested the actor for parts in, amongst other projects, two pictures planned by Group Three, a production company set up in 1951, funded by the National Film Finance Corporation (i.e.

government grants) to knock off low budget features stocked with new (i.e. cheap) talent. Sellers didn't need much encouraging to hie himself hither to Beaconsfield Studios. 'As an actor,' he panted, 'I have always wanted to plan a career, distinct from Goonery, in films'—and he made a start in *Orders are Orders*, as a batman (a kind of military gofer), and 'going a little further along the same lines…*John and Julie* provides me with another character part into which I felt I could get my teeth…'

What other performer would have used such tiny rôles as an opportunity to stretch himself? Hancock certainly didn't bother. He's in *Orders are Orders*, fat, slouched, and liverish, as Lieutenant Cartload, the despairing conductor of the military brass band. His scenes are not the least bit funny, though they are designed to be. A little of his round-shouldered grimacing, when the musicians hit sour notes, goes a long way. (Eric Sykes, credited for 'additional dialogue', is on cymbals.) Sellers, however, in a background rôle as Private Goffin, bored to death behind the bar in the officers' mess, is full to bursting with inventiveness and assurance. Hugely bloated, Goffin is not immediately recognisable as Sellers—he has no vanity here. He has a terrible haircut, with various shaven patches, and speaks in a North London whine. When there's nobody special about he is slow and sullen; if an officer appears he jumps to and is ingratiating—his voice, suppressing a giggle, is virtually Bluebottle's.

Sellers is able to convey how Goffin feels when he's abashed. Another actor might have made the batman sly or sneaky; Sellers' Goffin is a mock-innocent. What he enjoys best about the film crew which has invaded the 1st Battalion, the Royal Loyal's barracks, is the chance it offers him to, first, get one over on the likes of Colonel Bellamy—played by Raymond Huntley with his impeccable, customary sneer—and, second, dragooned as an extra, he can dress up, play-act, and have adventures, which is precisely what Goffin is in the army for. Attired as a Martian and toting a cardboard gun, Bluebottle's games are complete.

The idea of a movie mogul muscling in on people's lives, causing maximum disruption, is one Sellers himself would return to in *After the Fox*, when Aldo Vanucci infiltrates an Italian town with his floodlights and cameras. We do not, however, attend much to either the film crew or Col. Bellamy. They are upstaged by Sellers. He does nothing more than float by, bearing a teapot, yet it's only his reactions which give the farce any perspective or depth. That's to say, only Sellers gives an original performance.

Sellers takes over his sections in this film, spreads across them, just as the movie makers insinuate themselves into the army camp. What makes his performance noteworthy is that the liberties he takes, as an actor, perfectly match the calm and quiet insurrections of the character. In this film orders are bound by social class—and the underlying scheme of *Orders are Orders* is everybody in the audience's experience of the war and National Service. What could have been a satire on the imbecilities of obedience, however, is not undertaken. The joke is on the flummery and excess of film-makers, *American* film-makers, no less, and not on the army as an institution.

◆ ◆ ◆

George Brown Collection (Group 3 Ltd.)

Author Collection

(Top) Pte. Goffin in *Orders are Orders* (1954)

(Bottom) Young Scarface: Sellers' makeup
test for *The Ladykillers* (1955)

If *Orders are Orders* relied on everybody's brush with the call-up and being in uniform, *John and Julie*, the other Group Three effort, leans on the recent quasi-mystical ritual of the Coronation. The story, about a young brother and sister running away from home to see Elizabeth II crowned, ought to be (as Constance Cummings says) 'unbearable goo from beginning to end'. Actually, it is a hallucination of the early fifties, and it is full of golden, harvesty colours. Perhaps the film succeeds because it has the inner-strength of a fairy story? The two blonde children (played by Colin Gibson and Lesley Dudley), journeying alone across the English countryside, are resourceful and good, like Hansel and Gretel; they are babes in the wood, drinking from streams and hiding amongst the trees.

Intermixed with the tale is documentary footage of the Queen processing to Westminster Abbey—she is the goddess Gloriana in her coach. We see the yellows and scarlet of the carriages and soldiers, and posters of the Queen, in a buttercup ball gown sparkling with canary jewels, in shop windows. All this creates a landscape that gleams and glows—and Sellers, as the young Dorset bobby on the children's trail, is named P.C. Diamond.

Again, it is a background rôle which he turned into a commentary on the foreground action. Cheerful and chubby, with brown, steamed hair, he ambles so slowly, he might be in a trance. Sellers has Diamond caught up in the film's fairy-story mood; he is bewitched, as the entire sceptre'd isle is on Coronation Day, and as such not once does he voice a fear for the children's safety. Diamond is full to bursting with composure and confidence; he quietly enjoys the adventure. Sellers makes him seem almost blessed. Round and snug, to use a phrase of W. H. Auden's, in the den of himself, he is an early version of the Rev. Smallwood or Chance the gardener: characters with an inner, spiritual radiance, which Sellers could project in his performances, but could never attain in real life.

In *Orders are Orders*, Sellers' grins are ironic; Goffin is pleased to be doing something which will hurl one past the officers. In *John and Julie*, P.C. Diamond grins with happiness and jollity; and where Goffin unobtrusively mocks his masters, Diamond is amused by unfounded fear and concern—he seems to be in a wistful world of his own, listening, perhaps, to Eddie Calvert's trumpet wailing away on the sound track, a waltzy, lyrical theme, which merges into William Walton's uplifting Coronation marches and pomp. (It is the music of the spheres.)

It is an indication of Sellers' achievement that we never think that the policeman is an incompetent. Somehow, Sellers holds the spell together; and there is much about *John and Julie*, especially its tone, which could never be recaptured now and must have been a gamble then. The children are enchanted, and even London, which blazes with ruby reds (buses, hats, lipsticks, flags), is free of danger for them. As they move through the crowds and brawls they pass Marne Maitland, who'll play the crooked Indian Maharajah in *I'm All Right, Jack*, and Katie Johnson, the old woman in *The Ladykillers*, who is gazing with adoration at a statue of Queen Victoria.

◆ ◆ ◆

The dated decency and virtue of *John and Julie* only add to its charms. These days, moreover, child actors don't need to pipe up with such pert, posh voices; Colin Gibson and Lesley Dudley seem to have spent their entire waking lives in elocution lessons. Only Sellers sounds unmannered, and he was anxious to learn how people thought he'd fared. 'It's early yet to assess the reaction to these films,' he wrote in *Picturegoer*, in February 1955, 'but would you let me know how you feel, about this "new" career in films. Will [the public] accept Sellers the "straight" character comedian? ... I hope the verdict will be fair to a funny man.'

Work did not flow in as he'd hoped—and it was during this period, when he was desperate for a film career,* that he fell out with Milligan more often than usual and began misbehaving during radio and television broadcasts. 'Doing "The Goon Show" series,' he explained in March 1960, 'had some drawbacks. As far as filmmaking is concerned and as far as one's part in films as a character is concerned, many filmmakers tend to think of you as a funny-voice man, instead of being a serious actor. Consequently, if anything comes along, unless it is grotesque, they don't offer it to you.'

Sellers' solution to the problem of how to break out from the clamour of radio to the acclaim of films was ingenious—he decided to experiment with some silent movie shorts. If, before, all he'd been was a voice, now he'd try and convey life in all its facets by not saying a word. Back he went to the Marylebone Studios, to make *Dearth [sic] of a Salesman*, *Cold Comfort*, and *Insomnia is Good For You*. The first was directed by Leslie Arliss, who had worked in some capacity on *Orders are Orders*; the others were directed by James Hill, who'd direct Sellers in *The Dock Brief*; and they were written by Lewis Greifer and Maurice Wiltshire, who'd adapt 'The Goon Show' scripts for 'The Telegoons'.

Also dating from this era is a twenty-six minute romp called *The Super Secret Service*, written by Milligan and co-starring Dick Emery and the Ray Ellington Quartet. Sellers was a bowler-hatted City gent involved in (another) secret formula plot. Apparently, the celluloid was junked at some point. Graham Stark recalls seeing shreds and tatters of it being utilised at Pinewood as grist to test Movieola editing machines: 'Made in a basement studio in Dean Street ... it's black and white, with sound, and it's absolutely terrible ... Peter [was] running about the West End, willing to work for fourpence [peanuts] providing it was a film.' So I have not seen it; nor have *Salesman* or *Insomnia* surfaced. But I did discover *Cold Comfort*, and it is both low-grade and brilliant.

Sellers' bowler-hatted City etc., who appears in all the little films, was called Hector Dimwitty; the idea was to parody government information newsreels. The sight gags and nicely timed farce are overlain with a bright-voiced documentary scientist type, who tells us that (for instance) many of us will catch a cold today and fail to go to work—so instead of being spick and span on his commuter train,

---

* Q: Was it obvious to you that you were going to be the one out of that Goon group to really excel?
  A: It was to me, because I was determined to have a film career.

Rolling Stone, April 17, 1980.

with the other Mr Nobodies, Sellers is seen as a dishevelled, heavy wreck in his storm-tossed single bed.

Dimwitty makes his way myopically and wearily to the bathroom to examine his furry tongue and stinging eyes. He is the image of flu-wracked forlornness. He opens the window—his pyjama trousers fall down. He nips out to get the milk—door slams shut behind him. He's locked out and at once it starts to rain. He manages to tip the milk over his head. The simple pratfalls seem to be succeeding because Sellers doesn't race through them; he doesn't let his arms and legs spring everywhere, like many comics do when basically having to mime. He knows, as Ted Ray did on radio, how long to prolong a pause (it's for Dimwitty to have time to ponder)—how to react to absurdity, rather than to think you have to be the cause of it. Sellers has learned that trick of sufferance here, though he cuts Dimwitty's recoil back to the bare essentials, giving weight to the details: Dimwitty's slight, but constant, nervous fumbling with the edge of the bedsheets; or, short sightedness having been established earlier, it is doubly funny when he squints at the label on the nose drops and ends up by squirting a jet clear into his eye.

It is credible comedy. Yes, you feel, it could happen this way, if you were ill. The only off-putting note, oddly enough, is Sellers' urgent narration. 'Any fool can catch a cold,' we are informed, 'but it takes a real expert to hang on to it.' That dud aphorism squats miserably over Dimwitty's going to answer the phone in a draughty hall—and suddenly he has knocked over a vase of flowers and it is dripping on to his bare feet; so he hops onto the prickly stems and scattered blooms, to protect himself from 'a germ-laden floor,' and continues with his (unheard) conversation. Clouseau himself was never more deftly clumsy, nor so nonchalant.

◆ ◆ ◆

Cold Comfort, which in itself is nothing really, happens to encapsulate something of Sellers' genius in a way superior material, or a better quality production, often does not. I mean his ability to slow a film down. He's at it as Dr Pratt in *The Wrong Box*; in the scene where Fred Kite has been abandoned by his family in *I'm All Right, Jack*, and plods in and out of his living room and kitchenette, knocking his fists against his thighs; and in *Lolita*, when Clare Quilty is first introduced to us at the school prom, and he is intent on a hypnotic, lazy, dance routine—a heavy, sluggish sort of salamander's twist. It is the actor's confidence in setting, through the character, his own rhythms, which comes across. Sellers, of course, had been a drummer. The gift of comedy is related to a physical sense of beat, pulse, and measure. What makes such people artists, what empowers the best of them to deliver a gag (vocal or visual) so that it hangs in the air and sets off resonances, is that they involve their nervous systems—their work (in Wordsworth's fine phrase) is felt along the heart, impudently, or emotionally, or with an edge. They whip up a rapport with us and leave us elated. The beauty of Sellers' next rôle, in *The Lady-killers*, is that Harry, the Teddy Boy, seems to be listening to rock n' roll melodies playing inside his head. He moves about Mrs Wilberforce's villa with the lumbering tread of a spiv trying to cut a dash in a dance hall. It adds to the characterisation that Sellers is at least a decade too old for an authentic Ted—yet they do exist, these elderly Elvis fans and the hipsters that time forgot, and Sellers anticipates their creaking, shoulder-wiggling, self-conscious mannerisms.

All the characters in *The Ladykillers* are anachronistic, out of their element, era, or minds. Alec Guinness' Professor Marcus is a German Expressionist comedian; Danny Green's hulking One Round seems off either the pages of Dickens or a thirties boxing picture distributed by Warners; Herbert Lom's Louis twitches and glowers like a Chicago hood in King's Cross; and Cecil Parker's Major Courtenay, in a camel-hair coat and a luxuriant moustache, is the embodiment of every gentleman con-man that ever tried to outwit the taxman or sell properties in the South of France to which he does not hold title. Hiding in the little old lady's house, where the clocks stopped when 'someone came in and said the old Queen had passed away', the gang masquerades as a string quintet and Boccherini's tiddle-iddle-pom-pom-pom minuet underscores the film. The robbery is quite consciously set to music—Prof. Marcus is both enraptured and maddened by the violins on his horn gramophone, and when Sellers' Harry is killed off, the genteel tune modulates for a moment into a burst of the blues. *The Ladykillers* is a comic chamber opera—and as such was adapted by the Czech composer, Ilja Hurnick, in 1967, as a piece called *Dama a Lupici*: 'The Lady and the Robbers'.

◆ ◆ ◆

'The first *real* film I made,' he said, 'was *The Ladykillers*. I can remember all of that very well. I used to watch Alec Guinness, who is an absolute idol of mine, do everything, his rehearsals, his scenes, everything. It was fascinating ... Not that I could hope to be as good as Guinness. But he is my ideal ... and my idol.'

After Milligan, Guinness was indeed Sellers' great life-long inspiration and irritation. He wanted to have a film career like Guinness', and did; he wanted to do the equivalent of *Kind Hearts and Coronets*, and use the technology of cinema to play lots of rôles and encounter himself on screen, and did—in *The Mouse That Roared*; *Doctor Strangelove*; *Soft Beds, Hard Battles*; etc. (Through the agency of special effects the world could see how full of himself he was.) *Kind Hearts and Coronets* amused him, in addition, because one actor reappearing in a variety of minor rôles, which in the cinema won you praise for your panache, had long been a tradition in tatty music hall, circuses, and Rep. When Sellers met Guinness he felt he'd lunched with a demure one-man Rep. Company. 'You cannot believe how quiet this man is. He's shy! He's got a switch inside. He turns it on, and another person pops up!'

Alexander Walker, who is a film reviewer for an evening paper, has said that Sellers, when abroad, would often call him up in the small hours, just as a new film of Sir Alec's was about to open, to ask 'How is Guinness? How is he really?' He was praying for flops. Wolf Mankowitz told me that 'towards Guinness' talent, Sellers was absolutely cravenly attentive and admiring. I remember we went, with our wives, to the first night of Rattigan's *Ross*. Probably the worst performance ever given by Alec Guinness ... an absurd performance—and Sellers was happier than I'd seen him for a long time. This capacity for doing a *Kind Hearts and Coronets*—he was always coming back to that, always jealous of that film. He was never really able to do it because he was such an inventive mimic, and he assumed that that meant he did-n't need scripts—his improvising would always compensate. Well, all that Sellers' in-vention does is destroy the structure. So you either have to be a writer, or get one ...'

Sellers' party-turns were of Sir Alec—the impersonations of the Rev. d'Ascoyne, telling Dennis Price about his West Window; and Prince Feisal, in *Lawrence of Arabia*, coping with a corpsing O'Toole and blowing his lines about the Koran. One of his records contained a parody of a Guinness profile—under the non-disguise of Sir Eric Goodness—'I took it down to the theatre to play it over to Alec. It was while he was in *Ross**... He laughed. Then he said, "The im-personation is very good, but, you know, I don't think the *material* is very funny!" ... Of course the whole idea of the record was that it was an actor giving one of those completely pointless interviews, saying absolutely nothing.'

And, to give one more example of a Sellers/Guinness conjunction, in the re-shoot of *The Fiendish Plot of Dr Fu Manchu*, Sellers' oriental sage, in the new, in-serted scenes, suddenly slaps his thighs eagerly and laughs in Sir Alec's rich, full-throated guffaw. Coming out of the reed-thin Fu's devil doll mouth, like that, it is a spooky, devilish act of ventriloquism.

◆ ◆ ◆

These are all facile Guinness gags; they show Sellers delighting in derision, and do not hint at how he was gripped. When Sellers expressed his envy, what he had in mind were not the classical stage appearances (Hamlet, Lear's Fool, Aguecheek, Richard II), but things like Fagin, Herbert Pocket, Disraeli, the d'Ascoynes (of course), and the heroes in *The Lavender Hill Mob* and *The Man in the White Suit*; Guinness was a star character actor, who found, through the dif-ferent parts he played, a means of using up his anger and energy—converting these qualities, indeed, into vitality and flexibility. The Guinness whose magic op-erated on Sellers was the one whose imagination (like Shakespeare's) could en-compass saints and sinners, the restrained and the grotesque. (Sellers, however, thrilled by the amorality of the artistic impulse, made the mistake of applying it to his private life, and this is what undid him.)

Sellers makes an appearance in the very first paragraph of Sir Alec's autobi-ography, *Blessings in Disguise*, which is clue enough to the shared feelings and ex-perience of the two men. 'Poor, rich, exceptionally brilliant Peter Sellers never seemed to get himself sorted out in spite of the fact that, apart from upset mar-riages, there didn't appear to be much confusion in his life,' whereas Guinness was born out of wedlock and hidden in creepy hotels on the Cromwell Road, had a vi-olent step-father, and a mother who took his few possessions to the pawn shop and left him a legacy of unredeemed tickets and unpaid bills. Indeed, Sellers' fre-quent bleating about his identity crisis ('As far as I'm aware,' he told *The New York Times Magazine* in 1960, 'I have no personality of my own whatsoever') comes to seem a bit pathetic when compared against the hard facts of Guinness' bastardy. Never certain who his father was, no wonder he is drawn to Dickens. Over the

---

* 1960, at the Haymarket Theatre, London.

years, he has been approached by weird women who claim to be his half-sisters, or by other spectral types who say they have news of his origins, and 'I began to feel I was playing some minor character part in *Bleak House* or *Dombey and Son*.' His mother refused to enlighten him. His domestic upbringing was the opposite of Sellers'—Sellers, who was loved not wisely *and* too well.

All the frenzy and disorder that spilled out of Sellers, Guinness keeps inside. It is what can break loose in the Ealing classics, for example, when his bank clerks or scientists, forced by circumstances to be humdrum, suddenly rebel and give in to the irrational. No matter how outwardly docile his characters, you sense great impatience and temper lurking beneath, which are being actively controlled. (As a child he directed his hurt and frustrations into crayon drawings of exploding battleships and war scenes.) Smiley, for example, the spy catcher, exemplifies this. That's as minimalist an outing as Sellers' Chance. Smiley's brain, behind that dusty face and those polished spectacles, flickers and fizzes, solving puzzles, making links, trusting nobody. Chance has no brain to speak of. He has the attention span of a bird. Both parts needed geniuses to play them, to lift Smiley clear of being a boring, over-shrewd civil servant and to stop Chance from being embarrassingly mentally handicapped.

◆ ◆ ◆

Unlike Guiness, whose eventual conversion to Catholicism has protected him from chaos, Sellers, from his days at St Aloysius', never had the patience to adhere to a single religion; he wanted miracles to take place here and now and prayers to be answered instantly—if not, well then, God? Ha! Ha! During the speeded-up sword fight on the pirate ship in *Ghost in the Noonday Sun*, Dick Scratch withdraws to his cabin to pray for divine assistance. This is what it says in the battle-scarred copy of the script which Peter Medak gave me:

SCRATCH is kneeling before a crucifix. For a moment we think he is a reformed man. In the various corners of the room we see the God of four different religions—a Hindu god with many arms—a Buddha with incense burning around it—a prayer mat with symbols of the Koran. As he turns from one God to the other he is seen in the appropriate costume of the priest of each religion.

Because of the fast-motion which prevails in the finished film the scene makes no sense. In any case, the cabin set was far too cluttered for us to make out the various altars; and Sellers, doing his best to be awkward, refused to don the different clerical vestments. So it goes for nothing; and Sellers, too lazy to bother with the holy quick-changes, threw away a little homage to *Duck Soup*, where Groucho keeps appearing in different military uniforms (including that of a Roman Centurion and a Confederate General) from shot to shot.

The scene, as glued in the script, was typed on tissue paper and dated November 3, 1973. It is thus one of Milligan's contributions, Milligan having been brought into the production well after shooting had commenced on Cyprus, his mission being to inject some Goonishness that would entice Sellers out of his depressions. He clearly wrote in for Scratch one of Sellers' traits—the tendency to worship all manner of strange gods. Did Sellers pick up on the personal allusion, resent it, and was this behind his non-cooperation?

'I've no idea which emotional compass point he was on in his life,' Spike said to me. 'No idea. He went sideways. I once bought him a menorah as a Christmas present. You know, one of those seven-branched candelabra things used in Jewish worship. When he opened it he burst into tears. He was haunted by yesterday, yesteryear. Always telling Anne he wanted to come back to her; or that he wanted to see his mother again—all that lark.'

If Sellers lacked the discipline to think through individual religions, preferring instead to borrow the colourful highlights of several and inaugurate his own sentimental cults, he was at least aware of his divine urgings. 'Yes, I was religious,' he said. 'What I have to do is find my own way to pray to the God I believe in. I was very much interested at Haifa in the Bahia sect...I should say there's a strain of Buddhism in their beliefs...Jesus said, didn't He: Pray behind your doors. I feel one shouldn't make a public show of praying, of being religious...But...One ought to want to do something *for God*.

'I don't really believe in organised religion. If you fast for a day, that may be good for self-discipline, but...I can't believe God takes much notice. It's the same with confession. A man goes and confesses: I've done this and that, I'm sorry...All right, I absolve you...I can't see how anybody has the right to say that. It simply means that the man feels he can go out and do it again.' Sellers himself, under such circumstances, would no doubt have felt that he personally was free to sin and be shitty as soon as he was out through the door. This is the instant forgiveness Sellers wanted; it was a celestial version of his mother's letting him get away with murder.

The first perilous divulgence of his madness came during the period of *The Millionairess*. 'I remember once after the film had come out an Indian came up to me in the street and said quite seriously that I was the new Messiah, that I should lead India into new paths.' Instead of shaking off the fellow as a crank, Sellers was receptive to the message. (Sellers was the crankier.) 'Oh, I suppose it's quite common for an actor to identify himself with the part he's playing. But I really do find myself living the parts I act.' Ergo, he quite likely was the Second Coming. It meant a lot to him, Chance's walking on water at the end of *Being There*. 'People are always saying,' he said, '"what is this guy all about, anyway?" Why don't they leave you alone and just accept what you do? That's one of the things I like about Chance. Who the hell is he? Is he God? Is he sent by God? Is he a moron, or what?' Sellers' final rôle, Fu Manchu, was played as a living God; the plot, if you can bear to sit still and wait for it to emerge from the shellac, concerns the search for an elixir of everlasting life.

◆ ◆ ◆

Guinness doesn't mock or reproach. Guinness is as arrested by weaknesses and foibles as he is by the exotic; he is curious about people's psychological side-alleys and self-importance—in the follies that make them unique and of interest. The detached and humble attitude he personally takes—or which comes across in the theologically entitled *Blessing in Disguise*—is that of a parish priest. An actor, he actually says, is 'a kind of unfrocked priest,' who celebrates mysteries, concocts rituals, and convinces audiences that they can see things which aren't there.

It must be said that this kind of stuff can make for coyness and the solemnity-cum-spirituality in Guinness' performances can be tiresome, rather like the metaphysical passages in Iris Murdoch's novels which we all skip past when they start shimmering in. Guinness has made recordings of T. S. Eliot's poetry and such are his canonical tones, the maundering banalities ('All shall be well and all manner of things shall be well'—plagiarised from Julian of Norwich) are uplifted and virtually make sense. Guinness brings a gravity and decorum to his work, and this can take over. Back in the days of *Kind Hearts and Coronets*, the weightiness could be used for fun. The surviving d'Ascoynes, in church for the funerals, already strike marble attitudes in their pew—they don't flinch and so merge with the figures on the ancestral tombs. But Guinness' Charles I, in the otherwise clunky *Cromwell*, is so much the image of a royal portrait, the actor seems to be posing for Van Dyck.

Guinness' saintly stillness, which in *Little Dorrit* was used to suggest William Dorrit's bloated idleness, already seemed to be parodying itself by *Tinker, Tailor, Soldier, Spy*. When George Smiley was held in all those close-ups, we had world enough and time to notice how the make-up artist's face powder had settled on cheeks and crevices—like a patina of flakes and flour blown on to a statue during renovation work in a Cathedral. The light, glinting off his glasses, made the character additionally ceramic. Yet, somehow, the brilliant inner-life is conveyed. Immobility was one of the secrets of comedy, Sellers believed. John Bird once asked him straight out, what's the trick? 'He gave me some advice which I never followed. He said: *Keep your head still*. If you look at him, he does that. Everybody else is acting themselves silly—he is the centre of balance, like a dancer.' Then Bird added (without being prompted by me), 'Guinness' technique is not dissimilar ...'

Which is true, because in *Murder By Death*, as the blind butler, Bensonmum, answering the door and taking the guests to their rooms, and staring at the world-famous detectives with eyes which look but don't see, Guinness has made himself so stately and still, he's hieratic—with his close-cropped white hair, his head is huge, like an Emperor's bust. Maggie Smith, Peter Falk, Elsa Lanchester, and the rest of the cast scamper around him, like acolytes in olden days, skipping and strewing the place with petals and garlands. Except for Sellers. Sidney Wang, in ceremonial robes and monster teeth, is another totem—a stick-puppet. Bird summed up: 'You look at Sellers' work, you think: What is going on? Why is he so good? Despite the keeping still, and so on, there's nothing obvious that you can copy and make use of yourself. As with Guinness, it is great acting, and the greatness defies analysis.'

◆ ◆ ◆

With serenity, motionlessness, and basilisk stares to go on, we have at least made a start. Clouseau might be Smiley's accident-prone cousin, for they both bring evil-doers to justice and have withdrawn, sombre personalities. They interrogate; they are underestimated; they are conscious of their dignity. They are stilled points in the turning, duplicitous world. In attempting to solve crimes and expose lies, they are agents of order—or disorder, in Clouseau's case, for he cannot leave a house without first dismantling it, or Herbert Lom's office without igniting it. But there is no doubting his authority, which seems supernaturally abetted. (The fact that it's stuntmen who really do the work has its aptness: Clouseau splits up into doubles and doppelgängers like a subdividing angel or demon.)

Sellers and the spirit world is a large subject. Guinness, too, was prone to occult experiences at one time. He once owned a picture by Bernard Meninsky. In the manner of M.R. James' tale 'The Mezzotint,' the canvas began to alter, and trees and bushes, in the landscape, started to writhe. All was (apparently) explained by the oddities having occurred on the anniversary of the artist's suicide. Other 'phases of near-psychic experience' included Guinness' premonition about James Dean, whom he met in Hollywood. 'It is now ten o'clock, Friday, 23 September 1955,' he warned, in the manner of Obi-Wan Kenobi counselling Luke Skywalker. 'If you get in that car you will be found dead in it by this time next week.' Dean was pranged. Guinness was right—the Force was with him.

He also took to consulting the Tarot cards—and must have become a serious student, because his fear, when aroused, was sudden and total. He threw the deck, wand, books of spells, and other unspecified impedimenta onto a fire. This rough magic he abjured, it would seem, just before his conversion to Catholicism. The Tarot's symbols, he quite rightly saw, the chalice, spear, tree, and spiky crown, blasphemously alluded to the Crucifixion.

Sellers never ceased his explorations of necromancy. There was always some table-rapping, tea-leaf examining, ouija board session or voodoo rite afoot in his residences. 'I do indeed believe in extrasensory perception. It happens to me all the time. When I'm driving I can tell if a man is going to cross the road in front of me, even if he's nowhere in sight. When I was a kid in Ilfracombe I got to know... Estelle Roberts, the medium... She was extraordinary. While she was talking she'd suddenly turn away and ask: "What did you say?"—to the empty air, just as if someone were standing there beside her. She began talking about one of my uncles. She wanted to know if I had a picture of him. As a matter of fact I... had a snapshot in my wallet, he was in a group of people. I showed it to her. She picked him out at once; that's the one, she said. How could she have known? I'd never talked to anyone about my uncle. She really was extraordinary. She'd say: "*Nobody's dead.* There are no dead people, just people living another parallel life with us."'

Sellers' predilection for the signs and symbols directed at him from beyond the grave, his reliance on spirit mediums and the voices of the dead, all imply his basic contempt for human life and reason. His insistence on taking the advice of fortune-tellers was one more way of being unmanageable, and by deciding he had an aversion to certain colours (green and purple mainly) had a way of getting sets repainted, costumes remade, and bystanders in clothes of offending hues forcibly removed. As he said, the flapdoodle began in Ilfracombe, but it was in his bloodstream long before then. The backstage world, in which the Rays lived, and beyond that the worlds of the boxing and circus rings, are full of superstitions.

Though things like not whistling in dressing rooms can be ascribed to the prohibition on noises which would confuse the stage-hands and scene-shifters—for, originally, ex-sailors worked the ropes up in the flies and, as on a ship, whistles were used to signal to the men up in the rigging—many of the creeds and pieties seem nonsensical. When a cheeseboard fell on Sellers' head, he couldn't rest until he'd found out the reason why—an open umbrella drying in the boiler room. When one of his children fell off a horse, or if he had a bump with his car, it was because a bunch of keys had been left on the hall table. Michael remembers seeing his father look up at a flock of fan-tail doves cooing contentedly on the gables. 'Dad's face darkened. "It's those bloody birds. We've got to get rid of them—they're bringing us bad luck."' Sellers went to fetch his shotgun and blasted them to bits. 'I turned on my heel,' says Michael, 'and ran back to the forecourt to see the poor birds pitching off the tiles like broken shuttlecocks.'

It wasn't only the fowls of the air which Sellers found ominous.* He took against the children's first nanny, Frieda Heinlein, because she had once been a Lutheran nun and had asked if she could take her charges to Sunday School. He started calling her a 'German swine' and set about her constructive dismissal. 'You needn't say goodbye to Frieda this morning,' he told Sarah, in front of the good woman, 'Because she won't be here when you get back.'

Nanny Heinlein's replacement fared little better. (He seemed to resent seeing his children being cared for competently.) In fact, rather worse, because Sellers tried to murder her, believing her to be a witch. He collected a carving knife from the kitchen, and yelling 'I'll kill you, you cow,' stormed towards his employee's private quarters. He embedded the knife in the locked door (much as Milligan had done during another homicidal attack) and Nanny Clarke leapt out of the window, her fall broken by a rose bush. According to Michael's account, she hobbled to a neighbour's, was taken to hospital, and informed the police. Sellers told the constabulary that the woman was deranged, and they believed him. The violent scene, in retrospect, resembled nothing so much as a farcical set-piece invented for one of his films. (What was tragic in life was imitated for comic effect in his art, e.g. Mr Martin trying to stab Constance Cummings with an egg whisk in *Battle of the Sexes*.)

Since he was convinced that people were flashing him the evil-eye, or somehow in conspiracy against him, Sellers' paranoia was fed by the paranormal. But it had long been convenient to blame his screw-ups and terrible tempers on crossed knives and spilt salt. Anything external or other-worldly that could take the blame for his own mood swings or sense of disaster was conscripted—it was quite impossible for him, Peg's invincible golden boy, to find or admit to a murky source within himself. (Milligan said that Sellers 'thinks he's the only clean man in the leper colony.') The crystal-gazers and horoscopes, he maintained, put him above suspicion and absolved him from having to take any responsibility for his actions. Even his big 1964 heart attack, he reckoned, was preordained and a privileged preview of Heaven: 'I do remember one thing clearly,' he said of his death and resurrection, 'a feeling that I would expire, but I wouldn't actually die. I re-

---

* When I told Michael that one of my sons was born on Friday the thirteenth, he joked 'My father would have had it strangled.'

member there being a sort of large, strong, outstretched arm, pulling me—I knew as long as I clung on I wouldn't die...'

He'd been saved from his heart being drowned, and he believed 'I shall live till I'm seventy-five and will die in my sleep shortly after that. I know that. I suppose I knew all the time I would never die during that Hollywood business. But you have to watch things. Even so, I think I shall most probably die about then, seventy-five, that age.'

Sellers' premonitions were out by twenty-one years.

♦ ♦ ♦

If the occult was expedient, something you blamed bad luck and being a shit on, it was also a means of stretching credulity to the breaking point. 'Every time he went to see Doris Stokes he tried to get in touch with his mother,' says Milligan, 'but instead he got in touch with his dog, Chussy, a little white-haired Maltese terrier, who said it was very happy.'

The Land of Far Beyond was that of the Goons. When he was living in Ireland with his third wife, Miranda Quarry, he kept chickens. One day a hen went missing. 'I thought the fox had got it, but as Miranda was distressed,' he said, 'we had a séance. When Peg came through, I asked her, "Do you know where the hen has gone?" "Of course I do," she said. "It's up in the rafters of the stable."' The next day he found his stray hen. Up in the rafters.

The crotchety banter is like that of Tony Perkins and his mummified man in Bates' Motel. When she was dead, what with spectral pooches and disappearing chickens, Peg couldn't have had much peace. Sellers' séances interrupted her repose as his telephone calls at all hours of the day and night did back when she was alive. Indeed, his séances often *were* telephone calls. ('I still speak to my darling every day,' he said chirpily, a dozen years after her exit.) He'd ring up Maurice Woodruff, Doris Collins, or another of his witch-doctors, and they, with one hand on the ouija board, would relay his mother's messages and advice. Sometimes the psychic bulletins were further filtered through Bert Mortimer, Sellers' valet. Bert would ring up Maurice, who'd issue instructions, which were then relayed to Sellers, who'd be across the room doing things with a Tarot pack. These telephone calls, from anywhere in the world, would go on for hours until Sellers received the predictions he wanted.

The despatches wouldn't have much mattered if Peg had confined herself to domestic pets. But unfortunately, her chatter started to interfere with Sellers' work. On *Casino Royale*, the film company built a set at enormous expense, but Sellers had a nightmare about it in which his mother came on to the studio floor and said she didn't like it, so he insisted it be torn down without being used. If you ever dare to over-stimulate yourself by watching a video of *Ghost in the Noonday Sun*, you will notice a discrepancy in Sellers' character's name—Scratch in one scene, Scratcher in another. This is because Sellers had Maurice with him during the filming and the soothsayer took him aside and explained that Scratch was an ancient name for the Devil (a euphemism or synonym common enough to be listed in *Roget's Thesaurus*).

'I now know why all this bad luck is being visited on the production!' the actor announced. 'The Devil is blighting the film—so I want every scene in which I'm called "Scratch" scrapped. Every copy of the script which refers to "Scratch" must be destroyed. From now on he's Dick *Scratcher*.' Medak's ring-binder file, with its scotch-taped insertions and febrile ballpoint alterations, bears witness to this decree. Maurice also kept saying to Sellers that 'Today isn't a good day for being near water,' which, given that it was a pirate romp they were making on a reconstituted galleon out in the Aegean, only aggravated matters, to pitch it no higher.

Robert Parrish, a director who, like Medak, was abandoned in a foreign field to cope with a lunatic, estimated that Sellers' inner voices cost Warner Brothers, backers of *The Bobo*, approximately $71,428.57 for each day that the star declined to appear for work at Cinecitta. It was the same story on *After the Fox*, *I Love You Alice B. Toklas*, and *The Fiendish Plot of Dr Fu Manchu*, amongst many others. It all became too much for one executive. After stomaching delay after delay and the flimsy excuses of adverse ghostly prognostications, the producer took Sellers aside and said: 'Listen, Peter. It's very strange. But I've been hearing voices too. And you know what they told me? They told me that if you're not in tomorrow and ready to go, both your legs will get broken.'

The story may be apocryphal because most of the time Sellers got away with it. 'He got away with it time and again,' Milligan told me, his eyes glowing with amazement. 'He had a magic touch. He had a very bad name in the film world for being awkward, but he always got by. They kept using him. He never stopped working.' The reason he was indulged isn't so very difficult to address. *The Return of the Pink Panther* cost three million dollars to make and grossed a profit of thirty million dollars in the first year alone. Sellers' misbehaviour cost money, but it was written off as an investment.

Charles K. Feldman shrugged off the insanities of *Casino Royale* because he wanted Sellers to beget another world-wide smasheroo like *What's New, Pussycat?* And so it went on, money being hurled at him in the hopes that he'd get his creative juices flowing. It made him the more disordered. He was the superstitious actor who was partly genuine, partly posture. Sellers' caperings were something he developed to fill the gap where opinions or a considered personality should have been. If he was anxious, uncertain, bored, or feeling malicious, he'd allow something ugly to occur.

To give *The Prisoner of Zenda* its lavish Ruritanian look, Walter Mirisch had arranged for a beautiful steam locomotive to be restored to its full period splendour and brought from the Austrian Railway Museum to the location, outside Vienna. When Sellers, who had the say-so on everything, saw it, he said: 'Are you trying to destroy me?' It was green, of course. Universal, the film company, obliged and repainted the thing brown. They then had to re-repaint it the original emerald before it could be sent back again up the line to the engine sheds.

By 1978, and *Zenda*, he was mad; but he could use his madness, too. He was calculating about these outbursts. They were worked up like a child showing off— and here is the link, once again, to Peg. He always wanted his astrologers to dis-

cover what his mother would have said, what her opinion was, and in a twisted
sort of way, his caprices continued to be a way of trying to impress her. His bad
behaviour was a reflex action of his desire to please.

Peg never let him go.

♦ ♦ ♦

Spiritual matters, which gave Guinness his core of faith and security, made
Sellers fly apart. He chopped and changed from Judaism to Zoroastrianism to
Vendantism; he travelled from Israel (where he found people 'almost anti-
Semite') to India ('I went to see a lady... the other day who deals in numerology
and she told me of my various incarnations and what Karma I had to work off in
this life') to the Philippines (to meet a sect which cured all known ills by poking
around in chicken livers: 'These people are performing miracles. One day the
medical profession will recognise their work'). And the quests had the frantic ardour of his constant exchange of motor cars and his trading-in of wives.

Guinness made his submission to Rome ('I felt I had come home') at St
Lawrence's Church, Petersfield, Hampshire, with sober-sidedness and dignity.
Sellers' flirtation with Catholicism (after his St Aloysius' interests) took place in a
suite at the Palace Hotel, Gstaad; and this episode, more than any other, demonstrates the differences between the two men—and points to their divergence as
actors. Sellers, on his wanderings, had met a priest in Mexico who claimed to have
cured himself of cancer by constant prayer. One day, out of the blue, Sellers decided he wanted him at his side. Many hours of transcontinental telephone calls
later, involving embassies and consulates throughout Central America, the holy
man was located and persuaded to fly Swiss Air first-class to Geneva.

Thirty-six hours after Sellers had concocted the plan, the priest was installed
in a suite at the grand hotel. Another suite, at Sellers' command, was converted
into and consecrated as a temple. 'Only days before,' says Michael, 'Dad had been
placing orders with room service for champagne, caviare, club sandwiches, and
cartons of cigarettes. Now he was galvanising porters into preparing the rooms
for Communion.' Life-size plaster statues, a wrought-iron crucifix, pews, and a
pulpit were installed. Sellers fixed up his hi-fi so that it would seep out woozy organ chords. The effect must have been of a chapel of rest.

The priest was 'quietly impressed by my father's spiritual feeling', and
planned Mass for seven o'clock the next morning. Sellers' face fell at the news of
this early hour, so he telephoned Michael at six-thirty and insisted on his presence
as well. 'I'm asleep,' said Michael. 'This has nothing to do with me.' 'Of course
it's got something to do with you. What in name's sake do you think I flew the
priest over here for? I'm not going to celebrate Communion on my own.'

The next afternoon, the priest was winging his way back to his peons.

♦ ♦ ♦

Sellers' deep frivolousness and impatience, his need to receive instant pleasure, are worlds away from Guinness' modesty and quiet. (Can you imagine Guin-

ness taking a priest to a press screening, as Sellers did, to bless the film and ensure glowing reviews?) But in making an obvious enough moral judgement we
must take care not to throw in any counterbalancing aesthetic measures. Guinness
is the nicer man; he is not necessarily the superior actor. It is simply the case that,
after encountering Sellers and seeing the advent of Sellers' career, he became a
different one. His vigorous characters climax with Professor Marcus in *The Ladykillers*. After that, the insidiousness, the baroque flourishes, disappear. In the mid-
fifties, Guinness turned his back on the exaggerations which were once part of his
appeal. It is impossible to conceive now that he's the same artist who had played
Fagin with such relish. The Guinness admired by Sellers was capable of sinister
transformations. His Ealing heroes and villains are people brimful of japes and
stratagems; they keep us wide awake with their flashes and spurts. They seem
spontaneous. After *The Ladykillers*, though, as none other than Sellers observed,
'Alec likes to work out just what he will do before he starts. I have to "get inside
the part"—feel it from inside.'

What I am building towards here is the idea that Sellers destroyed Guinness
as a comic actor. Perhaps Sir Alec was already finding his own brand of exuber-
ance a dead end? (He worried that Professor Marcus was too much of an Alastair
Sim part.) Or perhaps in Catholicism, which he embraced a few months after the
premiere of *The Ladykillers*, he found a form and channel for his tremendous
drive; henceforward he didn't *need* acting in quite the same way? He makes the revealing observation in *Blessing in Disguise* that he has been known to break into a
run to reach a church, arriving to pray 'in a state of almost sexual excitement.' It
can be safely said that Guinness' later rôles are invariably sexless—Obi-Wan
Kenobi, Smiley, Reilly, and Monsignor Quixote, for instance, go one better and
are actually celibates. This doesn't mean they are hollow and dry. On the contrary,
sex has been superceded by piety and intellectual resource. (Guinness couldn't be
more different than his confrere, Laurence Olivier, in this respect, who turned
into Zeus as he aged, and gave erotic undercurrents to the versatility of his rôles.)

Whatever happened, whether it was religion's becoming more important to
him than theatricality, or whether Sellers was the catalyst in his change of direction,
Guinness got rid of his gaiety. When he was sent a script containing a part 'tailor-
made' for his talents, he'd send it back by return, pettishly making the observation
that 'nobody has been to take my measurements.' He was David Lean's third or
fourth choice for Col. Nicholson, in *Bridge on the River Kwai*, but this was the kind
of rôle—hard, undemonstrative, distant—which he now sought. 'False noses,' he
said despairingly, 'are too easy.' The putty protuberances, and all that went with
them, were appropriated by Sellers.* He it was, sniffing and sneezing with ambition,
whose restlessness and energy now found form in darting from one character part
to the next; and whilst he was about it, as we'll see in the next chapter, he revitalised
British cinema virtually on his own. Sellers may have been a trifling, arbitrary man
in real life, but before he lost his sense of control, his irresponsibility, as far as acting went (and no further), was a virtue; it made him the actor he was. It's his own

* 'The man with the longest nose sees furthest.' *Russian proverb.*

mercurialism which he puts on exhibition; his mystical thoughts and haphazard nature which filled out unremarkable characters in remarkable ways; his prodigality which revels and recoils around the remote mental crannies of Fred Kite, Mr Martin, Clare Quilty, Dr Strangelove, and the Lord He Knoweth Who else all.

◆ ◆ ◆

Sellers was a *commedia del l'arte* Alec Guinness. The sheer glee he brings to (say) Mr Topaze's discovery of crime, or the Rev. Smallwood's astral hymn singing, or to General Fitzjohn, high on his white charger, his eyeglass trained on the promenading schoolgirls giggling and romping in the dead bracken, contains the top-spin of an extra, sly joke. He seems to be sending a signal to the audience which says, in effect: Here is the Sellers version of Sir Alec! I'm out-Guinnessing Guinness! This message would have come across strongly when Sellers' films were first released, for every reviewer made the comparison and rubbed in who they thought he was emulating. In fact, the homage might more accurately work the other way about. If you look at Prince Feisal in *Lawrence of Arabia*, Lieut.-Col. Jock Sinclair in *Tunes of Glory*, Hitler in *Hitler—The Last Ten Days*, or the Earl of Darincourt in *Little Lord Fauntleroy*, the accents and appearance Guinness adopts are Sellers'; there must be people across the world willing to swear on oath that, in David Lean's *A Passage to India*, the part of Professor Godbole is played not by Sir Alec Guinness but by Peter Sellers.

But before Lean, there was Alexander Mackendrick, the Scot with an American passport who'd directed *Whisky Galore* and Guinness in *The Man in the White Suit*. This 'sophisticated grown-up Peter Pan,' in Guinness' description, was a combination of scepticism and eagerness, of 'caustic wit and chuckling irony'; and all this, plus Guinness himself in his rococo mode, plus a thirty-year old Sellers ready to show willing and as yet free from too many overt emotional blights, comes together in *The Ladykillers*, a masterpiece of fairy tale telling.

Many and various have been the commentaries evoked by *The Ladykillers*. Charles Barr, for example, in his history of the Ealing Studios, regards the film as political allegory: 'The gang are the post-war Labour Government. Taking over "the House", they gratify the Conservative incumbent by their civilised behaviour (that nice music) and decide to use at least the facade of respectability for their radical programme of redistributing wealth...' Gavin Stamp, in an essay printed in *The Times* on November 3, 1990, thinks the film inadvertently records the vanished charm of fifties' London. He has made blow-ups from stills and uses them to illustrate his lectures on the urban history of King's Cross.

If Barr's paragraph is gibberish and Stamp's architectural nostalgia, if not irrelevant to explaining the film, is at best incidental (though I share his enthusiasm for red telephone kiosks and 'the surreal desolation of a Victorian railway landscape'), Stamp has at least put in some legwork. Lots of it. He informs us that the robbery was filmed outside Stanley Buildings, in Cheney Road; that the crooks loiter near the Jesmond Dene Hotel, on the corner of St Chad's Street, when they are waiting for the arrival of the loot; and that Mrs Wilberforce's lopsided house was constructed 'about a mile further north', on Frederick Street, off the Caledonian Road: 'It is still possible to stand above the railway tunnel and see the strange, smoke-filled panorama.'

It says much for the enchantment of *The Ladykillers* that it can induce such pilgrimages and detective work; and it is true that, here and there, beyond the actors, Betjeman's London is going about its business. But to seek 'the real-life setting' for the film, to try and recapture the spirit of place, makes about as much sense as those tourist trails for Sherlock Holmes' sleuthings. It is not that Mrs Wilberforce, One-Round, etc., never lived, because Katie Johnson, Danny Green, Guinness, Sellers, and so on did indeed walk upon those pavements pleasant in ancient time; it is simply that we are dealing here with make-believe and illusion, and if Mackendrick used a street directory it was only to transfigure it. *The Ladykillers* has all the solidity of a pop-up book—unlike *Passport to Pimlico*, say, which is actually about a London which is as lost as Atlantis, and where a Gavin Stamp-style analysis would be central to its meaning and not a gripping footnote.

◆ ◆ ◆

The story had appeared to William Rose in a dream: 'I woke up one morning, at about one or two o'clock, and wakened my wife, and said: "I've just dreamt a whole film…"' Mrs Wilberforce, Professor Marcus, the raid on the security van, taking strongboxes to King's Cross, the stringed instrument-playing masquerade… Everything. It is thus Philip Kemp's account, in his critical biography *Lethal Innocence: The Cinema of Alexander Mackendrick*, which is the most enlightening. 'Perhaps Mrs Wilberforce,' he suggests, 'has fallen asleep within earshot of a radio and conjured up the gang from the depth of her psyche.' The violence and murder mood is thus 'an emanation from the dark underworld of Victorian morality.'

Well, yes, it might be. But (as in Dickens), the characters don't need to have bizarre, hidden, or ugly thoughts and inklings; they don't need to possess inner-lives at all. Eccentricity and goodness are there, stark, on the surface. We know Mrs Wilberforce is a one-woman protected species, a fairy, because she carries a wand—her parasol, which she keeps absent-mindedly losing. We know Professor Marcus is a troll by his outsize teeth and goblin's gait—he is as real as Rumpel-stiltskin. They are all exaggerated for gothic effect. Lom's Louis doesn't stop glowering; Cecil Parker's Major's moustache and canary-coloured waistcoat are out of a *Punch* cartoon; Danny Green's giant old lag, in his prison greys, seems carved out of rock; and Sellers' Teddy Boy, full of apprehension, pretends to be dipping and diving to Bill Haley and his Comets, or some such grandfatherly pop music. His Harry Robinson is totally jittery.

Sellers, as we know from his own mouth, watched Guinness like a kestrel. He was also, according to Tom Pevsner, the Assistant Director, 'very nervous and un-certain, and looking to Sandy [Mackendrick] for reassurance all the time.' His in-security was noticed by Michael Balcon, too. 'He was desperately anxious. He kept asking: "Is it all right? Am I any good?"' It is just this lack of confidence which comes across in the character—and it is ideal. Sellers may well have been 'utterly sincere and genuine' (Balcon's words) when questioning his work, but underneath the prevarications, Harry was taking shape. He's always looking over his shoulder, or pretending to be walking away; he gazes at Professor Marcus, eager for instructions and desperate to be emboldened. Harry, wanting to learn from the master criminal, is Sellers himself, absorbing the craft of a master-mummer; he plays the rôle as a London Jew—as near as he dared to the son of Peg, his own hair slightly curled and a duelling scar added to his cheek. It is Harry who tries to ingratiate himself with the old lady, helping out with her parrots (which Sellers voiced): 'You leave it to me, Ma. I'm very good with birds.'

It is not hard to imagine Harry as a mother-fixated East-Ender; and when Mrs Wilberforce creates the chaos with the barrow boy and the street marketeers, it is he who comments with amazement and awe: 'All of them out of business in ten minutes.' Katie Johnson's character is supernatural—her lightweight toddle is a hint that any moment she'll whirr aloft and take flight. Her face makes babies scream in their prams; her voice makes horses bolt. In the original script, she was to have been narrowly missed by a wrecker's ball on a building site, which swung past and crushed a car. Oblivious to it all, she's obviously Inspector Clouseau's fairy godmother.

Her house, a lopsided fairy-tale cottage, is a setting for shaping fantasies and fancy's images. There's no more marvellous sequence in British cinema than the one where Mrs Wilberforce's chums come to tea—a conclave of trim, elderly fairies—who have popped up through trap doors, chattering non-stop and bearing tidings of the robbery in King's Cross. Their costumes of feathered hats and pointy shoes—and parasols—are Victorian-era crossed with Walt Disney.

The robbers are powerless before this massed band. Instead of stamping out the little old lady infestation, which size for size would be no contest, they are spellbound. The next thing we know, everybody is in the parlour, the Professor hunched over the pianola, Louis backed into a corner, and Harry, up against the door, has a cup and saucer in one hand, a scone on a plate in the other, and he has absolutely no idea how to get either of them up to and in his mouth. It is then that they start to sing—the quavery women, the flat and defeated men:

Darling, I am growing old,
Silver threads among the gold,
Shine upon my brow today:
Life is fast fading away.

◆ ◆ ◆

Inside the house, where the music we hear is that Boccherini minuet, often scored for a music box's tinkle, the light is mauve and lavender—a soft and cool glow. Outside, where objects are in harsh silhouette and the night skies are a dark blue, the soundtrack is full of trains screeching and trucks being shunted. *The Ladykillers* is one of the great railway movies, like *The Lady Vanishes* or *Murder on the Orient Express*. But chuff-chuffs are no more realistically used than the London street locations. Mrs Wilberforce's villa, lying in the shadow of Sir Giles Gilbert

Scott's St Pancras, a forest of red sandstone, looks like a turret that has dropped off the station; similarly, Professor Marcus is a liberated gargoyle.

The steam trains are the film's dragons. They send clouds of sulphurous vapour billowing about the house. When the Major is pushed off the roof, Harry is brained by One-Round, Louis is killed, and the Professor crowned (by the railway signal), smoke and gasses cover the violence—we never see anything nasty—and the bodies are taken, one by one in a wheelbarrow, across the vegetable patch to the viaduct; they are then tipped over to the tracks, far below. It could be where the souls of the dead breathe out of the tunnel and tombs. The trains whoosh in the mist and their lights shine and blink like dim yellow eyes.

If the house is a bit of broken gingerbread, the backyard a haunt of hydras, and the looming edifice of Kings Cross a wild wood of twisted pinnacles and branches, the film's calamity—One Round's tugging at his double bass case and all the stolen money spilling out—has the beauty of falling leaves. The large white notes flutter from the cobalt sky in silence and slow motion. The men are mesmerised, as they were by the sudden appearance of the flibbertigibbets. There's nothing for it but to dash back inside the funhouse and plead for sanctuary. They wheedle; they cajole; they threaten blackmail. Mrs Wilberforce is adamant. The money must be handed to the police. They try sob stories:

[*The* PROFESSOR *calls in the* MAJOR *like an orchestral conductor.*]

MAJOR: [*In emotion.*] No...no...I...

PROFESSOR: [*Gently insistent.*] Tell her.

MAJOR: [*Reluctantly.*] Oh, well—it's just that—well, at this very moment, Mrs. Wilberforce, there is waiting an invalid—a dear sweet, little old lady, not, may heaven bless her, unlike yourself. Waiting with patient serenity but with high hope, that she has nothing more to fear. [*Pause.*] My mother.

[*The* PROFESSOR, *behind* MUM'S *back, nods to* HARRY.]

HARRY: [*On cue.*] With me, it's my little sister. She married a trapeze artist, Mum. Forced her into his act he did, a hundred feet up and no net. I told her I'd get some money to buy a little place for her and the kiddies. When I think of her up there, swinging to and fro...to and fro... [HARRY *sees it in his mind's eye*]...and her scared of heights, and all her little kiddies watching with their little eyes, holding their breaths...Just a little place on the ground, that's all she wants...

PROFESSOR: Each of them can tell a similar story. I planned the robbery, Mrs Wilberforce. [*Simply.*] I wanted to help them.

[*A long pause.*]

MUM: No.

HARRY: Eh?

MUM: No. I don't think—even if what you say is true—I still don't think it can be said to be enough justification.

MAJOR: In the name of all that's *holy*, Madam! Have you no decent feelings whatever?

[MUM *walks back into the hall.*]

I have quoted from the scene at length because we don't get to see much of it in the actual film.* *The Ladykillers* was thought to be over-running, so chunks were lopped off by (as usually happens in such cases) the studio janitor. 'You know,' said Sellers, 'I might have got somewhere with *The Ladykillers*, but forty minutes were cut. A lot of *me* was cut with that forty minutes.' If you watch what is left of the above carefully on your Ealing Greats videocassette, you'll notice a clumsy leap from the Major's 'My Mother' to the Professor's 'Each of them can tell a similar story.' Sellers was furious at having his big moment cut, and he lost confidence in the production.

'I myself was in *The Ladykillers* to get away from having to say the same lines every night for two years in *The King and I*,' Herbert Lom told me at the Reform Club. 'I'd taken over Yul Brynner's part and my head was shaven—that's why Louis wears a hat all the time indoors. Peter turned up in my dressing room after the show and *implored* me to get him a job on another film. He was convinced *The Ladykillers* was a disaster. He was sure of himself as a mimic, but not as an actor. As an actor he thought he'd be out of work.'

Since we now know what is missing, it is hard to be satisfied with the gap. It yawns. In fact, the rhythm, the absurd build-up, is wrecked; and Harry's 'Eh?' after Mum's 'No' loses its force—he's meant to be incredulous that his yarn hasn't won her over. I'd give a lot to have Sellers' little high-wire fantasy restored. His speech takes the mood off to a Goonish dimension, to a facetious realm which Mackendrick and Seth Holt, the Associate Producer, big fans of 'The Goon Show' itself, had wanted him to supplement the film with when he was originally cast; it's why they lobbied Balcon for Sellers and not Attenborough, the young scarface of *Brighton Rock*. And of course it is 'The Goon Show', whimsical and fantastic, with its psychopathic undercurrents, which lies behind *The Ladykillers*, linking them both together and to their fifties era. Major Courtenay is Major Bloodnok; Mrs Wilberforce is Minerva Bannister; Professor Marcus, twisted and decrepit, is an Emett or Searle drawing of Henry Crun, his madcap plan worthy of Grytpype and Moriarty. One Round is the brainless Eccles and Harry is Bluebottle—when he's alarmed, his voice *is* Bluebottle's. If the technology had existed, Sellers could have played them all—and in a way, he did. Michael Balcon, reminiscing in 1960, said: 'It would be easy for me to say now that I always knew he was brilliant. But that was not so. I admired him, thought he had possibilities. I didn't realise then what I now recognise, that he was a near genius, perhaps a whole one. Genius is a much-abused word, but I think Sellers and Guinness have it... One day we were all sitting in the studio canteen when over the loudspeaker came what sounded like the soundtrack from the film. But it wasn't the soundtrack. It was Peter impersonating all the actors himself on a tape recorder, including the camera director's remarks as well. People still talk about it in the studio—we were quite shaken.'

---

* My source is the original shooting script, housed in the archives of the British Film Institute. My thanks to Philip Kemp for fishing it out.

Chapter Eight

♦ ♦ ♦

No, Not Ealing

I admired his talent—which had flashes of genius—enormously. I worked with him only twice and always found him personally agreeable and friendly, but I never got to know him.

During the making of *Murder By Death* he had become pretty odd—measuring his caravan with a tape measure to make sure it was larger than everyone else's; deciding his mood by the colour of a stone in his ring; not turning up for shooting—saying he was ill—but seen lunching by David Niven in a Beverly Hills restaurant; making extravagant demands on the management, etc.—all tiresome stuff which made me think he had become a little unbalanced. I had the impression he greatly feared death but can't remember him actually saying so ...

Yours sincerely
Alec Guinness

♦ ♦ ♦

Of the two British character actors who have managed to become sound-era film stars of world renown, one went insane and the other is cordial. Guinness exchanged his briskness (Herbert Pocket) for a serenity (Smiley) and dispassionateness (William Dorrit). Sellers, by complete contrast, was never able to curb his nervousness and restlessness, and he used acting, along with his transient enthusiasms for a variety of women, religions, and residences, as a means of exploring all the misshapenness that loomed inside himself. Morbidly self-conscious, he was a man inordinately concerned with his own lack of colour, so he put himself, and those within his force field, through a series of tests and cues. He wanted to witness *reactions*—and, missing nothing, prove to himself that he existed.

His arrival on Cyprus, for *Ghost in the Noonday Sun*, in 1973, illustrates what I mean: 'We rented an incredible villa for him,' says Peter Medak, 'an *incredible* villa. But trouble started immediately. Peter turned up with his chauffeur and two hundred pieces of luggage. Before he did anything ... he brought out the most sophisticated Sony stereo system ... "Wait a minute, baby, I've got to put my stereo together." Then I tried to show him the ... house. He took a compass from his pocket and ... ended up in the maid's bedroom. "That's where I'm going to sleep because this faces to the East." ... Then we went downstairs and ... he said, "Let's look up the credits of the producers in a copy of *Who's Who*." ... He put the book down and said ... "I've got to get rid of the producers." A week later he created a situation whereby the producers were fired by him; but I'm sure they would have quit or resigned anyway.'

He'd been similarly destructive and mistrustful (i.e. paranoid) on *Casino Royale*, about six years earlier. 'One of the problems that blew the film apart,' says Joe McGrath, 'was that Orson Welles and I got along really well... Sellers then got annoyed. "I didn't think you and Orson would take sides against me." "I'm not taking sides against you, but Orson has the same feelings that you have—that there's a chance we can come up with some funny stuff." "Well, I'll only attempt to come up with funny stuff so long as *he's not there.*" So he and Orson came in on different days. He was frightened of the *scale* of Orson: his legend; literally his weight and immensity.' He was willing to sabotage the entire movie if it meant appearing in a scene with Orson and being outclassed.

Immediately he arrived on a set, Sellers was foreseeing problems—in the early days, because he was conscious of his high artistry and didn't wish to compromise; later, because he wanted to preserve his fame and status; and finally, because only the deployment of crazy laws and the wielding of absolute power gave him any sort of sensation. There'd come a point, which harked back to Nero, where he'd refuse to look at the colours green or purple. I have already mentioned the Ruritanian train story. His secretaries and personal assistants had to pre-inspect visitors and divest them of the offending hues; should you have turned up for a meeting in the wrong shade, back out through the door you went. And why?

'Green has been a superstition of mine for a long time and purple was laid on me by the late Vittorio de Sica. We were working one day and his script girl showed up wearing purple. De Sica went into a foaming rage and sent her away all the time doing this [the warding-off-the-evil-eye hand signal]... Then he told me. "My dear Peter. Purple is the colour of death."... Being a bit superstitious myself, I latched on to it myself. I figured de Sica must know something. And green. From my mother. She told me. It's certain shades of green. The hard, acidy green is bad. I pick up strange vibrations from it. It disturbs me.'

There are hundreds of people who'll testify to his outlandishness. 'We were to do the restaurant scene in *Hoffman*,' says Alvin Rakoff, 'and Peter wouldn't walk on the set, because there were purple tablecloths. We compromised. "They are definitely not purple. Those cloths are lilac."' Sellers refused to meet Blake Edwards' mother-in-law because she owned a purple coat. On *The Prisoner of Zenda*, one Friday, Lionel Jeffries said, 'Well, Peter, I'm glad that's over.' They'd been shooting in an underground casino, in stultifying heat. 'So am I,' said Sellers. 'But have you seen the roulette wheel? It's *green*...' The scene had to be done again—which is why the green baize in the film is now blood red.

I must add that Sellers didn't only come out with these superstitious fears when he had an audience to impress. His private life was blighted by similar stipulations. In the summer of 1979, he moved to the Hotel Crillon in Paris. His suite consisted of a hall, a sitting room, a study, and a bathroom. There was a double bedroom leading off the sitting room, beyond which was a second bathroom. However, the second bathroom was tiled in a light duck-egg blue which Sellers decided was a shade of green. 'If you don't want it to make part of your suite,' he was therefore informed, 'you can use the yellow bathroom you first saw, and we can block this second bathroom off.'

Sellers got them to do better than that—the offending ablutions block was bricked up. These bouts of Roman Emperor-standard improprieties, I think, are all part of his search for a retreat—a place within himself, immured by fads and caprices, where he could feel safe. Chance the gardener was his perfect refuge in this respect. R. D. Laing, talking about schizophrenia's being the ultimate refuge of the super-sane, has argued that the mad go into that private world to hide themselves—their fantasies are their protective armour against the sensitivities and hurts of everyday. Chance represented the ideal—Chance is in total control of his own limited little world. He can make things happen or make things not happen in it by wielding his remote-control zapper. No wonder that Sellers spent eight long years endeavouring to interest a studio in letting him make the film and play the rôle. Chance's winter garden was Sellers' great good place.

His enthusiasms were violent and short-lived. Herbert Kretzmer witnessed a revealing scene:

> I went to dinner with Spike Milligan one night, to Peter's flat in Stag Place. It was dominated by a huge photograph of his swami. He was utterly mad and impossible. Nothing had been prepared—no dinner. We were sitting around and a lot of Indians arrived from the take-away ... bearing tinfoil trays, which Sellers dumped on the smoked glass coffee table. There was no wine—he hadn't done anything at all, except fuss around putting on rock records so loudly nobody could speak ... He had no time for conversation. There was no period during that evening when there was any quiet or exchange; it was like we were humouring a drunk or a lunatic ... he'd spend a lot of time ... wandering in and out of the room and disappearing. He had one of the biggest and most powerful telescopes money can buy. It was trained on Big Ben, upside down. Any distraction—to avoid being normal, attractive, and possibly revealing.
>
> I called Peter the next day to thank him for the evening. 'Wonderful, your phoning,' he said. 'When one goes to a little bit of trouble to set up a dinner party, it's nice for people to appreciate it.'
>
> I'd never known a man to take less trouble. 'It was good to see Spike again,' I said. 'Yes—but he's turning out to be a bit of an oddball, isn't he?' And Spike had been perfectly coherent, sunny, wise, witty, when he got the opportunity amidst the clamour. Sellers was the oddball—but he'd reversed this in his mind ...

◆ ◆ ◆

The telescope, topsy-turvily fixed on the inverted clockface of Big Ben, is symbolic, surely? Sellers always wanted to outwit time; to show himself indifferent to its destructiveness. He began, as a drummer, by literally beating time; and he believed that if he behaved heedlessly, irresponsibly, time would be knocked out of joint for him. He'd thump it into submission. He'd be Peter Pan, never growing up, never hastened out of childhood and away from Peg. After he'd dumped Anne, Michael, and Sarah ('No one is going to catch me, lady, and make me a man'), he decided to enjoy the mad streak. He dieted. He popped a lot of pills—to get this gaunt, Don Juan look (on view in *Casino Royale* and *There's a Girl in My Soup*). He drank. He did an enormous amount of fucking, at which (according to Wolf Mankowitz, who'd broached the subject with Britt Ekland) he was not all that good. Later, there was a hefty use of cocaine, because somebody had told him it would improve his potency, enabling him to retain an erection all night. He used to smoke pot, and during the years he was in Ireland, he was really living in outer space. He seemed disembodied and, when people went to see him, he was so drugged and slurred, he was existing in slow motion. He'd got time to stand still.

'I could hardly make any sense out of him,' says Leslie Linder, a producer who flew to Dublin with a proposal for a film called *The Phantom versus the Reich*. 'I went over to see him with the writer Clive Exton. Peter was stoned out of his mind. He and his girlfriend were so far gone, they couldn't prepare lunch. They couldn't work out how a fridge door opened, and Peter gazed with rapture at a tomato ... It made communication with him impossible. Everything was slow-paced. *Interminable* ...'

It wasn't only marijuana and Bolivian Marching Powder making him like that, in all fairness. He was never an addict—drugs were simply a way, like going into a yogic trance, of taking a leave of absence from reality. Sellers was also stuffing himself with prescribed medicaments for his angina—though that condition, a by-product of his first coronary, was, in effect, self-induced. After having lured Britt, the young Swedish starlet, into his bed at the Dorchester, in February 1964, he began, once they were engaged, to guzzle and snort ampoules of amyl nitrate. These opened his valves and ventricles, increased the gush of blood throughout his anatomy, and enriched his orgasms. By Tuesday, April 7, his heart had pumped itself inside out and it gave up the ghost.

Because he recovered, he believed more than ever that he had totally created and recreated himself: the fat boy who had slimmed, the radio mimic who was a film star, the written-off patient who came back from the dead. Henceforward, he thought, if he kept himself busy, he wouldn't (as it were) have the time to die; or else, by attending to tinklings from mystical bells, and going in for supernatural manifestations and premonitions, he'd do his best to ensure he was not there when it happened. As much as he was obsessed by Sophia Loren, he once refused to fly to Rome for lunch with her because the newspaper horoscopes that morning had said 'this was not a good time to travel.' (Sellers was actually going up the Alitalia jet's steps at Heathrow before he decided to double-back.)

When time's arrow eventually did strike him plumb in the heartstrings, at 12:28 A.M. on Thursday, July 24, 1980, he was setting up *The Romance of the Pink Panther*. It was conceived for stunt-men, reverse angles, and long shots, and Sellers himself would barely have featured in it. It would have thus proved his transfiguration—he'd have been starring in a film and yet only appearing fleetingly in it, like a wraith. (The man-who-never-was as the man-who-was-not-there.) The conceit was taken over by Blake Edwards, who cobbled together out-takes and a compilation of unattributed highlights from previous Panthers to create the illusion of a new feature film, *The Trail of the Pink Panther*, in 1982. Sellers' double, John Taylor, the man who had actually done many of the heavy make-up scenes in *The

Fiendish Plot of Dr. Fu Manchu, because Sellers was either absent or ill, was hired, on minimum Equity rates, to impersonate Clouseau for a morning of linking shots. The result is ingenious and a shambles, but it does convey the impression that Sellers had continued to materialise in films after he had cooled.

♦ ♦ ♦

Of course, his dodges to use up time and to waste time, with his moods and fads, nymphs and narcotics, all imply a fear—the fear shrewdly scented by Alec Guinness—rather than an attitude for genuine disdain. It was bravado. This man in Peter Pan was as fretful as Captain Hook, forever hearing his nemesis, the crocodile, creeping towards him, the clock ticking louder and louder in its belly. Sellers knew his time was running out—we all do, so why did the concept particularly pain him?

Part of what made him mad was that he was insulted at not being made immortal. He had such a high opinion of himself that he couldn't accept that one day he'd cease to exist; that he'd wake up and not be there and that his eyes (in Emily Dickinson's phrase) would not see to see. He couldn't accept decay, age, feebleness. Thus his preference for keeping company with machines, which indicates, at least to me, that in seeking to invest objects with the potential for infallibility, he was somehow transferring to them a little of his contempt and dismay over human frailties and lacks. He wanted things to be brand new and to retain their newness, but they never could, and their appeal quickly wore off. This went for cars; it went for women: 'Every man's dream,' he generalised, 'is still, I'm sure, finding a virgin. The original idea was that the girl had never been with anyone else ... that to be in love with the girl of one's dreams ... was the ultimate happiness. I still want to ... discover the ideal woman and undress her, reveal her, in this fantasy of mine ...'

That is a repulsive fantasy for a variety of reasons, Sellers' sounding like Humbert Humbert being only the first of them. It wasn't exactly purity he was after, but power; and if he believed that young girls and virgins were spotless and innocent, like newly hatched eggs, he was either stupid and ignorant or a misogynist—and Sellers' vanity was one of his most overwhelming traits. Clearly, all he expected from a woman was that she should serve him. 'He had,' Michael told me, 'a number of older women friends, but they wouldn't stand for his crap and fickle nature; whereas young girls, he thought, would be totally besotted'—by his fame and will, if not by his physical frame. *There's a Girl in my Soup* and, especially, *Hoffman* (which was originally, unbelievably, entitled *Call Me Daddy*) pick up on the incestuous, predatory vibrations. In the former, Sellers, as a flamboyant TV gourmet, seduces Goldie Hawn, who leaves him when she sees through him. (Women, to Danvers, are nothing but side dishes or fast food.) In the latter, Sellers traps Sinead Cusack in his gloomy apartment for the weekend—*Hoffman* is beauty and the beast, where the beast is no handsome prince in disguise. He is morose, unleavened.

Sellers' final marriage, to a former child actress, was a fulfillment of several desires which were detected immediately by Lynne's mother, Iris, who was naturally extremely alarmed at the idea of a prospective son-in-law being older than she herself was. '... What mother can be expected to approve of the marriage of her daughter to such a man?' Outside of some dragon queen in the court of the Emperor Tiberius, not one. Mrs Frederick and the last Mrs Sellers were not fully reconciled until after the actor's death, when they clutched at one another for comfort at his funeral.

That Sellers' girls got younger as he grew older is another function of his attempts to live in a time warp; he wanted to think of himself as a dashing young blade, and hide the fact that, when he stared at a mirror, he saw one of the (his words) 'awfully strange brigade of pudding faces who melt in the crowds. I hate seeing myself. I'm not pleased with what I see in the mirror. I'm just disgusted, watching a bit more of the ageing process.' He had a horror of the flesh; so virgin's blood rejuvenated him? Sellers didn't even pretend to want to educate the nymphets (as the Woody Allen character does with Mariel Hemingway in *Manhattan*); it was enough that he expected them to look up to him, and in gaining possession of them he was trying to demean them.

◆ ◆ ◆

Woody Allen, Chaplin (all those blind flower girls), Polanski: the artists Sellers resembled or befriended all collected maidenhair, and had no qualms about putting their nympholeptic dreams into their films. Allen's *Husbands and Wives*, returning to a strand of plot from *Manhattan*, has a college professor leave Mia Farrow for a student named Rain in his own creative writing class: 'I feel myself becoming infatuated with a twenty-year-old ... I'm sleepwalking into a mess.' Allen's character, who claims 'I don't want to hurt anybody or be hurt,' seems to find the company of young girls bracing—as Allen the director and author does in real-life. Sex aside, Allen seems to enjoy pixies (if his own films can be said to contain clues) because being accepted by them is therapeutic. They are not psychologically bruised, like everybody else in his rep. company. They are dew-fresh.

Nobody would make the mistake of thinking that all Polanski wants is to be accepted by youngsters—his drives are carnal and avid, and he is still a wanted man in America, having once jumped bail when he was accused of committing a lewd or lascivious act with a thirteen-year-old schoolgirl. After having had Miss Farrow fucked by the Devil in *Rosemary's Baby*, he replayed the rape fantasy in *Tess*, when Nastassia Kinski, she of the crushed-strawberry lips, was defiled by Alec D'Urberville. And Sellers himself comes somewhere between these angels and demons.

He was not a rapist; he was not a nerdish neurotic pretending to be led. He was manipulative; he was an enervated vampire; and by the time he reached Lynne Frederick, there was not enough healthy blood left in his veins to sustain a hard-on. Between the *cardiac glycoside*, used to increase the heart's contractions, and the *glyceryl trinitrate*, a coronary vasolidator, used to lower his blood pressure and reduce the heart's work-load, his valves were popping open and shutting like the mouth of a goldfish, and the hydraulics in his loins clogged and wilted. 'We would try,' said Lynne, 'but it was difficult. He frequently felt he had failed in himself and would say "I can't look at you" ...'

The sexlessness, Sellers' genitalia a withered pear, dry and droopy, is horribly fitting. All his attempts to speed up his life, or to slow it down; his anxiety to buckle and pound the calendar, tackle tempo, and silence the clock's tick; his hallucinogens, gadgets and strange gods, come together in a single object: a need to return to the past and, if possible, begin again. To rewind the tape; to go for another take. And why? Because as a child he'd had to act older than he was. Precocious as an infant, he was childish as an adult—and in his attitude to women, it was the safety of the pre-pubertal relationship which drew him deepest. He wanted to run along back to the childhood he'd never had.

◆ ◆ ◆

Was a pre-occupation with the loss of innocence at the bottom of it?

'When his mother died,' Anne remembers, 'I had a children's shop in Hampstead called "Lollipop", and he suddenly arrived at the door—I was long remarried—in a terrible state. "Will you come for a drive with me?" We went on a long trip down Memory Lane. The flat where I'd first met him with Peg; his old infant school, where his first girlfriend was; the flat where I'd lived when he'd met me; where his uncle and aunt had lived... He was very sentimental about his past—he lived mainly in the past. After we'd split up... he cast me in the Peg rôle. He used to bring all his new women to meet me. He brought Britt. I must say, of all his wives afterwards, she was the best... [W]hen he was married to her and I was married to Ted... he did a number on her about me, like he had on me about Nora Barnacle—except that this time it was an open threat.'

The Sellers who traipsed the geography of his childhood and restructured his memories was remarked upon, too, by Milligan: 'Peter will never be at peace, never be happy,' he commented in 1969. 'That's why he is devoted to the past. He needs the past to bolster up the present before he can even look at the future. Even bad memories are inverted as good ones—if they were in the past they were wrapped up and finished with: he came through that period and survived, and he gets an illusion of security. He cries for yesterday and this has made him very lonely.'

◆ ◆ ◆

In the same way that Sellers did not acknowledge contractual commitments, if they got in the way of his whims, Sellers did not believe that death put you beyond his reach. He chewed the fat with both Joseph Grimaldi (1779–1837) and Dan Leno (1860–1904) on various occasions. 'Do you hear his voice the way you hear my voice now?' inquired Peter Evans, about Leno. 'Yes, absolutely as clear as that,' replied Sellers, 'I mean a clear, clear voice, as if someone is speaking, but in *here*,' and he tapped his skull. 'Is the voice spontaneous, unpredictable, or must you call on it, summon its presence?' continued Evans. 'Sometimes I ask for help, sometimes it just happens. It can happen anytime, anytime at all.'

The inner voices made him next start to believe in the transmigration of souls—he had *been* Leno in an earlier existence—and this theory he put about during the making of *The Optimists of Nine Elms*, which is full of authentic Leno jokes and songs. (I increasingly think of old Sam as the greatest performance, mainly because, in the teeth of a plot about children and animals, Sellers totally avoids the sentimental, to which he was otherwise so prone.) When he starred in *The Bobo*, Sellers thought he'd been possessed by the spirits of gored bullfighters and, whilst on location in Italy, he decided he'd had something to do with the Colosseum and that he'd probably 'been a priest in Roman days.'

Sellers first set about earnestly communicating with the past when Larry Stephens, the Wingate Raider, Goon collaborator, and uncredited tinkerer with *The Ladykillers* screenplay, died at a young age. Sellers had been pleased with his material and wanted him to continue with their working relationship. He got Stephens, on his deathbed, to agree that 'when he died he would make every possible effort to get back. One day I just had a feeling that he wanted to contact me. So I went to see Estelle Roberts with that in mind...' As usual, her room was packed with ghosts. 'She suddenly turned her head and started to speak to someone... "The young man you wanted to contact," she said, "has only been over this side a very short time and he's somewhat confused, so he's got nothing to say to you other than to give you an identification that you will recognise." I asked her what it was. She said, "Fred", which is the name we use as a Patron Saint. All things are built around Fred! I knew then that it *was* Larry. Estelle said that if I made further attempts later on he'll have many things to tell me...'

When it came down to it, Sellers had no confidence in the present and refused to stay there. As I argued in Chapter Four, 'The Goon Show', a bow window to exhibit his paranoia and render it comic, mocks nineteenth-century ideals of heroism. It is a look back in anger. Then, becoming a film star character actor, and being able to keep changing his own face, obviously satisfied a need; and I wonder if, in some obscure way, the versatility and the fear of death (i.e. Sellers' mourning in advance over his own disintegration) are connected? And did the mysticism and langour, which went on working underneath, and the commingling of his identities, which is what went on when he was acting, have a sensual significance? If his watching his mother in 'Fire and the Woman' was the formative experience I think it was, the answer to both questions is yes. 'My mother used to appear in sketches,' he said in 1962. 'There was an act in which a girl dressed in white tights stood against a screen, the coloured slides were projected onto the screen, so that she appeared to be wearing various costumes—she might be Britannia, for instance, or she might be a butterfly. I used to see my mother doing that; she looked very beautiful.'

It was as if Peg had lived for millions of years, and had been every heroine and brilliant creature; and between the clicks of the magic lantern, she and the screen were suffused with eerie, pearly light—she was a white goddess, pure and chaste. Sellers tried all his life to join her in everlastingness. His wives were foster-mothers; his acclaimed character, Chance, a spotless child grown to a man's dimensions, was a dutiful and docile son (and he's blissfully impotent, as Shirley MacLaine's Mother Eve discovers).

'He was still a child,' says Milligan, 'running away from its mother, who keeps looking back, seeing how far he can go before she stops him. "How far can I get away?" he's saying, "and still be safe?"'

◆ ◆ ◆

But his favourite time-machine, the toy which really warmed his heart, was his camera. 'I love the workings of a camera,' he cooed. 'I always want to open it up while it's working and watch it. I've ruined more film that way!'—which was a pity, because a camera, with its dials, levers, cogs, springs, and motors, is clockwork that retains the past, as Sellers knew.

'He had a habit,' Simon Williams told me, 'of holding up conversations or outings we were on to take pictures. "Quickly, quickly, take a photo! *Now!* We're all so enjoying ourselves!" He *loved* taking photographs. It was as though he didn't want to have anything to do with the moment *now*; he wanted to look back and see people and places with the benefit of hindsight. He was retrospective. "Sorry, it doesn't seem to be focusing," I said, when he'd thrust this solid gold Olympus at me. You see, in the view-finder he had his own prescription lens. In all my imaginings of the trappings I'd have as a rich person, I'd never have thought up that one.'

As Sellers had always felt lonely, at a distance, he naturally had an affinity with a camera, the voyeur's gadget. (When his aunt gave him his first Box Brownie, 'I felt a magical thrill running through my body.') On the obvious level, he enjoyed the technology and the jargon; the speed at which you could create; the images bubbling up like magic from the tanks and acid baths in the darkroom. But on a deeper level, as Williams perceived, Sellers was responding to photography's mortuary aspects. Freezing the frame, arresting time, the cameraman makes little bits of the past, its images and occurrences, safe. You are able to attest, later on, that something happened; that you existed. Looking over an album (or screening your old movies), you can watch yourself ageing and dying. An odd effect in the patchwork quilt that's *The Trail of the Pink Panther* is Clouseau's weight fluctuations from scene to scene, as the editor embroidered material gathered from across a twenty-year span.

Photography, which gave Sellers what Roland Barthes, in his book *Camera Lucida*, calls a 'certificate of presence'—ocular proof of being there—also served to remind him that he'd once been younger, happier, than he was now; less near the grave. So his archive, accumulated to confirm he'd had a past and to authenticate his fun, didn't make life any more acceptable to him. Indeed, as a man always foreseeing his own death—with soothsayers and all the rest of it—photography added to his agony. Before he left for London, the Dorchester Hotel, and his dying day, there were bonfires amongst the snow and ice of his Alpine retreat. He destroyed all his souvenirs. Having laboured to recreate and conserve the past by recording the present, he suddenly had a new horror—that the albums, etc., would outlast him. When he looked at his snaps, all he saw (Barthes again) was 'what is dead, what is about to die.'

Some items survived the inferno. Sellers had a commission once, straight out of *Lolita*, to photograph famous people's teenage daughters. I have a magazine clipping of one in the series: Jennifer Selznick frolicking on a beach. A girl is wrapped in layers of shawl and chiffon, she waves a hat, and she is chasing a pelican. Sellers has bled away the colour and the background. The girl is about to vanish into her capes, and the whole thing is sunless, flimsy, fading out. Elwood Rickless, Sellers' executor, remarks that 'Peter was only able to express himself through photography. At the chalet in Switzerland, there was a photo, taken in Sweden, of an old lady looking forlornly out of a double-paned window. Symbolic, I now see; for, like Sellers, she's totally cut off.'

He let the lens tell of his loneliness. Steven Bach, the United Artists vizier allocated to *The Romance of the Pink Panther*, detected something of Sellers' troubled spirit reflected in a blown-up still. Bach was taken on a tour of La Haute Grange and recalls that its master 'displayed quiet pride [in the] professional-quality photographs, one of which I especially admired, a nature photograph of a bird in flight, backlit by a starburst sun…' A little after Sellers had died, Bach received a cardboard tube in the mail, with a note from Sue Evans, Sellers' secretary: 'Mr Sellers wanted you to have this.' It was that silhouetted summer bird, cold and sharp.

The few Sellers pictures I've personally seen all oddly mapped his isolation: he took snaps of lonely creatures and abandoned, ruined things. As I look at the half dozen prints beside me as I write, their mournful message is unmistakable. If Sellers intended to speak from beyond the grave, he does so in the play of light and shadow on these crinkled leaves. The photographs are desolate, yet somehow pensive—Sellers has become the ghost in the machine. (He *was* a camera.)

The human story in the café scene is a sad one—all those empty tables and couples hurrying past. Sellers has no company except the ice bucket. Five people are glancing or staring his way, but a tall girl in dark glasses looks in the other direction—haughtily so, perhaps. The camera here is a Peeping Tom. But it is not the girl who captures my interest; it's the left-overs and ephemerality, which get in by accident, which I find rather telling.

For sheer bleakness, there's nothing to beat the portrait of a gnarled tree trunk, a giant piece of driftwood, striated and embedded with pebbles. Sellers was evidently fascinated with the shape and texture of the broken roots and branches. The object is almost alive. The effect is not of something worn and neglected, but of majesty and power (like Henry Moore's bronzes), and for a long time I thought that was that. Sellers had found and photographed a totem, a symbol of his aloneness and desire for preservation. (He had his name down for his corpse to be cryogenically suspended when he died.)

As I gaze at the photograph anew, however, I don't see Sellers identifying with the ancient storm-tossed megalith. I think that when he came across it, so concentrated and growing out of the shingle, his emotion was more like envy and resentment. He had no strength against it. The beauty of the object, twisted and blackened and crooked, is that it doesn't need to know what to do with itself; it is an image of soullessness. Greyness and cold are the subjects of the other pictures, too. Sellers seems to have gone out on his own very early one morning to take shots of lakes and ponds. Threadbare trees, in which no birds sing, criss-cross the photographs. (The woods are made of skeletons.) Wispy briars and branches and the ripples from the water further scratch and splinter the scene; there's a line of iron railings, like needles, and, in the distance, some sort of knoll where a goblin, or changeling, seems to be dancing. It is the Peter Pan statue in Kensington Gardens, and it looms out of the fog as a tiny angel of death.

'Sellers' photographs,' I said to Milligan. 'These gnarled trees and deserted beaches, and the desolation he managed to convey in his pictures of the Peter Pan are pictures of what was going on inside him...'

'His inner world, yes. Photography—the art of loneliness in pursuit of the lonely. The only things that didn't let him down were his gadgets. Cars fitted with tape recorders, televisions, telephones. He had to surround himself with material gadgets to make him forget he was alone. The films; the salary; the fact he got a long way from Southsea, where he was born; a long way too from touring with his parents' vaudeville act; the RAF; India and Germany; six weeks at the Windmill; seven [sic] years with 'The Goon Show'; three children; plays; pantomimes—yet it all came to nothing.'

◆ ◆ ◆

The dust-and-ashes scenario has a romantic appeal, but it is not quite accurate. His look of being alone was part of his genius as a performer. So many of his characters are stranded—the librarian, the old general, the union boss; or consider Mr Topaze, in the forgotten feature film Sellers directed and put much of himself into, standing on the chilly château terrace. 'Has your money bought you happiness?' asked Tamise, chancing by with a party of school children. 'I'm buying it now,' says Topaze, cynically. 'Then I'll leave you to your shopping,' says Tamise—the last line of the film, given a push and plangency by Michael Gough. Gough wanders away with his pupils; and it is Sellers (not just Topaze) who is left in a corner of that great cinemascope screen; a tiny figure, marooned and morose.

How else could Sellers have been? What else could he have done? His relationship with Milligan, during 'The Goon Show' years, was marked by envy and suspicion. He never had humility (like Guinness) and his attempts at self-abasement (yoga, gurus, etc.) come across as conceit. Auberon Waugh was surely correct when he remarked that, when Sellers was eulogising the Swami Venkesananda, 'I could not avoid the suspicion that part of his fascination is that Mr Sellers could study his accents, his intonations and gestures, and practise them quietly to himself in the bathroom afterwards.' He was always acting, acting, and in the end he was as mad as the vexed sea.

Sellers' selfishness and sullenness may have been connected with his being a whopping case of arrested development; he may have presented himself as the put-upon clown: 'People are all wrong about me... They think I'm a pretty funny feller. So they ask me to bazaars and cocktail parties and dinner parties and expect me to be funny all the time. Don't underestimate the effect of this, day after day, on the nerves and the patience.' He may have been quick to take offense and yield to a nervous frenzy, but a lot of it was pseudo-immaturity; behind the blankness he could be cunning, and he was quite aware of the apologies and allowances people were making on his behalf. And to say that his life and work all came to nothing except loneliness is contradicted by the facts. Nobody said to me, during the four years I spent on this book, 'Peter *who*?'

Sellers goes on. His children have had children and they all walk the earth (Michael's son is named William, for his great-grandfather); they have survived, and 'no one can deprive us of our memories... and we bear the name of Sellers with pride'. Secondly, over a dozen years since his death, every day I seem to meet somebody who had a brush with him and did not forget it: I have come to believe that everybody in the world had a chance encounter with my subject. Sellers, when he wasn't at the centre of your attention, getting himself over-wrought, was most likely the other side of the revolving door, or getting up to leave just as you came in, or alongside you at a hotel waiting for the lift. (Sellers, with an accomplice, would ride up and down in elevators pretending to pick pockets.)

At the edge of the frame, just out of reach, making his departure: Sellers seems to have been both omnipresent and insubstantial. The despot, the prankster, the rakehell; the lunatic, the lover, and very likely the poet as well, playing hide-and-seek. 'All you could do,' says Milligan, 'was watch him. Meeting him was like interviewing a ghost: "Will he turn up tonight, emotionally?"' There is, at least, for posterity his body of films and sound recordings; cryogenics notwithstanding, Sellers is unlikely to succeed in repossessing or altering his work at this late stage. Though he was the first to suggest things be abandoned midway, he always found it difficult to accept that a film was finished. *I Love You, Alice B. Toklas* and *The Prisoner of Zenda* he tried to have reedited; *Hoffman* he wanted to buy and destroy; *The Fiendish Plot of Dr Fu Manchu* he insisted on re-shooting.

◆ ◆ ◆

Since he died forever in 1980, he has been an effigy, reliant on the TV transmission of his films and availability on videotape to be given the illusion of life. The ghostly traces and hidden presences revealed in photographs are one thing, but if you really want to summon up remembrance of things past, look at old movies. In their diffusion of light and masses of shade they are little poems about life and death. Fred Kite's gaslit living room; Mr Martin's dreary counting-house, with its creaking floorboards and retinue of goblinesque clerks; the bunker in *Doctor Strangelove*, created out of deep and bold shadow; in *The Blockhouse*, a candlelit crypt. Morganhall, in *The Dock Brief*, is as pale as a dead leaf, his skin the same grey wash as the prison wall behind him; in the morning-after debris of Clare Quilty's gothic mansion, the melancholy mood seeps out of, or into, the black and white film stock. And Sellers could be frostbitten in colour, too: General Fitzjohn, for example, his scarlet tunic unbuttoned, framed against a marble grate (in which no fire flickers), tells his doctor that 'I make a noise, frightening the housemaids, Lord of the Manor... and the world says "what a man." But I'm empty, my friend. There's nobody inside. I'm alone... I'm afraid.'

Behind the voice, a clock ticks slowly, immutably. Sellers' head is held in close-up and in profile, and it is one of those moments in his films when his own intense personal conflicts are being confided. (Wolf Mankowitz wrote the screenplay for *Waltz of the Toreadors* and he knew exactly what to get Sellers to draw on.) If he did his best, with toys and tantrums, to evade having to live a real life, he could, at least, when these gambits failed, transform his life, work out his problems, by pretending to be somebody else. Sellers' films are particularly elegiac because, cast often as shuffling, wheezing grandads and crotchety fogies, he plays an age on the screen he never managed to reach as an individual. When he was young he enjoyed looking old, and he didn't get to be old.

There'd been the disturbed childhood, with none of a child's habits. He was like a dwarf—little, but treated as if he was cocksure and big. So when he was big he was (privately) childish and (professionally) a veteran; when he talked about his childhood what mostly came back to him were the smells—especially the pomade and toilet water, the mildew and rot, the dirt and decay, of backstage at the music hall: a catacomb smell?

'Peg,' says Milligan, 'sacrificed her responsibility to her husband and made Peter the head of the household. Any time of the day or night, he would call out "Peg, Peg," and she'd drop everything and come running immediately.' He'd never been a real child, as he was never allowed to play or develop; and precociously invested with a patriarch's power, he could be intensely infantile, and get away with it, as a Roman Emperor would. Perhaps only in acting *very* old indeed could he envisage a spot of calm. Henry Crun's senility is the obvious comic example. He's so dotty, he's in a world of his own, filled with Victorian bric-à-brac and weird inventions. Then there's rheumy William Mate Cobblers, over-extending his official powers as commissionaire or car park attendant. But, leaving these caricatures to one side, what concerns us now is the twilit atmospherics in the films which followed *The Ladykillers*, and the way in which Sellers seemed to be trying to be on good terms with death—so that it would be like a continuation of life. He was a man who played old men when virtually a juvenile; he was a man who kept prophesying his own death, even in his early years.

◆ ◆ ◆

Possibly he felt that, if he was elderly in his films, he'd stay young in real life—his films functioning like Dorian Gray's portrait. It comes as a shock, watching *The Mouse that Roared*, to see the owlish milky-pudding that's Tully Bascombe. Sellers is suddenly playing a character of his own age (thirty-something), and it must be said he's rather unsatisfying. The romantic scenes with Jean Seberg make us want to look away, they are so gauche. But Sellers was thrilled to be doing them at the time. 'I hear you have a love scene,' said a journalist. 'Is it serious?' 'Quite serious,' replied Sellers.

But Sellers lacked the pungency to be valiant, solid. Infirmity, indeed, is necessary to his style of acting—the ability to slip and slide and adapt. What Sellers seemed to think all kissing and cuddling on the screen required was that the folk up there doing it be good-looking; he wasn't worried by context or emotion. When

The Mouse that Roared was completed, therefore, and he inevitably disowned it, it was his vanity which was affronted. 'I enjoyed myself more as the Grand Duchess than I did playing myself in the love scenes,' he commented truthfully.

The Grand Duchess, as I've said elsewhere, is Crystal Jollibottom and his own grandmother; Count Mountjoy, the Prime Minister, is done as Alec Guinness. With this pair Sellers is rambunctious. He didn't make a sloppy Tully Bascombe mistake again—not until he was rich, famous, and emaciated, when he did it all the time.

Sellers started to avoid his genius when he began to fancy his chances as Cary Grant or Gary Cooper. Observers like Milligan must have encouraged him in this ambition, for Milligan said to me that: 'With his degree of artifice ... he was uncanny. An uncanny actor.' Milligan is in the right of it about the spectral quality, the illusionism, but Sellers, even at his most trim and debonair, could never have the self-assurance and glow of a matinée idol. Some things cannot be imitated: when Sellers turns on his wan charm and opens his brown faraway eyes wide, we are in for mush and gracelessness. He's trivialising his talent. When it comes to the yearnings and reveries of duffers, nuts, and clumsy chaps like John Lewis, however, and the actor in him is not erecting ornamental facades, Sellers is just about the most rhapsodic operator of his generation—and of the previous generation, which is where he insinuated himself.

◆ ◆ ◆

The Ladykillers was his finishing school. He was the apprentice, Guinness (his nearest contemporary in the cast, being only a decade his senior) the sorcerer. Harry Robinson, as a crook too old for the modish togs he affects, is almost a satire on how Sellers might have dressed for Peg, suppressing his real age. (Sellers would like to have been the man that time forgot.) 'The first actor I found who was really wonderful to work with was Alec Guinness,' said Sellers. 'Although I didn't have much to do with him, the little I did was a great help ... But I wasn't particularly good, and nothing else happened for about a year.' Well, only 'The Goon Show' and other radio appearances, all the television experience and the modest one-reelers, which I have dealt with; and there was *The Smallest Show on Earth*.

Conceived by William Rose (who'd dreamt up *The Ladykillers*) as a local riposte to Cecil B. De Mille's *The Greatest Show on Earth*, the film is muted, monochrome, and, where De Mille was overblown and festive, an object lesson in the art of film acting. Modesty and quiet are its virtues, decay and moribundity its moods, wet and cold its setting.

As the story of a crumbling pleasure palace, the Bijou Kinema, its fate, and its inhabitants, *The Smallest Show on Earth* neatly encapsulates the themes of stopped clocks and revenants which I've been running off at the mouth about in this chapter. Sellers plays Percy Quill, the projectionist, and he's one-of-three alongside the veteran Bernard Miles, as Old Tom, the commissionaire, and Margaret Rutherford, as Mrs Fazackalee, the pit pianist during the silent movie days and now the lady in the box office. The plot, in which Virginia McKenna and Bill

Travers, as Jean and Matt Spencer, an insipid couple who inherit the fleapit from an unseen shag called Great Uncle Simon, do their best to flog it to developers who'll pull it down and build a car park, need not detain us long.

Luckily, we can look behind and beyond the Spensers and their dignity to take in the true star of the film—the Bijou itself. Whether or not the original audiences, back in the fifties, were meant to agree with Matt and Jean that it's a derelict and worthless place, that's not how it comes across now. It is a tiny, lost, Edwardian paradise, tucked under a railway arch, wreathed in smoke and brimstone from the passing trains. The cinema, a domed and ornate Moorish temple with barley sugar pillars and gloomy framed pictures of forgotten idols from the infancy of the flicks, seems cut out by scissors from the shadows and black air. 'It was a theatre way back; then a music hall; then an electric theatre,' Mr Quill and his cohorts explain; they are the resident spooks.

The cinema is an architectural fantasia, like Mrs Wilberforce's villa in *The Ladykillers*. In *The Smallest Show on Earth*, Mr Quill's projection booth is out-of-kilter. As he gets increasingly crotchety over the capricious levers and knobs, popping light bulbs, and clanking magic lanterns, Sellers' character feels the need to take sustaining nips from a whisky bottle. The cracked lenses, mismatched canisters of film, and lost spools are the little cinema's equivalent of a senior citizen's decrepitude, hearing impairment, and dimming eyes; Quill loves and adores his equipment as he would if nursing his own dotard of a relative. He is the only man in the world who can keep the junk going. He is married to it.

If you wanted a single instance of Sellers' superior skills as an actor—some proof that he's in the first rank—you need look no further than his scenes with Margaret Rutherford in *The Smallest Show on Earth*. It's not that she doesn't swamp him, or that he successfully conceals the fact that he is three decades her junior. It has nothing to do with technique or tricks. What we notice is that Sellers and Margaret Rutherford can invest the material with more hush and resonance than perhaps its writers were aware of. There's a drollery about what they do; a fine, intuitive grasp—a clairvoyance, if you like. Dame Margaret once said that 'I am always surprised that audiences think me funny at all'—and it is similar, slightly whacky sincerity which Sellers brings to his work, and it turns his acting into a series of miraculous moments.

In *The Smallest Show on Earth*, Quill, Fazackalee, and Old Tom don't walk in and out of their scenes and cubby holes; they seem to shimmer, disembodied, from the other side of mottled mirrors; they are at one with the dust and flecks of paint and shadowy alcoves. Quill enjoys himself, in his eyrie, projecting *Killer Riders of Wyoming* and *Mystery of Hell Valley*; but there are never many people out front. Mrs Fazackalee, squat in the guichet as if it was a sedan chair, doesn't sell tickets, she accepts poultry or vegetables as barter.

When the Express whistles across the viaduct, Quill's apparatus has a seizure; on another occasion, the three old eccentrics, having the place to themselves, watch a silent movie, Cecil Hepworth's *Comin' Through the Rye* of 1916. Margaret Rutherford strums Chopin at the piano, Bernard Miles, on his own in the stalls, strokes the Bijou's cat, and Sellers, transfixed, moves out of the darkness to explain what's afoot to the young couple, who realise they've blundered in on magic— 'classics, you might say,' says Quill, with tears in his eyes. The caption on the screen in front of him says: 'When you return this rye will be harvested, and this field as empty as your heart.'

Like the influx of fairies, singing and gossiping, in *The Ladykillers*, the scene's arrival is both a surprise and inevitable, and it is enchanting in more ways than one. The surprise is that there was room for it, amongst the gathering plotlines. The inevitability lies in the fact that Sellers, Rutherford, and Miles are so well fitted for it; it extends and deepens the mood their characters would otherwise only give us in glimpses. The scene stands alone, and *The Smallest Show on Earth* would be nothing without it. Quill and his colleagues seem to have floated off the silver nitrate, tricks of the light. As they enjoy their session with sweet silent films, time is hanging in the air. Everything is evanescent, tenebrous.

We can only guess at the reverberations *The Smallest Show on Earth* set off in Sellers personally—decaying vaudeville venues of his youth, come back, as it were, to haunt him. But though Quill is tetchy, snappy, there is no bitterness—only nostalgia. As Milligan discovered, Sellers only really believed in yesterday (when all his troubles seemed so far away); '*Yesterday*,' Sellers once yelled at him. 'I get upset thinking about yesterday, because it's gone and it's so bloody buried, so irredeemable, and nobody seems to care. I can cry for yesterday.'

You can bet that he did give way to such jags of self-pity, and he'd have enjoyed monitoring himself being so moved, too. But though the general uncertainty over where his acting stopped and real life resumed was going to be a big problem, we can at least acknowledge that, when fully inhabiting a character, as he does Quill, Sellers, convincingly old before his time, can put his neurosis to beautiful use. When asked, in March 1959, which was his favourite rôle to date, Sellers said 'Peter Quill' ('with an affectionately reminiscent smile'). That he misremembered the name (it's *Percy* Quill) and substituted his own is a slip I'll leave the followers of Dr Freud to elucidate.

◆ ◆ ◆

The Smallest Show on Earth is quaint, as is *The Ladykillers* (for all that Professor Marcus' scarlet-rimmed eyes peer minatorily from the mauves, lavenders, and violet tints). The films, along with *Battle of the Sexes* and *The Mouse that Roared*, are quintessential Ealing comedies—except that only *The Ladykillers* is officially in that category. Sir Michael Balcon had sold his studio to the BBC in December 1955 (the very month in which *The Ladykillers* was released), for £350,000 (almost three-quarters of a million dollars), bringing to an end what Philip Kemp has called 'the faintly public school, all-together chaps flavour,' which had given the populace *Passport to Pimlico*, *Whisky Galore!*, *The Lavender Hill Mob*, and (famously) *Kind Hearts and Coronets*, as well as making heroes out of John Mills (*Scott of the Antarctic*) and Jack Hawkins (*The Cruel Sea*), among much else, mostly involving Alec Guinness. Artists and technicians had enjoyed the security of permanent contracts, and with the dispersal of the cottage industry to Pinewood (run by the Rank Organisation) or Elstree and Borehamwood (MGM), a certain confident and elegant tone left the British cinema forever.

Sellers, therefore, got the benefit of the last five minutes of Ealing proper and made use of its graduates and faculty before they themselves spun off into outer space and variously fragmented. What did linger longer was what Balcon called the 'spirit'. Meaning what? At its worst, a wartime patriotism that verged on xenophobia; at its best, a send-up of the British citizen's belief that the world begins and ends in London. As Constance Cummings (an American who now lives in Oxfordshire) said to me: 'Those films are so *English*. Their saving grace was their small-scale and inner zaniness. There was a zany sense of humour, no matter how *straight* they were done.' Perhaps, to foreigners, there's something automatically hysterical about John Mills' and Jack Hawkins' imperturbability? The way emotion is suppressed and valiant deeds are shrugged off as being of no consequence? The magnificent modesty?

It took Guinness, a knight of doleful countenance, a reincarnation of Sir Andrew Aguecheek, to imply the anarchic streak that lay beneath the orderliness and punctuality, the uniformity and discipline; he brought out Ealing's, and therefore the gentlemen in England's, latent comic spirit. (He is even kitted out, in *The Man in the White Suit*, in quilted home-made armour, and he brandishes a round table as a shield, as if purposely alluding to the chivalric theme.) Sellers, drilled in the violence and riot of 'The Goon Show', took the midsummer madness one stage further. If Guinness' characters were singular, dignified, then Sellers', once he started to receive star-billing, would be selfish and grasping—and I'm chiefly thinking, here, of Wee Sonny MacGregor in *The Naked Truth*, the film which followed *The Smallest Show on Earth*, and for which Sellers held high hopes: 'I want to be a star like mad,' he said. 'This is my first starring rôle in a film. I hope it clicks, because then I can get my teeth into other interesting rôles. That's what being a star means to me—being able to pick and choose.'

First, he had to seek permission from the BBC to be released from his radio commitments, so he could go to Walton-on-Thames Studios for the make-up tests. If this might seem a courteous enough request, it wasn't the way Sellers handled it. He wrote for the dispensation on May 21, 1958. The make-up test was the previous Friday.

◆◆◆

Had you been leaning over the railings on the little footbridge that crosses the River Windrush, upstream from Ascott-under-Wychwood, sometime towards the end of the last decade, you would have seen an interesting sight. Along the edge of a ploughed field two characters approach, gesticulating and talking at the tops of their voices. Kenneth Griffith is remembering his old colleague, Sellers; his companion on this occasion—namely, the present author—is doing his best, whilst clambering through bush and briar, to take mental notes on the speech.

'I remember him with great joy; and one of the most interesting aspects of it personally, these days, since he's *died*, is I quite often, when I observe something that is very funny, I long for him to be there—because his appreciation of it would be so extraordinary, and would add to my *own* appreciation ... And of course he could be ridiculous himself. Whether Peter ever saw himself as funny, I don't know. I think he probably did. We never discussed this.'

'There's a vulnerability and sadness somewhere in his life that comes across,' I said. 'We see it represented in *Being There*, and in *Only Two Can Play* there's a melancholy about that man's life and situation that Sellers gets at. Otherwise it would be an ordinary British comedy about adultery and it's not ...'

'Kingsley Amis' original novel, *That Uncertain Feeling*, though pretty heavily done over by Bryan Forbes. But of course Peter was like that, too. He was most of the time melancholy and troubled by his own fate. He had ... terrible doubts ... so I don't think he ever tackled a job, so far as I know, without this compulsion that he couldn't do it, and he must get out of it. Which included, of course, *Only Two Can Play*—but every film, and I was in seven films with him, starting with *The Naked Truth*.

'The first time I ever saw him, I was walking up Shaftesbury Avenue, and ... it was very early on in his career; he was just beginning to make a name—and Sellers was quite clearly delighted with me, and he showed that right to the very end, and I can recall two specific occasions. Once, on *I'm All Right, Jack*, when I had to report to Mr Kite that so-and-so had been working hard. Sellers says "Very commendable, lad."—*Very commendable*, was it? Wonderful!—Well, at the end of my little bit of terrible sneakery ... Sellers started to clap his hands. He did it again on *Only Two Can Play*—my first bit of filming on the terrace coming out of the house in Swansea, and I did something spontaneously eccentric, which was rather nerve-wracking, because I wasn't a star like Sellers who could do what he wanted ... And as my character left his house, swerving down the street, one arm swung and the other didn't, as he went off, and Sellers again applauded. "How *did* you *think* of that, boy?" Fascinated. Tremendous encouragement, from one who insisted that I was his peer. In fact he treated me better than that. His acts of generosity ... And on *The Naked Truth* I had an *astonishing* experience with him. I was his slightly gay dresser.'

'The relationship between the two of them is ambivalent,' I said. 'I think that's what gives Wee Sonny a certain strangeness.'

'Yes, yes, the characters do obviously care for each other in their own frigid manner ... But the experience was this: I went to view the rushes one day, and I was *appalled* at myself ... So all I could do was walk onto the empty sound stage in a state of *shock*; and I found Sellers there, in a terrible mood ... I'd never seen him in a bad temper before—and I said "What do you think of the film?" And he said coldly ... "What do you think I think of the fucking rushes? *Terrible*." ... I said: "Well, I must say, I was very shocked at what I'd done ..." He said "*What?* ... You were fucking marvellous—*that was the trouble*. ME. Did you see *ME*! It was *terrible*. What do you mean 'You'? You are what's made it worse for ME ..."

'Very interesting. I still believe I'd done something I shouldn't have chosen to do in a scene; but it was his *deep distress* which amazes me to this day. But... we became very close friends. On *The Naked Truth*, because he had a car and a chauffeur, I travelled with him a lot. He took me home... to my little mews cottage in the only poor part of Belgravia, from work one day... and he was in a very gloomy mood about his agent. So I told Sellers about John Redway, with whom I didn't hit it off very well. He was not a deep man, and if your face didn't immediately fit he could ignore you a bit, which was very serious for an actor/agent relationship. Anyway, I preached his virtues to Peter, who... said "Do you think John Redway would look after me?" Now by this time, of course... he was famous. I said, "Peter, I'm sure he would."... So I phoned up John Redway immediately with Sellers sitting there, and I remember it very clearly, because John said... "Are you serious?" "Yes." And Sellers brought Dennis Selinger with him, who was his personal manager, I think, from the Grade Organisation.'

'Did you know Sellers socially?'

'I knew him and his first wife very well as a couple. Anne... was, as could be said, his best wife. Good, loving, caring. She talked to me quite often about how, once he'd got a lot of money, that everything became nothing; she said, "If I wanted a mink coat, he said 'get one'." So all treats disappeared. I talked to them *both* about keeping their feet on the ground, and I urged them both to travel on public transport, to which Sellers thought, immediately, that's a very good idea... So of course he takes Anne on the Underground, and she's wearing a mink and he's Peter Sellers... And that would be it. He'd do it once. That would be it.'

◆ ◆ ◆

Sellers acted the rôle of being a star long before he officially was one—though nobody seems to have objected. That limousine, for example, which collected Kenneth Griffith and took him to the studios for *The Naked Truth*, was actually a Hillman Minx piloted by Sellers' cousin, Ray Ray; each evening, having dropped Kenneth Griffith off at 'the only poor part of Belgravia' (Pimlico), Sellers returned, not to a mansion with swimming pools and orgy rooms, but to 83, Oakleigh Avenue, Whetstone, N20, whither he had moved, on July 15, 1956, from Muswell Hill. The house, mock-Tudor and suburbanly nondescript on the outside, was soon gutted, painted bright colours, and turned into a personal nursery. 'It was virtually a semi-detached place,' recalls Peter Evans. 'A little house full of expensive camera and hi-fi equipment, a drum kit, and toys for the children—all in the most appalling taste, and in such abundance you couldn't get in through the door.' When the local picture palace was demolished, Sellers bought the blue velvet seats, and other odds and ends, and built his own private Bijou Kinema in the attic—except that he called it the 'B. Jew,' and had this name stencilled on the beams. Here, pretending to be Louis B. Meyer, or some such magnifico, he arranged for screenings of the classics, in eight millimetre. (There were electrically operated curtains, organ music, the works.)

'It was a very modest house,' recalls Ian Carmichael, 'with... a cinema up in the loft, up under the eaves. He used to hire films. "What would you like to see next weekend?" I said "Audrey Hepburn and Fred Astaire in *Funny Face*," which he loved.'

The film would have been not only unspooling there in his own house—it was also right up Sellers' street. *Funny Face*, directed by Stanley Donen in 1957, is a musical based on the antics of Richard Avedon, the photographer (played by Fred Astaire). Astaire goes off to Paris to shoot a fashion spread with Audrey Hepburn, a bookshop clerk duckling he's turned into a swan. What we (or Sellers) will have noticed, in watching it, is the discrepancy in ages: Astaire was thirty years older than Hepburn. When his desiccated nimbleness and her gaminesque charms come together, we think of a hypnotist and his victim; the young girl is brought out by the old man in disturbing, psychological ways. As Astaire's character literally has (Givenchy) designs on Hepburn's, the magical transformation of appearance and personality has a sinister, rapacious underside; the how's-your-father plot of *Lolita* is not far away at all.

With visions of Hollywood, flashbulbs popping, and spinning *Variety* front pages dancing under the pantiles, Sellers thought he'd best start dressing like a star, and: 'You never saw such a bloody mess,' remembers Milligan. 'He was mad to look good and wore every accoutrement from the tailor except the ticket of sale. He wore gloves, a trilby hat—if there'd been a face-mask he'd have worn one of those as well. He'd leave his raincoat open to show that he had a single-breasted jacket underneath—thereby getting his inner self wet at the same time.' The ambitious poseur was noted by Peggy Mount, too.

'We first met', she tells me, 'because we were both handled by the same man in the Lew and Leslie Grade Organisation, Monty Lyon... Sellers had a small part in the Palladium pantomime. He told me that his performance had overrun the night before, so he met with a certain amount of verbal criticism for doing so. Peter was put out. "I'll show Val Parnell when I'm a star," he said. "Go on!" I replied. "You'll never be a star any more than I shall." Fate decreed otherwise and, as you say, we met again making *The Naked Truth*...'

It was also to be Sellers' first film with Terry-Thomas. Thomas had been born and bred in Finchley and hated the place. He also hated his family for not being posh. 'I was ashamed of the lot of them,' he said, 'I just hated listening to their ill-formed vowels.' His double-breasted blazers, carnations, suede shoes, monocle, and cigarette-holder were all attempts to appear a gentleman—though, of course, he failed miserably and simply came across as exaggeratedly genteel; that was all right by Hollywood, of course, who eventually made him their (his words) 'favourite silly-ass Englishman'. He was a beautifully-dressed bounder, who played scoundrels on the screen and was a shit in real life. He held it against Sellers that he resided in Oakleigh Avenue: Sellers 'seemed just a typical suburban father. Perhaps that was because he lived in Barnet, which to me was another Finchley—*dreadful!*' That wasn't all. He also disliked Sellers for being a Jew. To Thomas, the adoption of 'very old-fashioned manners' meant you didn't really approve of Jews. He complained to Stanley Kramer, the director of *It's a Mad, Mad,*

Mad, Mad World, that as 'I am the only non-Jew in this huge cast, it's pretty tough going.'

Thomas' contempt expressed his fear of competition. He took rôle after rôle in Hollywood, as gentlemen's gentleman, cads, or Colonel Blimps, saying 'I'd hate myself forever if I turned them down—especially if, for instance, Peter Sellers took them.' Nevertheless, he believed Sellers' vocal dexterity 'a bit of a waste of time,' and he at no time took the trouble to see that his rival had a skewed, intense manner on the screen, which made audiences keep wanting to watch him to see what he'd do next. There's something uncharted about Sellers. But Terry-Thomas was Terry-Thomas. He had no mystique. He never gave a rôle any shading.

The difference between them as actors (and as temperaments)—Sellers' sombreness and giddiness, Thomas' sneers—is exploited in film after film, starting with *The Naked Truth*, and going on to include *Tom Thumb*, *Carlton Browne of the F.O.*, and *I'm All Right, Jack*. Thomas' Lord Mayley can't abide Sellers' Wee Sonny MacGregor, the arriviste. He says things like 'My wife enjoys watching you on the television—I can't think why', and 'I never could stand you, MacGregor.' If Thomas ever did manage to rise above his habitual slick bullying, he did so when putting plenty of resentment into such lines as those. We might almost suspect him of being headlong and personal.

◆ ◆ ◆

In that he was given the chance to don a number of disguises, *The Naked Truth* is Sellers' *Kind Hearts and Coronets*; he also inherited Dennis Price. This time around, however, it is Price who is to be the murderee, not the Guinness equivalents. Sellers had been apprised of the forthcoming film by his soothsayer, Maurice Woodruff. 'You will work for a producer with Z in his name,' decreed the clairvoyant. Who could that be? Darryl F. Zanuck, of Twentieth-Century-Fox? Franco Zeffirelli, the opera director? Adolph Zukor? Florenz Ziegfeld? No. Mario Zampi, the Italian responsible for Alastair Sim's *Laughter in Paradise*, in which a practical joker leaves money to four relatives in his will, and they can only claim their inheritance by making lavish fools of themselves.

Sellers didn't get along with Zampi, finding him indecisive. 'The way you are making this film is ridiculous,' he exploded one day, exasperated by the dozens of takes. 'I know much more about the camera than you do. I'll give you one more take and then I'm off.' For once in his life, Sellers may have been right. *The Naked Truth* is poky to look at; the simple plot (the bumping off of a blackmailer) is unnecessarily complicated; there are too many characters; the whole thing lacks style. The premise, however, was a good one. Dennis Price, pretending to be the editor of a scandal sheet in which the ghastly secrets of prominent people will be revealed, bravely confronts his intended victims and explains that, for a few thousand pounds, he'll keep mum. 'Pay up in a fortnight,' he says, 'or I'll publish in a month.' What seems to me to be original about the film is that it has no hero (or heroine). They are all shits. Terry-Thomas is a racketeer and an adulterer; Peggy Mount's detective novelist, Flora Ransom, is a plagiarist and, in the long ago, was a prostitute in Shanghai (striding through her scenes in satin pyjamas, she's the only person in the film who seems wide awake); Shirley Eaton, as the model Melissa Right, is not the spotless innocent her Texan billionaire boyfriend believes her to be; and Sellers' Wee Sonny MacGregor, the much-loved television personality, is a slum landlord who charges his elderly tenants extortionate rents. In other words, the blackmailer's targets are themselves crooks—fully deserving the exposure and humiliation which ought to be coming their way, MacGregor especially.

If there's one thing Sellers never worried about as an actor it was winning the audience's sympathy. He doesn't make Sonny in the least bit nice. Off camera, the TV host's smarm instantly evaporates—it's not a commodity he wants to waste.

How much of Sonny, in fact, is Sellers? Shirley Eaton, who (as we know) had worked with him at the Palladium in *Mother Goose*, believes that the actor and the rôle were closely interlinked: 'Peter was like his *Naked Truth* character. High-spirited, taking off like a small unguided missile; he was easily upset and he'd keep interrupting conversations to open and shut windows or to move to different telephones. Peter was a curious personality—I liked him, for his vulnerable nature, and of course for his genius as a comedian; but like most people of genius he was at times very difficult. He was taken in by false admiration, and in the end he forgot the reality of himself...'

I don't think Sonny is a genius—his problem is his mediocrity, which prevents him from being a proper actor, hence the rubbish game shows, etc.—but he is played by one, and as a portrait of a neurotic who behaves badly, and who knows exactly what he is doing, Sonny is a major creation. The problem, simply, is that Sellers' spookiness and powers are too much for the little post-Ealing comedy in which they are unleashed. Sellers is overqualified for what's demanded of him— or, as he put it at the time (allowing us to read between the lines), 'I believe that directors shouldn't interfere with an interpretation of a performance. Mario and I have had differences of opinion. But then it makes life more interesting.'

Sellers even quotes from *Henry VI, Part Three*. Sonny, deciding that he'll pretend to be somebody else when carrying out the killing ('Any one of a thousand characters I can create—and then destroy, just like *that!*'), glides about his dressing room, crooning Gloucester's terrifying speech (it could be Sellers' personal motto):

Why, I can smile, and murder whiles I smile;
And cry content to that which grieves my heart;
And wet my cheeks with artificial tears,
And frame my face to all occasions.

Paradoxically, when Sonny reframes his face, all the impersonations are so fluid and shameless, it is Sellers who has become those different characters; Sonny is bypassed.

There is some severe logic behind summarising Sellers' contribution to *The Naked Truth* as a series of quick music hall (or television) sketches. In terms of the storyline, that's all Zampi will have wanted from him. But Sellers goes well beyond the clumsily-executed farce: Sonny's malignancy is beautifully shaped. He's much more the cheat than poor Dennis Price who, as a performer, has lost all the cunning he had as Louis D'Ascoyne Mazzini eight years previously. Now (and for the rest of his career—he died in 1973) all he can manage is haughtiness and/or superciliousness. His faintly Byronic good looks have disappeared, too. Where once he was curly-topped and well-fed, in *The Naked Truth* he is puffy and slightly flaccid—completely middle-aged.

The scene where he confronts Sonny about the Eastditch slums, however, is one of the most mesmerising Sellers ever played. He has little to do except walk from the stage door to Sonny's waiting taxi. On the way he is mobbed by fans and Price comes forward, wanting a quiet word. Sleepily, seamlessly, Sellers is ten different people within five yards. As the crowd engulfs him, a bird-like old lady (Edie Martin, who was Lettice, one of the fairies in *The Ladykillers*) shouts 'God bless you, Sonny!' and Sonny responds with a warm Scottish chuckle (he's every mother's favourite son), 'You tae, ma!' A pretty girl asks for his autograph, and he's suddenly smooth, telling her to call him; a plain one makes the same request, and he brusquely sees her off. Mario Fabrizi, a skinny would-be actor with a luxuriant moustache, whom Sellers actually employed as a handyman around the house and put in the background of a number of his films, says how marvellous he is—Sonny is all collusive smiles. He gives out kisses and rebuffs. Then Price appears and Sellers says with Grytpype Thynne silkiness: 'I'm so sorry I can't see you now.' Price mentions Eastditch, and Sonny's face falls.

It all happens in a few seconds, from leaving the theatre to getting in the car. It is a throwaway scene, for the blackmail threat itself is made in the ensuing footage over at Sonny's flat (with Kenneth Griffith flitting around as a witness, like a minor devil hunting for his trident). Our doubts about Price really start to pile up when he says, without irony, what a luxurious little pad his victim possesses—it is meant to be conclusive proof that Sonny has the means to meet the disbursements.

Sonny is upset about the blackmail. Not because of the money or because he is remorseful, but because he is caught out as a hypocrite. The idol of the poor old folk, who keeps the old folk poor in an insanitary block at Eastditch. His next guest, on *Here's Tae Ye*, is a fat old fellow with white hair from Eastditch, 'and what a horrible place it is …' Sonny cuts him off. He goes berserk. 'Shut up about Eastditch. *Shut up about Eastditch.* SHUT UP ABOUT EASTDITCH.' It is very ugly, and goes on too long even to begin to be funny. Sonny's rage boils out of nowhere—it's Sellers'. There's no Scottish accent, or Londoner whine, or anything like that. The sound we hear is of a crack appearing in a frozen river, and we suddenly get a glimpse of the icy green waters rushing and seething up from deep below. It is out of proportion, and yet proves how inseparable Sonny and Sellers had become. The rôle is giving tongue to the actor's feelings.

The anger is frightening (it rocks the film), but it wasn't the only time Sellers let himself fly off. In *Casino Royale* it was nearly lethal. As Joe McGrath told me: 'The first thing that happened is that he hit me, the director of this picture. We

had a fist-fight in the caravan. He threw a punch and I hit him back. We got separated by Gerry Crampton, the stunt coordinator, who saw the caravan jiggling
on its wheels… Sellers could be very nasty and surly. He hit one of the actors.
He pretended it was a mistake… but he meant it. He should have thrown a
punch, as Evelyn Tremble, and missed this guy, in one of the scenes, but Sellers
was so fed up he hit out for real. He was particularly nasty to Jacqueline Bisset,
in that scene where she holds up a bottle of champagne and he shoots the cork
out. He actually threatened her with the gun before we did the take. I said,
"Look this is being stupid, it's only a movie!" "She can't get this right," he said,
justifying himself. She really was afraid—when a gun is pointed at you it's very
definitely not funny.'

It was almost as if, as he (in Shirley Eaton's phrase) lost the reality of himself,
he'd try and push people over the edge; only then could they join him. 'You always had to watch him' says McGrath 'and figure out what mood he was in, which
way he'd jump. He told me years later, "I don't have an awful lot of friends; but
there are three people I can trust. Milligan, Harry, and you. Because we've been
through hell together. You've actually faced me and thrown a punch at me. I know
you won't put up with any shit. We know each other well enough."'

Thus spoke another Daniel Mendoza.

◆ ◆ ◆

Though, to Sellers, it was always other people who were hell, what he could
never acknowledge was that the hell they often had to endure was exclusively of
his own devising. 'I'm the one who finally has to be in control,' he said of *Casino
Royale*. 'When we were making that film, people were falling over everywhere.
Charlie Feldman was in a corner ranting and raving. Joe was in another corner in
tears—and I picked that picture up by the scruff of its neck and said: *This is what
we are going to do…*' Well, that was the version of a man who only ever believed
in his own desires and appetites. The reason that Feldman, the producer, was in
the corner ranting and raving and Joe McGrath was in tears was because Sellers
wasn't turning up, or learning his lines, or doing what he was supposed to do for
his million dollar fee. By any stretch of the imagination, there was only one person responsible for the destruction of that picture—and Sellers walked off the set
for good, eventually, after refusing to share a scene with Orson Welles.

But he never admitted to any of this. The closest he came to accepting blame
was to complain about the huge amount of money he was paid—a back-handed,
round-about sort of admission that he'd yielded to temptation and shouldn't have
done: 'I've certainly proved that I have my price. I proved that with *Casino Royale*.
I was offered a million dollars to play James Bond. And I said "You must be out
of your bloody minds, because what about Sean Connery?"… And, much, much
later, I was in Rome and they came along with a new idea that Wolf Mankowitz
had thought up—but that wasn't for a million dollars. That was only for seven
hundred and fifty thousand dollars, which wasn't enough. So every film actor has
his price…'

The more he was paid, the worse he behaved. That's about the closest we'll get to adumbrating a general rule about Sellers. If you have ever whiled away a Sunday afternoon watching *Casino Royale*, and wondered why it doesn't make a bit of sense (scenes out of sequence, the disappearance of leading actors, the attenuation of plot strands, etc.), it is because Sellers never completed his rôle. Ken Hughes, one of the many directors called in to salvage a film out of the hours of meaningless footage which had somehow accumulated, summarises:

> *Casino Royale* came to a ghastly halt. Sellers stated that he was no longer pre-pared to complete the movie. Feldman was left with a few scenes shot with Sellers but no movie. He now had to consider either closing the film down or continu-ing. Big money was involved, and he decided to go ahead... [T]he writers were writing like crazy, trying to save the day, and Feldman is hiring everyone in sight including Woody Allen... and Charles Boyer; and to save time on production he engages five directors: John Huston, myself, Bob Parrish, Val Guest, and Richard Talmadge.
>
> The result was *total chaos*. Units were shooting in three separate studios... And none of us ever saw a completed script... I only saw the producer when I sent him a map of how to get to Shepperton Studios, and he dropped in for a day. But no single director knew what any of the others were doing, and not until we all sat down and saw it all cut together did we realise we had been conned into a total pile of garbage.
>
> The result speaks for itself. A mishmash that came into being because the star had walked out. Feldman said that Sellers had pulled out in breach of all manner of contracts; and I know for a fact that Feldman had a heart attack in the middle of all this and the general opinion was that Sellers was responsible...

Hughes adds that they had to '"skate around" Sellers, and use doubles to cover him in unshot scenes... I myself never met him. Indeed, I shot a scene with Orson Welles in which I used a double for Sellers... The two never came face to face. This is evident in the cutting.'

◆ ◆ ◆

Sellers' fingerprints are all over *Casino Royale*—he it was who got it to slip its sprockets. And he did destroy Feldman's health—something he maintained Feldman was getting him to do on purpose. 'Charlie Feldman is going to die,' he confidently predicted, 'and the reason he'll die is so that he can blame me—he'll say, *"There! Sellers killed me!"* He'll do it to spite me.' You have to be a special sort of raving lunatic to believe that people will actually drop off the twig to get one over on you. But, sure enough, a few months later, Feldman made the an-nouncement that he was suffering from terminal stomach cancer; and, sure enough, he told anyone who'd listen that 'It's that bastard Sellers. *Sellers has done this to me.*'

Sellers at the very least was ulcer-inducing, and he'd aggravated Feldman's condition. He continued to show only scorn for the producer's plight, and if he couldn't quite blame other people all the time for the befuddlements he person-ally was causing his films there were always, of course, the portents, magic spells, omens, and coincidences to wave a finger at. And, where *Casino Royale* is a few reels of obscurity owing to Sellers' absence, *Ghost in the Noonday Sun* is chockful of ennui because he made sure he impaired the takes by sticking around to upset his co-star, Anthony Franciosa.

In the story, Dick Scratch and Pierre are rivals, each wanting to be the pirate king. Sellers took this to mean he had to drum up animosity towards the other actor—he had to hate Franciosa for real. 'I saw a rough cut,' says Dick Vosbrugh, who wrote a hearty ballad to go over the titles, 'which included a take where Sellers insulted Franciosa—calling him a "two-bit Hollywood wop bastard." He came quite out of character with a genuine and shocking snarl; and Franciosa looked back angrily at what was so plainly a personal taunt. I couldn't believe it: Sellers' naked hatred printed and put into a rough cut. But Gareth Wigan, Columbia's executive, seemed proud of having been able to trace enough usable film to assemble any sort of a version at all, and Medak said they'd get Peter back to re-dub the line at a later date.'

The chances of recapturing Sellers and forcing him to make good his errors and wrecks were remote. He was up and away playing Queen Victoria in *The Great McGonagall* and having speaks with Lew Grade and Blake Edwards over staging a reunion with Inspector Clouseau. (*Ghost in the Noonday Sun* was wrapped at the end of 1973; *The Return of the Pink Panther* was put in celluloid in July 1974.) Instead, Medak was compelled to use reverse angle shots, long shots, shots with stunt doubles, etc. when attempting to camouflage the sections where Scratch's colourful rascally Irish cursing had overstepped the mark. It was *Casino Royale* all over again, except instead of being merely uncooperative, Sellers had now been actively seditious. 'His scheme was to do anything and everything to sabotage the film,' Medak told me. 'He set this in motion—by getting the producers fired; he had the cameraman fired—Larry Pizer, who'd worked with him before on *The Optimists*. He was Peter's personal choice. Then he tried to get rid of me ... Three quarters of the way through the film, he came over to me on a beach in Cyprus—everybody had been there since six in the morning, and they'd had to get to this bay by boat as there wasn't a road; and he turned up at eleven, without his make-up, which took two hours usually to apply—and everybody was dying in this hundred and ten degree heat ... He put his arm around my shoulder and ... said: "Why don't you quit the film? ... I have director approval, and. I'm going to reject every director they are going to suggest. I will get paid off— and I'll give you half the money." I turned to him very gently and quietly and said: "... You signed your name to a contract. So did I. The only way we are going to get out of here is to shoot our way out. You'd better go and put your make-up on."'

Sellers comes out of the episode even worse than this, if such a thing is possible. He was lying to Medak about not wanting to accept any replacement director. Night and day he was pestering people like Joe McGrath: 'I got these phone calls from him ... He asked me to take over *Ghost in the Noonday Sun*; and he'd ask Bryan Forbes to take over the films I did with him. Forbes and Dick Lester were both asked to do *Casino Royale*. I also got phoned about *After the Fox*. Peter wanted me to take over from Vittorio de Sica. They were filming in Ischia. Sellers insisted that they flew British bangers [sausages] in to the unit.'

♦ ♦ ♦

Can Sellers' Roman Emperor quality caprices be traced back to a source in (say) *The Naked Truth*? Did he learn something about himself back there? Given Sellers' hatred of being bored, his general impatience, and contempt for others, the sluggardly pace was agony. 'I remember one very difficult episode,' says Miss Mount. 'We were doing a very demanding shot... Nothing went right. There were some noisy bees on the set; an aeroplane went over; the camera squeaked; and on and on... just when we thought we had got it, a man in the gantry gave out a very audible snore. The comments were explicit, much to the annoyance of the union man on the spot who promptly called a strike in protest. The strike lasted another five days. We were eventually coming to the end of the sequence which required Sellers' false moustache to fall off, and it wasn't doing so. In desperation, and unseen by the camera, I blew hard in his face and, thankfully, the moustache fell off...'

Sadly, for all their efforts, the scene is a shambles. Zampi had made his cast go over their movements and dialogue so many times that the final effect is inert and zestless. As farce, it seems under-rehearsed, it is so torpid; and as for Miss Mount's heavy breathing: Joan Sims, kneeling over Sonny, who has collapsed after taking a glass of drugged Amontillado, shrieks something like 'Oh look, his moustache has dropped off!' Peggy then sighs heavily, and the moustache floats half an inch up Sellers' nose. It's hopeless. How did Sellers himself refer to the experience? Offhandedly: 'One day Mario Zampi offered me a part. I was to play five different characters. I thought: Good! I shan't be typed... But they were very dull...'

He did, however, retain a fondness for Sonny's Dubliner disguise: 'One of them was an Irishman—there's a still which I think is very funny; it's the epitome of all the Irishmen in their square-shouldered suits standing about in Mornington Crescent...' In the photograph, Sellers' eyes are porcine and stupid and his nose so large and lumpy that it seems modelled on the snout of a bullock—Sellers has turned himself into Brendan Behan, whose drunken brawling and carousing he spoofed as 'Mr Bedham,' the impossible playwright.

The 'Mr Bedham' language, the colourful phrasing and distortions, is what Scratch's became when Sellers went for Franciosa and took the button off his foil. It wasn't as simple as Sellers coming quite out of character; it was more that he had melded into another, related, and more deadly one. Thoroughly disturbed, his aggression was released by acting—and yet not all of it was acting. Whilst he could pretend to himself that his outrages were acceptable if conducted on a movie set (where it could be argued that it was his inventiveness carrying him away), underneath there was real disintegration and formlessness. When they were making *The Naked Truth* he told Terry-Thomas, 'I've come to the part of the film which is scaring me to death. I'm supposed to use my own accent. And I haven't got one.' Hence the medley of Scottish, Irish, Cockney, etc. which pours out of Sonny. His shifty personality is exhibited in his shifting voices, in the way he's charming or arrogant, as it pleases him. There's nothing about him you can trust. He *is* the thirty-something Sellers, slowly suffocating.

◆ ◆ ◆

There are a few rather more transparent effects of *The Naked Truth* than mysterious, autobiographical hints. First, Zampi, the hands-in-the-air film director, voluble and short on talent, was impersonated by Sellers, as Aldo Vanucci, in *After the Fox*. Flamboyant, cocking a light meter as a monocle and having lenses slung around his neck like an alderman's chain, Aldo minces up and down and to and fro in the world as if it's still the eighteenth century. 'We film directors must give vent to our feelings,' he states, before throwing piles of a policeman's papers in the air, adding, 'And I have just vented!' (If the idiot foppishness is Zampi's, the fit and squeal are Goonish.) Second, the experience of the strike at the studio, during *The Naked Truth*, and the irrational power of the unions they all had a taste of, gave Sellers his material to draw on when putting Fred Kite together in *I'm All Right, Jack*. He much admired the stubbornness of shop stewards, their self-satisfied sulks and tantrums, which had more to do with upsetting the master-race than spreading brotherly love amongst the workers. Third, the vituperative relationship between Sonny and Lord Mayley is repeated and exaggerated to out-of-scale pantomime proportions in *Tom Thumb*. Despite Mayley's snobbish class consciousness, he and Sonny are similar under the skin. They are both grifters. So it made sense to team them, in vaguely Laurel and Hardy fashion, as a pair of comic baddies.

First, however, there was *Up the Creek*, a nautical revel sponsored by Mountbatten. Again, Sellers plays a double-dealer; but Chief Petty Officer Dockerty is all speed and adroitness (he's like Phil Silvers' Bilko, awash with scams), where Sonny left us with an impression of lassitude and sneakiness. Suddenly, Sellers is invigorated. His eyes sparkle. Maybe it is the strong Irish accent which he enjoys? Or the naval uniform, which makes him look a lot snappier than in Sonny's dull and shapeless charcoal suits and narrow collars? He's still very fat, with chins galore, but this gives him authority, presence. We quite believe he's the brains behind *HMS Berkeley*'s sharp practices. He has charisma and an answer for everything.

HMS Berkeley is a non-seaworthy sloop, anchored off Meadows' End in Suffolk. The navy has forgotten about its existence. Dockerty and his crew of motleys keep pigs and chickens on deck; a public laundry operates in the boiler room; they make wedding cakes and other fancy pastries for the villagers—the ship is an enterprise zone. They sell navy-issue rum and cigarettes to the local pub (Dockerty says that the HMS imprimatur means Home Made Smokes), towels and soap to boarding houses, gun-metal paint to the hardware stores. 'The navy never pays in this place!' a visitor is told proudly, for the navy is the supplier of bounty; their rate of exchange is barter or grateful gifts.

Sellers, his face transformed by a pair of oval tortoiseshell spectacles, delivers his speeches as patter. 'We might as well be flying the skull and crossbones,' he says, surveying his accounts ledger, totting up the profits. Indeed, Dockerty could be Dick Scratch's quick-thinking brother, for the *Berkeley* is being run on benign piratical lines. The people being robbed and swindled are the paymasters back in Whitehall. What goes wrong with the bamboozling idyll is what goes wrong with the film as a whole ('A good idea insufficiently developed' was Sellers' accurate verdict): the arrival of David Tomlinson's Lieutenant Humphrey Fairweather. Fairweather is one of those wet and chumpish upper-class officer types usually played by Ian Carmichael. But where Carmichael conveys a sort of dreaminess, Tomlinson's reactions are a bit tetchy and exasperating. Noël Coward once described the actor as resembling 'a very old baby', and I think I can see what he meant. Tomlinson's full lips have a downward curl; he looks as though he'll stamp his foot in a rage. He is a ditherer always on the edge of being huffy, but too well-bred to show it.

The relationship between Dockerty and Fairweather is more superficial and immediate—Fairweather never gets far beyond exclaiming incomprehension. Sent out to *HMS Berkeley* by the Admiralty, which has discovered its oversight, he is easily fooled by the shyster he meets. His own extra-curricular interests in ballistics are too boring and contrived to concern us—except to say that it is one of his rockets which blows the ship up and gives us an ending.

When Sellers' Dockerty is in full panicky flow ('we couldn't very well *give* government property away, could we sir?'), his Londonderry accent is musical; his voice weaves in and out of the sighing which issues from Tomlinson and the grumbles of the crew members who come up to him with their fears. He copes; he soars. When Sellers scurries along the gantries and through the hatchways, the soundtrack cheekily toots Laurel and Hardy's 'Cuckoo' theme—cheeky because, though Sellers does have Olly's burliness, and the plot is another fine mess, Dockerty is no cosmic stooge, slipping and sliding and falling over. *Up The Creek* isn't slapstick; it's a chance for Sellers to exercise his helter-skelter rhythms. Physically, as he glides about on his secret errands; and of course vocally.

To practise the voice, he bought one of the earliest reel-to-reel tape recorders. Doing the Irish brogue didn't present a problem; what Sellers wanted was to get the raciness right, so that when he poked the Able Seamen in the chest for emphasis, or looked mock-innocent when interrogated, his words and sounds would fit how he looked and moved. 'He was determined,' remembers Tomlinson, 'to be taken seriously as an actor and not just as a clown who did funny voices.' Sellers asked his co-star, pointing to his gadget: 'Haven't you got one of these?' A few days later, he left a big parcel for Tomlinson backstage at the Aldwych Theatre. 'From a friend', said the enigmatic accompanying note. The recipient spent a year puzzling out who had sent it. Two decades on, in Paris, Tomlinson took delivery of another box: 'It's about time you had a new one,' wrote Sellers. It was another tape-recorder, the very latest and most expensive.

In the early days, Sellers confided his creativity to his tape machines; along with the camera equipment and motor cars, he could zoom about in, and try and control, time and space. Later, wives and children having been sent away, machines were his sole company. Yet even the tape spools, purring backwards, were no comfort. I asked Tomlinson what it was like to have known the Sellers who was first coming into his powers, in *Up The Creek*, and then encountering him again, on *The Fiendish Plot of Dr Fu Manchu*, after the end: 'If he liked you, he was wonderful, generous, funny. He never bothered me with talk of monumental depression—though I was aware that, in some mysterious way, he was *damaged*. He never read a book; he never went to the theatre or to the movies. He'd just sit on his own in the dark and brood ... Had there been a way of making films without make-up, without even having to turn up and be before a camera, he'd have been on to it. As for *Up The Creek*, that only cost about £150,000 ... Val Guest, the director, worked very hard, was very organised, and made himself a lot of money.'

The last point Sellers also made himself, in 1959: 'It was cheap to make and its takings have been fantastic.' (Translation: Though I'm not personally pocketing the door-money, millions of people are starting to go out to the flicks to see me.)

♦♦♦

The varying of himself in criminal rôles was enlivening; at his best, in such parts, he was quick and controlled. He was born to play Clare Quilty, Nabokov's 'grease spot of mirth ... this semi-animated, sub-human trickster.' Something of his own wildness could be communicated when he also became Mr Topaze, going from schoolmastering to embezzlement; or Dodger Lane, nipping in and out of prison; or Pearly Gates, calling a meeting of the underworld fraternity and chairing it like an antic Pluto. Sellers would have made a definitive Father Brown (the detective priest played simperingly by Alec Guinness), because he, like no other actor, could have shown the way Chesterton's character subjectively imagines himself to be the murderer he's out to catch—he could have dramatised Father Brown's paradoxical process of 'feeling his remorse beforehand.'

Crooks and swindlers, with their front of normality, their alibis and insurrections, appealed to Sellers not only because of their slipperiness and dark secrets; he also identified with a hooligan's concept of social justice—he always put himself in embattled, aggrieved positions, so as to be able to fight, scheme, try and claw back what he believed was rightfully his: i.e. anything of yours he decided he wanted. This could range from your cuff links to your car to your wife. When he was making *The Wrong Arm of the Law* he decided to add Nanette Newman to his collection. Michael Sellers says he remembers how it happened: 'My father offered to do a trade with Bryan Forbes. He rang him up and said, "I'll give you mine if you'll give me yours." Bryan said, "No, Pete darling, we can't do that," or something mollifying. Forbes didn't get angry.'

He'd have known there was no point. 'He was always searching for a home,' Forbes told me, 'and he'd come to our house and look about him and plead, "How did you get this to look a *home*?" I'd answer: "Because all our things have accumulated over thirty years of marriage. We haven't had an interior designer in to choose everything, right down to the ashtrays"—which was Peter's way. He envied us our stable domestic life. He thought if he could marry Nanette, it would be his, too. He asked me if I'd mind if he married Nanette. I said, "It's not my de-cision—let's ask Nanette..."'

Once he had realised that this was one citadel he'd not prise open, Sellers van-ished in some style. He invited the Forbes to spend a holiday with him on his yacht: 'His yacht!' Forbes exclaimed. 'It had more power and gadgetry than the *Queen Mary*. It slept six. It had a full crew and a cellar stocked with vintage Dom Perignon. It cost Sellers about £90,000, and yet he still had the engines replaced with Mercedes diesel engines—incredible luxury. And he never turned up—there was a note saying: "Have gone with Bert to Vienna to learn the zither. P.S., re-garding the map, the brown bits are the land and the blue bits are the sea." The Captain would say to us every morning, "Where'd you like to go?" We'd go off to Portofino for lunch. But Sellers was never there.'

Apart from a deep desire to knock everybody out (all credit to the Forbes' for withstanding him), there was nothing else about him you could predict. Why was he so aggressive, exploitative, covetous? 'I find,' he said, 'that I have been disap-pointed so many times in people, that I've become, not bitter, but I tend to ap-proach people warily—in case they are going to clobber me. I find,' he added, with no justification that I've been able to see, 'that I get clobbered a lot.' The snivelling tone is a performance. If anybody did any clobbering, literally or figu-ratively, it was Sellers. Other peoples' fear, especially, in mad-dog fashion, set him off. But such was his degree of mental topsy-turviness, and his sympathy as an ac-tor, that to achieve what he wanted, and to impose himself on the world through chaos, he seemed to almost completely become the people he was abusing.

His most frequent victims were his children. 'At eleven o'clock in the morn-ing he'd love them,' says Forbes, 'and by mid-afternoon he'd be disinheriting them.' He hoped to extend his sufferings and moods by working on theirs. It wasn't enough that he was ruining his own life. He expected them to feel how he felt. He wanted, as it were, to spread his sickness, like a vampire. This was his power; this was what he reckoned on as his right. 'I can remember times,' Sarah Sellers says, 'you'd be sitting there with somebody, and he'd get irritated with them, and all of a sudden he'd become them and talk back to them in exactly the same voice—awful, but amazing. Not just imitating the voice, but posture, looks, everything. It was hilarious and very embarrassing.'

Bloodcurdling is the word that comes into my mind. In James Hogg's novel *Confessions of a Justified Sinner*, a parable of egocentricity and demonic possession, first published in 1824, the religious maniac, Robert Wringhim Colwan, meets a master-mummer who turns out to be Satan, who says: 'My countenance changes with my studies and sensations...If I contemplate a man's features seriously, mine own gradually assume the very same appearance and character...I not only attain the same likeness, but, with the likeness, I attain the very same ideas as well as the same mode of arranging them, so that, you see, by looking at a person attentively, I by degrees assume his likeness, and by assuming his likeness I attain to the pos-session of his most secret thoughts.'

This could be a description of Sellers' necromancy. Alexander Mackendrick once hoped to adapt a film from Hogg's book. Sellers would have been ideal for all the doubling and disappearing—and the novel, being about split personalities and paranoia, would have suited him in many troubling ways. Robert Colwan and the Devil: a gift of a part for a delirious actor who (in Hogg's words) 'by setting his features to the mould of other people's, entered at once into their conceptions and feelings.'

◆ ◆ ◆

Had we been given the chance to wander around the sound-stages when they were making *Tom Thumb*, we might have felt plunged into a lunatic's landscape— everything so massively out of proportion, elephantine, that the human figure, small and undistinguishable, shrank away to nothing. The purpose of the enormity was to diminish Russ Tamblyn, the twenty-four-year-old American tumbler cast as Tom; and playing the part in tight orange breeches and a slit white shirt, he's Peter Pan. (Is it my memory playing tricks, or does this Tom have a dagger slung across his hips?)

The myth which underlies fairy tales like *Tom Thumb*, *Pinocchio*, *The Gingerbread Man*, etc., stories about changelings and childless couples, is that of the infant Christ—immaculately conceived, raised by wise and simple peasant folk, the boys are led into temptation, or they fall amongst thieves and devils, and, their innate goodness shining through (aided and abetted by various angels or diaphanous fairies), they rout evil-doers and restore order, virtue, happiness, and such. This, certainly, is *Tom Thumb*, the most sentimental rendering of the lot. But, luckily for us, Tamblyn's impish Tom goes against the grain, not by being brattish or ungovernable, but by having a certain sex appeal. This diminutive sort-of Christ figure, with his golden head of hair and twinkling eyes, overflows with boisterousness and has a dancer's awareness of his own body—Tamblyn is limbering up for the Mercutio rôle he played a few years later in *West Side Story*. As he darts through keyholes and penetrates locks (at the behest of Sellers and Terry-Thomas), you think: this Tom Thumb is a liberated flying phallus, a crowing cock.

What cannot succeed in the film in that case, Tamblyn's Tom being so knowing, are George Pal's celebrated puppet sequences. Tamblyn has to do a lot of acting alongside models and back projection screens. When the toys come alive in his nursery, ostensibly to amuse him, we wait patiently for all the hopping and leaping routines to be over, so that we can get back to Sellers and Terry-Thomas and their nefarious deeds. Ivan (Terry-Thomas) is the ultimate ne'er-do-well. As he puffs on a double cigar-holder, his black curls framed by a pointy Pied Piper hat, and his long flapping frock coat tailored, it would seem, for a foppish snake, he's every cheat and bogus gent Terry-Thomas played brought together in one place and cranked up for caricature, so that Ivan is a showman out of Restoration drama.

If Terry-Thomas is a fox or a serpent, Sellers' Antonio, big and round, is a bear. Fat as Sellers was, he's still padded out—he's spherical, an effect accentuated by the large, curved, bashed Roman priest's hat that he wears. His leather coat, trimmed with clumps of mangy fur, is sewn together from innumerable hides. Rotund, therefore, and carrying a caveman club, he's the hench-person, the stooge, and Sellers opts for Italianate, deep, ursine growls. 'Let's get reed of da kid now,' he suggests, 'so he don't open hees mouth.' He is couthless where Thomas is all politeness. Thomas, indeed, over-enunciates to such an extent, he seems to be singing. The film's best moments are the nods and winks which go on between them. Sellers, especially, his grizzly voice almost a whisper, does wonders with a brown-visaged scowl, a blank or collusive look. Where another actor might use the garishness of the production as an excuse for an outsize performance, Sellers, remarkably, underplays.

It is in *Tom Thumb*, therefore, that the lessons of 'The Goon Show' are seen to have been learned. On radio Sellers created characters and gave performances in which there was a big discrepancy between the calculated silliness of the story-lines and the genuine eccentricity of what he personally managed to accomplish. It's almost eerie, the way he touched in the foibles and curlicues, the psychology if you like, of cartoons. (He gave cartoons a third dimension.) As Antonio, a big blob of greed who doesn't know how many beans make five, he's similarly weird and stirring. For example, there's a terrific pantomime scene set in a ruined castle. The robbers are attempting to count their swag and Tom nips in amongst the coins, knocking over the piles of gold and hiding and meddling with the doubloons, so that Antonio and his colleague start to suspect one another of cheating, and a fight starts: 'There's a crook in here, Ivan, and it's not me,' says Sellers. We can see and feel the dinosaurian reflexes and the primitive befogged brain cells which have had to crank into life to come up with that calibre of deduction.

During the battle, which Tom has inculcated, Sellers is oddly nimble. He uses his rotundity to become a rolling stone. He bashes Terry-Thomas with a chairleg, a broad sword, and a shield. He jumps over tables and makes a passage through the cobwebs with a firebrand. The violence seems to get things going inside his own head, for suddenly, banging Ivan's noggin rhythmically on the marble floor, he can count! And he does so with a vengeance, getting his own back on a fellow cut-purse who has no doubt sneered at his ignorance for years. All of Antonio's humiliations, defeats, resentments come out and are appeased. Clonk! Clonk! Clonk!

◆ ◆ ◆

Up The Creek was released on November 11, 1958; *Tom Thumb*, six weeks later, on Christmas Eve. Would a tolerably aware contemporary picturegoer have noticed that Bosun Dockerty and Antonio the brigand were played by the same person? The one is all speed and unscrupulousness, the other all blockishness. What an early student of Sellers' performances may have noticed is that, no matter how crude and simple the surrounding film, the actor himself is tenacious about giving his characters conviction, verve, interest. Already he had proved that, on the cinema screen as on radio, he could alter himself totally. He was a shadow now, as well as an echo. And, active creatively, in his private life he was restless and changeable. Soon it would be clear that he made the sort of films he did because of the kind of man he was—a man tortured by his search for a rounded identity, who needed to be free, and who, hardly of this world, disrupted the lives of those who tried to love him or work with him—because (says Michael) 'freedom to my father meant laying his hands on whatever he pleased and doing whatever he wanted all the hours there were.'

He was always on his way to somewhere else. What made him worth watching as an actor undid him as an individual, for as an actor Sellers could signify the things which were on his character's minds (Kite's dreams of Russian cornfields, Nayland Smith's duels with Fu's spiders, Dr Strangelove's bunker-room orgies) without ever standing still to know his own. At a certain moment, in the reproductive, mimic-prone world of acting, Sellers would make an imaginative leap— and it would be art. To achieve this, he was filled with a nervous tension; the nervous charge which we, his audiences, carry away. And the endless effort of it hollowed him out.

Chapter Nine

♦♦♦

A League of Gentlemen

The ethos of Ealing and its derivatives was of an England as a land fit for heroes; of the English as respectable and innocent; of Englishness as a relentless chirpiness (amongst the lower orders) or a muted and noble state of mind—a condition which is quintessentially symbolised by the game of cricket. Sellers, in fact, was not in the least bit interested in cricket, though he pretended to be. It was expedient, and good for a gag, as in the scene he improvised with Peter O'Toole in *What's New, Pussycat?* O'Toole, playing a wan-faced satyromaniac whose bodily fluids have been pumped away, attempts to convince Dr Fassbender (Sellers, at his most Germanic and nutty) that he is not a pervert, that he can exert restraint, and that he is a gentleman. How can he prove he is a gentleman? Because he knows the rules of cricket. Cricket is all the therapy the well-brought-up need. 'Is there any sex in it?' asks the doc incredulously. 'Cricket is a game played by gentlemen for gentlemen,' retorts O'Toole. 'Then it is sick, *sick* ...' says Sellers, vigorously shaking his head.

Cricket, so cunning and forceful a pursuit under its serene surface, was a game he felt he ought to affect enthusiasm for, being a Totteridge and Whetstone ratepayer; more to the point, a local charity side was captained by John Boulting. Sellers anticipated that, if he turned up and offered his celebrity services for a match, the conversation might swing around to an offer of work in a Boulting Brothers film. It went better than that. John and his brother Roy put Sellers under a five year contract worth £100,000. At the press conference, convened to announce the deal, the actor smiled wanly as the twins went on about how they'd 'signed him up because he is handy with a bat and can talk cricket.' Sellers didn't demur. He gave every appearance of agreeing with them—'not because I had to' (he explained later) 'but because it seemed the right thing to do at the time.'

Eventually, however, Sellers' apparent capitulation to the arcane rules and rituals could not be taken straight. To the cricket chat, which he'd come out with when around the cricket-mad twins, he'd add a white jersey or he'd wear a cap. The satire culminated in his turning up, whatever the hour or venue (the Jockey Club, Washington, for instance), attired in white flannels, pads, gloves, spiked shoes, and visored helmet, and he'd be waving a bat. It was the equivalent of throwing your voice back at you—Sellers would throw your habits and hobbies back at you. Or he might retain some of them.

Being identical twins, John and Roy Boulting were accustomed to seeing double; with Sellers they were suddenly triplets, though Sellers did his best to modify his performance. Except for the cricketing masquerade, his efforts, in the Boultings' presence, to be phlegmatic, crisp, dithering if needs be, had an undercurrent of yearning. 'He was very aware,' Anne told me, 'of not having had any education. This was a terrible hang-up. When we went to the Boultings for dinner, and he met intellectual people, Peter was really out of his depth. Afterwards he'd say to me "Was I all right tonight?"—like he was doing some play-acting. His life was theatre. He became even more insecure, meeting John and Roy and climbing up. He was neither well-read nor intellectual, nothing. He was nothing.'

◆ ◆ ◆

'My whole life,' Sellers told Jerzy Kosinski, the author of *Being There*, 'has been devoted to imitating others. It has been devoted to the portrayal of those who appear to be different from what they are.' Thus, his dreamers and romantics, his mock heroes and monsters; the believability of Fred Kite, say, grows out of the fact that the character's malapropisms and genteelisms reflect Sellers' own fears about his suavity being exposed as a sham, the mirror crack'd from side to side. There's a breach between what Sellers' characters actually achieve in their lives, and what they think they are achieving: all those old actors and music hall crooners with the stuffing knocked out of them, thinking themselves to be in the noble service of art and illusion; time's passage and youth's being the stuff that won't endure gets to be the subject of *Waltz of the Toreadors*, *Hoffman*, and *There's a Girl in My Soup*. In those, Sellers' characters appear to be successes; inside, they are desolate. As he was.

'Success hasn't enabled me to find out anything about myself,' he said with surprise and indignation. 'I just know I can do certain things. If you go too deep into yourself, if you analyse yourself too closely, it's no good for the job. You can either act or you can't. If you analyse yourself and your own emotions all the time, and every doorknob handle, you know, you are up the spout.' Well, he could and he did and he was. He could act too well. He was always, as David Tomlinson said, brooding. He was also aware that, in terms of his high-powered career, his disaffections were necessary: 'I know that in this business success is so short-lived, so brief. It's not like being a part of [another sort of] big business that you're with for the rest of your life. That would lead to tranquillity. *But then I don't really want tranquillity.**I almost want the whole thing to crumble around me... Being well-known is a problem to me. Whatever you do, somebody wants to say something about it or photograph it... You're stuck with it... I can't achieve what I want to achieve. There's this constant gap between what one does and what one wants to have done.'

Divisions are what unified Sellers: the man in Peter Pan (there's a line in *Hoffman* which bounces off the screen as autobiography: 'There are two people in all of us. The child in the snapshot and the monster the child grows into'); the success who feared the boredom and meaninglessness of success and who was just about the best actor since Chaplin at portraying people with awkward and shapeless lives. He greatly feared death (as Alec Guinness testified) and yet courted it with spirit

---

* Italics added.

mediums and séances; and he died at least twice from heart attacks—on the first occasion emerging from hospital to say: 'I wasn't dozing off—I was dying. You'd feel okay...then you'd suddenly feel, "Ah—here we go again"—and that was death...' He didn't like time to pass, he sentimentally looked back and re-imagined events and the very next thing he'd do would be to whizz about in fast cars, doing his best to use up time and speed ahead: 'Yes, I've got this car thing...Since 1948 [he said in 1962] I've had sixty different cars...It's a search for perfection. Probably there is a link between this search and the other one, the one in my work. One is a search for perfection in a machine, the other stems from a great sense of depression at being unable to supply what I know I should be able to deliver.'

The man who switched cars also switched women and addresses—was always in panic and flight: 'My idea of permanence is about five years. I've always been restless. My grandparents were the same. Always on the move. I certainly have inherited this lack of a foundation, this lack of roots...I think being half-Jewish has a lot to do with it. That and the business. I have a feeling I'm not going to stay anywhere for very long...'

He was a collector who never kept anything. Once he'd bought and renovated a property, its appeal had evaporated. Herbert Lom recalls:

> Sellers spent more than half his life in hotel rooms. All film actors do, of course, but Peter preferred this sort of existence. Elstead, in Surrey, was as close to a home as he ever had that I saw. But it was like a well-furnished film-set. I had a home in the South of France...Peter bought a house nearby and it took him six months to move in. Though it was a brand-new house, he had to have it remodelled, refurnished, refurbished. Finally, he moved in. I telephoned him from along the coast to wish him a happy home:
>
> 'We're moving out,' he said. 'We don't really like it—and anyway, we don't like the French.'
>
> 'Why ever not?' I said. It typically didn't occur to him that I had a French wife.
>
> 'We don't like the French because they don't speak English.'
>
> The day he moved in, he moved out. Then he tried Gstaad because Blake Edwards was there, Curt Jurgens was there. Peter had to prove that he too could afford to live in Switzerland—and then he hated that.

Sellers' chalet, La Haute Grange, in the thin winter air of the megastar community of Gstaad, was a mausoleum—chilly and devoid of life, it belongs in the annals of gothic horror, right up there with Northanger Abbey and Bleak House. It was described for me in 1989 by Elwood Rickless, Sellers' lawyer and executor: 'Sellers...was never able to settle. He heard people say Switzerland was the place, so he repeated the sentiment—and...for tax purposes, Sellers decided on Gstaad—because Blake had a chalet there, and Sellers was always wanting to be... better than Blake. It was hugely expensive, the chalet he decided he wanted; and we, as his lawyers, were told we *had* to find the money. He was resolute. We tried to negotiate and reduce the price, but the vendor could see a sucker, and Sellers ordered us to pay.'

Lynne then spent another fortune on interior decoration. The chalet stood on a hill—most conspicuous, with ornate gables, and so on, all in contravention of strict planning regulations—but as far as playing king of his castle went, Sellers didn't move in the same social set as Blake Edwards, and he had no idea how to play host in his own home. He never had people over. He had no friends. So he and Lynne were always taking off—which raised problems for his lawyers and accountants, because a residency permit is very hard to obtain and Sellers was not clocking up enough days. The upkeep was vast. The house was cleaned three times a week. The lights came on automatically at seven and went off at one in the morning. There was nobody there.

It doesn't take much to imagine the light sinking in the hushed rooms, the curtains gliding open and shut on pre-timed electrified tracks, or to hear the sound of soft music tinkling automatically and forlornly from the hi-fi—like the breeze in the organ pipes in *Sunset Boulevard*. La Haute Grange is a haunted house, and it always was.

◆ ◆ ◆

At the end of *Hoffman*, the enervated figure Sellers plays is having a dream house built in Hampstead—another vampire's lair. Benjamin Hoffman will have all he wants: a well-appointed pad *and* Sinead Cusack to be his Wendy Darling. Yet still he slumps in his chair, very alone, half gazing at the night sky, heavy, weary, depressed about the state of the 'soul behind this bloodhound face'—hangdog, more like.

But if that image is rather a subtle instance of Sellers' use of division and discontinuity—having all you want and it's still not enough; being disenchanted when dreams come true—then he was quite able, elsewhere, to make broad slapstick out of the appearance *vs.* reality conundrum. Inspector Clouseau is the world's greatest detective as well as being the world's greatest idiot. His skills at detection are inadvertent, and yet if people try to assassinate him, they bump off themselves; if they try to outwit him, they tie themselves in knots. He turns incompetence into a virtue. He is charmed—a Holy Fool.

Clouseau's Irish cousin, another ostensible failure who paradoxically succeeds, is Dick Scratch, the mangy ship's cook who becomes captain, wears a bejewelled turban, and thinks of himself as Douglas Fairbanks Jr. Though Scratch stumbles upon buried treasure, loses it, reclaims it, loses it again, etc., he is lucky, (or unlucky) rather than perspicacious. In the world of slapstick, actions are mechanised, engineered; there's nothing much you can do if, as in the Panthers, your folding bed springs back, demolishes the wall, and precipitates you into the Seine, or if you charge at a locked door, hurl through it, fall out of a window, and splash into a fountain. And like Clouseau, Scratch is never in total control—but things fall his way (figuratively) or fall on top of him (literally). No wonder such characters are disjointed, dazed.

◆ ◆ ◆

It's Sellers' gallery of crooks which gave him the fullest opportunity to demonstrate how people are often not what they seem. The model prisoner who is simultaneously at liberty stealing a chest of jewels in *Two Way Stretch*; the gangster who runs a dress shop, in *Wrong Arm of the Law*, or a lock-up garage, in *Never Let Go*; the escaped convict who pretends to be a film director in *After the Fox*, and who wishes, along with all Sellers' rebels, 'If only I could steal enough to become an honest man.'

Criminology is a series of false fronts. At its most crude the concept is exemplified in a dragged-out sketch which appeared on the brother-and-sister sitcom 'Sykes', sometime in the early seventies. Sellers erupts into Eric and Hattie's life as an aged East End ruffian, Little Tommy Grando, who purports to be an ex-school chum who ran away to sea. It must be one of Sellers' worst performances—he barely suppresses his smirks, he is obviously enjoying himself and he signals this in a way that is amateur and boring. Sellers, brandishing weapons and being obnoxious, is back in the underworld of *Never Let Go*—he's verminous, and we can see what his Fagin could have been like. Sellers had such sinister reserves.

What was benumbing and foolish in 'Sykes', however, was revealing in *Lolita*. Quilty 'is not a starring rôle, but it attracted me in my urge to play parts that are always different from the others I've had…' In this, the first of the two films he made for Stanley Kubrick, the actor's frightening ability to slip from one identity to the next is the essence of the performance. Quilty is quicksilver; he's the mask behind the mask. Sellers is able to be different within the same movie without, technically, splitting himself up as the components of a crowd. Quilty gives us the creeps, and I don't think he does anything much worse than win and ditch the girl Lolita. Is it because we see him through James Mason's paranoid eyes? Or that his appearances and scenes, with their improvised speeches, are so unexpected and inconsequential—Goonish, but without Secombe's healthy laughter to draw their sting?

Watching Quilty, or watching out for Quilty, it is Sellers' own malleability and disquiet which we sense are being revealed. The very first scene, with Humbert Humbert arriving at the fogbound, gothic castle, hunting for his enemy, seems to take place at a permanent, hung-over party going on to celebrate moving-in day or moving-out day. We can almost choke on the stale cigarette smoke and the general airlessness and satiation. All the guests have gone. Quilty, like Sellers, is best imagined amongst the leavings of an orgy: the overturned sticky wine glass, the dirty plates, the refuse of a meal. As in the sight of shuttered music halls or out of season holiday resorts, there's melancholy symbolism (almost a *memento mori*) in the image of yesterday's decaying food and unwanted drink.

It is a great scene—Sellers' whole disconnected, wandering, and impossible nature is summarised in under ten minutes. Quilty is a patchwork-quilt of personality types, accents, and attitudinising. At first you think he must be drunk, he's so dishevelled and all over the place. But no sooner does Quilty remind you of one facet of Sellers than he's gliding away to try on another face and inflexion; as brilliant as the broken-up, mad mimicry of Quilty is—his performance-within-a-performance—the point of the scene isn't the actor's virtuosity or flightiness. It's the way that what emerges from the litter and turbulence on show is a very strong and coherent sense of menace. Quilty, and by inference Sellers, are of diabolical origin, their courtesy a bogus thing.

He seems lazy and drained, and he assumes Humbert is a gatecrasher, or a guest who won't go. Then, noticing the pistol ('that's a darlin' little gun'), it dawns on him he's about to be killed—a Roman senator in the presence of his assassin. Humbert is so focused, intent on talking about Dolores Haze; Quilty shifts and shimmers, and the camera tracks his desultory progress around the room.

It isn't only a confrontation between men who loved and lost Lolita; it's a duel of acting styles. James Mason, classically trained, highly intelligent and cultivated, with his lusts and yearnings kept under severe control; Sellers, loose, improvisatory, with an ungovernable genius.

Mason is the man in the white suit, whom Sellers defiles—and, deep down, Mason wants to be defiled and to let go: this provides the dramatic tension. Humbert is humbled by seeing his troubles and desires acted out for him by Quilty, and he is incited to murder. (He's like the dry Salieri jealous of the inspired Mozart in *Amadeus*.) As an overly-fastidious man, he has written out, in a neat hand, a letter or list of all the crimes and humiliations Quilty is guilty of: it is a death warrant. Mason starts to fire off the gun and he gets the victim in the leg. 'Gee, you hurt me, you really hurt me!' Quilty is incredulous, as he scurries amongst the shambles of toys and gadgets. He has discovered, against all expectation, a new sensation.

◆ ◆ ◆

Sellers wasn't a gentleman. Mason's acting relied on exploiting the difference between a well-mannered, well-spoken surface of Englishness and a bosom filled with the poisonous fumes of contempt and guilt. He was always careful of how he'd look. Sellers, by contrast, never feared degradation. He wasn't aware that such a concept existed, and what this meant in practical terms was that his irresponsibility and shabbiness added up to an ebullience against which Mason, and people like him (i.e. people who were careful and indirect), would blunder.

You'd never get your bearings with him; there was nothing you could grasp. He may only ever have seen things from his point of view, but that perspective was always changing. Says Joe McGrath, 'This is why he identified with Sir Guy Grand in *The Magic Christian*. Sellers had this feeling in his mind that he could do all those humiliating, mortifying things to people. He had a cruel streak and enjoyed setting people up, getting them to swim through shit. He was cruel with Cleese ... In front of the crew and everybody, Sellers said "Jesus Christ, *what* are you doing?"'

John Cleese was fired at the end of the first day of *The Magic Christian*. He went over to McGrath and said 'I'm so sorry—I'm just so nervous when I'm actually up against *him* doing a take.' Sellers was merciless. 'Remove him. Get rid of him. Get somebody else for tomorrow.' McGrath said 'Who?' 'Anybody—we're never going to get anywhere with him.'

Cleese was reprieved, so long as he came in early the next morning to rehearse privately with the director, who explained that 'then we'll get Peter in and try out some business.'

McGrath and Cleese shot for two hours before Sellers displayed himself. The scene was cut together later in the editing room and Sellers said, 'All right, leave it', but he was never happy with it. Why? Not because Cleese was especially incompetent, but because Cleese, as an obsequious salesman at Sotheby's, was more convincingly upper-class than the star, whose Guy Grand is meant to be a loopy aristocrat, and who comes across, unfortunately, as a bit of an arriviste. When Sir Guy says he wants only the nose from a Rembrandt, and takes a pair of scissors to the canvas, Cleese's whimpers of pain at the cultural devastation, mingling with his sobs of joy when pocketing the bribe, create a new noise: the strangulated cry of Basil Fawlty, swallowing his principles. (Cleese performs an Englishman's neuroses as comically as Mason did tragically.)

'Sellers wouldn't hide his annoyance with another actor,' says McGrath. 'He wouldn't put himself out to help anybody else's performance ... Sellers would ... lay them waste ... If they couldn't do a scene his way—out. Now, he'd been the first to say, "Let's get Cleese" and the first to say "Let's get rid of him." He had no allegiance.'

◆ ◆ ◆

When the bodies were falling during *Casino Royale*, Peter Evans asked him outright: 'What is this compulsion you have for sacking people?' Sellers said to him, quite hotly, 'I would get rid of my own brother, if he was not delivering the goods. If your sister had made you a typewriter, and it didn't work, *you* wouldn't use the bloody thing. If I find myself surrounded by incompetents and stupid people, I want to get rid of them.'

This striking disclosure is more than an admission of ruthlessness—Sellers comes clean about wanting every resistance removed. By drawing an analogy between other actors and home-made Olivettis, and the like, he is saying that, to him, co-stars and colleagues were simply machines, objects without feelings, which he could throw into a scrap yard the instant they displeased him. You prod and punch them; they do your bidding. He seems to have willfully confused the tools of the trade with being creative; typing is not writing and acting is not mechanical, but he pretends that there is a connection. Furthermore, why did he, an only child, bring brothers and sisters into it? Of course, he was *not* an only child. There was that still-born elder brother to haunt him—some innocent thing who had been dead all these years. Sellers, however, wanted to rid himself of relatives (and rivals) on any pretext. (He rather fancied being a displaced person.) His isolation and the satisfaction he gained from violence was the result of a desperate attempt at self-possession—he wanted to be more than a novelty, the music hall child good at funny voices. He had to assert his strength and independence. He was miraculous; out of nowhere.

One way he exhibited this was to refuse to be with his mother when she was dying. (Peg joined the Choir Invisible on January 30, 1967.) He remained in Rome, stirring up hostilities on the set of *The Bobo*. He resented Peg for being frail, old, mortal; he decided he hated her for reminding him of where he'd come from, and this was a theme which had been gathering momentum for some years. Michael recalls that when his grandparents called, his father would often lock himself away in the darkroom and refuse to come out; or Peg would be taken for a drive in one of those limousines where a sound-proofing panel could be raised to cut off those in the back seat. Imprisoned in her glass and upholstery capsule, the poor dear would then notice all the window panes gliding down automatically, as her son revved up and accelerated through the North London suburbs. The blast of cold air and slipstream flung Peg about, cannoning her off the minibar and armrests like an untethered marionette. Peter would have his little joke!

If the g-forces weren't matricidal, Sellers next tried neglect. Hattie Stevenson, his secretary for seven years, told me that 'Peg was only brought out to see him during his guilty moments. He wanted her in America, during the shooting of *The World of Henry Orient*, so I had to fly to London and accompany her back to New York on the *Queen Mary*. She was a very difficult person, an impossible person. She used to try and get around everybody by saying, "I'm Peter Sellers' mother, darling, and I want the best." A very embarrassing old bat; all the same, I was quite fond of her...Anyway...I was to be Peg's Travelling Companion—because *he* couldn't be bothered to take her out with him to America himself, or anything like that...When we arrived, she stayed all of two days, and he made me fly back to England with her because he couldn't stand her any longer.'

'What did she do to get on his nerves?'

'No idea. No reason for it...She'd pushed him on in the early years, and that's why he was so stony-hearted with her in retrospect—she'd made him an actor, so if anything went wrong in the acting world, he saw it as her fault. She was an awful stage mother...We used to have to shop at Harrods. I used to have to go on these expeditions. Again, she [would be] showing off to everybody. She used to charge his account—and he accepted this.'

'What about when she was fatally ill?'

'He thought she was crying for attention—because she did use to do that, and he used to do that. You see, they were like twins.'

◆ ◆ ◆

Sellers, when he confessed to Kosinski that he'd given his entire life to copying others; that he could have played any of us (rather better, no doubt, than our own efforts at being ourselves); and that his speciality was people who were not quite what they seemed: he may, I now see, have been referring exclusively to his own off-screen existence, dispersed and scattered, and full of fraudulence, as it was. When Peg died he was elaborately grief-stricken. He didn't care who saw him sobbing. As he wrote to Herbert Kretzmer, on February 3, 1967, acknowledging a consolatory cable: 'It was, of course, a terrible shock to me as I was devoted to my darling Mother, but it's comforting to know that she died happily, and very proud of me.' Once she was safely dead he could control his reactions to her, and start to misremember her. By the time Auberon Waugh located him, in July 1980, the song of lamentation was well perfected. 'Within minutes of meeting me, he told me that he was completely devastated when his mother died, rather as one might ask politely after a guest's journey...That was thirteen years ago, was it not? I said, putting on a sympathetic face.'

Sellers was in his element with the cult of the dead. Sentimental and sadistic, there developed in him an idea that other people's distress and exits would enhance his own power and renew his strength—abandoning his mother, dumping wives, jettisoning children, firing colleagues, kicking dogs, it was his version of a pagan's human sacrifice. He even reached the point of trying to destroy people *before* they were to work for him, as is exemplified by Jonathan Miller's story: urgently summoned to Hollywood by Sellers. Kept waiting for a week in the Beverly Hills Hotel with no word from him. Reduced to rage and despair. Then limo'ed to the studios. There's Sellers on the set, shading his eyes to peer past the lights at this new arrival, and crying gladly: 'Jonathan! Long time no see! What are *you* doing here?'*

Admittedly, he hadn't always been as scheming as that, but the Boultings revealed great clairvoyance when they'd put him under contract back in the fifties. They could see how to make use of Sellers' sinking and whirling temperament. For, if Ealing films were all about decency, respectability, and conventions temporarily flouted, the Boultings, who succeeded Balcon as purveyors of Englishness, turned England upside down. In a typical Ealing production, like *Passport to Pimlico*, people never defy authority for very long; to the Boultings, in *Brighton Rock* (adapted from Graham Greene's novel), or *Lucky Jim* (adapted from Kingsley Amis'), it is authority itself which is revealed as corrupt and substanceless. England's military (*Private's Progress*), judiciary (*Brothers in Law*), big business (*I'm All Right, Jack*), etc., are rotten to the core. Yet, though it is always said that the Boultings satirised institutions, like universities, the church, or Whitehall, I don't see it quite that simply. It's the individuals who make up the Establishment and fill the august professions which they had a go at; the sods and the worms out to impress, with their veneers and repressions. The message is clear: this land, dear for her reputation through the world, is populated almost exclusively with the covetous, the greedy, the hypocritical, and the perverse.

Conduct unbecoming is what the Boultings took as their theme; and if they did deride one occupation more than most then, paradoxically, it was the actors they employed whom they lampooned, for Roy and John, in inheriting Ealing's sterling cast of characters—Cecil Parker, Terry-Thomas, Dennis Price, Raymond Huntley, John Le Mesurier, Irene Handl, Margaret Rutherford, Miles Malleson, Wilfrid Hyde White, and so on endlessly—created a rep. company of snobs and shits, cowards and swindlers, who had never aged. Those who had been gallant and sound under Balcon and his kin were now encouraged to pick apart their impeccable drawing-room manners to show the bounder and blackguard beneath. And, to anatomise the avarice and selfishness of the English sensibility, it was almost as if the Boultings played a game with the fact that actors, as part of the job, manufacturing emotions, speaking beautifully, and pretending to be other than

---

* My thanks to Michael Frayn for this anecdote.

they really were, were confidence tricksters and counterfeiters by other means—
and none more so than Sellers. Having attended to his work on 'The Goon Show'
and television, and having seen all his films, they knew that behind the veal-faced,
tense, and reserved chap on the cricket pitch, who had all the appeal of a civil servant shut in an office with sick-building syndrome, there lurked something hostile and ambivalent. He had a free-floating, absurdist capacity, which was exactly
what the twins needed to galvanize their ensemble of genteel light-comedy performers. By giving his drive and exhibitionism a chance, they made him a star, and
in making him a star, they unleashed his meanness and spite.

◆ ◆ ◆

Being generous, I suppose you could say that there was nothing wrong with
Sellers that divine intervention couldn't fix.* I mentioned as much in one of my
letters to Roy Boulting; I also said something about Sellers and the price he had
to pay for being a creative genius, and 'When I think of Sellers, I keep wondering, was he Doctor Faustus?'† I was immediately upbraided, and rightly. I received
a postcard dated August 29, 1989:

> Stop wondering about Sellers and 'is he Faustian?' When your research is done,
> you will probably know. Develop a theory now…and you are likely to find your-
> self trying to fit Sellers-the-man to that theory. And both 'artist' and 'man', by the
> way, constitute highly complex indivisibles.

The interfusion of on-and-off screen performances is clearly manifest in
There's a Girl in My Soup, as Sarah Sellers had immediately observed. When I
asked her how does she think of her father now, a dozen years after his death, she
said: 'I like the older films—bits in all of them are hilarious, but other bits are flat,
aren't they? I don't tend to watch the films as films—I watch *him*. The bits I notice—his temperament coming through. *There's a Girl in My Soup*—I can see a lot
of him there. Expressions, gestures, mannerisms. Definitely.'

If Roy Boulting is correct, Robert Danvers was not a part requiring much
out-of-the-way research—and Sellers did aspire to being debonair. When he
started to lose weight and traipse around nightclubs with dolly-birds (ingénues),
being debonair was an all-consuming performance. How did he prepare for such
a rôle? No doubt the same way as ever: 'I start with the voice. I find out how the
character *sounds*…After the voice comes the look of the man. I do a lot of drawings of the character I play. Then I get together with the make-up man and we
sort of transfer my drawings on to my face…After that I establish how the character walks…And then suddenly something strange happens. *The person takes
over*…I suddenly seem to know what sort of life that man has had and how he
would react to a given situation.'

In knowing his characters inside out, in his being aware of what his characters were like and how they felt above, beyond, and behind the lines of dialogue

---

* Alexander Woollcott on Oscar Levant, the original of *Henry Orient*.
† Thomas Mann's.

with which they were provided, Sellers, at his best, was thorough and scrupulous. So why do I find that little discussion of his methods bleak and shadowy? By bravely entering a new element, and transmogrifying, it is as if dark waves and blind surges have closed over his head, and have devoured him. Sellers has described his own annihilation. He speaks like somebody who is already dead.

◆ ◆ ◆

'As John Boulting always says, "Let's get down to the serious business of making a comedy." And he's absolutely right,' said Sellers. 'I've a great respect for the Boulting Brothers, and what they try to do; indeed, what they *do* do. I don't agree entirely with everything they do; I don't think that any one person who is interested in films can entirely agree with everything anybody else does.' From Sellers, high praise—though hedged about with plenty of double negatives and abatements. The first cab of his off-the-Boulting rank was *Carlton Browne of the F.O.*: 'I had a great time... I play a Prime Minister of an ex-British colony, a bit of a rogue,' Sellers chuckled in the month of the film's release (March 1959). Later he was more dismissive, telling Terry-Thomas that he hated it.

The actor who might more justly have claimed to despair of it was Thomas himself. By the first day of shooting, at Shepperton Studios in September 1958, Thomas was already a prisoner of his own image. The rôle of upperclass nincompoop, this time called Cadogan de Vere Carlton Browne, is the one he'll reproduce time and again. The Foreign Office functionary, essentially idle, able to fake eagerness, and be consistently sly, allowed him to combine the scheming robber from *Tom Thumb* with the disdainfulness of Lord Mayley from *The Naked Truth*. His career, like a jelly plopped out from a copper mould, was now set. Sellers, by contrast, had liquefied and remade himself. As Señor Amphibulous, top banana on the atoll of Gaillardia, a marmalade dependency which Britain has forgotten is part of its Empire, he is all three Marx Brothers at once.

If only the film had much more of the Marxist medley. The idea of a tiny British colony lost in the fold of a map, still existing in some distant ocean with its Victorian rituals intact, has mouthwatering comic possibilities. *Carlton Browne of the F.O.* almost predicts the Falklands War: insignificant and distant outpost, a windswept sheep farm, which only comes into prominence when invaded. What is it that the Argentines knew that the British didn't? 'If there's anything there worth having,' says Raymond Huntley, the Foreign Secretary, referring to Gaillardia, *'we're* having it.'

The theme of *Carlton Browne of the F.O.*, like the Falklands War, is exploitation and possession. The Russians and the Americans both have spies on the island and intend to get what they can out of the ignorant natives. The British, meantime, putting on a show of goodwill and munificence, demonstrate the biggest imperialistic joke of all: that when the Union Jack flew over a distant country, and it was added to the long list of British territories, the remote populations were looked down on as outsiders within their own boundaries. In the Boulting film, Ian Bannen's young King of Gaillardia is tolerated, earns respect, and keeps his cool because he was educated at Oxford—he is virtually a gentleman. The unreconstructed exotic alien, the wog, is Sellers' rôle. With heavy lidded eyes and black oily hair, he has thick Latin blood pumping through his anatomy. Alone amongst the cast, Sellers is sultry—if he lopes, like Groucho, it is because he is bent nearly double from the heat. Sellers acts as if there's an equatorial sun in his sky, and it has made him dishevelled. Amphibulous is the only character who seems to be aware that Gaillardia is in the tropics, or anyway abroad.

Sellers, therefore, gnawing his cigars, dreaming up ways to make money for himself and his nation's exchequer, moving his shoulders and fingers in ways that are *foreign*, is out-of-key. He is a maverick. And there is thus an understanding between himself and Bannen as actors. Their few scenes together—a new, green King and an experienced politician—are the film's high spots. (Why not accept a few bribes, Amphibulous counsels, 'You get the Rolls, I get the Cadillac, and the people—they get the lavatories.')

Unfortunately, the film doesn't allow for these two actors to go very far with their bits of business or rapport (Sellers, as later with James Mason, is brought out in new ways when teamed opposite an actor from a different, straighter tradition); we have to swerve off to slapstick military manoeuvres in the jungle and to the long sequence of the procession, when Terry-Thomas takes the salute: the Gaillardian Armed Forces comprise a biplane pulled by a donkey, a gun carriage pulled by mules, and fat smiling girls on bicycles. At the climax of the scene, the VIP dais collapses, resulting in a tangle of arms, legs, and medals. 'My brother-in-law promised the rotten wood would only be used for the public,' apologises you-know-who.

♦ ♦ ♦

Carlton Browne of the F.O. is disappointing because it augers so well. For some reason, however, Sellers chose to remake the story time and again. In the course of the shooting of *Carlton Browne of the F.O.* he was appearing at the Aldwych, soon to be the London headquarters of the Royal Shakespeare Company, in a play called *Brouhaha*, directed by Peter Hall, and which had opened on Wednesday, August 27, 1958. During the run of the play he also made *The Mouse that Roared*, which was released on July 17, 1959. All three dramas had to do with quaint wee lands of far beyond; their common theme was, if you like, the spirit of independence—or, as expressed by Sellers, with his overtones of shamelessness, the spirit of anarchy.

His weekly schedule was hard-fought. He set out for the studio at six-thirty in the morning and arrived back at the theatre for curtain up at seven each evening. If he was shooting on location, he'd be driven off in his Rolls after the performance and he'd bed down for the night in his car. (The Duchy of Grand Fenwick was some woodland near Southampton.) On Sundays ('I used to live for Sundays, you see. Those Sundays, after a week of misery like that...') he'd rehearse and record 'The Goon Show' or work on his songs and monologues for gramophone companies. His dressing rooms were thronged with hangers-on, discarded costumes, and wigs, and there were always telephones ringing. When he spoke, Sellers assumed the voice and unruffled charm of Grytpype Thynne. He seemed to enjoy the turmoil—it meant he had no time to think.

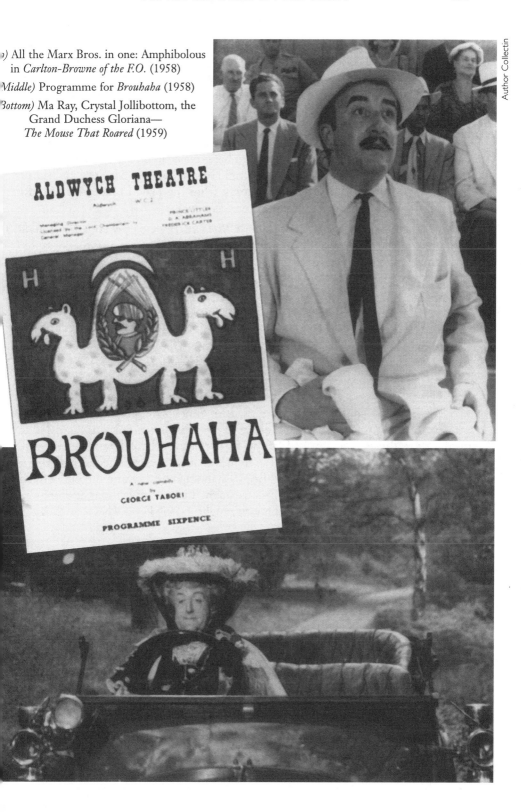

) All the Marx Bros. in one: Amphibolous in *Carlton-Browne of the F.O.* (1958)

Middle) Programme for *Brouhaha* (1958)

Bottom) Ma Ray, Crystal Jollibottom, the Grand Duchess Gloriana— *The Mouse That Roared* (1959)

ALDWYCH THEATRE

BROUHAHA

GEORGE TABORI

PROGRAMME SIXPENCE

If, during daylight, the Boultings were restricting or editing down his hyper-active talent, at night his gallivanting and his looseness went unchecked. That was the joy of live theatre. There was nobody to yell 'Cut!'; nobody to trim his per-formance afterwards with a pair of scissors; nobody to restrict him. Short of or-dering the fire screen down or implanting him with a knock-out dart aimed from the rear of the stalls, his jazziness and impudence had an ideal showcase. 'Peter was outrageous,' says Anne. 'He took his camera on stage with him and snapped away at the other actors. He pretended to bang his head on the "fourth wall". He made up half of the script as he went along. He grabbed Leo McKern and started dancing with him—Peter just danced away from the play. Lionel Jeffries didn't like it at all. He must have thought Peter was bonkers.'

He'd have been in the right of it there. *Brouhaha*, by George Tabori, was about a sultan who, with the object of attracting superpower intervention and capital, goes about secretly creating disturbances, making trouble, and instigating rebel-lions in his very own country. He thinks that if he fakes a revolution, his kingdom of Huwayat will be put on the map. Sellers, as the potentate, had the Ian Bannen rôle; but, instead of being regal and commanding respect, he made his ruler into a man who was startling and reckless. The sultan was capable of anything and everything—and what the character did to his country, Sellers did to the play.

'All kinds of things used to happen,' he confessed, 'and in those days it was taboo to do any improvisation... The first act was very good, the last act wasn't too bad, but it really took a dive in the middle—and I was determined to try and beat this... I was bawled out I don't know how many times—and in fact I was told it was *not done* in the West End to do the sort of thing I was doing. But, this night I man-aged to get through it, until we came to the scene where I was dancing with Hermione Harvey. I took two or three steps too many towards the footlights—and I just went straight over... eight feet from a standing position into the pit, with her on top of me. *Wham!* It was an enormous laugh. They must've thought there were mattresses down there and we did this every night. I don't know what they thought.'

♦ ♦ ♦

Sellers' retrospective version of events, in which he reckons he was heroically giving everybody a good time, differs markedly from the recollection of his co-star. I met Hermione Harvey, who now lives in Menorca, for toasted scones and almond tarts at Brown's Hotel, Dover Street, on one of her rare visits to London:

> Before the off, Sellers staggered on to the stage, in front of the tabs, and an-nounced, 'Ladies and Gentlemen, I am pissed. I have an understudy who is poised ready to take my place. But those of you who would prefer me to soldier on—say AYE!' There was, of course, a roar of AYE!
>
> Well, by Act III it was obvious that he was more peculiar than he was normally. In this scene we had to dance to a horn gramophone: 'Shall we dance, Alma?' This time we danced the wrong way round—he reversed, tripped, and fell over the edge into the pit, dragging me on top of him. He was a heavy man in those days. The audience laughed, thinking it was meant to happen. There was no actual orchestra there, just a lot of ladders and equipment from the Old Vic Company, which used

to rehearse at the Aldwych. And then he said in a very loud voice, 'Where the fucking hell are we now?' 'We are in the pit,' I said. He decided he'd hurt himself. I felt that the show must go on. He, however, had had enough. He climbed back on the stage and started to stumble off into the wings—ever the gallant, he'd forgotten about me and had left me down in the darkness. I called him back—and he did come and pull me out; and he momentarily returned to the play. The next line was 'Let's throw caution to the winds, Alma!' which got a big laugh. We finished the scene and he went off to his dressing room, locked the door, wouldn't answer it to anybody, and wouldn't appear in the rest of the play. Poor Colin Ellis had to go on and finish for him. The press were there immediately. I wasn't allowed to say Sellers was drunk. I had to say it was an accident.

On the last night, Noël Coward, Milligan, Secombe, everybody was there, and Sellers insisted I had a moustache. 'You must have a moustache. It's very funny.' He painted this on my face himself... Richard Waring was furious, 'How dare you come on looking like that!' 'I couldn't do anything, *he* insisted.' Sellers would override you. That night he came down from the flies on a rope. I just gave up. Afterwards, Graham Payn and Noël Coward held a party at Cheyne Walk. Sellers, the guest of honour, sat in a corner and sulked. He pretended to read a book until somebody gave him orange juice mixed with champagne, when he perked up, jumped into his Goon characters, and was happy.

Sellers was unbelievably unprofessional. He'd cut half the dialogue so he could jump to the end of a scene and go home. He didn't care about the other actors; he didn't care about the audience. He was more than eccentric. The way he went on, it was as if he was virtually insane. The whole cast would stand in the wings to see what he would do next.

Which might only have encouraged him in his excesses, of course...

◆ ◆ ◆

Brouhaha was Sellers' playpen. Those who turned up to applaud his antics did duty for the cousins and the aunts of the Southsea childhood, who had urged him on when (said Uncle Bert, perspiring at the memory) 'he was just a horror.' All eyes were on him. His wife saw the production over thirty times—she chaperoned him like a nanny. David Lodge had seen the play enough times to be able to turn to her and ask, as Sellers capered down to the front of the stage and clung there for a perilous instant before disappearing: 'Is this a new scene they are working into the show?' (As for Milligan, his comment was metaphysical: 'You don't think that orchestra pit got there by accident, do you?')

Sellers tried to justify his boredom by saying (to Pierre Rouve) 'I don't like to remember where to be on a stage. The stage is constricting. You can only face one way.' He also fulminated (to Dilys Powell) against long runs: 'I once saw an Agatha Christie play after it had been running for years—the poor actors seemed to be dragging through their parts... Long runs! Eight weeks is enough... I got into great trouble when I was playing in the theatre; I was badly misinterpreted. I said an actor only gave two performances a week. Well, it's a fact: an actor is really on top only about twice, perhaps only once in the week. You *try* your best every night. But it's only once or twice a week it works. And you know it the minute you walk on to the stage...'

If the Aldwych routine was draggy and stale ('I don't like the theatre,' he admitted finally), the character of the juvenile sultan was a rôle with which Sellers, in his slithering and comprehensive way, could completely merge. He appeared on the television current affairs programme, *Tonight*, for example, in full Valentino fig. If Cynthia Judah and Ned Sherrin, the producers, had expected him simply to be subjected to a few minutes of interview-cum-plug for *Brouhaha*, they were in for a shock. Sellers arrived, in brownish make-up and billowing oriental robes, expecting to be treated and talked to as a Middle Eastern oil sheik. His assigned four-minute slot extended to nearly a quarter of an hour, as he improvised opinions and pontificated about Egypt, the Suez Canal, pyramids, sand, Lawrence of Arabia, etc. The interview was conducted straight-faced and for real—only when they'd got him finally off camera did somebody feel they ought to explain that 'That was Peter Sellers, who is appearing in…'

How could people have known, in 1958, that there was the virus of disaster lurking within the put-on artistry and success of Sellers' ten-minute extemporisation? That *Tonight* spot was the limit of his attention span, and that's why films would suit him perfectly. 'He'd do two or three takes,' says Joe McGrath, 'and he'd get depressed if it wasn't working. He'd *never* want to try and figure out the faults. He'd want to stop, abandon ship. "Let's forget the whole thing." He never wanted to rehearse or to discover any depth or new approaches. Peter wanted, by living on his instincts alone, to do it and to be fully creative and funny; or else…'

◆ ◆ ◆

After the low Gaillardian skies and Huwayat's sickle moons, his next (or overlapping) fantasy island was Grand Fenwick. It is meant to be situated in a valley off the French Alps, but, like the other sheikdoms and emirates, its precise location may best be said to have been right inside Sellers' head. He was lured by tales of remote kingdoms (they include Fu's Tibet and Prince Rudi's Zenda). He could identify with beleaguered and self-sufficient city states—they were places where his alienness had a home.

In Grand Fenwick, large and containing multitudes, he's not only Tully Bascombe, the Hereditary Grand Marshal; Count Mountjoy, the frock-coated and monocled Prime Minister; and Gloriana, the Margaret Rutherford clone; he is also the model for all the pigeon-flecked statues in the town square. The country is a single extended family—an ancestral Sellers has managed to spread himself everywhere. He is a body of people. (When, by means of cinema's special effects, Sellers has a conversation with Sellers, or Sellers encounters Sellers, it is like witnessing black magic at work.) Is the eugenic dispersal, or dilution, the reason why there has been no social or scientific progress since the Middle Ages? Grand Fenwick's army wears chain mail and the longbow is the national weapon; Gloriana and Mountjoy are costumed as Irene Dunne's Queen Victoria and Alec Guinness' Disraeli in *The Mudlark*—they exist not in the real medieval period but in a nineteenth-century reconstruction: Ruritania. Here, all is pageantry and purposelessness. Nattily-attired brass bands march up and down, people wave banners embroidered with double-headed eagles, bunting is ever-present. It looks idyllic, but the populace is bored. How may they galvanize themselves? Why, declare a war.

If, originally, *The Mouse that Roared* was a satire on the postbellum replenishment and wealth of Germany and Japan ('We declare war on Monday, we are defeated on Tuesday, and by Friday we will be rehabilitated beyond our wildest dreams'), the film now seems more to be about deviousness and greed; its plot (the staging of a flop) prophesies Sellers' admiration of Mel Brooks' *The Producers* (where instead of phony war games we have a phony Broadway musical, which unaccountably takes off, as Grand Fenwick's belligerence does). True, the cunningness at the story's core is well disguised. Tully, in particular, soft and fat and clad in a yellow shirt, looks carved out of cheese. He's a frightful nerd to have as a hero.

Tully and his chums, with their bows and arrows and suits of cardboard armour (they are amateur dramatic Robin Hoods), set off across the Atlantic in a rusty tugboat to attack the enemy in person. They arrive in what is meant to be New York and there is nobody there. Hardly any wonder; the New World, in this production, is glued together from model shots, primitive back-projection, and stock footage. The result of this economising is that America looks less real than Grand Fenwick.

However, we must suspend our disbelief and pretend that the shabbiness is anti-naturalistic and done with intent, like the cellophane seascapes in Fellini. What would take mass hypnosis to get us to accept, though, is the romance between Tully and Jean Seberg's Helen. Seberg, a waif-like actress in the Mia Farrow mould, is utterly lacking in lightness and giddiness. This was tolerable in *Saint Joan*, where her dullness could seem like a martyr's earnest truth-telling, but the solemnity is hopeless in a comedy, and her sincere manner quite defeats Sellers. He is conscious, anyway, of his doughy body, and in his wobbling and wavering scenes with Seberg he keeps glancing away; he's awkward. What they seem like to me is an early, crude version of the courtship rituals essayed with such agility by Woody Allen. With the real, flexible, elvish Mia Farrow as his muse (or before that, the scatterbrained Diane Keaton), Allen overcame his unattractiveness and, in *Annie Hall*, *Manhattan*, and *A Midsummer Night's Sex Comedy*, he's quite the Priapus. (Indeed, he always gives himself beautiful co-stars, who adore him.) In film after libidinous film, goblinesque boy gets elegant and neurotic girl, with wise-cracks.

◆ ◆ ◆

Allen's cinema career began in Sellers' shadow. He wrote the original screenplay for *What's New, Pussycat?*, which Sellers broke up and waylaid with his precious improvising, and in it he played the part of Victor Shakapopolis, a backstage gofer at a strip club. ('How much is the salary?' 'Twenty francs.' 'Not much.' 'It's all I can afford.') During the shooting, in London and Paris, he was frequently mistaken for Sellers. 'Britt said it was weird when I walked into the room where she was reading,' recalled Allen, 'because for a split second she thought I was her husband, and she even said "Peter?"' Worse was when it happened the other way around, and Sellers, then at a pinnacle of international fame, was mistaken for Allen, the neophyte who'd never been further east than Long Island. 'One day,'

Clive Donner recalls, 'an executive producer came into the foyer of the Dorchester, where we were all staying, and he saw Sellers there and he mistook him for Woody, and he said "Don't worry about that guy Sellers. We'll take care of him..." And Peter immediately became and played along as Woody...'

To be avenged, Sellers' impersonation, or rather his expropriation, went further than the foyer. He took over the lines and situations in *What's New, Pussycat?* which Allen had carefully devised for himself. 'They would say "That scene between you and Peter Sellers or you and Peter O'Toole. We're going to let the two Peters do it."' What should be Shakapopolis' sexual frustration, as he gathers up the discarded g-strings at the Crazy Horse Saloon, turned into Fassbender's—who screeches to his valkyrie of a wife, 'I have hated you from the moment I first married you,' a classic Woody Allen quip. Allen was downgraded to a subplot; Sellers, who was only meant to be a guest star, having recently had a heart-attack, allowed his rôle to bloom and spread. 'There were fewer scenes in it for him when he accepted the part. That was one of the reasons he had decided to do it—it wouldn't overstrain him,' says Donner, 'but something curious happened... We did improvise a lot and Woody was petrified...'

Unless there was anything in the rumour that Allen was to have portrayed Sellers in a biopic produced by Robert Evans, he encountered his sort-of double for the second and last time on that (Woody's words) 'unredeemingly moronic exercise', *Casino Royale*. And, wouldn't you know it, *again* there was the case of mistaken identity, *again* in the foyer of a hotel—the George V in Paris, where Sellers was accosted by Leo Jaffe, the chairman of Columbia, and informed: 'That son-of-a-bitch Sellers is causing us nothing but grief on this picture. I wish to hell we never had signed him. You, Woody, are a gentleman.' Sellers, transforming his voice once more into Allen's, agreed with every word, disappeared into the night, and was next heard from in Sweden—he'd gone into hiding with Britt Ekland's mother, and he refused to return to the film.

◆ ◆ ◆

Which transports us back to *The Mouse that Roared*. Sellers' sallow Tully meets Jean Seberg when he blunders into an Institute of Advanced Physics and captures her father and his new hydrogen bomb—a fizzing rugby ball capable of destroying two million square miles. (It is a Doomsday Machine, and Dr Alfred Kokintz—'He's eccentric. He likes to work alone'—as portrayed by David Kossoff, is a benign Dr Strangelove.) That is why, by the way, the Fenwick army finds New York deserted. An air raid or fire drill is in progress and the half dozen extras portraying the American population are hiding in a cellar. They are very cheerful—they love the bomb, because 'whoever has the bomb has the world by its tail.' At school you will have been taught to underline those words in pencil and to write DRAMATIC IRONY in the margin.

On the boat back home, with the nutty professor and his daughter as hostage, plus their ovoid high explosive, Grand Fenwick now 'controls the destiny of the world'—but what of it? When we get to dry land and meet Sellers' other characters again, they are not the sort of people to be much interested in a hectic plot. Gloriana, swathed in blue chiffon and ostrich plumes, is simply and resolutely in a cuckoo-land of her own. Facts of history and chronology are not her concern—she's beyond them. Similarly, for Count Mountjoy to have to scamper around the castle, to a silent movie piano yet, is demeaning. He seems to want to find the bomb and give it back or let it off, or something tedious. As Sellers conceives him, his slightly exaggerated sleekness and purring voice gesture in the direction of Hercules Grytpype Thynne, no less; he ought to be besotted with a totally lunatic scheme out of 'The Goon Show', not stooping to a television sit-com chase, which climaxes with four-star generals from the world's big nations chucking the bomb, one to the other, in an American football game.

The director, Jack Arnold, was best known for his science-fiction films, like *The Incredible Shrinking Man*; that's what he does to Sellers' flamboyance—he miniaturises it, puts it up against a broad and coarsening New World *vs.* Old World polemic, which leaves me, for one, perplexed. The film is full of inconsistencies, logical jumps. Not only is the love-affair between Tully and Helen implausible because the performers lack the vital chemistry, but also, why does the Kossoff character decide to stay when he's been so badly treated?

I don't think we are meant to question, or even to acknowledge, the hole-riddled cheesiness that's *The Mouse That Roared*. It is a film people always remember fondly, despite the fact that its execution is such a shambles; it's the fancy behind the way the story is told which grabs the imagination. Grand Fenwick taking on America and accidentally winning, by default or what-have-you, is an underdog fantasy. But if you dwell on it, and actually sit through it again, the pro-quaint-wee-country and anti-superpower stance isn't handled very sensitively. 'The little nations of the world,' the film concludes, 'should be in charge of the bomb.' Oh yes? Libya? Iraq? Uganda? Haiti? Little bits of what was Yugoslavia?

♦ ♦ ♦

As prophecy and political satire, therefore, *The Mouse that Roared* is sentimentalising gibberish; its romantic scenes are limp; and simply in terms of cinematography it is uncraftsmanlike. Nobody was more surprised by its success than Sellers himself: 'The film that has really done incredibly well [in America] is *The Mouse that Roared*, for what reason I don't know, because I didn't like it very much. But over there in the first four weeks it took over a million dollars, which is more money than any other British picture ever to play there has taken in that time … And I suppose that that is the eventual answer. You can't argue with the distributor and say, "But I didn't like it"; he will only reply, "I'm not interested in whether you like it, my boy. I've got the money to prove that the public likes it." There's absolutely nothing you can say.'

Well, there are one or two things. There's no mystery as to why the Americans lapped it up. As a continent of plainsmen and little old world villagers, uneasily federated, they quite identified themselves with Grand Fenwick, the small and spunky lonesome state. That America itself, in the film, is meant to be a nebulous and slightly menacing Big Brother, indistinguishable from Russia, could easily be over-looked, for what do the stereotypical big-chested CIA colonels and Washington bu-reaucrats (who believe 'we've always been nice to little countries all over the world') have to do with real, individual American citizens? Real Americans, seeing 'a bunch of fifteenth-century Europeans' coming down the street, toting crossbows and hal-berds and using Thomas Cook's *Guide to New York* as the campaign plan, saw in Sellers one of the Pilgrim Fathers. He wasn't an invader—he was an ancestor.

It is muffled, but inside *The Mouse That Roared* is the spirit of adventure—or adventurism. The film was about chicanery and topsy-turvy bravery, which was fine. But what of the deeper drives of wilfulness and deceit which Sellers, who was never straightforward, could convey? *The Mouse That Roared* is over before it ought to have begun; with Fenwick, a speck, in charge of the entire planet, we might have had some true Goonishness and hazardousness. But the actor isn't given the chance to try things out, and, as he said himself, 'I can imagine seeing myself in that film in America and saying "Hmmm…"' Nevertheless, the picture did occasionally insinuate itself during Sellers' future career.

The kidnapped, bearded professor, beautiful daughter, and Doomsday Device plot is duplicated in *The Pink Panther Strikes Again*, where, for the second time, it lies inert. Yet, if the prof and the bomb routine wasn't enough to pilfer from *The Mouse that Roared*, how about putting Clouseau in chain-mail and getting Sellers to revert to being Tully, running around in an Alpine hunting lodge set?

Tully, as you'll by now have gathered, is perhaps Sellers' least entertaining performance; but it was a rôle (part Bluebottle, part mock-innocent) which he found useful to adopt in real life; women would be drawn to what seemed like his helplessness, his passivity—they'd want to mother him. He even favoured archery as a hobby and filled his garage with painted straw bulls-eye targets and quivers of arrows. Word of this reached Michael Bentine, who decided they ought to visit Robin's Oak, in Sherwood Forest, and practise their skills in the shadow and at-mosphere of the legendary bowman. 'I think that branch up there,' said Bentine, taking aim at the top of the tree. Years later, when the tree was pruned or felled, the Nottingham locals were delighted to find the arrowhead embedded in the bough—it was conclusive evidence at last…

Once Tully had aged, however, and his mildness had thickened into an atti-tude or outlook, the character he becomes is Chance, in *Being There*, shuffling through the dead leaves. Both speak with Stan Laurel's flat, dopey lilt; both are failures who paradoxically succeed—Tully being appointed Prime Minister, Chance being considered Presidential material. Compare and contrast the two performances and you'll see the differences between the early and late period Sellers. As a young man, playing a young man, he was featureless, blobby. We wait, in vain, for the inspired silliness (which was his gift on radio) or for his sad-ness (which emanated from his oldsters) to spurt out. Twenty years on, again play-ing an opaque character, there is mystery, rather than weakness and numbness; Sellers, who allowed himself to revert to his youthful plumpness to look like Chance, is no dead weight. He is affecting—the last thing his performance is is slack. Moving with the slowness and tentativeness of an oriental sage (we can see why Fu Manchu had to come next), with each gesture and banality counting for something, we yet get the impression that Chance is peculiarly loose and free. Kosinski (his name is Polish for *nothing*, incidentally) was thrilled by the portrayal: 'Peter Sellers understood my character of Chauncey Gardiner better than I, for good reason...He has no interior life. No sense of himself. No notion of what he was or who he would like to become...He is, in fact, beyond definition by himself and entirely defined by society, which perceives him for what he is not.'

This string of epigrams, describing a personality so adrift and distilled it must be mad, literally unhinged, is, as a description of Sellers, only partially accurate. For, despite his pains to commandeer *Being There* and everything pertaining to it ('I liked when they said in the film that the computer can't pin down where he comes from'), Chance was not Sellers as he really was, but as he'd liked to have been. It was the ideal of the empty space; degree zero; every moment, as reality erased itself, a fresh start. As with Tully's gormlessness, the wistful nullity of Chance was another fiction, a device with which to hide the truth of his paranoia, avarice, and calculated nastiness. To give a small but representative example of how Sellers was Sellers, not Chance the bowler-hatted gent: on *Being There* there was a runner who prepared and brought his lunch. Steak and salad every day at one P.M. sharp. After a month, Sellers suddenly turned on this chap and said 'What's this?' 'Your steak and salad.' 'You *know* I'm a vegetarian.'

He was so suspicious and disenchanted, and so lonely and full of waste, having driven wives and children off, he had to pay somebody to keep him company. I asked Michael Jeffery what it was like, this rôle of salaried chum: 'It took me at least four years to get over his death. I'd have recurring dreams—because we used to go to Golders Green a lot to see the rose bush for Peg and Bill, and I dreamt he'd appear from behind the tombstones, in disguise, saying, "It's me. I just had to get away from people." I had this nightmare for at least a year. I'd been with him for over four years—and towards the end it was twenty-four hours a day, seven days a week. And I'd never lost anybody close to me before. He fed off your energy. Everything I did was for him...'

♦ ♦ ♦

'What are your immediate film plans after *The Mouse That Roared?*' he was asked in the Spring of 1959.

'I'm making *I'm All Right, Jack*, with the Boulting Brothers,' he replied.

In the character of Fred Kite, the Boultings, who could see Sellers for what he was, made full use of their actor's obduracy (which is not the same as strength) and infantilism (which is not the same as childlikeness)—the extreme points, or twin peaks, towards which Sellers would always veer, as an artist and as a man. Wily and, when you tried to get the hang of him, far away from everything, Sellers was brought out by Kite—'a very serious part,' he said, 'and the only way to tackle it was seriously.'

Sellers maintained that he'd been offered a new beginning; and when, in later years, he roved over his career, he wiped out what had gone before, as if it had been of no consequence. ('My first real chance was *I'm All Right, Jack*. Fred Kite was a good character to play. Those days were wonderful days.' Etc.) In fact, the rôle grew out of his early work, where he'd learned that humour and comedy was not the same as plain funniness, and Kite was far from being a sudden new direction. He himself described the part as 'that hard-headed trier Fred Kite—on the surface such an infuriating old blockhead and yet, somehow moving—who did his best according to his own lights', and it was clear to the Boultings that there was no actor living *except* Sellers with the psychological quality, the furtiveness and strangeness, for the rôle.

'The Boultings wrote him an amazing part,' says Ian Carmichael. 'We were all reproducing our characters from *Private's Progress*, but Fred Kite was new and Sellers took it with both hands. The Hitler moustache was his idea. The mangling of the English language was his own—that wasn't on the printed page as I remember. Kite poured out of the Boultings; they loved writing that part and Sellers loved playing it, when he got into it—which he did, very much as a straight actor. John Boulting continued to keep him on a tight rein and Sellers was lucky to have such a director.'

◆ ◆ ◆

Carmichael is correct about the lower-middle-class Hitler moustache—'a stroke of genius' in Milligan's opinion. ('He must have chosen that because he did all his own make-up.') Sellers also allowed himself to be scalped. 'I really did live the part. I had my hair cut Gestapo-short and rarely went out,' he said. He still had to sally forth to record 'The Goon Show', however, and on the sleeve photographs for Parlophone's *The Best of the Goon Show*, Volumes I and II, you can see what he looked like with his brutalist barbering. (He looks like a mad monk.)

And the malapropisms and mispronunciations were Sellers'—one source of inspiration being his own mother. 'Oh Spike,' she'd once been heard to say, 'I'm very fond of... reading friction.' Kite, in full sail, says 'jeropadising,' 'revalant,' 'sitawation,' 'indawidawal,' and so on; and Sellers copied this from a chief grip at the studio who said 'prosholium' for 'proscenium,' and who, when Sellers once tripped over a cable, came up alongside and said, 'Can I assist you in your predicalament?'

Sellers enjoyed putting Kite together: 'Kite came from my watching television clips of various members of the TUC* coming and going from Downing Street, and fellows holding up microphones: "The situation, as I see it, is that the negotiations have reached a point of stagnation and all that can happen now is that they will reverberate to the detriment of the masses. All I am prepared to say at this juncture is that my colleagues and I are going to withdraw and consult." Kite was built up from a collage of that sort of people.'

Kite's voice is low and clipped, formed by a lifetime of whispering secrets and strategies to a huddle of like-minded factory foremen. He is so enraged by the exploiters with carnations in their buttonholes, who own the workshops and

---

* The British equivalent of the AFL-CIO.

foundries, that his speech is strangulated; he is pop-eyed with indignation. He also does his best not to be gruff. The Dennis Price, Terry-Thomas, etc. characters aren't only hatefully richer than Kite, and of a higher class, they are also more eloquent. Kite's ludicrous misuse of words occurs when he tries to rise and out-match these paymasters, and there is something very unpleasant about the scenes where we see that his snarls and follies simply amuse them.

'I had a bit of luck with the character of the shop-steward in *Jack*,' Sellers said, continuing to identify his raw material. 'There was a trades-union official I used to know at one of the studios: "I've seen 'em all come and go, you know," he'd say... He was the type who always... rushes about with a little notice board in his hands and a list of names on a sheet of paper fastened on with paper clips—I'm sure it's completely useless. I suppose I modelled the character from [all] these sources.'

Trades-union congressmen, studio henchmen and bureaucrats (who, during *The Naked Truth*, had called that strike which Peggy Mount mentioned), and the television news, however, were simply stimulants and residues. Kite was more a product of Sellers' own numberless facets and urge to prevail. The understanding went well beyond the staccato voice; it involved those beady, yearning eyes and the way Sellers knew that his character would wear his watch on the underside of his wrist. Kite's loose and flapping wrists become a significant mannerism. They thrust his hands at right-angles to his arms and body—like claws or stubby flight-less wings. Kite, after all, has an office. He pushes paper. He is proud of being able to wear that lumpy double-breasted suit, weighted down with propelling pencils. He *doesn't* work with his hands or have to don proletarian dungarees. You could almost regard him, with his big, moony baby cheeks and perspiration, as a crea-ture in mid-metamorphosis from the factory-floor underclass to the managerial level. And this, the sense we get that he wants to better himself, gives him a curi-ous rootlessness and anguish.

One of the merits of *I'm All Right, Jack* is that it doesn't take sides in the class war. Indeed, under the coverings of their respective languages and costumes, the bosses and the labourers are much of a muchness—they are all shits, lying and toadying. Except, of course, for Carmichael's decent and dreamy Windrush (he's Lord Peter Wimsey as a young man); and, in a more inscrutable way, Kite, who is suspended between the genuine menials and tycoons. Windrush, 'a university man... brought up as a gentleman,' wants to escape the hypocrisy of his tribe and live amongst what he imagines are the virtuous poor. He purposefully travels down in the world. Kite, similarly romantic, keeps himself going with reveries of Soviet Russia ('Russia, Russia, it's all we ever get in this house,' complains Irene Handl, as Mrs Kite). The astonished and faintly embarrassed meeting between the two men, who are each out of their natural element, gives the film its focus.

◆ ◆ ◆

Whenever I see *I'm All Right, Jack*, I'm surprised anew at how *un*focused it is. The film is as convoluted as Kite's diction and grammar; the plot 'reverberates back to our detriment.' And what a long time it takes before all that plot is given a push. Eventually, perhaps forty minutes into the film, we reach the domain of Kite and his cohorts. When Sellers comes on it is exhilarating. After having been lulled by a lot of fatheaded stuff about Windrush's incompetence, suddenly here is energy, here is assurance. Kite, his eyes as bright as glass, marches across the yard, in close formation with his comrades (including Kenneth Griffith and Cardew Robinson), to confront Major Hitchcock (Terry-Thomas), and we are held by him. What is the management up to, employing Windrush, an obvious twerp? It is 'bare-faced provocation of the workers.' Okay, says Thomas, in his card-sharp way, let's sack him. Kite continues to stare and blink into space. He's achieved what he demanded, but something isn't right. 'Incompetence,' he announces at last, 'doesn't justify dismissal.'

If the film was nothing more than sallies of this kind, it wouldn't be negligible; but what makes it a classic are the bits between the industrial relations jokes, the bits underneath the surface. Sellers was so smoked and kippered in the rôle of Kite that the home life scenes, with Irene Handl, stout and boisterous, and Liz Frazer, blonde and pneumatic, were to remain amongst the best he ever played. In the factory, amongst his troops, Kite's music, on the soundtrack, had the bounce and spring of a military band. Home again, however, in his parlour at the end of a busy day, he is fagged and faded—and the music, too, sags. The drums and trumpets slow right up and are vaguely bluesy.

Kite may succeed at work by blowing his whistle and *stopping* people from working ('The natural rhythm of the British worker,' says John Le Mesurier's time-and-motion inspector, 'is neither natural, rhythmic, or much to do with work'), but at home, or as a man rather than a rank, he is defeated. Sellers, without recoursing to any sentimental ploy, conveys the man's essential loneliness; when the womenfolk walk out on him, Irene Handl accoutred in a cloche hat, he is crushed. To the noise of their offstage packing and door-slamming, he droops and slouches. (The drums and trumpets aren't bluesy, they are simply listless.) He decides to hold a press conference, is puffed up again by the sight of a throng of reporters, but once more he is disheartened, his thunder stolen by Windrush, to whom the hacks really want to speak. Kite prowls around the knot of journalists, with their flashbulbs and notebooks, being ignored, and he is flabbergasted.

Abandoned in his own house, everybody—the journalists, Windrush, his wife and daughter—gone, he soon converts and reduces it to a masculine piggery. The sink is full of dishes, there is toast on the floor gathering fluff, and partially full bottles of rancid milk abound. At this point, totally dejected and wearing a pinafore, he is interrupted in the washing-up by Terry-Thomas. At least it will be company, of a kind. ('Do you imbibe?')

Hitchcock comes to see if Kite can get the workers back to work. The two men, who are enemies, achieve a rapprochement (after a few drinks) and, by the end, the Major is darning Kite's socks. Kite keeps his apron on throughout, and the atmosphere of the scene is cosy and domestic; the incongruousness of it is perfectly understated. Suddenly, these men who are so mighty and full of themselves are playing house. And Kite, at his moment of greatest power, in command of a General Strike, is actually feeling very hollow, very bereft. 'Have I managed to live my own life?' he seems to be thinking. 'Have I been simply an egotist, peering only after destiny and fame and my name in the newspaper?' The rhythms of the scene, coming after Kite's other disillusionments, imply these ruminations. Kite also seems to sense, in the shadows stirring in his room, that he is quietly growing old. When he glances at his wedding photograph, the face reflected in the glass is weary and bloated, past its prime. It only lasts a fraction of a second on the screen, but we know that Kite is overcome by the bitter taste of failure and incomprehension.

It is impossible to believe that Sellers was only thirty-three.

◆ ◆ ◆

I'm All Right, Jack concludes with a riot in a television studio; it is something of a cop-out, like the turmoil at the end of *Casino Royale*. Crude as this method is, we can at least now be sure that the Boultings intended their satire to get at the violence and barbarism within the English sensibility—the inward aggression which is outwardly manifested in the forms and rituals of, say, cricket. We can see what generals and judges and gentlemen actually are: they are people who enjoy being rude and unaffectionate.

Sellers himself would return to the subject in *The Magic Christian*, a decade later. Sir Guy Grand, a megalomanical practical joker, uses his money and ingenuity to humiliate, disconcert, chasten. The mercenary motive melts and warps the most honourable heart. Grand uses his aristocratic position, his sense of being superior, to wage a malicious war. He is a scourge—unscrupulous and cynical. Sellers' favourite scene was the anti-Satyajit Ray one where Grand constructs a large tank or vat, pumps it full of greenish-yellow ordure, scatters cash across its surface, and then invites the citizens of London to come and collect their FREE MONEY. Hordes of bowler-hatted gents (they look like Fu's thugs) have no compunction about diving into the mulligatawny soup. And if you think it sounds puerile and less than subtle, you'll be in good company. Irene Handl phoned up Sellers to say, 'Peter, you know I love you, but the other day I saw *The Magic Christian*, and you know when that scene with all the excrement comes on at the end?...I don't honestly think people want to see excreta on the films.'

'But the point was, love,' said Sellers, 'I know it was a hard-hitting scene, but it really meant that people will swim through shit for money. Which is absolutely true.'

David Frost—who'd marry his widow, Lynne Frederick—once asked Sellers, 'Do you think money is the root of all evil?' Sellers replied in a voice which had the trace of a lisp, a becoming impediment put on to indicate humility: 'I think you can do just about anything with it...You can buy anything with it, buy anyone with it. I started without a penny to scratch my backside with, like most of us. So I gathered around myself a lot of material, unnecessary things, to begin with. Until I found they were useless. They didn't bring me happiness. And it is a quest for that that I think we are really talking about, aren't we?'

◆ ◆ ◆

With the success of *I'm All Right, Jack*, which won Sellers the British Film Academy's Award as the Best Actor of 1960 ('I would like to say on behalf of me mum and dad that I am very pleased to return to the villas with the prize,' he told the mystified Duke of Edinburgh, who was presenting the trophy), he decided to move from middle-class Whetstone to the gentrifications of the Home Counties. Before he left London, however, Sellers organised a firework party at his old house—he would send himself off with a bang. It was to be his farewell to (half-way) ordinariness. He'd never again live in a street.

As Angela Morley, the former Wally Stott, explains: 'Around 1960, when 'The Goon Show' finished ... Peter ... decided to have his fireworks. Mario Fabrizi and such people were in the garden with rockets, lining them up. Peter was inside the house, looking out, shooting all this stuff with his Arriflex 16mm cine camera. One of the rockets fell over after it had been ignited and headed straight for the plate-glass window—smashed through that and set fire to the living room and dining room, singeing Peter's drums and doing considerable damage ...'

The inadvertent bombardment, the miscalculated pyrotechnics, are somehow apt; a warning signal. (Did the episode inspire the exploding firework factory sequence in *The Revenge of the Pink Panther*?) Sellers was migrating to a level of stardom, wealth, and international recognition which would give him all the personal satisfaction and pleasure of Dante's first circle in Hell. But being handed something or achieving something only to find it is not quite right is the Sellers hallmark. He derived humour from the way his characters tried to overcome, by fast-talk or pure ignorance, life's various calamities, choices, and limitations. Clouseau, for example, carefully examining a fizzing bomb before it goes off, as he expects, right in his face, is left none the worse for wear than being streaked with soot.

Sellers' characters absorb their hurts and pangs—perhaps they are repositories for the actor's, too? Kite, whose dreams of glory break over his head like rain-clouds, would certainly fulfill this function. 'I don't think I've ever met anyone who is completely happy,' Sellers once confessed. 'I don't know whether it is possible to be completely happy, because either one is terribly happy, I mean as far as one's business life goes—that goes marvelously well, and it seems that one's domestic life doesn't. I've never met anyone yet who could honestly tell me that *both* were going absolutely marvelously well ...'

Follow his pro-and-contra, home and work, argument to its end, and the world is doomed to cancelling itself out. Sellers himself, in being never acquiescent and in always demanding *more*, never struck the balance; he feared the boredom of it.

Part Four

◆◆◆

His Marvellous Years

ANNE: *I would I knew thy heart.*
GLOUCESTER: *'Tis figured in my tongue.*
ANNE: *I fear me both are false.*
GLOUCESTER: *Then never man was true.*

Shakespeare, *The Life and Death of King Richard III*

Chapter Ten

♦ ♦ ♦

Chipperfield Circus

I f the last the cinema-going world saw of Fred Kite was his expression of wonder and worry during the tumult at the television studio, that was not quite his positive final—or most excessive—appearance. A group of people, perhaps numbering no more than a hundred, saw him take form, like an unbottled goblin, on the island of Cyprus in 1973:

'On the second day of shooting *Ghost in the Noonday Sun*, by lunchtime it was incredibly hot,' recalls Peter Medak. 'I was in my trailer asleep, and I suddenly awoke to all this laughing and shouting—and I start listening, and I thought it was Peter entertaining the troops and giving an imitation of Fred Kite. As I listened more and more ... I started to wonder, what was going on? I went out. He had gathered all the actors around himself, he'd elected himself the shop-steward, and he made this insane speech about how everybody is incompetent ... He was doing *I'm All Right, Jack*. I'll never forget Peter Boyle's face—he was dumbfounded ... Then the entire crew gathered around—and Sellers said there should be a vote taken: hands up those who believed that the director was incompetent? About a third of those present—make-up people, all his flunkeys ... raised their arms. I was so furious, I jumped into a jeep, drove off at a hundred miles an hour down a dip, and shouted: "You are out of your fucking minds, the whole bunch of you!" There is one thing I can do, I thought: go back to Hungary; and so again I yelled *"You can go and fuck yourselves! the whole bunch of you!"* I drove off in a jeep to the sand dunes and then wondered what to do next. My whole crew is back there! I had to continue ...'

It should be noted that the film had been Sellers' project for years; that he had been billeted in one of the grandest villas in the Aegean (certainly the only one on Cyprus with green grass in its garden); and that he had a luxury yacht moored alongside the pirate ship set for his personal use. He'd never wanted the picture to succeed—it was simply an exercise in power and paranoia. He manipulated people; put people up against each other. If you wouldn't side with him, if you disagreed with him in the slightest, he'd take against you; you were justifying his mistrust. Peter Boyle, to this day, has never seen manoeuverings to compare with it: 'We got along fine, but there was a point where he went absolutely crazy. He staged a giant tirade. He'd called a meeting and he insisted on everybody's presence—*everybody* had to be there, including the rival Turkish and Cypriot drivers. When everybody was there he told us that everybody was incompetent—*everybody!* It was magnificent. I still remember this incredible scene—the wackiness of it! It was great acting. The epic and dramatic nature of it ... The whole thing—amongst the dunes, the exotic setting; the caterers, drivers, producers, the director... "If you don't all shape up, I'm on the next plane out of here!" Sellers was both scary and ridiculous. I got the feeling that, though he was a genius, with his mimicry, voices, dialects, he didn't get any reassurance out of comedy. He didn't see much that was funny. His life was no laughing matter. But even his mad speech was inventive. He couldn't stop being inventive.'

◆ ◆ ◆

Excessive, suspicious, and delusion-crammed as Sellers was once he'd become an international star, the forces which destroyed him were the forces which had created him. He was constantly playing some new part, except that, like Barrie's sentimental Tommy, 'playing is hardly the word... for into each part he puts an earnestness that cheats even himself, until he takes to another...' Sellers was intoxicated by the novelty and freedoms of acting, the deep and ever-widening sea in which he was immersed; to revert to 1959, when he was teetering on the brink of triumph, Sellers must have known that the scene in the house with Terry-Thomas darning the socks was important and rich in meaning, because he insisted, some weeks later, that the Boultings return to it and re-attempt it. He had to taste Kite fully. Sellers 'made a thing' about this, according to Thomas; and it was a huge request. The Kites' interiors had already been dismantled and it was no joke re-assembling the set and carefully matching the muffled, carboniferous lighting tones with previous shots. 'This re-take was the one used in the film,' said Thomas, 'but in all fairness to Peter, I couldn't see any difference [in his] performance [which], to me, seemed identical to the first one [take].'

The lesson we take away from *I'm All Right, Jack* is that Sellers, by making his rôle so his own, was finding a way to enlarge his imaginative experience. Next to him, the rest of the cast, whilst full of interest and intensity, have the unambiguousness of medieval puppets. Sellers, however, has singularity, abandonment. He's not like the rest of them. Sellers is the embodiment of magic realism. It is little wonder, then, that when trying to come to terms with the strength of his identification with a character, with his own plenty and consummations, that Sellers should invoke the paranormal. How else, and why else, should he be, like Bottom the Weaver, so *translated*?

It is during this period, the late fifties, that Sellers had started to rely on soothsayers, signs, and tokens: 'He was a great believer in spiritualism,' Ian Carmichael reminded me. 'I lived in Hampstead in a house opposite Maurice Woodruff's, a man who devised horoscope columns for the London evening papers. Peter's car was there... a *lot*. Peter wouldn't make a decision without consulting Woodruff... He thought Larry Stephens was trying to get in touch with him—he felt *very* strongly about this.'

Sellers said of his Woodruff visitations, in 1959: 'It's like a drug. The man's fabulously accurate. I keep on going to find out... to find out.'* Whether or not

---

* Wolf Mankowitz described Woodruff less caressingly: 'He was a really unattractive little homosexual personality who had a strange hold on a lot of show business people; they went to him before any deal and he'd fix their astrological charts.'

he needed the guiding hand of a collaborator from the early 'Goon Show' days as he began to flourish as an actor is dubious. Sellers didn't particularly want to see into the future; he wanted Stephens to help him keep a grip on the past—Sellers, the instant nostalgic. But much more to the point is the analogy he perceived between Woodruff's procedures and his own: 'I act as a medium, if you like, and let the character come out through me…I think there is something psychic about my acting to a certain extent, yes…'

Acting, for Sellers, had now gone well beyond mimicry or the expectations of caricature and satire. He wasn't copying whatever material came his way; he was transfiguring it. He could get a character's aspirations across—that's to say, he could convey what wasn't actually spoken or said or made explicit. Sellers, who had overflowed with accents, who possessed oceans and cataracts of trills and warbles, could be evocative with a look, a gesture, a sense of remoteness. Not just Kite, plodding to answer the door bell, but hundreds of examples: Clouseau, holding a bomb and waiting patiently for it to go off; or Clare Quilty, at the school prom, photographing Lolita; or Juan Bautista, observing that he was turned bright blue; or Old Sam, standing to a salute in the pet cemetery…About the last, Anthony Simmons has said to me: 'Sellers had grown tired and bored with the film. He wanted to get away and begin *Soft Beds, Hard Battles* with the Boultings. His mind was on that. So they are meant to be in the graveyard, and Old Sam sees what the kids have done for him, and the girl looks at him—Danny Kaye said they should kiss. "It is a love story, about a father and a daughter," he claimed. Well, I couldn't accept any kiss, but there is a *look*; and Sellers could imply all the emotions you wanted in a simple glance. Anyway, we were shooting in Hyde Park, with the horse guards, and I received a message that Peter was ill. I carried on filming with the children—so that that rather moving glance of Old Sam's was shot on a different day, from a different angle. Sellers and the girl, Donna Mullane, never actually looked at each other. But it works on the screen.'

It's all done by necromancy, illusionism.

♦ ♦ ♦

Sellers, in reconstituting himself and unbosoming himself, made acting hallucinatory—'an affair of ghosts,' if I may use V. S. Pritchett's phrase, coined to describe the novels of Henry James. James, incidentally, once remarked that 'To project yourself into the consciousness of a person essentially your opposite requires the audacity of great genius.' Sellers, beyond question, had the audacity, and the genius; he could body himself forth as other people, variously near or far from his own branch of solitude. What's at issue is the quality of his consciousness, its continuities, its brittleness, its incongruities, and its lapses. And with regard to extrasensory perception and the calling-up of spirits, let us continue for a moment with *The Optimists of Nine Elms*, which Sellers made fourteen years after *I'm All Right, Jack* (i.e. when he was, at forty-seven, nearer to Kite's probable age—though to play Old Sam he gave himself another two decades again).

It was for this production that he decided to be possessed by the soul of Dan

Leno, who'd played before Edward VII, and who later went insane. Simmons gives us an idea of how and why the haunting happened:

> He had decided on a flattened Yorkshire accent for the voice. For the face, Stuart Freeborn prepared the makeup of the slightly protuberant teeth and a pair of false ears, and he built all this on a model, on a plaster cast of Peter's head. We showed him this. Then we took him to Berman and Nathan's for the costume. Special shoes, with a hump in the soles, to create that funny, rolling walk. Gave a similar effect to long clown shoes... So the character gradually built up. A nagging process. We found that big, flapping coat, which could be turned inside out, and the lining was of many colours. We spoke to his chauffeur, his various girl-friends, his wife, his soothsayer, getting them to give Peter plenty of encouragement. I found him some primitive microgroove records of Dan Leno, which nearly put him right off—because Leno's voice was so non-resonant, like a cracked bell. But he became obsessed with Dan Leno. He simply felt he was the spirit of Dan Leno reincarnated. A medium, who didn't know what we were doing at the time, put him in touch [sic] with Dan, to give him the right sign. Sellers had to go through with this rigmarole before he'd broach the issue of a contract...
>
> We were *prepared*—and he could have no cause for losing confidence in the material later on. When we started filming, I'd be told by the third assistant when he was in a fair state of mind, and I'd go and see him in his caravan, early in the morning. It had to be before the teeth went in—the moment the teeth went in, he was no longer Peter Sellers; he'd become Old Sam. I'd go over the day's work with him. I'd then rehearse with the children, leaving Peter quite alone. The camera would be rehearsed. Peter then came out and did the scene. This was our routine. He'd walk through it—no rehearsal.
>
> He loved an audience—he loved getting a laugh. On the second or third day, he was to busk [as a street performer] outside Fulham football ground, with the real crowds... Peter sang and danced, ukulele numbers of his father's, he said; and the children did their stuff, passing round the hat. After the match, the children follow him through the park. The scene was shot the same morning... We shot the scene and the extras applauded. From then on it was marvellous. He knew he had the part in the palm of his hand...
>
> Sellers was a lonely man. I'd work with him in the evenings; and the producer's secretary would have to come in and hold his hand until the early hours for him to go to sleep. He was very odd.

♦ ♦ ♦

The false teeth were the source of his happiness. He was delighted in Battersea market, for example, when he was approached and asked 'Where can I find Peter Sellers?' People not with the film unit had no idea of his identity. He was in the character fully; there was nobody else. Picture, then, the panic when the choppers went missing. 'Only one set was made, for some reason,' says Larry Pizer, the cinematographer. 'The teeth had vanished from the dressing-room trailer. They'd got thrown out somehow when the caravan was cleaned. It was a serious and yet strangely stupid moment. Sellers was totally disabled without those teeth.'

Sans teeth, sans everything. Lacking the dentures he lost the character; and in the absence of the character, who was he? Suspended between rôles, he had to struggle against anonymity: 'Who can you talk to? Who'd understand your problem? Who can you unload your mind to? Then, after a few days, you get over it. I...drive; I try to lose myself in something, anything...'

Whatever went on in Sellers' head, he was incapable or unwilling to share with those around him. He didn't like to respond as a human being to other human beings. He preferred his motor cars, his clockwork and robotic things; and then there were the distractions of his disguises. Hattie Stevenson says that 'I shall never forget—while he was making *Doctor Strangelove*—he asked me to pop down to the studios with some letters. I walked onto the set (the very lavish one they had when he was playing the bald-headed president)—they had just broken for lunch—and I walked straight past him. Having worked for him for two or three years, I didn't even recognise him.'

And if you encountered him elsewhere, when he was ostensibly off-duty, still he'd be pouring himself, from hour to hour, in and out of dramatic poses. Simmons once saw him at a dinner party chatting up a young woman. The concentration and devotion Sellers brought to bear on the task were remarkable: 'He could turn his charm on and he could equally easily turn it off—because, you see, he'd not be involved with the lady...Just like *There's a Girl in My Soup*. He had to feel that everybody was concentrating on him...He came to our house for Christmas lunch, with his children, and he was...hilarious company. But it was, like his womanising charm, switched on, done for the moment. We didn't exist for him as individuals—only as an audience. He was pitching to an audience.'

Did the floor-show ever abate? On the whole he didn't dare allow many curtain drops. Audiences, any non-particularised mass, fed his egotism. Whether you were in the cast of *Brouhaha*, the stalls during his early music hall days, the crowd thronging the recordings of 'The Goon Show', the suffering crew on his international film sets, or his family recovering from an outrage and goggling at one another in amazement, you were meant to surrender to his private games. Otherwise he felt unsafe and exposed. He felt diminished, and he complained about this until his dying day. 'I tend to be rather disappointing, socially. If people are looking for a laugh, they've invited the wrong person,' he stated in an interview published a week *after* his death in 1980. 'They should invite someone like Peter Ustinov, a very fine raconteur, a very funny fellow, who doesn't mind being the life and soul of the party.'

There is a world of difference between Ustinov, an entertainer who is like Father Christmas at his post-prandial ease, and Sellers, who was either manic, mesmeric, or sulky and wanting to walk out. Ustinov's film performances, too, have an air of the after-dinner speaker (urbane, apparently effortless, faintly bored); he is always, you feel, beneficent and responsive. He lacks hostility. And like Robert Morley, Sellers' co-star in *Battle of the Sexes*, who was admittedly more brisk and shrill, Ustinov is not an actor who'd benefit from any form of disguise; he doesn't need make-up, vocal variations, or any other sort of metaphorical trapdoor to fall through and be taken out of himself. Whether he's Captain Vere, Charlie Chan, or Hercule Poirot, the rôles he plays are thrown over his own temper and breadth of mind with the lightest pressure. It all adds up to an uncomplicatedness. Sellers, however, much more crabbed and sorry for himself, clung to his transformations.

◆ ◆ ◆

Not even the company of Milligan, the man who understood him best, could alleviate his self-involvement. Indeed, when they were together the garrulity, japes, and palaverings were non-stop. It was almost as if, seeing in each other one of na-ture's solitaries, and mindful of the occasion when Milligan had wanted to kill the star (the abstracted celebrity that Sellers had become), the two men did their best to *avoid* a normal confrontation; they didn't dare meet as their real selves—they had to put on a double act. Leslie Linder remembers an occasion in their company which quickly turned into the semblance of a sketch from one of the 'Fred' shows. 'I spent a crazy evening with Peter and Milligan, but the funny person that night was not Peter, it was Spike. Peter was driving and we came up behind a Securicor [armoured] van that had these watchdogs in it. Milligan hated the idea of animals being locked in a vehicle, so we stopped the car and he and Sellers crawled along the ground and opened the back of the truck and let the Alsatians out... They had a strange relationship. Spike was a good conversationalist, but it was Peter who, by the end of the evening, would have everybody's attention because he'd simply imi-tate everybody who'd been there. Quite remarkable; quite sinister.'

Sellers' talent was diabolical; he could be everybody except himself—and thus did he assert himself. With Milligan, he'd pretend not to be competitive by com-municating in the code of 'The Goon Show'. (They had to have fictional crea-tures interposing.) 'We really cared desperately about the characters,' said Sellers in 1971. 'They became real, so real for us, as they are now. I get letters every other week from Milligan, addressed to Bloodnok—because Bloodnok we keep alive regularly. Moriarty and Thynne are more or less dead now through hunger... I still get and send letters from and to Hen and Min. We had special notepaper printed. Whacklow, Futtle & Crun, solicitors at law. We send them occasionally to odd people when they don't pay us for odd moments.'*

The Goons were their go-betweens, and they both kept an eye out for Goon-ish manifestations in real life. If a chat show tried to pair them, they'd do their best to be daft—predictably daft. They'd switch chairs, mutter and screech as Hen and Min, Bluebottle and Eccles; Sellers would sing tunelessly ('I want to be un-happy, but I can't be unhappy, until I've made you unhappy too-oo-oo') whilst Milligan did trombone noises. Anything to deflect a serious conversation. When an interviewer once asked Milligan, in Sellers' presence, whether 'You recognised and were seeing a reflection of yourself at all' in the sombre documentary he'd written for Tony Palmer, *Will The Real Peter Sellers (Stand Up)?*, he couldn't bear to be drawn. 'No,' said Milligan, 'I was pissed.' (In the documentary, which Sellers tried to ban, Milligan had said: 'The real Peter Sellers won't stand up until he's dead'.) And if the talk started to concentrate a bit much on the international film

---

* The 'Authentic Inter-Goonal Correspondence' is published in *The Book of the Goons* (Robson, London, 1974)

scene, with which Milligan had no connection, he might interrupt Sellers (who'd be saying that 'Satyajit Ray, you know, he is a very sensitive and brilliant and wonderful man') and chip in with a few dud limericks, which he claimed he had just composed there and then—emphasising that he had been feeling left out.

The dynamic duo rose, or fell, to new levels of mischief when interviewed by David Frost just prior to the release of *The Magic Christian*. Milligan, ignoring his cue, sloped from behind the scenery and, with Sellers' encouragement ('come in, Min'), made gun-shot noises and jumped up to touch and grab the sound boom. Sellers then joined him in imitating monkeys and chickens, before launching into a song: 'Jews and shepherds come away, come away...' Milligan, going over to sit on Sellers' lap, next pretended to be a ventriloquist's dummy. After that, they came to rest as Eccles and Bluebottle.

Listening to their mugging, to the contrived chaos and the slobber of shouts and goonery, what I personally detect is that, first, both Milligan and Sellers believed it incumbent upon them to rebel against the manners and customs of a television talk show; they feel obliged to deconstruct it. Second, submerged in the mass and welter, concealed amidst the leaping and bounding, is their great and abiding rivalry. They try to outdo one another, top one another. 'I thought I had the same comic ability as Peter Sellers,' Milligan said in 1987, 'because I used to match him in the Goon Shows, but the cards fell right for him when he went into films and never came right for me.' But Milligan, surely, would be the first to admit that he is not anything of an actor; what he is (like Ustinov) is a personality. He almost parodies acting, hence the garish, gaslit, music-hall artificiality of *The Great McGonagall*, a film I love. (Nobody else does, however. 'There was a ghastly silence on the first night. I've never heard a silence like it. You'd think we'd made a film about a leper colony,' its star recalls.)

Milligan's gift is for comic conceptions, rather than performance; he is crammed with ideas which worked when set free on radio and in snatches on television, but would, he has always believed, be snuffed out by the heavy industry of cinema. 'Peter and I did phone each other a lot to exchange comedy ideas,' he told me, 'and I miss that. I don't know anybody his equal in comic ideas. We used to say, oh let's film this! But we couldn't. Too exotic; too exquisite.'

Sellers, who had been given, as I argued in an earlier chapter, structure and form by Milligan—he was, in many respects, minted by Milligan—would never have returned the compliment. In fact, his statements about Milligan (whom he did call 'a near-genius') are the reverse of generous. They are anti-tributes. 'I think he feels that all the things that have happened to Harry and me in the way of success should possibly have gone to him.' Asked, in the mid-1970s, if there would be any more Goon shows or similar collaborations, Sellers said: 'Spike has this enormous ego these days and it would be difficult to work with it. He seems to be uniquely jealous of me as a person...'

◆ ◆ ◆

What is the state of mind behind this remark, to which my immediate response is simple disgust tinged with disbelief? Sellers was speaking to Alfred Draper, author of *The Story of the Goons*. They'd met at the actor's penthouse flat in Roebuck House, Stag Place, SW1, which was decorated with photographs of the Queen Mother and Prince Charles, a yoga shrine, a pair of plimsolls mounted and glazed, and the famous Cape Canaveral telescope, through which the master watched the expanding universe. Sellers, as so often when stalled between films, was bed-ridden with a virus—he had completed *Murder By Death* and he was soon to begin *The Pink Panther Strikes Again* (during which 'he got stranger and madder', according to Blake Edwards).

Also in the apartment, and what a significant souvenir it must have been, was the framed wedding day photograph from *I'm All Right, Jack*—the very same snap that Kite himself glances at during his darkish night of the soul. Kite, in his Sunday best, looks at the camera proudly; his Hitlerian moustache is neatly brushed and his boutonnière consists of a large fern and a frilly bloom. He is militarily correct and old-fashioned, with his rounded collar and shiny shoes. Irene Handl, as the blushing bride entwined with orange blossom, is either only three feet tall or she's kneeling down besides her lord and master. The formality of the pose, and our being uncertain as to whether she has fallen over or is a dwarf, gives the picture its comedy. It is authentic thirties, and yet full of concealed ridiculousness, as well as being very human and poignant—people do look awkward and over-done for their marriages. It's the difference between Kite in this photograph, plump with promise, and Kite during the sock-darning evening, when he realises, in a flash, that the life he has led has failed him, that gives Sellers' performance its great interest and mystery. He would return to the drama of a pale and wasted life, and give it extended treatment, in *Hoffman*, at the end of the sixties—a film in which 'he did himself' (or so Milligan said to me).

Sellers was always swinging between doubt and elation. When Draper encountered him, he was bitter that he was only newly rich because of Clouseau's resurrection. He was aware that his experiments in serious rôles had (commercially) flopped—i.e. *The Blockhouse* and *The Optimists of Nine Elms*. His hopes, if he was to break free from slapstick and cartoonery, were already pinned, as fixedly as Kite's fern, on adapting Kosinski's novella, *Being There*, which he had been given (by Victoria Lindsay-Hogg) on its publication in 1971; and where he will have read that:

> with all its life, even at the peak of its bloom, the garden was its own graveyard. Under every tree and bush lay rotten trunks and disintegrated and decomposing roots. It was hard to know which was more important: the garden's surface or the graveyard from which it grew and into which it was constantly lapsing.

If it was indeed the case that Sellers, as he admitted, 'read the book every six months,' then he will have been well aware of this passage; and he will also have perceived that, in terms of his own existence, in relation to his own brooding and backward-reaching temperament, it was an apt metaphor. He himself, despite his need for fresh starts, fresh wives, fresh homes, fresh characters, was more susceptible than anyone to the call of the dead—to the tangle of pugilists and music hall troupers, radio waves and assorted phantoms out of which the creature Draper

Mr and Mrs Fred Kite (1959)

met in 1976 had sprouted. The forthcoming *The Pink Panther Strikes Again* was not only a replay of *The Return of the Pink Panther* of the previous year, but also that that money-spinner itself branched off from *A Shot in the Dark* and the original *Pink Panther*, both released in 1964. Sellers was imitating his own ancient imitations. And now here was Draper wanting to dig up 'The Goon Show', and asking if the likes of *The Last Goon Show of All* will be repeated... Sellers felt himself to be running, jumping, and standing still.

◆◆◆

It is one thing to be sentimental about the past, and to put on demonstrations of weeping and wailing that would have silenced Donald Wolfit, ('Oh Christ,' he once gulped to Graham Stark, 'whatever happened to Aircraftsman Sellers?'), it was quite another for the critics and the public to accept, or lament, that he was going backwards. And so he lashed out at Milligan, the instigator, the inspiring principle, the wonderful talker; and he also said to Draper: 'I disagree with Spike that tomorrow can never be as happy as yesterday. I live for today and tomorrow.'

With that comment, what it is that Sellers is up to comes across with a horrible candour. He was projecting his own perniciousness and envy onto Milligan—imputing to Milligan his own shudders and chill. He was intent on this, spreading discord and trying to absorb Milligan's life into his own, back on *Ghost in the Noonday Sun*. As Medak explains, 'Spike is the most organised, level-headed, kind-hearted person I have ever come across—whether it's towards individual people, or trees, or animals.' This is true (in its own way). He has made people aware of the unnecessary vivisection carried out for cosmetics, and he was thrown out of Harrods when he tried to stuff twenty-eight pounds of spaghetti down the throat of the Food Hall manager, in protest against the force-feeding of geese for pâté de foie gras.

'He'll always go out of his way to do something good,' Medak affirms. 'He came to the film late on to jazz up the script and to put one-liners in it, which he's brilliant at. He wasn't there to accommodate Peter, so Peter turned on Spike, and there were days when they wouldn't speak to each other. Spike tried to get him to do things—everybody's complete effort went into keeping Peter alive, into keeping him functioning.'

I think I can understand, at last, why Sellers wouldn't go along with the *Goons at Sea* concept; why, divided and frustrated, he was determined the film should be a fiasco. He couldn't bear it for Milligan to triumph, for Milligan to hew laughs out of the heat and dust. Which Spike might well have done, because his ingenuities and suggestions (all, of course, ignored or botched in the execution) are light and frisky. *Ghost in the Noonday Sun*, with a budget of two million dollars, could have caught fire and been 'The Goon Show's' cinematic breakthrough; crammed with a bit more corniness and loopiness, its plot, about lost treasure and idiotic desperadoes, is ripe for Ned of Wales—a thought which crossed Dick Vosbrugh's mind: 'I said, "If you would just hire a studio for a day, and get Secombe, and have a Goonish preamble—I could go through all the Columbia pirate pictures, and do a *Hellzapoppin'*, with Sellers providing a voice-over."'

Sellers would not cooperate. But the idea stayed with him. After the shooting of *Being There*, when he was hot and nominated for the Oscar, he attempted to personally buy back the negative from Columbia—and he said to Medak, 'I would love you and I to reedit it, get Spike back to do a narration, and we could get it released.' He tried to purchase a work he had hated because the origins of his hatred were so complicated; his motives receded, like tendrils, to the start of his career and the beginning of his fame. 'There is such brilliant stuff in the film, we can make magic out of it,' he kept saying. 'We really ought to put our heads together.'

Columbia wouldn't part with the material, even though they had never distributed it. The most likely explanation of this is fiscal—the costs of the film had been written off against tax, and it would be an accountant's nightmare reopening the books and seeing if it could turn a profit. Economics aside, however, Sellers' change of heart is what's of interest. To Medak, it is final proof that 'he was definitely schizophrenic,' and not simply cussed or conventionally *difficult*. 'His switches of mood were terrifying. One day we got off the boat at this lovely harbour in Kyrenia. He came and put his arm around me and said, full of calm menace, "Why don't you quit the film?..." "What are you talking about?" "I don't think you are enjoying this movie, why don't you just *quit* it?" And he stalked off. An hour later at dinner he'd treat me like his long lost brother and best friend. He really was quite insane.'

◆ ◆ ◆

Milligan describes his experience on the picture as 'like being given a statue. Chip this away, a bit here and there, and make it look better. I did a rush job. I wasn't working—I had to make a living—so I went out there.' He needn't be so dismissive about his (unutilised) contribution. I particularly like the harkings back to Eccles and Bluebottle logic ('Smoking stunts your growth. But for this [a hubble-bubble pipe] I'd be seventeen feet three'), and what about a flashback to Scratch's youth, as the pirate tells Jeremiah, the cabin boy, of his father's great estate (we were to see a grotty field) and how he helped him to supervise the farming (we see Scratch in harness pulling the plough); and how he serenaded a princess (a toothless crone) from his white charger (a donkey); and how he duelled with a King (an old codger who belts him); and how he ran off and became a buccaneer (policemen chuck him off a pier)?

This sequence, which exists solely as a yellow, crumbling leaf, dated and gummed into the script on November 3, 1973, would not only have been a neat superimposition of sound and vision, it would also have been a jibe at the tendency, Sellers' in particular, to romanticise, change, and puff up one's past. It was a little scene designed for a fantasist; this is only my personal impression, but as I examined Medak's own copy of the script, a binder of faded coloured paper, crosshatched with doodles and pencillings, it dawned on me that Milligan's rewrites ('I had to rewrite every morning. I'd be woken up—"Can you rewrite this?"') seem to encipher, through Goonish rant and subconscious touches, his intricate and perplexing relationship with the star.

◆ ◆ ◆

'Peter and I are like Gilbert and Sullivan,' Milligan had said in 1960, when 'The Goon Show' had ended and the 'Freds' fizzled. 'We love and hate each other at the same time...It's just a matter of chemistry I suppose. We have a completely opposite approach to what we want to do, but by hammering it out we come to some agreement. But it's hellish going. When we get together we smoulder...You see, I'm deeper than he is. He takes things seriously—but in a quite different way...I think humanity's a failure, but he doesn't care to think about that. I think he's an enigma...and I don't think he understands how much talent he has got. We always clash about the quality of perfection we want to achieve...Basically he is uncertain of himself and that makes him more sensitive as a performer.'

Sellers' wandering consciousness mutated from rôle to rôle, from film to film, caring for and believing only in his own interests and amusements; always, underneath the arrogance and the dashing about, he was afraid of his inability to understand what he was doing. Do you know that cartoon, attributed to Einstein, of the rock climber? The think-bubble, above the figure's head, as he clings to the precipice, is filled with a succession of incomprehensible formulae, which turn out to be advanced mechanics for the transferral of centres of gravity within the joints of the human body. Half an inch up or down? This way or that? Apply this to Sellers' performances: *he* is the one clambering nimbly, ascending, levitating, in defiance, it would seem, of nature's laws; *we* are the ones working out the formulae. Strange things happen in readjusting one's balance—and Sellers, with his intuitive torrents, had that ability to a degree which was a miracle.

At least he did in the late fifties and early sixties; after that came the boring international capers, bad behaviour, loads of money, parties which lasted for days in a row, the chance to fuck beautiful young girls, etc. Sellers didn't have enough personal resistance to such luxuries (would *you*?); never having appreciated his own capacity for either dedicated serious work or indolence and hedonism, he'd say to a journalist: 'I feel that I want to be very, very, very discriminating...I have great, great, great ambitions to do something as an actor which I will leave behind me, because...I *know* I have it in me', and follow this up immediately with *Where Does It Hurt?*, a dismal hospital farce, notable only because it connects with Sellers' morbid interest in heart attacks and the blissful vegetative existence of a patient; *Alice's Adventures in Wonderland*, which, though full of marvels (Ralph Richardson, Robert Helpmann, Sellers' March Hare), totally lacks zest; and *A Day at the Beach* (unreleased), *The Blockhouse* (unreleased), and *Ghost in the Noonday Sun* (unreleased).

Sellers' rise and fall and then his rise again, in the marketplace with *The Return of the Pink Panther* and as an actor with *Being There*, is out of a fairy tale—the more so as the archetypal, mythological cycle was about to turn once more, with *The Fiendish Plot of Dr Fu Manchu*, Sellers' final and, in my view, megalomanical attempt to obliterate his feelings for Milligan with a super-dooper version of 'The Goon Show'. As Piers Haggard explains, with regard to Sellers' last gasp: 'I got a call from Orion. My name had come up as a last resort on a project they were in deep shit with, *The Fiendish Plot*...I was summoned to see Peter Sellers, one of my heroes, at the Inn on the Park in May 1979; it was there I learned that there had been a script already, but that at some point he'd decided it was rubbish and he wouldn't do it; he had written a slim number himself which he pressed into my hands. I later discovered that the script he'd hated, Orion had been extremely pleased with, and very hopeful of. He'd taken against it. I read Peter's script... some of which was funny. I detected a sort of innocence and charm about his story... a balloon drifting across, a flying English cottage, a wistful English detective. A germ of a comic fantasy narrative, set in the past...'

The reasons why it all went wrong are not difficult to discover. 'Orion, who had spent over a million dollars already, were trying to hold on to Peter Sellers... They were willing to do almost anything to please him... Everything was gift-wrapped to be sold to Peter, in the most elaborate way. Increasingly, I, as the director, became angry and despairing at not being able to have a normal relationship with my leading actor... I wanted to be able to help him, but he would not open himself to me; wouldn't trust me—even though he'd said to Orion "I'll only do the film with Piers, so fuck you." And then, shortly before we began shooting in Paris, I finally had a meeting with him on his own—with the intention of discussing the myriad artistic details to do with making a film. Well, my first proper meeting with Peter was also my first experience of Peter in depression, which was puzzling and frightening. He was sitting in his dressing gown over near the window and the room was, or felt, very dark. He looked dreadful and sad. He sat like a graven image, very sombrely. He was on his own. I later looked back and saw this moment as a premonition of the insanity I had got myself into. Because from that point everything became *worse*.'

♦ ♦ ♦

If only he'd died after *Being There*, for his own sake. He cannot have been pleased with himself for living life as it should not be lived; for behaving as one should not behave. The fear of life, the fear of death, the fear of human contact, the fear of loneliness. The sadness is in considering how gifted he was, and how much mental disturbance and unhappiness there was by the end. (His fate ought to put anybody off wanting to be a star.) And the story, as if it wasn't operatic enough already, doesn't even end with *The Fiendish Plot of Dr Fu Manchu*. Sellers was reaching new and spectacular peaks of fever and frustration on *The Romance of the Pink Panther* (which was to be his revenge on Blake Edwards). I will simply drop into my cauldron this excerpt of a letter from Steven Bach:

> Clive Donner* is a lovely man and a good filmmaker who was ideal in one sense for Peter: he is a gentleman who would not inflame Peter's never-very-latent paranoia. On the other hand, Clive's very decency was a disturbing factor to Peter who had worked it out in his head that if you weren't overtly trying to fuck him you were doing so covertly, so there was simply no way of winning with him. I think Clive knew all of this, and he probably knew that deep down Peter had the bully's mistrust and

---

* Donner had last worked with Sellers in *What's New, Pussycat*. He was to direct *The Romance of the Pink Panther* and was present in Gstaad both for discussions with Sellers and to meet any United Artists personnel. (Bach was at that time the company's Senior Vice President and Head of Worldwide Production.)

contempt for anyone who gives in to him, out of whatever compassionate or human ground or need. Clive did that—as Clive out of compassion would—and somewhere Peter saw that as a) duplicitous and/or b) weak. These may sound mutually exclusive, but nothing was so logical with Peter as to have been governed by normal patterns of thought. He was, quite simply, deeply unbalanced, if not committable: that was the source of his genius and his truly quite terrifying aspects as manipulator and hysteric.

My personal fondness for him and my admiration for him as an actor do not override my feelings that he was on very important levels a monster, and I try to say that with all the compassion I may possess.

◆ ◆ ◆

This is the tragicomic culmination of Sellers' proclamation, in 1960, that he intended 'to become so successful that I can name the *parts* I want and play them the *way* I want.' And who would have gainsaid him that ambition back then, with *I'm All Right, Jack* making his name and *The Mouse That Roared* making money? And who would have regarded the following, from 1957, as minatory: 'I've got an awful lot out of life—a beautiful wife, lovely children, a pleasant home. Being a star couldn't add much to that. It's the power that counts'?

The power, which to Sellers meant seeing how far he could go in abusing people's patience and demanding homage, certainly didn't reinforce or augment either his professional standing or his personal happiness. Power, i.e., the opportunity to be intemperate, wrecked film after film, marriage after marriage. He never saw it this way, of course. He saw himself as Prince Valiant. Around about 1970 he said: 'I'm going to defeat all these berks [morons] that are around me. And I'm going to *do* it...very soon, because I'm getting that way *now*; because I have a name for being very difficult. I'm not difficult at all...It's just when people just don't seem to *know* or have the basic knowledge of what makes A and B tick, that gets me. For example, I am written up as being *nasty* on the set. I'm not nasty on the set at all. It's just that when you try and argue a point with someone, not argue, discuss a point...' And so wheedlingly and endlessly on. Sellers' wantonness was often carried out under the guise of rectitude. He alone was trying to appear strictly professional; he alone was aiming for the heights: 'I am a very ambitious person... And no sod is going to kill it in the future because I'm really...'

Fade out Sellers, mix in Milligan for a concise summary and translation: 'He hated people, you see. He hated people because they used to stop him from doing what he wanted.' Not that he knew what he wanted particularly, beyond everybody capitulating and acknowledging that he must never be curbed. His loathing extended from the studio, to his behaviour off-screen, where, as we know, the self-recreations didn't cease, to his having it out on inanimate objects. (Sellers was a barnstorming version of Clouseau: a man whom the universe seems to be *against*.) Herbert Kretzmer recalls an evening when Duke Ellington was in town, 'and I managed to get tickets. We went off in Peter's Rolls to the Royal Festival Hall. He couldn't find a place large enough to get the Rolls in easily—there were plenty of parking spaces, but they'd have called for some manoeuvering. And an astonishing change came over Peter. He decided to forego the concert. "To hell with it, there's no place here for my [car]. Let's go back to my place and I'll run *The Pro-ducers.*" This hadn't been released yet, but he had a sixteen millimetre print. He was clearly in no mood to be argued with over this. An evening with Sellers was an evening with Sellers. It was of absolutely no consequence to him that the rest of us were missing the concert. We went to Clarges Street, where he lived with Britt. He set up a projector and the screen—and he didn't have a take-up spool. He spent the next hour and a half, obsessive, on the telephone, looking for a take-up spool. He tried to track down Tony Armstrong-Jones. We sat around with drinks and cigarettes. Finally, he got hold of a nightwatchman at the Technicolour Laboratories in Hounslow—"I'm only here with the key," said this William Mate Cobblers type on the other end. Peter then started to describe what a take-up spool was to this idiot. He wanted this fellow to go into the factory, find a take-up spool, phone him back, and he'd send a car for it. Needless to say, we never saw the film, we never saw the jazz concert. A totally wasted, pointless evening, be-holding this madman. It put him in a terrible temper...'

◆ ◆ ◆

In two weekends in 1959, between the end of *I'm All Right, Jack* and the start of *Battle of the Sexes*, Sellers put his random, startling, and unpremeditated way of doing things to lasting use in *The Running, Jumping and Standing Still Film*. This eleven-minute opus must be the most successful home-movie ever made. Leonard Mosely, from the *Daily Express*, heard about it and said he had a friend who was gathering material for the Edinburgh Festival—where the film won a prize. It went on to the San Francisco Film Festival, and won first prize, The Golden Gate Award. Then it was nominated for an Oscar.

It is often slipped into television schedules to this day, and it was a particular favourite with the Beatles, who invited Dick Lester, who'd helped to edit it, to come and direct their own Goonish features, *A Hard Day's Night* (which in turn inspired Sellers' Shakespearean rendition of the soundtrack) and *Help!*

'There was never any attempt during the filming of it, or during the post-production of it,' says Lester, 'for it to be of any commercial use at all—it was re-ally just a chance for Peter to play around with his camera.'

Whether he was mucking about or not at the time, Sellers would speak, after the fact, as if he'd fully intended and had personally masterminded a miniature epic. 'If I can get a footing with my films such as *The Running, Jumping and Stand-ing Still Film*,' he pontificated in March 1960, 'which I only made as a demon-stration to show what can be done without dialogue, I want to inject this type of thing into a British screen comedy...'

'We got away with it, with that little short,' Milligan said to me. 'It's the only example of Sellers' real sense of humour. His sense of humour wasn't Inspector Clouseau—it was much more abstract than that.' Abstract? It was the very word Sellers himself had used. 'I find this abstract humour very pleasing. There's noth-ing to worry about, to think about. Things that happen in it either amuse you im-mensely or don't amuse you. It's a fantasia in a way, you might even say it's bizarre.'

What was a delightful stream of consciousness for Sellers was hard work for other people. Lester's testimony is revealing on this point: 'Peter relied a great deal on Spike in our period—Spike was the creative force, Peter was the performer. I think Peter envied, in the best sense, Spike's ability to create. Peter was a wonderful adaptor of other people's ideas. He honed them and made them into something infinitely better... but in terms of raw creation, certainly Spike was the creator of almost all the ideas that came up.'

John Browell, producer of the tenth and final series of 'The Goon Show' in 1959, has said that *The Running, Jumping and Standing Still Film* 'was being made during recording periods... Very often Sellers and Milligan were rehearsing ideas for it while we were trying to rehearse in the Camden Theatre, and sometimes I was not quite sure what performance I was rehearsing for.' Those cavortings are lost to us, of course. *The Running, Jumping and Standing Still Film* is the only complete example we have of Sellers and Milligan functioning together frictionlessly outside of 'The Goon Show' proper (for all that *that* series was replete with tantrums and for all that I'd take grave issue with Lester's sub-clausal 'in the best sense,' above). Or, to put it another way, their friction is concealed—and *The Running, Jumping and Standing Still Film*, however it came into being, and at whose instigation, is a transubstantiation of Goonish sound into Goonish image.

◆ ◆ ◆

'*The Running, Jumping and Standing Still Film*,' said Milligan in November 1987, 'I made that with my ideas. That was me. And it was perfect.'

It wasn't, as he explained to me three years later. 'I had to go to Australia, and Peter handed it over to Lester, who clouded it by putting a jazz tune on to it. A fatuous soundtrack, which has nothing to do with the film.' He is right, the bird-whistles and snare drums are monotonous and tarnishing. What is instead required, to set the vanished past to music, is a plangent silent-movie piano theme composed by Erik Satie; something that would grace a Sunday in the park with Sellers', and the others characters', meaningless pursuits.

It was indeed when Milligan was in Woy Woy, Sydney, that, on Sellers' instructions, they must have added the credit titles—which would bring a blush to the chartreuse cheeks of Mr Toad: 'A Peter Sellers/British Lion Production,' 'Devised by Peter Sellers,' 'starring Peter Sellers,' 'produced by Peter Sellers.' ... Sellers, in fact, in his squirearchical tweeds, could be said to prance through the film as Kenneth Grahame's conceited amphibian from *The Wind in the Willows*. He hops into most shots, toting a gun or a camera; he lurks in the undergrowth and the background, scanning the other clowns suspiciously. He doesn't want to be left out. And Mr Toad, bounding from hobby to hobby, not willing to be censured by Badger or Rat, spending money freely on himself, having adventures with motor cars and donning disguises, is the creature whom Sellers now became. 'Do you tend to spend freely on yourself?' *Playboy* magazine asked Sellers in 1962. 'Yes, very freely,' he freely replied. 'I used to think, one day I can buy this and that, and now I can. Buying what I want is not really extravagance. If you bought what you don't need, that would be extravagance. But then I can always persuade myself that I need what I buy. I don't believe in being the richest man in the cemetery...'

Sellers' income had risen from £17,000* a year in the middle-fifties to twice that by the end of the decade. He'd received £7,500 for *I'm All Right, Jack* and would be paid £9,000 for *Battle of the Sexes* and £15,000 for *Two Way Stretch*—which means that, by the early sixties, when he had films opening every other month, the least he was looking at was £150,000 a season; in fact this figure edged towards the quarter-of-a-million mark by 1963, when, for *Doctor Strangelove*, his fee was £1,600 a day for eleven weeks. The big money had started with *The Millionairess*, in May 1960. As Wolf Mankowitz explained to me, 'Sellers...was getting relatively quite small money for his films; I believed that if we developed significant properties for him, we could push his money up—make a package deal and get part of the producer's percentage profit... So I started to develop various ideas; and one brought to me for Sellers...was for *The Millionairess*. I put the suggestion of Loren and Sellers starring together...to Sophia and Carlo Ponti...and they seemed pretty interested... Sophia had seen some of Peter's things and thought he was the funniest man living; she was very keen to play the part... On that basis...I made the deal, with £50,000 for the two of us. Sellers had £37,500 and £12,500 was for me—and I wrote the screenplay. That was more than he'd ever received up until then...'

And he needed it. 'Peter has always overspent himself,' said Milligan at the time. 'He realised early on that he was never going to be happy unless he spent and spent and still had money left over, and this must always be part of his pattern.' His chief means of indulging his squandermania, in December 1959, was to leave the firework-charred Whetstone property for The Manor House, Chipperfield, Hertfordshire—and everything about him changed. His acting had always transcended the film studio because of whatever he did, was up to, was interested in. Now Mr Toad had acquired Toad Hall. He altered his walk, his laugh, his wardrobe, his demeanour. 'The graciousness with which he now entertained' recalls Peter Evans, 'had no connection with the informal, suburban dad in Oakleigh Avenue. He was Lord of the Manor and Anne was the châtelaine.'

Chipperfield was a Crazy House. Schizophrenic to begin with, being Queen Anne in front, Elizabethan at the back, the property was quickly re-shaped to suit its new master. 'I have only to hear about a new electric oven with a built-in fridge, and I've got to have it,' said Sellers. In addition to such appliances, he had the lawns mined for a swimming-pool and the outlying tithe barns restored, one to be filled with a large set of trap drums, the other to contain his five hundred metres of model railway track. What was the library he turned into a stereophonic workshop, called The Gramophone Room. Though he possessed thousands of jazz records, it's not accurate to say that Sellers actually managed to listen to any of them; he never relaxed to Ellington or Basie. He was the sort of infuriating knob-twiddler who, never satisfied, kept jumping up to adjust the treble and bass levels. Needless to say, the sound system was coordinated to flickering, psychedelic lights.

---

* The dollar equivalent is approximately twice the amount in pound sterling.

Like expenditure, which rises to meet or exceed revenue, the more space Sellers had available to him, the sooner he filled it with his Mr Toad toys. 'I *cannot* walk past a toyshop,' he admitted. 'It has a fatal attraction to me. Hamley's in London's Regent Street is a Utopia.' And of course, poop! poop!, there were the cars. Chipperfield had ten bedrooms and two garages, and obviously this should have been the other way around. Sellers had owned fifty-two cars since the end of the war. His fifty-third, bought to adorn his new house, was a blue Cadillac convertible with a black hood. (It was parked alongside the giant mechanical elephant which Sellers had acquired in 1958.)

Sellers also installed another of his smallest-shows-on-earth, a 16mm cinema complete to the last detail. After the success of *The Running, Jumping and Standing Still Film*, the most commonplace home movie had to be preemed, to use a *Variety* word, before 'anyone who's silly enough to accept an invitation to the house.' And accept they did. Sellers played the grinning host at weekend parties for Kubrick, Sophia Loren, the Boultings, and Bryan and Nanette Forbes; Wolf Mankowitz, Herbert Kretzmer, Graham Stark, David Lodge, and their wives, would often be present, playing cricket or sipping drinks.

Sellers employed a Spanish gardener ('we call him Dirk Bogarde'), a handyman named Dewberry (whom Sellers put on a record album as a Flat Earth Society member, raging against balls, bottoms, breasts, and other sundry spheroids), a butler, Bruno, who clanged his head on the cast iron chandelier when serving dinner ('Any minute now ...' Sellers would whisper expectantly), the German nanny, various kitchen maids and scullions; and he had also opened his London office at 37 Panton Street, Haymarket, SW1. Here Hattie Stevenson, his secretary, and Bill Wills, his accountant and manager, were encamped.

'I'd never had a job before,' says Hattie, 'I was straight from secretarial school, and a friend who knew Anne Sellers said, "Why don't you have a go?" I didn't know he got through a secretary a week—if you *stayed* a week you were lucky ... So I went down to the studios where he was making *The Millionairess* and met Ray Marks, known as Ray Ray, his cousin ... "Bad luck," I was told. "He's in a filthy mood. He's got a headache. Filming hasn't been going right." But all Sellers said to me was "Hello Miss Smith,* when would you like to start?" No interview—and having said that, he was notoriously bad at making snap decisions. But this one worked very well because I stayed for seven years.'

♦ ♦ ♦

The empire had formulated itself quickly. Owing to the success of *The Mouse that Roared*, which took over two million dollars during its eight-month run in New York, offers of work were starting to arrive from America—Sellers was asked to consider a £25,000 fee to play Mephistopheles opposite Laurence Olivier's Faust on network television, for example. It was one of the many tantalising projects which Sellers rejected. I mentioned a few of these in my Introduction. The

---

* 'Miss Smith' is what the Sinead Cusack character is called, every other few seconds, in
  Hoffman—she's from the office typing pool.

Beckett, Pinter ('I should like to play in Pinter'), and Brecht ('I was offered *The Good Soldier Schweik*') plays; Julius Caesar in Elizabeth Taylor's *Cleopatra*; the stuttering, shuffling emperor in a John Mortimer adaptation of Robert Graves' *I, Claudius* (the rôle abandoned by Charles Laughton and played on television by Derek Jacobi); Captain Hook in *Peter Pan*—I personally sat through Spielberg's *Hook*, in which a great subject was thrown away, despising every moment of Dustin Hoffman's mewling, runty performance. The rôle cried out for Sellers—a notion alluded to every minute Hoffman was on the screen, because he was made-up to resemble, and his voice tried to imitate, Terry-Thomas.

Sellers was John Huston's choice for Freud, in *The Secret Passion*. 'I am jolly interested in the Freud idea for John Huston,' Sellers told Roy Speer, in March 1961, 'but I don't know how I can fit it in this year. I have two interesting subjects to do—*That Uncertain Feeling* [which became *Only Two Can Play*] and *Waltz of the Toreadors*, so I can't very well do Freud until the end of the year, but maybe Huston can't wait that long.'

He couldn't—Montgomery Clift played the rôle, bringing to it all his introspection and agony. How would Sellers have fared? He did his best to get out of his other commitments to find out. As Leslie Linder, who worked for John Redway, recalls: 'Two weeks before shooting started on *Waltz of the Toreadors*, Sellers said "I've had an offer from America and it's a lot of money—it's a smashing part." I said, "How can you even consider it. You've signed a contract to do *Waltz of the Toreadors* which *you* desperately wanted to do. You can't walk out. The whole crew is ready; it's ready to go ..." He said, "Well, if I was with MCA ..."—the biggest and most powerful agency in the world. "Look, Peter. You know where they are. When you leave this building, you turn right at the entrance and you go to MCA. There's nothing we can do about it." He stormed out, and though he came back a couple of days later, he'd been very angry and he even took legal advice.'

He would have liked to have played Freud if he could. It would have been his first encounter with a director of undeniable diamond-hard vision and first-rate artistry. Afterwards, Sellers' career might have followed a totally different path—for, in the days before psychoanalysts meant Dr Fritz Fassbender in *What's New, Pussycat?* and anybody vaguely Viennese or German meant Dr Strangelove; when Sellers was as subtle as a sphinx, and didn't feel, as he did towards the end, that he had to be dressed as a Nazi stormtrooper to get laughs (and to get by); *then* he would have been ideal for the stubborn Jewish revolutionary, full of possibilities. It's not so much that Sellers' Freud would have been a way of facing up to his feelings for Peg and Bill; it's more that, with Huston as his guide, Sellers would have created a character whose off-centre nature and essential loneliness (and arrogance) chimed with his own zig-zag mind.

What Sellers' miscarried or ploughed projects suggest is that producers and writers were thinking of him for extravagant, despotic, showy rôles; it was recognised that he could bring, or touch, with his instinct and innovation, a sense of torment under the sovereignty, or he'd convey a softness, where another actor might be straightforwardly rigid. Sellers had a shifty, pulpy genius (which Kubrick snaffled up), but he was not keen on being reminded of this. 'I've never played me, not at any time, so there's no such thing as Peter Sellers' rôle,' he once snapped—unable to perceive, as others could, that it was precisely for his superabundance, the multiplication of his aspects, and for his deceitfulness and guile, that he was wanted.

'I don't even bother reading scripts anymore that are sent me with an accompanying note: "This is a typical Sellers,"' he continued, implicitly conceding that he'd deny himself the very characters best suited to his mentality. That's why Clare Quilty stands out amongst the wasteland of cops and robbers flapdoodle (which he entered into freely because 'it keeps you in touch with a certain section of public'). Sellers' vanity and hypocrisy are used in the Nabokov rôle and were not the forces ensuring he'd swerve away from it—as was the case with *Expresso Bongo*. Wolf Mankowitz, who always had a novelist's regard for Sellers, once calling him a cockatrice (a fabulous reptile hatched by a serpent which deposited its eggs in or on the larva of another lizard or insect as on the spot food for its own progeny), invented the rôle of a rather openly opportunistic theatrical hustler, who takes a huge percentage of his young client's earnings and whose speech patterns, ingratiatingly and automatically, adapt and meld with the accent of the people he's talking to. He is foxy; he uses others ruthlessly—and Sellers considered the offer of the part an impertinence: 'I turned down *Expresso Bongo*, the part that Laurence Harvey did, because I didn't like it. I thought that it was an incomplete part; I didn't like the script, although Wolf's a great friend of mine ... It was a two-dimensional character and wasn't real. I know these characters very well ... and this fellow wasn't true, wasn't right ... And so therefore, without a major rewrite, it would not have been possible for me to play it truthfully. I couldn't have ... shut myself up and thought, "Well, you know, it's a part." I can't do that. And so I turned it down [in favour of *Two Way Stretch*].'

◆ ◆ ◆

Wasn't real ... wasn't true ... wasn't right: Sellers' phrases are to the point. He was quite aware, if the above speech is any clue, that the deficiencies in Mankowitz's fictional character were actually reflections of the faults and flaws to be found in his own real personality, but he did not want to confront this, or to know about it. Thus, as I said, Quilty aside, his feckless lack of moral quality was deflected and concealed behind gold bullion raids, jail breaks, scams, stings, and harmless jewel thefts. The criminal fraternity, in Sellers' films from the middle-sixties onwards, represent fun and freedom—life as a spree, a giggle. Dodger Lane, Pearly Gates, Aldo Vanucci, and their gangs, belong, like Scratch and his pirates, in the tradition of loveable rogue. Sellers gives these figures texture and he plays them as befits a virtuoso, but film after film was (his words) 'another romp like *Two Way Stretch*.' When he was successful and internationally known he avoided, like a sleepwalker keeping away from the top of the stairs, putting much of his improbity before the public.

His reaction to Mankowitz, who'd seen into him and through him, was more true to form: 'He [Sellers] took vengeance on me and at the time I thought his gesture totally selfish, malicious, disloyal, dishonest, and stupid. What happened is that, as I had found him biggish money for *The Millionairess*, I received his go-ahead to build up Sellers-Mankowitz Productions Limited. He designed the stationery, incorporating his Daniel Mendoza portrait, and he briefed his bankers, lawyers, and accountants. I personally, on the basis of Sellers' name, had made arrangements with half a dozen very important artists who'd be associated with us—like the early United Artists, when Mary Pickford, Douglas Fairbanks, Chaplin, and D. W. Griffith made and distributed their own films. We'd have been artists in association who could make major deferments and therefore get some money for films which would be controlled internally. Dream stuff, because if you are successful a major takes you over, and if you are not successful you'll disappear anyway. But that was the idea. With projects in hand, such as *The Survivor*, a story about an Austrian undertaker; *Memoirs of a Cross-Eyed Man*, a satire on show business, being written by Frederic Raphael; some adaptations of my own novels; and Joyce's *Ulysses*, with Sellers as Bloom, I had got finance—£250,000 in cash which was also being met by a bank; so we had half a million set with which to make relatively low-budget, high-quality films. Of this company, Sir David Webster was going to be the Chairman; Jack Hylton was putting up some money; Howard Samuels, who was a socialist millionaire, was putting up money; and Lord Goodman convened the meeting. A morning meeting. Sellers and I were to attend and have all these arrangements finalised, at the Royal Opera House in Sir David's office. That morning I received by hand, half an hour before leaving my own office in Piccadilly, a letter from Sellers withdrawing from everything—on the grounds that he couldn't afford the £10,000 which he was meant to make by way of a deferment, which was nonsense; and he blamed me for doing too much, for doing too many things.'

♦ ♦ ♦

Like Alun Weaver in Kingsley Amis' *The Old Devils*, Sellers was not a man you should rely on for anything more important than the way to the Gents. His treatment of Mankowitz replays, in essence, his behaviour towards Milligan, and of anybody else with talent and individuality. He had to destroy them.

Here is the document Mankowitz received on the fateful morning:

Dear Wolfie,*

Since I saw you, I have been thinking a great deal about your new company and it doesn't seem to me, on very full consideration, that it is going to be the right step for either of us if I become a member of it.

First of all, I have got to concentrate on being an actor...

Secondly, even if I became merely a director of your company in name only and have no other involvement, people seeing my name on the paper will think otherwise...

The third point is that of money and it does seem clear to me at the moment that I can't afford the sum of £10,000 to invest...

I value my association with you in a way which we both realize...

---

* When Sellers tried to soften you up with a coy endearment trouble was on its way.

It wasn't only the timing of this letter which was implacable; its actual content doesn't add up. Why should Sellers, who never cared what people thought, care what other people might think if they saw his name printed on the stationery? How does that diminish him in his own, in anybody's, eyes as an actor? And hadn't Mankowitz, with *The Millionairess*, actually demonstrated that the route to riches was to receive a percentage of the producers' take? As for £10,000: Sellers always had £10,000 for another motor car...

♦ ♦ ♦

For all his avowed professionalism in his letter ('I have got to concentrate on being an actor'... 'I value my association with you...'), Sellers, in private, was pleased with his own vengefulness. Under the guise of a 'career objective', and seeming a saint when most he played the devil, he had been quite consciously spiteful; he had found a way, by leading Mankowitz on and then abandoning him, of appeasing his jealousy and arbitrariness.

'Wolf and I couldn't find suitable subjects to work on together,' he lied, adding, 'Wolf is doing so many things it's difficult to keep track of him. In my opinion, though I doubt whether Mr Mankowitz will much value it—he has too much on his plate. He is a very strange person with so many things on his mind. In my view he should concentrate more on one thing, like screenwriting, and leave the impresario business alone.'

As when he complained about Milligan, Sellers' words are impeccable, irreproachable—as a *self*-diagnosis. (He thinks himself the physician; actually he's the foul disease.) Mankowitz, neither at that time nor later, made any attempt to dissemble about his own disappointment. He had been a classic gull and didn't see any advantage in pretending otherwise: 'He's not exactly on the dole, is he?' he said of Sellers in the autumn of 1960, when the press heard of the split in their indissoluble partnership. 'The truth is he has taken over Sellers-Mankowitz completely and I leave it to you to guess who got pushed... For six months I have devoted myself to forwarding the Sellers-Mankowitz operation and its collapse leaves me free. I am unbusy. I can tell Mr Sellers—actor, producer, director, script-writer, and recording star—that I shall be glad of the rest.'

Sellers' response to Mankowitz's comment was as straight as a hazel-twig: 'If you are sufficiently well-known and in demand you can have freedom anyway—you can set up a good subject very easily, with anyone.'

♦ ♦ ♦

Whatever other relevance the foregoing little demonstration of power might contain, it is proof enough that Sellers, as a wheeler-dealer, and hence as a popular star, was not going to remain at the level of offbeat, whacky one-reelers like *The Running, Jumping and Standing Still Film*, despite what he said: 'We may do a series of short abstract comedies,' he announced in March 1960, when news of the Golden Gate Award came through, before, in the next breath, completely changing his mind: 'Financially there's no money in them. From that point of view they are a waste of money and time... I would like to make a full-length one, not necessarily abstract comedy but a silent film in that respect, with some music and sound effects ... *The Running, Jumping and Standing Still Film* was done on 16mm, but we are going to do the next one on 35mm because it is so much easier.'

On standard-gauge celluloid, non-abstract, and with a soundtrack (because 'these things build up atmosphere enormously'): Sellers was veering back towards the conventions with which *The Running, Jumping and Standing Still Film* had broken, and he was also getting away from any dependence on Milligan, who'd expected a breakthrough in his own career on the basis of that little short: 'I'd hoped people would take me up on it and use me in films for ideas,' he said to me. He recently amplified the remark in a television interview: 'I tried to say to people, "Look, you don't need ten million pounds to make a film, you can make one for as little as fifty pounds." I thought someone might take me up on that and say, "Hey, if you can do that, hey, he's our man." But that never happened.'

When I visited Milligan for this book, in his spotless, waxed and polished house, where all the pictures are screwed to the walls with little shiny brass brackets, and where the Victorian horsehair and button-hooked chairs and couches float on two acres of snow-white carpet, like boys and girls changed and immobilised by a witch's spell, he made one remark which particularly stuck in my mind: 'Funny about Peter—Peter never ever came to me for a film script. He never said "Spike, write me a film." I don't know why'.

When Milligan spoke these words, in his slightly tremulous thousand-year-old man way, his mood was not resentful or bitter; he was intent on conveying something much more like regret—even of concern. Not a regret for himself and his own loss, or chagrin because Sellers never made any effort to put him on a Hollywood studio's payroll. Nothing so vulgar and imputable as that. His tone, I'm convinced, was sorrowful *for* Sellers, and there's a connection with what he went on to tell me next: 'He spoke to me on the phone from Paris. He said, "I'm a bloody fool. I've left my children nothing in the will at all." I said, "That's terrible, Peter. You work all those years and leave them high and dry." "You're right, Spike. I'll have to leave them in it." I told Lynne Frederick this, but she wasn't interested.'

His own children; Milligan as mentor; Mankowitz as a partner: Sellers rejected them all out of the same underlying principle—mad, calculating, and self-protective, he had to expel those who were not malleable or who might surpass him by, say, living longer or by being more greatly loved. He got rid of people one by one; and then, his heart being his own executioner, he got rid of himself.

Chapter Eleven

♦ ♦ ♦

Bubble Bubble

It wasn't Milligan, therefore, who was able to capitalise on *The Running, Jumping and Standing Still Film*, but Blake Edwards, for the short was 'one of his favourite things' and it inspired the structure of *The Party*, nine long years later. 'The idea that Blake had,' said Sellers, 'was that we should just have an outline, and work around it, and try and think things up. He's very good at thinking up ideas and bits and we used to work together quite well. We took for a theme an out-of-work Indian actor who's gone to America to appear in a television series, and... he rolled up at this huge Hollywood party and nobody recognised him. There were some remarkably good things in that film. The end went wrong— mainly because Blake was at that time busy with getting *Darling Lili* together... He couldn't concentrate on what we were doing.'

One of the visitors to the studio, as we know, was Satyajit Ray, who to his dying day couldn't understand why Sellers had failed to grasp the feebleness of the material. *The Party* is indeed rather slow and (the chicken portion pinned to a tiara; the ever-unspooling toilet roll dispenser) dogged; and Hrundi V. Bakshi, Sellers stained a coffee colour, is a sub-continental Clouseau without a case to solve. The film unfolds in a Californian ranch house crammed with gadgets. I'd say that the location for the party is the star of *The Party*. The building is a mixture of Ancient Rome, sixties Americana, and Sellers' own gimmicky taste. When Hrundi fiddles with an electronic console, flames roar in a distant grate, the burbling brook becomes a torrent and the gentle fountains turn into geysers, the drinks table rotates and a public address system blasts people with muzak. It is a booby-trapped pad. Hrundi is the booby.

Like many of Sellers' characters, he is also an innocent. He slinks about the house, dignified, his hands behind his back, the very soul of courtesy. When he smiles his big toothy lop-sided grin, people are compelled to respond civilly. *Is he an idiot*, they seem to be thinking, *or a genius?* Hrundi, as an Indian, is automatically the outsider at this Hollywood reception, but he's more than foreign. He's an alien—virtually from outer-space, the way Sellers plays him. Sellers throws himself into these passive rôles so completely, it really does seem as if he is photographed by accident—he is not, you'd swear to it, aware of being spied or eavesdropped upon. (This is how his violent characters operate, too, by being indifferent to others.) In the midst of the cinema screen, and within that, in the hurly-burly of a movie studio with all the heavy engineering of artifice, Sellers can look totally alone and forlorn. Not even Chaplin could manage that; he always had a winsome

Sellers (as Hrundi Bakshi) and Britt watch a playback of a take on the set of *The Party*.
Photograph taken by Satyajit Ray (1967)

and dewy eye on the audience. He was ever ready to acknowledge applause. Sellers, by contrast, creates an impression of privacy (and of mystery). Might this have something to do with his radio apprenticeship, when he'd been all-powerful, absent-yet-present, and when nobody could see him at the end of the microphone?

♦ ♦ ♦

The Party wholly lacks the nineteenth-century surrealism of *The Running, Jumping and Standing Still Film*: what it chiefly has in common with the short, in that case, is a looseness of form and a looseness of content, which all adds up to something inconsequential. That's not a totally pejorative remark. The drifting, desultory behaviour of people in their leisure moments, off-duty in the park or mingling and gossiping at a soirée, would seem to give the films whatever links to intelligibility and sense that they may possess. But the one hour and thirty-six minutes of *The Party* on Warner Home Video lasts a very long time indeed. (It is a short stretched out to feature length until it snaps.) Hrundi could have reduced people, indeed, to the naked barbarism and whimpering madness of Dreyfus, in *The Return of the Pink Panther*. Instead of which, and God knows how, the film ends with a painted elephant being given a bubble bath—i.e., with whimsicality, and nowhere near the grotesque.

It is also virtually a silent movie. Long stretches contain no dialogue or anything much beyond a soft hubbub. If, as Sellers said, 'Tati's an idol as far as I'm concerned, he's a great, great, great filmmaker,' then why didn't he purloin a few more hints and signals from the master, not just the obvious swipe of a character (Hrundi; Clouseau) who is clumsy and choreographed at one and the same time?

◆ ◆ ◆

With Fred Kite's heavy-set melancholia still upon him and *The Running, Jumping and Standing Still Film* (which 'as it happens...only took two days') in Lester's care, Sellers left for Scotland on June 6, 1959. He was to spend a week, with Constance Cummings and Robert Morley, shooting location sequences, under Charles Crichton's direction, for *The Catbird Seat*, as *Battle of the Sexes* was then called. The alleys near Edinburgh Castle were used for the situation of Mrs. Barrow's flat; the hills and fields on the city's outskirts, at Arthur's Seat, became the remote island dwellings of the crofters and their spinning wheels. (The remainder of the film was made at Beaconsfield Studios, near London.)

Sellers was now white-haired, stooped, neat, mild, and attentive. Mr Martin's veins seem to contain not blood but a mixture of milk and water, for Sellers almost glows, he is so snowy and pale. 'I personally think it was about the best performance he ever gave' said Crichton. 'He hadn't had...a leading part, and he took it very seriously. I didn't help him enough; I didn't reassure him enough. Did anybody, in fact?...But I think Mr Martin was *the* most considered performance he ever gave. It was poignant. He was far better at these sorts of rôles than the flamboyant parts, which I think coarse, but which did make him rich and famous. He was also very inventive. That scene where he's backing towards the kitchen door and he pulls out the knife—but it is an egg whisk. All Sellers.'

Battle of the Sexes was the first outing for Sir Michael Balcon's gathering of independent producers, Bryanston Films. Were they hoping for an international or transatlantic subject? 'Harold Hecht in Hollywood had rights to the story and he invited me to America to direct it,' says Crichton. 'I arrived in Los Angeles and... didn't have a single dollar in my pocket. I borrowed some money to call the studio, and got Hecht's office. "Sorry Charlie, didn't anybody tell you? We've given it to somebody else." They had a plan of combining it with another Thurber story. "It's all nonsense," I said, "You'll never make it." For once in my life I was right.'

The story had begun a life as a four-thousand word New York fable by James Thurber; you'd not expect that it could have been successfully transplanted to Scotland—and yet it does work. Mr Martin's self-effacement is a strength and virtue in Edinburgh; he has Presbyterian restraint and reflectiveness.

The ballyhoo about Sellers' involvement in the post-Ealing company reached the front pages of not only *The Bristol Evening News* and the *Brentwood Gazette*, Essex, but also of the *Johannesburg Star*, South Africa, and the *Malay Mail*, Kuala Lumpur. He was getting known. As an individual, however, getting to know him and trying to fathom him was proving increasingly uncertain.

'He was a little bit vacuous,' said Constance Cummings. 'When he was not playing a scene he sort of disappeared, like a mirage. He was not a man to hurl himself about. He took the greatest delight in Mr Martin and in these characters he played...And Peter was a quiet man. I got the impression that he had this longing, this yearning. He felt himself to be inadequate and he was conscious of having been disadvantaged as a child. He spoke of his sad life as a child. But we never met outside of the film.'

Sellers also shrank from Crichton.

'I never knew him socially. He didn't keep up any contact with me. He was very keen, at one time, that Danischewsky, the writer and producer, he, and I should continue together and make more films. I don't know what happened. He lost belief in all of us, and *Battle of the Sexes*, before it came out. Then, years afterwards, Princess Margaret said it was the best thing he'd ever done ... and then perhaps he regained his belief?'

Constance Cummings was not aware of any of Sellers' doubts or denunciations. Indeed, it is quite clear that, around her, Sellers carefully kept himself secretive and in character—except once: 'Yes, he was charming, and so *quiet*, and also a great giggler. There was a scene we had where a blind man walks down the stairs ... The blind man's dog was a retired police dog—so he was trained to cope with every dangerous eventuality. They'd built this rickety staircase without banisters—because the camera was meant to follow us up and down. And they got this dog, Astor ... and he was meant ... on *Action* ... to start guiding his master down the steps. Well, this retired police dog took one look down this staircase and just crouched— as if to say: "That is too bloody dangerous. I'm not going down *that*!" Still makes me laugh to think about it. Peter and I began to giggle ... finally they decided that they would shoot silently, with the trainer at the bottom hissing "Seek, Astor, seek, seek!" trying to get this dog down the stairs. And Peter and I were standing there waiting ... and the dog wouldn't budge. Peter absolutely *went*. He lost all control and just dissolved. He had a sense of humour which simply couldn't resist something like that. Charlie got very cross with us, not with the dog. We were helpless. We'd be standing quite po-faced [solemn-faced], but the minute the clapper went and Charlie said *Action* ... both of us, *helpless*. "Seek, Astor, SEEK, *SEEK!*" The dog never did do the scene; but if Astor had, *we* wouldn't have anyway ...'

'I had heard that Sellers, even then, could be difficult. A bit uppity,' says Crichton, 'but on the whole of that picture I had a ten-minute argument with Constance Cummings, because she and Sellers kept corpsing, and that was all.'

◆ ◆ ◆

'My rôle in *Battle of the Sexes* is a serious one,' offered Sellers. 'I spoke to a chappie the other day who said, "Oh yes, but it is funny isn't it?" So, perhaps I am wrong ... Here again there are things in it that I'm not entirely happy with; but then I don't suppose I'll ever find anything that I'm entirely happy with, even in my own stuff...'

Disregarding Sellers' grumbles of dissatisfaction, it's not that Mr Martin is not funny because he is serious; it's more that he is undemonstrative and the humour derives from his calm looks and glances of reproach. Like Clouseau, Mr Martin, during the period of time covered by the film, is finding that his life has been booby-trapped—and he reacts with a cunning that he didn't know was in him. I don't think he's heroic, exactly; it's more that, confronted by circumstances which are horrible and boring (Robert Morley's pompousness, Constance Cummings' hollerings), he can apply himself to sorting it all out. And, realising that 'you can always rub out an error,' he is as agile and unruffled planning a murder as he is totting up columns of figures in his office. He doesn't, therefore, become a new or different person—he simply develops or enriches what's already there in essence.

As in *Two Way Stretch*, which followed immediately after *Battle of the Sexes*, Sellers, by some instinctive means, keeps very still and quiet, lets everybody else strut and fret, and steals the scenes. (He casts himself in a silent movie again—we watch, and register, his meditations becoming visible.) He is a particularly effective focal point of a steadiness and nonchalance when the supporting cast includes a high-spirited circus elephant like Morley. Clad in a kilt which contains enough tartan to curtain and carpet Skibo Castle, he resembles, more than ever, one of Dr Moreau's mutants—a turtle crossed with a Cavalier King Charles spaniel, blown up to monster size.

That Sellers' restraint, in the face of Morley's fuss, never looks like discomfiture (we don't feel he's in retreat); and that his expressionlessness is, paradoxically, expressive, is a great achievement. As soon as we see Mr Martin, a cloth-capped figure tapping his way along the street, grey-haired and never catching anybody's eye, we register his diffidence—and also his control. He is not shiftless. He is not nervous. He is careful—at the wake for old Mr Macpherson, when the others are deeply into the whisky, for example, he sips at a glass of ginger ale. He also flinches from any gossip about girls and family. Mr Martin belongs to nobody.

Mr Martin's office is piled high with ledgers, parchment scrolls, and bushels of quill pens; his underlings are goblins out of a fairy-tale forest and cousins of Henry Crun from 'The Goon Show'. Mr Meekie and Mr Munson, talking in whispers and wearing wing-collars, scurry though the undergrowth of papers and sit in their little dens and cages; they have eyeshades and little cardboard sleeves on their forearms, to protect their cuffs from splatters of ink. They are Santa's elves.

Into this tottering edifice of speaking-tubes and controlled chaos ('I don't suppose you'd call it a system, but we do find what we want when it's needed') come Cummings and Morley. The lady is an advocate of efficiency and the application of 'psychology to business'. Having, in thirty seconds, wrecked the cross-reference and card-indexed order which had taken centuries to form and grow, it doesn't take Mrs Barrows longer than a quick-fade and dissolve before she has insisted that MacPherson 'break with tradition' and replace the Victorian furnishings with fifties junk.

Mr. Martin could probably adapt to the technology; what gets to him is Mrs Barrows' personal manner. She treats the men like naughty boys. MacPherson loves this bossiness—Morley's eyes gleam. Constance Cummings is a nanny fantasy. Mr Martin, however, is starting to calculate inwardly. Crestfallen, because he's just been called a 'fossil', a 'Rip Van Winkle', he can see that a nasty modern ceramic, on the other side of the room, is about to drop off the mantelpiece accidentally. He makes no move to save it. It smashes—and he allows himself a tiny grin. It is an omen. He will rebel.

◆ ◆ ◆

As the film chunters on, Morley's performance becomes increasingly wayward. You suddenly think: The House of MacPherson is endangered not by that meddlesome woman but by this basket case. Charles Crichton agrees: 'The picture was damaged by Robert Morley, who *overflows*. Constance hit the right level. Morley plays it like a great baby. He's not right. But at the time he was much more famous than Peter Sellers ...'

What in another's hands might have been a straightforward operation is, in Sellers' performance, quite a set-piece—and this is what happens in the remainder of the film, once the formalities, motives, etc., are firmly in place. Sellers is given long scenes in which he can luxuriate in his character; he tries out variations on his character. As a result, drab little Mr Martin is gripping (in a way Morley's MacPherson, monotonously petulant, is not) and it is a pleasure to see him tuning the nightwatchmen's radio to a Strauss polka and throwing files in the air and snipping name tags with a pair of scissors, his midnight anarchy *choreographed*.

Unlike Kite, who is embarrassed and humbled if left in solitary confinement, Mr Martin doesn't mind his loneliness. When he allows himself a sword-fencing flourish of his umbrella at the marble busts of the MacPherson ancestors, we can see how happy he is, not being watched. (He can be himself when he's on his own.) His elation continues the following day. Morley is going bonkers, in his mission control, because the intercom's lines are all crossed (he wants Mr Meekie and he gets the tea lady), when, to add to the chaos, dozens of packing cases are delivered. Mr Martin smiles with pleasure at the confusion. 'You're a canny man you are, Mr Martin, you are that,' says the porter. 'Aye,' he responds, inaudibly. As the rest of the staff exit, and MacPherson and Mrs Barrows go off arguing, he does a little pirouette and tosses a handful of the sawdust packaging (again) into the air. It is an inspired, eloquent moment—and Sellers doesn't have to utter a sound.

Mrs Barrows escalates her side in the war: sack the oldsters. Hearing this, Martin, too, is galvanised. If he bumps off Mrs Barrows and purposefully scatters false clues about—whisky, cigarettes—he'll be the last person the police will suspect (his transition to master criminal may be compared with John Cleese's development from barrister into jewel thief in *A Fish Called Wanda*); his preparations for the deed result in dialogue which can only be called Goonish. When he's standing on a chair and preparing to club Mrs Barrows, she moves out of range with a millisecond to spare (it looks as if he is merely uncorking a bottle); he goes to stab her and the connecting door in the kitchen swings shut, and the knife is embedded in its panels (it looks as if he'd been using the knife to dislodge the icetray in the fridge). The scene is a dance. Mrs Barrows is brisk; Mr Martin is thwarted. He is about to push her out of a window when Morley arrives. Sellers speeds about the flat retrieving his umbrella and cap, planting his evidence and covering his tracks. We never know which door or hatchway he will be behind—it is scrupulously done.

'My favourite scene—when he wants to murder me,' remembers Constance Cummings. 'He thinks about pushing me out of a window; he gets the knife and sticks it in the door. That was great fun to do. I always loved that complicated farce. You had to be very meticulous to do it all absolutely dead in the right sec-

ond—has to be neat, neat, neat. Peter kept thinking up things to do. He did it *very*
seriously. Much of it Peter invented—he *took* to that. He was a genius and he had
a neatness, in the way he moved and in his words. I'd say he was a miniaturist, with
his love of precision.'

◆ ◆ ◆

It was a love he would stop labouring for and lose. The later series of Pink Panther films are hardly anything more than slapstick sequences, for example, but the
richer and more famous Sellers became, the more lethargic was his acting. Sometimes, in the martial arts scraps with Cato, the houseboy, we see four people, if not
more, doubling for Sellers. In his contract, at the behest of his insurance company,
was the phrase 'The artist shall not be required to do scenes of a hazardous nature.'
Define *hazardous*! To Sellers, by the middle seventies, getting out of a parked car he
considered hazardous. You never knew what he'd refuse to do or on what pretext.
As Burt Kwouk, who endured the karate chops and explosions, recalls: 'Peter was a
genius, and one of the reasons I say this is because he was capable of giving wonderful performances and he was also capable of giving the most god-awful things
you ever saw in your life—this means that, to me, the line is very fine... Because he
was a major star, and the person with the most clout... he was expected to have control, a say on this or that. But as an actor *he* needed to be controlled. He went in and
he did it and everybody deferred to him—which is wonderful if you are insecure,
like Peter. Everybody flattering you. But he *knew* in the back of his mind that it was-
n't quite true... So he was suspicious of praise—and very suspicious, it must be
added, of criticism. He couldn't *understand* why people disagreed with him; he was
volatile. An up and down performer. He'd had an uneven life—and so he also had
an uneven career. He had an uneven personality—all part of Peter Sellers...'

If the producers chucked money at Sellers, in the hopes of coaxing his talent
and inventiveness into being, it ought to be mentioned that John Taylor, who was
passed off as Sellers-and-Clouseau in the grave-robbing *The Trail of the Pink Panther*, was remunerated with zilch and treated without ceremony; still, he's no better
or worse than the master (and his stunt doubles) when it came to falling over a lot.
Which speaks volumes about the extra aura Sellers must have had. As soon as
Sellers had died, and the decision was made to concoct the film from old out-takes
and new linking material, 'they were pressuring me to get down to Pinewood that
same afternoon' says Taylor. 'No formal proposition was put through my agent.'

Taylor was considerate and professional—two qualities which Sellers, because he
was a star, i.e. because he didn't need simply to be competent, had abandoned. As
Blake Edwards puts it, when Sellers' career was at a low ebb 'he'd be co-operative
and wonderful to work with'; but the moment he became famous, he was 'a monster... angry, sullen... He wouldn't show up for work and he began looking for anyone and everyone to blame, never for a moment stopping to see whether or not he
should blame himself.' Hence, for *The Pink Panther*, his first adventure out of
England, he did his best; for *A Shot in the Dark*, which followed the acclaimed *Doctor
Strangelove*, 'he just got bored with the part... and the shit hit the fan.' Sellers then
made his less-than-magnificent continental films, *After the Fox*, *The Bobo*, and of

course *Casino Royale*, so crept back to Edwards and made *The Party*, on which 'our...
experience had been a good one.' *The Return of the Pink Panther*, five or six years later,
rescued Sellers from his string of unreleased features, and after that 'we got very
rich'—and Sellers remained ungrounded for the rest of his life. 'I mean,' says
Edwards, 'Sellers was a pretty strange gentleman to begin with, but that awful heart
he had apparently affected his memory. If you gave him any kind of intricate physical moves in scenes in which he also had lines, he became literally incapable of doing both... We got more and more away from Clouseau's character involvements and
we put in more and more physical comedy so that we could use doubles for Peter.'

Sellers' dependence on, and his periodic rejection of, Edwards and Clouseau
follows the pattern of his behaviour towards Milligan, Mankowitz, and the
Boultings: he was industrious and/or perfidious as it pleased him, his mood swings
being dependent on his sense of power. If he felt he didn't need you, he'd misbehave to make up for the times when he did have to be compliant—and the sever-
ity of his agitation and exhilaration was manic depressive. Psychoanalysts would
say that Sellers had turned the director-actor relationship into a version of the
mother-son bond, with all its love-hate ramifications. Cognitive psychologists
would argue that, on the contrary, Sellers' problem was that he found his career
and existence unrewarding and he was therefore full of self-disgust. Other sorts of
therapists might say that Sellers' early experiences, traipsing England's music halls
with his parents, had instilled a sense of helplessness.

Whatever the students of the mind might come up with, the fact remains that
on *Battle of the Sexes* (to round off my discussion of that film) his ability to go from
being the elderly shag with a walking stick at the start, to doing the nimble jigs in the
middle of the film, and then to pull off the full-dress mazurka at the end; to make the
adjustment from muffled clerkiness to sombre-countenanced would-be killer; to
make his characterisation coherent, credible, and to get us incontrovertibly on his
side; and beyond these basics, to imply that, hidden inside Mr Martin are other Mr
Martins: this is the performance of an actor in his prime. And, as in the Keats poem
about the ripe fruits, ready to decay, the plump, gambolling lambs, ready to be meat,
the bee's store of honey 'o'er brimming their clammy cells,' Sellers' moments of perfection were in a conspiracy also to be the commencement of his rot.

◆ ◆ ◆

'Damn it! If I'm ever going to be happy surely the time is now?' Sellers said
angrily to Herbert Kretzmer, at Chipperfield. 'I've got everything... Why can't I
be happy now? What am I looking for?' At first he thought his goal might be financial. 'I think the ideal thing,' he told *The New York Times Magazine*, on March
27, 1960 (when *Battle of the Sexes* was about to open in America, and when *I'm All
Right, Jack* and *The Mouse that Roared* were still doing brisk business), 'would be
to... have enough money—say £200,000—to sit back and think, "I don't have to
work anymore."'

When Sellers allowed himself the leisure to meditate, however, he achieved
no complacency, but other things. He was bent on making his aspirations and de-

sires into anxieties; and even happiness was to be feared and could induce a depression, because (a) it wouldn't last and (b) if it did, he'd get jaded: 'I tried to think about what is happiness, and I suppose it is those brief moments that come to you—that you can say, "My God, I'm really happy today," or something's happened ... And then it goes—and I suppose if you had happiness all the time, you'd probably get blasé with it; you'd never appreciate it when it came along.'

Sellers talked of happiness as an object, a possession, not as a condition or a state. Death, similarly, if his talk about being quick-frozen and warmed up by scientists at a future date is to be believed, was another commodity—an optional one at that. Death, indeed, he took as a personal affront. It implied how little he counted. Hence, I think, during his marvellous years, 1959 to 1963, his decisive efforts to summon up remembrance of things past. He'd outwit time by going back in time. 'How do you fancy a weekend in Paris?' he asked David Lodge. 'I'll take Annie, you bring a girl, and we'll recreate some of those times we had at the end of the war.'

John Osborne had written *Look Back in Anger* four years previously as an invective against the hypocrisies and illusions people take out of the past; Sellers looked back angrily too, but his rage was the rage of the sentimentalist who *wants* to impose false colours on yesteryear, who *needs* to deceive himself that he can grow young and fresh by retrospection. Sellers booked rooms at the Hotel Favart, by the Opèra Comique, where he and Lodge were quartered a decade and a half ago. His Rolls took his party to London airport, and on arrival at Orly, a Columbia limousine transported them to their billet. They had lunch at La Fouquets, went to a cabaret at the Chantilly, and then moved on to hear some jazz at the Blue Nun. *Up the Creek* was unspooling in Montparnasse and Sellers was met and made a fuss of by Kenneth Hyman, the executive producer from Allied Artists and Seven Arts (for whom he would eventually make *Lolita* and *I Love You, Alice B. Toklas*).

Such a trip would make anybody walk tall—not Sellers. Despite the retraversing of his past in order not to feel an erasure, all this new opulence and applause did was serve to remind him how tenuous was the hold on fashion and fame. He knew he could lose it as quickly as it had come to him. 'I accept myself,' he said uncertainly in December 1959, 'but sometimes I get worried. It's success that does it, I suppose. You worry about how long ... it's going on. And you wonder how long *you're* going to go on.'

When the band of brothers called the Goons broke up, and he moved out of London and onto the international circuit, Sellers repined for his early gigs as a drummer: 'I'm not really afraid of being poor. When I was poor I was happier—I didn't worry. [Now] I get ... *terribly* depressed; suicidal; black!' He took out his frustrations on the fabric of Chipperfield Manor itself. 'This is quite perfect,' he announced, showing a visitor the blossom in his garden in June 1960. He then insisted that all the beautiful apple trees lining the lawn had to be cut down. 'Why weren't they with the rest of the fruit trees in the orchard?' he complained, very testily, when people objected to his vandalism.

Chipperfield's sense of history, the spirit of it as a place which had persisted across the centuries, started to irk him. Sellers remembered that, when he visited the empty house to arrange for the rewiring, somebody had said to him: 'It will be ten years probably before the villagers accept you.' He returned to this comment and took offense. He started to resent his wife and colleagues who had 'talked him into going on with' the purchase of a stately home. *Ten years!* He wasn't going to wait ten minutes: 'One tries to create roots,' he said 'it's vital for the children... But they've probably inherited my restlessness. They never seem to mind moving.' In other words, Sellers was going to unseat and disorient his brood whenever he felt like it; they were assumed to have no opinions which might diverge from his own.

'He was monomaniacal,' Michael said to me. 'The world did revolve around him, especially as brought up by Peg. So it's not a case of saying fame made him lose touch with reality. He'd never had much to *do* with reality. And suddenly he went on private jets... then decided he had a fear of flying, so we went to Rome on the train—fabulous luxury. When he was doing *The World of Henry Orient* in New York, we went on the *Queen Mary*—and on that ship the second-class and the first-class couldn't swim together. They used to empty the pool and refill it for the first-class passengers...'

'He'd have wanted the pool emptied and filled yet *again* for his personal use,' I suggested.

Michael laughed and then said, 'My father wasn't actually with us on those trips. He'd have summoned us but we'd be on our own; or with his secretary or a nanny. We turned up on his boat the year before he married Miranda, 1969; I was fourteen or fifteen. I arrived in Venice for a cruise with him around Italy to Monaco. We got a water taxi which took us miles to his yacht. We drew up beside the boat, he was on the deck and he threw *his* bags into *our* taxi. "Where are you off to?" I said. "Back to England." "But I've come to be with you—and to see you." "Sorry, love. I've got to go." With that, he disappeared.'

◆ ◆ ◆

Sellers behaved as a potentate. That was fine in the context of *Brouhaha*, or in any of his other Ruritanian or Arabian fantasias; it was a bit harder to take when he was autocratic in his home life—his imperialistic attitude extending towards, and encompassing, even his guests. 'In the early days he was wonderful company' says Herbert Kretzmer, 'especially at Whetstone. But come Chipperfield—he wasn't a lot of fun to be around eventually. He became increasingly friendless. There were a lot of people he'd *known* for a long time, a Peter Sellers "crowd" or "gang" that was often at his country house, but he began to go out of his way to hurt people.'

Wolf Mankowitz, who remains unforgiving over the saga of the Daniel Mendoza colophoned production company, would agree with this assessment: 'Sellers very quickly started to live a very expensive and expansive life, and he was spending money on a large scale—so he suddenly started to look as if he was a much bigger star than he was. One of the shittiest effects of his sense of elevation was that he began to regard the rest of humanity... as his own personal court of performing dwarves.'

Mankowitz was *used*; Kretzmer had a taste of the fitfulness, too. 'Sellers would encourage and more or less commission projects. People would get put to work in a fever of enthusiasm and then, Sellers' own enthusiasm not lasting the night, he'd get Bill Wills to be the bearer of bad news. I went through one of these experiences. We were going to record an album of children's comedy songs, and on the day he came to hear them at a flat in Queen's Gate that had a piano, almost the first thing he said was, "Right, let's get on with it. I've got a driver outside." People had been so excited to know that he was coming. It was impossible to get anything going with a man who has got a car waiting outside. We'd anticipated, and deserved, a couple of hours to play a dozen songs.'

These songs, incidentally, would have involved the same team as 'Goodness Gracious Me,' the duet Sellers had sung with Loren, in their characters from *The Millionairess*, and which had earned him five thousand pounds in the first few weeks of its release on disc: 'I mean, what would bring in the same money?' he said. 'And, let's face it, it's bloody good money.'

'He tried to get out of doing "Goodness Gracious Me",' recalls Kretzmer: 'He didn't want to do it finally, though the theme of the heartbeat and the doctor, and the idea of a song to push the film, was all his inspiration. He'd liked it originally, but he went off it. He'd even insisted on a B-side, "Bangers and Mash," because he'd taught Sophia Loren some Cockney slang. It was George Martin who said, "We've got Sophia Loren coming to EMI Studios at ten o'clock on Saturday morning, and I'm coming to fetch you at nine." He was dragged into the studio.'

◆ ◆ ◆

Sellers' contempt was severe—abnormally severe. There was no healthy scepticism or wisdom about his judgements. He was simply easily piqued, disbelieving, resentful. He was 'basically not a nice man,' says Blake Edwards with commendable understatement. 'I would defy anybody to tell me what was nice about him.' The best illustration of this, in the Chipperfield period, is the famous Graham Stark-in-boot (trunk)-of-car story. The full dress version goes like this: Stark receives an urgent phone call from Sellers in the early hours of the morning; he puts a mackintosh over his pyjamas and whizzes over; Sellers is standing next to his new car, holding a piece of chalk and a flashlight: 'There's a rattle or squeak coming from the rear of the car, I can't place it, can you help me trace it?' (Those sorts of things always made Sellers crazy.) Stark has come all this way, is relieved that there was no genuine emergency, and says, 'OK, let's get on with it.' Sellers says, 'No, you've got to climb in the boot.' One thing leads to another and Stark does indeed end up in the boot, with Sellers driving around North London, steering on and off the kerbs to accentuate the squeak—meantime Stark, using the implements he'd been handed ('Take these'), the flashlight and the chalk, is making little circles and crosses where the sound was coming from; and of course the experiment had to be at dead of night, to cut down on any competing traffic noise. 'They had gone four miles down the road,' Michael tells us in *P.S. I Love You*, 'when Dad was stopped for speeding by the police'. In Stark's own account of the episode,* he says he had been persuaded ('in a moment of weakness') to climb into the boot because Sellers had

---

* To be found in his book, *Remembering Peter Sellers*, pp. 40–41.

called him a 'fellow lover of fine machinery, a connoisseur of quality merchandise *and* his closest personal friend.' (Italics in original.) It is impossible to imagine Sellers using such words without, at the very least, the hint of sarcastic edge. Only when the racing vehicle came to rest at a red light did Sellers remember that Stark was still concealed in the luggage compartment, conscientiously doing as he'd been bid, with flashlight and chalk. Now, whether it was night or day or whether people were actually wearing pyjamas, it remains that the story is not apocryphal.

Milligan, incidentally (and this ought to be of interest to a psychiatrist), has at least twice claimed that *he* was the dupe. On 'The Don Lane Show', recorded at the Comedy Theatre, Melbourne, sometime early in 1980, he was entertaining the audience when Sellers appeared via satellite from London. Milligan proceeded to tell the squeak-three-A.M.-call-out-car-boot story: 'This is true, for God's sake believe me…' 'That's right, Spike,' responded Sellers flatly. The second occasion he projected himself as the stooge was in a story called 'Peter Sellers' Rolls-Royce Christmas',* and this time around it is December 24 and snow is falling yet. A policeman opens the boot 'to find an unshaven tousle-haired man…in his pyjamas on his knees drawing little white crosses on the floor… "Oh, it's *you*. Merry Christmas."'

To Milligan, the point of the story is Sellers' formidable single-minded nuttiness; it is a gag from 'The Goon Show' come to life. (He refers to 'my lunatic friend Peter Sellers', 'my loony friend', 'what *was* he getting at?') Sellers is crackers, you feel, but also mesmerising; you, too, would have been tempted to become a party to his schemes, because you'd want to discover how the surrealism will be resolved. You are in the presence of a magician—one who can turn an accomplice into a gull. Sellers is hurtling along, oblivious to Stark's discomfort; and what all this indicates, plainly and horribly, is that human beings were a stage further back in his concerns than machines. The car had a squeak; so what if Stark was bruised and asphyxiating? This is also the lesson the reader takes away from Stark's own paragraphs: Sellers considered himself a perfectionist. If he hadn't solved the problem of the rattle, he'd have changed the car. If anything went wrong with his possessions, he'd throw them away, his patience would snap.

Taking these variations and facets together, there is still one element missing: Sellers the prankster. I cannot but suspect that a large part of him thoroughly enjoyed the thought of a poor boob being locked in the trunk. Similarly, when shooting the scene, in *The Pink Panther Strikes Again*, where Stark is a Bavarian innkeeper puffing on a meerschaum, Sellers 'went into convulsions' because the pipe had been surreptitiously filled with marijuana. Stark, who didn't discover the reason why until months later, says his head 'felt as if it was stuffed from ear to ear with cotton wool, and as if the tympani player from the Royal Philharmonic was…thumping both my temples.'

People skilled at practical jokes are the reverse of good sports; they enjoy watching the suffering they inflict on the nice and the innocent, but is there any-

---

* Collected in *Scunthorpe Revisited*, edited by Jack Hobbs, London, 1989, pp. 11–13.

thing else they gain by it? W. H. Auden, in his essay on Iago, 'The Joker in the Pack,' has this to say:

> The practical joker despises his victims, but at the same time he envies them because their desires, however ... mistaken, are real to them, whereas he has no desire which he can call his own. His goal, to make game of others, makes his existence absolutely dependent upon theirs; when he is alone, he is a nullity. Iago's self-description *I am not what I am*, is correct ... If the word motive is given its normal meaning of the positive purpose of the self, like sex, money, glory, etc., then the practical joker is without motive. Yet the professional practical joker is certainly driven, like a gambler, to his activity, but the drive is negative, a fear of lacking a concrete self, of being nobody. In any practical joker to whom playing such jokes is a passion, there is always an element of malice, a projection of his self-hatred on to others, and in the ultimate case of the absolute practical joker, this is projected on to all created things.

◆ ◆ ◆

There we have Sellers. His complaint (or boast), in a thousand interviews, that 'I have no personality of my own. There is nothing I put forward as specifically me'—his credo of dullness and blankness—is actually the most dangerous thing about him. By insisting that he was the actor's version of the writer's empty sheet of paper or the painter's dun canvas, he wasn't telling us what an expert artist he was, getting all those different voices and expressions to peter across his face; he was telling us how alienated he was.

'Though he was different in every film,' Miss Cummings said to me, 'you knew it was Peter Sellers. This recognisability, when they are transformed, marks out the greatest actors—Larry Olivier, for all his false noses—you never said, who's *that*? If Peter kept himself to himself, when I worked with him, it's because, behind it all, he was afraid he'd be *found out*, in real life, as an unfunny man. I thought he was a bit like Willy Loman, and he'd have been terribly good in that play, wouldn't he?'

Olivier fondled the idea of being in *Death of a Salesman*, too. Willy Loman's contradictory mix of heroism and phoniness, sentimentality and flashes of nobleness; his crassness, his lying, his despair, his sheer *talkativeness*, has an instant appeal for any actor (the play is mid-afternoon soap opera blown up to Shakespearean size), but it wasn't Arthur Miller which Constance Cummings sent Sellers' way—it was Marcel Pagnol. *Mister Topaze* had been translated and adapted by her husband, Benn Levy, and made into a film with John Barrymore in 1933.

'*Mister Topaze*,' she explained to me, handing over the crumbling folder containing Levy's original notes, 'is about a very mild schoolteacher ... [who] gets corrupted. Finds he has a hidden talent for shady deals. Becomes a dynamic man, through deviousness—not honesty. *Perfect for Sellers*. He must have recognised something deeply congenial in the material, for he directed it ... So *right* for it.'

◆ ◆ ◆

Mr Martin gives thought to murder, Mr Topaze to fraud. The romp which Sellers rushed into making immediately after *Battle of the Sexes*, however, was *Two*

Way Stretch, in which, as Dodger Lane, he's an habitual, not a new or would-be, criminal. It was now December 1959. He'd made pictures at such a lick, there was skirmishing amongst the people who fixed schedules and premières, and *Two Way Stretch* beat *Battle of the Sexes* to the screens by a fortnight. Sellers was in the middle of shooting *Battle of the Sexes* at Beaconsfield Studios when his previous film, *I'm All Right, Jack*, had its preview in Soho. Anxious beyond measure to see how it had turned out, Sellers organised a fast car to take him to the Beaconsfield Cricket Club ground when his day's work as Mr Martin ended. From there he was whisked, by specially chartered helicopter, to the South Bank Heliport, where another fast car was waiting... The dash cost him £200. (Approximately a year's wages for a girl shop assistant.)

As for *Two-Way Stretch* itself, it was not stretching, but it is revealing. Sellers is stripped of makeup and eccentricity; he does not add decades to his demeanour, and his voice is unreconstituted Cockney. Dodger needs a haircut and to go on a diet—and so might he therefore resemble the real, young, flabby Sellers? Indeed, instead of ageing himself for once, Sellers is going in the other direction. Dodger's giggles, the pettiness of his crimes, his one-track mind in respect to his girlfriend, Ethel, all suggest a juvenile offender. If, at first sight, Sellers doesn't seem to be exerting himself much, on second glance we can appreciate that, to knock a decade and a half off his real estate (thirty-four), all his skills as a dissembler are being employed. And he holds our attention, this sagging, plump Peter Pan, by keeping still; he makes lethargy dramatic: we sense the craftiness which has gone in to getting people to wait on him.

Sellers spread easily into the part. 'You *feel* with Peter as he reaches for a character,' said Robert Day, the director. 'He works his way towards the perfection of the rôle.' Which he must have reckoned he'd reached without ado, because the actor certainly enjoyed showing visitors the set ('come into my cell') and explaining the plot, not something he'd normally do. 'I'm afraid I am rather an unrepentant law-breaker. I like my comforts, as you will observe.' The contraband in the jail, the cooking outfit, the wine and spirits cupboard, the well-stocked larder and portable radio: it was like Peg the hoarder's flatlets during the war. Sellers continued. 'I have two cell-mates, Lennie and Jelly... Soapy (Wilfrid Hyde-White)... is one of our former confederates, and has plans for a million-pound robbery. He has a scheme to smuggle us out of prison.'

Hyde-White, like Cecil Parker, was at his best when playing a caddish variation on his gentlemanly screen persona. (Like Major Bloodnok, he had the affability of a man who'd not think twice about robbing the regimental cash box.) But what *is* distinctly unusual, in all this exegesis by Sellers, is that no mention is made of the character, and actor, which bursts through the film like a shipwreck flare— Lionel Jeffries' Sidney Crout. Crout, the martinet prison guard, not only has the best line ('Silence when you are talking to me!'—appropriated by Sellers in *What's New, Pussycat?* when Fassbender hurls the logical conundrum at his wife during a fight); he also has the best comic sequences, e.g. the dynamiting of the quarry. 'What are you afraid of?' he sneers at Dodger, Jelly, and Lennie, as they dive for cover. 'A little bang?' Crout emerges from the explosion and smoke, his clothes in ribbons, his face streaked with soot—exactly like Clouseau, in *The Revenge of the Pink Panther*, who survives bomb blasts with his dignity intact, and whose still-smouldering uniform ignites Dreyfus' office.

Sellers was jealous of Jeffries' crackpot performance, and no wonder. Crout's normal level of speech is a scream—he's a screaming skull—and far from being 'over the top' (as Sellers sneered), the point of the characterisation is that the man's anger has to be contained. As much as he'd like to, he can't run amok. It is a brilliantly strangulated performance, and Sellers made use of it twice. The correctness, the observer of protocol, the man who remains exact and diligent in his job, no matter what disasters befall him, is clearly Clouseau, as those scorched pants signified; the high-pitched rage is Dr. Strangelove. The Nazi inflections breaking through; the rogue arm flying off to give a salute: these mannerisms derive from Crout, sitting in Commander Horatio Bennet's office, and having to listen to a talk about the rehabilitation value in basket-weaving, using all his powers of will to prevent himself from having a fit.

Crout is a demon in a pantomime, yet also curiously credible, i.e. unique. His drive to hunt down deviants, and his serpentine walk, which intimates his inner twistedness, are the Marquess of Queensberry's, whom Jeffries had recently played in *The Trials of Oscar Wilde*. Jeffries, you'd be forgiven for thinking, was getting more like Sellers than Sellers in respect to the outlandishness of the parts he took, and this wasn't lost on at least one of the pair of them. They met again on *Wrong Arm of the Law*, another mirage of Ford Consuls, Jaguars, and Sunbeam Rapiers. After the first fortnight, when Sellers had been playing the gangland dressmaker, he realised that the best rôle was Jeffries' policeman, Nosey Parker—infuriatingly so, because Sellers had originally been given the choice of the two parts. He suspected Jeffries of again stealing the film. 'Lionel, I've made a mistake—it's *your* film. I've picked the wrong part.'

Sellers, as ever, was avenged. After his heart attack in 1964, he asked Ray Galton and Alan Simpson if they had a quiet little story which would suit him. They had a draft screenplay handy called *The Spy with a Cold Nose*. 'We arranged to meet Peter Sellers, now married to Britt, at Elstead, one Sunday,' recalls Simpson. 'We gave him the script and he started falling about at the first gag. He was giggling so much we thought he'll be having another heart attack. He loved it: "We'll produce it ourselves ... We'll have Lionel Jeffries and myself as the vet and the doctor ..." Then he couldn't decide which was the best part to play and he kept excitedly changing his mind. He got as far as hiring a studio and we were very excited because he was so keen. Then we had a call to see Bill Wills... "Peter said to tell you he can't do the film. He's already under contract...[to make *What's New, Pussycat?*]" ... Typical Peter Sellers... For three or four weeks he had us all running around. Then, again typically, he didn't tell us himself he was out. It was very frustrating and annoying.'

◆ ◆ ◆

Sellers avoided Jeffries until 1978, and *The Prisoner of Zenda*, when, suddenly, 'he claimed a paternal relationship with him,' says Simon Williams. 'He would phone Lionel at all hours of the night, saying he wanted advice on this and that. He treated David Tomlinson in exactly the same way on *The Fiendish Plot of Dr Fu Manchu*.' The odd thing about this is that Jeffries was actually a year younger than Sellers (and Tomlinson was only eight years his senior); but nearly two decades on from *Two Way Stretch* and *Wrong Arm of the Law* Jeffries had changed out of all recognition. The thin, angular, manic tenor of Crout and Parker was now a bewhiskered, baritonal old codger; and Jeffries had (like Guinness) relinquished his fervour. And therefore (to Sellers) he was no longer competition.

It was not uncommon, however, for Sellers to be exceeded. George C. Scott's ape-like General Buck Turgidson, in *Doctor Strangelove*, is funnier than the President, the RAF officer, even the mad doc himself; and Sellers, who was meant to play the Texan pilot, too, 'was infuriated, really frightfully angry', says Hattie Stevenson, 'that Slim Pickens played the part so well in the end.' When I watch the later Pink Panthers, it is Herbert Lom's repertoire of nervous ailments which I look forward to most, by way of laughs; and for sheer, immediate mirth, it is often not Sellers who is the cause of the tomfoolery. In *Mister Topaze*, for example, he is upstaged by Leo McKern's bumptious M. Muche, the headmaster, who roves about the ramshackle school pocketing stray pencils. Ernestine, his daughter, played by Billie Whitelaw, is a caricature of pertness. Michael Gough, as Tamise, Topaze's fellow academical

George Brown Collection

Topaze and Monsieur Muche (Leo McKern)

clerk, is so abstracted, he has his head in a Latin grammar when he's doing the cooking; and Martita Hunt, as the (farting) Baroness, almost seems in drag.

Given that Sellers directed the film, and therefore masterminded the stage effects, we can see how he pushes his cast into giving redoubled, vaudevillian performances. Indeed, what with the music-hall-sketch structure of the scenes, the exaggerated silent movie melodramatics of the acting, the preposterousness of the costumes and the painted decor, the film, all crazy appearance and surface texture, has been assembled from a wicker basket belonging to the Ray Bros. Except, that is to say, for Sellers himself. Topaze, who says 'I am completely alone in the world,' is also alone in avoiding the artificiality which otherwise, and elsewhere, prevails. Sellers has surrounded himself with flamboyance; he remains muted and small-scaled: the very thing he's *not* is frenzied. And he's the one we watch. He's kind and scholarly, and looks for the good in people, and the object of the film is his refusal to be degraded. 'A lot of things are different,' he says at the end, when he is wealthy, 'but it doesn't matter so long as the man inside is the same.' Of course, without it's having to be said out loud we can sense that the inner man has altered—he's become disillusioned. All he has to do to get people to throw away their principles is to say 'How much?' *The Magic Christian* is thus the sequel to this film. *Mister Topaze*, in spite of its French carnival background, gets to be bitter and dark.

Sellers, by being unremitting, has made acting itself a form of detachment. Topaze is at the centre of the story, and yet also, implicitly, commenting upon it, above it. And this is an extended example of what happens in other films. Sellers has the ability, paradoxically, to be the focus of attention at the same time as he's diffuse. Other actors are full of comic flourishes; he is the one who stays in the mind. At his best he was always the straight-man. In *The Millionairess* he's the straight-man to Sophia Loren; in *Woman Times Seven* and *Being There* he's the straight-man to Shirley MacLaine; in *There's a Girl in my Soup*, he's the straight-man to Goldie Hawn. There's nothing chivalric about this. Sellers doesn't peaceably step aside and allow these ladies their laughs. On the contrary, he is very much in evidence, implicitly mocking feminine silliness—especially that scene in *Being There*, when Shirley MacLaine's Eve is masturbating with a vengeance, rolling over the rug and rubbing herself obscenely against the bedpost, and Sellers' Chance looks away, to find the television more interesting. (The scene is *effortlessly* Sellers'.)

When he is forced into slapstick, however, in the later Pink Panthers, or in *Waltz of the Toreadors*, in the scenes where General Fitzjohn falls off a balcony into a waterbutt, something essential to Sellers' talent is getting demeaned. Where his skills lay was in apprehending some other person's quirks, turning them over in his mind, and reacting. He reacts at top speed in (say) *Lolita* and *What's New, Pussycat?*; he reacts with dinosaurian slowness to the world about him when he's Chance the gardener. What I seem to be leading up to saying here is that Sellers, the one-time radio voice and mimic, was able to convey, to perform, the shiftings and changings of thoughts and dreams, i.e. things that are outwardly neither noise nor movement. He stands there and his inner turbulence is registering.

◆◆◆

Sometimes it was Sellers' personal sensations which got in the way of his characters' consciousness, as he admitted. 'I'm thinking, when I'm working, only about that work,' he said, referring specifically to his glazed expression on and off the set during *Being There*. 'Shirley MacLaine couldn't figure me out at all; she just couldn't. But Jack Warden did; we were great buddies. And Melvyn Douglas, jeeze, I found myself in scenes with him where I was so carried away with the force of his acting that I forgot my lines. Almost by just looking at him. The whole experience of making *Being There* was so humbling, so powerful. And I'd often say "Cut!" and people would come running, saying, "Is anything wrong? Don't you feel all right?" I've just never seen anything quite like this film.'

In other words, Sellers' receptivity to another actor's versatility had very definite limits. If Douglas was excelling, Sellers would ruin the take by coughing, drying, or coming out with some gobbledygook excuse. It had for a long time been thus. The all-star bill of *Murder By Death* was a torment. ('Maggie Smith's a dear girl. She lets me shine her Oscar twice a day. Even tips me for polishing the bloody thing. What more can you ask of a co-star?') It wasn't so much that he was competitive; the problem was that he was such a bad sport. 'He was very envious, Sellers, of other actors,' says Wolf Mankowitz. 'I'll never forget the occasion when Orson and I, two rather large fellows, were travelling down in the lift one day in Grosvenor House. The door opens and Sellers was there... He wouldn't go down in the lift with us. He said it wasn't safe. Orson was very pissed off, "What the fuck is he talking about?" "I think he means the combined weight, Orson" "What the fuck does he weigh anyway? Skinny as a shrimp. *Looks* like a shrimp, come to think of it."'

Sellers ranked his dieting amongst his major achievements, not that being slim and slender improved him as an actor. Maybe a lot of what was unpleasant about him can be traced to his vanity. 'I used to write his fan letters and sign them,' confesses Hattie Stevenson, 'but he used to sign all the photographs. He was very, *very* fussy about what picture to distribute... Actually, he didn't like any of the ones that were taken of *him*, as opposed to him playing a rôle. He wanted to look dashing and debonair... He hated himself as chubby and bespectacled. He was really unhappy with himself. Later he nearly had anorexia, in a male kind of way: "Look, Hat, I'm so *thin* now."'

Sellers was happiest when he felt superior. He claimed to hate it when strangers tried to speak to him: 'They'd shout to me, "'Ullo Pe'er', 'ullo Bluebottle."'... Taxi drivers would say to me: "I seen you. Harry Secombe: very funny it was"—even the name would be the wrong name.'

The way Sellers went on, you'd think he was the only famous man in history to be misidentified. The journalist David Lewin was once alongside him walking down a London street. 'Are you Peter Sellers?' asked a woman timidly. 'Not today' snapped Sellers, refusing to break his stride. This rather goes against the grain of his belief that he was 'so plain-looking, so average, I don't see how you can tell me apart from anyone else in a crowd'. He was, in fact, punctilious about how he was to be approached and addressed. 'In private I always called him Peter, but in the office and in company he insisted on "Mr Sellers,"' says Hattie

Stevenson. 'He was adamant about this. He used to get cross about the familiarity of the "darling," "love", "Pete" stuff of the film studios. Didn't like that at all. He absolutely *hated* to be called "Pete".'

Sellers wanted the respect and awe accorded to a god. He was absent yet present; invisible and anonymous, yet also needful of ceremony. Simon Williams recalls the 'regal feeling' which swept the ballroom and coronation sets during *The Prisoner of Zenda.* 'The lights and the camera, the extras and the supporting players, would be prepared. The cast would be called in ascending order of importance, Lynne Frederick being beckoned penultimately. Then Mr Sellers himself would deign to grace us, surrounded by this train ... He'd start losing his temper, twitching in annoyance, and a real Sellers accent would spurt out—he'd be sounding like the Jewish boy from Finchley, instead of upper-class like Jeremy Lloyd.

'Sometimes he simply didn't materialise, in any shape or form ... without explanation ... Richard Quine [one of the directors] ... was an old man, broke, he hadn't worked for years. Sellers was nothing but nasty to him. We all felt acutely embarrassed, and Quine did commit suicide soon afterwards ... Sometimes he'd radiate displeasure and you'd wish you could say "What is it you don't like about the way I'm doing this scene?" He wouldn't help. And if you were obviously good and funny he'd let you know he felt threatened by it. "Come on—you can't have it both ways," you'd feel ...'

Both ways? Sellers wanted it every which way; by the end, there was no pleasing him. Piers Haggard, who'd watched helplessly as Sellers systematically destroyed the script, the shooting schedule, the performances of other actors, and just about anything and anybody not nailed down during *The Fiendish Plot of Dr Fu Manchu*, says that the star had overshot any normal definition of madness; Sellers was in a fairy-tale region all of his own—and the worst thing was, he was bolstered, and encouraged to stay there, by the spinelessness of the producers, who'd have let him get away with murder so long as he completed a film. 'Nobody would say to Sellers, at any time, "if you do not turn up you will be sued." Nobody, at any point, did anything stronger than threaten to phone Marty Baum, Sellers' agent in Los Angeles ... It was like the Court of the Mad King—where, if the King says "it's black," it's black; if the King says "it's white," it's white ... Whatever it is the King wants, is enacted; whatever it is the King might want, is imagined; and whatever it is the King wanted yesterday—it is remembered, in case the King might want it today, or tomorrow. And everybody at the Court of the Mad King is reduced to a neurotic gavotte to no purpose—and that is what it was essentially like working with Peter Sellers.'

◆ ◆ ◆

The Court of the Mad King was underway nineteen years earlier, at Chipperfield, where Sellers had installed (in miniature semblance of Charles Foster Kane's private menagerie) two dogs, a cat, a goose, and an aviary of songbirds. He also wanted to add people to his collection—a human zoo. Kenneth Griffith—on anybody's estimation a most brilliant creature—could see what was going on and didn't seem to object: 'There was an area where he admired one as a curious person; and he had great imagination, and he wanted to express affection and professional respect, because he'd take to you as a *character*. He was an inspiration; he made you laugh. He was audacious. He had a creative vision that soared above most...'

Yes, indeed; but he'd also devour you, given half a chance. Herbert Kretzmer had noticed that Sellers no longer invited his guests, he summoned them or, worse still, he was starting simply to expect their presence: 'I remember one night in Harry Saltzman's flat in Adam's Row where he got insane. "I don't see enough of you," he said. "Why don't you come out?" "Peter, all you have to do is phone and I'll gladly come out...I just don't want to hang around..." That angered him. He actually bunched his fist and hit the wall between us. I mean really *very hard*. "Life has been difficult," he said by way of explanation. "Why don't you show more sympathy?"'

Sellers never appreciated that other people might have an existence beyond the compass of his own. One of his persistent anti-social habits was to telephone people when he knew they'd be asleep. The most extreme example of this egocentrism would be funny if it wasn't proof that he was completely off his head. Sellers threw a tantrum because Piers Haggard was in the lavatory. 'Very late one night, I was in the bathroom and the phone rang and it was Peter. My wife answered and said something quite harmless and really normal, like "Hold on a minute—I'll get him." I came to the phone, but telexes flew to his lawyer, agent, Orion about how my wife had been rude to him. We got calls all through the night about this, from anxious executives in Hollywood, and my wife had certainly not been rude to him. That is a vivid example of how *insanely* touchy he was.'

On another occasion he kept Lord Snowdon on the phone for hours. Snowdon eventually terminated the conversation as gently as he could—it was nearly dawn—and a telegram promptly arrived: 'WHY DID YOU HANG UP?' Another time, because Lynne Frederick, who was living in Los Angeles, wouldn't answer her phone, Sellers sent Michael Jeffery, who was with him in Gstaad, all the way over to California by jumbo jet to knock on her door. ('She was still out,' says Jeffery, 'so I stuck a note on her car.')

As he floated out of reality, it became increasingly impossible for him to have friends in any normal sense of the word. He was unknowable, like a phantom. You never knew what form he'd take—or how he'd sound. 'So many people ask me why it is my voice constantly changes depending on whom I'm talking to at the time,' he said. 'It's because I don't have any actual voice of my own. I don't ever do it intentionally, but it happens. It's very difficult to sustain a voice for any length of time without letting it tail off after the first week.'

Constancy was obviously an intolerable effort. He set up any number of false appearances and employed Theo Cowan, a publicity agent, to help with the circumvention. Cowan, who told me that the press were always after Sellers, helped to nurture a popular and likeable image. He fended off newspapers in the midst of his client's marital mishaps and heart attacks ('I told the press that Peter was fit and that "he went cycling yesterday"'). He protected Sellers from the kind of profile-writers who'd have exposed the Arch Goon as a shit. Cowan saw his job not as generating gossip and news breaks, but (as he said to me) 'in husbanding the garden, getting Peter to avoid storms.'

Behind the facade, or back in the potting shed, as it were, Cowan knew all too well what a monster he had germinating. 'You could never plan ahead. For twenty years I worked on an hour-to-hour basis. I got used to his reneging, in the morning, on a promise he'd made the night before. The secret, if you were to ride with him, was to listen first and gauge his mood. You'd say, "Let's think that over, Peter..." He was not a man who could deal with permanence. Everything was *now*, how he felt *now*. His mood could change in the middle of a sentence.'

By his very nature he was friendless—not because he was loutish and tactless particularly (qualities which, in any case, it is possible to put up with); or because he was implacable and distrustful. He was isolated because, as Milligan put it when Sellers was still alive: 'He wants to be accepted as normal when he knows he's not... The real Peter Sellers will have vanished long before anyone gets too close—perhaps the enigma is more real than the man himself.'

To give this will-o'-the-wisp at least the appearance of being functional, Sellers had business colleagues, executives, and agents extracting their percentages—but unless he felt you were a subordinate he was filled with apprehension. Thus the importance to him of his secretary and valet—the people who were paid to keep him company. 'He never wanted you to have time off,' says Hattie Stevenson. 'He wanted you to have no life of your own. I was sacked so many times, you wouldn't believe it, and always over the most idiotic and footling things. He'd lose his temper, or if things weren't going right, then you were out... [Once] he fired me in front of the whole world. It was the *Waltz of the Toreadors'* première. The reviews were being dictated to me over the telephone from New York and I... only got half of it down. I said "Leave it with me. I'll type what I've got and call back." I arrived at the première and he bellowed down the stairs with all the stars there, including Royalty, "Have you managed to read your own shorthand yet?" If he was in a foul mood, you just *ran*...'

Hattie's male counterpart in Sellers' entourage was Bert Mortimer, who approached his women. 'I... got the job of obtaining the phone number or address of a girl he had heard about. Yet while I was ringing around getting the information, he would look into the mirror and say "Why do they want me? I'm not handsome."' Mortimer, a big strong bloke, also fetched and carried for him, drove for him, cleaned the cars, cleared up after him generally, bailed him out, and covered for him every day between 1960 and 1977. He was Sellers' bodyguard, and if nobody tried to attack him, Sellers would try and create complications to justify the incumbency. One night, for example, they were out dining in Cyprus with Titi Wachmeister, the daughter of the Swedish ambassador to Washington. When a middle-aged man at an adjoining table, quite innocently and civilly, leant across to speak to Titi, Sellers flew into a jealous rage. He made Mortimer drive him back to the house. He shoved all Titi's belongings roughly into a suitcase, and they returned to the restaurant, Sellers by now foaming at the mouth. Titi, embarrassed at having been abandoned, had joined the man and his girlfriend, and the three of them were now confronted by Sellers, who resembled a Hogarth portrait of a Bedlam inmate, brandishing the suitcase above his head. 'In a blind rage,' says Mortimer, 'he threw it on top of their food and wine and ordered Titi back to England on the next plane.'

As he knew that Mortimer would always spirit him to safety, Sellers could luxuriate in violence, or threats of violence. Mortimer was a form of conspicuous expenditure, conspicuous consumption—Sellers consumed another man's life with his own puny desires. (Mortimer used to joke: 'My wife said that if we ever divorced she would cite Sellers because I spent more time with him than with her!') Another formidable person he tried to exploit, though he was never on the payroll, was the stuntman Gerry Crampton.

'I'm not an actor, so I was no threat to him,' this courageous operator told me. 'And I didn't need him, because my speciality is big action films. I knew Peter from *The Millionairess* onwards. We had a great time on Ischia doing *After the Fox*. He... just liked me around, Peter. He asked me to be on all his films. I'd say "Peter, I'm a stuntman, what can I do?" On *Ghost in the Noonday Sun*, I organised five stuntmen and we played pirates for five months.

'But mainly I was always getting Peter out of scrapes; somebody would upset him on the set, or in a nightclub, and he'd call "*Gerry.*" He used to ring me up at all odd hours. I was at the Britt wedding and the Miranda wedding. I was invited to the Lynne wedding, but I was in India. Lynne, when she found out about me, said "He's just a stuntman!"... And then I was the usher at his memorial service. I showed Olivier in. "Who are you going to put me next to?" I sat him down next to Bernard Cribbins.'

◆ ◆ ◆

Cinema may be a world of illusion ('magic time' in Jack Lemmon's irritating phrase), but as illusionists go, Gerry Crampton and his team-mates actually have to do all the brave and death-defying things which the actors get given the credit for on the screen. Sellers, when he wasn't treating them as his personal Praetorian Guard, was shrewd enough to know that the stuntmen made him look good, and he liked to believe he was in league with them, could knock about with them. Stuntmen appealed to Sellers because they were the cinema's link with circus and tumblers—i.e. with his own origins as a descendant of Daniel Mendoza, the showman boxer. The last film he saw, on television at the Dorchester, the day before he died, was John Wayne's brutal and shameless *Brannigan*, in which the Duke, as a Chicago cop, chases around modern London wishing it was the Wild West. 'Father identified many of the stuntmen appearing in it as those he had worked with at some stage in his career,' recalled Michael. 'His mood brightened...'

Crampton, when he was in charge of the dare-deviltry, would often put Joe Dunne in a shot to double for Sellers. ('Joe could imitate his funny walks'.) Dunne and his family now live in Hollywood, and they remember Sellers with amazement. 'I saw what he could be like,' Joe said, pointedly, in a letter to me. 'I never socialised with him outside of work, ever... In Cyprus... he constantly had arguments with Tony Franciosa, on the set of *Ghost in the Noonday Sun*—so much so, that eventually Franciosa's close-ups were shot over my shoulder, with me doing Sellers' dialogue. The stars wouldn't work on the same set together...

'After *Ghost in the Noonday Sun*, Sellers...insisted that I was on every one of his pictures...He said I was his "good luck charm" and that he had to have me... When I visited Los Angeles, sometime in 1978, I left a message for Sellers to say I was in town. He called back a few days later, very early in the morning. He was just off to start *Being There* (a movie which obviously required no stunts) and he ended the short conversation with "I'll talk to you when I get back." We never spoke again. I'd suddenly fallen out of favour and was no longer the "good luck charm". Once Lynne Frederick entered his life he dropped people who'd had a relationship with him that was longer than his new wife's...* But he continued to send Christmas cards, written in his own hand, as if nothing had happened. When he decided to make *Romance of the Pink Panther*, he suddenly decided he couldn't make it without me. I was his "good luck charm!" I didn't want to work with him again—so instead of turning him down flat...I asked for an enormous amount of money. The producer said he'd get back to me. He called the next day. Sellers MUST have me. They would pay me my fortune. I still didn't want to do the movie, and of course it was never made...'

Mathew Dunne, who today is Blake Edward's assistant director, has a signed photograph on his wall—a still from *The Pink Panther Strikes Again*—which bears the inscription: 'To Mathew, with sincere wishes, your dad's double, Peter Sellers.'

◆ ◆ ◆

Picking people up and discarding them; behaving wretchedly and expecting others to cope with the mess; cancelling, or simply not turning up, for flights and cars which had been booked by Theo Cowan (a minor sin in the scheme of things, but crappy and symptomatic); the importance of a valet; duplicates, doubles, decoys: Sellers, bolstered by his retinue, was monarchical. And his largesse was monarchical. Kenneth Griffith tells a story of when he was filming *The Bobo* in Rome. On Griffith's birthday, Sellers chauffeured him in his Rolls to the Gucci shop where he went to extraordinary lengths to buy a uniquely monogrammed leather briefcase as a gift. As Griffith recalled the occasion, he confessed, 'Tears touch my eyes at the memory of the man, for all his failings and the things you hear against him...'

Was it generosity? Or an inducement to make Griffith think well of him? Once Sellers started to be able to support his fantasies he splashed jewels and presents around—not because he was generous, but because he had no sense of the reality of money. As Blake Edwards says, Sellers was very, *very* selfish: 'I mean he was generous—quite often he would give all kinds of gifts—but they were bribes. He was generous in material things, not really generous in his heart because he really didn't know how to do that. When I say "generous", he was generous because he had his chums, he would see to it that they were hired. That was to ingratiate himself and make himself liked, among other things.' As Griffith

---

* Bert Mortimer, after sixteen years of service, was dismissed in a curt letter, handed to him by a hotel chambermaid when he was getting ready to join Sellers and Lynne on a yacht.

concedes, there was possibly an ulterior motive tucked away inside the Gucci briefcase—but when Sellers tried to collect the favour he now considered owing to him, he found he'd picked the wrong man:

> On *The Bobo*, whatever Peter said, was ... One day I came to do a scene and Peter was directing, and Robert Parrish [the director] was sitting in the background. Nothing was said to me—no explanation. *Nothing*. And so I carried on ... until the end of the day. I was disturbed by this ... and I thought I'd go and look for Parrish. I knocked on the door of his office ... 'Bob I'm troubled. No one has explained—what's been happening today?'
>
> 'Well, Ken, Peter decided to take over the direction of this film.'
>
> 'What! Did he discuss it with you?'
>
> 'No. He just said he was taking over.' ...
>
> I was very sympathetic because I was very fond of Robert Parrish ...
>
> Back in London, Theo Cowan came to see me. 'Peter wants you to write a piece about what you think of him as a director on *The Bobo*.'
>
> 'I can't do that, Theo. It would imply that I had accepted what happened to Robert.'
>
> 'Kenneth, every other actor has done it.'
>
> 'Well, I'm sorry, Theo. I can't be a party to this—unless I can write about what really happened.'
>
> For six months Peter wouldn't speak to me. Once, in Leicester Square, I was with my last wife. In the middle of the square, there's Peter and Britt Ekland. He cut me dead.

◆ ◆ ◆

It is this sense of volatility, of a character who was both heedless and absorbed, which comes across in Dodger Lane. Sellers managed to rebut Jeffries' Crout's rococo rage, and salvage *Two Way Stretch* for himself, by reclining on his prison cot, or by leaning against a wall, becoming the very image of mock-regal indolence. Dodger is a man who has used his quick wits to get everybody else chasing their tails, doing everything for him—a master-delegator, waited upon hand and foot. It is, like the armed forces, a closed society of men. Dodger doesn't much mind this—he's too desultory to think ahead about marriage or anything appertaining to it. 'We've been engaged for five years,' Ethel tells him, 'and I got nothing to show for it.' 'Then you're dead lucky, aren't you,' comes the reply.

Liz Frazer, who plays Ethel, the girlfriend, was Sellers' daughter in *I'm All Right, Jack*; and Ethel's mother, Mrs Price, is another petite dynamo set in motion by Irene Handl, who'd been Fred Kite's wife. I mention this so as (a) to marvel retrospectively at how convincingly Sellers had aged himself in the earlier film, and (b) to remark that, whatever the type of person Sellers was playing, there was always an underlying intransigence. The intensity of that self-will, much muted in Mr Martin, hidden behind insouciance in Dodger Lane, was about to burst through the surface—of both Sellers' life and his art.

Early in 1960, *Never Let Go* was made between *The Two Way Stretch* and *The Millionairess*. Richard Todd tells me that Sellers had originally been cast as the meek little salesman, the Willy Loman-ish John Cummings; but he insisted, instead, on being the psychopath Lionel Meadows, so he and Todd exchanged rôles. It was one of the most extraordinary self-revealing parts he ever did—equal and opposite in every way from Chance the gardener. Chance is empty, bereft, dead already; Meadows is zestful and an incarnation of the devil. Chance is Sellers at the end of his life; Meadows is Sellers at the beginning of his international fame. Perhaps Sellers wanted what he deemed to be a Lionel Jeffries/Sidney Crout rôle; a pantomime genii, after the inwardness of Mr Martin and Dodger Lane, and the preceding shuffling old figures? His need for variety in his work ('I don't particularly want to do any one thing for too long') matched, as we shall see, his mood off-screen. Sellers made *Never Let Go* in what he called 'a black hell of depression,' i.e. he was beginning to go mad—and this darkness is all too visible.

◆ ◆ ◆

Todd (echoing contemporary reviews) also told me that Sellers, as Meadows, began on an outrageous note, and that there was simply nowhere to go after that; the audiences laughed in embarrassment. In fact, Sellers starts over-the-top and just keeps on levitating and magnifying. It is beyond question a performance to set beside Olivier's Richard III—indeed, as a result of *Never Let Go* 'I was going to open the Mermaid Theatre with Bernard Miles in *Richard III*, but we did not have the time to prepare it...' Like Richard, Meadows is an exercise in horror-comedy, acted out with great glee. The problem is simply that the surrounding plot has not been devised or written by Shakespeare.

The plot, as the original posters and press advertisements left you in no doubt, concerned THE CAR RACKET EXPOSED. Cummings, a cosmetics salesman, has his under-insured Ford Anglia pinched, and so, as A MAN WITH TOO MUCH TO LOSE—AND A NEW LIFE TO GAIN, he sets about trying to find the damn thing. In a HIGH-TENSION THRILLER THAT PINS YOU TO THE EDGE OF YOUR SEAT FROM START TO FINISH, he descends into the criminal underworld and confronts YOUR FAVOURITE STAR, PETER SELLERS, [WHO] HAS A CHANGE OF FACE IN HIS LATEST FILM. SEE HIM IN A NEW TYPE OF RÔLE IN HIS LATEST FILM. SHOWING AT THE REX ALL NEXT WEEK.

As in *Death of a Salesman*, Willy Loman-Cummings is made to bear all the world's problems upon his weary shoulders. He's not doing too well toting his case of lipsticks and face creams around the department stores; he hopes that by splashing out on a little car he'll be able to whizz around more shops in more towns. The increase in his commissions will earn the money to pay off the debt incurred by the purchase of his wheels—so his careeristic dreams are compromised instantly by a spiral of debt. Going with the financial insecurity, of course, is a personal uncertainty, and Cummings' job requires him to project a breezy, joshing kind of confidence. A salesman, first and foremost, has to sell himself—and this, we quickly deduce, in itself is an affront. It is emasculating.

Had Sellers played Cummings, as originally intended, when John Guillermin

'He became whoever he was playing' (Anne Levy): Lionel Meadows in *Never Let Go* (1960)

and Peter de Sarigny's script was called *Moment of Truth*, I daresay there'd have been more to the rôle than cold sweats, fear, incredulity. Todd's conception of the rôle is emblematic. Cummings is weak; he is tested; he is strong. He simply needed a bloody nose to bring him out. Sellers, by contrast, would not have implied a moral judgement on the salesmanship side of the question. He'd have been much more ambiguous about the posturings and little subterfuges needed to get by in everyday life, and how slight adjustments to the kidding and disingenuousness make you a failure or make you a success. For to get by it is necessary to act—to hide your boredom with your boss, your contempt for your friends and colleagues; there is a difference between how you seem and what you are—and keeping the two going, keeping faith to both, is an effort. Hence Meadows' power, or advantage (as Sellers plays him—I can't think how Todd would have played him). He finds the effort easier because inner and outer man are totally fused. He has a tenacity (he never lets go); and it's tenacity, his grip on the rôle he has assigned himself, which Cummings develops and strengthens. (Ideally, Sellers should have taken both rôles.)

◆ ◆ ◆

In the film as we have it there are no parallels, or psychological overlaps, between Meadows and Cummings; there is no subtlety. (The film is in every sense black and white.) If Todd represents mankind as the bare, forked, gibbering animal, who turns out noble and a bit trite, Sellers is the vindictive deity, hurling thunderbolts and causing tempests and eruptions (the characters are unattracted opposites); and as befits a red-hot savage, and a tale about the underworld, the film begins with bonfires and welding-torch sparks. The smoky scrapyard is Meadows' kingdom. Meadows' henchmen, flitting about in the sooty rain like demons, are busy reconditioning the stolen cars. In fitting old vehicles with new identities, there is more than a suggestion of the fake passport and false papers plot of *The Man Who Never Was*.

Who cares about the cars? What matters is not poor old Cummings, the travelling salesman who can't travel, who trudges about on buses and is late for appointments. (Todd semaphores the man's frustrations without ado.) What is transfixing about *Never Let Go* is not sympathy with the downtrodden, but Sellers as a force of evil. 'I know how to handle people, you see,' Meadows says to Tommy Towers, one of his minions, played by the nineteen-year-old Adam Faith. To demonstrate what he means he crushes the boy's hand under a record player lid.

As in *Richard III*, the antihero's own enjoyment of his excesses bespeaks more energy and liveliness than all the lamentations of the virtuous. Sellers even invents a special voice for his villainy. Words squeeze down his nostrils and out through his clenched teeth; it is the sound of a creature more used to breathing flame than having to talk. You feel that when Meadows is off-screen he'll be lubricating his larynx by sucking boiling water from a copper kettle spout. It is a voice incapable of not sneering. 'Me, I'm in the garage business,' Meadows says at some point, '*legitimate* business.' Never has the word legitimate, spat out slowly, a syllable at a time, seemed so ominous and diabolical. His face, too, is framed to make no expression other than a snarl. Sellers, utilising his punch-drunk boxer's build, seems hewn from a misshapen and discoloured rock. Like many spectacularly ugly people, of course, he is very vain. He is dapper in his bow tie and blazer. In every scene he courts the amorous looking-glass. The devil is a dandy.

When Meadows clips over the cobblestones we know there is a cloven hoof inside those brogues. His spruceness ('I like to see everything nice and clean and tidy') and his avowed perfectionism and business philosophy ('I've learned that money makes money, Tommy') deflect attention from his corruption and inner squalour. He is particularly despotic towards his women, whom he calls his tarts. Nothing pleases him more than to devise punishments and tortures for them.

The cops, however, remain offstage and we are made to follow Cummings, the vigilante, on his quest: 'I've got to hang on. I've got to see it through.' And instead of Meadows, with his grinning menace, representing the fears inside himself which Cummings is being made to confront, the film develops into a basic man in a white hat versus the man in black, who has to be vanquished. Despite Cummings' victory, however, I can't recall his achievement. I don't remember feeling joyful for him. This is because Sellers' performance is so hypercharged, you feel Meadows could rise from the dead (you almost want him to); only an exorcist could get rid of him.

◆ ◆ ◆

As when Alec Guinness, in the final, annoying, shot of *The Lavender Hill Mob*, gets up from the café table, handcuffed, so the ending of *Never Let Go* is the one demanded by tradition. Sellers' exhibition of dementia begs to break with such rules and conventions. Meadows is the kind of jeering and lewd bogeyman who won't go away; he incarnates, or focuses, a spirit of arrogance and self-reliance that is abroad, pervasive—especially in Sellers' career. The power of the imagination which created the part, such that we can clean forget about the complacency and sentimentality of the film he was actually in, lies within the grandiosity of Strangelove, the causticity of Quilty, the vanity of Henry Orient, etc.; but, more interesting, I think, are the bonds between Meadows' self-determination, and isolation, and Sellers' ostensibly mild characters. It is not that the likes of Sellers' Dr. Kabir, Rev. Smallwood, Hrundi Bakshi, Benjamin Hoffman, Mr Martin, and so on are deceivers and libertines; what I mean is that each of these reserved men has a measure of fundamental obstinacy. They will not give in. They are in worlds of their own, mentally and often actually, and they want to stay there. Clouseau's obliviousness is really only a farcical egotism. He's wrapped up in himself—as is Chance, who looks as if he'll become President of the United States, his benign self-centredness having been mistaken by everybody for spirituality and wisdom.

Chance's early try-out, Smallwood in *Heavens Above*, also never loses his radiant and seraphic grin, even when the howling mob attacks him. He seems to enjoy the humiliation—it's a saint's pride—and as the Bishop of Outer Space, up in his rocket, he is gloriously alone. There's nobody in sight to try and contradict him. Likewise, Juan Bautista, in *The Bobo*, is peculiarly private. He quietly exults in the fact that his skin has been dyed an indelible bright blue. It is a stigmatum—

visible evidence of his difference, his isolation. When he walks off out of Olimpia's house, children bait him and dogs bark at him; we zoom aloft for an overhead helicopter shot of his progress through the city's sunny boulevards. If it is meant to be a funny ha-ha conclusion to the film, it isn't. Bautista is turned into a freak—and he retains his dignity. He is thus doubly saddening.

How much does it take for gravity, dispassionateness, inscrutability, etc. to become botherations, aspects of selfishness? If Meadows, a character crammed with nastiness, is one extreme, and Chance, as one of the walking dead, is the other, then a mingling of chemical components from them both will produce the raw emotional material for Sellers' rôles. And he veered between the poles himself. If, as Bautista, he was all graciousness, as the star actor-cum-unofficial director of *The Bobo* itself, he was all tempestuousness. 'I'm not coming back after lunch if that bitch is on the set,' he stated. 'Tell me which one and I'll take care of it,' said Robert Parrish, who had already had to sack the script girl. 'The one over my left shoulder, in the white dress...' Sellers was referring to Britt Ekland, of course.

◆ ◆ ◆

Vladimir Nabokov, in his careful study of Stevenson's *Dr Jekyll and Mr Hyde*, points out that Hyde isn't a separate entity who comes and takes over the good doctor; he's an amplification of the hypocrisy and spite that is already present. We see enough of Jekyll, before he starts experimenting with potions, to know that he is unforgiving and capable of skulduggery. Hyde is this side of him which 'chained down, began to growl for license.' Exactly the same thing happened to Sellers. The plucky young actor, who had to hate restrictions and proprieties if he was to survive, deliberately chose to play a deeply unsympathetic character. What this suggests to me is that Sellers needed to give shape, form, and expression to his quarrelsomeness and yearnings for destruction. Something lurking in him wanted to make use of Lionel Meadows' malevolence. Where was he in his psychological development at this point?

A clue is given by a remark Anne made to Peter Evans. Evans, invited to Chipperfield, had been taken on a tour of the tennis courts and swimming pools. 'You're very quiet this evening,' he said to his hostess. 'With all this excitement [Sellers' established reputation, the forthcoming film with Loren, the money and the trappings of fame, etc.] you should be bubbling with excitement.' Anne, staring at the blue floodlit sheet of water, said: 'Bubble, bubble. Isn't that the noise people make when they're drowning?'

Thirty years after hearing those words, Evans said to me: 'Such was Sellers' nature, he had the Star Syndrome very badly from about 1960. He was moving on, and upwards, and Anne was going to be jettisoned. The big time. He was getting a very firm view of himself which precluded old baggage—his nice wife, the kids, things like 'The Goon Show'. Hollywood beckoned; Sophia Loren was coming to work with him. It is hard to remember now just how hot he was at that time. In terms of the sixties, and as far as showbiz and money went, Sellers was as hot as you can get—hotter than Satan's bollocks [testicles]. He was in the same class as the Beatles.'

Anne is philosophical about the transformation of her former husband from actor to icon: 'I was the only one who knew him from *before*—and I don't honestly think I'd have wanted to cope with him as a superstar, which is what he allowed himself to become. The fat impressionist from a variety family, who toured the music halls, who was ugly—suddenly to become a leading man: it's like a film, isn't it?'

♦ ♦ ♦

Because Sellers was bored with Anne and the children, and was ready and waiting to fall in love with Epifania Parerga (Sophia Loren's character in *The Millionairess*), it was convenient and easy for him to think of his family as enemies. Instead of *Never Let Go* being a catharsis, however, an outlet, the violence in the film was continued and extended behind Chipperfield's iron gates. Acting all day with Richard Todd didn't deplete him, it fired him up. Anne used to have to get the children fed and out of the way before he returned from the studio. During this period, she recalled for me, 'he was totally impossible. The rôle and the man became indistinguishable—he acted the rôle of Lionel Meadows even under his own roof. He became very aggressive. Particularly towards the end of our marriage, and then ever afterwards, he'd *be* whoever he was playing; he'd come home as the person. Yes, for *Never Let Go* he was *very* aggressive.'

Having found it, he couldn't lose it—the rôle would never let him go. He'd always been touchy when he was preparing a film, walking around the house, trying to find the voice, movement, look. He spent a lot of time acting in front of mirrors, and now the evil reflection wouldn't fade. For once in his life he (backhandedly) admitted as much. Asked by an interviewer whether the complete identification with his performances affected his home life, he first said 'Not at all' (meaning that he himself was what he was); then he added: 'My wife is aware of it, though, especially when it's a nasty part, as in *Never Let Go*. I was sort of edgy with her while we made that film. Then, while I was making *The Millionairess*... I was very serene.'

Oh, well, that's all right, then. *Edgy?* When he saw Anne calmly leafing through a magazine he flung a vase at her; he ripped a chromium towel rail off the bathroom wall and bent it into shapes; he smashed the pictures in the bedroom; he did his emptying-milk-bottles-on-the-floor bit. Another evening, he tore up his wife's best frocks, because he didn't like it that people complimented her on her appearance. He plucked apart a mink hat and snapped a string of pearls. (He later decided that 'pearls were for tears' and wouldn't allow Britt to possess any.) Anne became a prisoner, as Michael records: 'As long as she was in the house and giving him her undivided attention, then Dad would be content. If he was working in the studios he would ring three or four times a day to check her movements. If she left the house even to go shopping she would be subjected to interrogation.'

Once, she tried to have an hour or two to herself—she came back to Chipperfield to discover the contents of the drawing room in fragments. Porcelain had been ground into the carpets, the tables and chairs were matchwood, unread leatherbound classic novels were ripped to confetti, and cushions were disembowelled. Then Sellers started on Anne herself. 'My headboard and my parents' bed were separated by a thinnish wall,' Michael told me. 'I remember my mother pleading with him to stop—to stop hitting her and to stop threatening more and more violence, I learned later. What I learned was that he wanted to kill her. He was in the middle of making *Never Let Go*. He made me sit down and watch that film. I was frightened by that fight scene between Meadows and Richard Todd— he assured me that there were plenty of crew members standing by to prevent the swinging chains and winches from actually hurting him.'

His father involved in mock-battles at work; his mother covered with real bruises at home (no stunt doubles deputising for her); Michael was six years old when he was subjected to all this.

Chapter Twelve

◆ ◆ ◆

The Spirit of Romance

Sellers' attention was only held by what was in prospect—by what (for the moment) he did not possess. The rest was dross, and dulled his blood. His demands could be quite small (a weighing scales, a jar of royal jelly, a toaster), though they were often still very far from being reasonable. When he was making *The Pink Panther Strikes Again* at Shepperton, he needed such an amount of waiting-on, he had his own personal props buyer—a chap on hand around the clock to whizz up to London and obtain whatever the master wanted, at whatever cost. His dressing-room trailer was a self-contained luxury flatlet on wheels, where the star had already installed a white-liveried chef. Sellers didn't care how much money disappeared—getting his way was what counted. 'Peter always knew what he wanted and because he was so definite we all hated to ask him to compromise,' a former member of his staff told me. He was the Mad King in a fairy story, who sends people scurrying off in all directions on an impossible quest. While he was making *The Party* he decided he wanted a Pontiac. He made a list of the exact colour, type of brakes, level of air-conditioning, and the pattern on the tyre treads which the car had to have—or else. When, after a hunt across America, a vehicle fitting his specifications was found, Sellers (still dressed as Hrundi Bakshi) delightedly ran out of the studio, hopped behind the wheel and drove straight back to the house he was renting on Bedford Drive, Beverly Hills. (Whatever vehicle had brought him to work that morning was now simply abandoned.) Sellers then spent the remains of the day taking hundreds of photographs of his new bauble. One week later, however, he was saying 'I hate this terrible car. I've got to get a Corvette. It must be white, with hard and soft top, FM-AM and all the extras...' This time the car was airlifted from Detroit.

And as with cars, so with women. He sprang from model to model as the novelty wore off. 'When a marriage or love affair is over I just have to get rid of everything associated with it,' he said. As Bert Mortimer said soon after his ex-master's death: 'Many of his women he treated in the way a child plays with a new toy. After showering the lady with flowers, gifts, and compliments he did not want to know when the conquest was made.' Once somebody had been appraised, anticipated, and controlled, like a machine, there was nothing left for Sellers except dissatisfaction. The experience of Trudi Pacter, a journalist whom he met after the break-up of his marriage to Britt Ekland, would seem to be indicative.

'There will be a lot of pretty ladies in my life now,' he told her. 'I like pretty ladies.' Their first evening out together was a success—Pacter found Sellers completely charming. On the second evening, however, when the maître d' asked 'In what name is the table booked?' Sellers screamed: 'Who the bloody hell do you think the table's booked for? For Christ's sake, don't you know who I am?' From then on, nothing was to his liking. 'This just isn't good enough,' he said, hurling the dishware to the floor and stomping out. He later tried to make it up to his date by organising a private party in her honour at a Chinese restaurant in Kensington. Pacter spent a lot of money on a frock because Sellers had said, 'Put on something nice. It's important you look beautiful for my friends.' When she made her entrance, the rest of the company were in more casual attire. 'Don't you think you are a little overdressed?' said Sellers, in a way that should have made bystanders want to hit him. 'Why don't you pop home and change?' She did just that. Roman Polanski drove her there and back. She returned to find Sellers going on about his death and resurrection: 'I died once in my life, and it could happen again. I live in fear that every day could be the last one.' A doctor present, believing that Sellers was fishing for sympathy and expecting a contradiction, compliantly said, 'Peter... that heart of yours is as strong as anyone's in the room!' If this was what Sellers had wanted somebody to say, another part of him hated the rebuttal and coded it as hostile. So (Pacter reports) he stood up, walked over, and slugged the man into unconsciousness. And was this demonstration of physical strength meant to prove, or disprove, the doctor's comment about his ticker?

Polanski, in his memoirs, *Roman* ('Frank, Shocking, Revealing'), records the episode slightly differently. He names the doctor as Tony Greenburgh. The discussion was not about Sellers' heart and his day-return to the Underworld. They were arguing, instead, about a doctor's moral responsibilities. If (said Greenburgh) a patient was intent on destroying his health by smoking and drinking to excess, then a physician cannot be held accountable for any subsequent respiratory illness or liver and kidney failure. Sellers was so incapable of accepting criticism, or liability, even infirmity and ageing had to be blamed on the negligence of someone else. (He point-blank refused to see that he was a participant in his own dissolution.) His voice rising in pitch and volume, he countered by yelling: 'You're wrong, doctor. You're wrong. *You're fucking wrong.*' Only when it became necessary to enlist help in prising Sellers' fingers from Greenburgh's throat did Polanski and the other guests see that this was not playacting or an elaborate joke but that, far from it, Sellers was truly demented. 'Tony was choking and turning purple as Peter genuinely tried to strangle him...'

Later, in the car going home, Sellers reverted to his hideous little-boy-lost performance; he blubbed and pretended that being grown-up was all too much. 'They don't understand,' he wept to Pacter (it was always a comfort, his belief that he was misunderstood). 'How can they? They're all so much younger [Polanski by a mere eight years] ... I play their games. But never will they accept me. I'm just an outsider, a middle-aged man [he was forty-four] who pays the bill at the end of the evening.'

Pacter never saw him again, which must have been a relief. Sellers went on to spend Christmas with the rest of the evening's company in Cortina. He had another bout of boiling and bubbling, got depressed, and returned to England on Boxing Day.

◆ ◆ ◆

That women, like cars, were in the category of mechanical things is illustrated by another anecdote involving Stark. He once sent Sellers a letter purporting to advertise a plastic kit which, when assembled and rigged up to a small battery-operated engine, turned out to be a life-sized horizontal doll complete with all moving parts. 'Just think what we can do with it!' said Sellers, apparently taken in. 'Especially when we get the motor going!' Only when Stark started guffawing did he realise the hoax. ('He joined in the fun but his laugh didn't cover the disappointment.')

Sellers should have played a megalomanical inventor like Dr. Coppelius in *The Tales of Hoffmann*—an evil genius in an opera cloak who creates a robotic beauty. 'I'm continually searching for this woman ...' he said in 1969. 'I keep reading of the great women behind great men: they mother you, they are great in bed, they are like a sister. They're not there when you don't want to see them; they are there when you do want to see them. I'll find one one of these days.' And once he had got it to sing its clockwork aria he'd have been free to smash it to pieces. Why was Sellers like this? Why did he want to despiritualise his relationships? The reasons are fundamental. As Milligan had said: 'He can never be happily married because the person on whom he most depended is dead. He was an only child, and his mother naturally wanted him to have the best in life ... When she died he lost the perfect set-up—except that this boy never really got over it.'

I don't believe that Peg's death was the problem; it was the pressure she exerted when she was alive which did the damage. She'd made her son incapable of loving anybody. What he required, instead, was that women should be seen to love him— more, to adore him. (Similarly, with blokes he wanted not friendship but loyalty.)

Sellers, sick with self-love, couldn't see that it was his own twisted up narcissism which blighted his liaisons before they had begun to bloom. As everybody attests, he was an expert at the gigolo part. The wooing; the courting. He enjoyed that. Bouquets; gifts. (When he was making *Hoffman** he invited Sinead Cusack out to dinner. She asked where they were going. A helicopter was heard flapping and descending near at hand. 'Paris,' said Sellers.) But afterwards? What rôle did a husband play?

He addressed the puzzle whilst deciding what to do about Lynne Frederick. 'I've learned that I'm obviously a difficult person to live with, and I've chosen the wrong ladies to make that work—because they were probably all very fine in their own way, but not with me. I now know that I have to be ... *terribly* careful, because ... every time that paper's been signed it has changed everything ... My ideal has always been achieving the ideal marriage—the great romance that lasts

---

* Could the title (the name of Sellers' character) conceivably be an allusion to the Offenbach opera or to E. T. A. Hoffmann, the German romantic poet of unrequited love?

throughout a great romantic marriage... But I'm so scared of it now. I'm afraid I might go and lose what we have simply by saying "I do" all over again.'

Wedlock was the devil. If Sellers couldn't see, more and more clearly as the years went by, that his cycles of obsession-leading-to-boredom were getting repetitious, he must have been blind on purpose; and you'd have thought even he might have perceived that marriage, meaning a commitment (to someone else; to the future), was not a state his grasshopper mind was cut out for. Sellers liked to try and exist in a permanent, heedless present-tense, as Chance does; as he gained power in the cinema industry, always wanting to re-shoot or abandon ship, so did he try and wipe out mistakes in his private life, by starting over. You re-wind the tape and have another go.

Which is not to say that he blundered into one pair of arms after another, totally open-faced and hopeful; and he never did a single blessed thing against his will. I think that, cruel and manipulative, he actually liked this pattern in his life. Since he treated women with the flippancy that he gave to trading cars, it gave him pleasure to see an attractive woman, an ambling status symbol, submitting to him—just as, later, during the inevitable roundelay of squabbling and forgiving, he would wonder at how easy it was to stand outside of another person's pain and distress; which would lead to his next, inevitable thought: How lonely *he* was! And for a while he would be dejected, claiming (as he did in 1963 when the divorce from Anne was declared absolute): 'I no longer get any kicks thinking about falling in love or the great glamour of the great chase... Sometimes I figure that women are basically all the same... There's nothing more I want in my life than to love somebody and be loved. But I haven't ever been able to get it excepting, of course, from my parents. But that's a different thing.'

◆ ◆ ◆

Never Let Go, a horror-comedy about a man who hates himself, starring a man who loved himself, was, Anne can see in retrospect, 'the beginning of the end of our marriage—when his career was on the up; then he did *The Millionairess* and thought of himself as a romantic lead; and he had an affair with Loren... I don't think it came to anything physical—though he swore to his dying day that they did... It was purely mental, in all senses. He was *mad* about her. He used to chase her around everywhere and ring her up at all hours. She had a great affection for him and humoured him. But... he insisted on coming home and telling *me* about her, like I wasn't his wife... Wolf Mankowitz said "What he wants is a mother"; I said "Well I'm not his *bloody mother* and he can *piss off* as far as I'm concerned." ... And Peg was still alive, but if she was aware of Peter and Sophia she'd just think "Oh well, that's just Peter! He's having a nice time." She'd go along with it. She'd not see that it wasn't easy to live with.'

Mankowitz confirms that Sellers was going bonkers on purpose:

> He started to get disturbed in the course of *The Millionairess*. I have pinpointed the very moment when, in my opinion, he started to let go. I used to drive back from the studio with him in a Rolls he'd got at the time. He stopped the car... and

said, 'Look, I've got to tell you something. I'm in love with Sophia.' I said, '…Naturally, that's the idea. Everybody should be in love with Sophia.'

'No, no—this is serious. We are in love. I'm going to get together with her…'

'Really? Does she understand this? Does she want to leave Ponti? That's most unlikely…'

'Well, she doesn't know about it yet.'

'Okay, fine. If you can make it, make it. Somebody might one day—but don't talk about it. Tell me, but don't tell everybody.'

'I've got to tell Anne…that I'm in love with Sophia, and I'm going to do everything I can do to make certain we can be together.'…

'What for? I beg you—don't. She adores you. You've two children…I want to tell you, Peter, with the utmost confidence and conviction: *all this is a fiction*. Sophia will never leave Ponti. She has all sorts of reasons—psychological as well as financial ones—for staying with him…He leaves a Sicilian armed guard to sleep across her threshold. You don't know what you are getting into.'

'Yeah, but she adores me. She told me so—and she's very sweet to me. We have great fun together.'

That very night he told his wife about this, and the marriage relationship started to degenerate fast…This is when it first became perfectly clear to me that he was losing the ability to differentiate between fantasy and reality. Everybody goes mad about a woman every so often; that in itself is not a certifiable form of insanity. This was more than that…This was dangerous. And he started to chase her around a lot and he became quite a nuisance.

◆ ◆ ◆

Loren was born in the bastards' ward in Rome, in 1934, and raised under a volcano, in the Naples slums. Her mother (like Peg) was a thwarted actress, who encouraged her daughter to enter beauty contests and to seek work as an extra at Cinecitta. (Loren is in the crowd scenes in Mervyn Le Roy's *Quo Vadis*.) The movies were seen as a means of overcoming poverty—as a gateway to something magical—and in Loren's case this is not a sentimental overstatement. From a childhood filled with the problems of basic survival and sacrifice—her neighbourhood was bombarded by battleships during the war, and the Germans destroyed the water mains—suddenly she had mansions all over Italy, France, and Switzerland.

She met Ponti when he was adjudicating one of the Miss Rome beauty contests in 1950. He was a producer, wheeler-dealer, agent, and lawyer. Affable and tenacious, he became her sugar-daddy (he's over twenty years her senior) and gave her confidence and security. 'Without him I am nothing,' she said, 'I have no intention of giving myself to any other man.' They were married in Mexico in 1957, and it's at this point that her life-story started to get complicated. Ponti had been married in the long ago to one Giuliana Fiastri. Though he had been divorced from her, Vatican officials did not acknowledge the separation—and the wedding with Loren was condemned as bigamous. The couple were threatened with excommunication and jail. To establish the legitimacy of their relationship, and to be able to have children who'd not have outlaws for parents, therefore, they had to take French citizenship—which Ponti did in January 1965, and which Loren did in June of that same year. (Divorce remained illegal in Italy until 1970.) They were remarried—or legally married, in the eyes of the church—in April, 1966.

The above paragraph is a laughable simplification of legal-papal-bureaucratic shenanigans which dragged on for years, generating mountains of dossiers and a king's ransom in costs. It is sufficient to be able to grasp, however, the conscientiousness—doggedness—with which Loren and Ponti set about becoming orthodox and dignified. They had no intention of being bohemian or rebellious; Loren, in particular, had no wish to replicate the lackadaisical atmosphere which had existed between her own mother and father. This was the set-up which Sellers thought he could so easily overturn, the citadel which it would be a piece of piss to penetrate.

He met her on Wednesday, May 18, 1960, two weeks prior to the release of *Never Let Go*. He was on the platform at Victoria Station to receive the Golden Arrow, and his first words to her were: 'Welcome to England. I've never had it so good.' The pair were transported, like Royalty, to the Ritz; and at the party which then took place, to celebrate the commencement of *The Millionairess*, Loren was heard to comment: 'He's so shy, don't you think? So different to the ordinary man. So shy, so gentle... I'm sure we'll get on well together.' Sellers explained that 'I don't normally act with romantic, glamorous women. You'd be scared to. I'm more an introvert than an extrovert. She's a lot different from Harry Secombe, you must admit.'

Sellers then moved across to Loren and kissed her on the cheek—fifteen times. ('But it was only for the photographers' sakes,' he emphasised.)

◆ ◆ ◆

The Millionairess, according to what its producer, Pierre Rouve, told Paul Sherrif, the production designer, 'should be set in a kind of no-period, where orchids in one's buttonhole were not viewed with envy, where tipping with gold sovereigns was commonplace, where people, rich beyond one's comprehension, loved the idea of being rich beyond one's comprehension, where "to be" or "not to be" were worlds apart. In the period, in fact, where millionaires were millionaires and loving every minute of it.' Or, as Rouve said to me, 'The film is a parody of thirties opulence; everything is heightened and artificial.'

Perhaps the artificiality is not heightened enough? Or was it that Anthony Asquith, the director, was literal-minded and not the man to bring out any surrealism, any screwball zest and spontaneity? (That Katharine Hepburn had played the rôle on stage, and wanted to do so on film, suggests the material's potential for eccentricity.) Or is it Shaw who is the dud? He could never overcome his intelligence and the expected—and therefore never reached the hyper-intelligent realm of Wildean folly and paradox. In any event, instead of an erotic charm and sheen, *The Millionairess* is full of airs and ostentation, and is really a series of tableaux to show off Loren's looks. She appears in one damned wide-brimmed hat with a lace veil after another (the Cinemascope screen functions as an art gallery frame) and these pink or blue or peachy vast puffy creations are teamed with elaborate furs and stoles. Thousands of arctic foxes and poodles must have laid down their lives for this production. It isn't drama, it's millinery.

The problem with *The Millionairess* is it is not a musical. It ought to have been; what survived of the Loren-Sellers partnership is the song 'Goodness Gracious Me' (with its unlawful pregnancy allusions: 'Oh doctor I'm in trouble' etc.) —though it is not actually sung in the film proper. As Herbert Kretzmer, the lyricist, recalls: 'Sellers called me one day—and it was all his idea; a very good idea. "There's a scene in the film I'm making with a very glamorous patient. I'm the doctor and I'm quite indifferent to her but I'm fascinated by her heartbeat—and I was thinking, if you could come up with a song around that idea of the heartbeat and an Indian doctor—then Sophia and I, she's got a sweet voice, could do something."'

Sellers, who had lost his heart to Loren, was explicit about the cardiological chorus (and the boom-tiddy-boom on the soundtrack is a bit spooky in view of his recurrent heart attacks); but with his genius for how things were heard—for atmospherics—he could tell that the film would be flat and stillborn without some melody. He had already refused to play Kabir as Arabic. Indian, which he remembered from the war, had a different combination of sonorities. Rouve's job was to convince the Society of Authors, on behalf of the Shaw Estate, that the character could be altered. 'They said, yes, because it had been a disaster when Robert Helpmann had done it on the stage. He didn't have a musical delivery— the language wasn't able to sing.'

And yet does it this time around? Sellers seems to mumble his way through the film. He has darkened eyes, a copper complexion, jet black hair, and he thrusts his lower jaw out, to get his tongue and teeth around the Hindi. Shaw's repartee— the soulful doc versus the cold and spoilt bitch—is a load of blah. Sellers is more himself, which is to say his character comes alive, not when he talks, but in the silent throwaway glimpses—in the big, echoing, empty hospital he smiles quietly to himself as he experiments with the electronic automatic doors. He is amused by the nonsense of it, the magic of it. He's more absorbed by those doors than by Epifania, and who can blame him? Epifania is bored by her wealth, and Loren, a consummate artist, plays her boringly. Kabir is not interested in her capitalistic creeds and Sellers, equally consummate, plays the part unengrossingly.

What went wrong? 'It was hoped,' Rouve explained to me 'that Asquith could balance Sellers and Loren without commanding them—because they were two difficult creatures...Appalling! They froze! Sophia was so frightened—yet she was supposed to play somebody who was so totally self-assured...Peter was equally...nervous of Alastair Sim, who plays the slightly corrupt lawyer, until Sim went over to him and said, "Look, I am an admirer of 'The Goon Show'." The problem was to make the film without going into any discussions of...anything slightly academic, it would have had Sophia and Sellers running, howling...Nor were either of them happy about the film's mockery of money. I remember very distinctly hearing Peter say one day, between takes, "All that money—you don't give money away. You feel superior when you've got money." And Sophia started to talk to him about the post-war poverty of Naples; and she said how she, too, had learned the importance of money—it got her away from her beginnings.'

♦ ♦ ♦

There was more of a George Bernard Shaw comedy going on between the stars off-camera than ever found its way on to the screen. 'After all those marvellous men you've acted with—people like William Holden and Charlton Heston—I must seem almost insignificant,' said Sellers. 'Peter—how little you know. It's what's behind the looks that counts,' Loren replied. It was during their confidence-building chats, whilst they lounged in the studio in their name-stencilled canvas chairs, reminiscing about how they had got going in show business, that Sellers began to get woozy. 'She really threw me,' he told Donald Zec, Loren's biographer, in 1975. 'I thought then, and still think, that she was the most beautiful creature I'd met in my life.' Because his co-star started to give him reassurance, by laughing at his funny voices, he wildly over-interpreted it. He decided he was suddenly aware of a different atmosphere with Loren—who was at her best, at her grandest, and using all her seduction. To his way of thinking, she was continuing to be the millionairess; she represented energy and vital forces.

'I adored her' he continued to Zec 'and I had the feeling all the time that it was mutual... One day... she came on the set in a... wistful mood. I said to her, "Anything wrong? Has anything upset you?" "No, no. I'm fine... I love you, that's all." I believe if Carlo went tomorrow, God forbid, she'd come to me. I tell you straight. As it is, I'm happy that she is fulfilled. She has what she wants... Sophia is a marvellous actress who still hasn't reached her true greatness. I love her and always will.'

The infatuation with Loren was due not only to her overwhelming sexual presence but there was also a parallel between their careers. She was the girl who had made it on a world-wide scale; and she, more than anybody, encouraged Sellers to embark on the search for international fame. 'All the hidden dreams of Peter Sellers seemed to coagulate around Sophia. All his confused aspirations,' says Rouve. Sellers also revealed that his favourite line in *The Millionairess* came during the big-new-hospital sequence. Epifania is boasting that there are beds for more than five hundred patients. 'Ah,' says Kabir, 'but would you know their names?'

That was the one thing he'd brought out of the film—the nameless boy, from nowhere.

♦ ♦ ♦

But what about the love affair? 'The woman the least interested in sex that I have met in my life is Sophia Loren,' Rouve vouchsafed. 'Sophia had had unspoken-about traumatic experiences as a young girl in post-war Naples; and just about the one thing she would *not* do is sex—because it connects with the one moment in her life which she was striving to forget... Too many elements which kept her away from sex. Sellers wrapped himself up in a complete fantasy. She... was close to him—and she likes laughing. Peter would reduce her to hysterics with his complete repertoire... She creates a mood of warmth and understanding—she brings people out...'

(Top) Goat's Cheese and a She-Wolf: Sellers and Sophia (1960)

(Middle) Poster for *The Millionairess*

(Bottom) Dr. Strangelove receives direction from Stanley Kubrick

Michael Sellers Collection

George Brown Collection

Many of her leading men had been enchanted. Clark Gable said, 'This girl makes you think all the wrong thoughts'; Alan Ladd entered the *Dictionary of Quotations* with his comment: 'Working with her is like being bombed by watermelons.' But these sorts of courtesies are in the category of teasing and joshing ('I love that cow!' said O'Toole, after *Man of La Mancha*); and she has been able to shrug it all off, saying: 'Maybe actors have been in love with me, but there was never any danger...'

Sellers, however, was disquieting and anguished. Though he claimed he had turned into the Indian, which was crackers enough in itself ('I even began to feel that I could heal people'), it wasn't Kabir's purity which was coursing through him but Epifania's fury and fatuousness. Her fondness for electrical gadgetry and orange bed sheets—Sellers' taste; her tendency to telephone people at half-past four in the morning—a Sellers' trick; her huge sulks when she can't get her way—Sellers' traits, as also her alternate giggling and glaring. Kabir says that Epifania is the kind of grown-up brat who 'demands toys—then tosses them aside without unwrapping them,' a description which matches Sellers to perfection; and Epifania's way of degrading people with her wealth is an anticipation of the sour everyone-has-his-price ethos of *The Magic Christian*: 'Is there nothing one can get with money, except more money?' asks the doctor sadly. To which the millionairess's shitty reply is: 'Well, one can get most men, yes.'

And, as Epifania over-dramatises her reaction to Kabir's rejection of her advances—she's suicidal—so did Sellers become increasingly frenzied and insufferable. Especially with Anne, who was getting cold-shouldered. 'It was total madness the way he kept blabbing to me about Sophia Loren. Total and utter madness... He'd lie in bed and say "I can feel her spirit coming into the room"...And he'd spend our money on her—because she had some jewellery pinched, he toddled off and bought her some very expensive pieces. He was totally, totally obsessed with her—in a way which was a madness. This was the start of the real break-up of our marriage. It had always been up and down...I'd been brought up in an old-fashioned way that meant once you'd got married you stayed married, for better or for worse. Divorce was never in my mind. It was when we moved to Chipperfield and he started *The Millionairess* that it all got too much—the obsession went on long after he'd finished the film. He'd still be ringing her up...I'd hear all this patter and canoodling...I decided I was going to leave—he was doing *Waltz of the Toreadors*... I couldn't stand it any longer, and he said, "Well I'm not going to work." He refused to go. Bill Wills rang and said "Would you stay on until he's finished the film? Because he won't come in to work and we'll all be in terrible trouble." So I stayed. It was always some form of blackmail. When I did leave I had to do so in a very sudden way, finally—when he was away...I was scared of him, you see. He was physically violent when he lost his temper. We had rows that went on for hours—for fifteen hours I think there was one. I'd go to sleep in the middle. It was a nightmare, because he was mad. You can't put it in any other way. He was quite mad.'

◆ ◆ ◆

Because she was unobtainable, Loren stayed Sellers' ideal woman; even from beyond the grave he was faithful to her memory and inspiration. Interviewed through a ouija board by a psychic named Micki Dahne, he said, 'Sophia was my ultimate woman, perfect in my eyes. I dreamed of her constantly. One of my only regrets about my life is that we did not marry. I would have made any sacrifice to have had her as a wife.' When he was still with us on the ground, Sellers was equally as effusive—almost as if he was setting out specifically to disregard Mankowitz's advice about shutting his trap: 'I was never in love as deeply with any woman the way I was with Sophia,' Sellers told Zec. 'One day Basilio Franchina [a Ponti henchman] came to me and said "When the husband he finds out about this there will be trouble ..." I told him, "Well if he has to find out about it, it's just too bad."'

Sellers cast himself in a bedroom farce—Loren's own *Marriage Italian Style*, perhaps. While he was making *Mister Topaze* in the Loire Valley, 'he used to cry a lot,' Michael Gough recalls, 'because he couldn't get through to Sophia Loren— she was closely guarded. Sellers said that they couldn't ever go to his place, nor to her home, and hotels were out because tongues would have more than wagged— so all their "courting" was done in the back of his car.' The delusionary life was still being lived during *The Dock Brief*, in the Spring of 1962. One of his many anxieties (according to John Mortimer) 'was that he was being pursued by the Mafia because of his undoubted affection for Sophia Loren.'

When a journalist asked him, eleven years after *The Millionairess*, whether it had been a professional love or a spiritual love, Sellers said: 'Both. We had the same sense of humour, in fact we had a lot going in common, and we fell in love— just like that.' That must have done wonders for your ego, said the reporter. 'It certainly did,' confirmed Sellers. 'I was about two stone [twenty-eight pounds] heavier than I am now, and most unattractive. We're still great friends. Yes, I would make another film with her if the right subject came along.'

It never seemed to do so. Sellers wanted her to be in *A Shot in the Dark* and *Casino Royale*. He had himself photographed as Napoleon, in order to get a part in *Madame Sans Gêne*, which was made near Bari in 1962. The part went to Robert Hossein. When the casting was announced for *A Countess from Hong Kong*, Sellers longed to play the valet, Hudson, a rôle conceived for the unavailable Noël Coward. Chaplin, however, thought that with Loren and Brando, and Margaret Rutherford as a dowager, his tale of a shipboard romance was already getting top-heavy with stars. The part went to Patrick Cargill.

But if Sellers and Loren were not fated to be conjoined professionally, Sellers did his best to try and meet her on location in a private capacity. He haunted the set of *The Fall of the Roman Empire*, in Madrid (where he was cross to ricochet into Dick Bentley); and when Loren returned to Italy, he turned up at the Villa Ponti and begged to be able to install the hi-fi, hiding speakers and tape decks behind the walls. (Was he in disguise, like Clouseau in *The Return of the Pink Panther*, calling at Christopher Plummer and Catherine Schell's villa to repair the telephone?) Most embarrassing of all, he couldn't be shaken off during the shooting of *Two Women*, which was being made between Venice and Naples. Loren was renting a large house and Sellers arrived and moved in.

The actress wanted to concentrate on her rôle—of a careworn mother who is raped, along with her daughter, by Allied Moroccan soldiers at the end of the war—and she would waddle off to her bedroom at nine each evening, bolting the door. She barely spoke to Sellers, who'd sit eating spaghetti and shellfish with Rouve and Vittorio De Sica; but he still hung about for three long weeks. 'In Italy, with Sophia next door, he'd...endeavour to be noticed by making jokes and doing his Goon voices. He'd show off—but De Sica, Sophia, and the young Belmondo *they* were all show-offs. It was difficult for him to compete. I would occasionally translate for him,' says Rouve, 'and after a while he'd sit there and drink.'

Sellers was finding the repudiations a new experience—like being shot is a new experience for Quilty. He saw much more of Loren's sister, Maria, who was engaged to Romano Mussolini, than he did of Loren. Maria, too, had wanted to be an actress. Paramount had even offered her a script, on condition that she had plastic surgery. Romano, the son of *the* Mussolini, was a competent jazz pianist. At the party to celebrate the successful completion of *Two Women*, Maria encouraged her fiancé to play something. After listening to the music, and deciding he was enthralled, Sellers felt he ought to express his appreciation. He sauntered over to Romano. 'Gee,' he said, 'I'm really sorry about what they did to your Dad.'

◆ ◆ ◆

Sellers took his fantasticated indiscretions to elaborate lengths. To prove to Milligan that 'he and Sophia had a thing going between them' he took his chum all the way to Rome for an afternoon out. 'He wanted to see Sophia Loren in Rome, and he asked me to go with him. He did his best to canoodle with her—looks and everything. I had to go all the way there, wait in a hotel room, and then fly back to London. A bit much, isn't it? ... He was very excited about Sophia, I do know that. He grew a beard—for this'—and Milligan tapped the back of his hand under his jaw to indicate Sellers' double chins.

And indeed, on *Mister Topaze*, which was made next, Sellers is heavily be-whiskered. In the original Pagnol play, when he gets to be a businessman, Topaze is a celebrity; he is invited back to his old school to present the prizes on Speech Day. Tamise, his former indigent colleague, is asked if he'd like to come and be his secretary. In the Sellers version, however, Topaze is alone in his castle and Tamise walks away. The impression conveyed is one of loss, lucklessness, idleness; of gathering gloom. 'Being rich,' he says, surveying his new palace, which gives him no joy, 'is the only thing that gains one respect.'

The line (Rouve wrote the screenplay) could be from *The Millionairess*, and there are other, more private, allusions. When Loren first met Ponti, and was asked to make a screen test, the cameraman said: 'She is quite impossible to photograph. Too tall, too big-boned, too heavy all round. The face is too short, the mouth is too wide, the nose too long...' Ponti discussed this report with his future bride thus: 'Would you consider doing something to your nose and maybe losing twenty pounds or so off your weight?' That is why, in *The Millionairess*, there's a (non G. B. S.) scene where Epifania, having been rebuffed by Kabir, goes to see a psychi-

George Brown Collection

Sellers with Anne and Michael on the set of *Mister Topaze* (1960)

atrist, played by Dennis Price. 'How can I be more attractive to men? Should I get my nose fixed?' Ponti, incidentally, came to see that scene being shot, and Rouve had to whisper a running translation to him—'and he shot bolt upright at that line.'

In *Mister Topaze*, Sellers is the one who gets his physiognomy scrutinised. At the expensively designed movie-set garret where he lives (fogged window panes, rusting boilers and pipes, a clutter of dusty books and old clothes), Tamise tries to galvanise his friend's courtship of Ernestine, the headmaster's daughter, by saying: 'You have a commanding nose…a learned brow.' Topaze takes up the theme (Sellers appears to improvise—the words come out so naturally): 'My nose is commanding from the front, not from the side.' Sellers, who of course directed the film, included the interpolated scene solely as a homage to Loren.

But there is more to it than Sellers' appropriation and replication of Loren's conk complex. As a director, Sellers impersonated De Sica, who, as we know, Sellers had watched handle the megaphone during *Two Women*, for which Loren won the Oscar. Sellers had noticed that Loren was basically an imitative actress, which is why De Sica, who couldn't really direct so much as act it all out, was for her. And this is how Sellers tried to take charge of *Mister Topaze*—as if it was a Sophia Loren film. The De Sica style had percolated to him. 'He never came to terms with what cuts into what, the technical side,' recalls Rouve. 'With that he had to be helped—but only to the extent that a typist has influence on the work of a novelist.' The actors and the casting were all Sellers' ideas. McKern as the headmaster; Herbert Lom as the swindler—Lom, who had a semi-heavy attitude in *The Ladykillers*, here does a spoof on the Lom of his previous films (and prepares the way for the twitchy Dreyfus). Sellers knew what he could extract from such performers by acting things out for them. And what of his characterisation? On Topaze's desk, during his affluent phase (his secretary, Colette, is Joan Sims, still a bag of nerves from *The Naked Truth*), there is a bronze figurine of a Greek youth escaping from a nymph. The symbol can be decoded to mean that with money now at his disposal, and with material luxuries as palliatives, Topaze hopes that he will somehow be above, or absolved from, base and bodily cravings—he's monkish and withdrawn; he has leapt free.

It is not difficult to see that Topaze on his terrace, moping and believing that he is enlightened at last ('I'm just beginning to learn how the wheels go round') is Sellers himself, beyond the touch of ordinary humanity, and continuing to get crazily self-absorbed. As he said to Herbert Kretzmer at the time, with his marriage disintegrating and Loren distant: 'I had nobody to talk to... I've never been so low in my life. The days were all right... I worked non-stop. I set out to *lose* myself in work. I made film after film, almost anything to take my mind off Anne and the kids... At night it wasn't so easy. I got so dejected and introspective that I would sit at home alone for hours, going over my childhood days in my mind, trying to fathom things out.'

◆ ◆ ◆

What was Loren's reaction to Sellers' crack-up and amorous seizures? Mostly, it would seem, she kept mum; and in any event, as nothing had happened between herself and her quondam co-star (whom she privately referred to as 'Goat's Cheese'), there was nothing to document. Hence the omission of his name from her autobiography, *Sophia: Living and Loving*, ghosted by A. E. Hotchner in 1979; and thus there is nobody playing him in *Sophia Loren: Her Own Story*, the mini-series for television based on the memoirs, made the following year.

He was furious at the inexplicable absence of at least one long chapter dedicated to his grand passion ('Sellers is outraged by this dismissal of an event that he believes changed his life,' said *Time*); and when his own biographer, Peter Evans, had a conversation with him in 1980, and asked 'Do you manage to stay friends with your lovers, wives, and girlfriends after the event', Sellers said (pointedly): 'Certainly with Sophia, we are great mates now.' It was a remark (Evans tells me) 'which fell very naturally into our chat'; and Sellers towards the end of his life started to assign blame: 'After all, our relationship was one of the things that helped break up my first marriage. Miss Loren was *always* phoning me and I'd go rushing all over Italy to be with her. It's odd that someone who apparently meant so much in her life—or so she *said*—should not figure in her life story. The only reason I can think is that she was married at the time. But it's not as if her husband didn't know. Carlo knew *very* well...'

But Loren has not been totally mute. As long ago as 1962 she was telling Lillian Ross: 'I hate to hear actors say things like "when I play a King, I *become* a

King," because to me this is really phony talk. You feel what the character you play feels, but not completely. You never lose control. When you kiss on the screen, you don't really kiss.' That is an implicit and effective demolition of Sellers' style and pretensions, don't you think? And when Zec's book was published, the actress took explicit exception at last. As Zec said to me: 'This is the one area that Sophia Loren was upset by. She questioned the assertions and comments that Sellers had made—especially his claims that there had been a love affair. She didn't like the implications of what he was saying. She is a moral lady; she hates cheap gossip, and she thought that whole business lacked dignity—it implied she could be frivolous in her marital relationship, and she was hurt for the embarrassment it caused Ponti. She also feels that she has been falsely implicated in the break-up of Sellers' first marriage.'

Well, no one could accuse him of ever behaving rationally, and obviously his excitable claims about Sophia Scicolone coming close to being Sophia Sellers are so much moonshine. The piteousness of that is no surprise. He had dreamed it up—the wishes and longings were father to the thoughts. But what began as delight—the fat radio Goon co-starring with a world-famous broad—quickly became nightmarish and absurd, and deeply-embedded psychologically. Sellers was 'a crazed manic figure' according to his son, Michael, in the aftermath of the Loren passion. As proof of this he sold Chipperfield Manor, without asking for Anne's opinion, and shoved the family in a hotel. This peremptoriness did not go unnoticed by the press, to whom Sellers explained: 'We left our house at Chipperfield because we simply couldn't get proper service there.'

Sellers' problems of domesticity and daily living were maniacal. He was subjecting Anne to endless tyrannies. 'I went to stay with my mother when we separated. My mother lived in Bovingdon. Peter was in Hampstead, and he asked if he could come and see me ... "You'd better come in," I said when I met him, because he seemed to be in a terrible state. He was dazed and blank. Don't forget, I'd known him since I was about seventeen; I was now thirty-one—and he suddenly looked at my mother and said "Who is that old lady?" ... He'd known her a very long time. He was so odd, I said: "I think I'd better take you back." I drove and ... he kept asking "Who am I? I don't know who I am." He went into this whole speech about dark green, which he called Levy green, because Ted [Anne's second husband] had used it to decorate his house; and he kept asking who I was, who he was—a whole performance like he'd lost his memory. I drove him from Bovingdon to Hampstead, took him to the flat. He went in, slammed the door, wheeled round on me and said: "Right, you're not getting out ... *I will not let you out.*" It was then four o'clock in the morning. I had to phone the doctor: "You've got to come over. He won't let me out—and I want to leave." He came and stayed with Peter and sedated him. It was *terrifying.*'

♦♦♦

And the terror predicts the mood and plot of *Hoffman*, which was made in 1969, by which time Sellers had repeated with Britt, and others, the sorts of horrors he had perpetrated on Anne. In *Hoffman* Sellers is depressed and sluggish, and yet he also suggests a terrible repressed energy. His eyes seem hooded and his long face is dark bottle-green and blueish, like an El Greco. It is almost a ghost story—Sellers creeps about the shadowy flat and the shuttered rooms as Nosferatu, the original bloodsucker. 'How attractive you look in the fading light,' he says to Miss Smith; and when, later on, she complains of a sore neck and he applies it with liniment, ('your neck…so young and defenseless'), we fully expect him to sink his fangs into her throat. Instead he sings a song—a dolorous vampire's love lyric:

> Once I knew a pretty girl
> I loved her as my wife
> But I put my hands
> About her neck
> And robbed her of my life.

Sinead Cusack's meek little colleen, in her neat wee beret, is a lamb-to-the-slaughter. 'I want to eat you,' says Hoffman, 'I want to consume you—what do you think of a man who wants to do that?' You'd think she'd want to be going a long way somewhere far off to avoid such an epicurean nutcase, but it is too late. She is a prisoner. She flees to the stairs—but Hoffman sails serenely down in the elevator and reclaims her. 'I do have full use, Miss Smith. Any man suffering massive sexual frustration would be out of his mind if, on getting the girl of his dreams, he didn't put her to *full use.*'

Sellers' Prince of Darkness doesn't get to release his tensions in any normal (or violent) way; instead he toys with the girl and prolongs his own agony. (The film has a sado-masochistic undercurrent.) Sellers, however, is sinister not through any cackling, hooting, or exophthalmic virtuosity; he is the more scary for being solemn and correct. He is full of silent staring and noiseless snooping and slinking. It is as if his permanently twilit apartment has been purposefully designed as a voyeur's maze. We are never quite sure which door he will come through—some locks fail to click; some thresholds seem to materialise in solid walls. And though, with his unexpected entrances, he is in every single scene of a one-hundred-and-eleven-minute movie, the character can slip out of sight, too, just as abruptly as a revenant would.

Sellers' stillness is utilised, for this one occasion in his career, as a source of fear. The level of intensity on offer is like Lionel Meadows'—the difference being that, in *Never Let Go*, Sellers did not hold anything back. Here all is muted, crepuscular. There's not another performance to compare with Benjamin Hoffman until the courtliness of Sir Anthony Hopkins in *The Silence of the Lambs*, and that psycho-thriller's juxtaposition of eating-sex-death-cannibalism is predicted here. 'Hurry,' says Hoffman, 'Life is awaiting us. Eat or be eaten.'

That, in addition to everything else, Hoffman (and *Hoffman*) is repellently misogynistic is hardly an observation that needs making. He trots out dozens of automatic put-downs: 'It is not only homosexuals who don't like women. Hardly anybody does,' for example; and what we hate about it all is that Miss Smith accepts these judgements. She succumbs to them and makes herself available to him, even though the script has required her to deliver home-truths like: 'Look at you! Who

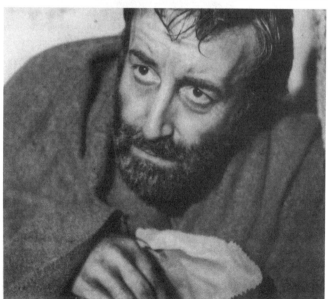

(Top) Nosferatu the Vampire: Sellers as he really was—*Hoffman* (with Sinead Cusack as the recumbent virgin)—1970

(Bottom) A Living Death in *The Blockhouse* (1972)

wants you? You are mad and you are ugly.' But Hoffman's problem isn't a straightforward hatred of women. What he hates most is that part of himself which needs
them (for sex and other domestic duties); and he hates women the more when they
yield. It is the hatred of a man who is dependent on his victims, and yet who wishes
to be celibate and aloof: 'Every girl is a flower garden with a compost heap at the
bottom. And many a noble man has had to drown his dwarf wife in a zinc bath or
strangle an idiot girl on a muddy common in order to draw attention to himself.'
Slaying women, or at the very least subjecting them, is the male's rite of passage.
When a woman is dead you possess her wholly—she has no independent life left.

Sellers' phrasing here is masterful. He pauses, potters about the flat, moves
from thought to thought, adds to his idea. It is the key-speech in *Hoffman* (and, not
incidentally, it expresses Sellers' own view of women); it's the moment when the
central character realises that he is disgusted by what he craves. ('Lips that touch
kippers shall never kiss mine,' he says riddlingly.) To try and cope with the temptation and lusts, he reduces women to their component parts—he verbally dis-
members them: 'You are here to be two arms, two legs, and the bits that fit in the
middle,' Miss Smith is informed. She stares with terror into his big sad eyes. Miss
Smith is a virgin-defilement fantasy who might have stepped from the shiny,
coated pages of a holiday brochure or soft-core magazine. 'To awaken one morning and find a strange and beautiful naked girl asleep by your side. My dream, every
man's dream,' her possessor says. (She is like Sellers' dream of a mechanical kit
model girl.) Hoffman can hardly believe she is real, and neither can we. 'You don't
seem to like women, do you?' she says eventually—and incontestably. 'Yes, I am
filthy, yes,' he responds, before letting fly some self-pity as he stares in the mirror:

> My maniac face. Girls all over the world are afraid of men with my expression. Plain,
> sad-faced men. Mature, sexually starved men. In offices, busses and trains. Men
> who've missed the boat. Their day is coming. Their revolution is almost upon you...

◆ ◆ ◆

If Oscar Wilde is correct when, in the preface to *The Picture of Dorian Gray*, he
says that 'To reveal art and conceal the artist is art's aim,' then it is apparent that
with *Hoffman* something has gone wrong. Contempt; fastidiousness; anger; humiliation; sullying and being sullied: the moods and nuances in the work make it less
of a film than a confessional, as Sellers knew. 'It's the first time I've been called on
to play what *they*—the producer, the director, the author—call *myself*. It's a very difficult rôle to play. It comes out of a lot of anguish.' Just how much anguish Ben
Arbeid, Alvin Rakoff, and Ernie Gebler were shortly to discover: Sellers tried to
buy the negative and destroy it. He was confronted by a self-portrait, which revealed his internal monstrousness, and, like Dorian Gray, he wanted to plunge a
dagger through its heart. As Arbeid explained to me: 'Benjamin Hoffman is very
lonely, very insecure, very self-deprecating; and these were all terms used by people to describe the real Sellers. So there was much of the character already in our
actor. The part called for that vacuum factor of his—his way of filling himself with
everybody and yet being nobody.

'This was not the sort of rôle that would normally attract him—he usually went for bravura stuff. Hoffman was not that at all. He had to play the internal self which wasn't there to start with. He couldn't rely on mimicry, and he went through the torture of not knowing who Hoffman was because he didn't know who he was ... He was so good, so convincing, he tried to buy the prints and burn them. Not because he was ashamed of the film, but because he recognised aspects of the inner man he thought he'd hidden forever ... But it was impossible for him actually to purchase the negative. The company—Anglo-EMI—had accepted the picture. He had had ample opportunity to discuss the film with me before it was delivered to them as a finished piece. Sellers just wanted to *eliminate* it.'

In the event, political manoeuverings at the studio resulted in the burial of the film, which was barely advertised or distributed. (Few people today have heard of it, let alone seen it.*) As Arbeid explains the palace revolution: 'There was a conflict in the executive corridors of the film company as to who was in charge; a personality clash between the man controlling the studio, and with whom I made the deal to make the picture, Bryan Forbes, and the man who was then chairman of the parent company, Bernard Delfont. It was almost as if the projects Forbes had instigated were deliberately not being promoted ... Very easy to do with *Hoffman*, because it was an unusual piece; not what you'd expect of a Peter Sellers performance ...'

That it was not what Sellers had expected from a Peter Sellers performance, either, was evident very early on to Alvin Rakoff, who went to meet him in Clarges Street:

> He greeted me—wide-eyed, hypertense, slightly manic, with an Austrian accent. And his first words to me were the first words of the film. 'Miss Smith, come in.' ... I said 'I don't think it needs to be an Austrian accent ... Why can't you just do it straight? You can, you know.' This was the biggest sales pitch, director-to-actor, that I did ... In order to make this eccentric, sinister man work, he was going to play it full of laughs ... So I had to calm him down—and the opposite happened. Peter, having always played comedy, wanted a tragic edge. He went the other way—his Hoffman is dark and slow. I kept trying to get Peter to do it faster, but he wouldn't ... He argued for this brooding quality. 'I'm waiting for this moment to arrive. The girl of my dreams. I'm opening the door. I would be in this terrible state.' That's why he is so black and cringing.
>
> There were strange imbalances in the man. Manic depressives could have taken lessons from Peter. One day he had a scene in the bed when Miss Smith is leaving him. He couldn't get the lines right. He started screaming—then he couldn't stop laughing ... Then he got bad tempered and left the studio. We didn't know if he'd come back the next day or not. He did return, as a matter of fact. We were to be given a bonus if we finished on time and on budget ... We brought it in—and the upper echelon had been so concerned about Peter's misbehaving. Everybody remembered *Casino Royale*.
>
> He became Hoffman ... he could do subtleties and variations, thousands of gradations, in a characterisation. An extraordinary talent, and as a director ... you had to decide amongst the eight different ways he'd want to do a two minute se-

---

* The great photograph by Roy Jones, which adorns the cover of this book, was taken in Sellers' dressing room at Elstree during the making of *Hoffman*.

quence. 'Which one do you want?' he'd say…He knew that he was always in turmoil; he was going through a metamorphosis of some kind, starting on the path
that leads to *Being There*. Death obsessed him. He kept thinking about it, because
he didn't want to accept it. He said he'd set aside the money to be frozen when he
died. He told me all about this, and he wanted to know why I wasn't going to do
it…I said, 'Peter, suppose you are thawed out in a hundred years time—maybe
even longer; suppose it is *several hundred* years. The world will have changed. You'll
not fit into it anymore. You'd be in a zoo, a freak. Or like meat in our deep freez-
ers, you'll deteriorate.' None of this could dissuade him at all…

Of course not. He knew all about being a freak, a misfit, and far from disintegrating further, the ice would arrest his decay.

♦ ♦ ♦

The beauty of cryogenics, to its proselytisers, was that you could control your
going hence as well as your coming hither—you could outwit 'the fellow in the
bright night-gown,' as W.C. Fields always referred to death. Suicide only deals with
the first half of the promise, but the principle of management is the same. You reg-
ulate your own exit—nothing is left to chance. Seven or eight years prior to *Hoffman*, when Sellers was ridding himself of Anne, so that he could be born anew as a
young romantic leading man, he tried to give the impression that he was happy: 'I
was amazed by the reaction *The Millionairess* had on women,' he explained, 'I suddenly found myself receiving extremely pleasant fan mail. Believe me this was quite
a new experience. I've never considered myself to be at all the romantic type. And I
wouldn't argue with anyone who described my looks as homely. But I must say I do
have a giggle whenever I read these rather flattering fan letters.'

But behind the scenes, suicide was his constant threat: 'And with Peter, you
never *knew*' says Anne. 'I remember he once asked me over to his flat with the
children, and he said, "Right, if you leave this flat, I am going to jump over the
balcony. I'll meet you downstairs."…It was mad, and calculating, because he
knew I'd never take the risk that he wouldn't leap, especially with my two children
in the flat…But in the end he didn't do anything dramatic—he just killed himself
slowly. He used drugs, too, when he married younger women. Sexually he
couldn't make it like he wanted to. When I was with him, he never took drugs and
he drank very little. After he had his first heart attack, he was on cocaine a lot.

'When I was married to him, any studio or newspaper publicity was about
"Sellers the family man"; until we split up there was never any *strange* publicity.
Then we split up; Bill died; Peg died. He had no family. He'd been called the Arch
Goon—and once he started to get into films, he didn't want to be seen as the Arch
Goon. He wanted to be regarded as an actor…There was always a fight in him—
perhaps because of his over-possessive mother. It must be a hell of a fight for a man
to be totally dominated, like he was for so long. Maybe he thought he could dominate me, to make up for it, which was to be true in the end, because I gave up the
theatre in desperation…And then I had Mike. The funny thing about Peg was,
when Peter and I split up, she absolutely begged me not to go…Once Michael was
born we'd sort of made it up—it was too much for her, a grandchild, she had to come

and see me. I can't say I ever liked her, but we did tick along, and I liked Bill tremendously. And I remember Peter telling me his parents did split up at some point.'

That evidently clutched at his heart. Why? I think it is because, when he was reaching back, searching for lost time, he could see that that was the moment in his life when he learned about disharmony and division, and it left a profound impression. Bill's absences hadn't been noticed; it was his new, crestfallen presence which had been so off-putting. Was Peg going to share her tenderness? Was Sellers expected to? 'When I first met Peter, he was twenty-two or twenty-three, and he was already focused on his childhood,' says Anne. Her future husband was already trying to see what it was he had lived through—and he never was able to resolve his sympathies and emotions about the past. His father's humiliating return, the falsity of the unity his parents subsequently presented to the world—and all this overlaying the instability of his here-there-everywhere boarding house infancy: Sellers was aware that ordinary domesticity was not something he had ever known; and maybe, as his mind was flooded with memories and comparisons, he realised that it was not something that was for him at any stage.

'My father liked one-off payments', says Michael. 'You settle a bill, an account, and that's that. The continuous expenditure a family involved upset him—a continuous drain on his [emotional] resources.

'He'd forget about us for months on end, if he was away doing a film; and then, when he'd run out of other people to amuse him, and he was lonely—then would come a phone call. But never any apology or explanation for the long silence or neglect.'

When Anne left he grew bitter and retrospective. As he confessed to Herbert Kretzmer: 'Why, I wondered, does one marry the wrong person? I began keeping a kind of diary...It kept coming back to the same questions. For instance, when I met Anne Hayes, why did I rush all over the country trying to persuade her to marry me?...Anyway, I never found the answer.' Well, no. He'd never in a million years have admitted any blame—he could not see that Anne left him because he was psychotic and violent. But there is more to it than this. When he and Anne swung apart it was like when Peg and Bill swung apart—and this was one way of bringing the past up to date. It was also one way of getting close to a side of his mother that was a mystery to him—how she'd felt when she was walked out on. And had her sense of grievance (mingled with gladness) communicated itself to him? Because the ironic twist in this tale is that Sellers, though he had tormented and victimised Anne without stint, felt himself to be the victim, not the aggressor. It had never occurred to him, when he was inflicting his tortures, that Anne might move on to have a happier life elsewhere—or that she'd find her protector in the very man whom Sellers had hired to decorate his flat, Ted Levy.

◆ ◆ ◆

The fact that Sellers had bought a seven-year lease on a top-storey flat (for £31,000) and had disposed of the freehold security of Chipperfield (sold for £41,000) is evidence enough that he intended reverting to a bachelor existence, though he pretended otherwise: 'My wife and I recently sold our home in Chipperfield and for a while we lived at the Carlton Tower Hotel. That was a sort of clearing-house while we looked around,' he told *Playboy*. 'I liked living at the Carlton Tower. I liked the atmosphere. Now we've taken a flat in Hampstead.'

West End hotels and penthouse apartments were luxurious versions of his childhood boarding houses. As the manager of the Dorchester said to me: 'Mr Sellers was such a regular guest; he was in and out quite a lot at all hours... It was more or less his London home, and he knew all the staff—they were almost like his own personal staff... He liked the twenty-four hour service. Being Mr. Sellers, he would want breakfast, say, at any hour of the day or night—and it would be brought to him without any problems.'

Sellers could pretend he was a sultan—the sultan from *Brouhaha*, perhaps—and a hotel's liveried servants did duty for the admiring aunties backstage in Southsea and Ilfracombe. Though he knew that this sort of limitless pampering was what he wanted, he still went through the motions of hunting for a fixed family abode: 'Houses! You wouldn't believe the places I've looked at lately. And the estate agents [realtors]—I must do an estate agent one of these days... "What would you say to a bungalow by the river, kitchen garden, boat-house?"... Yes, I really must do an estate agent one of these days.'

He didn't (insofar as I am aware); but he did find himself imitating the fellow who was putting the finishing touches to an eagle's nest in Northwood Lodge, Oak Hill Park, NW3. 'I am a person who has no real voice of his own,' said Sellers, as ever trying to imagine what it would be like not to exist. 'I'm like a microphone... I pick it up from my surroundings. At the moment I've got a South African architect working on my new flat in Hampstead, and so I tend to speak in a South African accent all the time.'

To discover that he was in the presence of a curious echo was disagreeable; to find that his vocal double was maltreating his wife and children was insupportable. Ted Levy had to intervene. 'In South Africa, all Ted's generation wanted to listen to was 'The Goon Show', so Peter Sellers was Ted's idol when he came over to Britain and designed our Hampstead flat,' says Anne. 'Ted didn't notice me—he was far too overwhelmed to meet the legendary Peter Sellers—but then he saw how he behaved... Ted thought that, in real life, Peter was *disgusting*. He was his greatest fan—and then, well...'

What happened is that, to make the best of living in a flat, and to try and keep the family together for a little longer, Anne threw herself into decorating the place—into trying to make it a home. She therefore accompanied Levy on expeditions to look at furniture and ceramic tile samples. When they returned, Sellers accused them of having an affair; so relentless was his campaign, he achieved what he feared—he pushed them together. This (in circular fashion) justified his rage and dejection. 'The evil forces consuming Dad,' wrote Michael in his book, 'were to make poor Ted pay a horrendous price for what Dad termed an "injustice".' The children almost became accustomed to their father raving that 'Ted Levy has destroyed my life. He has taken your mother away from me. I'll kill him, I'll kill him.'

Levy did indeed think his hour had come. At two o'clock in the morning, Sellers discovered where his enemy lived and set out to confront him. He hammered on the door until Levy was roused from sleep and let him in. Sellers was wearing a heavy overcoat and gave the impression he was armed. 'He wore an expression of hate, anger, and frustration, the like of which I'd never seen on the face of any human being before. I was convinced now that he was going to murder me.'

Levy, as calmly as was possible under the circumstances, said that he was not the cause of any marital bust-up, and that surely the Sophia Loren episode hadn't helped. He also pointed out that Sellers had already started to sleep around, and that if Anne wanted to leave or stay with her husband, given those sorts of circumstances, it was none of his, Levy's, business … and so on. Sellers left around about then and returned to wherever Anne and his sleeping babes were abiding. Michael told me, 'I remember he said, up at the penthouse, "You'd better not be here when I get back—or I'll kill you."' And off into the dark he disappeared again—but at least that request and threat made a change from the one where he wanted to keep Anne a captive.

Arguably, the psychological harassment of his children was as bad as his physical maltreatment of his wife. He constantly dragged Michael and Sarah from their beds to tell them he hated their mother and was going to divorce her. Once, because it was about four o'clock in the morning and his solicitor didn't seem to be in the office answering the phone, Sellers pulled his infant son from his bed and told him he had to remember everything that was being said, that he was an official witness. One such statement which Michael obliged by not forgetting was (to Anne) 'You must get out of here and never come back.' A similar scene took place with Peg present. As Michael told it to me: 'She was never nasty to us—she reserved her scorn for my father's women. She came to our aid a lot of the time, especially when there was an argument before he was to go off to America. My birthday is in April, and he said quite kindly: "Are you coming out for your birthday?" "No, I want to stay here for my birthday." "*How dare you!* I'm your father. I'm going to give you a ticket, and if I say you'll come, *you'll come.*" "All my friends are here. I want to have a party here with my mates." It went on and on, and eventually he threw me out—out of the Dorchester, in fact. His finale was to demand, "Who do you love the most? Me or your mother?" So Sarah goes, "I love you both the same." Nice and cool. But I said "My *mother*." By then I'd had enough. I wasn't going to play his games. I didn't feel like placating him after what he'd just put me through. So—"Right. *Out.* All your stuff will be turning up at your mother's house soon."

'Peg made the peace for us. "Calm down. Let's have a cup of tea," she'd say.'

But it wasn't peacefulness, as such, which reigned. Sellers was simply diverted into ranting about something else. He'd always say his children didn't love him, that they were all against him and using him, none of which was true. (It needs to go on record that it was Ted Levy who—voluntarily—paid for their education and who supported them: Sellers was meant to pay ten pounds a week maintenance, and only when the arrears totalled two thousand pounds, and he was threatened by court action, did he grudgingly cough up.)

Sellers' persistence in putting his children on trial ('Which of you shall we say doth love us most?') made him a mad and modern Lear. Far from showing a loving nature, his demands (like his mother's) expose a jealous and selfish brooding—and Michael, whose obstinacy was feeble compared with his father's positive derangement, did have to go to America, of course he did. ('Right. That's it. He's going to America'), where he was left in the care of Bert Mortimer and Hattie Stevenson.

♦ ♦ ♦

Sellers played the rôle of aggrieved innocent and deceived nearly everybody, himself included. He invited Herbert Kretzmer up to the penthouse, showed off the stained wood ceilings and matching fabrics, and then said: 'I can hardly wait to get all this Ted Levy stuff out... I can't live in this place the way it is. It holds too many memories. I'm going to pull the whole lot out by the roots and start again. I want to see nothing around me to remind me of Anne, or that man, or the life we used to live here. In any case I never really liked this place... It's so... like a hotel or a ship... Over-masculine. It's just not me, love... Anne, of course, loved... this chap's designs and colour schemes. They kind of overruled me, always around, the two of them, buying wallpaper and wood and stuff. Gradually I caught on... [to] what was happening, but I didn't want us to break up. I bought Anne a house near here so we could separate. I thought it would be a solution if, maybe, we didn't actually live together for a while. I desperately wanted Anne back, well, because of the children and because I was still in love with her...'

To find another monologue that so craftily interweaves lies, hypocrisy and all-over baseness, you'd have to go back to the dramas of Molière. The masculinely drab decor, like the idea of the flat itself, was his own inspiration. The hotel-cum-ocean liner effect, again, had enthralled him; and as for Anne's enthusiasm, she did well to try and make the place comfortable, within the limits of Sellers' instructions, especially as she'd rather have been still at Chipperfield or perhaps Whetstone. Sellers' threats that he will tear the place apart are simply spiteful (wouldn't it be simpler and cheaper to sell up and move on?); the comments about still loving Anne and how much he loves the children are sentimental and hollow; and is it possible, logically and practically, to 'separate' and yet also not to 'break up'? But to dissect the speech in this manner is all too easy. That, to Sellers, love was an issue of power and will—part of his compulsion to possess and dominate—is by now very clear, and this would never alter. So what interests me about the performance is whether or not he was aware that he was giving one. Did he not realise the situation? The bulk and gist of his words, which complain about his isolation and urge us to picture his injuries as a new couple were off gallivanting, make sense only if they can be imagined as being voiced by Anne, had she wanted to describe what it was like when Sellers was doing his utmost to give the impression that he was gadding about with Loren.

In talking about Anne and Levy, therefore, Sellers is referring to himself and his goddess—and he did so in a deliberate parody of his wife's grief. For as Anne said to me: 'When he was having his affair with Loren, nobody mentioned it to me, and I thought in my stupid way, if nobody is talking to me about it, it isn't going to happen. I really cared about his career, and I cared about him as a person. I gave my *time* to him—but I should have seen what was going on. The first time Loren came out to Chipperfield, we had to have a huge party—Peter spent the afternoon filming it and taking photographs. She arrived in a yellow dress and a vast *My Fair Lady* hat covered with flowers. Michael said, "I don't want to meet her. She looks like a chicken!"—which I loved! Another time I had to go into town and meet them for dinner. Michael looked at me and said, "You look like a fairy princess, Mummy, you look beautiful"—which is an unlikely thing for a child to say, and I thought he's the only person who's going to say that tonight. Because I know my husband won't. He's with his girlfriend. Michael had intuitively picked up that something was going on. But with Peter, he was playing the part of a romantic actor, and playing it in real life; and I always felt there was much more to Peter than one ever saw.'

♦ ♦ ♦

When Sellers' first marriage broke up, he was left broken up—and if he didn't know Wyndham Lewis' admonition that 'in order to live you must *remain* broken up'—which means, I presume, that if you are not to ossify and grow dull it is necessary to keep on the move and to search for constant stimulus—then he certainly showed a marked fidelity to such a concept. Yet—and this is the great paradox with Sellers—what was divisive in his life was put to creative use in his films. Out of the welter of projects now offered to him, in the wake of the release of *The Millionairess* around the world, he chose those in which his struggles and uncertainties could flourish (or at least be mimicked). Asked, at the time, did he feel a compulsion to work, Sellers said: 'Well, what else is there? I don't really want to do more than two pictures a year. That's the ideal... But I don't relax easily. And the moment you do stop work, they all descend on you—you get all the moguls with ideas; producers, they come round and they say, this is good, Peter, this is wonderful, they say, we must do it right now, and you say, all right, and most of the time there isn't even a script...'

There was a script for *Only Two Can Play*, however, and Sellers was fascinated by it, mightily so. John Lewis' relationship with Mai Zetterling's Elizabeth Gruffydd-Williams is a carnal version of Dr Kabir and Epifania's serenades; beyond that, Lewis' restlessness and his sense that he is trapped and is being worn down chime with Sellers' own fear of boredom, stability, and a settled marriage. Elizabeth Gruffydd-Williams, in floral headgear and clutching a topiaried poodle, stands in for the full-of-poise Sophia Loren.

'When I was first asked to make this film I was a little doubtful about it,' said Sellers. 'I'd read the original story, and I don't mind admitting that I wasn't too keen about it. I was handed a film script and after I'd read it I couldn't resist playing in the film. It was such a wonderful and funny script' by Bryan Forbes, who tried to improve on Amis' original by incorporating some gags of his own. The scene where Sellers is trying to seduce Mai Zetterling in the American convertible, for example, and the car is mobbed by a herd of Friesians, was based on a real experience of Bill Kerr's—whose coitus was made interruptus by cows when he was in the RAF near Peterborough. Another interpolation is the bit on the crowded early morning bus to work, when Sellers, to goose the bosomy typists, cops a feel and then pretends to have a withered arm, like Richard III's. 'He'd get stuck on a line or stage direction like that,' Forbes told me, 'and he'd be *helpless.*'

Only Two Can Play differs from *That Uncertain Feeling* in that the former is a simple seven-year-itch sex romp ('as you say, it was just a romp,' Sellers said to Dilys Powell a little peevishly), and in the latter libido is a symptom and not the cause of the hero's desire to have an adventure. In Amis' original, Lewis is a man who is in the process of discovering that he's no longer young. 'Now don't stand there giving me that little-boy face, you're getting too old for it,' his wife shouts, when she confronts him with his womanising, i.e. his disloyalty and selfishness. That line isn't in the film (though Jean's harassed anger is), and the miracle with Sellers—his genius—is that he can imply all the feelings and guilts which are in the book but which the film otherwise leaves out. The way he yawns, the way he slouches around his kitchen, the way he leans on the counter and against the shelves at the library: we can see that Lewis, suffused with tediousness and staleness—with a lassitude so extreme it is almost languorous and pleasurable—is on the brink of going to seed. In other words, though this is a film, and one designed as an adulterous farce at that, Sellers is incapable of being superficial. His performance has a *novelistic* spaciousness and reticence—almost as if Sellers' underlying processes were like Henry James', who'd only need the tiniest glimpse of an idea—half an anecdote overheard at a dinner party, say—to be able to worry it into a full-length drama. There was no need for research, and with Sellers (at any rate) what he accomplished did not require an analytical brain. His understanding was instantaneous. Whatever outrages and mess he committed in reality, when it came to his art he could be sympathetic and unifying—his puerility and crudity were transformed.

◆ ◆ ◆

There is a particular scene in *Only Two Can Play* which gets it all across—when Lewis attempts to perform his ablutions in the squalid bathroom, with its steamed-up mirror and rust-pocked sink. He is preparing to shave, and is squinting at the reflection of his dewlapped face, when an old man emerges from behind the partition which hides the jakes [toilet]. Coughing and wheezing, the codger exits, leaving behind what must surely be a radioactive pong. The plumbing is primitive and the chain for the flush cistern is situated above the basin (we might have mistaken it for the light-pull switch), where Lewis is now stooping, gazing at the gray scummy lather he is about to apply to his skin. He glances at the gently swinging handle on the chain as if hypnotised by it. A few seconds later he grabs it and stills it; he also pulls up the tab on the Air Wick to maximum length. His failure and despair crystallise in that moment. He is overweight, zestless, underpaid, with a wife and children to support. Did he get to be a graduate (BA, Univ. Coll., Swansea) for this? Jean, in her turn, is fast losing her looks (Virginia Maskell's bony, wan prettiness exactly fits Amis' description: 'It was saddening to remember how lustrous, as well as abundant, her hair had been before she'd had the children; to know how necessary that careful make-up was, and how angular her hips and shoulders had become'). She is wearing herself out in the top-floor

(Top) 'Now don't stand there giving me that little-boy face, you're getting too old for it': John Lewis in *Only Two Can Play* (1961)

(Bottom) *General:* 'My God, woman, I hate you.'
Emily: 'What difference does that make? I'm you wife.'
Waltz of the Toreadors (1961)

Michael Sellers Collection (photo by Norman Hargood)

Michael [Sellers Collection (photo by George Ward: Rank Productions Lt.)

flatlet, surrounded by soiled diapers and no hot water. There is also no fridge, phone, or television set.

The appearance of the Mai Zetterling character, therefore, is to Jean an affront (Elizabeth Gruffydd-Williams is rich, shiftless, childless) and to Lewis an avenue of escape. The white goddess brings out in him what he might have been like when he was younger. Sellers, as with Kite, doesn't allow caricature to warp his performance: when Lewis is aroused by a dream girl what we register is the extent of his self-delusion. He thinks he can rush about like a horny teenager, and then again he knows he can't. We sense Lewis' own ironic awareness of his plight—and this is where Sellers finds the comedy: in the division between a desire to be irresponsible and the knowledge that his character is too mature (i.e. basically decent and moral, i.e. cowardly) to set himself free.

Off the set, Sellers constantly carped about Virginia Maskell and wanted her removed from the film. (Her confidence duly undermined, the actress made one more film and killed herself in 1968.) Was he treating her like that because he was treating Anne like that? Did Sellers, whose domestic problems were enciphered in the film, try to duplicate those problems when he was making the film? (Lewis himself, by contrast, is tender with his wife: 'Her face is one that I can never see without wanting to smile for one reason or another'—another sentence of Amis' which Sellers, sunk in the rôle, communicates on the screen without having to say a word.)

If he stored up (unjustified) rancour for one woman, he doled out (unwanted, unreciprocated) attention on the other, for he decided to have a shot at romancing Zetterling, as if she were an encore of his antic hey-hey over Loren. Luckily, Amis himself came to her rescue, though he may not have known this. When Sellers went off into this funny voice routine, which had worked so well during the leisure moments on *The Millionairess*, Amis interrupted him with impersonations and gags of his own. The distinguished novelist in his younger days was evidently a one-man version of 'The Goon Show', and he much impressed another writer who has always fancied his chances as a comedian, Clive James, who has reported that 'Amis' mimicry is not quite in the same league with that of Peter Sellers as to accuracy, but the mind and invention behind it make it a feast for the gods. He is a brilliantly entertaining man.'

That established, here is how Zetterling recalled the behind the scenes socialising in Swansea: Sellers and Amis 'tried to outwit each other with reminiscences and dirty jokes, Kingsley punctuating his with resounding farts, to everyone's embarrassment...'

Thus was Sellers' frantic ardour dispersed.

◆ ◆ ◆

Bottom burps and imitation games to one side, another reason why Sellers would have hated Maskell is that she, like him, was giving a vivid, downbeat performance. Jean is flustered, cross, and left on her own to cope with the kids all day. The half-bottle of sour milk on the food-cupboard, the sticky lino floorings, the coin-in-the-slot gas heating: the domestic surroundings in *Only Two Can Play* could have come from a Ken Loach or Lindsay Anderson docu-drama about life in a sooty city, and Jean and Lewis add up to a realistic portrait of an airless, wormy modern marriage. That's what is in the book; that is what comes across on the screen. Sellers, however, was simply envious of his co-star's skills, and as a manipulator he didn't like having to share being at the centre of things. No doubt he'd have preferred Lewis not to have had a visible wife at all. Is this what he was scheming for? An off-camera She Who Must Be Obeyed? A Her-Indoors? Could Lewis' home-life have been signalled simply by the little brown paper parcel of sandwiches he totes to work?

Such attitudinising works against Sellers' discreet, diffident Lewis, and perhaps another actor would have been demolished had he accepted the part and then been thrown in the ring with a lot of busybodies and comedians. Sellers, however, makes the fact that he does not properly belong the key to his performance. His own dissociated sensibility is shaped to Lewis' quiet, suggestiveness, and cynicism. Lewis—indirect, infectiously humorous, and imprisoned by home and job—gives grudging acceptance to the fact that there is not, after all, going to be much more to his life than respectability.

Lewis is related, in Sellers' canon, to Dodger Lane, who is literally in prison. Dodger is one of Sellers' most domesticated characters, and he hopes against hope that the jewel robbery (which of course is bungled) will be his means of escape from a domineering Irene Handl and a shrewish Liz Frazer. The little photoplay would have been a negligible prison caper without Sellers; and Lewis, too, without Sellers there to convey the self-mockery and the genuine frustration, would have been a bit of a bore in a boring film. As it is, a film about boredom is exceptional and interesting. Sellers could take an ordinary man and convince us that, inside his head, some of the brain-waves are floating free. Now that I come to think of it, many of his characters are dreamers—men inspirited by romance. If it weren't for their fantasies, they'd be defeated, tragic. Morganhall, in *The Dock Brief*, for example, fools himself into believing he'll be a great advocate.

We see him, in a flashback, at Oxford during a 'beautiful long summer'—but as the others go off for picnics on the river, the young law student is left behind in his rooms, struggling with his Latin textbooks. As the years pass, he remains in his chambers all alone, doing the crossword. The title sequence unfolds over images of caged birds—and who is the more constrained? Henpecked Mr Fowle (Richard Attenborough), who kills his hooting and guffawing wife because she wouldn't leave him, or the barrister, who needs the criminal classes because they are his livelihood? The film is full of cages, locks, bolts; when the sunlight shines on a wall the striped shadows form bars. Sellers is wonderful at oscillating between Morganhall's hopefulness and hopelessness—and when he says 'Oh, Fowle! The wonderful new life you've brought me!', we know that he'll screw up on his big day in court. And he duly does lose his papers, drop his legal tomes with a clatter, and forget his speech—he dries, like an actor, and he is derided by judge and jury. 'I had only to open my mouth,' he says later, 'and pour out words.'

It was Morganhall, not the defendant, who was really on trial; and when it came down to it, and his dreams of glory were set to come true (Morganhall becoming a rival to Sir Edward Marshall Hall), he backed out—as Lewis backs out of having an affair with Elizabeth Gruffydd-Williams. Faced with the choice between romantic yearnings and their fulfilment, Sellers' characters often seem to need to recoil. 'Reality,' as Hoffman says, as he shifts right across the bed to avoid touching Miss Smith, 'betrays us all.' Reality is contingent, it is crammed with unknown variables, like other people and their inner mysteries; it is intrusive and inadequate.

Though Sellers' characters often fear failure and rejection, therefore, they fear the actual and the responsibilities of commitment more. 'There are ways and ways of losing,' commiserates Fowle—who is set free, not because of his counsel's forensic brilliance, but because Morganhall was deemed incompetent. The old barrister can never be free, in that case; he is hampered by his humiliation. And we can sense that, though permanently crestfallen, there is something in his nature, which makes him accept solitude, that is rather fearless. Morganhall could be seen as a sombre version of Clouseau, who likewise learns to live with ridicule—to such an extent, indeed, that ridicule becomes a consolation.

◆ ◆ ◆

Sellers instinctively feels his characters' slights—the obvious examples are Juan Bautista, when he is dyed blue; Henry Orient, after his calamitous piano recital; and the Rev. Smallwood, when he is stoned and thrown on the dustcart. But what interests me at the moment is not so much the proud outsiderishness—the embattled martyr element when they muff things—as the rather more compelling suggestion, lurking under the surface, that Sellers is trying to come to terms with his own experience of being a fool. He was mortified over Loren, and in the films that followed on from *The Millionairess*, foolishness is a sort of shelter: for Topaze, Lewis, Morganhall, Smallwood, Henry Orient, and so on it doesn't much matter if people think them clowns. They themselves are indifferent to the sniggering—for they have mysterious imaginative lives, a private wildness inside, where the limitations of the world may be overcome. Such was Sellers' virtuosity that he could make the quality of this interiority seem virtuous, or arrogant, or vain, or deluded, by turns; when Emily asks General Fitzjohn: 'Inside your head—what's going on in there?', he is thrilled to be able to respond 'My head, madam, is out of bounds. It is the only place left where I can get a bit of peace.'

To each of his characters, Sellers gives a little of his personal instability and erratic nature. The way he was becomes the way they are. But did his receptivity to derision—which made him all the more stubborn when it came to his saying that he and Loren loved each other—in fact reach further back to his music hall childhood, with its twilit old actors? His parents, playing the piano and ukulele or dressing up and disguising themselves as a cossack (Bill) or national heroines (Peg), earned their living by appearing before audiences and asking to be loved. This is certainly the atmosphere of *The Dock Brief*. Sellers plays Morganhall as a silver-haired leading man down on his luck; his posh, dark voice has a note of apology in it—he's like the sort of leading man who'd have toured provincial theatres during the war, exempted from military service by a wooden leg or a buggery charge.

'A sad and tired look': Morganhall in *The Dock Brief* (1962)

When Morganhall is handed the brief, he is so delighted he is flirty, seductive, gay (in the original meaning of the word); he flourishes the bat-wings of his gown as if he is soliloquising on the cardboard mezzanine at Elsinore, and when he practises his speeches in the empty well of the court he is a classical actor rehearsing. Then, after curtain up and he gets stage fright, he more or less gets booed and pelted with rotten eggs and tomatoes—as the ropey, grave, and dignified tenor does on *The Sellers' Market* album, when he warbles a few bars of 'Only a Rose,' accompanied by an out-of-key honky-tonk piano.

Sellers saw himself in these permutations. In *Waltz of the Toreadors*, which was made after *Only Two Can Play* and before *The Dock Brief*, he plays a man who plays the part of the great seducer, and General Fitzjohn, when he goes a-courting, does the equivalent of falling off the stage and crashing into the pit. He gets drunk in the bar of Ghislaine's hotel, finds her bedroom, and falls off her veranda. Then again, counter-poising the farce is a sense of elegy. His lost love, when she reappears, makes the General think of the wasted years and the problems of ageing— and as Sellers himself said: 'The thing about Anouilh is he can be tragic, then in the middle of a scene he can turn to comedy—and back again.'

The film, directed by John Guillermin, who'd allowed Sellers to be so demonic in *Never Let Go*, suffers from just this commutation. One minute the General is poetic and rather moving, as he tells us about his suffering and sense of mortality; the next minute he is Major Bloodnok, storming into Dr Grogan's house and fighting a duel with his furled umbrella. Perhaps *La Valse des Toréadors* had a Gallic charm and lightness of touch, a way of intermingling farce and tenderness that was urbane and not coarse? Perhaps General Saint-Pé, as Fitzjohn is called in the original, was coherently tragicomic, his fate bittersweet? Translated into *Waltz of the Toreadors*, however, the film is broken-backed—and Fitzjohn, who wears the full scarlet dress uniform and medals of a Grenadier Guardsman in every scene, seems to have come adrift from a D'Oyly Carte touring production of *The Pirates of Penzance*—he's another of Sellers' old troupers.

In fairness, it should be noted that the film suffered at the hands of a timorous producer, Julian Wintle, who cropped Margaret Leighton's miserable-and-abandoned-wife speeches and interspersed them with back-projected sequences in which she is meant to be at large on her bicycle, her nightdress and waist-length grey hair streaming in a studio wind-machine hurricane. (Emily is a former opera singer, and her antics make her madder than Donizetti's Lucia di Lammermoor.) The attempt to make a serious character silly is artless, benighting; after another burst of bleakness ('I'm dying for want of your love'), off she bolts on her bike again, this time to get involved with a fox hunt—and the fox takes refuge in her pannier. None of this is funny, and instead of ameliorating the film's gloominess— or figuratively shedding light on it—the indecisiveness of the film's style, tone, and intentions is simply affirmed.

It was a mistake, from the beginning, to Anglicise the original material. Promiscuity and sexual consummations do not belong to the English comic idiom. In French farce, the running in and out of doors and windows mimics the antic penetrations of love-making—all those fissures and holes in the body begging to be filled. In Britain, by contrast, humour derives from sexual failure and frustration: there is too much guilt and embarrassment built in to the national character to allow for much pleasuring. Hence, where General Fitzjohn, because he has an eye for bottoms and breasts, seems lecherous, General Saint-Pé, his continental counterpart, was curiously pure and enviable. His tragedy—though that is too strong a word—was that he felt the life-force to be ebbing. He is having to cut down on his daily quota of orgasms. General Fitzjohn's fate, by contrast, is more melancholy. He is not only sexually impeded (his impotence being signalled to us by one of Emily's arias: 'I know what a woman feels when she's left unsatisfied'), he is also encumbered with regret about a missed opportunity—the way he had failed to 'live in the sunlight of a glorious love,' with Ghislaine. We are presented with the big English romantic theme: loss.

◆ ◆ ◆

To the English, happiness survives as fantasy—a dream of the Golden World past, a mingling of memory and desire. To the French, happiness is appetite—an expression of vigour. *Waltz of the Toreadors*, which is often stilted when it tries to be pensive, and dull when it opts for slapstick, is also uncertain—preposterous—in its tone. As a French (copulative) farce acted out with such Englishness, what might have been ribald in Anouilh either now strikes us as out of key or as plainly vulgar. If Grogan and the General were French, I'm sure I could accept their chit-chat

('Fascinating how these ancient machines still work so efficiently,' one or other of them says, referring to a veteran car, leaking steam and exploding, though of course the innuendo is obvious); between Englishmen, however, of the Edwardian period in which the film is set, but not only then, comments like these provoke a snigger and a blush: 'Well', says the General, giving the doctor permission to minister to his hypochondriacal wife, 'you'd better go up and lubricate my old heap…'

That would be a nice line if Sid James said it to Kenneth Williams, with reference to Joan Sims; in the context of a film that is trying to create a climate of sophistication and disenchantment, though, it is a music hall gag. On the other hand, it is apt for Sellers, for whom cars and women were synonymous; and Sellers, like Ralph Richardson, who played General Fitzjohn on Broadway, had the talent to imply mystery and helplessness under the surface defiance and swagger. But he is on his own. Cyril Cusack as Dr Grogan really only exists for the General to have somebody to talk to; his sympathetic presence prevents Sellers from having to spout what are technically soliloquies.

Over balloons of VSOP the General complains about his wife and expresses regret about his mistress, and he is correct to be exasperated on both counts. The former, when she is not bicycling, is made to shriek and moan like a Greek Chorus. Of the latter, and the romance at the Cavalry Ball, whilst the band played the schmaltzy 'Waltz of the Toreadors,' and he was a dashing dragoon, he says: 'It all seems to me, Grogan, like some fantastic flight to the moon.' (As I suspected, Fitzjohn is a visionary in the tradition of Baron Munchausen.) Ghislaine, who does not seem to have aged in the intervening seventeen years since the precipitate bunny hug, reappears wearing huge fancy hats and elaborate lace pantyhose—costumes perhaps discarded by Epifania Parerga—and she keeps pretending to commit suicide, again like Epifania Parerga (even to the extent of jumping into a lake so that she can later parade in her scanties to get dry).

Here we have the appeal of the story for Sellers. Dany Robin, in her lime-green and peach Zuleika Dobson outfits, is playing Loren (in Sellers' imagination) and Margaret Leighton (again to Sellers) was standing in for Anne. He had filtered his fantasy life through *Only Two Can Play*; here, in another man-wife-mistress triangle, he was doing it again—and much more rancorously.

◆ ◆ ◆

The film everybody else is in was not the film Sellers is in. When General Fitzjohn decides to write his memoirs—an account of his soft beds and hard battles—and takes refuge in his private chambers, the completeness of Sellers' self-absorption is profound. Dr Grogan has no access to these scenes. Nobody has. In *Only Two Can Play*, the aspirations and despair of the librarian, and his dream of fair women, ironically cut across the actor's own domestic drama, and he took comfort in the rôle. In John Lewis, we had watched Sellers' vulnerability and absurdities, sure enough, but the mood was softer, more amiable, and we could respect the hero because he knew himself to be idiotic. When General Fitzjohn goes upstairs to his lumber room, however—to a castle-within-the castle, with its wide staircases, its wax-encrusted chandeliers, and its draperies and damask—he is torpid and knotted-up. If the decor is meant to suggest grand opera, it equally implies the theatricality of horror movies.

Lewis learns a few adult lessons—that 'Ye trancèd visions, ye flights ideal' (Keats) must yield to real everyday pressures and responsibilities; that the search for personal happiness can depend on, or involve, the pain it causes to others, so you must learn restraint and self-sacrifice—and part of the film's success lies in our knowing full well that Sellers himself could never face up to an awareness of this kind. (*Being There* works in a similar fashion: manic Sellers camouflaging himself as moronic Chance; and *There's a Girl in My Soup* does, too: unsavoury Sellers coming on as Don Juan.) But the thing about *Waltz of the Toreadors*, when General Fitzjohn is walled off from the world in his gothic web, is that all the moping, the deep jealousy, the aridity, the hysteria, is authentic. Sellers, like his character, was dooming himself to disintegration. Sellers' mind is on display up on the screen; we are on the other side of his craziness with him—and when the General and Emily indulge in the following exchange, it is impossible not to feel very ill at ease:

> GENERAL: [*Whispering and then rising in intensity.*] I want a divorce…Damn you… Damn you. I'm leaving you.
>
> EMILY: [*The opera diva artificiality giving way to sincerity.*]…A woman belongs to whoever takes her and keeps her…
>
> GENERAL: [*With extreme loathing.*] My God, woman, I hate you.
>
> EMILY: What difference does that make? I'm your wife.

♦ ♦ ♦

There is always a chance that the above dialogue could be put across as a leg-pull—the badinage of a couple who trade insults as endearments. Sellers, however, is completely bitter and exhausted. It is one thing for the film to be muddled about its pan-European pedigree, and for it to have endured producer interference; it is quite another for its star to wrest certain scenes and to fill them with his personal malignancy. For, I am convinced, the power of the harangue is coming from deep inside. Elsewhere in the film Fitzjohn is variously genial and/or sorry for himself. Nothing prepares us for the spitefulness of this particular confrontation; nor do attempts to defuse it later succeed.

It is one of those moments—like the temper tantrum I discussed in *The Naked Truth* [see page ???]—when Sellers goes beyond acting, to achieve a pitch that is unconnected with the rest of the film, or with his conception of the character, and which is insane. It happens in *The Bobo*. He and Britt (who is playing 'the most desirable witch in Barcelona') have a scene in a furrier's shop. Olimpia wants a mink coat. She is accompanied on her expedition by the mild matador—except that, inexplicably, as Olimpia examines the pelts and talks to the manager, Juan Bautista starts to behave very meanly and petulantly. (He is *out* of character.) There is a distinct cloud across the scene, as if Sellers couldn't stand being ignored a moment longer. Sellers delivers his lines with an angry rap. And then we cut to the street, and an exterior location, shot on a different day, and Sellers and Britt revert to having a kindliness between them. Inside the shop, Sellers grabs Britt's wrist; outside, they are holding hands. There is a lightness in the air which, after the foregoing agitation, is equally ruffling. (There is a discontinuity of mood.)

There is a similarly overheated atmosphere in the early part of *After the Fox*. This time Britt is Sellers' sister, Gina. He, having escaped from prison, heads home and is disgusted to learn that she has designs on becoming an actress. Aldo Vanucci's jealous rage, however, is a husband's. When he grabs Gina from the set and frog-marches her back to the Roman apartment, the argument which ensues is a marital row. Sellers' own contempt and cynicism get in the way. 'Harlot' and 'starlet' are flung about as interchangeable terms of abuse. Then Aldo asks the momma to turn away so that Gina can be thumped: *'You will do what I tell you,'* brother dins into sister. She disregards him, goes back to the film set, and he storms after her again: 'This time I kill her!'

As we know from the testimony of Kenneth Griffith and Robert Parrish, this is the gallant way Sellers treated his wife in real-life. Michael, too, recalls his father screaming at his step-mother: 'You're a lousy bloody actress. Can't you get one scene right? Why don't you listen to what I tell you?' Britt's additional problem was that Sellers wanted to turn her into Sophia Loren—a scheme which is about as mad as Caligula deciding he'd make his favourite horse a consul. It is not my intention or concern, in making such an allusion, to denigrate Britt's career and capabilities. Sellers himself did enough of that, especially in his later years. 'A professional girlfriend and an amateur actress.' What amazes—and amuses—me, quite simply, is how he thought an incredibly beautiful blonde from the frozen North could be converted into a raven-haired she-wolf from the Mediterranean. But still he advised his bride 'if you do the *right* films at the *right* times then you could be bigger than Loren.' He made a start on this by getting Britt to dye her hair black—though he had to be satisfied with a wig—and then they made *After the Fox* and *The Bobo* in Rome because 'I love acting there. Rome is one big open-air Actors' Studio.' And Cinecitta was convenient for the Villa Ponti, where Sellers was always angling to get invited—and where Britt (who felt herself to be 'the little Swedish mouse' in the Great Presence) noticed that Loren could never relax: 'Every appearance she made, even within her own household, meant that she had to be properly dressed and made-up.'

Is this what Sellers wanted for Britt? That her naturalness be replaced by a stately mask and that her every appearance become a grand entrance? Whatever, the Italianising of Ekland proceeded apace. *After the Fox*, he said in November 1966, 'is a return [after his heart attacks] to the ambitions I have for Britt... Britt had to wear two wigs at once for one scene—a red one when playing a part in the film-within-a-film, with the brunette one under it... you couldn't get angry with Britt as a blonde. But you could slap her around when you see her as a Roman *raggaza*, all teenage cheek.'

Hence the authenticity, and offensiveness, of the surliness in the brother-sister encounter which I described. All Sellers' resentments came out: he hated Britt for not being Loren; he could shout at and hit Britt as if she was Loren. He made it quite impossible for her to succeed; no matter how good she might have been if left to her own devices, he had to undermine her. He knew best; he could not allow her any independence, whether in judgement, thought, or deed. As Britt herself said as long ago as September 1966, before she was willing to admit what a mean-spirited warped egomaniac she was lumbered with: 'Peter...saw a scene I had done when he was not on the set. He came home and told me it was the most terrifying thing he had ever seen, that it was really awful. It was like someone just put a big foot on me and crushed me to the ground because up till then I was convinced that I was just marvellous and...how easy it was! I got so unhappy.'

To further build up his wife's confidence and self-esteem, Sellers resorted to what we might call the Lionel Meadows tactic. He intimidated Britt to such an extent (by throwing chairs at her, for example) that she had to flee their villa in the middle of the night and seek refuge with Neil Simon and his wife, Joan, who had rented a house across on the Appian Way. When they all went to Ischia, for six weeks' location work, Sellers sulked in his room at the Hotel Regina Isabella, and expected Britt to remain caged with him. He wouldn't allow her to see much of her family, who had come from Stockholm to join her, because they tended to babble away in Swedish and he felt excluded; he was even suspicious if she went into the nanny's suite to check on baby Victoria. 'There were perpetual rows,' Britt has written, 'and sometimes our precious furniture got broken. In one row I chipped one of my front teeth. The flaw is still visible today.'

Apparently, Sellers had upended a bed, which very shortly before Britt had been asleep in, and one of the castors clonked her on the mouth. He also disassembled her Cartier watch without telling her, and it was a bit of shock seeing the little cogs and springs eddying in the toilet bowl, like coral fragments at the bottom of a reef.

◆ ◆ ◆

To adapt a line from *Carmen Jones*, once he'd loved you, that was the end of you. 'I loved them all', he confided in the spirit medium, Micki Dahne, after he'd died. 'I adored women and constantly need [*sic*] to be with them. They were the driving force of my life—my work was only a means to be with them.' There was, however, sadism in Sellers' attitude to sex and women. He wanted his partners to suffer because he despised them for yielding. Better, by far, was to have remained absent and indifferent—like Loren: 'above them all stood Sophia—she was my Goddess. I dreamed of her constantly. I prayed that we would be together one day...' However, he reiterated before the astral signals faded at last, 'I really loved all the women in my life when I was with them...' Quite so. Once they'd quit his pad in the service elevator, they would already have started to cease existing.

With Sellers, after he'd had you and, as a possession, you were relegated to a lower order of being, he was, as General Fitzjohn says of his particular liaisons, 'bored to death'; and, like the unhappy hero of *Waltz of the Toreadors*, who believes himself to be encumbered by wife, family, and the obligations of rank, so did Sellers consider himself inconvenienced. He looked at Anne and the children and blamed them for his own staleness. He identified with these saturnine aspects of the rôle to such a degree, he marred the film—the scenes with Margaret Leighton, as I argued earlier, are *too* powerful.

'He wanted to play General Fitzjohn desperately,' recalls Leslie Linder. 'But the producers were very worried about him, having heard that he was difficult. Eventually, after weeks and weeks, we talked them into it.'

Julian Wintle and Peter de Sarigny, the backers, were correct to have misgivings. As Anne Francis, Wintle's widow, remembers: 'From the outset of production, Julian was bedevilled by the problem of attempting to control ever-rising costs. Sellers, engaged in domestic arguments, moodily, and too often, kept the film unit waiting.'

I pointed out to Anne (Levy) that the domestic arguments *in* the film seemed to impinge on the domestic arguments *surrounding* the film, and she readily agreed with this: 'Things going on in his private life did tend to come out in his films—because in *Waltz of the Toreadors* you have an old soldier trying to disentangle himself from his wife to chase his girlfriend—abandoning his family security—and, by coincidence, all this was happening to Peter. We were at the Manor House, or had just left it, and I went to see him on location. Had a *terrible* row there.'

If the animus for art was being provided by real life, Sellers, when he granted an interview to Herbert Kretzmer, and had seemed to talk so openly and wrathfully, was actually requisitioning lines of dialogue from the film to describe his own feelings: 'I wasted eleven years of my life with the wrong woman. No. I mean that. Something has been wrong with us for a long time. Did you never notice it before?' That's what the General says to Dr. Grogan. How aware was he of the source of what he was saying?

Anne told me about how upset she had been by the publicity surrounding the divorce—and at the miraculous way Sellers had posed as and convinced the public that he was the injured party: 'How dare you write this about me! I said to Herbert Kretzmer, when that article came out... People only wanted to know about the star, and I felt it was a betrayal of friendship—but I did realise, when Peter and I split up, that there was no such thing as loyalty. It was all down to work and money. The only... [people] I remained friendly with... [were] Spike... and Theo Cowan... None of the others came near me after I'd remarried—one of his cronies told me: "I can't see you because Peter doesn't want me to." Peter told everybody: "Don't have anything to do with her." It all swung around later—and he resented it that I'd been snubbed. He then didn't like it that they'd done what he'd told them to do, which was to have nothing to do with me...'

Part Five

♦♦♦

The Afterlife of Peter Sellers

Why is it that one runs to one's ruin? Why has destruction such a fascination? Why, when one stands on a pinnacle, must one throw oneself down? No one knows, but things are so.

Oscar Wilde

Chapter Thirteen

♦ ♦ ♦

The Crack-Up

Lis attitude to women, therefore, is to be hit upon in *Waltz of the Toreadors*—as it was to be again in *There's a Girl in My Soup*, which exposed his shallowness and vanity, and in *Hoffman*, which dealt with his bloodlessness and predatoriness. His wandering loyalties and strange vulnerability; his changeableness and fight to be free; his miraculous way of putting innocents in the wrong; these are the irks which course through the General's rain-lashed house. Sellers' affinity with the character even extended to his eyeing up of the nymphets in the cast—one of whom grew up to be Prunella Scales: 'I am, of course, only admitting to being sixteen years old at the time of *Waltz of the Toreadors*' she told me. 'I remember Peter Sellers being very serious and helpful; in the lunch breaks he would sit and improvise scenes from the General's life with me and Denise Coffey—and Peter did, one evening, ask me to go to the cinema with him. To my eternal regret I said no, because I had a date in London. Heigh-ho...'

Sellers was evidently intent on reviving himself with young company. He'd do this with increasing regularity—clear his life and fill it with new friends who'd not last long enough to become old friends. His psychic surgeon, Doris Collins, witnessed a revealing scene in this regard: Sellers giving a double performance on the telephone, speaking in one voice to a girlfriend, in another, with his hand over the mouthpiece, to Mrs Collins. Both speeches, says the medium, were made with total conviction.

If the future Mrs Timothy West/Sybil Fawlty gave him the cold-shoulder, he had better luck with the former child actress Janette Scott (a daughter of the magnificent and still-going character actress Thora Hird), who was thirteen years his junior. The point is, for all that Sellers had his dream-figure in Loren and kept making films that expressed either his solitude or the pitfalls of romantic entanglements (real and fanciful), intermittently, in the holes and corners of his life, he gave vent to his lust and emotional sado-masochism. The clandestine relationship with Janette Scott underpins everything that I have been unfolding:

> Peter, not long after we'd started going out together, mentioned Sophia Loren, and said he'd thought himself so unattractive a person, he was totally bowled over when she came up to him on the set one day and said 'I want to roll in the hay with you!...' The moment changed his life—and he led me to believe he'd taken full advantage of the invitation. But he was probably just trying to impress me and had made the entire saga up.

> I'm sure...he gave Britt the same story. You realise that it was Epifania, in the

film, who goes on about making hay whilst the sun shines? That wasn't actually Loren talking at all.

In those days I was a very big name in this country; I'd started starring in films when I was nine. By the time I met Peter, in the year he made *Doctor Strangelove* [1963], I had grown up in the public eye—as everybody's favourite girl next door; and this image was carefully guarded—and having down-to-earth parents, they'd have not wanted my name in the papers, romantically linked to Peter Sellers...

We were aware of each other. I had gone to the first night of *The Bedsitting Room*, at the Mermaid. There was a party afterwards on the stage. Amongst the guests were Peter Sellers and Dennis Selinger—my agent, Peter's agent—and the next day Dennis Selinger called me up and said, '...Peter Sellers wants to know if it would be all right for him to ask you out.' I was so amazed he'd gone through Dennis, I said 'Would it?' almost as if I was asking him for permission. 'What do you mean?' I continued. 'Is there something weird about the man?' Dennis didn't sound absolutely certain it would be all right, but he didn't specify anything...

And so it was a secret romance. I wouldn't go out anywhere in public with him; he wasn't about to force the issue himself. I was living at home with my parents, because my house in Stewart's Grove, Chelsea, was being redecorated. Peter was very generous—he never arrived at my parents' house without bringing gifts, for my parents as well as for me. He was very keen on photography...but because I spent my professional life being photographed, although he often asked me to go on photographic expeditions, I never went. But he was *always* wanting to photograph me...

He moved me into a flat at the top of the King's Road, which he said his company owned...About this time [March] he started *Doctor Strangelove*. Whilst it was being filmed, on several nights he'd arrive for dinner, but neither of us would eat anything, because he was so upset. He'd break down and cry, and say he didn't think he'd be able to go on with...the strain of doing the film. We went out to dinner several times to Stanley Kubrick's Victorian flat in Kensington. Everything was very nice and friendly—but not too close. They were not buddies. They rarely spoke of the film.

On other evenings, we'd be at his penthouse in Hampstead—at the top of an ugly modern tower block. Peter was inordinately proud of it. I found it as cold as cold could be...there wasn't a speck of colour. We might as well have been in a hotel lobby. Anyway, I acted as hostess for innumerable dinner parties there—Kubrick, Sterling Hayden, Robert Wagner, George C. Scott...Peter was a good host, but...I got the impression that the meals were gone through out of policy and courtesy, and not out of any pressing need to get together with friends. Sterling Hayden...didn't get the gist of the fact that I was with Peter. He insisted that I went out with him. Both Peter and I were rather insulted by that. But the vast majority of evenings, it was just the two of us in the flat off the King's Road...

On weekends he had access to the children and he was as good a father as it was possible to be: (a) for him; (b) under the circumstances. Michael and Sarah would come along, and we'd put on pretend shows, or record pretend radio programmes. Peter had enough equipment to run a real radio station. He always showed off his gadgetry to visitors. I must say, I felt closer in spirit to the children than to Peter...

Anyway, I felt I was able to cheer Peter up. During these crying spells it was obvious that he got depressed either very easily, or that there were deeper, psychological reasons. I understood any technical problems that would bother him about filmmaking—I could explain those away—and for the first couple of months he was generally happy and wonderful. He started talking of marriage. He wanted us to go to Japan the following Spring and to marry when the cherry blossom trees were out in full flower... But little by little, the ploys I was using to cheer him up weren't working so successfully. Bert called me up late one night. Peter had locked himself in the bathroom and refused to come out—and he was so worried about him, could I come over and help...? I drove over there and sat on the floor outside the bathroom door, until daylight...

He was threatening suicide. Our talks didn't make a great deal of sense—he went on about this overwhelming weight he felt; everything was too difficult... It was always the burden of his work he talked about. I tried to tell him that no film on earth could be that important; that if he tried, he couldn't be bad. These rambling conversations went on from eleven-thirty until the dawn. A lot is said, and yet nothing is said, because nothing really works. Twice this particular all-night suicidal session took place—once in the bathroom, once in the bedroom. Finally, he'd come out and put his arm around me—more big-brother-and-little-sister than lovers. 'Sorry if I've put you through it.' ...

Peter then started not turning up for dinners I had cooked... A couple of times I called the Dorchester late in the evening, and they referred the call down to the restaurant. This hurt me dreadfully. As I was about to move back into my Chelsea house, a letter arrived: 'Jannie—it just isn't working, is it? Dreadfully sorry. Love you a lot, Peter.'

A few months later I met David Frost [who many years later would marry and divorce Lynne Frederick].

Curious, the movement of the chess pieces. I lived with David for several years. I was in New York meeting my agent and David was setting up *That Was The Week That Was*. I got two phone calls in rapid succession from two of Peter's friends, both of them saying: 'Jan, Peter met this Swedish girl a few days ago, and he's going to marry her. Please come back and talk some sense into him.' ... I decided to have nothing to do with it. You could have been entangled in the ups and downs of Peter's emotional life forever if you didn't draw the line.

What I discovered is that greatly manic-depressive people need you to think of something *new* that will cheer them up—they *drain* you. I have rarely been so emotionally drained as I was by Peter. He left me an emotional husk. He was so self-centred, he couldn't see any hope outside of himself. He began to use me—and he became resistant to me, as to a drug...

I think now that, in some strange way, he enjoyed all these crying jags—self-indulgence and self-pity, which he carried to extremes. He'd like to surround himself with people who'd make a fuss of him when he was down—which gave him a false sense of reality, because he'd worked hard at being unhappy. Could it be that, as a child on tour, he'd gained attention and affection from his mother only when he was unhappy? He mentioned his mother often. Mort Sahl said to me that what you've got to do, as a Jewish son, is to be angry. In your mind, you try your mother; you convict her; and then you forgive her.

Years and years later... when he was married to Miranda, and I was married to Mel Tormé, he telephoned me in Beverly Hills and we went out to dinner, along with my parents. Miranda wore a see-through blouse and my darling Dad could not take his eyes off her titties the entire evening... None of us could understand how Peter could be at ease with the effervescent, amusing Miranda...

They just weren't a couple. I couldn't see it at all. A few months later I read they'd split. Peter's parents were not dissimilar to my own—my father was a drummer in the pit when Thora Hird was on stage in *The Desert Song* at the amateur dramatic society. Peter was really happy with my parents, and in a strange way I was only ever part of a package that included them. They represented his own background to a certain extent. I can see him now taking off his glasses to wipe the tears of laughter away after something my mother had said—something about her overhearing a woman on the bus say: 'See that over there? That's the second largest power station in the north of England. And what's more, *I* know the manager.'

♦ ♦ ♦

Doctor Strangelove—or *Dr Folamour*, as they call it in France—lives up to its title. From the fornicating flying machines over the title sequence to the crazy Kraut's yanking himself up and out of his wheelchair in the final scene (the flaccid graveyard worm is suddenly *homo erectus*), the film is filled with strange, dehumanising kinds of loving. The red alert is sounded because a General, suffering from impotence, finally flips. 'Women sense my power and they seek me out,' he says with quiet psychotic reasoning. 'I do not avoid women. But I deny them my Life Essence.' Believing that his sperm count has dropped owing to secret chemicals pumped into the water supply by the Russians, he pushes the end-of-the-world buttons. Up in the B-52, the pilot examines the emergency ration packs—an over-sexed adolescent's dream-kit: chewing-gum, condoms, lipsticks, nylon stockings. 'Gee,' he says, 'a fella could have a pretty good weekend in Vegas with all that stuff.' Over at the Pentagon, Buck Turgidson keeps getting calls from his floozie ('Look, honey, I can't talk now—my President needs me'), who won't be put off by any silly war games ('Of *course* it isn't only physical,' he implores); and the Russian premier, when he is located, appears to be in a bordello. The theme of gonadic stir-craziness peaks when General Ripper's HQ is finally taken: Col. Guano is reluctant to let Mandrake use the phone—he thinks the British officer is in drag, a 'deviant prevert [*sic*]'. 'What do you mean suit?' retorts the pukka officer. 'This happens to be a RAF uniform.'

What with Strangelove's dream of fertilising women down the mineshaft (and gorging himself on the animals which 'vill be bred unt *slaughtarrh'd*); the chaps flicking through *Playboy* in the bomber; General Ripper's obsession with his infertility; Turgidson's mistresses; the guns spurting out spent cartridges; the Coca-Cola machine spraying Col. Guano full in the face; the nervous chewing on phallic cigars: men at war and men and sex are one and the same. In *Doctor Strangelove*, the characters seem to fear it, or are useless at it—so they take out their frustrations in bringing about the apocalypse (the ultimate orgasm). The nuclear bombs go off, and the popping mushroom clouds are like those close-ups of delayed-action blooms and pollen puffs which use to be cut in to B-movies, along with waves breaking and trains entering tunnels, to mimic the agonising ecstasy of coming. (Kubrick's symbolism is on a level with the imagery in *The Blue Lagoon*.) The irony, of course, is that *Doctor Strangelove—or: How I Learned to Stop Worrying and Love the Bomb* is not about love, but death; not about insemination, but annihilation; and this is its only irony, in fact. I find it a suffocating, portentous film, and its fascination—which is therefore considerable—principally lies in what it reveals to us of Sellers' own extremely post-adolescent view of a world he was not terribly happy about inhabiting. For, as much as there was a screenplay and a structure laid down in advance, 'during the shooting many substantial changes were made in the script,' Kubrick has said. 'Some of the best dialogue was created by Peter Sellers himself.' And if many of the scenes in the film were improvised—and Sellers *is* the film—all that material has had to erupt from somewhere, surely? *Doctor Strangelove* (and *Lolita*, too) gives outward form to its star's anger and madness.

◆ ◆ ◆

Asked, towards the end of his life, what he was most proud of having done, Sellers said *I'm All Right, Jack* ('I loved doing that'), *Only Two Can Play* ('I loved the Kingsley Amis book which Bryan did the screenplay for ... A fine movie. That really stands up'); but his chief conjunction, he knew, was 'my meeting with Kubrick, who is a god as far as I am concerned, and you can watch *Doctor Strangelove* now and it is even better than when it came out. It is a *remarkable* film.'

Apart from Peg and Loren (his goddesses), Kubrick would seem to be the only personage in the Sellers line-up who managed to escape from censure and the after-effects of disillusion. Kubrick was his ideal, and he testified to this in hundreds of interviews across a seventeen-year period: 'I take my hat off to Stanley...'; 'I think I've enjoyed working with Stanley Kubrick more than any other director, apart from John Boulting...'; 'I think Kubrick is one of the five great directors in the world...'; 'I'd do anything he wanted to make...'; 'I admire Stanley Kubrick so much—he is a painstaking, brilliant and generally self-efficient director...'; 'Kubrick is marvellous to work with...'; 'Stanley Kubrick ... understands me. [He] seems to know what goes on in here ...' (said Sellers, tapping his skull).*

And so on fulsomely. What Sellers had found, for the space of two films, was a serious-minded Milligan—though perhaps this mentor (who in photographs resembles Dame Flora Robson in a frizzy black beard) wasn't *that* serious-minded, if what Shelley Winters says is true. She recalls that, when they were shooting *Lolita*, Kubrick always arrived at and departed from the studio by bicycle, whatever the hour or weather. She kept trying to offer him lifts in her chauffeur-driven limo, to no avail. 'Shelley,' she was eventually told, 'Stanley Kubrick two years ago decided he would not fly in a plane. Last year, he decided he would not ride in a car. He will only trust his bicycle.'

Whether by accident or design, Kubrick (b. New York) is an English director—and his work shows an interest in the English sensibility, in peculiarly Englishy themes: class, chivalry, hypocrisy, repression, patriotism, xenophobia. Which was ideal for Sellers—the actor had returned to the climate of 'The Goon Show'—and where Milligan's scripts had a dream logic, Kubrick's films have nightmare logic, which similarly liberated him. In one particular instance, 'The Goon Show'—or, to be accurate, one of the 'Fred' shows—specifically overlapped with, or inspired, a great screen moment: 'In one of the Freds,' explained Sellers, 'we decided to see

---

* Sellers' sole disparaging remark was also his most hilarious ever. He claimed not to have liked *A Clockwork Orange* because 'surely we've had enough violence for a while ... I used to enjoy seeing the odd gangster film a few years ago. But I am a Yogi—and am against violence completely.'

what we could do with the glove puppet idea…so a shot was set up of someone who, to all intents and purposes, was Harry Corbett with Sooty.* Sooty kept hitting him and "Corbett" was saying "Stop that, little Sooty! Stop it!" But little Sooty wouldn't stop, so suddenly he gets a slap and…drops out of sight while the man says, "He is a naughty little Sooty doing that, isn't he?" Then Sooty comes up with a gun in its hands and fires and the man slumps forward. Then the camera crabs round and you see that "Corbett" himself was being worked by someone else with his hand up the back of his jacket. He looks round, startled, and says "Oh!" It was a very weird moment. One day, Stanley suggested that I should wear a black glove which would look rather sinister on a man in a wheelchair. "Maybe he had some injury in a nuclear experiment of some kind," Kubrick said. So I put on the black glove and looked at the arm and I suddenly thought, "Hey, that's a storm-trooper's arm." So instead of leaving it there looking malignant I gave the arm a life of its own. That arm hated the rest of the body for having made a compromise; that arm was a Nazi. When it tried to choke Dr Strangelove, the other arm had to hit it. It was the same thing as the Sooty sketch—the arm or hand having a life of its own, hating the rest of the body.'

Despite Kubrick's grimmer air, the prevailing belief that man is not a deeply rational creature is the same as Milligan's philosophy; the rowdiness, mutilations, and explosions are the same; the asperity is the same. Underneath the surreal antics and jokes of 'The Goon Show', Milligan never lost sight of the war; he created humour out of shell-shock, combat fatigue, dirt, and danger. And, if one of the purposes of war is the chance it offers chaps to assert their manhood—they can come of age by being violent—this, Goonery's great satirical theme, is the theme, also, of *The Killing* (with Sterling Hayden), *Paths of Glory* (obviously), *Spartacus, Doctor Strangelove, 2001: A Space Odyssey, A Clockwork Orange, Barry Lyndon*, and *Full Metal Jacket* (again obviously). Armies, duels, weaponry, thuggishness, machismo, and power: this is Kubrick's world—a world (like that of 'The Goon Show') without women, on the whole. (Shelley Winters and Shelley Duvall turn up not as women but as banshees.)

◆◆◆

The patriarchal spirit (Kubrick seems to be saying) is basically destructive, predatory. (What the matriarchal spirit might be like we are never told.) Hence *Lolita*, which is about the perversion of the father-daughter bond. Humbert Humbert moves in on the Haze household, and goes through with marrying Charlotte (Shelley Winters at her blowsiest), the better to ambush the prepubescent Dolores. Nabokov's original novel intermingles several skirmishes: Humbert *vs.* his deviancy ('We are not sex fiends!…We are unhappy, mild, dog-eyed gentlemen…ready to give years and years of life for one chance to touch a nymphet'); Humbert *vs.* Charlotte ('You're a monster,' she tells him, when she finds out his secret and his calculation. 'You're a detestable, abominable, criminal fraud…');

---

* Corbett was very popular on television in the fifties in Britain. Sooty was a little bear-puppet; his sidekick was a little black dog-puppet, called Sweep.

Humbert *vs.* Lolita, who is incapable of returning the intensity of his possessive love ('Even the most miserable of family lives was better than the parody of incest, which, in the long run, was the best I could offer the waif'); and Humbert *vs.* Quilty, his sinister double ('To know that this semi-animated, sub-human trickster who had sodomized my darling—oh, my darling, this was intolerable bliss!').

The film,* however—not surprisingly for all those decades ago, and total paedophiliac candour would be more than a challenge today—doesn't do much with the forbidden fruit element, and Sue Lyon, in a large floppy sun hat, whilst pretty and teenagery, would not be mistaken by anybody for a child. What this means, in effect, is that an atmosphere of warped, dangerous eroticism is lost; the specific act of child molestation is lost; so Humbert's guilty passion is lost. *Lolita*, the film, has as much connection with *Lolita*, the novel, as a production of *Othello* in which the Moor is portrayed as being white; and the sexual relations between James Mason and Sue Lyon, in fact, far from making us retch at the idea of the beast with two backs, are less off-putting and more chaste than Audrey Hepburn and Fred Astaire in *Funny Face*.

Kubrick's *Lolita*, therefore, comes down quite fast to rather vaguely being about James Mason's ability to show what a man's face looks like after years of secret suffering. Mason's Humbert Humbert is a creature of bad temper and moods, all right, but so would you and I be if wedded to Shelley Winters' Charlotte—a terrifying portrait of a suburban vulgarian in a leopard-skin belt ('culturally we're a very advanced group, intellectually'). Their scenes are a straightforward—bitter, recriminatory—battle of the sexes. They more or less go for one another in slow-motion, and once 'the noxious mama,' 'the stupid Haze woman', 'the brainless ba-ba' has been killed off, the girl and her stepfather drive away, and Mason's cause for concern, and reason for frowning, is his ward's consumption of chewing-gum, milk-shakes, and trashy magazines. (Lolita is going to mature into a double of her mother.)

♦♦♦

So, unless the viewer wants to decode Mason's grimace, and attribute reasons for the suppressed violence in it—is that why Quilty's murder is shifted to the start, so that we do not forget that this silky fellow can kill?—*Lolita* avoids what it is meant to be about. Except that then there is Sellers, so full of implication and outlandishness that Winters was moved to say: 'Peter Sellers seemed to be acting on a different planet.' This is a very perceptive remark, and the extra-terrestrial origin, as we know already, was 'The Goon Show'. Quilty fools Humbert with false identities and funny voices; he scampers across the film exactly like the young Sellers himself, free-associating behind the microphone at the Camden Theatre, twitting Wallace Greenslade or the dyspeptic producers. (It is as if somebody had already made the James Mason-Shelley Winters-Sue Lyon film, and then elves and goblins got at the negative and interspersed it with Sellers.)

After the evocative prologue, in which he plays ping-pong and is gunned down ('the first five minutes are pretty stunning,' Sellers always conceded) Sellers'

* Made in the winter of 1961/62, between *Waltz of the Toreadors* and *The Dock Brief*.

character not only keeps reappearing, in disguise, to gleefully upstage Mason; there is also the sense that his mutations, by being so fluid and imperious, are in themselves a form of hostility. Quilty (at least in the novel, which is presented as a madman's paranoid fantasy) is meant to function as Humbert's liberated double and Id ('instinctive impulses of the individual as part of the unconscious', *OED*); he is his tempter and tormenter. It is perhaps easier to see Mason as the unwitting stooge in a music hall act—like Grytpype's Moriarty.

We first see Sellers as the distinguished author at a High School prom, going through the motions of slow jazz steps, a shuffle really, and looking at his watch. He is bored and cynical and can't recall anything about Charlotte except that didn't she have a daughter with 'a lilting, lyrical name?' I don't think his nibs was ever as authoritative and frightening as he is in a long shot in this scene, lazily dancing, absorbing people's high regard for him; Quilty is nasty, supercilious, and as bloated by fame as a television personality. His 'toad of a face' (Nabokov) thus connects very well with Wee Sonny MacGregor in *The Naked Truth* and Robert Danvers in *There's a Girl in My Soup*—other men who succeed at appearing charming and normal, whilst underneath there is rottenness and revulsion.

Thus, the significance of *Lolita*. Quilty, a man who is always trying something on, and who is ungraspable, embodies a lot of the personality of the actor playing him. Sellers has said that he never met Kubrick until 'right before *Lolita*. He came straight to me and asked me to play Quilty... To me, that was an enormous honour'—and I must say it was a casting decision of genius. (I'm not so certain about his original choice for Humbert: Noël Coward.) Kubrick could evidently discern that, behind the levities of 'The Goon Show' there existed a talent towards which we react with both admiration and animosity; Sellers is so quick and ticklish—one moment Bluebottle, the next Bloodnok, etc.—that he can never be totally trusted. He enchants us and baffles us, and his endless re-creations also implicitly criticise the rest of us for being rigid and conventional, for being stuck with who we are. And this is how Quilty mortifies Humbert: he mocks the complacency of his self-estimation and forces him to reflect upon his own vileness and falseness.

It is apt, therefore, in a parodic way, that Quilty next appears as a policeman—as a guardian of law and order he cuts a devilish figure. The cop's apparently innocuous chatter, which drones on, like muzak in a lift, is full of innuendo and taunts: 'I enjoy judo. The pain. I lie there in pain, but I sort of love it. I lie there hovering between consciousness and unconsciousness. It's really the greatest.'

Humbert puts up with the smirching, and does his utmost to be civil, because he is wary of being arrested, his perversions exposed. He knows sooner or later he will be disbelieved—and Quilty knows he has this fear, and pumps him further for information. Humbert, not to appear rude, starts to vouchsafe one or two things about himself, such as Charlotte's recent death, to which Quilty responds: 'Gee, fancy, gee, a normal guy's wife having an accident, gee... Gee, I keep getting carried away, me being so normal and everything...'

When Sellers, fiddling with his spectacles, faces away from Mason, and leans over the balcony towards us, his whole boxer's body is made ogreish by the shadow. The contrast between the bulk and the benumbing feminine singsong which pours from his lips adds to the grotesquerie—for Quilty's ungainly monologues more than comment on Humbert's thoughts; they *are* his thoughts. They are his hysteria breaking out. 'Are you with someone?' Humbert eventually struggles to say, desperate to be polite and to withdraw. 'I'm not with someone,' says Quilty, in a line to give us the shivers. 'I'm with you.'

◆ ◆ ◆

When Humbert comes to rest after this trans-American voyage, it is to teach at Beardsley (as in Aubrey) College. (The name is a joke, like Camp Climax for girls was a joke.) He and his child-mistress rent an old dark property, and the more he complains about untidiness and cooking, the faster the romance withers: 'You just want to keep me locked up with you in this filthy house,' she shouts, with complete justification. Humbert won't let her mix with her classmates and speaking to boys is forbidden. Under the guise of an autocratic father he is getting to be the insanely jealous lover, the girl is getting shrewish (i.e. like Charlotte) and it is not long before the campus psychiatrist, Dr Zempf, pays a call. Lolita is starting to behave oddly, he says. Does she know the facts of life? The curves of her body are beginning to attract the interest of young chaps at her school, but she is not responding. Her boredom with sex is not right. 'She is suffering from acute repression of the natural instincts.'

The Freudian gobbledygook, like the speech about martial arts and normality/abnormality ('Gee, I wish I had a lovely tall pretty small daughter like that') glistens with sarcasm; again, however, Humbert does his best to hear his visitor out respectfully. The prying policeman seemed to know more than he let on; so does the psychiatrist. Humbert is so relieved not to be charged with statutory rape and unlawful sexual intercourse on the spot, and hoping to allay Zempf's threat 'to investigate thoroughly ze home situation,' he agrees to allow Lolita to take part in the end of term play, which happens to be a production by Clare Quilty… The demon is closing in—and there he is again, in person, taking photographs of the satyrs and shepherdesses from the wings…

He is not seen thereafter. Paradoxically, his presence is the more spooky and intensely felt for this absence. Humbert decides to make a run for it from Beardsley, and then Lolita herself is spirited away, making Humbert's deepest fears come true: the graceful and baleful rival has won. We flash-forward a few years. Lolita is tracked down, married and living in poverty as Mrs Richard F. Schiller. Bespectacled and drab, she is no longer the nymphet. Humbert can't decide whether to kill her or bestow money on her and try and forget her. ('I was weeping again,' Nabokov has him say, 'drunk on the impossible past.') What he does is to inquire: 'Who was Clare Quilty?' 'Why,' says the girl, amazed he hadn't known, 'all of them, of course.' At that moment Humbert knows Quilty must be killed—executed. 'He wasn't a normal person,' Lolita continues, not realising the effect her words are having, 'he was a genius. I guess he was the only guy I was ever really crazy about…' Quilty is her lost love; she is Humbert's. In *Lolita* the characters are dispirited by romance.

◆ ◆ ◆

Like Quilty, Sellers was not normal; and his genius, too, lay in being able to produce any one of a thousand different convincing faces or voices from up his magician's sleeve. But was it really *genius*? 'Peter could be every living, breathing thing,' said Milligan, who once stated that Sellers was more than a genius—he was a circus freak, or sideshow, or psychiatric specimen. Pressed as to what exactly he meant by this, Milligan continued: 'Peter had such a large area of unexplored emotionalism within him, in which he could drown. He's always on the edge of ferment, of tears, of hysteria. The actual business of living made him afraid...'

Hence the recourse to magnificent, limitless dissembling. It is important to see that this is not the same as saying that Sellers was an impersonator, and that was that; nor was it simply the case that, having found Quilty and Strangelove, he himself then retreated behind them. 'Many people claimed he hid behind the characters he portrayed on the screen. That was absolute rubbish,' said Lynne Frederick soon after her husband's funeral. 'Peter regarded those kind of remarks as a big joke'—despite the fact he had laboured long to palm journalists off with them. The truth is that Sellers was not only a chameleon, he was 'an *emotional* chameleon,' as Milligan explained to me; his rôles were coloured by his own rage and disingenuousness, and so it is no wonder that he affected to dissociate himself from them. How could he admit, whilst he was alive, that the will, energy, and desires of his characters spilled over from, and revealed, his individual consciousness and lack of inhibition?

This is especially the case with the Kubrick films, because what might have begun with mimicry was let loose by improvisation, as Sellers once explained: 'While we were making [*Lolita*] with Stanley Kubrick...we did something interesting. If a scene didn't seem quite right, we'd read it from the script and pick out the parts which went best. Then we'd sit round a table with a tape recorder and ad-lib on the lines of the passages we'd chosen; in that way we'd get perfectly natural dialogue which could then be scripted and used. It's the spontaneous to-and-fro, waiting to hear what the other person says; no matter how good an actor is, he can't get that effect if the dialogue isn't right.'

In terms of *Lolita*, though, it was not *dialogue* which was perfected but *monologue*; Kubrick purposefully encouraged Sellers to go too far, so that the actor's bamboozling of Mason, Winters, etc., represented Quilty, the character's, spell-bindings. 'I could never connect with him,' Winters has said of Sellers, 'and whenever I complained to Kubrick...he would agree with me. But he didn't change [Sellers'] performance, and this very frustration that I had in real life was what was so sad and funny about Charlotte. I never felt anyone was listening to me when I talked...I didn't understand the lonely quality it gave me until I saw the film.'

Quilty is the great solipsist—or egotist, if you want to put it no higher. But where have we heard all this stuff about improvisation and tape recorders before? Why, at Grafton's during the Sound Mirror days. ('When we used to meet we all got high,' said Milligan looking back in August 1980, 'but not on drink. It was the sheer adrenaline that did it—the fun of being together.') Kubrick had given Sellers back the psychological atmosphere of 'The Goon Show'. He steered him toward making full use of his imaginative faculty—and Sellers, with gusto and assurance, leapt into his own unconfined inner-labyrinth, a place full of sunshiny and snowy memories; a silver-grey grotto of neuroses, crammed with dream-visions and ghosts. But Sellers' imagination was not fixed, like wax flowers under a bell jar. It was aggregating and modifying. In the workings of his mind, Sellers re-shaped, fused, and blended the patterns of his life and temper; the result of this free activity (as Kubrick himself has said) was that 'he could certainly play any conventional rôle, but his real genius lay in embodying over-the-top, larger-than-life characters and pulling moments of pure comedy out of them. It's true that he could start first from the voice, but he achieved far more than vocal authenticity and dexterity. He was also the only actor that I ever knew who could really improvise… Sellers… even if he wasn't on form, after a time fell into the spirit of a character and just took off—it was miraculous. A good part of Dr. Strangelove came from his inspiration. I filmed him with many cameras, never less than three, so that I lost nothing.'

◆ ◆ ◆

Sellers' tragedy is that, such was the pitch of his hypersensitivity, fact and fiction intermingled. What he dreamt up about people he proceeded to believe was real. We know that from his reactions to the Loren business. On the other hand, there came a time—worse, in many ways, than when he was maniacal—when his imagination failed to be excited and he became sullen and lethargic; his hypersensitivity was replaced by—or exposed as—touchiness and vanity. Such was the case on *Casino Royale*. Peter Evans, who had watched the disaster unfold, told me: 'The genesis of the failure of *Casino Royale* is in *What's New, Pussycat?* In the latter, they gave Sellers his head, allowing him to ad-lib and mess about with O'Toole. There was a lot of spontaneous so-called creation on the set, and they got away with it (to Woody Allen's dismay). *Casino Royale* was not intended to be free-wheeling, but… what Peter wanted he got, and that's when it started to go badly wrong. It was a very big example of how dangerously crazy Peter could be. He completely and utterly destroyed that movie. People were sacked, scripts were abandoned… Columbia… [was] floundering, and yet because it would have been too expensive to close the picture down, they parted with more and more money. Peter was coming into the studio and having wonderful ideas, and they'd be building the sets in the afternoon; the next morning he'd come in, and they'd have dressed the set, and he'd have changed his mind—he didn't want to do that scene anymore. And Charlie [Feldman] believed Peter's genius could pull it together.'

It didn't—and Sellers kept plummeting. Because he came increasingly to rely on his unique slant and intuitions, his conception of a rôle had to come together all at once or he'd panic. Permanently anxious about what was happening to him, his only reality—his only existence—was to be found in what automatically bubbled up from his lower depths. And there started not to be anything there—the quality of his creative imagination deteriorated. One of the saddest, maddest exemplifications of this happened during *The Revenge of the Pink Panther*. The idea was for Clouseau and Cato to enter a night club, disguised in zoot suits and Afro dreadlocks. 'Peter,' says Blake Edwards, 'was then supposed to come out with a lot of what Clouseau thought was very hip black street lingo and, of course, screw it all up. Peter absolutely couldn't *get* it. That made him very angry and resulted in a very unpleasant day on the set. About two o'clock in the morning, though, Peter telephoned me, as was his wont, to say, "Don't worry about tomorrow... I've talked to God, and he told me how to do it."... The next morning, he came in and wanted to do the scene immediately... Peter made his entrance at the top of some stairs—and it was perfectly obvious that he didn't have *anything* planned. He just believed that by some miracle he'd do something brilliant, but what he did was awful. Afterwards, I said, "Do me a favour, Peter. In future, tell God to stay out of show business." I did it as a joke, but it didn't work. Peter drifted off into such a depressed, morose state that you could hardly hear him when he performed, and his whole physical being seemed to wither. We had to cut the entire sequence and replace it with a new one... in which we used a double. It was very sad.'

It was bad enough, towards the end, when directors like Richard Quine and Piers Haggard tried to sort him out in advance by asking him to rehearse. Sellers, who got so that he couldn't step into the same performance twice, could not repeat material. Everything had to be accomplished in one take. He was completely desaturated. As Jeremy Kemp (who played Duke Michael) told me: 'I'm afraid that by the time we came to make *The Prisoner of Zenda* he'd *gone*, really. He had a very poor view of the director, Richard Quine, a man who had not made a film for several years— but this was an excuse. Sellers was simply not functioning... It wasn't laziness—he was ill, physically and mentally. His mind... was disintegrating. He was going insane... There were many delays. I was thoroughly aware that all was not well. Peter

Off his head in more than a manner of speaking: in Vienna for *The Prisoner of Zenda* (1978)

Author Collection (Univeral City Studieos Inc.)

came over to a group of us by the caravans and said "How terrible that Quine has kept you waiting. I'll talk to him about this, the bloody useless article." But the delays were all caused by none other than Sellers. Lionel Jeffries, in particular, was very upset and concerned that such a once great talent had lost all sense and control.'

Simon Williams, who reminded me that *Being There*, with its hollow man, had intervened between his first experience with Sellers on *The Prisoner of Zenda* and his second on *The Fiendish Plot of Dr Fu Manchu*, said that 'there were days when we had to pretend to corpse. One of Peter's great pleasures in life was giggling— so we'd not only have to act in a scene, but act breaking up, just to prove to him that the old magic was there, which it wasn't. A very unreal experience.'

The Prisoner of Zenda, with a script by Dick Clements and Ian la Frenais, lost momentum quickly. 'The Frewin character,' says Williams, 'became lugubrious. Maybe Peter was playing about with how to portray Chance? Find a heavy pathos? I don't know, but something was going on in him. And the scenes as Prince Rudi in the casino—there were endless delays, because he wouldn't have green within a hundred miles. The set was re-dressed and re-dressed ... On another occasion he suddenly said "This is not funny, it's boring. It has lost everything"—and he ordered everybody to have Vitamin B12 injections. He made people do this a few times. He said it would perk them up. Or he found a tape called *The Legend of Gunga Din*, which is where the idea for *The Party* came from. Galloping, with pauses and gunfire, then it carries on; cannons and machine gun fire; more pauses, and then the galloping starts up again—and so on and on and on. Sellers had Quine play this tape in the studio. We all got bored with it, but Peter would do the full crying-with-laughter, wiping-tears-from-his-eyes routine. He had to have these ways of getting in the mood. He had to feel funny to act funny ...'

But how could he, with his presumably baroque apparitions of standing before the mouth of an open sepulchre, and the hooded skeleton there pointing him down into the darkness? 'He'd often talk of his interest in being frozen when he died,' continued Williams, 'and he was frightened of death. He told me about the experience of soaring above himself, when he had a heart attack, and he'd be watching the doctors jumping on his chest, wondering what they fuck they were doing. When he was Fu Manchu, he gradually got to be quite godlike and immobile ...'— as if all the conduits of his blood were iced up; and with his stringy white Oriental beard, this grained face of his was hid in sap-consuming winter's drizzled snow.

It was with an intensified stillness—an effigy—that Haggard had to contend:

> It became clear that Peter didn't know what he wanted, except to disagree vehemently with the suggestions of people he'd decided to take against. Which was everybody. Problems in the script were never solved. I left new pages at his hotel, but he refused to collaborate with me over them; 'What shall we do here?' I'd ask, referring to various scenes—but if the experience of preparing the film was misery, shooting it was worse ... Sellers wasn't actually available for work of any description—he'd gone to London, for advice on his impotence, and hadn't returned. We were all expected to swallow this. There was a struggle about Fu's eyes. In the script, Peter had written 'yellow eyes' and he said 'I'll wear contact lenses.' ... We did some tests, and suddenly during shooting he said 'I don't want to do it like that any more.'

Like an idiot, I kept waiting for the thunder clouds to pass and tried to find ways of being positive...He didn't seem to want to try—and this seemed to me very unusual, not to say tragic, behaviour. It was as if he wouldn't allow any artfulness—from anybody. The problem...was that his sense of timing had gone. He was slow and whispery, and taking too long...No adroit editing in the world could pull this together. So I was not succeeding in directing him—there was no performance there to shape...

We carried on—but...it was never really any good, and I was clearly not in the process of making a good film. I'd want to try something out. He'd say 'I don't think so.'...He slowed right up, and wasn't always available. Nobody censured him. The belief back in Hollywood was: 'We have a Peter Sellers film shooting in Paris. We're bound to get something out of it.'

I never saw him socially. He never allowed me to have a relationship with him. I soldiered on and shot nearly everything, and actually there's some good stuff which Sellers had destroyed when he had me sacked...Anyway, we had eight or nine days left, but decided to shut down over Christmas. Peter and Mike Medavoy wanted to look at all the rough-cut film, and...after that session, Peter said he didn't think he could work with me anymore. This was after four months, with only a little bit to go...He realised he'd not been doing well—and I'd completely failed to get a performance out of him. Normally, you find ways of working with people—but he was unable and unwilling to do this. So I was fired from the picture. He had Lynne Frederick brought in as producer, and it was somehow edited and finished off and released after he'd died. I didn't supervise the cutting. The stuff he shot—for I did see a rough cut: Orion wanted my comments—was a bit silly. He had a lot of footage where he is swooning in Helen Mirren's bosom. He also re-shot the scene in the doctor's surgery, where Sir Nules Thudd is strapped down and examined for 'elephants on the knees'; and I saw a memo—'Piers's version of this much funnier than Peter's'. The sadness is in considering how gifted he was, and how much mental disturbance and unhappiness there now was, at the end.

◆ ◆ ◆

The Fiendish Plot of Dr Fu Manchu is no worse than *The Pink Panther Strikes Again* or *The Revenge of the Pink Panther*—it is rather superior, actually, what with Alex Trauner's magnificent sets: Chinatown, opium dens, dragons, abundant baskets of orchids, a Himalayan palace, underground laboratories. As Haggard suggested, however, no editor could salvage a coherent film from the spools as exposed at the Studios de Boulogne, Paris, the crack cinematography and the scenery notwithstanding. The Edwardian interiors, with their candelabra, mirrors, marble busts, and carved ceilings, have a French fuss; Fu's headquarters has a vast, polished, red, blue, and yellow mosaic floor—but what of it, when Fu's long black fingernails come and go from shot to shot; when references are made to George V's equerry, whose scene (with Eric Idle) has been excised; when the thugs are all suddenly bandaged and bruised, and we have no idea why; when the Fu of the Tower of London scene is such an obvious double, we wonder if this is intended as part of the plot; when Sellers' own voice, barely disguised, issues forth from dubbed minor characters...? And so on and on. Despite the background opulence, the overall effect gets to be rather shoddy.

The interest of the film, therefore—over and above its being Sellers' termi-

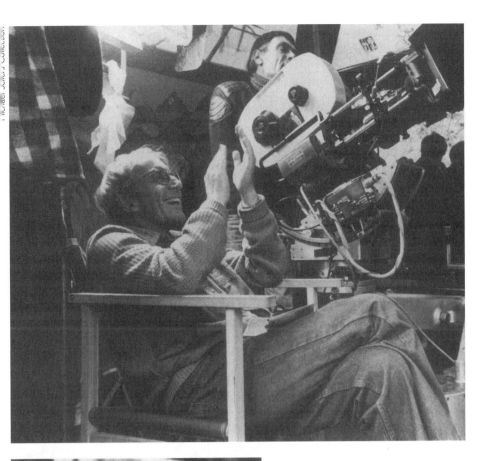

(Top) Directing in Paris—having sacked
Piers Haggard (1980)

(Bottom) Nayland Smith in *The Fiendish
Plot of Dr. Fu Manchu* (1980)

nus—must lie in something other than its execution, and so it proves. *The Fiend-ish Plot of Dr Fu Manchu* is a summary—virtually an anthology—of Sellers' life and work. It was as if, by alluding to all his other films and experiences, he hoped he could agitate, stir up, his imagination and prove that his wasting lamps had yet some fading glimmer left. (It was like trying to give emergency treatment to stimulate a stopped heart.) Thus, David Tomlinson has been brought in from *Up the Creek* and John Le Mesurier from just about everything; Steve Franken was the waiter in *The Party*; Simon Williams reminded Sellers of Ian Carmichael; Clive Dunn is a beefeater, as he had been in Michael Bentine's 'It's A Square World' on television, in which he had also played Fu Manchu, setting sail in a war-junk up the Thames to bombard the Houses of Parliament with cannon fire, 'and Peter must have remembered this'; and Burt Kwouk, renowned as Clouseau's houseboy, makes a brief appearance as Fu's servant ('Your face is familiar').

David Lodge was summoned to play a policeman—the desk sergeant he had been in *After the Fox* and *The Naked Truth*. ('Who wouldn't have accepted the invitation for an all expenses trip to Paris?' he said to me jokingly.) He had to organise an identification parade, and Helen Mirren, disguised as Queen Mary, sailed in to examine the line-up. The entire sequence, lasting approximately seven or eight minutes, was later discarded, as were whatever contributions John Antrobus had made to the screenplay. Sellers, who was too proud and jealous to allow himself to go cap-in-hand to Milligan, tried to do the next best thing—and he hired the co-writer of *The Bedsitting Room*. (Antrobus also contributed to the script of *Wrong Arm of the Law*.) He spent a long time at the studio, only to be informed, on June 25, 1980, that he was to be denied any credit. 'In my opinion,' Sellers told him, 'it is to your advantage not to have your name on the picture. Because of the dreadful cutting insisted on by Orion, I have now removed my name from the film—other than my acting credit, which I'd also have removed if it had been possible. I am deeply disappointed with their final version which bears very little relationship to what I had visualised and worked towards.'

It was typical of Sellers to blame others for chaos he'd created. For the record, I asked the editor, Russell Lloyd, for his opinion of the film, and he said: 'In the cutting room we had a good relationship. Peter listened. But he was very intolerant with... producers or directors, and he'd made life *very* difficult for Piers. However, as I cut the picture, it was clear that Piers had a great eye for the photographic. We used most of what Piers had shot—except for an elaborate theatre scene, which Peter decided was too farcical, too contrived. He wanted everything to look natural, and for the humour to come from that... He was very ill during shooting. The doctor would say "He'll be well enough by Thursday"—when really he needed until Monday, but he kept on going...'

There are citations, even, to cardiology in the film. Indeed, Fu has to devise his fiendish plots because his elixir vitae—his supply of heart drops—has run out. (Kwouk's character smashed the last bottle of this specific when his sleeve was ignited by birthday cake candles.) Periodically, and in the absence of medication, Fu experiences breathlessness and faintness, and he fends off unconsciousness, and gets his blood circulating, by zapping himself in an electric chair: 'It might keep me going a few days longer,' he says. Sellers felt the same way about his pacemaker, which was implanted and replaced three times in 1977 alone. It was his least frivolous gadget. The pulse generator, containing batteries and electronic circuitry, was employed to treat the heart block which lingered from his acute myocardial infarction—his heart attack of 1964. The exacerbation of his angina was a sign of a worsening condition and Sellers' death resulted from blood pressure so low it dropped off the scale. When Fu receives intensive boosters, therefore, by putting his fingers in light sockets and by standing between a pair of fizzing, spitting Dr Frankenstein-sized AC-DC transformers, it is not really a gag; it is a straightforward dramatisation of cardiopulmonary resuscitation.

Sellers showed more jocosity the following Spring—in April 1980 (just prior to his departure for Cannes)—when he was shooting a television commercial in Ireland. He was pedalling an old bicycle and was hit by severe chest pains. He spent six days in the coronary unit at St Vincent's Hospital, Dublin, being looked after by nuns. Joe McGrath, who was directing the million-pound ad for Barclays Bank, went to see him, thinking he could be of service. 'Can I do anything for you, Peter? Make some telephone calls, or whatever?' The waxen-faced Sellers, lying on his bed, near to death, said: 'Yes, go over to my briefcase. Inside you will find a pair of gold Gucci jump-leads. Put one end on your heart and one on mine, and give me a start, will you?'

One is reminded of the lines in *Love's Labour's Lost*:

> To move wild laughter in the throat of death!
> It cannot be; it is impossible:
> Mirth cannot move a soul in agony…

—as Sellers discovered. Though he filled *The Fiendish Plot of Dr Fu Manchu* with purloined gags which had amused him, or with personal references which meant something to him, and all the music hall nostalgia ('the music hall has been one of my pursuits and delights since I was a young man,' says Fu, perking up): despite these spindly props and talismans, Sellers was aching for air, medically and metaphorically. And so of course his forlornest hope was that he'd be oxygenated by 'The Goon Show'—'Yes, it's like the early "Goon Show",' he freely confessed of his ambition for the film. 'It has all the comedy of the ridiculous.'

'The Goon Show', for all its tangents and flim-flam, used to succeed best when there was an underlying storyline. Episodes may have given an impression of being slapped together by a pack of kindergartners, but the material had been carefully composed and run-through beforehand; and Sellers, sulky even in those days, would always abide by producers' decisions. (Was he storing up resentments for later life?) In his dealings with Pat Newman or Peter Eton, there was a definite tension—Sellers' unruliness was never very far off—yet when he made 'The Goon Show' (or films with the Boultings or Kubrick) he was still a professional and (grudgingly) one of a team, and that is why the recordings may still be listened to (and the early films watched) with pleasure. Sellers was not—as so often later—spoiling things for everybody (himself included) *on purpose*.

Two decades after 'The Goon Show' had ended, his ambition had carried him far beyond crappy things like co-operation or conceding points. (There are plenty of flunkies, lawyers, and tycoons to back up a film star if he wants to be a bully.) If ever challenged, the ghost of Daniel Mendoza would rise and walk, and Sellers would get sickeningly self-righteous: 'A lot of people believe or feel that if you get into an argument on the set with them, they are to go stark raving bloody mad for some reason... I've had that [the luck to work with great directors]... on two or three occasions. The rest of the time it has been a bit ropey. But it won't be in the future, because... whatever I have... I'm going to put it up there... and *do it*. That's the way I feel about it right now anyway.'

Translation: nobody was going to stop him from doing exactly as he and he alone wanted; and, indeed, the first thing to go when he was a star was his fragile self-control (a faculty allied to judgement and conscience, which Sellers never had). And so, if Goonishness fizzles in *The Fiendish Plot of Dr Fu Manchu* because Sellers couldn't see that the all-important fifties post-war context—in which it had flourished, and of which it had been so much a part—had disappeared, is there any other incongruity, or autobiography, which he imposes on the film and which, likewise, won't flutter into life?

Yes: Sellers abandons the entire concept of Fu's machinations, which may have been amusing and, throwing away what the film is meant to be about, fills the space with the spirit of romance—all those dread seduction scenes with Helen Mirren, which Haggard mentioned seeing. Decrepit as he (and Fu) was, Sellers still had to inflict his supposed irresistibility on his audiences. (Fu's long hair could be Robert Danvers' grey locks in need of a trim, and his boudoir has a big circular bed, like the one at the centre of the set in *There's a Girl in My Soup*—which, in its turn, with its automatic curtains and mirrors, was based on the Hampstead penthouse.)

◆◆◆

It makes no sense, and serves no purpose, in the film itself, when Alice Rage, saxophone-playing policewoman and Queen Mary impersonator, goes over to the enemy side (Fu has her kidnapped, and when she is unbundled in his den she doesn't object). Mirren tried to explain her character's motivation by saying: 'There is a scene in which Fu is ageing fast, and I promise to do everything in my power to make Fu young—or at least *feel* young. The thought kept flashing through my mind, "Am I *really* saying these things?" But I *was*, and the feeling was rather good.' Gerontophilia like this replaces Sax Rohmer's fondness for poisonous orchids, scorpions, and clockwork tarantulas. Sellers, having rid the project of Haggard and of any residual controlling intelligence, decided that he wanted to be 'doing something outrageous in the name of Fu'—and what this meant, in effect, now that he commanded an entire film crew and could act out his mad impulses, was allowing himself to become a lover of little girls. Fu's voice grows dark and chocolatey, owing to his 'extraordinary sex-appeal. After all, if you've devoted 150 years to devilish cunning, you're bound to get good at it,' said the star.

The way Fu lopes around his apartment, inspecting the drugged chalice and the fragrant bath oils, recalls Danvers' half-crouch, half-run, as he checked appurtenances like fresh bed linen and the champagne bucket. The compulsive or would-be skirt-chaser, however, whether John Lewis, General Fitzjohn, Clare Quilty, Henry Orient, Fritz Fassbender, Evelyn Tremble, Juan Bautista, Harold Fine, Mr Hoffman, or the womanising late-period Clouseau (whose fervour is checked by knotted belts and ties) is always an aspect of Sellers himself—who once said: 'I don't think it's possible to have women friends. I don't believe in platonic friendship with women. Sooner or later something springs out of it.' And who also said, when reference was made to his weight loss: 'That was in an attempt to become more attractive to women, I suppose, and to be able to wear more attractive clothing. But it is difficult—I adore chocolate and good food.'

Fu doesn't list the eating of human flesh amongst his diabolisms, though it would not be out of place. *Hoffman*, in which digestion equals sex, is full of slurping, cooking, feeding imagery. ('Women are always hungry. Fallopian tubes with teeth,' is one of Ernest Gebler's witticisms. 'A man is excited by splendid breasts, Miss Smith. He gets an instinctive feeling of well-being, of food in the offing', is another.) On a rare foray beyond the fortress of the flat, the two characters visit the Harrods Food Hall, and Miss Smith, as Hoffman's sacrificial victim, is posed beneath mutton carcasses and serried ranks of feathery pheasants and grouse.

The gastronomy metaphor of *There's a Girl in My Soup* would seem more playful by comparison—light and airy like a soufflé, after *Hoffman*'s bloody innerorgans, nutty gizzards, liver slices, and fried hencod's roes. But, in fact, the underlying philosophy, that women are kitchen utensils, or platters to be scoffed and then spat out, is common to both films—they are misogynistic, and surely not only because, two decades later, we are more enlightened about feminism and justice for all. Hoffman lacks confidence; he is nervous of what will happen 'if the prisoner within me has escaped'. Danvers, by contrast, has nonchalance to burn—but the two men intend gorging on females, and the sweetmeats they capture don't really mind.

In *Lolita*, when James Mason mounts Shelley Winters, he stares hard at a photograph of Sue Lyon on the bedside table; in *There's a Girl in My Soup*, when Danvers squirms on top of Gabrielle Drake, his eyes stray to the television screen, where his own smarmy face is on, telling housewives the recipes for banana splits and skewered chicken. The real Danvers then turns back to the girl and he says 'You have a delicious flavour ...' If he is Narcissus, the TV is his pool. When he is presenting his programme he wears velvet coats and curled, Roman-consul hair—he affects effeminacy; in the privacy of his own bathroom, however, we have the chance to corroborate Britt Ekland's statement: 'Sellers' hairy-cladded chest did much to perpetuate the argument of mankind's evolution from the gorilla.' In the last shot of the film, he is slapping cologne on his chops when he catches sight of himself in a mirror and murmurs 'My God, but you're lovely!'—his catchphrase. Hoffman would seem to believe the opposite of this: 'A man's face doesn't matter all that much,' he says plaintively. (It is a line Charles Laughton would have relished up in his bell tower.) In fact, he is equally vain; it is simply that his shames and emotional problems are on show. Danvers is superficial, the public image; Hoffman is the man behind the mask.

Both facets are wrought into *The Fiendish Plot of Dr Fu Manchu*—Sellers tried to give the Oriental mastermind a comic neuroticism. Sax Rohmer meant him to be the supremely confident 'Lord of the Fires'; Sellers had the possibly excellent (and anyway undeveloped) idea of making him not unlike Clouseau—the wicked criminal who, for all his posturing, is a flop. Fu could have joined Old Sam, the Shakespearean music hall artiste who is now only a busker; or Fred Kite, Mr Martin, Morganhall, etc. in Sellers' gallery of dolorous clowns. Instead of which, there are these Fu/Alice Rage scenes, which are lewd—a bit gross—and go right back to the old days of *The Millionairess*. 'He once said to me,' says Joe McGrath, 'that he'd reached a stage in his career where he could have been Cary Grant for the rest of his life. After *There's a Girl in My Soup*, he said "They are paying me a lot of money just to be Cary Grant..."'

As far as Sellers was concerned, Cary Grant never had to make any effort to do anything; he merely had to turn up—he had no ugliness to overcome. 'I'm not a star,' Sellers complained a thousand times, 'I'm a character actor. The character actor must tailor his talent to the parts that are offered. If I were a leading man, a tall good-looking sort of chap, you know, a chap who has a way with him, who gets parts tailored for his personality, like Cary Grant, then I could regard myself as a star. I'm not a star because [*altogether now*] I have no personality of my own.'

You have only to see the sogginess of Sellers the seducer to appreciate the ruinousness of his Cary Grant-style aspirations. As a great screen lover Sellers does not ring true. In *Casino Royale*, for example, he is slim, lit carefully, made up with lip gloss and a hint of mascara, but he is also pallid and very, very dull. (When everything stops for Sellers and a co-star to get romantic, it has all the joyfulness of those wretched Nelson Eddy-Jeanette MacDonald duets.) What Sellers enjoyed, I think, and thus had no compunction about pouring on to the screen, was his playboy affluence—a rôle he maintained in reality with his penthouse pads, mews cottages, hotel suites, and private jets. (He wanted to be glamorous—couldn't he see that this turned him not into Cary Grant but Clare Quilty?) In 1962, when at his peak as an actor, he said that if he ever played James Bond he'd satirise the machismo: 'I should like to make a comic film from one of the Fleming books...Bond ought to be not one of those mammoth characters, like Mr Universe, but some great flabby type...' Five years later, when just such a project was meant to come about, Sellers, thinner, vainer, married to Britt, and determined to make us understand that he now thought very well of himself indeed, had quite forgotten his original scheme. He didn't want to parody urbanity, he wanted to be regarded as urbane—and his ordering of *forty-five* changes of costume for himself for *Casino Royale* is a sign (or symptom) of his rampaging pompousness and swank. (The tailor, Douglas Heyward, invoiced the film company, which refused to pay, arguing that the clothes had not been authorised. When Heyward complained, Sellers said: 'That will teach you never to make anything without a contract.')

To be Cary Grant requires more than immaculate threads and an excellent set of manners; you need assurance and you need to be able to tantalise, and Sellers is at his worst when he tries this on, without irony, without self-mockery. As a romantic he has no warmth—and so he suddenly has no depth. One of the paradoxes of Sellers is that when he was hired to play a caricature, he was unpredictable, resilient, full of humanity and/or scoundrelism. Deciding, in the sixties, to idealise himself and be expensive-looking—both in art and life—he robbed himself of his wit. As a cartoon, he'd found recesses, juice; as the man about town he was mediocre and flat. He'd got rid of his soul.

◆ ◆ ◆

The only beneficial effect of Cary Grant on Sellers that I can see is that he encouraged him to quit, if not heart attacks, then smoking: 'C. G., Cary Grant, did that for me. He said: "I don't know why you smoke, my darling. You're all you've got." He always called me that. That's my real name. My Darling Peter Sellers.'

Grant did well to appeal to Sellers' ego—that, unique unto himself, he must preserve himself; on the other hand, that Sellers was only Sellers, and that he did not actually double, split up, scatter, and divide off simultaneously into new and multiple selves—this, the fact of his mortality, was one of his great disappointments. He was all there was, all he had to go on. 'Honestly, I don't really know what I'd have done without films,' he confessed—without a medium to make him unreal. 'It's true,' his son Michael told me 'that his characters were much more full of life than he ever was. Far more interesting than he was as a person, as an individual.' And Sellers himself once said that, as an actor, he left a copy of himself at home— the version he saw in the mirror, who was ageing and ordinary: 'There are many men like me,' he wailed, 'some of us sit in Tubes [the subway], some are faceless...' Whereas the Sellers who flamed into being at the studios, by contrast, after a short journey in a chauffeur-driven limousine, was full of eagerness and unfading.

The concept is vaguely vampirical—Sellers in his coffin or frozen in his tomb all day whilst a supernatural emanation is off regenerating and having a good time. It is also inaccurate. The point about Sellers, before his vaingloriousness got in the way, was that he could give a character poignancy and a degree of nobility not by ignoring dishevelment and the effects of growing old, but by drawing on just these feelings and observations. Sellers raised the profile of nondescripts. They had quirks, oddities. But by the time of *Hoffman*, say, a definite, contemptuous edge—a streak of bitterness—had come to the surface. (He'd become inhuman.) He used to play old when he was young, and he was happier in those rôles; and by wanting to look twenty-five when he was middle-aged he was simply continuing the trend of living his life back to front.

Sellers' main characters are lonely—or loners. They are entirely themselves. It is impossible to imagine Dr Strangelove, for example, as having any family or progenitors. (He sprang from a nuclear accident, similar to the airborne bacilli which created Lionel Meadows.) Hrundi Bakshi, in *The Party*, is self-sufficient (that's why the flirtatiousness with Michele seems so tacked on); Inspector Clouseau is in a world of his own (the assistant he's saddled with, Hercule, in *A*

Michael Sellers Collection

Peter Medak

Peter Medak

(Top) Homage to the Music Hall: Old Sam in *The Optimists of Nine Elms* (1973)

(Middle) Insanity on Cyprus (a): Sellers snoozes alongside Peter Boyle. Peter Medak shakes a stick (1973)

(Bottom) Insanity on Cyprus (b): Milligan and Peter Medak attend to the script whilst Sellers sulks

Shot in the Dark, was a mistake not repeated); and who can forget Dr Pratt, in *The Wrong Box*, wreathed in cats and fantasies? If the Sellers and Loren relationship worked in *The Millionairess* then it might have had something to do with the way Dr Kabir rejects Epifania. The film is not clouded or sentimental. Kabir is left to his solitude, as Topaze is (the threatened romances with Nadia Gray and Billie Whitelaw do not take place), or as Old Sam is, in *The Optimists of Nine Elms*.

In the latter film, dressed in a turban and a coloured coat with crested moons and frilly sleeves, Sellers is a dream-figure out of Dickens. The London locations (as photographed by Larry Pizer) are Dickens'*—the poisonous skies, the pipes and sparks of the steelworks, the teetering bridges and catwalks, the bonfires along the river's edge, the dust carts and garbage-laden barges, the fences, chimneys, weed-clogged railway tracks, and the fog; and the music, by Lionel Bart, is hurdy-gurdy music hall, like from *Oliver!* 'Peter first saw the final cut one Saturday morning when he was still freshly in love with Liza Minnelli. They both loved it,' says Anthony Simmons. 'At that stage the film only had a rough piano score built out of a few Lionel Bart songs … Later, when … orchestrated and dubbed, the film changed. We never got back to the raw emotion of a single old piano.' But most of all Sellers is Dickensian because nothing is concealed. The huge nose, the teeth, the little jig of a walk, the outlandish costumes (Sam is a dilapidated dandy for whom all-the-world's-a-stage) are fantastic and exaggerated—but what is being exaggerated (or enhanced) is the truth of the character's nature.

His hovel (which he might have inherited from Fagin, along with the flapping coat) is like a theatrical warehouse, with scrapbooks of press clippings, yellowing and disintegrating posters (advertising THE HALL FAMILY & LITTLE SAMMY), and a lot of Sellers' own past seems to be stored here: the Dan Leno-ish little rhymes and sayings; the Russian dirges and balalaika, from Ma Ray's shows; the banjo playing and Formby songs which Sellers had learned from Bill; the wardrobes of Pierrot suits, ruffs, and parasols, which Peg was once mistress of. But beyond the bric-à-brac, there's Sam's fear and mistrust, and his protective brusqueness. The loneliness which comes across in the film (and which, free of self-pitying and sorrowing, is allied to independence) is at the root of Sellers' discontent, and is what made him an actor. As a child (like Little Sammy who grew up into Old Sam) Sellers had been isolated, and his entire career was a means of expressing that isolation. Left in the care of households of aunts and landladies, whilst his parents were away pursuing a different life before audiences and in pubs, he had known abandonment; and when his mother returned, and overdid her affection, he knew the opposite extreme, a possessiveness which was pathetic and horrible. One way and another, the buffetings and experiences boxed him in and made it impossible for him to return love—and what he expected from others was a total, uncritical adoration. As Milligan mused: 'His second wife, Britt Ekland, he married eleven days after he met her—no wonder it didn't last, people said. But he wanted the security his mother had given him, and so naturally he thought it must come through

---

* Sellers', too: 'Makes a very good Grand Marnier soufflé does the chef 'ere,' says Old Sam, as he and the children trundle past the Dorchester.

marriage. He was always trying to replace the security of his mother—and that se-curity was a dream. It bore no relation to the real world, where people are hard. The real world, full of obligations and liabilities, was like a violent attack on his warm, glowing mother-son relationship. It hacked him to pieces.'

◆ ◆ ◆

The deep appeal of *Being There*, with its Little Boy Lost hero, can immedi-ately be understood. Chance isn't shy or mute, or a zombie, he is a child—the child trapped in the big body ('You's always goin' to be a little boy, ain't you?' says Louise the maid). To acquire the novella's film rights, Sellers set about bewitch-ing and bewildering Kosinski. 'It started in 1971 when I was in London,' said the author. 'He left me a message saying C. Gardiner had called. It turned out to be Peter Sellers. For seven-and-a-half years he sent cables [such as "Available my garden or outside it"], letters on special headed paper, and left baffling messages on my answering machine. Gradually we became friends and whenever we met he would do a Chauncey Gardiner act. I gave in finally.'

Sellers, to get what he wanted, serenaded Kosinski as he would a woman (he once sent Britt three consecutive telegrams: I, LOVE, and YOU); it is no surprise to note that, after *Being There* had been wrapped, Sellers saw no need to continue cordiality, and he pissed on the author without stint: 'Jerzy Kosinski wanted the part himself. That's why he wrote it for a young man of Olympian, god-like beauty. I saw Chauncey Gardiner as a plump figure, pallid, unexercised from sitting around watching television. Too old? A lot of people said that. I just told them "You're wrong, I'm right." Hal Ashby managed to bring it off. Jerzy? He has always wanted to be in films. He is now appearing with Warren Beatty. [As Lenin's chum Grigory Yevseyevich Zinovyev in *Reds*.] Huh!' Sellers sensed Kosinski's vanity—and it was similar to his own vanity. It was Kosinski whom Sellers blamed for breaking the sen-sitive news of his surgical tucking and patching: 'I suppose it makes interesting read-ing for some people, but it infuriates me. It isn't true.' (It was, as we know.) Sellers' revenge was idiomatic. He added to his repertoire of party tricks the very Polish Kosinski trying to get his tongue around the very Anglo Saxon sound of 'Fuck off.'*

During the run up to the film, however, he was careful only to be serene. 'I re-member after years of telling me he could play Chance...once, in Malibu, he

---

* Some months after originally writing this page, I came across a description of Kosinski, by Paul Theroux, which is so apt and illuminating I have to quote it:

He seemed a bit paranoid and insecure, and vain in an unexplainable way. One night in Berlin he had gone back to the hotel and put on a type of male make-up, giving his pale Polish complexion an instant tan. What was that all about?

He told me that he was afraid of assassination attempts, of being the object of sin-ister plots. But it was the opposite that he feared—not notoriety. He was afraid of being ignored, not taken seriously; he could not stand being regarded as insignificant, or of his gifts being belittled... He liked power. He wanted to be respectable. When he ceased to be respected—in the end he had actually been mocked for being a lightweight... he killed himself.

The Happy Isles of Oceania (London, 1992), pp. 615ff.

proved it,' said Kosinski. We were walking in a garden at a friend's house and he saw a small tree that was drying out. Dying. He bent stiffly, picked up the hose, and began watering the little tree. Very quietly. Complete contentment on his face. He *was* Chance. Nobody thought Chance was even a *character*, but Peter *knew* that man.'

The rôle was Sellers' melt-down—he put all the nothingness he had into it— and his sense of exclusion, of being impossible to reach, went back a very long way. In 1962, when Anne left, he felt somnambulistic; it was as if he was staring at a void, and that death was at the centre of his life: 'I'm nothing,' he'd say, 'I wasn't baptized. I wasn't Bar Mitzvah'd. I suppose my basic religion is doing unto others as they would do unto me. But I find it all very difficult…' He had no faith ('I'm not comfortable about organised religion'); he had no interest in current affairs ('I have a Victorian outlook'); he had no connection with other people ('I don't like taking part. Becoming part of some large group never does any good'). All he had was his mother. When she cooled, whilst he was making *The Bobo*, in 1967, he went into mourning and never came out: 'I remember when my mother died… even though I have children alive, she was my last close relative. I felt a great feeling of loneliness. I couldn't just pick up the phone and speak to her anymore. I felt that a lot.'

Well, there were the séances, which blighted his marriage to Miranda Quarry ('He spoke to his dead mother… He became very interested in psychic powers and often talked of the "voices" he heard,' she told a journalist); and there was a film to take to his bosom, and which he championed as he had *The Producers*—Hal Ashby's *Harold and Maude*. 'I thought, "Why is *Harold and Maude* playing to such a tiny theatre?" So I got a friend in L.A. to get hold of the distributors, and they didn't want to know, man. I offered to pay Bud Cort and Ruth Gordon's fare to London so we could launch the film properly…'

You don't need a framed psychoanalyst's diploma on the office wall to be able to see that *Harold and Maude*, a black comedy in which a twenty-year-old demented urchin and an eighty-year-old hag make whoopee, was *Peter and Peg*. The actors even resemble Sellers and his mother. Bud Cort, who was a pudgy-faced Peter Pan in the Icarus fantasy, *Brewster McCloud*, is now, having fallen to earth, merely goblinlike. Ruth Gordon, who had won the Oscar as a witch next door in *Rosemary's Baby*, is a thin painted bird—her flowery clothes and ponchos are her plumage. (But she's still a bad fairy.)

Sentimental and silly, freakish and charming—*Harold and Maude*, in which the hero finds a mother and a lover, was destined to appeal to Sellers' incestuous fantasies, and it duly and 'absolutely blew me out… So a few weeks or months later, when I read *Being There*, I thought, "Well, the guy to do this is Hal Ashby." I sent him the book with a note saying, "Need to see you, read this." He saw everything it had to say. We then started our quest [for backing and Kosinski's consent]… It was particularly difficult, yet I was going back to the old days, away from these Clouseau things I was doing—which are fine for what they are, but I found I was getting in a bit of a rut. I just wanted to break there, desperately, and do some other things. And do you know, I've been after this for six years. Hal Ashby had done *Harold and Maude* and I was going through a very bad patch. Nobody wanted to know me. They were crossing the road in order to avoid bumping into me at that stage. And Hal fell in love with it. And we made a promise to each other that if ever we got a break with it, he would come to me, or I would come to him. And suddenly Hal phoned me one day in Vienna, and said, "I hesitate to say this, but I think we've got it off the ground. It's really going to go." And I'm glad in a way it didn't happen before. Because those days would have been wrong. The progress that's been made, politically, economically, satirically since then has been enormous. So I'm glad it's been done now.'

◆ ◆ ◆

A development in world events aside (*Being There* became topical because Chance predicted President Reagan—an imbecile camouflaged in the White House), the chief advances, affecting the film's tonalities, were ones made by Sellers himself—i.e., he had travelled nearer to his death. As his executor, Elwood Rickless, said to me: 'From the time of *The Pink Panther Strikes Again*, in 1976, he knew he was dying. He knew he had little time left.' And this is apparent in every shot in the film; it is as if the picture is saying (with Philip Larkin), *beneath it all, desire of oblivion runs.*

Being There ends with a funeral (Melvyn Douglas') and commences with a corpse—that of Chance's (unnamed) employer, whose demise means that all the servants will have to be let go. ('It's like what he did to us,' says Michael, on behalf of himself, Sarah, and Victoria. 'A lawyer coming along and explaining "I'm sorry, there's no provision for you in the will. You have nothing.') Chance potters about a bit in the walled garden; he rakes the gravel and prunes a leafless bush; and then, when Louise, the maid, fails to arrive with his lunch, he packs his bags and, eerily calm, makes his solitary way into an overcast and windy Washington. This, we are meant to believe, is his first excursion beyond the old dark house, and Sellers is like a man who has just alighted on a new planet: motor cars, shops, muggers, the entire streetscape.

Chance's discoveries, however, are quickly cut short. Entranced by a bank of TV sets twinkling and winking behind a plate glass window, he steps back to get a better view—to a TV addict the display has the splendour of the Sistine Chapel (it is an electronic altar)—and is nudged in the knee by a huge black limousine, and out pops Shirley MacLaine. Assuming, from his bowler hat and dark grey double-breasted striped twill suit, that he must be a gentleman (doubtless she'd have instructed her chauffeur to step on the gas if the car had hit a poor black), she insists that Chance's contusion gets examined by her personal physician; so he is inside that funereal limo and being ferried off to be looked after, all within a few hours of leaving his old home.

The Rand mansion (which resembles Kane's swamp-enclosed Xanadu) is a shadowy labyrinth, not unlike the mahogany and marble place where he was raised (i.e., it is another mausoleum)—and cadaverous Melvyn Douglas, propped up in a glass oxygenated room, is a replacement for that sheeted, anonymous employer, whose nineteenth-century clothes Chance has appropriated. Chance, who does not have much of a long-term memory, probably fails to notice that he is living anywhere different; and his *indifference* is interpreted by his new-found (childless) friends and benefactors as well-mannered restraint. It is classy not to be impressed or gush over the palatial surroundings—it is alluring. Soon Chance's gardening homilies are being quoted as snippets of wisdom (like the sayings of Confucius or Fu Manchu), and his subdued merriment appears civilised and poised. Here we have, then, a mental defective who is considered innocent and true—a superior being.

At that point a satire on modern America, the cult of the celebrity, the prevalence of television, the conversion of news into entertainment, and God knows what else, could have taken flight; but, rather like *The Mouse That Roared*, a dramatic situation is constructed only to be ignored. This sort of avoidance wrecked the earlier film—it makes *Being There*. Off-stage, as it were, the President is dispatching his minions to discover Chance's background ('What do you mean he has no background? I quoted him on TV didn't I?'); and so with plot consigned to brief flashes and glimpses, we can see that the purpose of the film is not action and incident (still less satire) but reverie. Is it more obvious now, all these years after its release, that the film is an allegory of Sellers' own disconnectedness?

Sellers had no roots, no fixed addresses as a child, and so he had no roots of personality—no sense of *being there*—as an adult. As late as 1978 he was still saying: 'I don't have a home, don't have any roots. Which is nothing unusual. I've been a gypsy all my life.' Whatever characterisation he fancied, whatever mood struck him, he was; he became it utterly. If he played a blank, then he was a blank. He'd not shake it off until the next assignment came along—so from the little fat man in the snowy château he proceeded to be the gnomic Fu. It interests me that, for all the horticultural talk in the film, we see no blooms, no life. *Being There* is a winter garden; roots are snapped off.

Melvyn Douglas' Benjamin Rand is a dying plant; his personal hospital is like a greenhouse and, with his big bony hands and square, dislocated jaw, he resembles a pot lily. The dried flower arrangements which adorn the mansion are wreaths; and Johnny Mandel's theme music, picked out on a piano, sounds like the tinkle of icicles. We hear it a lot when Sellers and MacLaine tour the rose beds. MacLaine's character is named Eve, and this is a barren garden of Eden. We see acres and acres of brown nothingness and thorns. If it wasn't for Eve, however, the deathliness and decay would be stultifying; she's the only person with energy (it is on the cards that MacLaine will age into a human woodpecker like Ruth Gordon) and it becomes pretty clear early on in Chance's stay, when she floats into his bedroom wearing a negligee, that she is yearning for some sex. Benjamin, who is way past any stirrings in the trouser-snake department, tacitly gives Chance his consent to go ahead and give the lady what she craves, but he can't. He has no sex drive.

Chance cannot read or write, either; we almost feel he is above the need for such attainments. Similarly with sex. His impotence makes him holy (Catholic priests vow celibacy, but Chance is already an evolutionary step beyond them), and he induces impotence in others. The President is unable to make love to his wife after he has met Chance. We have a number of shots of Jack Warden's pale

Mr. Nobody: Chance in *Being There* (1979)

and puffy face as he tosses and turns in his bed; what upsets the President is that he has met somebody who is not corrupt. Eve, meantime, starts to glow, masturbating in Chance's presence. He gives up watching after a few seconds—he is far more intrigued by Bugs Bunny on the television. The scene goes on and on, though—MacLaine having convulsions on the carpet; Sellers watching the box.

Its function, in terms of the story, is that Eve believes she has made love to Chance without touching him—she is therefore not technically an adulteress; she may even still be chaste. What is actually at issue is Chance's vegetativeness. He's not interested in learning about things; in appearance, too, he is sleepy and amorphous. 'I had to put on a lot of weight to play Chance, and I cut my hair terribly short, because the kindly, efficient maid Louise used to cut it for him. I knew it was right for Chance. And I've had the most terrible battle ever since to get this fucking weight off. When you get to be my age it's so hard.' In the event, his wasting heart made him meagre. He suffered from chest pains, feelings of faintness and anxiety—and, as he explained to Max Geldray, in *Being There* 'I look quite plump…which was *deliberate*, I wanted the character to look stocky. However, now I have lost almost thirty pounds! and have made myself rather weak in the process, but it was necessary for Fu Manchu, or me maybe.'

Sellers' instinct was right to make Chance thick-set—he's monolithic. The actor has reverted to Daniel Mendoza dimensions, and I also think there is an echo, in the impassivity, of that uprooted tree trunk photograph, which I discussed in Chapter Eight as a symbol of the primitive and everlasting. Chance is white-haired and quiet, and there's nothing to him except the externals. He has no thoughts, no raging elements, which is why Milligan said 'almost miraculously… Peter Sellers himself seemed to be totally excluded.' For, indeed, who is this sweet-smiling agreeable creature, with Stan's voice and Ollie's build? Fuller of face, heavy of tread, Sellers harks back to Fred Kite, especially to the scene where the union boss, rigid and on his best behaviour, is quizzed by Malcolm Muggeridge on an ersatz-television programme called 'Argument'. But most of all, in portraying a character whose life is eroded of all except the essentials—Chance eats, sleeps, seeks shelter, parrots whatever he's told—Sellers had reverted to the safety of the nursery. Eve will protect him, mother him (she is, of course, Mother Eve), and their frictionless relationship is an idealised symbiosis of the bond between mother and child, a timeless Peter and Peg.

In *Being There*, Sellers achieves a state of perfect nostalgia. Exactly what this meant to him personally is something he tried to get across in an impromptu speech at the Cannes Film Festival in May 1980: 'This *Being There* film is the most unique film that has ever been made, and I mean has *ever* been made in the history of filmmaking.' Hyperbole, yes, but to Sellers *Being There* propounded his view of Heaven, and to most sane and normal people it looks like Hell. Chance's every need is catered for. The Rands, who function as parents, have limitless wealth and power. They do not try and unmask their guest, who is literally a foundling. The dark side of the idyll is that Chance had died but he's not dead; Sellers seems like a ghost returned to haunt himself and the huge house is a house of death, its grounds forever chilly. No birds sing; no leaves will sprout on those skeleton trees. It gives me the creeps, actually, the atmosphere of the Rand mansion, Chance's paradise garden—as it did an earlier guest. Henry James stayed at Biltmore, the Vanderbilt pile in North Carolina used for the location, and dubbed it 'impractically spacious,' 'a castle of enchantment,' 'a phenomenon of brute achievement.'

◆ ◆ ◆

The childhood Sellers regressed to, as Chance, is benign, but it is still autistic; the character has avoided (or been deprived of) social interaction, so he retreats to what psychiatrists would recognise as 'uninterrupted self-isolation … a life not too remote from a nirvana-like existence.'* Thinking about his own childhood, and what we know of it, I wonder whether Sellers' early years were blighted by unacknowledged mental illness? The term 'childhood schizophrenia' is generally applied, by the diagnostic system of the American Psychiatric Association, to any manifestations of 'autistic, atypical, and withdrawn behaviour; failure to develop identity separate from the mother's; gross immaturity and general unevenness and inadequacy of development'—and Sellers felt isolated from society long before fame, money, etc. allowed him to reserve secluded hotel suites, book private jets, and travel in darkened limos. It is not very surprising that sufferers from childhood psychosis go on to become adult schizophrenics, and Sellers could have checked off not a few from that sinister list above. He absolved himself from responsibilities—he gave up—and this rather feckless moral attitude, optimistically acted out as wistful idiocy when he played the Mr Nobody of *Being There*, meant something quite different in practice. It meant being appalling to his wives and children, alternately showering them with gifts or threatening to kill them; it meant divorces and disinheritance; it meant abandoning friends for years and then telephoning them persistently in the small hours; and it meant making life grim for people trying to help him, because he didn't appreciate presumption ('I never *tell* people to do anything, because I never do anything myself when I'm told to do it, only when I'm *asked*').

Heartless and sentimental (he died literally of a broken heart); generous and stingy; violent and crying easily; rancorous, hyperactive, or unresponsive: Sellers would have worn out teams of mind-doctors. By the time of *The Pink Panther Strikes Again*, says Blake Edwards, 'if you went to an insane asylum and you described the first inmate you saw, that's what Peter had become … He was certifiable, and anybody who says he wasn't just doesn't know … It manifested itself in the way he treated women. I don't think Peter liked women at all, and I think that had a lot to do with his mother … Peter had a classic love-hate relationship with her …' And, thinks Edwards, one of the reasons Sellers hated him was because they were dependent on each other for Clouseau's success. 'He must have loved me kind of like I loved him, and hated me to such a degree that it was kind of like [I was] his mom, that terrible tearing feeling. I know he had a big emotional in-

---

* My source for this scientific material is *Abnormal Psychology*, by G. Davidson and J. Neale, (New York), 1978, Chapter 15, 'Child Psychoses'.

vestment in me ... but he hated the fact that I was so responsible'—for scripts, direction, conception.

Edwards' words are corroborated by Herbert Lom in our conversation at the Reform club: 'Peter was a great imitator—to the extent that, when he'd thought out a character, he'd imitate himself in the part. Clouseau was always "him" or "he", never "I" ... He couldn't cope with fame, women, money—everything confused him. And that was his nice side. Little Boy Lost. A superficial judgement would be to say: You have fame, women, money! You have arrived! But he was always insecure. When he went to a party, he always thought everyone disliked him. So he surrounded himself with cronies. He referred to women only as "birds". On the day after he married I had lunch with him in Hollywood. He said he was off to Germany to see a bird. He was always on the lookout for a new distraction ... He didn't possess any culture, any background. Nothing to fall back on—to the extent that he never knew whether to accept or reject a rôle. He came to me once in a state ... [because] King Lear had been offered to him ... I advised him to turn it down. But he'd been thinking for quite some days, "Perhaps I'm Lear?" ... He had so little knowledge of himself, he didn't see how inappropriate he'd have been in a classical tragedy. He thought he should accept, but had he done so, it would have been a disaster.'

'Yet he became like Lear,' I suggested, 'dispossessing his children, banishing people, mad and foolish fond.'

'There is a difference between *being* Lear and *playing* Lear.'

'Was his emptiness almost innocence?'

'He was like the President of Czechoslovakia, years ago, when it was asked if he'd accept a book as a gift: "No," he said, "I've already got one."'

'He had a difficulty with abstractions,' I said, 'and a greater difficulty with people. He hovered between the two, certain only of his gadgets and the successfulness of his temper tantrums.'

'Peter was ... more talented than people gave him credit for, but Blake, for instance, had to give up directing him ... And for some reason they fell out ... in the middle of a film. Messages had to be conveyed by assistants. "Tell him to come through that door and sit on that chair." "Tell him I don't want to ..." We had to stand around. Embarrassed. Now I was sad about this, because I ... wanted the [Panther] series to run forever; so I tried to reconcile them ... And they did make it up and we made more films. But it was a shaky alliance. Blake showed me telegrams he had received: "YOU ARE A ROTTEN HUMAN BEING. YOU ARE A SHIT, AND I CAN AFFORD TO WORK WITHOUT YOU. I DON'T NEED YOU TO GET WORK. LOVE PETER."'

Chapter Fourteen

♦ ♦ ♦

Love and Death

In the midst of the craziness and ugliness, Sellers met Lynne Frederick.

'Lynne is different to all the ladies I've been attracted to. She's a good one, that girl; and a terrific bloody actress. I met Lynne at one of Dennis Selinger's parties... We were mutually attracted to each other... It's certainly working very well, and please God, if it goes on like this, it will be a real treat. I've known it very different in my time, as you know. On the other hand I think, why should we get married? I'll be in a better position to answer that in the New Year when... her film comes out... How will success affect her? Because she will come into her own when this film comes out—*The Voyage of the Damned*. I think she will become a very good actress in the full sense of the word actress. Although she doesn't want to be—she wants either to be a housewife or continue studying physics. Everyone I've met, including Malcolm McDowell, was knocked out by her performance in this film. I suggest she continues with her career and becomes very selective... She says... "If you want, I'll give it up." I just want to see how she takes to the applause... It's all very happy there. All very happy...'

The above monologue was recorded by Peter Evans in December 1976. He tells me that 'I'd had lunch with Sellers... He was on good form, telling his stories, outlining his plans. Lynne was present, and he'd be bringing her into the conversation; she didn't need a great deal of encouragement for that, which I thought slightly dangerous, knowing Peter. She'd step on his lines. But he was very tolerant, very loving, and very well-behaved... That evening I got a call from him... The calmness... and the amusement of lunchtime was... completely gone. He was in a terrible... worked-up condition. I had to promise him I'd not mention Lynne Frederick in any interview or piece I might be writing; that... "It has been a ghastly mistake and *she's out of here*..." That was within a period of three or four hours.'

Woody Allen, when he had to linger in London for months on end because of *Casino Royale*, said that the great thing about England was that it had all four seasons in a single day. Sellers, similarly, blew hot and cold. His relationship with Lynne, whom he married on February 18, 1977, oscillated from ardour to hatred, reconciliation, and remorse—and, of all his wives, she had the most consistently terrible time. (How could it have been otherwise, given Sellers' deteriorating condition?) When groom was in Europe and bride was in America, she'd receive telegrams signed 'Your nearly ex-husband'; then a dozen roses would arrive. Sellers would state categorically 'It's over', then he'd wax lyrically about how 'We met in a previous incarnation.' Understandably beflummoxed, Lynne gave an in-

His last young child bride: Sellers in the French Alps
with Lynne Frederick (thirty years his junior) in 1979

terview to Roderick Mann, in May 1979, in which she said: 'We have both consulted lawyers, though … neither of us have filed for divorce. We talk every day [by long distance telephone] and I know he feels just as badly as I do about the break-up. Peter says he thought it would be forever. But so did I … I know Peter is talking of a reconciliation, but I cannot predict what will happen when I see him … I knew I was his fourth wife … and my mother warned me against marrying him. But I was sure we could make it work. The age difference [she was now twenty-four; he was fifty-three] has had absolutely nothing to do with it. I've always preferred older men … Peter and I shared such a lot together: we went through so many highs and lows. And I still love him, of course … It hasn't made me bitter or angry, though. Just sad.'

Sellers' reaction to his wife's philosophic resignation was to accuse her of conducting an affair with Mann, the journalist who had done nothing more than take down her words. He also had her tailed by a private detective and told Michael: 'I can't take any more. She's messing me about. She's got the hottest pants in Hollywood. No wonder she doesn't want to come back here …' Michael told his father he was imagining things—which was to put it mildly. Sellers had always liked to accuse his other wives of infidelity. He was as operatic as Othello when it came to the strength of his jealousy; he would have kept his women locked up in a tower if he could. Now, however, he was exhibiting the histrionics and exaggerations, and holding the irrational beliefs, of a patient in the grip of dementia. 'He became very cruel, hurtful, and destructive,' says Blake Edwards. 'He was an emotional and physical bully, especially to ladies.'

◆ ◆ ◆

She was his child-bride, upon whom he showered furs and pearls beyond price; she, in her turn, was coquettish and lively—thrilled by the blood sports he took her to see, by the erotic pavanes at court, by the sudden attention of the powerful. When we see them in the bedchamber together, his impotent and ravaged bulk and her Pre-Raphaelite slenderness are an obscene conjunction—it is horrific to think of them having sex; and soon the old King, humiliated by his sense of failure, is raging and howling in the palace corridors, mad with visions of plots and disloyalty. Even when he's calmer there was always his melancholy disposition, his sense of being lonely within his rank, which would wreck what remained of any relationship. Quick to anger, ready to give ear to slanders and surmises, he interprets his new wife's natural flirtiness as inherent impurity; he allows her to be imprisoned on false reports and driven crazy by meddling lordships...

Lynne Frederick's rôle as Catherine Howard, in *Henry VIII and His Six Wives* (directed by Waris Hussein in 1973), was a frightening premonition of her life with Sellers: his paranoia, boredom, greed, impotence, fury, envy, and his reliance on the musterings of whispers, gossip, conjectures. Like Henry, Sellers was deplorable and improvident; he was not capable of love, only violation. His version of love was a clinging, a leeching—the unnatural demands of a creature totally obsessed with itself. Lynne, full of tenderness and pity, however, decided that what he was crying out for was protection—and as his daughter Sarah said to me: 'She took over the jobs and rôles of all those countless people he'd had around him—secretaries, chauffeurs, valets, cooks... She was totally dedicated to him.'

Sellers' helplessness became Lynne's inspiration—and she was right in one respect. Sellers, who was searching for Peg in all of his wives, wanted to be mothered. Finally, he'd got what he deserved, and more: 'I was his mother, his sister, his daughter, his lover, his wife,' said his widow towards the end of 1980, 'and he became for me my father, my lover, my friend.' What the pair of them mostly were in fact was patient and nurse. 'He was now sick enough, things had gone far enough, that he no longer wanted the hassle of running his own life,' says Michael. 'This is how it started. Bert Mortimer left, or was induced to leave; Denis O'Brien was dropped... Bert had been... with Dad for sixteen years, which was in itself a feat. He was the right-hand man. Drove for him, picked stuff up, liaison officer, an organiser... But Lynne took control, basically. My father thought she knew what was best for him—so he let her get on with it.'

Lynne had the good intention of managing Sellers' existence—of becoming necessary to him. 'Peter... was insecure about himself and his relationships with others, particularly women. He believed he did not appeal to women because he wasn't attractive... Gradually I helped ease his anxieties... I told him I found him very attractive, that I had from the beginning. I told him I liked his hair grey and he shouldn't tint it.'

First there had been Sophia Loren, re-awakening in him the adolescent idea that 'I am a child of the cinema.' Next came Janette Scott, listening to his midnight cries through a locked bathroom door; and now, the would-be suicide having gone completely off his rocker, it was Lynne's turn to minister to the lunatic in Intensive Care: 'The change I made was to help him even out the graph of his emotions: the highs got lower and the lows got higher. It didn't become a straight line of course—with his talent it couldn't.' Indeed not. The straight line would have been that of the electrocardiogram informing you that the patient is dead. Lynne did calm him down for a while—for the duration of the *Being There* shoot, for example, which was, however, ungraciously followed by 'one of his depressions... at the end of what he knew was his finest work'; and so the pair separated. 'We had been together solidly without a break for three-and-a-half years. And no matter how close, no couple can live in each other's pockets like that.' Piers Haggard told me that 'one of the troubles with *The Fiendish Plot of Dr Fu Manchu* was that... Lynne... was always somewhere else, and didn't appear until after shooting had started—and it always did him *good* when she was around. Got him going a bit.'

As that evidence suggests, Sellers put an incredible strain on his bride. It is no wonder they were to diverge. Sellers denied Lynne any separate emotional existence. 'He constantly needed my support to help him get through the day,' she said in August 1980. 'I felt it was my duty to boost his confidence.' Two years earlier, just before the start of *The Prisoner of Zenda* in Vienna, she'd voiced a similar opinion: 'Peter is a very dear person and he desperately... needs his confidence replenished.' This around-the-clock ego-massaging and shielding from reality took the form of never appearing to hold an opinion that was contrary to his, throwing away negative newspaper reviews, and seeing off people whose presence might have ruffled the star: 'He's not good at taking criticism,' Lynne told *Time* magazine four months prior to Sellers' death. '[S]omeone he thought of as a friend may do something which convinces him he never should have trusted him.'

Sellers was clearly a hopeless case. He scented betrayals everywhere. Nothing was trustworthy. He held other people in such contempt, I wonder whether hating others was what gave him peace of mind? Lynne, meantime, whilst having enough misgivings about Sellers-the-man to have signed a separation agreement on June 15, 1979 (which gave her a fifty-grand annuity and a million-dollar house in Los Angeles), continued to be faithful to Sellers-the-legend—to the *idea* of a wayward, wonderful stage-front genius. 'I feel it rather sad,' she said twelve months before they split up, 'that Peter reached his age while not being really happy. I am very young, and I am happy... He is young in mind, and I am old in mind, so there is a meeting someplace.'

Does any of this gush sound familiar? The Lynne/Sellers relationship, suitably idealised, is the one foisted upon us in *The Fiendish Plot of Dr Fu Manchu*. 'I don't think age matters,' Alice Rage coos to Fu and he, ecstatic, promises her the earth. 'You shall have everything your heart ever desired,' he purrs. When she strips down to her camiknickers, the better to blow into her saxophone, he murmurs, 'Don't mind me. I'm just a feeble old man.'

Feeble and sterile Sellers might have been, but he still had his wealth to deploy. In a Last Will & Testament dated July 27, 1979, drawn up by Alfred von Grunigen in Gstaad, Sellers stated that 'As adequate provision has been made for my wife *Lynne Frederick Sellers* in a separation agreement … it is my express wish that no provision be made for her in my Will.' After a few pecuniary legacies, the balance of Sellers' loot—his residuary estate—was to go to the British Heart Foundation. When Lynne returned to him, briefly, later on in the year, Sellers scratched all this latter bit out. In a codicil dated October 29, 1979, in Paris, the residuary estate was now to go to 'my wife, provided that she shall survive me by a period of thirty days'—so fuck the British Heart Foundation.

Quite who was to receive this-and-that and how much is not of significance to the present argument; what does matter is that we can see Sellers quite blatantly, and pathetically, trying to buy devotion. Lynne would not be a party to his wiles, though; and even when he made Orion (after Haggard had left) pay her seventy-five thousand pounds to be a 'production executive' for a mere three weeks ('She'll be helping generally where she can,' said the film company vaguely), 'the general feeling as regards Lynne,' says Simon Williams, 'was that she was not "with him".' The separation agreement was not cancelled and when *The Fiendish Plot of Dr Fu Manchu* wrapped, Lynne spent most of her time back in America.

◆ ◆ ◆

She was far from being the only woman who thought she could save him, and, when he was still alive, she was pragmatic about what the future might bring: 'I believe Peter and I were meant to meet, have a relationship, get married,' she said in 1978. 'But what will happen I don't know … There's nothing I can do about it.' Sellers underscored the suggestion that this was a transitory match—i.e. that his unhappy marriages would resemble each other: 'There's no telling how long a marriage will last,' he said, 'but I am very happily married.' And then, as we know, he'd be changing sides and informing Michael: 'I'm going to have to tell Lynne … she doesn't understand my way of life. I shouldn't have married her.'

Mr and Mrs did manage to appear together at the Cannes Film Festival, between May 9 and May 23, 1980. It was Sellers' final public appearance. He looked so emaciated that as he and Lynne strolled along the Promenade de la Croisette he resembled a reliquary being trundled out by a favourite nun. For the hacks and flacks who flapped about him, he said: 'If ever I catch a cold—it's a heart attack, seizure, head fell off, knee gone.' He snapped, 'It's not a festival, it's … a *bazaar*.' If an actor had thought Cannes *wasn't* a trade fair, this may have been a scoop. As it was, Sellers looked ripe to walk amok, throwing the money-changers out of the temple.

He was equally fissile in private, quarrelling with Lynne and (says his lawyer) 'just generally flailing. He was desperate. He knew he was going to die—this terrified him, and this was why he grabbed at projects: to keep himself going, to keep himself alive. United Artists were committed to *The Romance of the Pink Panther*, which Blake didn't want to direct; and though the script was terrible, U.A. were giving in to Peter on every point. Which was not the way to deal with Peter

Sellers. When he had complete control … the result was … disaster … During his last few months his marriage was in great difficulties … He was all over the place—ordering me to serve divorce papers, ordering me not to do so … Eventually he … went off on his own …'

By now he'd made sure he had no friends—only show-biz acquaintances and sycophants. There was nobody with whom to share his problems. Lynne, too, was treated like a retainer—doing everything for him, doing his bidding. ('He consumed every minute of my life,' she said the day after he died.) He would overpower women. He was wilful—which is not the same as being strong, as having strength of character. And as a starlet in her early twenties trying to cope with and run a homunculus practically foaming at the mouth, Lynne's experience was a reduplication of Britt's—a fact she was not keen to acknowledge. 'Britt Ekland!' she snorted on July 27, 1980. 'How could she understand him? They were married fifteen years ago, and Peter had changed a hell of a lot since those days.' Quite so. He'd got worse.

In 1966, Britt told *Photoplay*: 'When you are single you … seldom think of anyone else. But now I think in two of everything. Instead of making one cup of coffee, I make two. And I have to remember if Peter takes sugar! You become more concerned for the other person than for yourself … You mature because you have an enormous responsibility to the one you love.' If asked about the age gap (sixteen years), she'd say 'In Sweden we have a saying, "The younger the branch, the better it bends"'; and she'd add (in interviews conducted, like all of Lynne's, at the Dorchester), 'I am very careful about my appearance, especially for Peter's sake. When he comes in at night … I know he's been a whole day at the studio so I make myself look nice for him … I think everyone should do that for their husband.'

Britt had offered herself as a vassal only to have her self-sacrifices and compliance derided. It is rather a shame that the cosy scene she tried to create was spoiled when Sellers decided he liked stamping on her wedding ring until it was flatter than a squashed piece of bubble gum (this happened so often, Garrads grew accustomed to re-shaping it); or that he liked to threaten her with a double-barrelled shotgun; or that, when they were staying at the Excelsior Hotel in Rome, he decided to rip up her clothes, smash her cassette-radio, and rant and rave until three-thirty in the morning.

Looking back over their years together, Britt said, in the week of the funeral: 'Being married to Peter was like riding on a rollercoaster. One minute you were flying high, the next you were running low—and I'm sure that his other wives found that … Peter always felt insecure, about his physical appearance especially. He feared the macho-type man posed a threat to him, so he was jealous if another man even glanced in my direction … I am sure Lynne was a loving and devoted wife. We all were, but none of us could reach him. He was an unhappy, troubled human being. We wanted to help him, but he could not even help himself … I thought back to sixteen years ago … He had eight successive heart attacks [in 1964] that nearly killed him. For days he was on the brink of death.'

◆◆◆

Was he a homosexual?

A thread may be traced through the films. In *The Naked Truth*, Wee Sonny and his dresser bicker like a pair of old-fashioned queens. And then there's *The Magic Christian*. In Terry Southern's original novel, Guy Grand is a cynical Santa, a preposterous Puck. He maddens people. His pranks account for 'the faces, and especially the eyes, of people in the cities'. What Quilty does to Humbert, Guy does to people wholesale—he makes them paranoid. Sellers, however, loses this aggressiveness. His Guy has no glee. He is bored, listless—like himself. (Guy's house is full of discarded gadgets, games, a giant TV screen, etc.) In appearance, with his hair a tall, tapering quiff, he is an apathetic version of Robert Danvers; and if the film, lacking the panache of the novel, is inert and dumb, there is at least one new whimsy. Where *There's a Girl in My Soup* was about misogyny and automated humping, into *The Magic Christian* Sellers introduced a homosexual curiosity and undercurrent.

The film begins with Sir Guy picking up a boy in a park and adopting him—Youngman Grand (who does not feature in the book) is his catamite—and their pranks and bribes are queerish: enticing Laurence Harvey to play Hamlet as a male stripper; getting boxers to stop punching and start kissing; that sort of thing. Interviewed on the set, at the Theatre Royal, Stratford East, during the shooting, Sellers pretended to be an arts journalist ('This is Nudbolt Thules') telling us, in hushed tones as the lights go down, about the significance of what we are watching—i.e. sex in Shakespeare. 'In "To be or not to be, that is the question," he means "To be homosexual..." Or does he not? Only the viewers can decide...' So it goes on. Polanski is seen playing a hare-eyed loner propping up the bar in a gay night club. Yul Brynner, en travesti, sings Noël Coward's torch song 'Mad About the Boy'—or, to be accurate, he mimes to a track made by Miriam Karlin; and because *The Magic Christian* is rambling, episodic, and anything can be tossed into the stew, we are given glimpses, now and again, of near-naked Negro musclemen and, down in the ship's engine room, cracking a whip, the Queen of the Amazons, played by Raquel Welch, presides over a platoon of butch lesbians pulling at oars.

Sellers wanted to appear, in a subliminal shot, dressed as a nun and for the nun to resemble his mother. 'There's a very quick disco sequence when they are on the train going north; and there are nuns in it,' Joe McGrath explains. 'He wanted to dress up as a nun. On the morning we were doing it, he called me into the dressing-room. "Who is it? Who am I?" I said "Your mother". He said "I never realised until I started getting dressed up that I looked exactly like my mother." She looked exactly like him.'

◆ ◆ ◆

I don't think I want to let my mind linger too long on the significance of that. (It makes Sellers seem comparable with Norman Bates in *Psycho*.) Suffice it to say that to a psychoanalyst the problem would be as clear as day and homosexuality not an option but an inevitability: the seductive mother (Peg) and the distant father (Bill), and Sellers replacing Bill in Peg's affections to the extent that she discouraged any friendships or interest in other women (that's why 'birds' or 'tarts' were all right: they are a lesser order of being); and when he did go with them, and compelled himself to marry them, he was filled with guilt and felt degraded, and he had to get violent to assert his masculinity... Or something pseudo-scientific like that. Sellers, with Fritz Fassbender in *What's New, Pussycat?*, gave the world one of the funniest portrayals of a shrink who is more bloody barmy than any of his patients ('Why don't we all take off our clothes? It's so modern, you know'); and, in that film, the O'Toole character's compulsive promiscuity ('A little pleasure, a little pain, and then always back to the ladies') is a complaint Sellers affected to suffer from after the discarding of Britt, when he preened to the press: 'If one more doll just so much as makes a pass at me, I think I'll... leap into the nearest river.'

Which brings us to Clouseau—who is often drenched, doused, dipped, ducked, and dripping after an encounter with a woman. In *The Pink Panther*, the first in the interminable line, he is married to Capucine, who is classical beauty incarnate; her elegance extends to the slapstick routines with Sellers. The pair of them are foiled Gallic lovers. Clouseau's own pratfalls occur because of all his suppressed frustration and tension; he can't manage to get into bed with his own wife without hours of calamitous foreplay, as he trips and stumbles. If he goes anywhere near a bathroom, a sink, taps, or a water source of any kind, there'll be a biblical flood.

The character was conceived as a mockery of virility. 'I arrived in Rome to work for Blake Edwards... "How do you see Clouseau?" I'd read it once. "Well, he's a sort of below-par French detective." We later invented all his accident-proneness. It came out during the early discussions... I thought, Clouseau must have a thick moustache to prove to somebody or other that he's virile—and in command, you see. That would be the first thing. And the hair fairly short, you know. And he'd use this French/English accent.'

So what happens? He stands too close to electric fans and we hear a sudden *ping!*; billiard cues go for his groin; prongs and levers attack his crotch. He's always being threatened with castration. Then again, the joke of *The Pink Panther* is that it is a sex comedy in which the characters don't get to have any. Nobody succeeds in getting their rocks off—nobody manages to keep possession of the rock, the Pink Panther jewel itself. And it is Sellers' film for one big reason. Clouseau, by the look in his eyes, appears to believe he is fully rational and controlled. It's the rest of the world that is out of joint. Clouseau, scratching his violin (his homage to Sherlock Holmes), is magnificently pensive. Niven, Wagner, and the rest, are shallow and basic; Clouseau, by contrast, has a mind, a sensibility. 'There are people like Clouseau all over the world,' said Sellers. 'He's a man with great in-built dignity, you see... He's an idiot, and he knows that, but he won't let anyone else know that...'

What he doesn't have, after the first film, is a wife. Instead there is Cato, his houseboy, with whom he enjoys a comic sado-masochistic relationship. If, in *The Pink Panther*, Clouseau was an unsuccessful heterosexual—his bottled-up feelings making accidents occur almost telekinetically—later on his world is distinctly queerish. I don't simply mean that Cato hides in his master's bed and bathtub, or that Clouseau (like Holmes) is generally bachelorly in his habits and persnicketiness. (Women, in the later films, are just there to stand on the sidelines and gig-

(Top) His Nazi Fixation:
Sellers the Demon

(Bottom) An Inspector
Calls: Sellers the Innocent

gle.) I mean, rather, that there gets to be a preponderance of transvestite killers and fag jokes. Cato cross-dresses as a geisha; Clouseau is attacked by a transvestite in the Bois de Boulogne, and ends up in skirts and wig himself. In *The Pink Panther Strikes Again*, for example, there is a long, unpleasant scene in a gay bar. Michael Robbins is a transvestite butler who dances cheek-to-cheek with Clouseau, gets shot, and plants a big kiss on the Chief Inspector's lips before dying. And the film begins with an extraordinarily tasteless gag. Dreyfus, having fallen four or five times into the lake, is gasping for air. Clouseau pulls him on to the bank and sits astride his back, rhythmically pumping the water from his lungs. Cut to two old ladies regarding this with horror. Cut to their point of view (Clouseau and Dreyfus in the middle distance): they obviously assume some alfresco sodomy is in progress. Cut back to old ladies hurrying away.

◆ ◆ ◆

Though Sellers came to hate Edwards because he was jealous of him, there were odd moments when he was lucid and good-natured enough to admit that 'as far as fun goes, I think I had the most fun working with Blake... I'm pleased to say that wherever I go in the world I get the impression that [the Inspector Clouseau] films are probably the most popular things I've done. I'm always being asked to make another one.'

If it hadn't been for Sellers' truculence, it would have been the ideal working relationship: Edwards' knack for slapstick, Sellers' goonishness. But Sellers (as with Milligan and Mankowitz) would not be beholden; he had an aversion to the sharing and involvement connected with the word *rapport*—and as Lom said, it didn't take long before director and star were only communicating through intermediaries. Danny Shelmerdine, who worked as a clapperloader on *The Return of the Pink Panther*, recalls that the actor 'was very unreasonable—and quite oblivious to the ways in which his unreasonableness affected the life of the crew. He wouldn't turn up, when we'd spent all day preparing for a shot... Whatever he was obliged to be doing now, today, irritated him. It was difficult to get him going in the mornings—though he found that being Clouseau came easily and naturally to him. Then he'd start laughing at the potential of a scene—which Blake would have prepared—and he'd eventually *go*.'

Edwards (like Kubrick) would spend ages setting up multiple cameras for comedy sequences and Sellers would materialise and improvise his way through—and disappear again. By arriving on stage to execute a routine and make a quick exit, Sellers had imposed on the cinema industry the self-containment of a music hall act. (He'd returned to his origins.) The director would plan the next scene on the bill, and meantime use doubles and stuntmen and stand-ins. But it was not only the agreeableness of these conditions which suited Sellers (up to a point); Edwards' sly, sophisticated, cynical creative temperament was congenial. He is fond of filling his films with spies, gangsters, murderers, and madness. And he's very fond, too, of transvestism—the games people play with sexual rôles. Aberrant social behaviour (being a criminal) is connected with deviant sex—and this, again, Edwards has dealt with amusingly and bitterly.

Edwards sees the figure of the detective as a man who restores order to a chaotic world, who deciphers its puzzles and plots. (He is an unmasker.) Hence the spoof of Clouseau. The divisions and ambiguities developed and approached by Edwards in dozens of other hit-and-miss films—good and evil; niceness and squalor; sourness and sentimentality—now receive crude cartoon exploitation. Clouseau survives endless assassination attempts on top of all the scorn and derision, yet he's never less than heroic. Dreyfus, driven crazy watching a fool succeed, stabs himself, guillotines his thumb, shoots off his own nose—a gradual dismemberment which turns him into a cloaked phantom-of-the-opera, cackling at his pipe organ in a remote mountaintop castle. Dreyfus is France's most august policeman, the Commissioner; he is also a strait-jacketed bedlamite, scrawling KILL CLOUSEAU on the walls of his padded cell. Clouseau, in his turn, *is* as triumphant as Holmes, despite the setbacks. And, like Holmes, he loves disguises.

The Clouseau films do not address any remotely serious or deep issues connected with identity—on the contrary, Clouseau's carnival costumes debunk the very concept of a cop (or an actor) taking on the colour of his surroundings, melting into the night, and all that stuff. 'I glide through the underworld like a shadow,' Clouseau vouchsafes in *The Revenge of the Pink Panther*; and then we see him as Toulouse-Lautrec, a Hong Kong coolie, a Mafia Godfather, a Swedish herring-merchant, and as a Catholic priest officiating at his 'own' funeral. (Dreyfus gives the oration. His happy choked-back chortles are interpreted as grief-stricken sobs.) Like an exhausted, resentful music hall artiste, Sellers could no longer be bothered to stay in character consistently. Often, the clenched-jaw Gallic suavity just falls away; he stops being Clouseau and is bored, and himself: heavy, puffy, flashing his own chest hair and Shanti-Om medallion.

The later Pink Panthers are shoddy, plotless, hectic—they are revues. The best bits are those we know from Denis Norden's out-take compilations, *It'll Be All Right On the Night*, when Sellers got the giggles trying to talk to Dyan Cannon and when mispronouncing his lines, or the scene with the mobsters breaking wind in the elevator. I personally do not find the cutting-room floor material especially amusing, for the cock-ups weren't happy accidents. Sellers made his mistakes on purpose. 'I search through the scripts to find some words I can play with—"officer of the *law* [leu]" sets them off,' he boasted. In the finished film we see the results of the corpsing—scenes have to be trimmed back to virtual jump-cuts.

Clouseau, a conscientious cuckold in the original film, degenerated eleven years later into a clown, and the editing and continuity are home-movie standard. But the idea of these expensive productions looking so cheaply made; the notion of a brilliant comic actor being so bad *he* (not Clouseau) is the one who has to be hidden inside suits of armour and thick make-up disguises, and his appearances generally faked by lots of reverse angles and medium long-shots of decoys in trenchcoats: all this ingenuity and incompetence makes for clod-hopping camp. Allied with the cross-dressing and dozens of night-club locations, the fuddled, forced, sleepy atmosphere is almost decadent. Though as unsubtle as a circus, tacky and superficial, under the surface of this burnt-out group of films, therefore, is Sellers' fatuousness and stagnation.

◆ ◆ ◆

Yes, but was he homosexual? (It would have suited Peg if he had been.)

He couldn't cope with women at all; he couldn't cope with his daughters, he couldn't cope with his wives. If he suspected they were trying to outwit him, compete with him, or have thoughts of their own, he could always rely on his superior physical strength to regain the advantage and settle arguments. (Once, infuriated to hear Miranda Quarry justifying, on aesthetic grounds, Sam Peckinpah's use of screen violence, Sellers, the advocate of yogic calm, countered her claim, and put the case for nonaggression, by punching a hole in a restaurant wall.) Most married men, with families to support, knuckle down and accept a measure of responsibility, but to Sellers, responsibility equalled docility. The welfare of other people was not for him. He didn't want anyone near him who was an equal. He was as cold and lonely (i.e. as independent) as a homosexual—and as for his tomcatting? Didn't he work too hard at that? Didn't he dramatise his rakishness to disguise his aridity?

Sellers, cold and depleted, was on the alert only for new sensations. And he found one. His final years were spent living not so much with Lynne as with a man. It was not a physical relationship—which, since Sellers had lost the power of erection, was impossible. Rather, it was a curiously emotional association. Michael Jeffery was like his mother and a son-surrogate rolled into one. At last here was a marriage without the inherent ordeals of marriage. ('I think a relationship goes wrong as soon as you get married,' Sellers had always said.) Jeffery was womanish without the disadvantage of actually being female; he could fuss and cajole, henpeck and defuse tension—and as Michael Sellers, who witnessed the ménage at La Haute Grange, said: 'Jeffery got on well with Lynne, as well as with Dad, so he was taken on ... Michael Jeffery could *mother* him, which Bert couldn't; campish people can mother you. That was what my father wanted. They sent one another up something rotten ... It was a light, easy, dressing-room atmosphere.'

The master-servant distance suited Sellers. I went to meet his former cup-bearer at a flat in Chalk Farm, North London. I thought he looked like a buddah—and then I noticed, on a side-table, a number of squatting buddah figurines, so Jeffery was evidently living up to his bric-à-brac. There were also framed autographed photographs of Sellers, fragments of Fu Manchu's kimonos, lemon and red, and a book about garden gnomes on display. (The latter bore the flyleaf inscription: 'These will be better at the BOTTOM of your garden than those other things, Peter, July 1979.')

'I met Peter on *The Revenge of the Pink Panther.* I was employed to look after him, his costume-dresser; and before then I went to meet him at Stag House, Victoria, with the wardrobe supervisor, Tony Nichols ... We had a shirt-fitting. We all left, and Tony got a phone call from Peter: "Who was that young man you brought with you?" "That's Michael ... He's going to look after you on the *Panther.*" "Oh, is he? I'd better see him again, then." So I went back and met him again. I did the *Panther*. I came back to England, and...I kept getting phone calls in the middle of the night...[to] be on the next film, *The Prisoner of Zenda*, in Vienna. He...used to invite me out to dinner—every night when Lynne left. He insisted I appeared in the film—I was Oscar Wilde at the Café Royal...but this scene was later cut out. Then we went to Los Angeles...he said, "I'm staying here. Would you stay?" By that time I'd become a bit...like a Personal Assistant.'

Sellers was offended by the scissoring of Jeffery from the film. On March 27, 1979, he complained to Walter Mirisch about 'many of the worst imaginable [editing] errors...' that had been made: 'Why on earth,' he asked, 'other than your dislike of the reference to Oscar Wilde at the Café Royal was it omitted??? It MUST be put back.' It was not, all in deference to the ignoramuses in 'Arizona or Orange County,' Sellers alleged.

I asked Jeffery what being a P.A. involved doing.

> Not a lot. Really just keeping him company when there was nobody around... In between films I travelled with him as a companion. I used to cook, or take it in turns with Lynne, if she was there...He used to send me off to his soothsayers— I'd have to deputise for him at palm-readings and things, to find out his future.
>
> He and Lynne had Candice Bergen's house. I was with him—he'd phone up (I had the guest cottage in the garden) and take me to dinner or the cinema. Then came *Being There*, and...after the film we went on holiday together, without Lynne...He'd decided he and I would go...to Oliver Messel's house in Barbados— which Lord Snowdon had told him about. We flew on a regular flight to Miami; then a private Lear jet to the island. In the Bermuda Triangle the engines cut out... suddenly it was weird. No noise. We were bounding off the ceiling and hitting things. Peter started chanting...a mantra—and there was an awful cracking sound...I thought the fuselage was splitting. I really thought we were going to die...Eventually, the engine spluttered on again...By the time we arrived in Barbados it was late at night, and the...driver didn't think we were going to arrive, so he'd gone home. We had to get a taxi for the half-hour drive to the house—and the staff had gone home. Nothing to eat. It was night and we were expected in the early afternoon. Peter was livid—hopping mad. 'I know what we'll do,' he said, 'We'll go to London." The pilot, who was in a hotel in Bridgetown, was got hold of. 'Can you take us back?" Peter refused to go to bed...
>
> We flew to Miami, and on to New York, and just missed the Concorde. We had to stay overnight in the Kennedy Hilton, an awful place surrounded by barbed wire and guards. Again, Peter wouldn't sleep. Next day, we got on to Concorde with Dustin Hoffman and his mother and Justin Henry from *Kramer vs. Kramer*.* Hoffman and Peter were discussing doing a film together. In London, we discovered that all the rooms at the Dorchester were booked, so we had to go to the Inn on the Park, where Peter was given Howard Hughes' old suite. We still hadn't slept—because he wouldn't sleep in New York...It was the day of the General Election [May 3, 1979], so...we stayed up all night watching the results coming in. When Thatcher won he sent an immediate telex to Number Ten Downing Street asking her to reduce the income tax so he could move back into the country. There was a reply from her saying that the next few years will be very hard...

---

* Hoffman was to beat Sellers, and Chance, to the Best Actor Oscar for that grinding *feuilleton*.

We went off on the *Berengaria*, which was moored off Cannes and Antibes, in June; and ... he'd pour his troubles out. I was totally inadequate to solving his troubles ... [which were] mainly his impotence, the loss of his virility. He went and had acupuncture treatment in Geneva ... He wanted me to have it done first—to see if it hurt! ...

Once we started shooting, Peter wouldn't go to view the rushes—and then he decided he would, after weeks and weeks, and he stormed out again, this time off the entire film. He went to Switzerland. Mike Medavoy, Eric Pleskow, Zev Braun—all the Hollywood big-wigs came over. Peter was in Intensive Care, in Geneva. I was in Paris and his driver took me all the way to the hospital. He was all alone. To get in, I told the nurse I was Mr Sellers' son; *he* told them his younger brother was coming. I had to sneak back out and get him a hamburger at eleven o'clock at night.

Another visitor at the Geneva hospital was David Tomlinson, who sensed that Sellers was channelling his energies into, and keeping himself going by 'a pathological hatred of producers. When he had a heart attack, over Christmas, Zev Braun ... who was genuinely appalled at the thought of Peter Sellers dying—tried to see him in Gstaad. Peter said "The only person I want to see is David." I flew to Switzerland ... but I could not persuade Peter to be kind and rational towards Zev. I said "He's a decent, honourable man." Peter said "I think he's a sack of shit."'

The film resumed; Lynne arrived 'with a revised dissolution agreement, signed by her, with instructions as to how Peter is to sign so that she can hand-carry to Geneva' the legal memo; sets were rebuilt for Sellers' re-shoots; people were inconvenienced (Simon Williams, for example, who had a commitment in the London West End in January 1980, had to commute back and forth to Paris every single day for three weeks); and the lawyers declared 'a pure *force majeure* [unforeseeable course of events discharging people from a fulfillment of their contracts] situation.'

◆ ◆ ◆

When Sellers became the director, he found a (literally) touching scene for Jeffery. Elsewhere, the doubling had been done by John Taylor; but in the last sequence, when Nayland finally gives Fu the magic rejuvenating medicine, 'I played Fu's hand, with the long pointed fingernails. Peter thought Taylor's hands were too fat for a close-up. Then, after that, it was back to Gstaad ... Peter wasn't a skier. He didn't like being there in season ... A beautiful house, La Haute Grange, but very boring ... He'd be on the phone a lot in the late afternoon, early evening, at night, to America. He'd be on the phone to Lynne for two or three hours at a go. She was away a lot towards the end. If he was down, he'd be on the phone to Spike or Tony Snowdon. Peter and Michael, his son, were getting very close; he came to stay and we'd go to the English pub and play darts. The funny thing about Mike—he never cried when his father died. A long while after, we went out to dinner ... he asked me if I thought his father had loved him. I said, "Of course he did, deep down and in his own strange way." Mike said he had to go off to the loo ... He was gone ages. When he came back I could tell he'd been crying his bloody eyes out. This happened to all of us. We went through a lot mentally with Peter.'

His sickliness enveloped everybody and the atmosphere, during those last

months, compounded by his entanglement of guilts, was awkward at best. Michael
Sellers says, apropos his visit to Gstaad: 'It was the February of the year he died.
On the second night, I was knackered [exhausted], idly staring at my plate. I just
wanted to go to sleep. He took Michael Jeffery off to one side and demanded
"What's the *matter* with him?" In a way, he didn't allow for other people, if they
didn't fit into his plans; unless they did what he wanted them to do ... Not that he
was always clear about what his plans might be from moment to moment ... He'd
create rules for us, as children, and then admonish us for breaking them—but he'd
not have made us privy to what his rules were in the first place. We did whatever
he wanted to do, or he just left us; very rarely, if ever, would he bend to our needs;
we fitted in with his needs.'

◆ ◆ ◆

There were others flitting in and out of his life, too, as it drew wretchedly to
its close: United Artists personnel, somewhat grotesquely trying to force another
Clouseau out of a dying man (Steven Bach described him as 'a spectral presence,
a man made of eggshells'), and Jim Moloney, who came to collaborate on *The Romance of the Pink Panther* screenplay. In this script (for which Sellers received a
million dollars; he'd have received two million more had the film been made),
potty Peter built in a few references to lost time but, on the whole, if *The Fiendish
Plot of Dr Fu Manchu* was about music halls and shadowlands, then *The Romance
of the Pink Panther* would allude to Sellers' years of fame and emptiness. The locations would have been luxurious: that is, he returned to the idle-class ambience
of *Casino Royale*. And his baccarat-keen heroine, Clouseau's adversary, the 'International Arch. Criminal, The Froeg,' could have been Ursula Andress' Vesper
Lynd, right down to her Bond-ish walkie-talkie, secreted in her lipstick.

The film would have had no actual story; nor even scenes—just blocks of (supposed) action, where the stuntmen could exhibit their talents. There aren't any jokes,
either. There's little, here, which they hadn't already put onto the silver nitrate in the
silent-movie era, and Sellers' own international-transatlantic super-rich Monte-
Carlo-or-bust tone is very dated, very sixties. That is why he wanted Clive Donner,
of *What's New, Pussycat?*, to direct. Sellers, yet again, was trying to outwit his ageing
body and pretend, by glancing and gazing across all the come-and-gone seasons, that
it was really twenty years ago, and that he had twenty years yet to live.

But what of Clouseau, wouldn't he be cadaverous? Not necessarily, for we'd
hardly see him for his disguises. He'd be inside the springs and stuffings of an antique chair, in an albino gorilla costume, or made up as 'the famous English clown,
Grock,' or as a moustachio'd W. C. Fields. (It would have been John Taylor's film.)
What was quintessential Sellers, however, was the flirting and courting of Clouseau and The Froeg, which would have stopped the film dead—scene upon scene
of champagne toasts and sweet nothings; and, underneath the romance, the inevitable self-pity: 'I'm going to shock you, Cato. I know you have always thought
of me as being the irresistible, debonair, ladies' man. That is only a clever appearance. In truth, beautiful women have never been attracted to me.' Cato, who
was never the Inspector's confidant, is unlikely to have had any thoughts on the

matter, one way or the other; that is solely Sellers speaking. And how was Anastasia Puissance, The Froeg bride, envisioned? She was to be 'breathtakingly beautiful, her long, jet-black hair set off by alabaster skin and topaz eyes. She radiates a deep and mysterious sensuality, tantalisingly amplified by the outline of her perfect and long-legged body as accentuated by the tightly wrapped towel ...'

Beyond the eye-popping intensity of the adolescent prose—all radiation, amplification, accentuation—we can immediately picture Sophia Loren, Sellers' one big excitement. (Anastasia receives advice and hears ancestral voices from a family portrait, as Epifania does in *The Millionairess*.) The script, completed a week before his death and mailed off to United Artists on July 16 with a cover note from 'Peter Shakespeare' ('No joking, I think it's bloody terrific, and I hope you will' the proud author stated), was to be his final attempt at connecting himself with a woman whose presence had inspired and disturbed him. 'It shows a facet of Clouseau's character which hasn't been seen before,' he explained to Auberon Waugh. 'He has a real-life romance with a French countess who tempts him away from the Sûreté.' His irresponsibility, his hostility—his adherence to the pleasure-principle—went uncontrolled. He was careless and indignant—and, in a cartoonish lightweight way, Clouseau is glad to fall from grace and experiment with crime. Like Sellers himself, he gets to be conscious of his alienation.

In between uprooting the saplings of 'Peg's Tree', because the ominous crows had pecked at them, and lighting bonfires, during the last weekend in Gstaad—'He decided to get rid of all the photographs of Lynne,' says Jeffery, 'and anything to do with Britt was put on'—Sellers was having consultations with Clive Donner, who recalls that: 'There had been a final and irrevocable break with Blake. A curious relationship, extraordinary. Sellers was noted for developing a scene, seeing the rushes next day, and demanding it be done again. His personal doubts and insecurities cast aspersions on Blake's comic judgement—and this caused many a conflict ... Peter very much wanted to make *The Romance of the Pink Panther*. He said, "It will be the last one, the best one"—and he personally asked me to direct it. At Christmas 1979 I went to Gstaad; we met again in the summer ... But it was getting to be a complicated set-up ... Lynne was to be executive producer ... but she did not take part in these discussions. She was in America. I worked with Peter in Switzerland, trying to get a comic flow to the scenes in his script; United Artists were very keen for us to proceed. We spoke to a production manager, who flew from Paris. I had to get back to Los Angeles by the end of the week. Peter said, "I'll see you on Saturday. I could do with a few days in England first. I'm going to meet up with Spike and Harry on Tuesday." I remember flying with him in a private jet, early on the Monday [July 21], sitting opposite him, and he was wearing a tracksuit with a zip. I said to him, "Peter, where is your pacemaker?" "It's here!" he said, brandishing his scars. "And there's a new one coming out and I'm going to have that fitted." An extension of his gadget fixation. We met up again on the Monday night in London. On the Tuesday morning I spoke to him on the phone before leaving for Los Angeles. When I arrived in Los Angeles he was dead.'

◆ ◆ ◆

The narrative is picked up by Michael Jeffery: 'We spent our last afternoon on an outing to Gruyère. I took some snaps of Peter on the ramparts of the castle. The day after that we flew to Stanstead with Clive and Jocelyn [Rickards, the art director]. On the way to the Dorchester, we stopped at the crematorium. The times we'd been to the crematorium and got to the gate and he wouldn't go in! When we actually went in I was very surprised. We smuggled in our flowers, a rose for Peg and a rose for Bill; we lay them just under the bush and then we went to see the new plaque. "Do you want to see the ovens?" he asked. "No I *don't*," I said. We went on to the hotel. He saw Elwood Rickless that afternoon and we went for a walk around St. James' Park, and over the bridge where they did a scene for *The Magic Christian*.'

Rickless remembers his visits to the hotel suite:

He wanted to finalise a trust fund for Victoria, who was then aged fifteen. The figure of twenty thousand pounds froze in his mind. He didn't seem to see that, because of inflation, the twenty thousand which Michael and Sarah had received when they reached the age of twenty-one would now be worth a lot less. His attitude was: 'I started with nothing. I came up from nothing. They have had twenty thousand pounds, which is twenty thousand pounds more than I had.' And he was looking back happily to the days when he earned twenty-five quid as a stand-up comic. Even when he was capable of commanding millions, at the back of his mind he'd rather have been a stand-up comic. This was the impression he gave me, anyway—that he never came to terms with the demands of stardom.

He was flying to America partially on *The Romance of the Pink Panther* business, but chiefly for an angiogram and tests—all preliminaries to major open-heart surgery, which was his only hope of prolonging his life. (He should have had this sort of operation fifteen years earlier, but he had a dread of going under the knife.) He stopped off in London to see Spike and me. I saw him on the morning of the day he collapsed. He looked very unhealthy—ghastly, ghostly. At the same time he had a ruddy complexion and was wearing a tracksuit. He'd been standing on his head to give himself colour. He looked pale and sickly and flushed at the same time.

I must say, few people die as well-prepared. His Will and legal affairs were in perfect order.

Rickless, who had the task of arranging payment of his client's hospital bills, was told by a consultant at the Middlesex that had Sellers had the angiogram, he wouldn't have pulled through it; and Michael Sellers concurs with the gloomy prognosis: 'He was too ill to be saved, according to the doctors who examined him ... Only four years earlier, however, he'd met Dr Christiaan Barnard, was invited to South Africa, and agreed on a bypass operation. My father was allowed to photograph heart surgery in detail—and it suddenly dawned on him that *that's* what they'd be doing to him in the next few days. He went back to his hotel room, booked a flight, locked the door, wouldn't come out, wouldn't speak to anyone, and left. Subsequently he got ill again, needed treatment, and he and Lynne went off to meet those charlatans in the Phillipines, who extracted pigs' entrails from the ends of their fingers whilst they were massaging his heart. They advised him to stop taking medication, which he did. They said, "You're fine now. You're cured." He believed them, and he promptly keeled over. He was put in a proper hospital and fitted with a pacemaker.'

At the time of his death, his heart was as big as his chest—a huge swelling of tissues and tentacles, fluttering to little effect; a great, sad sea-creature, out of its element, a fish in air. 'He was having constant heart attacks—we were forever getting urgent calls,' says Rickless. What Sellers was growing accustomed to were Adams-Stokes attacks, mini heart attacks, during which he blacked out for a few seconds owing to ventricular tachycardia (excessive heart beats) or fibrillation (quivering and irregular beats). The pacemaker was meant to prevent these, but evidently complete cardiac arrest, and death's terror, was imminent.

'We had lunch,' says Jeffery. 'Dover Sole and salad. He had a second helping. Sue Evans, his secretary arrived. I went to get his clothes ready for the evening, and Sue suddenly yelled *"Michael!"* He was sitting at the table, his face bright blue, and he fell sideways off the chair ... The Dorchester's nurse was there within seconds; they called a doctor and Peter was given mouth-to-mouth resuscitation. It was pretty horrible. We followed the ambulance in the car to the Middlesex Hospital, a six-minute ride away. Michael Sellers arrived ... Yes, it was on Peter's mind that he would die.'

Sellers was on the Dorchester's sixth floor, in suites 611 and 612. Those rooms do not exist anymore. They were lost when the hotel was gutted and refurbished a few years ago. I would find it hard to explain quite why I find that so symbolic and right, but I do.

◆ ◆ ◆

A little before The Goons were due to arrive at the Trattoo restaurant, on Tuesday, July 22, Alan Clare, the pianist, received a phone call.

'Well, Peter won't be coming tonight,' said Milligan, at the other end of the line.

'Oh why? That's a shame,' replied Clare.

'Because he's dead.'

'Come off it Spike. Don't play games like that.'

'Well, he hasn't been breathing for about twelve minutes—doesn't that mean he's dead?'

'So he's died?'

'But Harry and I are still coming over, with Britt.'...

'*Tonight?* If Peter's just *died?* What *for?*'

'Well, I'd like to hear her side of the story.'

So Milligan listened to this long harangue about what a bastard Sellers had been to her. Secombe remained at home; and, Clare says, 'I was surprised when I met Britt. I thought she was just another toy which Peter had gone around the corner and bought; but I quite liked her—she was intelligent and nice.'

She had flown from Stockholm, with Victoria, the moment she'd grasped the gravity of the news ('I knew that my first duty was to bring Victoria to London. I felt it was right she should be at her father's bedside, like his other children'). Also jetting into town was Lynne Frederick, who had only said in an interview four months previously: 'It's a fifty-fifty chance whether we get a divorce.' Michael Sellers would put the odds much higher. During his last conversation with his father, Sellers had said to him: 'She annoys me. I just wish the divorce was over and done with.' He was worried about the forthcoming surgery and that Lynne would try and take charge of him: 'What if she shows up at the hospital? I don't want her there... She's bound to catch up with me.'

All Sellers needed to have done, of course, if he genuinely felt so oppressed, was to re-summon Elwood Rickless, add a new codicil to his will, and sign the papers. He did not—or shall I say, if such was his intention, he did not have time to act upon it. In the event, Lynne did catch up with him at the hospital, though hardly the hospital he had in mind. Despite what Milligan thought, when he dined with Britt and Alan Clare on the Tuesday, Sellers was not totally deceased. He was in a deep coma—and his brain, starved of oxygen during those bright blue moments on the Dorchester carpet, when his heart stopped beating and his breathing ceased, was now irreversibly vegetative. Lynne, landing in London on Wednesday, July 23, after an eleven-hour flight (arrival formalities were waived at Heathrow to get her to the Middlesex as quickly as possible), was confronted by a death-bed scene. Sellers had had emergency treatment in the ambulance, to combat the unconsciousness and loss of pulse; he needed further, or continued, resuscitation in the casualty department, and only then was he transferred to the intensive care unit. 'He is critically ill,' said Mr David Johnson on behalf of the hospital. 'He has received a lot of drug therapy in intensive care.' Later on Wednesday, a further bulletin was posted: 'There has been a deterioration in Mr Sellers' condition, which is now very grave.' He was hooked up to a life-support machine; an endotracheal tube was introduced to ventilate him; electrodes were glued to his arms and chest to relay plips and plops to computer screens—and his entire body was wrapped in foil, to preserve its heat. The effect was of a flimsy armour for the frailest White Knight.

'He is in a coma and unconscious,' Lynne told the press. 'But he had hung on for me to come. Of that I am sure... there is no clinical or medical explanation how he could have stayed alive with all his senses gone... He had worked so hard to stay alive until I could get to him, but finally it was too much.'

Perhaps, in one final crazy decisive deed, he intended gathering himself enough to spit in her eye?

◆ ◆ ◆

'After Sue and I were having lunch and he went blue and collapsed,' says Michael Jeffery, 'I lay on the floor of the hospital in the nurses' office for two days. The Sister [Head Nurse] said, "He's stable. Go and get some rest." And just as we returned to the Dorchester the phone was ringing. "He's deteriorated. Can you come back..." By the time we'd got back, he'd gone. It was terrible seeing him on that machine. We used to hold his hand and talk to him—Michael, Sarah, Victoria, and I, and then Lynne—there was a chance he could hear us. As it was coming up to the Friday, I suggested to Michael that we bring the shrine-photograph of Peg. But he died on the Thursday [just: at 12:26 A.M., July 24], and the funeral was on the Saturday.'

The committal was to take place on the Jewish Sabbath, but that didn't seem to matter. 'Mr Sellers' death was entirely due to natural causes,' said a hospital spokesman. 'His heart just faded away ... Every effort was made to keep his heart going, but ... there is a limit to what can be done.' In Malibu, the former Serpent of the Nile and Helen of Troy—she, who like the Mona Lisa, has been dead many times—sat up with a bolt. 'Something has happened to Peter Sellers!' said Shirley MacLaine. Later on, when a reporter telephoned to confirm her premonition, she thought: 'Yes, you probably think he's dead, but he's really only left his latest body.' Nearer to home, at Willen, a village near Milton Keynes, the spirit medium Doris Collins experienced heart murmurs: 'I heard a voice saying: "Doris, God help me." I would say it was Peter reaching out to me.' In London, Graham Stark left the celebrity party for Alan Parker's *Fame* because, though not a believer 'in extra-sensory perception, some hunch ... told me that this wasn't the night to go dancing.' He toasted his pal silently with a cup of tea: 'Here's to the memory of Leading Aircraftsman P. Sellers ...' And on a beach in Mallorca, Bloom Clare, Alan's wife, found herself crying and crying.

No doubt there were eagles and comets, lionesses whelping in the streets, and any number of portentous things as the great necromancer was flying beyond the sheltering sky. 'I'm well prepared for when I enter the after-life. My mother has talked to me about it frequently since she died in 1967,' he'd said whilst at the Cannes Film Festival, so very recently. 'I feel her through vibrations in my head. When I had my first heart attack in 1964 and was actually dead for almost three minutes, I saw my mother. It was just too early for me to die. She pulled me back from the grave. She is always here looking after me, helping me in a crisis. We're as close as any mother and son could be.' Peg must have been an amazing woman if she could march into the underworld and behave like a gliding ghost three years *before* she was actually grassed over. Indubitably deceased by 1980, however, she was able to warn Sellers that 'the day will come soon when she will tell me it's time to pack it in. It will happen simply and I have no fears.'

The paradox is, though he could act old, he didn't want to be old. He had a dread of being an invalid, and getting old and sick. He wanted to be forever young—but instead of remaining youthful in his enthusiasms, he grew spiteful, disruptive. He didn't actually care for (real) children, yet he'd aim to please, like a child, and mainly he'd aim to hurt. (Lynne, wise to the Peter Pan performance, would respond by being Wendy: 'I would just say, "You know, it's naughty to do things like that [*what?*] and I don't like you for it." But I never stopped loving him.')

◆ ◆ ◆

Sellers told Herbert Lom that he was proud only of two films: '*Doctor Strangelove*, in which he always believed, and *Being There*, where he walks on water at the end. Otherwise he was disappointed and mixed up.' I think it is possible to understand how these works are connected. They are about immaturity and morbidity. Sellers' films, from the early black-and-white efforts to Fu undergoing funny Adams-Stokes attacks, are often funerary and (fleetingly) poetic; and Chance in his winter garden and the politicians and soldiers willfully covering the planet with mushroom clouds symbolise a satirical extreme of sterility and dereliction. The atmosphere of *Being There* is passive, doped; that of *Doctor Strangelove*, by contrast, is anxious and busy. But in both, men behave like children; and is it a coincidence, or what, that the one was made at the peak of Sellers' early fame, and the other right at the end, when his lacks and losses were, miraculously, converted into an acting style?

Being There was a lullaby and a swansong, Sellers being the pale faint swan who chanted a doleful hymn to his own death; *Doctor Strangelove*, still in the nursery, is brattish. (The war room is a playroom where grown men can express themselves by smashing up the world.) The only tender—maternal—moment is the credit sequence, with the planes suckling—refuelling—in mid-flight. (The nuclear bombs, couched in the fuselage, are a pair of eggs.) After that, it's a Boy's Own story. George C. Scott sulks, pouts and interjects. Peter Bull, as the Russian Ambassador, is sullen and sneaky (he is covered with hidden cameras and espionage equipment). Major Kong, aboard the errant B-52, takes a childish glee in the gadgetry at his disposal. Doctor Strangelove himself is the class nerd, fiddling with his pocket calculator and slide rule; Merkin Muffley, the President, is like the weedy teacher's pet, left in charge whilst the adults are off elsewhere.

The performances are frenzied (and funny) because these grown men, with their uniforms, guns, and dens, take themselves so seriously—they don't realise that they are only six years old, mentally. No wonder the original idea was for Sellers to have taken on the whole kindergarten. 'In fact,' he admitted, 'I was going to do them *all*. Stanley Kubrick was convinced I could...And I'd say, "I physically can't do it!...I'll try and do the Slim Pickens thing, but I mean I think that's *enough*."'

As it turned out, Slim Pickens himself was hired to play the Slim Pickens rôle, Major Kong. Sellers decided he wasn't happy with his attempts at a Texan accent—though the official reason he gave for abandoning the sequence was a broken ankle. However, says Hattie Stevenson, 'it was *not* a broken ankle, but he still insisted on getting put in a plaster cast so he could get out of the part. He then became terribly sarcastic and nasty because Slim Pickens was so good.'

With infantilism prevalent on screen and off, Kubrick's decision to lop off the last reel is to be deplored. 'After a screening of *Doctor Strangelove* I cut out a final scene in which the Russians and Americans in the War Room engaged in a free-for-all fight with custard pies. I decided it was farce and not consistent with the satiric tone of the rest of the film.' Has ever a director so misunderstood and failed to perceive the drift and nature of his own work? The film builds to that pie fight—it should culminate in the children's delight in destruction. It was an error of judgement to deny us that; now the film ends abruptly, with Peter Bull going off to photograph the big board computers and Strangelove tottering out of his chair.

The person who recalled the pâtisserie tournament best was Sellers, who looked back in April 1980 with much merriment to 'the famous alternative ending...Stanley has a copy of it. The pie fight started with the Russian ambassador photographing the big board again, and George C. Scott rushes over and chases the scared ambassador behind the buffet table. The Russian says "You vill pay for diss!" And he picks up a large pie and goes to hurl it at George C. Scott. He ducks and it hits me, the President, full in the face. Scott says "Gentlemen, our beloved President has been struck down in the prime of life by *pie*! We demand merciful retaliation!" And of course, the whole army, air force, and navy hate each other anyway and they start on the ambassador, and then they start on each other. Strangelove eventually turns out like—you know when you see a bug and you spray it and spray it until it's slimy and can't move? Well, just everybody pelted him until he couldn't get up. And he's trying to get back on his chair and the more he grabbed it the further it went away from him. In this sea of muck, cake, and what-have-you, [Peter Bull,] George C. Scott and the President are seen in a corner like little kids making mud pies. Their minds are gone. Suddenly, you see a heaving mess drag himself out and it's Strangelove. He gets a gun and fires it in the air and says: "Gentlemen, gentlemen, don't you realise what will happen to us all in a moment? This pie is non-protective! We must go down to the shelter as quickly as possible. Don't worry about showers, we have plenty down there. Through the mine shaft!" And as they all go out of the room you hear the song "We'll Meet Again."'

♦ ♦ ♦

Sellers had clearly enjoyed himself; he'd been back where he wanted to be—in early childhood, engrossed and rampaging. As he did not take other people seriously, it never worried him that the rest of us were being denied the scene ('Well, Stan felt it was a bit long there.'). But if a missing ten minutes is a tantalisation, what about a missing whole feature?* *The Blockhouse*, which hardly anyone has ever seen, functions, in effect, as a sequel to *Doctor Strangelove*—it is about the candlelit years seventy-foot underground, with collapsed walls of a thirty-foot reinforced concrete thickness separating the survivors from any way of escaping back to the surface. One by one the men—yes, as so often in a commendable Sellers film, there are no ladies present—lose their reason and die off in grisly fashion.

It is a film of portraits; of icons, in a way. Down in the underworld, ravaged faces peer from the gloom: Charles Aznavour as a sharp-faced, beady-eyed chancer from Marseilles; Per Oscarsson as a weird blonde giant who thinks he can hammer and chisel his way to freedom; Jeremy Kemp, as a Polish officer who tries to keep his dignity, and who goes to pieces; and Sellers. It is simply a scandal that his performance as Rouquet, the schoolmaster, has been allowed to slip into oblivion—but that's by the way. The fact is, in terms of the pained, cheerless Sellers whom I have tunnelled out in this book, *The Blockhouse* is the crucial opus. It is about a living death. The men get more ill, older, paler; they don't know how long they have been trapped. Time no longer has any meaning. They put on blankets and come to resemble strange, hunched medieval figures; and, with all the candles, the bunker is like a cathedral under the earth. There is little action. The film succeeds in its mood—fear, claustrophobia, the endlessness of the webs of darkness encircling them—because of the feelings which emanate from the actors.

If Hell were photographed, it would be similar to these catacombs. Sellers'

---

* Of the many kindnesses I was shown as I wrote this book, one which stood out was the special screening of the single extant print of *The Blockhouse* which Clive Rees arranged for me.

Rouquet is the least demonstrative of its denizens. He's always quietly examining things: the ladder, the wine, the firebrands. He jots in a diary. He makes calculations. He's methodical, pedantic—ever the schoolmaster. By timing how long a candle lasts, he works out the passage of time—soon they have been buried alive for seven weeks, and excitement has turned to fear.

Rouquet, however, tries to stay alert. He recites the poetry he has memorised and chalks lines and rhymes on the walls. He plays chess with candle stubs ('There is no point playing with you—you always win,' he is told) and he organises a game of dominoes—in a speech Sellers improvised. 'The origin of the game dominoes—it sounds Greek, "dominos"; maybe it was discovered by an Englishman in Greece, and he brought it back.' Rouquet explains the rules—it is the longest speech in the film. It was the character's one lapse, which I think important, into being more typically Sellers.

"'It comes from the Greek dominos"—all that ... completely improvised!' concurs Kemp. 'He made it up there and then. It went on for ... several minutes—until I could bear it no longer. The wit and ingenuity of this attribution of a game of dominoes to the Greeks ... worked. Peter was able to give free range to his extemporising powers, but there was no sense of it being other than this man Rouquet, a schoolmaster from Northern France, doing the talking. He never budged out of character. Poignant, and rather beautiful—and the muted, detailed, miniaturist performance contrasts very sorrily with how he'd grown by *The Prisoner of Zenda*.'

As a prisoner in the sunless cellar, where they have forgotten what the progression of the seasons was like, Sellers is to be glimpsed in the background of most shots, punctiliously dipping his food in a pinch of salt (he's not a slob like the others) or trimming his beard, his big brown liquid eyes slowly taking everything in. After a while we notice that he is having trouble with his little spectacles, or is it his eyes? Down in the dimness, he is failing to focus on his disintegrating books. He huddles in corners. With a short tilting back of his head, he lets out a sigh. Suddenly, he has the screen to himself. He is looking at a sepia postcard. The creased picture is of the school where he'd taught. He puts the treasure back in his spectacle case, snaps it shut, and goes off, out of frame. We see him clipping open a bag of cooking flour. He cuts his wrists and plunges them into the powdery sacks, letting his life drain away. It is as if he is falling asleep. His life extinguishes with the last of his candles.

Sellers' character articulates the fact that, in extreme circumstances, it is perhaps better to end your life than to live on into further mental and physical disintegration. That is why he kills himself—which he does in the same neat, practical way he'd brought to everything else. Rouquet is a sensitive man—we pick up his emotions and what he is going through without there needing to be dialogue or interplay. As an experiment in what the art of acting can achieve, I'd rate it higher than *Being There*—perhaps because Sellers makes no attempt to dominate any scene, and *The Blockhouse* is not sentimental.

More true to form was Sellers' obliviousness to other people's feelings. He'd snap away with his stills camera or make his funny voices. As Rees says: 'He could be incredibly sensitive, and yet also be totally blind to things ... [Jeremy Kemp] found [the last scene] very hard to do. He ... was on the verge of a nervous break-down. Everybody knew how delicate this was. When Peter heard afterwards, he hadn't realised at all—and yet he'd be completely sensitive to other things.'

Though Sellers conveyed the impression that he could keep the mood jokey, by coming out with goonish rubbish between takes, entertaining the crew, he was equally distressed. On occasion he'd weep, owing to problems he was having with his marriage (to Miranda), people supposed. He'd fall into deep sleeps on the set—yogic trances, it was alleged. Bert Mortimer, who ran the household on Guernsey, where the film was made, had long been used to his master's threats of suicide—an old gambit 'to get what he wanted. It was a form of emotional black-mail.' But during *The Blockhouse*, suicide was no longer a game. Because he was on an island, remote from the world, and working in a deep cavern, where his char-acter was severed from the world, Sellers' strange, strong fears and sense of dis-sociation were intensified. 'He was so wrapped up in the part,' said Mortimer. 'I believed he might actually do it. And Peter was nervous himself that it might ac-tually come about. I was out of my mind with worry about it, because for many years I had lived with his suicide threats.'

Sellers didn't attempt anything dramatic—perhaps there weren't the right sort of people in the vicinity to try and impress? In default of suicide, it was as if he resolved to flinch, in the future, from the serious and confounding business of drawing on himself when acting; henceforward he would be shallow, vulgar, care-less (and intermittently brilliant). If films of the mid- and late-sixties were bad, those of the seventies were worse. Down in the blockhouse, when Sellers felt perdition catch his soul, instead of killing himself, he buried his career—though, in saying that, I am aware that I am talking about a man who gave more pleasure to the public than almost any other actor since the grafting of sound to moving pictures. What he achieved was more than most people manage—hence the huge scale of his failure, too. It was a failure, I think, of energy. Sellers lost his glint. The climate darkened. His paranoia, sense of futility, aggression, explosiveness, vanity, hysteria, procrastination, and intentional bad behaviour all got worse.

◆ ◆ ◆

Rouquet, entombed and watching the lights go out, one by one, is a symbol of what happened to Sellers, whose life showed not development but reduction. He began by aspiring, he ended by raging. (He attained what Samuel Beckett called a 'nullity of being'.) When Lynne met him he was already half a ghost, hov-ering in a Roebuck House apartment which she considered 'faceless—like a large Hilton hotel suite. Even the few paintings looked as though they had been moved in by a firm. The bedroom was functional, the walls were white and bare.' Thus the habitat, thus the man, who was as chilled as stone.

Conversation, too, between the young girl and the wasting man was of death or (a related topic) sterility. Michael Sellers once heard a harrowing tape his fa-ther had secretly recorded of a private phone call to Lynne, in which he told her about his horror of impotence and of a consultation with a Dr. Brock: 'I told him that the problem resulted in a rift between my wife and me and was causing an awful lot of pain and depression.' The journalist David Lewin was in the right of it when he said the marriage was not about beginnings—new starts, new hope— but endings—for Lynne had told him: 'Peter would talk to me often about what to do when he died and...he would go over and over the plans—almost like a dress rehearsal—for getting him back home, so he could be cremated in Golders Green, where the ashes of his mother and father are.'

When the day dawned to carry out the last wishes, on Saturday, July 26, 1980, it was as if Sellers, like Prospero, had bedimmed the noontide sun. London was plunged into a perilous night. The sky was full of flying shapes—witches?—the winds ripped at the trees and chimneys, and cross-blue lightning flashed upon the funeral procession as it headed, twenty-five minutes late, along the Finchley Road to the furnaces.

The fifteen-minute (Anglican) ceremony was conducted by Canon John Hester, who remarked: 'In its own way it was the right weather for the occasion, with a thunderstorm to give Peter a suitably theatrical send-off. It would have appealed to his sense of humour.' Fewer than thirty mourners were allowed to attend,* though approximately two hundred people gathered outside the chapel to pay their respects. Lynne, by making it an invitation-only do, had hoped to debar any ex-wives from the service. Britt, however, demonstrating the independent streak which Sellers had hated her for (and which any sane person can see is nothing but admirable), decided to break the embargo; she wanted to look after Victoria, who was sobbing non-stop—and also 'I went to the funeral to pay homage to a man whose life I once shared. It was my duty to show him that respect.'

Lynne didn't see it that way. As she made her way down the aisle, towards the oak coffin—was Sellers inside? I have failed to trace the undertakers. Had he been spirited away to a secret crypt and freeze-dried?†—she suddenly bridled. Later, in a reception at the Dorchester (which Britt steered clear of), she flew at Victoria: 'What was your mother doing there?' Michael Jeffery had to intercede: 'Please don't cry, Victoria. We all knew your father once loved your mother, so please don't pay too much attention to what Lynne is saying. She's too upset to know what she means.' Nevertheless, her anger—it was almost as if the prima donna resented being upstaged—was all over the front pages the next day. 'I certainly... didn't invite her,' Lynne was quoted as saying, from the Dorchester's Harlequin Suite. 'I was amazed when she turned up in the chapel.'

---

* They comprised: the widow and her immediate family (to whom she had very recently started speaking again after a four year estrangement. 'The bitterness is still there,' she was to say later); the three children; Jeffery; Milligan; Secombe; Bentine; Ve and Do (Mrs Vera Elmore and Mrs Vera Marks, the last survivors of Mr Herbert Ray's Company); David Lodge; Graham Stark; Alexander Walker; Evelyn de Rothschild; the Earl of Snowdon; Theo Cowan; Jim Maloney; Brother Cornelius; Dennis Selinger; and Britt Ekland. Plus assorted spouses.

† We may call into question the truth of this exchange:

  Parkinson: 'You were at the funeral, weren't you?'
  Milligan: 'Yes—so was Peter.'

The funeral service had included a reading from the gospel of St. John, Chapter XIV—verses normally designated for the Monday before Easter:

> Let not your heart be troubled, neither let it be afraid. Ye have heard how I said unto you, I go away, and come again unto you. If ye loved me, ye would rejoice, because I said, I go unto the Father: for my Father is greater than I. And now I have told you before it come to pass, that, when it is come to pass, ye might believe... Arise, let us go hence...

Before the congregation did so, Canon Hester explained that, in place of the normal hymns and arias, Sellers would trundle on to the pyre to one of his requested tunes—'In the Mood.' Michael Sellers had gone out and bought the LP the previous day. His father had always said that the big band sound was wonderfully inappropriate—hence, wonderfully appropriate—for solemn occasions. Bentine said it was Sellers' *least* favourite number—that, when he'd been a dance hall drummer, he came to hate it so much, he was, in retrospect, fond of it. Stark, too, said that only when 'In the Mood' started to pipe through the chapel speakers did a full sense of loss finally overwhelm him: 'There, in my mind... was Leading Aircraftsman Peter Sellers, smart as paint in his best Air Force uniform, confidently gliding across the dance floor at the Nuffield Centre, holding a pretty WAAF in his arms.' He felt that, had he but glanced upwards, a spotlit rotating sphere would have been dangling from the chapel ceiling.

The crowds, press photographers, and policemen in their rain capes pressed against the celebrity mourners as they quit the building and found their limousines. The following day, Michael Sellers, Michael Jeffery, Ve and Do, Sarah, and Victoria returned to Golders Green to examine the wreaths. They were surprised to see a long queue of people intent on the same errand. Jeffery went to the front and whispered to the attendant that 'Mr Sellers' family would like to come and see the flowers'—so they were ushered along, very conscious of being stared at. Messages scribbled on the cards were Goonish and Pink Pantherish: 'Farewell, Pink Panther'; 'Ying Tong Iddle I Po Forever'; Burt Kwouk's floral tribute was signed 'Cato', Harry Secombe's ('Bluebottle is deaded now') 'Neddy Seagoon'.

'I took Ve and Do to see the rose bush, which had had two fully-blown roses on,' Jeffery told me. '"One for Peg and one for Bill," Peter'd said. When I went up with Ve and Do, there were the two blooms still, and one bud. Peter would have loved that.'

◆ ◆ ◆

That's so fucking corny, I thought to myself, as I left Michael Jeffery's flat and walked to Chalk Farm Underground station, intending to return to Paddington and Oxford. Instead I rode the Northern Line three stops to Golders Green, crossed over to Hoop Lane and entered the crematorium gardens, where the recently-dead are sprinkled like slug repellent across the soil. Sellers' is rose bush number 39802. There is a small plaque nearby, placed by Lynne: 'My darling husband I will always love you'; and on the wall behind is the *Being There* gibberish:

'Life is a state of mind'
WITH EVERLOVING MEMORIES
PETER SELLERS
C.B.E.
1925–1980

I was aware of the corny impulse behind my own pilgrimage: Hamlet in the grave-yard, handling the clown's skull and asking it: 'Where be your gibes now? Your gambols? Your songs? Your flashes of merriment?' But when he was alive, Sellers wasn't Yorick, he was the prince—a mother-fixated man, 'Constantly occupied with the world within, and abstracted from the world without, giving substance to shadows, and throwing a mist over all commonplace actualities…His senses are in a state of trance, and he looks upon external things as hieroglyphics' (Coleridge); 'he who has felt his mind sink within him, and sadness cling to his heart like a malady, who has his hopes blighted and his youth staggered by the apparitions of strange things; who cannot be well at ease, while he sees evil hovering near him like a spectre; whose powers of action have been eaten up by thought; he to whom the universe seems infinite, and himself nothing; whose bitterness of soul makes him careless of consequences, and who goes to a play as his best resource to shove off, to a second remove, the evils of life by a mock representation of them—this is the true Hamlet' (Hazlitt); 'the whole drama is the tragedy of the convulsed reaction of the mind from the flesh, of the spirit from the self' (D. H. Lawrence).

I knew that my adventure was almost over, and that one of the meanings of Sellers had come to me. Looking at the flowers and leaves, the ashes and atoms, the memorial stone benches with cobwebs at their corners, and at the flakes and silt swelling into gusts of wind, I could see that Sellers, in the dissolutions of his personality when he was alive, and in the transmutations he continued to make after he was dead—into dust, blooms, obituaries, thousands of different, jostling recollections—had demonstrated the essential alterations—of one thing becoming another, and another—that (against the odds, given how I have belaboured Sellers the King of Shadows) are on the side of life. He was like a running stream. You only have to ask yourself 'Did Sellers have a death wish?' to grasp this. And of course he didn't want to die. He lived a pretty wild, unhealthy sort of existence, and it was his body and brain which let him down. But it was not a death wish—more like the opposite. He had a biological and constitutional tendency towards melancholia, and he fought against this and tried to be vivacious—indeed, his intractability (if you were not on the receiving end of it) could be deemed heroic. There was great comment in his work, especially in the forlorn characters. Everything he saw and heard he turned to mimicry, impressionism, immediately, like a reflex. His joy of observation, and his joy in expressing what he felt, may be traced right from 'The Goon Show' to *Being There*: when he looked at the world he saw its ludicrousness.

What my other conclusion was you may discover in the last chapter.

Chapter Fifteen

✦✦✦

The Evil That Men Do

The astute reader—and the root-faced reviewer—will have noticed that, what with all the digressions, diversions, curvilineations, and white-water pages, day-to-day detail was, with certain exceptions, let go in 1963. Here is why. On Sunday, August 12, 1990, I placed an author's inquiry in the *Los Angeles Times*. Amongst my many respondents was Michael Selsman, who had been Sellers' account executive at Rogers & Cowan, a public relations firm. He said that Sellers 'was an unusual client, even for an actor. Troubled doesn't begin to describe him.' For my interest, he enclosed a carbon of a letter he'd written, twenty-seven years previously, which contained some telling phrases:

> To answer your question, we do not intend to carry on as before. We intend to carry on a good deal better than before...
>
> I think, Peter, that... our immediate job is to re-evaluate the magazine situation and to initiate extensive text and photo pieces on your behalf...
>
> I think one facet of the trade press has been ignored and that is the editorial column which should point out your continuing and growing importance to the world film industry regarding the amount of business you stimulate at the box office and the image as an actor you project...
>
> We have not taken full advantage in the past of the very good relationship we had with Theo Cowan. I will endeavour to correct that...
>
> In sum, there have been whole areas of neglect which you can rest assured will be corrected...
>
> If you have any thoughts, Peter, about what I have said here, one way or another, or if there is something I have not said, please let me know and it shall be done.

We can see from this (propitiatory) letter—clearly sent in response to some complaint—that Sellers was a madman who thought he was Sellers. He had become, by 1963, the star he wanted to be, and he did not wish to resist his own legend. He was sucked into a machine that manufactured facades, false fronts; and the truth, the reality, of his nature and temperament was to be hidden. He would address long letters to newspaper reviewers, for example, not because he had any personal respect for them, but because he considered them an important component in his fame; their good opinion was worth fostering. (One, dated September 23, 1963, sent to Alexander Walker from New York, plugs *A Shot in the Dark*— 'we should be all set for a very good time, and a cracking film in the process.')

Peter Evans told me that Sellers had a brilliant nose for news, for getting himself coverage. 'It was Sellers who helped me to get that job [show business editor] on the *Express*. He kept giving me very good stories about himself and other people. I was selling these stories as a freelance. I could depend on a front page Sellers story about once a month.' Sellers trusted Evans, and later entrusted him with his life, or Life. 'As a showbiz columnist I consequently got to know Sellers extremely well ... In about 1965 we started talking about doing his biography—his idea entirely. Would I like to do it? The more I listened to him talking about himself, the more I realised that he had secrets in him, depths, and a history, and I hadn't realised this.'

My present point is simply that Sellers, under his apparent gregariousness and ingratiation, was quite consciously and cunningly furthering his own career. Rampant ambition is all very well, but Sellers was avid and devious. (As a character in *Sweet Smell of Success* says, 'I'm nice to people where it pays me to be nice.') He turned himself into a commodity. He stopped being real. How this contrasts with his first dealings with fame, when he'd visited America a few years previously, in April 1960. Then he had taken umbrage at being referred to as 'the property'. As he told Dilys Powell: 'It's strange the way people look on an actor. I went to America for the première of *I'm All Right, Jack* ... I was interviewed by everybody in America, so it seemed to me; if my friend Graham Stark hadn't been with me I think it would have killed me. When I arrived in New York ... my hotel room ... was crammed with people. There was one character on the telephone; just as I came into the room I could hear him say "I must get off the line, the property's arrived." That's what it is: one is just a property.'

It was the twelve days which shook his world. As Stark observed, all Sellers' high spirits and pranks for the camera aside, the New York adventure was 'a turning point. Up to then Pete was Pete. A carefree, comical lad. Now he was a valuable, must-be-carefully-nurtured asset that could make a lot of people a lot of money.' And Sellers slowly seethed over the evaluation for the rest of his life, and beyond: he stipulated that no American was to be present at his funeral. He decided that all Americans were commercially-minded vulgarians, who measured success in terms of money—they were 'immersed in the theology of making a fast buck' (*Sweet Smell of Success*, again); they were brash and insincere. When he was in the Hamshere House penthouse, someone said (one would imagine self-mockingly): 'Look down on the town, Peter. All this is yours now.' Sellers refused to collude. Remembering his overnight visit to America after a brief [1956] appearance on Toronto television, he said (with unmistakable coldness): 'I'm exactly the same as I was the last time I was here, and you ignored me then.'

He wasn't. First, between 1956 and 1960 he had accumulated a formidable list of achievements. He had made a dozen films, ranging back to *The Ladykillers*. Second, he was no longer the same because the man who had once said disingenuously 'Some people say I ought to aim at being a big international star. I don't think that works with a character actor. I think to do that you have to be another kind of actor: a hero-player, not a character player' had become the man who was now going to look ahead and 'see it this way. I'm thirty-seven and the next eight years are the most important for me. In that time I've got to internationalise myself. That doesn't mean I shan't make films in Britain. It simply means that I'll make only big films which get an international audience.'

As we have seen, in his drive to internationalise himself he destabilised himself. Out went Anne and family life; in came Britt—and then out *she* went. Out went intelligent, original, cagey black-and-white performances, full of rewards and mystery; in came the soulless rubbish of the Age of Aquarius. He wanted to empty his life and start again—to such an extent, he did not appreciate being reminded of who he was: 'Someone comes up and says, "Eh, ain't you that Peter Sellers?" And if you don't pass the time of day with them they say, "That Pete Sellers is a bleedin' big 'ed." So what do you do? You have to chat to them.' No you don't—as he shortly discovered. Money frees you from the need to mix with mortals, and as Paul Theroux says 'it is the easiest thing in the world to become corrupted by the good life … after you have tasted luxury, you are changed, and there is no cure for it.'

This is not totally true. Stark, who shared the New York pampering, showed no signs of corruption afterwards. He went on as before, a happily-married man working as a nice little comedy bit-player. He did not become habituated. Sellers, however, who had betrayed symptoms of being seriously unhinged just prior to departure, refused to treat the adulation and attention as a holiday from reality. He took it as his due—and in due course he would act the part of a superstar, with all his dolly birds, fast cars ('Cars are freedom,' he once said), and travelling everywhere unnecessarily. Sellers would take up residence in an invented world; and what was begun with Lionel Meadows—the unbottling of his ugliness and brutality—was transformed in America, when he was encouraged to believe in his own invincibility; and the process was completed on his return to England, when he met Sophia Loren—'and the biggest giggle is that … I've become a heart-throb … I guess women think that if I was good enough for Sophia I'm good enough for them.'

Sellers was a dedicated pleasure-seeker—and he was afraid that it wouldn't last: 'The public's very fickle … If everything came to a stop, what could I do? After all, I've got a wife and family now.' The hypocrisy of that last phrase fairly shimmers on the page. Though (as Leslie Linder puts it) 'all of us who knew him felt that his biggest mistake ever was leaving Anne, whom he then proceeded to treat as his mother, by taking his new wives and girlfriends to see her, looking for approval,' it is the case that Sellers was very intent on severing ties, fragmenting, and reconstructing himself; and it is also the case that he feared for the precariousness of his new life and felt the strain of upholding a playboy persona. (He removed his face to reveal his masks.)

When Peg and Bill reminisced about the old ghosts of music hall, therefore, Sellers envisaged himself amongst them. His, after all, was a music hall talent; 'The Goon Show' was music hall; and as an actor he adapted, or adopted, a music hall method. Is that why, in the sixties, he began to make this bad dream of obliteration come true? Was he guilty because he knew his acclaim wasn't deserved? He recreated the wanderings and rejections of his youth; he worked it so that people would loathe him, thus justifying his paranoia (I lost count of the people who confessed to me 'I ended up hating him'); he appeared to be self-destructive and heedless. Robert Graves was shrewd when he said 'Peter Sellers—I grieve for him! He must be a very unhappy man with so many terrific talents which he probably despises.' There was indeed a tension between Sellers' hedonism and hysteria, between his desire for liberty and terror of dissolution.

On the other hand, what if instead of desiring banishment from the acting profession, he was perhaps testing its limits? What he despised was the actor as dancing bear, doing what he was told, so he rejected artistry and the discipline that goes with it. What he enjoyed was exerting his own power—defiling, degrading—and once Anne and the children were gone, he became uncontrollable. He liked to insist upon hiring weak directors, because he could bully them (it is interesting that he never sought out Kubrick again); and yet, because he didn't know how to manage his gifts, and had no judgement, the bigger and brighter he shone as a star, the worse his films—and the more he thought people were trying to get him, were lying in wait for him, which they weren't. He shifted blame, went in for bombast, and came and went as he pleased. Robert Parrish, for example, who took over the helm of *Casino Royale* for a few days, found himself, Orson Welles, all the extras, and the crew made up and ready to work at eight forty-five in the morning, as per their contracts. Sellers did not arrive for another two-and-a-quarter hours—he'd stayed in his car, circling Shepperton Studios, wasting time and abrading people's nerves on purpose. (He had a telephone in his limousine and he kept calling a lackey on the set, for up-to-date reports on the general restlessness.) Welles spent the morning telling anecdotes about his favourite restaurants and practising magic tricks. When Sellers eventually arrived, ostentatiously dishevelled and un-Bondlike, Welles boomed 'Welcome, Mr Sellers! How good of you to join us!' He had arranged for a spotlight to pick out the wretched star. 'Let's have a big hand for Mr Sellers!' Sellers, momentarily startled and magnificently befooled, made himself into air, into which he vanished. Nobody heard from him for two solid days—though people continued to go through the motions of assembling on the set at nine, going for tea at ten, breaking for lunch at twelve, returning to their dressing rooms at two and leaving for home at five; and then he said he'd come back only on condition that he never had to see or speak to Welles, on screen or off, ever again. He claimed that Welles was trying to put a voodoo mind-grip on him.

◆ ◆ ◆

Sellers hated Americans 'with such a venom, you'd have thought he was Red Indian on his parents' side', says Milligan. They were competition. They were an entire continent of people magnified to be like him: unrestrained, driven, ready to put up a fight. After Ealing, the Boultings, Englishness, and leagues of gentlemen, Sellers, on a visit to New York, was suddenly confronted by what must have seemed like his own venality running wild. It was an ideal environment and society for him—so, peevishly, he affected to recoil from it in distaste. Sellers saw charm openly being deployed as no more than a cover for aggression and push; he saw mercilessness and aplomb; superabundance and psychoses. Hattie Stevenson, who was with him in 1963 for *The World of Henry Orient*, confirms the way Sellers was projecting *his* distemper and bad manners on to others: 'He didn't like

(Top) A Jewish Double Act: Sellers (dressed as Henry Orient) and Mel Brooks in New York (1964)

(Bottom) Poster for *Cassino Royale*

New Yorkers—he thought they were rude... There was a different law applying to himself, but... he'd detect slights and hostilities where there were absolutely none.' His paranoia was ever-increasing; and in addition to his philistinism, he imported, or imposed, his private collection of poltergeists and demons on America, too: 'He decided New York was too hot, so everybody had to move out to Long Island. We stayed in a clapboard traditional American house and Sellers was convinced it was haunted. Everything that happened in there he'd attribute to the spirits... It got to a pitch one night when it was a full moon. At two A.M. Sellers demanded that we... pack everything up, and we moved back into New York, to the Regency. Theo Cowan was amusing about the sudden flit and rang me every five minutes to find out if we were still there or if we had moved recently.'

Out of the twenty-three projects which Sellers was considering for his American debut (what were the ones he rejected, I wonder?) *The World of Henry Orient* is an odd and revealing choice to have made. The film was based on Nora Johnson's novel about Oscar Levant, a morose pianist and actor (*Rhapsody in Blue, An American in Paris*), who said of himself 'In some situations I was difficult, in odd moments impossible, in rare moments loathsome, but at my best unapproachably great,' and who also claimed 'I'm a controversial figure. My friends either dislike me or hate me.' In place of the whiffs of sulphur that such a choleric character suggests Sellers decided to subvert the megalomania. Henry is decidedly on the slide. He is vain and pompous, pathetically puffed up. As Sellers himself said—under no illusions about what he was trying to accomplish: 'I play a phoney... a concert pianist by profession and a woman-chaser by preference. He's a rogue and a liar, with his... charming words and ways, including a hint of a foreign accent, which he believes tantalises the ladies.'

Though this be Manhattan, Sellers is drawing on the strolling players and gypsy accordionists of the Ilfracombe substratum. (Orient's Italian accent is a put-on, like Waldini's Romany spielings.) Henry is not what he seems. The Latin lover antics are thwarted by the two young girls who follow him and plague him; his Carnegie Hall debut is a botch. He is at his best, alone in his apartment, a creature of fantasy, preserving his looks with a hair-net and red satin eye shades. Despite the clinches with Angela Lansbury and Paula Prentiss, this is another of Sellers' lonely-are-the-brave performances—perhaps a compendium of them. But where, in the past, there was a note of elegy, a pang of gloom, a sense of mooniness, in *The World of Henry Orient* Sellers seems closed-off. He is billed as the star but his scenes are cameos, virtually skits. He is brilliant in them—he just lacks resonance, all of a sudden.

His genius was to play failures in such a responsive way they became paradoxical successes; there was a division, which we could accept and enjoy, between their shallowness and Sellers' deep waters. He had the intuitions of a true artist—and these, once he had sought and been through the entrance to the VIP lounge, he denied. He no longer seemed quite all there—he was mad. Prior to *The World of Henry Orient*, Sellers was able to re-work, dwell upon, dodge, exorcise, or fictionalise the circumstances of his life. His ambition, hypocrisy, meanness, his mood swings from black violence to off-white innocence, as a marriage was running down, made him transform his being into his art—he was his own central subject. When he said 'I must tailor my talent to a rôle', that is precisely what he did. He elided with it, colluded with it.

Even after 1963, after *Doctor Strangelove*, in which Sellers took a childish rage to an extreme and symbolically annihilated the planet, this remained the case. The difference was that, now he had become an official celebrity—up for an Oscar indeed—instead of being an actor, and getting on with the job, he started to have a *conception* of himself as an actor; instead of having experiences spontaneously, he adjusted and stage-managed his life, and made his life theatre. *Henry Orient* was the first sign of this falsity, and the extent of Sellers' dissociation—to use the psychiatric term—can be seen by the way in which he believed himself to be Henry Orient away from the set.

'He decided he had to make conquests,' says Hattie Stevenson. 'A girl sent him her photograph—beautiful face. He made me arrange for a meeting at Grand Central Station. Bert and I were made to go along in case he didn't like her, and he hid behind a pillar. The girl appeared and she was totally huge. We had to go and say "So sorry he couldn't make it." She was very persistent, however, and in the end he proposed to her and gave her an engagement ring. That lasted all of a day. Then he got rid of her. He proposed to countless women.'

◆ ◆ ◆

Sellers returned to England on October 3, 1963 ('because I have had New York in a big way, mate. They are all too rude here for me … it's the man-in-the-street—or the woman-in-the-street because it's the women who run it here …' he jabbered to Walker). He took up residence in the Dorchester and began work on *A Shot in the Dark*—which in itself was an ominous sign: Sellers was starting to repeat himself. He expressed his anxiety and irritability by making everybody un-

Inspector Clouseau, Blake Edwards, and Elke Sommer on the set of *A Shot in the Dark* (1964)

Michael Sellers Collection

easy. Blake Edwards tried to put a stop to the nonsense by pushing a note under Sellers' dressing-room door: 'Come on, Peter, act like a professional.' It was not an appeal likely to have much chance of success: 'It was like punishing a bad little boy,' the director realised later, 'and taking a parental attitude about this whole thing. He pouted and went up and down with his attitudes.'

In fact, now I come to think about it, having followed Sellers on his way up to 1963—his marvellous years—and having seen him roll all the way down, towards death and disaster (his making and unmaking), I would go so far as to state that it was only repetition which awaited him in the future. As Wolf Mankowitz said to me, 'All his comedy goes back to his early radio days.' Quite so. You can line up the characters he subsequently developed—like Marcel Duchamp's *valise*—a miniature collection of all his works, gathered up and put in a box.

◆ ◆ ◆

Before he himself was gathered up and put in a box, and died forever, he had died a lot. (Death was an experience he kept living through; and his fear of death helped ruin his life.) It was always his heart. 'He used to think he was having heart attacks,' says Anne. 'I was driving home with him one day, from *Brouhaha*. "I think I'm having a heart attack.."..."Don't you think I should drive the car in that case?" I said. "No. I'll be all right, just leave me alone, I'll be all right."... He gets home and went straight to bed... I summoned Dr Studley: "It's the usual. He's having a heart attack at the moment." "Right," he sighed. "I'll be there." It wasn't.'

'I don't know whether I ever consciously worried about having a heart attack, as my ex-wife Anne says I did. I can't be sure,' said Sellers in 1965. 'True, my father had three coronary attacks, but it was actually prostate trouble that killed him.'

Bill had died in October 1962. He ended his adult life, as he had begun it, in a spirit of amiable sponging. The patronage of the Mendozas, however, was parsimonious compared with his son's handouts. Sellers bought his parents a flat, and (said Bill) 'Peter gives us an allowance and it's a pretty big one. He paid £1,500 for my operation in the London Clinic. He buys us a new car every year, and now he's sending us away for a very expensive holiday.'

As the dutiful son, Sellers was irreproachable. Peg and Bill, after all, were his most devoted fans. 'I know... my Dad always reads out my write-ups, but I'm sure he's pleased. My mother—I believe I've done all she hoped for me.' He didn't actually see them very often, but that didn't matter. He'd left what could be taken as a duplicate of himself in their care—what in spiritualistic parlance is known as a familiar: a parrot. 'I'm all right, Henry', it squawked... *Bollocks* [slang for testicles] was his favourite word. His owners delighted in his devastations. (They soon gave up confining him to a cage.) He ripped the curtains and pecked at the chairs; he disembowelled cushions and dive-bombed Peg when she was in the bath. He was rewarded with packets of seeds shipped from the tropics.

As an imitator and a conscience-free destroyer, it was like bringing up their poltergeist Peter all over again—and Sellers' real name, you may remember, was Richard *Henry*. In addition to his birds of the air and other gifts, however, Sellers also made at least one attempt to find his father a foot-hold in radio. Now that he was an established star, he'd hoped he could get Bill's songs broadcast—but it was not to be. The George Formby-Ivor Novello ditties, sentimental and winsome, were deemed derivative. Sellers received the politest of rejection slips from the BBC.

◆ ◆ ◆

The plight of the failed entertainer is at the heart of Sellers' work (Henry Orient is part of the pattern); his second film in America—his first in Hollywood—continued the trend. *Kiss Me, Stupid*, his next project after *A Shot in the Dark*, is about a songsmith and piano teacher—a small-town dreamer—who gets the chance to play his tunes to Dean Martin. (Orville J. Spooner's compositions are actually hitherto unpublished works by George Gershwin.) Martin's car has broken down in Climax, Nevada; he has time on his hands whilst the garage fixes it and he can be on his way; what else is there to do? He grudgingly agrees to go across the street to Orville's little house, which is flanked by two huge lolling phallic cacti, for an audition—and then he scents Orville's wife, Zelda, played by the beauteous Felicia Farr (her profile is Garbo's). Billy Wilder's film gets to be genuinely cynical and lecherous quite quickly after that. Orville's dilemma: does he allow this creature to flirt with his wife? Will that make him better disposed towards purchasing his songs?

Kiss Me, Stupid, is a slutty film, and yet it is also adult about adultery. (*What's New, Pussycat?* is puerile by comparison.) Zelda is aroused by the idea of breaking free for a little while, of being unrestrained and dominated. (Wilder seems to imply that within every prim provincial housewife there is a minx who wants to be slapped around.) Orville, in his turn, is a runty fellow incongruously married to a sweetmeat he can't handle and fears he'll lose. Martin's appearance, therefore, triggers his greatest fear (desertion) and dream (celebrity).

To complicate matters there is Kim Novak's authentic hooker, Polly the Pistol. She is constructed out of curves, undulates across the carpet, and looks like a human version of Betty Boop. If Zelda thinks 'it was fun being a hooker for one night,' Polly, who lives in a trailer park, yearns for a different kind of life. 'I'll swap you for the wedding ring,' she responds sadly. Under the cover of darkness, the women carry out what in Shakespeare's day was called The Bed Trick: they impersonate each other under the sheets, change places, and the men on top never know (lesson: all cats look grey in the dark).

It is a knavish, carnal story. There is no nonsense about Martin ('What's with the broads round here?') being gallant—he leaves a five hundred dollar tip in the caravan for Mrs Spooner, thus debasing her as a strumpet; and Orville is not only a pimp: something in him is attracted to, and revels in, the humiliation.

◆ ◆ ◆

Wilder called Sellers' Orville 'superb', and Sellers too, at least initially, was content. 'I might say that it's long been my ambition to work with Billy Wilder... I think Wilder is one of the greatest, if not *the* greatest, comedy directors... in the world.' The interviewer, Steve Allen, then asked what *Kiss Me, Stupid* was about and Sellers had to ruminate: 'Well, *Kiss Me, Stupid* used to be called—ah, now,

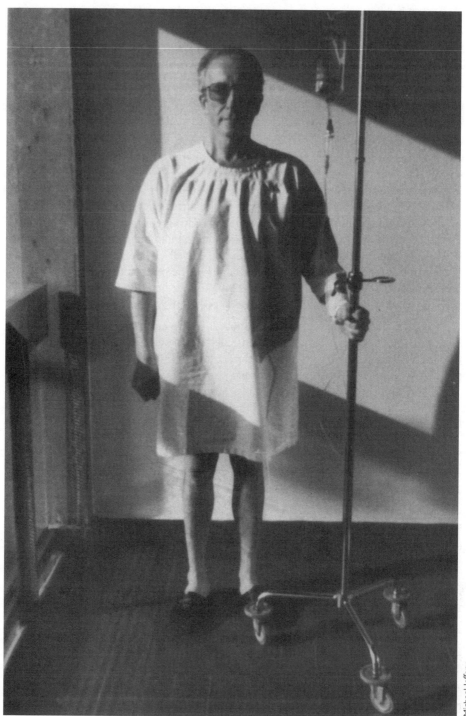

The fellow in the bright nightgown: Sellers awaits the inevitable (1980)

Michael Jeffery

wait a minute. What did it used to be called? ... Anyway, it doesn't matter. It's now called *Kiss Me, Stupid*. It's ... a wonderful opportunity.'

If indeed he ever had thought the opportunity wondrous, Sellers didn't seem to consider that to be the case for very much longer. These words were spoken on March 20, 1964. On April 7 he was wired up in the Intensive Care Unit of Los Angeles' Cedars of Lebanon Hospital. 'He will do anything to get out of being in this fucking movie!' one of the producers exclaimed. Wilder, apprised of his leading actor's collapse, said 'What do you mean, heart attack? You've got to have a heart before you can have an attack.' Sellers had arrived in California ready to be temperamental. The first problem was that Wilder did not welcome improvisations on the set. His scripts—written in collaboration with I. A. L. Diamond—were scripture, and how this differed from the spur-of-the-moment ideas and brainstorms encouraged on the studio floor by Kubrick and Edwards. Sellers, after having tasted a pell-mell approach, did not appreciate reverting to a more disciplined style—though it was, for example, the Boultings' style, and once-upon-a-time Sellers' inventiveness would have overcome restrictions, made a virtue out of them. But now, uncompliant, certain he had no more to learn, 'I ended up in the middle of the film becoming very ill, so it was never completed with me in it anyway. Perhaps you are just not meant to do certain things.'

Sellers' second complaint seems paradoxical in the light of the alleged constraints he felt he was under: Wilder, for all his dictatorial attitudes towards his actors—i.e. his expectation that they will be professionals who adhere to their lines—liked work to proceed in an atmosphere of high wassail. Sellers, who didn't have any friends in Hollywood, felt left out.

What dismayed him during *Kiss Me, Stupid* was that he was uncertain about overcoming resistance. Looking back in 1976, he claimed: 'I had a very sad and depressing experience working with a director whom I admired tremendously—Billy Wilder ... I realised that ... placing oneself entirely in someone's hands, even Wilder's, brilliant as he was, just wasn't right. He and Izzy Diamond's words were golden, but they were very set in their ways.' The real quandary, therefore, wasn't so much the disallowing of deviations from the script. This was symptomatic of a more general indignation—namely, Sellers' refusal to be beholden. He decided to be stubborn to punish Wilder for giving orders; and the more people cried shame on him, the more determined and cruel Sellers grew—until, in an astonishing outburst, he reckoned that it wasn't only Wilder and the cast and crew of *Kiss Me, Stupid* who were ranged against him and to blame for his unease: it was the whole of Hollywood. 'I have had Hollywood, love,' he told the *Evening Standard*. 'As far as film-land is concerned I've taken the round trip for good. The noise and, to coin a phrase, the people.'

He hated the East Coast; he hated the West Coast. Between his experiences on America's extremities had come *A Shot in the Dark*, which he had hated, too. What we are seeing here is a man whose vehemencies were ingrained, whose independence had become exaggerated until he was inaccessible and belonged nowhere, and whose dissatisfactions were destructive and no longer part of any drive to attain perfection: 'The trouble is,' he said in January 1963, 'you find yourself trying all the time for satisfaction and then never really being satisfied with yourself. I suppose that's ... a battle you can never win.' Where possible, the battle against himself was re-deployed as a battle against other people, to whose feelings he was always indifferent. It was with something like surprise, therefore, that he opened a telegram a few days after his anti-Hollywood babble had been printed, and read: 'TALK ABOUT UNPROFESSIONAL RAT FINKS'. It was signed by Wilder, Dean Martin, Kim Novak, Cliff Osmond, and others—good for them—of the *Kiss Me, Stupid* company.

As Sellers would have been aware, a rat fink is one of the terms of opprobrium used in the film by Polly the Pistol. Sellers couldn't see it, of course. He felt suffocated, persecuted, cold against them. In an attempt to broadcast his conviction that he was not the one in the wrong, the following notice appeared in *Variety* on July 1, 1964: 'I am [not] an ungrateful Limey or rat fink who has been abusing everything in Hollywood behind its back. I did not go to Hollywood to be ill. I went there to work and found, regrettably, that the creative side in me couldn't accept the sort of conditions under which work had to be carried out. This is a personal matter. I have no criticism of Hollywood as a place, only as a place to work in. The atmosphere is wrong for me. At the same time anyone is at liberty to say that I am wrong ...' And so, wheedlingly, on and on.

◆ ◆ ◆

The advertising space for Sellers' self-justifications cost him either £250 (Evans) or £750 (Walker); leaving aside the classifieds, do not his words and tone suggest he should have been certified? For, if his transgressions over *Kiss Me, Stupid* connect with his life-long dismissal of authority, his behaviour also—more specifically and interestingly—fits with the crack-up which overtook him in the early sixties, when he became unsettled in every sense: geographic, careeristic, spiritualistic.

Whilst it was possible to publicise his disagreements over Wilder's *modus operandi*, there were deeper, murkier forces at work inside Sellers which he didn't dare voice. The first of these has to do with Bill. In 1976, Sellers added another, new, reason for his unhappiness with the film: 'I couldn't make anything of the character,' he claimed, 'because I didn't know people like that.' The failed songwriter, the hen-pecked husband, the overlooked man, withdrawn and fidgeting, was somebody Sellers knew, all right. But if *Kiss Me, Stupid* alluded, unmistakably, to his father's prostration—to the life of a man who was not important—then, much more unnerving was Orville's overlap with Sellers himself.

Two days prior to his departure from England to begin the film, Sellers had married Britt. Less than a month prior to that he had met her for the first time. As he described the romance himself in 1965: 'The best thing that ever happened to me was ... [at] the Dorchester Hotel ... while I made *A Shot in the Dark*. I'd moved out of my apartment [in Hampstead] ... and I hadn't yet moved into [Elstead]. So there I was lording it in the giant Oliver Messel suite. Alone. One day I walked down the hotel corridor and there was this unbelievable chick coming the other way. "Who is that?" I said to Bert Mortimer, my chauffeur-valet ... "Britt Ekland", he said. "She's here for talks with Twentieth-Century Fox—I read it in the paper."…So the same night I sent Bert round with a note and asked her to come in for a drink. Which she did. I was…absolutely stunned…She was so great. She wore a simple dress and her hair was like sunlight. Unbelievable! Well, you know what a camera fan I am. I asked her if I could take some pictures of her. She thought it was a fun idea—and from that moment we were never apart. Three weeks later [on February 19, 1964] we were married. It wasn't until much later that I came across a slip of paper with the initials B.E. My friend Maurice Woodruff, the clairvoyant, had forecast six months earlier that I'd meet a girl with those initials and marry her—but I'd completely forgotten.'

Actually, Woodruff hadn't been quite that precise. What he had said was that a person with the initials B.E. would figure in Sellers' life in a general way. Woodruff, who was in the pay of film companies to steer Sellers in the direction of their projects, was meant to be laying the ground for the acceptability of Blake Edwards and *A Shot in the Dark*. The actor, however, failed to make that connection. He married Britt instead.

Notice too, in that self-pitying image of his solitude and abandonment in the luxurious hotel suite, how easily Janette Scott had slipped from Sellers' mind. He talks of himself as if he was haunting rather than living—and then along came Britt, for him to feed off. 'For two years, until I met Britt, I had been terribly despondent. I was working to forget how unhappy I was…I would sleep maybe for six hours, but…I wouldn't get any more than half an hour's real rest. So I was taking tranquillisers—I was getting into the pill area in a big way.'

Was it marijuana which made Henry Orient and Clouseau, in his second outing, look so glassy? The picture Sellers tried to project, of the lonely man-beast saved by a goddess of the Spring, is far from accurate (though he tried to repeat the fable again with Lynne Frederick). Sellers may have found Britt arousing, and he did want to enjoy her, but she was less of a real person, in his eyes, than the object of his brutish attention. He wanted to overpower her, and he infected her with his malaise. She didn't save him—he nearly destroyed her. 'Our moments of real happiness,' she was to confess, 'were rare and far apart.' Eventually she would try and take an overdose.

Britt, who was twenty-one and had barely serviceable English, had been offered a contract by Darryl F. Zanuck, and she was staying at the Dorchester pending instructions to fly to New York for screen tests. She remembers Bert Mortimer knocking on her door with his message, and she found him rather persistent. Sellers taught her how to smoke a joint, grabbed her and started kissing. The next morning, the contents of the Dorchester's florist stall—proprietrix: Miranda Quarry—were carried up to Britt's room, along with the card 'Hope you slept well—Clouseau.' Over the next few days, the young Swede was seduced with jewels and a Lotus sports car; Sellers took her disco-dancing and to expensive Mayfair eateries. Five days later, Britt was obliged to travel to New York, where she stayed at the Drake Hotel. Sellers telephoned her incessantly and informed the newspaper columnist Roderick Mann: 'I really believe this may be more than just a casual relationship…My trouble…is that I can only be attracted to pretty girls. And that's courting disaster from the start. Especially if you tend to be jealous, like me.'

Sellers' jealousy was Shakespearean—it was an emotion connected to his pride in the rights of property-ownership and his fears of a slave's revolt. As quickly as he could, he locked Britt up. He was at Heathrow on February 12 to meet her off her plane and give her an engagement ring. The marriage was held in Guildford Registry Office on the following Wednesday. Hundreds of people jostled outside, and the crowds followed the newlyweds to the gates of Elstead. (The next time Sellers drew the fans like that it was his funeral.) There was a smorgasbord luncheon and a supper later at the Tiberio restaurant in London. Sellers had the whole day filmed by sixteen-millimetre cameras and he later added a commentary and a musical soundtrack. Don't you find that an odd thing to do in itself? Sellers, by designing his day for posterity, and living his marriage through a lens, was already confirming the artificiality which was now gripping his life. He didn't believe he existed, except on the screen. That Graham Stark and David Lodge were cast as Sellers' best men added to the fantasy world. Microphones were secreted in vases and button-holes. Interviews were conducted with the principal players—and there, on what Milligan would call Minnie Mouse legs, was Peg, with her pterodactyl face. She'd seen Anne off—and now this, a girl-bride. Peg survived another three years, feeding herself on gin and cigarettes. To compete with Britt, she painted her face with lashings of Mary Quant mascara and rouge. The effect must have been like one of those pox-ridden screaming skulls in the Bedlam sub-plot of a play by Middleton & Rowley.

◆ ◆ ◆

Sellers was then bound for California and *Kiss Me, Stupid*; Britt, thrilled to be in possession of her Fox contract and a United Kingdom work permit (not easy to obtain), was due to appear in *Guns at Batasi*, which was being made in Britain by John Guillermin, the director of *Never Let Go* and *Waltz of the Toreadors*. Instead of a honeymoon, however, and the excitement of entering a new, strange life, Britt was chilled to discover that she'd been carried over the threshold into a nightmare. 'The true character of Sellers began to emerge. His incredible affection soured rapidly into an habitual jealousy which filled the first few weeks of our marriage with despair.' In the widening circle of Sellers' madness, the only constants were deceit and slipperiness (he assumed other people were just like him in that respect). His underlying bitterness and grievances came out, and he *was* Orville J. Spooner, who worships Zelda, but can't trust her. Sellers had spies on the set of *Guns at Batasi* and he himself telephoned Britt persistently, cross-indexing and double-corroborating the reports. 'I would have to describe my day almost minute by minute,' his wife said.

Sellers was convinced his pond was going to be fished. Like Orville, he snooped on his pretty bride, cross-examined her, and tried to have the mileage checked on her car. He accused Britt of casting-couch capers with Zanuck—he resented the producer for having discovered her first—and when he asked about her relations with John Leyton, the star of *Guns at Batasi*, his inquiries grew increasingly lewd: 'Tell me the truth Britt...Are you sure you don't fancy him?...You didn't have to kiss him...?'

Sellers' obsessive questioning suggests that, in spite of himself, he was thrilled

(Top) The White Goddess

(Middle) A Very Public Wedding: February 19, 1964

(Bottom) Sellers with his new wife and new father-in-law: note the microphones for the nuptial home movie

Hattie Stevenson

Hattie Stevenson

(Top) Ready, Aim, Flee!
Shooting Britt in Hollywood
(1964)

(Bottom) A Pained
Expression: Sellers in
Disneyland, a few hours
prior to his heart attack,
April 6, 1964

by the concept of cuckoldry. Was he uncertain of his manhood? Was it his latent homosexuality coming out? (Get busy, psychoanalysts.) He'd been the same with Anne, accusing her of falsehood, and he'd be the same with Lynne—when, beyond all shame, and much to his son's disgust, he set private detectives to follow her. He did not wish her to be seen talking to Simon Williams and Stuart Wilson on the set of *The Prisoner of Zenda*. He felt threatened by any male less antiquated than Mervyn Douglas—the exception to the rule being Michael Jeffery: 'Lynne and I had a dance routine and Peter used to get us to do it,' he told me. 'He used to love sitting back and watching us.'

Given all this psychopathology, it is little wonder that Sellers' work in *Kiss Me, Stupid*, despite his diversionary tactics and meannesses, was brilliant. So brilliant, he burned himself out, his heart a phosphorescence. When I watch the film today, I feel I'm being horribly unfair to Ray Walston, who took over the rôle of Orville; I keep wondering what Sellers would be doing, and how he'd be doing it better.* Walston's Orville is old-ladyish, fey. He is nervous, nasty, charmless, and shallow. Sellers would have been all these things, too, no doubt; but he'd have transfigured the rôle. The rage would have been real and unfathomable (instead of simply tetchy); the sinister sadomasochistic streak in the material would have been more strongly implied; and beyond all this, I think, there would have been some sympathy. There would have been a creepiness that was almost beautiful.

By 1964, however, it was too late. What made Sellers an artist on the grand scale was what made him mad: the intensity and excitement of his imagination. He passed between dreams and reality 'as through tissue-paper' (Barrie) and he could not sustain a performance of Orville's calibre; and in any event it was too close to him. *Kiss Me, Stupid* penetrated to Sellers' own fears, which he was not willing to explore; it resonated through to his subconscious. He was being prevented from breaking up the script into a series of semi-extempore sketches; and as each scene approached, his malignancy grew, his sexual frenzy grew, and he sent for Britt in person. He enticed her to Hollywood for an Easter weekend break and he wouldn't allow her to return to her film—he made out she was suffering from nervous exhaustion. 'Britt you are a sick girl,' he said. 'You don't want to crack up totally, do you?' He was going to keep her prisoner and wreck her work on *Guns at Batasi*—or, as he conveyed the drama to the papers, adroitly putting the responsibility for the flit on to Britt: 'Swedish Bride Flees Country To Be With Bridegroom'; 'Britt Flies To Her Man'.

Britt arrived on a Friday and she was meant to be back in Pinewood within seventy-two hours. She was not, and a writ for breach of contract was immediately issued. Sellers ignored it. He decided to take his family—Michael and Sarah were present—to Disneyland. They had stayed the night of Saturday, April 4 at a hotel, and on the Sunday morning they visited a cowboy ghost town in the Californian desert. (Sellers dressed as a saturnine gunslinger.) The staff (Hattie and Bert) then went on their way across the Mexican border; Sellers, Britt and the children re-

---

* If anybody knows of the whereabouts of any Sellers' *Kiss Me, Stupid* footage—he shot for six weeks on the film, after all, so there'd have been a great deal—do please let me know, c/o the publisher.

turned to Spyros Skouras' villa. Whilst his wife frolicked with Sarah and Michael in the pool, Sellers leafed through the script of *Kiss Me, Stupid*—he had a six A.M. start for the studio on Monday—and, once the babes were settled in their nursery (Michael was eight, Sarah four), he brought Britt to bed for rumpy-pumpy.

He had forced pot upon his bride; now he liked her to inhale poppers whilst he squirmed across her belly. Britt wasn't impressed with the aphrodisiacs. The chemical vapour reminded her of an operation she'd once undergone in Stockholm for her adenoids. Sellers, however, was transported. The drug (supplied by his diet doctor, incidentally) caused a dilation in the coronary arteries, leading directly to an increase in the coronary blood flow, which in its turn, after Sellers had had his orgasm, led to a sudden overload in the amount of blood leaving his heart and a corresponding reduction in the stream of blood on its way in. The heart, its rhythmic pumping action sabotaged, galloped, fluttered, and shut down. Sellers, still reeling from his ultimate come, was on his way to the bathroom when the fires in his chest started and pains flashed down his arms. He told Britt to phone the heart specialist, Rex Kennamer, who had been recommended to him by Elizabeth Taylor (one of our century's great sufferers). Kennamer arrived at the villa, took a cardiogram and gave Sellers a sedative.

The doctor then left. He returned within a few hours. The results of the electrocardiogram (ECG) had been processed and he said: 'You have had a mild heart attack'. He wanted Sellers to enter hospital for tests. The oracle had spoken. Sellers was curiously pleased. He had a good excuse for shirking Monday's *Kiss Me, Stupid* stint, Britt had a good reason for not flying back to *Guns at Batasi*; and so they departed for the infirmary immediately. The children were given to the maid. At this point, Bert and Hattie returned to the empty house and disbelieved the news.

For the first time since he had begun working and living in America, Sellers was happy. The New York flatteries and fawnings were nothing; the Hollywood party circuit was nothing; Billy Wilder was nothing ('I still have a few idols but now I consider them no more infallible than the man next door.). When it came to dying and not dying, though, America was really something: 'You've got to have top billing to get into a five-star joint like this,' beamed Sellers, as he checked in to the exclusive (i.e. expensive) institution. (This was thirty years ago: Sellers' room was sixty-five dollars a day, exclusive of medical fees.)

Britt backtracked to Hillcrest Road for a nap. The day was filled with a battle about the children. 'A real test of nerves,' recalls Hattie Stevenson. 'Sellers wanted them in California because he had just remarried; he wanted Britt to take over as their mother. Anne, meantime, wanted them away from the publicity.'

If Sellers' hospitalisation for observation made the London evening papers on the Monday, what happened next filled the front pages all over the world. In the early hours of Tuesday morning, a nurse making a routine check discovered that Sellers was 'unconscious with no blood pressure and no pulse.' Emergency cardiopulmonary resuscitation was applied. He was taken to the Intensive Care Unit—wittily known as the Eleventh Hour Ward—and re-connected to cardiograph machines, heart stimulators, and a ventilator. 'He has had a serious setback', said a hospital spokesman. 'This looks like a close one.' At four-thirty A.M., there was a second massive coronary attack and the word went out that Sellers was 'deteriorating'.

Britt was brought to the hospital and informed of her incipient widowhood. Dr Kennamer was joined by Dr Eliot Corday, America's foremost heart surgeon. 'Everything humanly possible is being done,' said Britt. 'But a few prayers would be very useful now.' In London, Ian Carmichael was urgently beckoned by Associated-Rediffusion—as he told it to me: 'When he was at Cedars of Lebanon Hospital he was not expected to survive. I was confronted by the television people. They were preparing a memorial programme for that evening because Peter Sellers would be dead. Would I be the anchorman and provide the linking commentary between the clips? Spike and Harry were also to appear…I was given a script. I had to read, "Today, on Tuesday, April 7, 1964, at [blank for time], in the Cedars of Lebanon Hospital, Los Angeles, Peter Sellers died." And it was macabre, because he was still alive. The producers were so wrapped up in it, I got the impression they'd be bloody annoyed if he lived—which he did. I met him later on. I never told him about it.'

◆ ◆ ◆

Sellers, meantime, like Orpheus, was in the underworld: 'It's weird when I think of it. That I was dead, I mean. I had eight heart arrests. After six…[the doctors] told Britt there was no hope. But it wasn't my turn for the wooden overcoat, apparently. The first time, my heart stopped for one-and-a-half minutes. If they had been a second later getting me down to the pacemaker machine, I wouldn't have been worth saving. My brain would have been damaged. Fortunately, I never knew what was going on. They kept me heavily sedated…The staggering thing, of course, is that when I thought I was just falling asleep, I was really dying…[I lay] like a collapsed puppet, with wires and strings all over me.'

Sellers was diagnosed as having endured an acute myocardial infarction with a complete heart block. 'After a period of rest he could be a new man again,' said Dr. Kennamer. 'His millions of fans will not be disappointed, provided he follows medical advice given to him.' Milligan and Secombe sent a telegram: 'YOU SWINE BLOODNOK. WE HAD YOU HEAVILY INSURED. HOW DARE YOU.' Sellers, or Bluebottle, responded: 'I AM DOWN HERE IN THIS HOSPITAL WHICH IS IN THE LAND OF AMERICA, AND I DON'T LIKE THIS GAME, NO I DON'T. I AM NOT DEADED, I TELL YOU, I'M ALIVE. THINKS "I HOPE SO".'

Confined to his bed, Sellers delighted in Goonery. By April 9 he was (in the hospital's phrase) 'holding his own' and he pulled funny faces for the nurses. He ate meatballs and rice and said 'I feel great'. Thousands of letters and messages were arriving from fans. 'A whole new world opened up for me,' he claimed, 'I didn't realise it meant so much to people whether I lived or died.' He was on top of the world: 'I feel like the Miracle Man who came back from the dead!'

The physiological and psychological impact of his heart attack on his re-

maining decade-and-a-half is incalculable. He was worried about his health—
what he should eat, what he shouldn't eat. He was very attuned to the problems
of his body—which would be hypochondria, except that he'd had that glance
across what he called 'the valley of the shadow'. But then the whole of his make-
up had *always* been sensitive. Anne told a reporter at the time: 'He took such care
of his health that when I heard the news I just couldn't believe it. It seems incredible that anyone so fanatical about health could be ill. He was obsessed with
physical fitness. But Peter lived at quite a pace, and ... was an obsessional worrier.'

She was not to know that the deciding factor—the trigger—was her former
husband's new fondness for narcotics, or that he'd had one chemically-exalted
fuck too many. But she did tell the press that: 'He was haunted with the idea that
he would die from a heart attack, like his father and several uncles. It was on his
mind constantly.' For Milligan, indeed, the heart attack was fated—almost psy-
chosomatically induced: 'Years before he had this heart attack he always worried
about it, was always searching for the bloody thing as if it were a letter that he
knew had been posted and hadn't arrived.' He was ill because of what he was.
Today, doctors would call such a condition 'cardiac neurosis' or 'neurocirculatory
asthenia'—palpitations, headaches, stress, dizziness, sudden fatigue. Then again,
all these symptoms could have been quite justly explained away as basic overwork: 'I used to work with a kind of frenzy, just ... to lose myself entirely in my
films. No holidays, reading scripts, rehearsing, always on the go.'

Yet he wanted to be like this; he had been busy since 1948, when he made his
first BBC broadcast. He could never stand being merely himself—contingent, relative, mortal—and vacations, the spots of time between projects when he was not
obliged to rôle-play, always made him malignant. Hence, the valium and tranquillisers he was guzzling assisted the process of getting out of himself; pills made
it easier for him to go on being a disturbing influence, claiming complete freedom. The capsules he'd inhaled with Britt were part of this pattern. This heartless man's heart attack, therefore, vindicated him. First, it came in handy as a way
of—retrospectively—making his enemies feel guilty. Second, it was a sign that he
was not inconsequential. Indeed, he claimed—like Lazarus laughing—that he was
immortal: 'One of the cardiologists told me that what I'd been through wouldn't
hit me till later, and it's true. The other day I started thinking, "Man, I died!"'

As for the after-effects, Sellers didn't change, as such; on the contrary, his
long-established traits were magnified: his torments and tensions, his deliriums.
As he grew older and more ill, the chief result of the Cedars of Lebanon adventure was the way it confirmed for him his earliest inkling—that he was marvellous,
eternal, everything that Peg had promised. He wanted to live *forever*. As an actor,
he was infinitely resourceful. When one character ran out, he'd assume another—
and this is how he wanted to be in reality. When one life expired, he'd be back in
a new shape and guise. 'It was virtually a case of having another time around,' he
said in 1971, 'because I did in fact die ... I suppose when you think about *that*, you
think to yourself—well, having come back from wherever it was ...' Sellers' voice
trailed off. He was trying to convey what it was like being a phenomenon. He was

eloquent elsewhere, however, in his films—when Clouseau survived death and destruction to bounce back time and again, when Chance walked across the waters, or Fu Manchu found that he could rustle up the secret recipe of everlastingness.

◆ ◆ ◆

Sellers very quickly came to the conclusion that he had survived because he was infallible. The first sign of a rift with Britt appeared when he took offence at her practicality. 'He was disappointed when I told him he had *not* died,' Britt explained later. 'He wanted to be able to tell people what it was like to be dead and then come alive again. But I convinced him he hadn't *really* been dead, even if his heart had stopped beating.'

She convinced him of no such thing. Sellers was far too enthralled by his own mythic, phoenix-like, version of events to want it sullied by crappy things like medical knowledge (the paroxysms are a condition called ventricular tachycardia); also, he believed that he had lived not so much because of the well-equipped hospital and professional expertise, but because the world downed tools and prayed. 'I mean, having thousands of people writing to you telling you they're praying you'll recover. God, it taught me a lot.' Not about humility, of course—Sellers, by contrast, felt messianic, justifiably not commonplace. 'I can't guess why I survived,' he fibbed. 'Thousands of ordinary people all over the world wrote saying they had prayed for me—so perhaps the power of prayer does do something when it is directed … I am not just another actor to some people; that they really care about me.'

They had as high an opinion of him as he had himself—isn't that what he meant? After a fortnight in the Intensive Care Unit, Sellers was moved upstairs to a private suite (number 503) for a further month. 'The decor is much nicer and I'm … off the critical list', he wrote to Peter Evans on April 21. (The letter ends with the solemn valediction 'God bless you.') He was discharged at the end of May (with a huge bill) and on June 4, two months after the start of his illness, he became the one-hundred-and-forty-sixth star to have his footprints set in cement outside Graumann's Chinese Theatre. He signed his name inside a Cupid's heart. 'I have given up … the frenzied film-making … I have got this lovely girl and I am going to relax now and see all the places I have never seen. Perhaps it takes the hand of death upon your shoulder to make you realise how wonderful life really is.'

He sketched his precise plans for the near future in—aptly—*Life* magazine: 'I live in one of the most beautiful parts of England. I have bought myself a red setter, to take long walks with. I also have a pair of matched palominos, for riding. I've ordered a nice, fast, new car—my eighty-fourth, a blue Ferrari.' Britt expanded upon the idyllic designs. The couple planned to go to New York to see Richard Burton and Elizabeth Taylor (and swap medical anecdotes); then they would begin a belated honeymoon in Switzerland, Spain, and the French Riviera.

None of this came to pass. Back in England, Sellers made those nasty comments which elicited the rat-fink rebuke. From his happiness in the hospital he plummeted into a depression which would never lift, except intermittently, for the remainder of his days. He was a messiah without a mission. 'I don't know why I'm here!' he said to Shirley MacLaine (a receptive audience). 'I can't figure out my purpose.' His problem was that, believing he'd had a glimpse of Heaven—'I looked around myself and I saw an incredibly beautiful bright loving white light above me. I wanted to go to that white light more than anything. I never wanted anything more'—there was going to be nothing *this* side of paradise which would gratify him. Think what it must be like to reach the Elysian Fields only to be turned back. You'd be pretty resentful. So it was with Sellers, a man unconsoled by earthly powers.

◆ ◆ ◆

His heart attack—that ecstatic moment when the attention of the whole wide world was upon him—became part of his long search for perfection—a cosmic variation on his struggle to find the flawless motor car, the non-hissing hi-fi, the optimum lens, the most desirable dwelling and the immaculate woman. (The consequence of his manic dissatisfactions was that he was increasingly startlingly imperfect as a human being.) He was soon untempted by Britt—and *before* she was induced to absent herself from *Guns at Batasi*, Sellers was sighted in Acapulco with Stella Stevens. He'd hired a private plane and the trip was conducted in great secrecy, naturally enough. Unfortunately, the Mexican night club had a house photographer.

Coronary problems recurred; bad marriages recurred—all problems, actually or figuratively, of a breaking heart. His muse-figures, who inflamed him with their unattainability, recurred—the Sophia Loren erotomania was repeated with Nanette Newman. 'He was in love with Nanette,' Forbes said to me, 'and he did want to marry her. Nanette was the only person who could talk him out of his black moods. She loved him, and does still, but as a friend—she was never in love with him.'

As when he'd allowed the plot of *The Millionairess* to overtake his life, so did Sellers extrapolate a romance from *The Wrong Arm of the Law*. Nanette played Valerie, a sweet and innocent supergrass. There are several bedroom sequences and Sellers was smitten. Nanette received the Janette Scott treatment—i.e. she was required to use up her energies explaining to Sellers why he needn't kill himself (he'd bought guns for the purpose on two occasions); and if he believed he'd found a Wendy for his Peter Pan, he was spot on. Nanette has a sympathetic understanding of a child's imagination.

Peter Pan is actually a psychopath ('I forget people after I kill them,' Barrie has him say in *Peter and Wendy*); so was Sellers. Britt, after a bout of maltreatment, would seek refuge at the Forbes' house near Wentworth. She'd pour out her heart to them and Nanette said firmly: 'You have no alternative, Britt. You've got to leave him.' Sellers then arrived, acting the rôle of abashed, conciliatory husband, and collected his wife. Alone in the car with Britt, returning home, he'd revert to taciturnity and abuse. Sellers, on anybody's estimation, was an arch-manipulator, Britt was an innocent victim of a monster, and Miss Newman, according to her own daughter, Emma Forbes, can only have descended from the Darlings: 'She is the sort of person who makes your pillows nice and plump and mixes up delicious honey and lemon drinks. She is ... an optimist and great fun to be with.' No wonder Sellers wanted her. He wooed her with furs, jewels, and an E-Type Jaguar. He tried to fight the flab. Forbes said to me, 'He saw a headline in the *Express*: "Mastroianni: Peter Sellers With Sex Appeal." He threw the newspaper down, went on a crash diet, and didn't want to be thought of as a comedian ever again. He was burly—never naturally thin—and all the drugs he took to lose weight must have shortened his life.'

In the end he began to get bitter, surrealistically vengeful. Because Forbes had complimented Sellers on the food one evening at Elstead, Sellers got it into his head that Forbes was going to try and lure away his chef, and that he was doing this because of latent homosexual tendencies. 'Sellers put forward this scurrilous and false rumour about Bryan,' says Hattie Stevenson, 'and it was crackpot, his indignation ... In his mind he convinced himself he had the moral right to acquire Nanette—and ... if ever Bryan phoned ... Sellers ... made me, completely innocently, imply that they were gallivanting off on afternoons together. It was total fiction.'

Total madness, I think Miss Stevenson must mean; but Sellers outdid himself with his next School of Sophia compulsion: Princess Margaret. 'Sellers used to say to me "Ring P.M." as he'd call her; and I'd say "It's not my place to do so." She had a direct line at Kensington Palace, a magic number, and Sellers knew what it was. She accepted all his funny phone calls and funny voices, but we had to ... keep to the proprieties. Sellers used to go out with the Snowdons ... and he'd come in late with the Queen's sister. I suddenly had to get up and curtsy. You are not meant to leave before she leaves ... and I'd be compelled to stay and have a drink. Even in an informal capacity she was very formal—in a Dorchester suite, with nobody there save herself, Sellers, and me.'

◆ ◆ ◆

To Sellers, the Saxe-Coburg-Gotha-Mountbatten-Windsors, with their long history of tours and public spectacles, were a show-business family, like the Mendoza-Marks-Rays. Britt has written that she would 'squirm with embarrassment at the demeaning lengths he would stoop to in order to ingratiate himself with the Royal Family. It was contemptible.' His behaviour may or may not have been contemptible, but it wasn't ingratiation. Sellers was being subversive. He was taking them on—proving himself superior to them. At one of those celebrity line-ups after a gala screening, when the princes and princesses shuffle along the foyer and have a brief word with each star, Sellers, when asked 'What are you doing now?', decided to take the Queen Mother literally and, grinning fit to bust, said, a bit incredulous: 'Why, standing here talking to you.' He was similarly obstreperous at the charity première for *The Pink Panther Strikes Again*. He wanted Lynne Frederick to be presented to the Prince of Wales. 'Make sure Lynne's invited and is in the line-up,' he told Charles Berman, who was organising the event. Her name was duly submitted to Buckingham Palace, and an equerry asked 'Is she Mr Sellers' wife?' She wasn't, at the time. 'Is she in the film?' Again, no. 'Well, she can't be involved.'

Sellers, as may be guessed, got the shakes but good: 'What you mean is that they won't have her…Well, I'm not fucking coming either.' He sulked in his apartment at Roebuck House and the evening went ahead without him. 'I think it was very bad form,' said Prince Charles, who after all was the one being snubbed, not Lynne. 'Peter was bloody rude.' Despite the ruckus, H.R.H. agreed to come back eighteen months later and adorn *The Revenge of the Pink Panther*.* Lynne, as the official Mrs Sellers, was guaranteed a place in the line-up, but what angered Sellers this time was the presence of Blake Edwards and Julie Andrews, whom he feared might upstage him and get treated as the leading lights. So anxious was he to position himself, and Lynne, at the head of the queue that he arrived at the Odeon, Leicester Square, an hour early. Having discovered the mezzanines and auditorium deserted, Sellers and his bride, fuming and perhaps feeling that they'd made themselves look like pricks, marched out again. Sellers was yelling 'I'll kill him! That fucking Blake Edwards! He got me over here [from Port Grimaud] and there's no one up there! Wait till I get hold of him!'

A search party had to be sent out into the Charing Cross Road, Shaftesbury Avenue, and the Strand to round up the dippy star. He was found in a pub near Panton Street (where his office had once been situated) and persuaded to return. 'Oh no!' Berman was thinking. 'Not again! We've got a repeat performance of last year. One prince and no star…It was a damned close-run thing.'

As a star, Sellers put himself above a prince—above everybody. He was super-human. The Royal Family evidently recognised (and were willing to countenance) his anarchic-genius qualities, for despite his effronteries (Princess Margaret called him 'the most difficult man I know') he was a frequent visitor to Clarence House and Windsor Castle. Sellers would get up from the dinner table and pretend to be Sweeney Todd: 'I wish the world was one big throat and I had the cutting of it!' he'd announce, curdling the blood and pretending to be an actor in an old-fashioned melodrama. The Duke of Edinburgh, not to be left out, set fire to the tablecloth.

The Royal Family need their playtime and private moments to be as organ-ised for them as their regimented official duties. They rely upon, like any inmate in a long-stay maximum security hospital, a vast staff of professionals and a rigid routine. Sellers functioned as the court jester, venting his folly. He wasn't given a bladder on a stick, but he was expected to throw himself into Charades (Britt had to mime being a lobster), Blind Man's Bluff, and other such games from the Ed-wardian nursery which forms the Royal Family's mental atmosphere. When he went water-skiing in Windsor Great Park he created hilarity by getting himself thoroughly ducked—their highnesses were not to know his incompetence wasn't being faked. 'He's fallen in da wahtar!' they squealed—a Goonish catch phrase. (Lord Snowdon, taking pity, invented an extra-long twin crossbar, so that he could stand alongside Sellers and offer instruction—to no avail.)

◆ ◆ ◆

---

* H.R.H. The Prince of Wales was willing to indulge Sellers because he adored 'The Goon Show'.

More in Sellers' line than parlour games was the regal theatricality. In 1974 he made *The Great McGonagall* at Wilton's Music Hall in the East End. This was a vision of Imperial England as vaudeville—with Victoria herself, the original royal enchantress, positioned on a dais in the centre of the stage, surrounded by cardboard hills and cardboard deer. It is possibly my personal favourite of Sellers' lost films; it is full of genuine cavortings. The film doesn't hide its artifices, yet has its own powerful logic. Apart from Sellers' Victoria (he named his second daughter Victoria because of the aura of dewy roses and nineteenth-century bric-à-brac) and Milligan's poet, the actors play lots of parts—this is a travelling rep. company from the nineteenth-century, lit by gas flares and footlights, hamming it up amongst flaking plaster thrones and bright red curtains, scaffolding and dust sheets.

If *The Great McGonagall* (which is virtually unknown) had been made by Czechoslovakians with unspellable names and brought to the West in a badly-dubbed scratched print, it would be regularly listed in the *Sight and Sound* poll of best films. Sellers was 'in his element,' McGrath told me, with the Goonish music hall and magic lantern style, with Prince Albert being dressed as Hitler, with Queen Victoria humming along to a jazz piano. This enthusiasm may have been due to the fact that ten years previously, for the real Queen's thirty-ninth birthday, he had made a fifteen-minute home movie which had utilised similar techniques. At a personal cost to himself of six thousand pounds—home-movie it may have been but, like the Britt wedding day photoplay, it was professionally edited and dubbed—Sellers had deftly interlinked his own nostalgia for ropey music hall sketches with the Royal Family's instinct for tableaux.

In the Queen's film, Britt played Queen Victoria and (or perhaps as) a silent-movie vamp; Lord Snowdon was a one-legged golfer and a queer gangster; Princess Margaret was Herself; and Sellers was Fred Thrump, an illusionist. He was going back not only to his Palladium act, when he'd been the hapless quick-change artiste holding a stuffed crocodile and claiming to be 'Queen Victoria when she were a lad'; he was also, as so often, tempting fate and reverting to (and mocking) the earnest vaudevillians who filled his childhood. (In many respects, as a man who alters all the time, he always was one of these quick-change artistes.)

Thrump did the standard sub-standard repertoire—Richard III, the Hunchback of Nôtre Dame, Captain Bligh, Toulouse-Lautrec—and then, after the 'Goodness Gracious Me' Pakistani doctor, he said 'I will now do, in what I can safely say is the world record time of six-and-one-quarter seconds, my celebrated impression of Her Royal Highness, the Princess Margaret.' Sellers ran behind a screen and threw coats, bloomers and baggy shirts into the air—and the *real* P.M. emerged. She waved to the audience, sashayed back behind the screen, and Sellers re-appeared: 'I broke the record! Six seconds!' The film ended—another homage to Sellers' past—with the entire cast singing 'We're Riding Along on the Crest of a Wave.' The film was less 'Goon Show' than Gang Show.

◆ ◆ ◆

As he had been capable of believing, with Sophia and Nanette, that a film-set relationship was a real relationship, it took no effort at all to believe that he was in love with Princess Margaret and that she would marry him. He sent her romantic letters (which at one point he wanted back, pending the day when they could be buried with him in his coffin); he tried to get his spirit medium, Maurice Woodruff, to predict the regal wedding day; and he gave Snowdon hi-fi equipment, cameras, a CIA bugging device capable of picking up conversations within a hundred-metre radius, and a Riva speedboat in what he hoped would be part-exchange. Princess Margaret, he said, wore the same size bra as Sophia Loren—what further possible sign and portent did the world need?

As crackpot behaviour it was well up to standard. Princess Margaret, as Sellers saw, was defenseless. Her life, like his, was histrionics. 'I've never known her especially enjoy protocol,' said Sellers, 'but she knows she has to live with it. Yet I have taken her out to lunch without a detective or chauffeured car and she simply doesn't enjoy that.' In other words, actually liking the bowing and scraping isn't part of the issue; she'd simply be unable to cope without it. To give the impression that she'd be adequately looked after, Sellers invited the princess to his house in Clarges Street and had tapes of chatter and hubbub playing so that it seemed an off-stage party was in full swing.

Sellers turned his pad into a theatre; the other place—or factory of make-believe—he often met the princess at was the studio, where she would be his special guest. He was most put out, on *Casino Royale*, however, when she seemed intrigued by Welles. Sellers had boasted all morning that she was due to appear. 'Then, Princess Margaret *came*' laughed Welles, 'and walked on the set and passed him by and said "Hello, Orson, I haven't seen you for days!" *That* was the real end. *That's* when we couldn't speak lines across to each other. He went white as a sheet because *he* was going to get to present *me*.'

Sellers was already adopting a proprietorial attitude; Princess Margaret's presence meant that he could compliment himself on his choice of powerful friends. Snowdon was a companion, too, in his own right. Both men enjoyed practical jokes; both, obviously, were passionate about photography. One of the reasons Snowdon's portraits are successful, I think, is that his work has a comic edge. Do his subjects collude? Do they know how much they are revealing about themselves? Above and beyond the technical expertise of his shots, we can detect an impish intelligence and imagination being brought to bear. But Snowdon never captured Sellers as Sellers, only Sellers as, say, Old Sam, in *The Optimists of Nine Elms*, pottering about in the mud on the edge of the Thames, flapping open his coat to reveal the Union Jack lining. In any case, 'we tend to put off taking photographs and talk endlessly about the latest cameras, electronic gadgets and fast cars,' he has written. '[Sellers] will go down in history as one of the great performers of our time.'

Snowdon also appeared on the *Casino Royale* set, much to the surprise of Joe McGrath and Charles Feldman, who had barred journalists and photographers from the studio. It turned out to be Sellers' doing. Snowdon took some snaps of Britt just prior to her wedding; and the Snowdons and the Sellers' went on holiday together in Sardinia as guests of the Aga Khan. Such a trip might well have symbolised Sellers' arrival in High Society, you'd have thought. But he was not satisfied. He wanted to be a renowned photographer—'If I hadn't been an actor, I would like to have been a photographer'—with an Earldom thrown in. Back at Elstead, at dinner, when the Snowdons were invited, Sellers was pleased to observe the marital friction. 'P.M. used to be very nasty to her husband,' recalls Hattie Stevenson. 'They used to say the most awful things to each other. I can remember dinner parties and they'd argue right across the table.'

Sellers didn't help matters when he instigated the Affair of the Mighty Mellotron.* (It rivals in absurdity 'The Mighty Würlitzer' episode of 'The Goon Show', in which Neddie Seagoon breaks the land speed record in a cinema organ.) What happened is that he was staying at the Dorchester, having grown bored of Britt, and to keep him company in his suite he had a mellotron. Eventually Peter decided he wanted to give it to Princess Margaret.

The mechanical monster—all tubes, flues, flashing lights, and gears ('It's capable of doing forty knots' said Sellers)—was delivered to Kensington Palace. Princess Margaret couldn't be kept from it. She perched on the stool and attempted Phantom of the Opera arpeggios. The trouble was, the instrument was a big souvenir of Sellers, there in the royal front room; it became a symbol of the couple's dissent. Snowdon moved out. Sellers did his best to move in. 'Once you've got over the fact that you are sitting down eating bread and eggs with the Royal Family, you realise the whole family together is just a very normal family,' he who had no conception of family normality bragged.

Unlike Sophia and Nanette, who did their best to put some distance between themselves and Sellers, with Princess Margaret, whom he was now calling 'Ma'am Darling', it was Sellers who retired. The official reason he gave was that he'd wanted to have an affair but 'couldn't because I knew I would never be able to look Tony straight in the eyes again without feeling guilty.' Sellers was not one to experience guilt or compunction, and the real reason for his withdrawal was that Princess Margaret refused to marry and ennoble him. 'She is a very resolute woman. When she decides to do something she goes through with it.'

Sellers was particularly hurt by the Roddy Llewellyn gossip—he wished that such rumours were accruing to him. 'I've never discussed Roddy Llewellyn with her,' he said sniffily, before having to admit: 'I've never noticed her show any sign of outward affection for him.' Sellers felt resentful, overlooked. He went to stay at the Royal Lodge, Windsor, and phoned Michael Jeffery asking if he'd ring back 'and pretend to call me away for an urgent appointment. Get me away from here. I am so bored.' The ruse worked and Sellers returned to Jeffery, at the Inn on the Park. The next day, Ma'am Darling's detective was downstairs at the hotel, returning Sellers' three-quarters empty bottle of shampoo which he had left in the bathroom.

Was this an example of regal waste-not want-not economising or, as I see it,

---

* A mellotron is a mechanical musical instrument which is particularly adept at mimicking strings and woodwinds.

an act of defiance? But then who precisely was defying whom? Sellers, in leaving indiscreet traces of himself in the private quarters? The princess, in pettishly signalling to her would-be swain that if he wants to clear out early, he'd better take his rubbish with him? They were obviously very aware of each other and had formed a strange alliance. Whether the relationship was actively sexual is almost an irrelevance. (One of her staff, questioned on this point on my behalf, answered snootily: 'Well, if she did, she had her eyes closed and she forgot about it immediately afterwards'.) The point is that Sellers had thoroughly enjoyed himself until her rejection of his marriage hints. Suddenly, it was as if he had never been important to her; he felt inadequate and disdained. He telephoned Kensington Palace and, pretending to be Snowdon, gave a lurid description of nights with Lady Jackie Rufus-Isaacs, Snowdon's current inamorata. She did not find this amusing, but neither did she retaliate. She was too isolated to feel the force of his coldness.

Sellers' final taunt came in June 1979 when he opted to squire her to Yul Brynner's revival of *The King and I*. He insisted on taking Michael Jeffery, too. Sellers bought the lad a full-dress Yves St. Laurent evening suit in Geneva. As late as he dared leave it on the day of the show, Sellers announced that he couldn't be bothered to go. He told his secretary, Sue Evans, to phone up Constance Spry for some flowers. He stood her up. He'd done his best to be incredibly discourteous, and he succeeded. He'd been so sensitive that he was not himself the man born to be King, he was senseless.

◆ ◆ ◆

Sellers' blue-blood fantasies went back a long way—to the remote Mendoza link with the Rufus-Isaacs'; to his belief that he was the Earl of Beaconsfield. Lady Jackie Rufus-Isaacs' brother, Lord Anthony, produced *The Blockhouse*, and he told me that 'when he came to dinner, he'd be playing a character, and he'd remain as that character throughout the entire evening. This enabled him to tell the most outrageous lies about himself. He was brilliant like that.'

It was an effort, though, and one wonders why he bothered. Revenge? In 1958, he had told Herbert Kretzmer: 'I hate that chi-chi set.' The resentments may be traced (like so much in his life) to the end-of-the-pier, when he had had to beat time in a dance band. He never forgave America for branding him with success; he never forgave England's hunt ball-types for treating him as a failure. Now, however, the class which had noticed him only to look down on him were attempting to flatter him, but Sellers wasn't to be beguiled. According to him, what his rich hosts and hostesses were commanding were performances from him for free—and doing him a service by receiving him. 'You find yourself sitting in a chair', he said, 'and people are crowding round saying "He's bound to come up with something… funny. It's only a matter of time. Turn away from him, and look back when he's funny…"'

He lampooned these sorts of condescending idiots as Prince Rudi in *The Prisoner of Zenda*, whose vowels are so plummy he has a speech impediment. It is fair to say, however, that Sellers' loathing for the nobility concealed a good deal of fascination. A famous man has access anywhere, and for all his mockery of 'the Eaton Square Mob,' he chose to run and mix with the clotted cream. When asked why, his answer was that of the detached actor, gathering material: 'I feel a completely new world has opened up, [of] people that I probably would never have met, and as an observer of human nature, I find this [*le mot juste*] fascinating.' I think Sellers the anthropologist can be quickly discounted. First, these were people (like him) above the common mass; second (unlike him) they were established—they had history, pedigree. Sellers, with his personal background of vagabondage, found this alluring. There was a strong suggestion of a different, better world. He wanted to acquire it; he thought that then he might no longer be in such painful flux.

And so he wandered in silk-lined rooms and perched on golden furniture— and he married Miranda Quarry, the step-daughter of Lord Mancroft. It was one of the worst decisions of his life, and proof of how berserk he was. He'd assumed that lords and ladies would pride themselves on knowing him, as he'd felt himself enhanced by befriending the palace. It was not to be. He was seen through and denigrated as never before. Once, invited to Mrs Desmond Guinness' stately home, the hostess greeted another of the guests, Michael Fish, the dressmaker, effusively: 'Mr Fish, I know exactly who you are!' She then glanced Sellers' way and commented, 'You must be Peter Sellers, Miranda's new husband. I'm afraid I've no idea who you are. You see, I never ever go to the pictures.'

There was going to be no prospect of his being appreciated as a source of reflected glory; and as a self-made man, concerned for his career, his money and flash were deemed infra dig. Instead of getting himself accepted by an élite, he'd further divided himself from people—he remained a stranger. 'I feel I'm a totally different person [with Miranda's crowd] to the person I am when I'm with my own friends. [*Who are they? The other Goons?*] ... I don't open up at all, and I think that must be very boring to them. I let them believe what they want to believe, and if they think I'm a bore then they must get on with it.'

◆ ◆ ◆

The two obvious cinematic results of Sellers-and-the-idle-rich were *There's a Girl in My Soup* and *The Magic Christian*. (In each he was superficial, glazed, languid.) The latter's première was held on December 11, 1969, at the Odeon, Kensington, and there was a gala party afterwards at Les Ambassadeurs, Hyde Park Corner. The guests included the Beatles and Britt, from whom Sellers had been divorced a twelvemonth previously. Princess Margaret and Lord Snowdon arrived separately at the bash—and the Earl went and sat at Lady Jackie and Lord Anthony Rufus-Isaacs' table. Miranda did not materialise: '[She] isn't speaking to me right now', Sellers explained. No matter; he played at being a King—Rex Finchley—with Ma'am Darling. It was all rather an extension of a film fantasia; Sellers had melted into the rôle of debonair man about town.

If Chance the living saint is Sellers as he wanted to be, Danvers was Sellers as he liked to think he was. It was brave of him, I think, to play an ageing playboy,

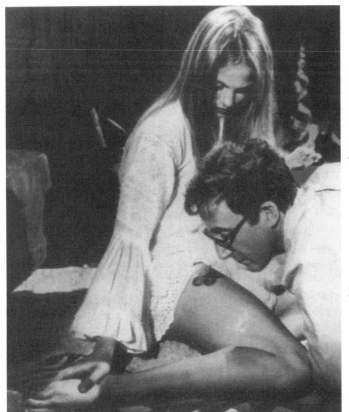

(Top) Sellers with a Britt lookalike (Leigh Taylor Young) in *I Love You, Alice B. Toklas* (1968)

(Bottom) Robert Danvers and his latest dish (Goldie Hawn) in *There's a Girl in My Soup* (1971): Sellers as he would have liked to have been, i.e. debonair

whose hairbrush is clogged, whose belly flops over his belt when he forgets to suck it in. He was parodying his own public image—the forty-something endlessly chasing the teeny-somethings. Danvers goes to society weddings like Harold, in *Harold and Maude*, goes to funerals—for the bodies. *There's a Girl in My Soup* begins with a swift seduction of the bride (Nicola Pagett) before she goes away on honeymoon, and barely have the credits finished rolling than our hero is in bed with a bridesmaid (Gabrielle Drake). Then comes the fling with Goldie Hawn—it isn't love; it is simply that Marion is always one up on Danvers' stratagems: she can see him for what he is, and this amuses him. The film concludes ninety minutes later with the approach of another bimbo—they seem to come off an assembly line—named Paola, played by Françoise Pascal, with whom Sellers proceeded to have an affair.

Françoise was currently being squired by Terence Frisby, who had written the screenplay. At a party given by Victor Lownes in the Playboy Club to celebrate the wrap, she met Sellers again. 'Do you want to come back to my place?' he asked. 'Sure,' she said. He made her sit through hours of tape-recorded playbacks of his Indian voices and throat-clearing practice. He produced marijuana and when she was doped he took her to his web. 'Peter was a nice guy,' she says. 'I only slept with him twice. He was an awkward man, even in bed.'

There's a Girl in My Soup conveys Sellers' predatoriness—the fellow with tons of money, who doesn't know what it is like not to be pampered, who does what he likes all the live-long day. Sir Guy, in *The Magic Christian*, is Danvers taken to a caricatured extreme: the upper-class accent is drawlier, the hair-do is more preposterously bouffant, the tedium at the centre of his life is more intense, and his pocket is deeper. Indeed money—what people will wade through to get it—is the film's motive. It is meant to be a satire on cupidity.

The film is a chain of bribery scenes. However, it isn't Sir Guy's victims who are exposed as wormy and cheap—it's himself. If you ask yourself who is the most culpable, the giver or taker of bribes, it has to be the former—he's the instigator, taking advantage of human weakness. Sir Guy's—and Sellers'—cynical empty-heartedness is revealed in every so-called gag. Sleepy-eyed though he be, at the core of *The Magic Christian* is the turbulent tempter 'ere the accuser of mankind: Satan. (Sellers has a silver streak through his hair—a devil's quiff.)

Was Sellers ever aware that Sir Guy's actions, which he endorsed, rebounded upon him? '*The Magic Christian* gave him the chance to express what he felt about the human race in a commercial film,' says Milligan. 'The whole thing could have been written *about* Peter instead of *for* him.' One of his pranks, which wasn't always appreciated—it illustrates his lordliness in all things—was to enter a cockpit after landing and to tip a pilot as one would any common taxi-driver in London or New York.

There seemed to be a confusion in his mind between his personal love of money—and the goodies and freedoms it allowed—and his contempt for those whose services or products he felt he needed, commissioned, and had to pay for. 'Now is the time to enjoy it,' he said of his loot in October 1962. 'If I see some gadget or car and want it—I buy it... I certainly haven't got a guilt complex about spending ... I don't believe in doing charity work publicly [*or privately, come to that*] ... I want to do it unseen, not to make my niche up in Heaven a little larger.'

The possession of large amounts of money, which started to come his way regularly in the early and middle sixties, unwrapped new temptations, principally the capability to get away from things, to become self-inclusive and unapproachable. The great evil of money, as applied to Sellers, is that he could dodge life. When he said—as he did often—'people will swim through shit if you put a few bob [shillings] in it,' Sellers unwittingly gave us an image of *his* avarice, *his* greed; this is how he soiled co-stars, directors and producers. He was thrilled and sickened in equal measure when folk obeyed him (weaknesses were confirmed). 'Deep down, Peter, too, has little regard for the morality of the human race,' Milligan has said, to no surprise.

◆ ◆ ◆

The Royal Family didn't get uppish with him (it was *he* who was uppish with *them*), but Sellers, according to the gentrified descendants of 'a Dubliner born plain Arthur Guinness whose grandpa, they say, got accidental eminence when he let the hops burn brown,' was deemed to lack class and breeding. The Mendoza and Rufus-Isaacs link was distant and tenuous, and anyway Jewish; and then there was the problem of his being an actor, an unholy, threadbare trade. Sellers tried to compensate for these lacks with his money—astronomical amounts.

His credo was put succinctly and honestly in December 1976, in the midst of a discussion about *The Pink Panther Strikes Again*: 'As Kubrick used to say, "Get some FUCK YOU money in the bank, then you can afford to mess about." He's proved that. Having earned my FUCK YOU money, has it made much difference? You see, I've never ... coveted money, like some people do ... I always knew I could take care of myself [but] I never knew I would get into this sort of league ... People somehow treat you differently. It's strange how in awe some people are of money.'

Miranda wasn't in awe of money, nor was she extravagant; she simply expected there to be plenty of it in the background or as part of the air she breathed. It was what facilitated leisure, which to Sellers looked from a distance like happiness. Sellers had met her at the London-to-Melbourne car rally at Crystal Palace in 1969. He fed her with marijuana-spiked honey and later, on another occasion, he tried to be impressive by consuming sugar lumps soaked with LSD, which made him sick. He was a middle-aged man in the Age of Aquarius, an era of Carnaby Street, sex, and drugs.

Dressed in loosely-knotted scarves and snakeskin jerkins, Sellers and his very youthful moll were familiar features on the Swinging London scene: Annabel's, Berkeley Square and Tramps, Jermyn Street—where Sellers and Miranda held their wedding reception. If peers and prosperous paupers met and mingled, our man was there, spreading the gospel of self-indulgence; he was frantic to be part of the frivolity. On January 16, 1969, he told a crowd of students: 'I've used marijuana with groups of friends and there's no harm in it ... It heightens the senses and one of the best ways of using it is when listening to music. You can hear music as you've never heard it before.'

One of the people influenced by these words and who tried to follow his example was his own son, who was suspended from school, King Alfred's, North London, for three weeks and threatened with expulsion. As Michael told me: 'He came up to the school where I'd been caught smoking pot and gave me this whole lecture in front of the headmistress: "You can't do that, it's against the law ... it's not right ... blah blah blah ..." Next day he's at the London School of Economics. They ask him if he smokes cannabis. "Yeah, it's great ..." Didn't do my case any good! He couldn't handle drink and drugs at all. It took him too far over the edge. It made him more ... reflective and introverted, and this induced his paranoia. Drugs wound him up, and he began to have doubts about himself and whether he could act. I've seen him take cocaine—especially when he was on the fringes of the pop industry. He had the same manager as George Harrison and ... became friendly with [Keith Moon] shortly before he died. Cocaine was free and running at those parties ... He was tempting fate. He didn't care. He was more interested in getting stoned and enjoying himself.'

◆ ◆ ◆

The sixties' combination of bliss and depression, insouciance and willed chaos, mock innocence and authentic brutishness could have been an emanation of Sellers' mood and toy-life. The relationship with Miranda was up and down, on and off. He was always arguing with her. He deliberately crashed his Rolls because of something she'd said—he didn't like women to have minds of their own. (She wouldn't retract, so he sent the car into reverse and rammed the vehicle behind as well.) He took her on his yacht ('I don't use it very much now', he sighed, affecting aristocratic disdain) and he introduced her to celebrities. He courted her for two years, spoiling her rotten with gifts—whilst simultaneously, though of course also separately, he romanced Francesca Hilton (Zsa Zsa Gabor's daughter) and Titi Wachtmeister (former girlfriend of Britt's younger brother), whom he thought seriously of marrying because the photographs he'd taken of her in the shower were 'beautiful'.

He cavorted like his James Bond character from *Casino Royale*: 'a bounder and a vulgarian, a joke-shop spy, a sexual acrobat who leaves a trail of beautiful dead women behind him like blown roses'—and it was Miranda whom he selected for capture on August 24, 1970. She was so surprised that she was going to be a bride, she didn't buy a special kaftan until the morning of the ceremony, which was held at Caxton Hall (where Sellers had married Anne nineteen years previously). The best man was Bert Mortimer, ever faithful, ever true. He married her to spite her—to spite everybody. He phoned Anne and Britt moments before the service began to remonstrate with them. 'Look what you made me do! I'm having to marry a third time because my marriages to you didn't work.' His conception of cause and effect was the wayward child's—shifting responsibility on to its elders for its own malice and misdemeanours.

The unrealities intensified. The Irish government had declared the Republic a tax haven for writers and artists. After a party at San Lorenzo's on March 25, 1971, Sellers duly moved to a palatial residence, beyond the reach of the Inland Revenue, in the village of Maynooth, a few miles outside Dublin. Here, surrounded by a five-mile stone wall, with five entrance lodges, was an estate fit for Rex Finchley and his queen. Carton House, Co. Kildare, was formerly the seat of the Dukes of Leinster. It abounds with colonnades, baroque plasterwork, and over a thousand acres of private park, containing cows, pheasants, and ducks 'reared to enhance the wild population'.

Miranda, he said, 'is rather a special type of girl insomuch that she is concerned with making a home.' Her concept of domesticity, however, wasn't connected to any innate motherliness. She designed water gardens and her taste for interior decoration tended towards psychedelic purple murals and ultra-violet lamps, which was all very hip and groovy. But what about washing up the saucepans? Where was her devotion? Where was Peg?

'Miranda we didn't really get on with,' Sarah Sellers told me, speaking on behalf of the whole family. 'She wasn't too crazy about us, either; but it wasn't malicious or intentional. She just had her life and ideas about how children should behave, and we didn't fit in very well.'

Neither did Sellers. His wife was alien to him. In London, there had been the clubs and the illusion of liveliness. Exiled in Ireland, away from excitement, he and Miranda were on their own as a couple for the first time and Sellers felt a sterility round him. Like many in her class, Miranda was courteous and cold. Her emotional relationships were with animals. She filled Carton House with yapping dogs, cats, and parrots; they were called her 'babies' and were almost encouraged to befoul the floors and furniture. They were fed on fillet steaks and roast chicken, and when Michael, Sarah, and Victoria came to stay, all Sellers' own real infants got to eat were Heinz baked beans.

If Sellers had hoped that his wife's affection for her pets would be superceded by a new slavishness towards him, he'd misread her strength of character. She was not malleable. The serenity and invulnerability which he had wanted to procure, defeated him. Miranda failed to notice him. Instead of being replenished, he felt belittled, subsidiary. The Anglo-Irish gentry, which she seemed to know already, he spurned as stiff and stupid; they (he guessed) considered him ridiculous and impudent. Sellers hardened. 'I'm pissed off...That's what you get for being such a bloody snob [*meaning himself?*] I think that all Miranda ever really wanted was a bit of rough, a stroll across the tracks'. How could he assert himself? He crept downstairs one night and strangled a cockatoo. He threw a puppy in a swimming-pool (whence it was rescued by Michael). He tore up the album of wedding photographs and confiscated Miranda's jewellery. He then decided to commit suicide.

♦ ♦ ♦

It all sounds horrible from beginning to end. There was never an atmosphere of trust and easiness, and Miranda told me that 'my marriage to Peter was a difficult and ultimately painful time in my life.' When he'd realised she wasn't under his influence, Sellers had done his best to tear her nerves. The paranoia which gathered momentum and destroyed the marriage to Anne, which had wrecked the marriage to Britt, and which would poison his relationship with Lynne, put paid to this alliance, too. Sellers was dejected to find out that he wasn't the person he wanted to be, so he reasoned that the people he was with weren't what he thought they'd be, either. Sellers started to eavesdrop on her phone calls and brought his usual gamut of groundless suspicions into play: Who had she been seeing? Was she having an affair? 'I want proof of your innocence.'

It looked like he was going to start getting violent. Instead, he was gripped with an ennui so stultifying, he thought he was dying. Was it, he wondered, his heart which was murmuring to him? 'I keep getting these moments of blackness,' he said. 'If you have thirteen [*sic*] heart attacks in a row, and the supply of blood is stopped for two minutes—I think something must happen. They did tell me I'd suffered no brain damage at all.' It was the nearest he came to confessing he was mad, that he needed psychiatric help.

Sellers took to his bed for days on end—the gentleman of leisure turned into a shuffling recluse, who made a dash for the refrigerator at midnight when the rest of the household was asleep. He refused to speak to anybody except Peg (through a ouija board). He played his private archive of radio tapes—'Variety Bandbox', 'Ray's A Laugh', and especially 'The Goon Show'. We can see, from what he'd told Barry Took at the mansion in October 1971, just where his mind was wandering—into the past. 'As a matter of fact, I have all my early recordings. I've got my very first broadcast... I've never thought of anything other than I miss doing 'The Goon Shows' on Sundays. The big thing in my life. If anyone said to me ... "What were your happiest days?" Well, they were the Sundays... [when] I was part of the Goons...'

Out of this longing came *The Last Goon Show of All*, recorded in London on April 30, 1972, with the Royal Family, Anne, the children, and Britt in the audience. Sellers, who had scaled every height and removed every human obstacle without compunction in order to get himself off radio and into films—because 'I always had an ambition to work in films as an art form'—looked to Goonery as a world without restrictions. Cocksure, standing behind the microphone, he had been fulfilled. 'The Goon Show' was the one great good place where his raging and destructive fantasies could be converted into comedy. Because he was a sentimentalist, he was quite able to forget how he'd rejected Milligan. Nothing mattered except that he was absorbed and never gave way.

But still the bitterness persisted. Finally, he opened a drawer and took out the kitchen scissors. He went back to his room and toyed with the blades. In a frenzied rage, he gave his arteries a miss and chopped off all his hair. 'He looked ghastly,' said Bert Mortimer. 'I said "God, what have you done?" Slowly he replied, "I think I'll become a monk—I'm going to join a monastery."'

It was this peculiar penitent who made *A Day at the Beach*; *Where Does It Hurt?*; *Alice's Adventures in Wonderland*; *The Blockhouse*; *The Optimists of Nine Elms*; *Soft Beds, Hard Battles*; and *Ghost in the Noonday Sun*. If Miranda was the wife people beneath the rank of baronet never knew, then these are the films hardly anybody saw. Despite this, the Aer Lingus shuttle between Heathrow and Dublin was laden with producers and directors bearing projects to Maynooth. 'I went to Ireland to show him the script of *The Blockhouse*,' says Clive Rees. 'Bert Mortimer said he was out shooting coot with an air pistol. We had lunch with him and he said "Yes". We came back to England and his agent [Dennis Selinger] said "The answer is definitely NO"...But Anthony Rufus-Isaacs rang him up direct and Peter said, "I'm going to do it. Don't worry."'

◆ ◆ ◆

Can a thread be traced through his Irish phase films, so to dub them? *Alice's Adventures in Wonderland* was Sellers' second outing with Lewis Carroll. His first, Jonathan Miller's television film of 1966, is one of the best literary adaptations that I know. (It is perfection.) Talk about 'Off with their heads', the characters here are off their heads. It is a crazy, beautiful interpretation of the Victorian mind, and it seems to be set in the park of a neo-gothic haunted house that is actually an asylum. (A prediction of Sellers' court at Maynooth?) The mood manages to be both languorous and feverish—i.e. manic-depressive—and Alice's pre-adolescent obsession with identity ('Who am I? That's the great puzzle') leads to the overwhelming answer: Nobody ever knows.

In this film, people's extraordinary gibberings, their energies and lassitude, are all seen as a means of avoiding stark reality and dread. Rules, regulations, laws (social and moral); religion and patriotism: they are structures created to give an illusion of order and purpose. If Carroll's fable has a message, it is that adulthood and/or maturity are not worth attaining. What awaits the keen and expectant child is disappointment, exasperation, despair. (Like *Peter Pan*, it is an indictment of adulthood.) Can anything have been more up Sellers' street? (Miller seems to be giving us a picture of the inside of Sellers' head.) 'I'm afraid I don't know just at the moment', says Alice, as the paranoia-inducing question *Who are you? Who are you?* gathers in intensity. 'I know who I was when I got up this morning, but I've changed several times since then...I'm afraid I can't explain myself. I'm not myself, you see.'

Sellers himself plays the King of Hearts. The other illustrious public rôle-players and inmates of the booby-hatch are Royalty. Much of the hymn singing and band music that fills the film flows from the King and Queen's processions. They are always having processions. (Pageantry joins pedantry as a way of using up time.) The institutions of power are in endless, flagging movement. Sellers, in an elaborate Austro-Hungarian tunic, totters and stoops in the rear column, his voice Henry Crun's. Confronted with the imbecility of the Knave of Hearts, he says 'But at least he's tall—very tall'. If everybody else in wonderland is strident, sure of themselves as madmen are, Sellers' King is dotty and bewildered. He's aware that he could be dreaming.

He's next seen at the trial—England's legal system, its arcana and pettifoggery being Carroll's final target. Sellers, in an outsize judge's wig and wielding an ear trumpet, presides. The courtroom is a dark theatre. In the galleries and boxes, people are taking baths, shaving, cooking—they live there. The King tries to keep order but he is ignored. He falls off his throne; he does bits of business with the wig and ear trumpet. 'Let's not have another witness—let's have a song,' he says,

(Top) The master and his state-of-the-art gadgetry (*c.* 1970)

(Bottom) A brilliant performance in a crappy film: The March Hare in *Alice's Adventures in Wonderland* (1972)

Michael Sellers Collection

and a gloriously discordant chorus of the 'Eton Boating Song' ensues, complete with poultry accompaniment and noises out of 'The Goon Show'. 'Ah,' he says. 'They don't reach verdicts like that any more.' He then sleeps, snores, makes animal noises, and collapses with a heart attack. It is funny, inventive, indulgent.

The feature directed by William Sterling seven years later returns to Carroll's text—from which Miller's film had taken wing—and quite misses its higgledy-piggledy spirit—which Miller had indisputably captured. It is leaden, as Sellers warned when he was interviewed on the set at Shepperton: 'There was certainly no improvised dialogue at all. The script was very straight'—and boring, he might have added. 'I've been trying to remember how old I was when I first read *Alice*. I think about fourteen. I re-read the book when I did Jonathan Miller's television version a few years ago. I wanted to see the difference between his interpretation and the original one.'

There is much in Carroll to appeal to Sellers, in addition to the identity crisis already mentioned. The whacky logic, the mathematics and conundrums suggest 'The Goon Show', as does the baby transmogrifying into a pig or Alice's alarming growth and shrinkage. The Duchess and the Cook, smashing plates and chucking pepper about, are a music hall duo, and many of the buffoons Alice meets are vaudeville or pantomime grotesques. There are sexual themes, too, in the story. Alice Liddell is Lolita, and Sellers' eye appraised Fiona Fullerton, who was golden-haired and budding: 'She's fifteen, and seems to be very confident of herself.'

But it is only really worth sitting through for Sellers, who transcends the puppet-theatre monotony: 'I chose the March Hare character ... I've studied the wild antics of live hares in the countryside round my home in Ireland. They do actually seem to go mad. It's part of the mating season during March ... They come up and look at you, then tear about all over the place at a most alarming rate.' Did he recognise a kinship, I wonder? The alternating mania and numbness?

Sellers came out with a deep, gurgling, twitchy voice—the exact opposite to Michael Gough, in the Miller film, who stammers and rocks back and forth, catatonically clenching his fists and jaw. Gough's Hare was clinically, authentically mad; Sellers' is gloriously eccentric. There is a moment in the trial scene, when he is sitting in the well of the court, and not particularly the centre of attention, which is simple and awesome: Sellers lets a quiver or shudder run along his spine that is exactly like a rabbit or hare. The detail is over in a flash, but I'll never forget it. Watching the wild things in the green fields of Maynooth paid off. Sellers is jiving, electric.

♦ ♦ ♦

In both of his *Alice* efforts, Sellers is clownish, out of vaudeville. It constantly haunted him, the side shows, the rough magic, and we can see how his memory worked. *The Optimists of Nine Elms* and *Soft Beds, Hard Battles*, with its multiple-rôle quick-change artistry, also see him seeking sanctuary in frowzy music hall. (After dinner in Maynooth he used to enjoy singing himself to sleep with the ukulele.) Though he'd gathered strength from it—and had surpassed it—he could not escape. It contributed to his feeling that he was going bad inside. By *Ghost in the Noonday Sun*, his mind was crumbling into so many pieces, he was swirling like dust.

It was that film, nevertheless, which restored him to popularity. He turned up at Kyrenia harbour during a night shoot and said he was going to make a commercial for Benson and Hedges cigarettes, to be produced by Anthony Rufus-Isaacs' company. He wanted Peter Medak to direct it. Medak told me, 'Needless to say I ended up doing it in Cyprus on our only day off. It won several awards. Sellers and Milligan are breaking into a customs warehouse where all this gold is kept; they stack the gold into Spike's pockets... Sellers orders Spike into the boat and he crashes through the bottom of it and it starts to sink... We had more fun with this commercial than on the whole movie. This is when Peter had the idea to revive Clouseau... Within six months he was making *The Return of the Pink Panther*.

'Anyway... Peter was to take out the Benson and Hedges packet and let it flash in the sunlight. "Oh, not me, daddy," he said, "I'm not allowed to touch cigarettes any more." Spike said he was chairman of the anti-smoking league. James Villiers was in it. He said, "Sure, lovey, anytime," and Jimmy was only getting two thousand pounds for this job. Spike got twenty thousand which he donated to charity. Sellers got a new Mercedes as his fee, and poor old Jim did all the work. The entire thing done in five hours.'

Whenever he didn't fancy putting himself out, which was often, there was his heart. 'On the first day of shooting,' says Medak, reverting to *Ghost in the Noonday Sun* 'the first scene was a long tracking shot... We were in the sand dunes, very isolated. After the second take, Peter, who was half a mile away, clutched his chest, and on the walkie-talkie he sent a message back that he had cardiac pains. Everybody panicked—everybody thought he was getting another heart attack... he was whisked away. So we then stopped shooting. The next morning I had the same tracking shot. He went insane. "How do you expect me to do this? I couldn't do this yesterday!" "Well, maybe you don't have a chest pain now—it is flat where you are—you just have to walk."'

It was nostalgia for his heart attack which drew him to the hospital comedy, *Where Does It Hurt?*, made in Los Angeles the previous year, 1972. The critics have buried it. ('Atrocious'; 'colourless, tasteless and... decidedly malodorous'; 'a dismal comedy.') In fact, though we keep seeing the tops of sets and the obtruding boom microphone, it isn't so awful. My complaint would be that it is not tasteless *enough*.

Sellers is Mr Hoffnagel, the corrupt administrator of Vista Vue Hospital. After so many suave rôles, it is good to have him back where he belongs, playing a twinkling shit. The voice he settled on was Nixon's; the walk, a lop-sided glide, is that of a shyster thrown off-balance by his own crooked schemes. Hoffnagel runs the hospital as a big business (or as Nixon ran the country), and illness isn't something to be cured, and the patient sent on his way. Illness is there to be cosseted, coaxed, invested in.

Where Does it Hurt? is a television episode of 'M*A*S*H' without the integrity; if Mel Brooks decided to spoof hospital sitcoms, it would be up to this standard. Like *Blazing Saddles*, which ends with a free-for-all, somehow the hospital is turned into a whorehouse ('Big, beautiful tits' lusts Hoffnagel), complete with a Mexican band, balloons, and streamers. Alarm bells and phones ring unheeded. The drunken doctors perform a circumcision on a young man ('Some day he might want to marry Barbra Streisand') and disinfect the snip with a splash of Bushmills. Hoffnagel sets up a secret camera to film the illicit fornications and general medical incompetence (blackmail material for later) and he has sex with a nurse in a linen cupboard...

Yes, it is slapdash in a way that isn't energetic. But Sellers breaks free, and his character is at a remove in any event. Clad in an immaculate brown suit and with brown lenses in his spectacles—he's a streak of brown lightning—he appears happy and comprehensively spurious as a minor Richard III, bribing and threatening. ('You are about to join the ranks of the unemployed,' he says to any member of staff who crosses him.)

He claims to be cursed with a 'shitty personality'; like Richard, descanting on his own deformity, he knows he is blessed. Hoffnagel is consummate. He loves himself. He loves totting up inflated bills and dreaming up forbidden activities. The last plot is seriously sicko—even without its connections to, and echoes of, Sellers' own sessions on a hospital slab. He decides he wants to be operated on. He'll then sue for malpractice, make a mint, and split the insurance payout with the quacks. The sight of Hoffnagel—or Sellers—bandaged for surgery, lying there in state, is disconcerting, to pitch it no higher. He is inscrutable—an anticipation of Chance; and he is also in position to be the mummified Fu. Hoffnagel disappears to be replaced by the Sellers who believed that death wasn't an opposite to life, but a status that shared the winter with birth.

◆ ◆ ◆

Is that what Sellers was, in the final analysis (not to say urinalysis): a shitty personality? A man who always had to have his own way? Who was averse to behaving naturally? In fact, to call Sellers a shit demeans him; his faults and cunning are in a different league. To call him mad, as I have often done throughout this book, excuses him ('Peter was psychiatrically cruel,' Milligan told me. 'His judgement was not that of a normal person'). What I think we need to do is revert to more ancient terminology, when summing him up. He had an evil streak in him. Sellers was evil. At the end of the last chapter, when I was in the graveyard, I promised you a further concluding point, and this is it. He was a destroyer. He was pandemonium.

Let us start with his invidious behaviour towards his children. It is possible to explain away his iniquities by saying, well, Sellers was a basic, crude performing mechanism. He simply played certain rôles. He had no idea of what a father was meant to do. What did it mean to be 'Peter Sellers' children?' He had no conception of domestic life—they don't show ordinary domestic life in the movies. He was no sort of father to Michael, Sarah, or Victoria because the part did not inspire him. They must have wondered who this person was, permissive and suddenly harsh, flying in and out of their lives for a few days at a time, wanting everything to operate in his favour.

Though there is much to recommend a mask-behind-the-mask-interpretation—Sellers, the compulsive mimic, who had no mind or philosophy getting in the way—it is too exculpatory and limited for my taste. He was ignorant, but he wasn't stupid. He never had any desire to put the effort into learning anything; he was an uneducated man who couldn't hold an intellectual conversation, but he knew what he was doing. He was no fool; he was egotistically sublime. He rejected his children because, by virtue of their very existence, they made him belong to material reality; they compromised, or revoked, his fantasy lives. They gave him a cold feeling—like a memento mori. They were also a boring responsibility, a bondage, and he wasn't going to accept that. There was nothing he could get out of them—no advantages. Any school achievements or gifts they might have made he mocked and threw out.* He had no use for his children, and his lack of consideration was completely consistent. (That they were left high and dry in his will quite fits the pattern.)

Victoria got the worst of it. Sellers didn't want her to be born. 'I've got Michael, I've got Sarah. I don't want any more children.' Only the intercession of Bryan Forbes and Nanette Newman prevented Sellers from ordering Britt to have an abortion. He was making *What's New, Pussycat?* when the baby appeared, on January 20, 1965. He was so preoccupied with the re-starting of his career—his performance as Fritz Fassbender being his first major post-coronary rôle—he dumped his wife on the pavement outside the Welbeck Street Clinic, without so much as carrying her suitcase in through the door. (Not for him any father-in-attendance rubbish.) Congratulatory telegrams arrived by the thousand, but Peg was not impressed. She only ever referred to Victoria as 'it'; Sellers seems to have followed this example.

The baby was raised by nurses and strings of nannies, and Britt had to ensure that Victoria was hidden out of sight and earshot by the time the master returned from the studios. He was so competitive, he was jealous if he sensed his wife used her energies up being a mother. She had to be all for him. Here's how, in 1966, she felt obliged to set her routine: 'In six months or a year's time Victoria will want more from her mother and I will have to give her more. That does not mean I will have to give my husband *less* time but that I may have to take more time off from my own career.'

No matter how conscientious or compliant Britt was, Sellers would have been dissatisfied. It had appealed to his vanity to woo and win a beautiful woman; but having made the conquest he was bored with her and wanted to kill her. Indeed, he despised her for trying to love him—he was both smart and twisted enough to see that as a flaw in her nature. (Also, young and gorgeous, she reminded him he was

---

* 'Dear Sarah, I have just been given what I believe to be your Christmas presents ... I know it is the thought that counts and not the money. But what a thought. Yours, Dad.'

growing old.) Many of the quarrels and fights, already discussed, which took place during the making of *After the Fox* or *The Bobo*, unfolded with Victoria present.

The innocent child in their midst was the battle ground (or battle trophy?). Victoria was to be victimised, as anybody could tell from the statement read out in the London Divorce Court on December 18, 1968. Mr Joseph Jackson QC, appearing for Sellers, said: 'They know that even if they have failed with their marriage they must not fail over Victoria. They are both devoted to her. They have her interests vitally at heart.' The judge gave Sellers and Britt joint custody of the girl, who was not quite four, but daily 'care and control' did go to the mother. Britt was granted a decree nisi on the grounds of her husband's cruelty— and Sellers, who was not in court, did not instruct his lawyers to deny that cruelty. Mr Jackson said: 'My client … is entirely satisfied that his wife will behave responsibly towards Victoria. I think that both of them have been very sensible over what I could call their "common asset".'

If only Sellers' learned friend had realised the implications of his little legal quip! Sellers felt he was being officially sanctioned to treat Victoria as a bit of impassive property. Famously crude and abandoned over goods and chattels, he consigned his flesh and blood to the ranks of cameras and cars (and dolly birds)—an object he could pretend to be occupied with and then neglect. As part of his courting of the Royal Family, for example, he gave Viscount Linley and Sarah Armstrong-Jones a palomino pony, Buttercup—Victoria's. Sellers' daughter went in the paddock one day and the animal was gone. Cruel? Thoughtless? Spiteful? It mattered nothing to him that his daughter might have feelings that could be hurt. In recent years, Victoria has tried to be understanding: 'I really missed that pony. But you just had to accept that that was the way Dad was'. She then added a gloss to the resigned remark which, subconsciously I am sure, goes right to the heart of her father's evil nature. 'It was an object to him, and he never got fond of objects. Once they'd stopped being new toys to him, he'd give them away or sell them.'

What went for Buttercup went for people; as if the Royal Family was short of nags! But he wasn't giving the Snowdon babes a present so much as hoping he could bustle closer to the throne. He was only generous if there was an end in view, or to get allies, or to get a reaction. Indeed, generosity was a perverted concept where Sellers was concerned—he felt momentarily better for the attention/gratitude he inspired; he liked having the power to spend and surprise; he was bragging (it was self-glory) and he didn't give a flying fuck for the actual recipients.

He resented spending money on his children, but he didn't stint on wasting fortunes, over the years, surging after Britt with solicitor's letters. He opposed all her ideas about education on principle, with the upshot that Victoria was frequently uprooted and made to traipse Sweden, England, and America in search of a suitable lycée. He called Britt filthy names in front of the child, to make her tearful, and he expected to get from her what Britt said about him, all the while scaring her 'by threatening to have Britt arrested and thrown into jail, and that he would seek custody of her; then she would live with him permanently because her mother was a bad influence…'

Far from his being interested in keeping Victoria, protecting her, or contemplating her welfare—she didn't exist—it was the act of throwing her back and snatching her away which provided Sellers with amusement. On one occasion, Victoria was on her way to the airport, with the flight tickets in her pocket, when Sellers cancelled a long-promised holiday.

They did, however, eventually reach a beach. 'The only time I really saw him militant,' Herbert Lom says, and he must have acquired a strong basis for comparison, 'was when he was fighting Britt for custody of Victoria. He was happy at the prospect of taking Victoria on holiday—a grand beach house was procured for three weeks. After three days he was back. "We grew bored with each other." Tragic. As a father I'm sure he was a monster.'

♦♦♦

And as an ex-husband. He commissioned a private dick to shadow Britt *after* the divorce. He intimated that he would apply to have Victoria made a ward of court if her mother took a boyfriend. Meantime, of course, Sellers was tom-catting like billy-o and telephoning his ex-wife to boast of his conquests. Mia Farrow, soon to be a famous Earth Mother, was in his harem. ('EXIT BRITT, ENTER MIA' blazed the tabloids.) They dressed in kaftans and beads, lit joss sticks, and watched the sky for UFOs. (On one trip into the desert to have a mystical experience, they were secretly followed by Roman Polanski, who threw rocks and made funny noises. 'Did you hear that?' whispered Sellers. 'What was it?' hissed Mia. 'I don't know, but it was fantastic. *Fantastic!*')

Sellers was fascinated by the flower-power paraphernalia of the sixties. (He could hide his evil behind it.) He burned incense and chanted sanskrit before a statue of Buddha; he acquired an altar, complete with a porcelain three-headed elephant and velvet prayer cushions. He was a proselytiser for Ravi Shankar. The film which exhibited much of the cock and bull—the pretences—was *I Love You, Alice B. Toklas*, in which the Jewish lawyer dropped out to become a hippie. 'It is really a full-blown story of a man and the metamorphosis that comes about when he is exposed to pot...Alice B. Toklas' chocolate brownies with hashish in them [are] the springboard for a change in the man,' explained Hy Averback, the director.

As it is possible to detect from this effusion, *I Love You, Alice B. Toklas* contained elements of documentary. It is Sellers' life and times which are on show. The guru's questioning, 'Who are you? Do you know who you are?' fits with Sellers' own endless ego trip; and Harold Fine, anxious, angry, Jewish, mother-dominated, is simply saturnine Sellers with a Californian accent. The satirical barb, too, hits him palpably: the successful man agitated because he thinks he is missing out. Harold grows his hair and walks barefoot, but he hasn't really altered his personality (only his wardrobe)—he is still possessive of Nancy, the girl he meets who munches oranges complete with peel—and who, as played by Leigh Taylor Young, is a dead-ringer for Britt. When Nancy is seen painting psychedelic mauve squiggles on another guy's body, he explodes. 'I like him,' the Lolita says ingenuously. 'Is there anyone you don't like?' snarls her Humbert Humbert.

For Harold, the hippie-business is street theatre, a dodge; the drug culture enables him to block out his family problems—he can't confront them, he still can't cope. Intoxicated by marijuana, he says he doesn't have 'hatred and violence' in his soul any more, but he does, and Sellers himself did. The hippie antics were completely bogus, the latest posture among many, as witness his anti-nirvana-like behaviour whilst making the film. He wanted the crew changed because he said they didn't like him and were leaking stories to the press. He had the script girl sacked because she was wearing a purple dress—the colour was giving off bad vibes, he argued. Bad vibes seemed to reach Sellers like a dog whistle. The air was full of pulses and wing beats, as Roman Polanski discovered: 'Peter's idiosyncracies could be a drag...I grew to dread the moment when, after ordering [in a restaurant], Peter would whisper: "Ro, I can't stand it. Bad vibes in here...Let's go somewhere else."'

◆ ◆ ◆

What for Harold was a masked ball and an affectation, however, with Sellers was hypocrisy. The yogic dumb-shows in the film are there to be laughed at; the standing-on-his-head and lotus position meditations, which Sellers went in for, were party tricks, too, but what bestowed a particular perfidiousness upon them was the way he pretended to have achieved the calm-dignity-grace of Buddhist ethics. (Sellers was a mock priest.) 'What I am aware of,' he stated as late as December 1976, 'is that I'm never one for feelings of revenge. It's anti my beliefs in yoga...I've got nothing to come out now. Nothing up my sleeve. I'm clean, bare, naked. That's fine.'

It was fine, too, to bring Victoria to Ireland and banish her to remote icy bed chambers; it was fine, if Britt remonstrated with him over the maintenance arrears, to send the child a letter saying she should no longer regard him as her father; it was fine, if she did come and stay, to 'let me do anything I wanted because that was his way of getting back at Mum...Then he could be completely cold and distant as though I wasn't even in the room.' Any discipline or routine Britt may have established Sellers delighted in wrecking—and he would have condoned his daughter's career as a nude model, we can be certain of that. 'Mum might freak out, so I'm avoiding her,' said Victoria, when her acceptance of a *Playboy* assignment was announced. 'But I don't think Dad would have been all that negative.'

The feature spread, with photographs by Richard Fegley, was published in the issue of April 1986, when Victoria was twenty. Had Sellers lived to see her thus exposed, I'd be afraid for her. The excuse for Victoria's strip-tease was Sellers' own *Playboy* pictorial of April 1964, called 'Sellers Mimes the Movie Lovers.' In that he (rather brilliantly) impersonated the likes of José Ferrer in *Moulin Rouge*, Rudolph Valentino in *The Sheik*, Bela Lugosi in *Dracula*, Cary Grant in *Notorious*, and then he was himself (as it were) in *The World of Henry Orient*. Needless to say, Sellers is completely clad in the various costumes; he stares at the camera in mute appeal whilst the playmates, with a hint of nipple, try to paw and fondle him.

Two decades on, the feature 'Best Sellers: Peter's Daughter Victoria Joins the

Family Business', is not only complementary; it is like delayed-action incest. Sellers' versions are reprised and inset, to look down upon Victoria—leggy and pawky—as (among others) Elizabeth Taylor in *Cleopatra*, Jane Russell in *The Outlaw*, Sophia Loren (*Sophia Loren?*) in *Yesterday, Today and Tomorrow*, Brooke Shields in *The Blue Lagoon*, and Kathleen Turner in *Body Heat*.

Sellers, in his assignment, had managed to spoof the notion of practised lechery. We admire his facial expressions first and only then hunt for the scarcely exposed knockers. With Victoria, breasts, bottom, and beaver push towards the lens, like plastic flowers seeking the sun. The emphasis on body parts is almost pornographic, or shall I say fatuous? Victoria doesn't resemble the screen vamps, nor can she get into the spirit of them. She seems to have nothing to bring out. Despite the elaborate sets, make-up, and general scene-setting, she does seem very young and vulnerable. What I see, behind her eyes and embarrassment, is her father and a process of dehumanisation.

So much for sex; now it is the turn of drugs. Narcotics gripped and blighted her life after Sellers' death. Following the funeral, when she had been screamed at unnecessarily by Lynne, Victoria went through a long period of uglifying herself as a punk rocker. In May 1986, she pleaded guilty to knowing about an international cocaine ring run by her violent boyfriend, Reed Wallace. The Assistant United States Attorney, Judy Russell, in consultation with the Drug Enforcement Administration, agreed to a light sentence on conspiracy charges after Victoria had promised to be a prosecution witness against the gang.

That the girl turned out this way can be no surprise.* Her ideas of right and wrong, good and bad, had been formed by a father who'd rant: 'As far as I'm concerned you can get the next plane and go home. I never want to see you again. Your behaviour is disgusting...' Etc., etc. Be on the receiving end of a repudiation like that, and what's the worry with real vices? Sellers had seen to it that his daughter was lurid and apathetic. He inspired a malaise. As Victoria's probation officer, James Brouchard, said, 'Our concern is not that she is not sincere in wishing to kick drugs, but that she is incapable.'

She has, in fairness, been rehabilitated somewhat, and in October 1992 she said: 'Drugs are behind me. They nearly ruined my life ... It's humiliating to have to keep taking drug tests but it's a small price to pay rather than going to jail.' Michael and Sarah were not corrupted by their father, but they were no less affected and shell-shocked: 'Having been brought up like that,' Michael said to me, 'unable to relax when he was around, the mechanism for dealing with ... people ... prevents me from being totally open, because I was emotionally trampled on when younger; I've been taken advantage of, and the result is I have few friends. I have no old school friends, because of the way he moved me around. I find it difficult to trust people and to make new friends.'

---

* It is common knowledge that Victoria has worked as a high-class hooker ('The guy wasn't repulsive and it was straight sex—which was over in three minutes. I remember taking a huge sigh of relief. I knew then I could do it. It was easy money.')

The evil that men do lives after them (the good is oft interred with their bones—though I'm not convinced of that, either). After he'd made *The Magic Christian*, Sellers, steeped in decay and gloat, evangelised as follows: 'Love, in the fullest sense of the word, contributes to my search for happiness. Not just physical, sexual love—I mean ... trying not to be uptight about people. You know when somebody says something that makes you rile a bit—trying to kill that if you can. I've been unsuccessful at this, but that would be my aim.'

Would be his aim, except ... : note that use of the conditional tense. In fact, Sellers had long before renounced love in order to gain power. That, I now see, has been the theme of my book; it is what gives Sellers' story a moral dimension. Even his money has been cursed. In the fifteen years since Sellers' death, his widow and the beneficiary of his estate has continued to live very much in his shadow. The money has done nothing for her. Lynne is shut off from the rest of the world, save for her mother and grandmother. A friend who has observed her plight told me: 'Hers is a tragedy, being swept off her feet at a very early age by someone who was both used to getting his way in everything and very aware of his mortality and fragility. She has had a rotten time of it for the past ten years and all that wealth has given her no satisfaction ... I think that one of the qualifications of artists should be a vow of celibacy. They should be confined to ruining only their own lives.'

◆ ◆ ◆

After the turning-point in the early sixties, when he zoomed from star to superstar status, his refractoriness intensified, and the destructive forces which made a hell of his private life created such despondency on his film sets that clearly the man and the artist were one. Roy Boulting has said that his relationship with Sellers during the making of *There's a Girl in My Soup* 'had been a very abrasive one. I emerged from it worn, shaken, and swearing that I would never endure such an experience again. What I did not know until later was that Peter himself was suffering domestic traumas at the time that left him nervy, irritable, and deeply unhappy.' Yet he always had domestic traumas on the go. He inculcated them; they were one of his diversions, thinking up new ways of being repulsive. It was his nature.

Fame facilitated the release of all the unpleasantness in him. His faculties, too, altered. He went from being the sort of actor who entered into his characters and revealed their oddities and quirks and became—or tried to become—the kind of performer who insisted on his own ego and vision. This is why, after *Doctor Strangelove*, characters come to resemble one another: Evelyn Tremble, in *Casino Royale*, is an Anglicised Harold Fine, from *I Love You, Alice B. Toklas*; Benjamin Hoffman and Robert Danvers are shadowy and sunny twins; Chance and Fu Manchu are serene and godlike, and there's *The Prisoner of Zenda*, which is about a pair of brothers ... Sellers was a one-man family, and he felt ranged against the world.

Once awakened, his evil nature created the problems he could then complain about. As Wolf Mankowitz says: 'Sellers' poor standards of behaviour would create the most unbelievable mess—because by *Casino Royale*, say, he was pretty well round the bend and couldn't function properly. He'd change the order of shooting on what might be very complicated films. He'd be 'unavailable' or he'd constantly change his timing, making it difficult to splice material together...The eventual film doesn't make sense...Charlie Feldman...agreed to anything to keep Sellers happy. He gave him a white Rolls-Royce on the first day of shooting, just as a come-on.'

If he had intended to bribe Sellers into being complaisant, Feldman found the opposite was happening. 'Feldman was glad to get Sellers at any price,' says Joe McGrath. 'He'd put up the money for Sellers' personal insurance on *What's New, Pussycat?*—after his heart attack, nobody would cover him—but Sellers wouldn't be beguiled. "Even at that time Feldman was devious," Sellers told me.' Sellers imputed underhand tactics to the producer, and his mistrust spread across the film like a cancer. 'I walked off the film after six or seven weeks' shooting,' says McGrath. 'I told Feldman, "It's pointless going on. There's no control. Nobody has any overall feeling for the film and what's happening".'

McGrath was responsible for the seduction scene, in which Tremble dressed up as Hitler and Napoleon to try and impress Ursula Andress. 'A typical Sellers scene,' says McGrath. 'Milligan phoned him up over *Casino Royale*, and said that the disguise sequence, where Ursula is photographing him, was wonderful. "Peter, what went wrong with the rest of the movie?" Our script [the Sellers-Southern-McGrath version] would then have had Peter playing a lot of other parts—disguises...I was meeting with Sellers and writing it at the Dorchester, and then shooting it.'

Or not shooting it, because his nibs had his little tantrum about Welles. Whatever it was that emanated from the hotel suite, it was nevertheless Mankowitz's job to try and coordinate it with his own proliferating draft screenplays. By June 9, 1966, *he'd* had enough, and he instructed his agent, John Heyman, to send Feldman the following letter:

> Wolf feels that there really is very little more he can contribute to *CASINO ROYALE*. He also points out that in the past two weeks he has done—
>
> 1) rewrites for the last sequence [the gunfight at the casino].
>
> 2) rewrites and cuts for the Tremble sequence which was in total chaos and is now ordered and effective.
>
> 3) new link scenes for Niven [in an office talking on the phone].
>
> 4) additional material for Cooper—which, even if it doesn't satisfy you, is the best he has been able to come up with.
>
> 5) some cuts on Mata Bond and story discussion with Karel Reisz [for scenes directed by Ken Hughes].

The problems alluded to in point (2) gave rise to all the other predicaments. Point (4), by the way, connects with a long memorandum, previously delivered to Feldman, in which Mankowitz outlined how a burly, middle-aged nondescript played by Terence Cooper could be incorporated into the story to fill the gap left by the errant Sellers. If you watch the picture, therefore, and wonder who this big boring lump is and what he is doing, he is standing in for Sellers. It is also clear, from my examination of the material edited and presented under point (2) that

Sellers didn't execute the photography sequence with that much dedication. Tremble dresses up as Hitler, Napoleon, and Toulouse-Lautrec—and that's it. He and Ursula Andress are meant to be discussing baccarat and working up to making love, but Sellers is glassy. He doesn't bother to speak in Germanic, French, or Groucho Marx voices, as indicated by the script. Nor did he pursue his original idea to make Tremble a boy from Birmingham: 'It's the most unattractive, the least sexy accent in Britain,' he'd told Joe McGrath. 'James Bond parodied as Black Country. The epitome of the Secret Service with a horrible whine—there are possibilities…'

'We could have done a whole sequence of him starting off with the Birmingham accent and then losing it,' says McGrath. 'When he's taken down to the basement of Harrods and they fix him up with the clothes and gadgets, they could have given him elocution lessons.'

Clearly, Sellers was more interested in making trouble than making a film—here's how the genesis of *Hoffman* was described to me: 'Between the time when I had been advanced money and supported by the London head of Columbia, and the time when the script was finished and I'd acquired the interest of Peter, the hierarchy of Columbia in London had changed,' explained Ben Arbeid. 'A…man… called John Van Eyssen, an ex-actor, had become Head of Production. As was my obligation, when the script was finished and the project was put together, it was submitted to Columbia for first refusal. Van Eyssen rejected it, criticising the script… By the end of the week, a new deal was signed with Bryan Forbes and EMI. I then had the job of informing Columbia formally that I was withdrawing the film… I had to inform Peter, because he was still expecting to work for Columbia, about Van Eyssen's coolness. "I understand," he said. "Don't worry—I think I know why… You know he was…a lousy actor? Well…a year or so ago Miranda and I were guests on Sam Spiegel's yacht at Cannes. So was John Van Eyssen…I said…'What are you doing, John?' 'I'm now the Head of Production at Columbia Pictures.' At which point I fell off my chair in hysteria, and…said…'You couldn't even act the part.' You can get an idea why he didn't want to do *Hoffman* with me in it."'

◆ ◆ ◆

On November 24, 1969, Sellers bought a page in the trade paper, *Today's Cinema*, and informed its readers: '*Hoffman* was not only a motion picture—it was an experience I will always remember'—with dread. 'He hated the film after it was finished,' says Arbeid. 'He wanted it burnt.' This was a frequent invocation, which had nothing to do with his retroactive wish that he'd done better. (A consistently crappy Sellers thing was his allegation that he was a perfectionist.) Sellers wanted to destroy his films because he saw, with considerable mortification, that they were self-revelations. As he put it, 'I'm too close to all of them to be objective. I couldn't stand outside any of those characters—I've got to *be* them. So I could never be "critical."'

To the present purpose, therefore, comes Lionel Meadows, from *Never Let Go*; the energy Sellers found for the character suggests a fascination with evil.

(Pasolini, the director of evil, would have relished Sellers, I think.) But after that film, he played it safe. He became more of a cartoon actor, throughout the sixties, and refused to allow the public to appreciate his capabilities—instead, his lechery was caricatured (*What's New, Pussycat?*), his vanity was mocked (*The World of Henry Orient*), his explosive temper was Latinised (*After the Fox*), his solitariness was made clumsy (Clouseau's appearances), etc. His propensity to go over the top for its own sake was often unrestrained, rather than inventive (Evelyn Tremble, in a related though opposite way, is so muted, he's bland—which is not the same thing as his being understated); or perhaps it was simply that, after his heart attack, he had to show-off and convince us of his irrepressibility. That may be why, in contrast to the black-and-white movies of the fifties and early sixties, he's often less than recognisably human.

Whatever, he was still egotistical beyond, and if his film rôles made comic capital out of the seven deadly sins—pride (Robert Danvers), anger (Aldo Vanucci), envy (Harold Fine), lust (Fritz Fassbender), gluttony (Danvers again, also Hoffman's food/sex imagery), avarice (Mr Hoffnagel), and sloth (Dr Pratt)—in real life he was increasingly disabled by his appetites. His versatility was compromised by pettiness and spite; his determination and ambition became a coarse kind of stubbornness; and his mercurialism and affectations, out of which he had once made art, left him dissipated. If, on the screen, his performances came to be self-indulgent turns, hollow at the core, that is because his juice was being deployed to spoil the films he was in, as he was making them—not only before or after the shoot, but as the cameras turned.

'The one thing he enjoyed was manoeuvring and manipulating,' says Peter Medak. 'He'd do a deal with a producer, and then decide he deserved more money. For *Ghost in the Noonday Sun*, he doubled his money, and the producers had to cave in or the picture wouldn't have gone ahead and they'd already built this pirate ship in Athens...

'To this day, the producers think I was a party to the games, which I wasn't. I tried to reason with Peter, but he wouldn't listen—and it suited his purpose— whatever that was—to create a situation between me and the producers... Sometimes he got carried away and started acting—sometimes, you can see it in the film, he'd switch off right in the middle of a scene—comes right out of character and stops acting... He had lots of problems—he'd just broken up with Liza Minnelli, whom he was infatuated by. He was on drugs—marijuana, I don't know what else... He alienated everybody.'

◆ ◆ ◆

The Minnelli episode, which wrecked the production schedule of *Soft Beds, Hard Battles* such that the Boultings were nearly bankrupted, in addition to imperilling *Ghost in the Noonday Sun* and the future career of its helmsmen, was a fast-motion version of all his other love-affairs—a world which turned from glee to wearisomeness. (He was still married to Miranda, but no matter.) He was glad to be with a show business creature again, after the blue-blood experiment and the

Irish exiles; and Liza,* who always has about her the flooziness of Sally Bowles, reminded him of a successful version of his mother—Peg, the cabaret performer, eager to perform, to give out... Liza, too, was a bird-woman—her eyelashes are like
the wings of an injured crow; and is Loren there, also, in those dark and lumpy features? In that automatic flirtatiousness? Yet where Loren plays duchesses, count-
esses from Hong Kong—millionairesses—Liza's public persona is vampish, a bit
sleazy; she is ripe and erotic, very much the daughter of the fag-hag of fag-hags,
Judy Garland.

Sellers was impassioned by these connections and reverberations. Liza had
opened at the Palladium on May 11, 1973, for three nights. Sellers was so excited that
he stood up at the première and began taking photographs, no doubt infringing any
amount of copyright laws. He came back for the second and third performances, and
similarly bounded about popping flash bulbs. Liza's reaction was magnificent. Since
Sellers was so keen, she invited herself and full company back to his bijou house, at
11 Eaton Mews North, and did a selection of her numbers specially for him in the
lounge-room. 'Peter was overwhelmed,' Bert Mortimer, who was also squeezed onto
the premises, commented. (I'm imagining something like the stateroom scene in *A
Night at the Opera*.) 'It was Liza's zany zing that really got to him.'

Perhaps because of her energy, perhaps because she was always aware of the
omnipresent camera, Sellers called her 'Flash'. He had this sobriquet inscribed on
a miniature tape recorder, which was one of his first presents. They attended Noël
Coward's Memorial Service together; they decided they were in love. Liza told
the press, 'I have always been an admirer of his wonderful talent and we both believe in humour and in having good times.' Sellers was now talking of marriage—
and a formal engagement had been announced on May 22. Liza, however, took
Anne Levy's chum, Loretta Feldman, aside and said: 'How the hell did he ever let
her go? He's got to be out of his mind!' (Well, yes.)

'During their hot, passionate... relationship,' Bert Mortimer said, 'they spent
virtually every night together'—not only in the obvious place, but at clubs and
discos. As a result, Sellers, who had six A.M. calls for the Boulting film, would
slump, snort, and snore in the make-up chair. Liza accompanied him to Shepperton and applauded his transformations into Nazis, Japanese generals, and French
persons. 'It is terrific,' she said, 'to find yourself in love with a genius'.

The production shut down so that the genius could recuperate and grow
bored with his new conquest. It was obvious to anybody that Liza's need for excitement upon excitement would pall on him. So it proved. He began to complain
about her entourage of secretaries and executive assistants—he didn't like his
queen to come with a court of her own. Liza wouldn't budge. 'These are my
friends, Peter. They're always going to be my friends.' By June 20, the two stars
had collided and left each other's orbit.

---

* My publisher's legal advisers have requested that I make it clear that this whole paragraph
  refers only to Liza Minnelli's characters. I am happy to assert this fact and to concur that my
  descriptions would be impertinent and misleading if applied to the real human being.

'It's over, but Peter is marvellous and we had a lovely, lovely time,' pronounced Liza. 'Regrets? No, I have none.'

The relationship finished as it had begun—five weeks previously—with a crowd of people present. 'When he parted from Liza Minnelli they had a rave–up at the Trattoo which went on for four solid days', says Alan Clare, who played the piano for those ninety-six hours. 'The entire love-affair was like a publicity stunt.'

◆ ◆ ◆

Sellers had enjoyed and encouraged the press attention—if he read about himself in the public prints, it had to be true. But Liza wrong-footed him when it came to announcing their dissolution. He hated it that the public were being told that *she* was leaving *him*. 'It's true, but it was for Liza to say so,' he pseudo-gallantly said when asked to confirm the news. 'We are finished, but it was not my wish.'

It was with an affectedly broken-hearted Sellers that Medak had to contend during pre-production. ('I wasn't sure he'd ever read the script' the director told me); but by the autumn of 1973, when they were in Cyprus, Minnelli's effects were wearing off. He gave himself booster shots of amorous wrangling by squiring Titi Wachtmeister, another Britt lookalike, but fresh sport was required. Sellers had to devise a new torture. Hence, his decision to harass Tony Franciosa. 'He mocked Franciosa without mercy,' says Medak. 'Franciosa came over to me and said "I'm going to fucking kill that son of a bitch—if he ... provokes me once more, I'll knock him out and not be responsible ..." He ... picked up his heavy sword and I thought he was going to cut Sellers' head into two halves ... I pulled Tony away ... "That fucking man tried to kill me," [Sellers] screamed. "Who the fuck does he think he is? I refuse to be in the same frame as him!" I reported that to Gareth Wigan, who said, "You'll just have to do it in separate frames, then, won't you?" There was meant to be a whole confrontation scene between the two characters at the end. How could we do it?'

It was a repeat of Sellers' Welles aversion. The duel, instead of being on screen, was between the actors on the set—or simply deep in Sellers' mind. I asked Franciosa for his recollections and the first thing he said to me was: 'Why wouldn't Sellers see a psychiatrist?' Then he went on: 'I was a great Sellers admirer. I was a fan. Then I was to work with him ... He just seemed to want to sabotage the production. Medak was shooting correctly. Everybody was doing their best, under trying conditions on the ship. Sellers wouldn't cooperate ... From my personal point of view, I spent a glorious two months on Cyprus with my wife and children—and I do believe that Sellers took against me even for this.'

I should think that Franciosa's ability to return to, and seek sanctuary amongst, a happy family atmosphere would have rattled Sellers no end. He'd have been convulsed with jealousy—and resentment that his attempts to undermine his co-star were not working. Franciosa had also refused to vote with him for the sacking of the director, and as he told me: 'Sellers was ... paranoid about people around him. If you disagreed with him at all, as I did over his desire to sack Medak, you were confronting his paranoia. He had profound problems!'

His immediate one was how to wreck the film if the director was staying put, his co-star remained relatively unflurried, and Gareth Wigan was keeping a cautious eye on all and sundry. Of course! Why hadn't he thought of this one before? Sellers sacked the cinematographer, Larry Pizer.

This was a particularly injurious and shitty deed, because Pizer had shot *The Optimists of Nine Elms* and Sellers therefore knew that he was trifling with a totally competent and distinguished technician. They'd parted from the earlier film on good terms and Sellers had said, 'I look forward to seeing you on the next one, Larry!' Work began and (as he told me) 'one became aware of a lot of tension on the set and a feeling of people being careful of what they said … and suddenly I was asked to leave. I'd been working fourteen-hour days in the heat and the dust. I remember a party with Peter—he was singing all his Old Sam the busker songs, and his daughter, Victoria, who was about eight, was on my lap, joining in … The following morning I was … handed a plane ticket for a flight leaving at midnight. They wanted me out of the place like I had some terrible contagious disease … I flatly refused to leave so quickly … but Sellers had wanted the director of photography to disappear off the face of the earth overnight. Cast and crew were indeed bewildered by the event; they clubbed together and bought me a brass ship's lamp.

'Peter had asked me to his party … [but] didn't say a word or indicate anything about what was going to happen. He clearly knew. His decision, the director of photography's going … Peter Medak was very upset, but … it had nothing to do with my work. They were thrilled with what I'd shot … I'd given my total dedication to … the director, and … I was busy making the picture look good—did my departure improve it?'

It was precisely because Pizer was making the picture look good, and heeding Medak's instructions, that Sellers had to have him exterminated—he was the strong link in the chain. That was devious enough. What was shabby to the point of criminality was the note which he sent to greet the chastened cinematographer on his return:

My dear friend Larry,

There is no *clear* answer to the reason for your going except that Medak was thought to need an iron willed cameraman because he is unable to make his mind up. Chaos is supreme here and I await Milligan (if he decides to come) with eagerness, as if all is not clear *then*—thank God we will all go home.

It's easy to say but don't be unhappy, it has NOTHING to do with you.

Your true friend …

Sellers refused to view himself as a participant in the dramas and upheavals he'd set going; yet he was at least in the right of it when he emphasised Pizer's innocence. Was he subconsciously admitting that it had EVERYTHING to do with himself? But it is shameful behaviour, unameliorated, as it turned out, by Milligan's arrival. ('Once Spike arrived he eased up a little bit,' says Medak, 'but then he got bored with that as well.')

'Nobody on the film was funny,' Milligan told me. 'Not the director, not

Tony Franciosa, not Peter, not anybody. Medak is a very lovely man, but because Peter kept leaving Cyprus to go back to England, the film was dead from the start ... But every day was a miserable episode. Tony Franciosa claimed that I was baby-sitting for Peter Sellers, which was a bloody insult. He threatened he was going to kill us. So I went up to him and said ... "If that's what you think, I'm leaving tomorrow." And I did. I got on a plane the next morning and that was it.'

◆ ◆ ◆

As we can see, Sellers was not lackadaisical or an eccentric; he was not careless, lazy, or simply childish. He was systematically destructive, putting a great deal of effort into his backstairs plotting. (It's where his audacity went.) He was amazingly inconsiderate—people would write scripts, build sets, prepare shots, and he'd disappear. That (as it might be) ninety crew members were sweltering on a galleon, getting it ready for his big scene, only encouraged him to whizz away from them in his luxury yacht. 'He did this because he enjoyed it,' a veteran key grip told me. 'On one occasion I had to build a long track for the camera crane. It took me four hours to carry the equipment across the dunes to the location. A big set-up rig. Just as I'd finished, a message came over the short-wave radio: "Wrap it. Sellers won't come and do the scene." This happened all the time. A nasty man. Even now I can never come to terms with how brilliant people say he was.'

After *Doctor Strangelove*, nobody, from the director down to the caterers' runners, was immune from his chicanery. You never knew when he'd become crackbrain. Clive Rees told me that, throughout the making of *The Blockhouse*, he was 'fully expecting typical Sellers bad behaviour at any moment—and this was a great strain ... At last it came—Sellers turned up in a kaftan and a long wig. He was also stoned. I decided to ignore him and eventually he fell asleep in a corner. He phoned me up at three o'clock in the morning: "You didn't like my wig?" ... "I hated it."'

Anthony Simmons had to endure a similar bout of unbidden inspiration. 'There was to be a busking sequence outside the ... Windmill Theatre. An expensive day for us, on our tiny budget, because ... it was a Sunday—overtime for the crew. I got a call at three A.M. Peter suddenly had all these marvellous ideas ... he was going to have Old Sam strip naked ... and do all his music hall act on this white horse outside the Windmill. "Fine, Peter. See you tomorrow morning." In the morning he'd totally forgotten all about it. We didn't have any white horse, but I fear if we'd been a big studio with lots of money, that's what he'd have insisted on—white horses. People gave in to his crazy whims.'

They did, always. If he had accomplished good work, he still liked to retain the right to go back and spoil it. He couldn't set fire to *Hoffman*, but he made sure he pooh-poohed it in the press. Likewise he decried *The Prisoner of Zenda* ('I advise people not to go to see it'), *Murder By Death* ('the epitome of eight millimetre home-movie making'), and just about everything else, including his own life, or Life. I'm referring to his behaviour towards Peter Evans and the composition of *The Mask Behind The Mask*, which was first published in 1968. 'I had nothing to do with the book at all,' Sellers claimed. 'It was Peter Evans' own brain child ...

I asked him to wait until much later in my career, and then to do one from the masses of notes on the things I've done and the people I've met and the incredible situations I've been in. At some time in my life I mean to make them into book form. The true story!...The book wasn't done with my approval.'

No more was ever heard of 'The Sellers Papers', if such an archive, or *nachlass*, existed, which I doubt. Nor was Sellers being fair to Evans' book, which is indeed a true story, insofar as it went. Where his comments verge on the definitely false, however, is the impression he gave of being completely asunder from the project. In fact, it was practically an authorised biography. As Evans explained to me:

> He was very excited and pleased that, by leaving my job at the *Express*, I'd have more time to work on his Life...Just before I started writing the book, having interviewed him extensively...my secretary phoned me and read out this letter:

> Dear Peter,

>> I have given a very great deal of thought to our proposed project on my life story, including dying and everything, and I have a strong feeling that this is not the time to do it, even though I think your idea for the general layout is the best yet. I won't bore you with the whys and wherefores; enough that you know, in the words of Fred Kite, that: 'I have withdrawn, meditated, consulted, convened and my decision has been democratically arrived at.'

>> I think later on, much later on, would be better for me—perhaps in about eight or nine years. Of course it may be that nobody will be interested by then, but the reverse also applies, and I know I am just coming into my most productive period right now.

>> I wish that you will understand my feelings, Peter, and not be disappointed.

>> All good wishes,
>> As ever,
>> *Peter Sellers*

> Just like that! He'd known I'd given up my job. He'd decided the time wasn't right! I was pretty angry—my first reaction—and apprehensive about my future. He was in Rome making *After the Fox*. I immediately flew...to see him. He was living on the Appian Way, a beautiful big film-star house, built by Mussolini. I turned up there unannounced at ten o'clock at night, and Sellers was sitting down with Britt in a huge fascistic-brutalist chamber lit by candles—all slanting shadows and pillars...'Hello, love,' he said. 'Fantastic to see you...' He didn't ask me why I'd turned up, and...instantly wanted to open the Dom Perignon...Finally, I said how upset I was by the letter. 'What letter? Oh, that letter. Well—you understand...' 'No, I don't understand...We have been working together on this project for nearly a year...I must tell you, whether you continue to work with me or not, I'm going to write a book about you. I have a contractual commitment...'

> It ended with his saying: 'Great, I'm all excited again. It's a wonderful idea—let's go forward together.'

> Until then I'd not personally experienced his betrayals and changes of heart. I came back to London; I went back to Italy and saw him on...*The Bobo*. He welcomed me, though I could see the picture was in a lot of trouble, and this was affecting him...The whole production revolved around him. Already he was having

trouble with Britt...He announced for a second time that he wouldn't cooperate with me, with the consequence that I informed him it would in any event be a better book without him in many ways...He was never threatening to injunct the book itself. He just didn't want to be part of it anymore.

He'd lost interest in his Life, or anyway in Evans' version of it. I suspect that Sellers had a fear of too many facts. A biography is an extended obituary—there you are, mapped out. His changeling fantasies; his sentimental revisions of the past: how could they stand up to scrutiny? Biographers have a habit of bringing their subjects down to earth, to make them a bundle of foibles, a string of causes and effects—just like you and me, with a bit of Freud thrown in the stew to explain away creativity. How could Sellers countenance any of that? How could he bear to have a stranger, assuming the vantage point of God, look down upon his life from above and confront him with his misdeeds? How could he dare be made explicable—levelled—by tabloid journalists? In Tony Palmer's documentary, *Will the Real Peter Sellers (Stand Up)?*,* Milligan, who is providing the commentary, suddenly rounds on the camera crew and says: 'How can you encompass a lifetime? Do you think that by showing his agony to other people you will in any way help him? In Peter's case this is crucial, because he's so emotionally defenseless...'

I am not so sure about the defencelessness—that's where the tantrums and shrewd bullyings came in handy. Sadism was his shield. But Milligan has a point about the biographical pursuit and intervention—the chase, the quest. For how *do* you tell the story of another man's life? If you want to know a man's heart, you have to find a structure and form that suits each individual subject—and out of this can come a dialogue (so to speak) between the author of a book and the person he is writing it about. That, anyway, has been my own intention. Unlike Evans, Walker, Stark, et al., I never knew Sellers personally. Now I know him intimately; he haunts me; he is always just around the corner, as a sly ghost. I have stood outside his houses and on the pier at Ilfracombe. I have visited his birthplace—at the junction of Southsea Terrace and Castle Road, Southsea; and I have seen the woebegone plastic plaque nailed under the eaves of what is now a Chinese Take-Away:

PETER SELLERS
Film Actor and Comedian
Was born in the flat
Above these premises
On 8th September 1925
Presented by the Post Office
1985

—I have tried on his old costumes...And all for what? To be as he was?

♦ ♦ ♦

He forswore Evans and Palmer; he relinquished his children and his films (his

---

* Q: Did you recognise yourself in that portrait?
  A: No, not at all, no. No.

brainchildren); he wanted to be strangely vanished. One piece of labour he did get his hands on was the album *He's Innocent of Watergate*, produced by the former ring-master of 'The Goon Show', Peter Eton. 'We did a thing on Nixon,' says John Bluthal. 'Six months later I'm in Australia and I see it in a record shop. I buy it. I listen to it. I had about two lines left. I came back to England. I see Spike. "Spike, what's this? This isn't what we did." "Oh yeah. Bloody Peter. He got a new cast a week later and re-did the whole album."'

That was unforgivable. Milligan had been part of the development side of the project, and Sellers overrode him. (He overrode Eton, too, who was so embarrassed by the tinkerings he removed his name from the sleeve. Now the disc is credited to Pismo Clam—an old W. C. Fields pseudonym.) Why did he re-record the Watergate spoof? Like the re-takes of the Cleese scenes in *The Magic Christian*, because Bluthal and Milligan were *too good*. Two tracks were deleted in their entirety.

I'm not suggesting that masterpieces in the History of Western Comedy have been lost; I am suggesting that there was a barely-hidden fury in Sellers, and you could never be certain when it would surface, or to what extent, or why he was getting into conflicts at all. Often, people didn't know that they were going to be his victims—or that he'd be having this sort of duplicitous exchange with Joe McGrath. It is three in the morning. The phone rings.

'Will you take over the movie?'

'No. Peter.'

'What you are saying is you're *refusing* to take this movie over?'

'Yes.'

'Why?'

'First of all, you didn't ask me to direct it or be involved originally; second, I haven't seen the script; third, I don't like taking over from other directors. You've got to have some sort of loyalty to your craft. People don't end up being directors as an accident, Peter. It takes time. If [insert name] has got a director's ticket, it means something.'

'You are turning me down.'

'Yes.'

'Right, I'm off.'

McGrath might not hear from Sellers for six or seven weeks. Then would come another inconvenient phone call from the hotel on location.

'Will you come over and take over the direction?'

'Look, I didn't want to even before you started shooting.'

'Well, it's just a disaster. I've got no confidence in ...'

'Peter, you haven't got confidence in *anybody*.'

Et and no doubt cetera. 'He had no conception of allegiance,' McGrath told me. 'He'd only have lost confidence in me as well, as on *Casino Royale*. "This isn't working out. I don't have any confidence in you." Totally self-centred. He'd get in a state if he couldn't control things, yet he'd have a big enough problem with his own part, let alone trying to control an entire production.'

It was megalomania. He disposed of people who displeased him. He trusted no one. Dr Thomas Stuttaford, in his column 'Medical Briefing' in *The Times*, on February 7, 1991, would seem to be trying to define a Sellers-type:

> They disregard the usual rules of society as they seek to achieve their own ends. They are impulsive and demand immediate self-gratification; if frustrated in their objectives, they will not respond to reason but are likely to become increasingly violent and aggressive; rather than capitulate they would prefer to sacrifice their own life ... or that of others ... [They] are sexually irresponsible, albeit successful, for provided that life is going their way they are often charming and plausible. These same characteristics can be used to manipulate the gullible, hence perhaps Hitler's love of the uncritical, whether unsophisticated children, impressionable women or fawning dogs.

Dr Stuttaford was attempting to describe the personality of a psychopath, with particular reference to Saddam Hussein. If this seems laughably hyperbolic in relation to a nutty actor with a weak heart who cooled over fifteen years ago, this is what Milligan said in 1969: 'First there was Hitler, who loved Wagner, children, flowers and sunset, and then he goes and murders six million Jews. Peter can't work off his madness—it's all bottled up in him. Peter's biggest rage is that he can't be violent like Hitler. Don't mistake him. He's full of ... the rage of a murderer.'

We must be grateful, in that case, that he was *only* an actor. What Sellers represented was an attitude of mind. He seemed to want to pay people back, get one over on them. It was fatal to try and be friendly. (He behaved especially badly to those who did the most for him—by being sympathetic, or in taking him at his word, they gave credibility to and confirmed his fantasies, depressions and fears.) His ambitiousness, which had made him, proceeded to unmake him—his destructiveness was the other panel in the diptych. His rage found its first pure expression in 'The Goon Show', and Milligan was right to say 'from it has sprung everything': the fifties fustian, the cackling demons, the Hitler jokes, the cockiness, the misanthropy, the irresponsibility ... That is what Sellers took away from his radio days, and it was made to conform with what I have chosen to call his evil dimension—his psychopathy—which gripped him after his first marriage, his first divorce, his first heart attack, his ending of the world in *Doctor Strangelove*—that period in and around 1963, which forms the bend in the river.

Epilogue

♦ ♦ ♦

Who's the Man?

I know him very well indeed. Sometimes he bores me, sometimes he frightens me. Frequently he bewilders me. Occasionally he astonishes me, and sometimes I think he's mad.

Sellers describing Sellers.

He had the lot—beautiful women (and he was either fat and plug-ugly or thin and goofy); great riches (think how he started, on the road with the saltimbanques); there was an element of fairy story in his rise (let alone the mythic themes of doubles and duality); he was world famous. Insanity was the last luxury left, the only blockhouse he could hide in.

What with the ferment going on inside him already, trying to cope with the flow of external phenomena, on top, was beyond him. He wanted to still it, as with a camera. He abused kindnesses, to see how far he could push people—like his wives or Janette Scott: they were subjected to crazy tests or psychological seige. He played practical jokes on those who might otherwise have been his chums, to show them who was boss.

The well-being of others did not concern him. Only a constant succession of toys—or the turning of individuals into automata—kept him happy. The inhumanity of machines, and the sets of data which he could reel off about them, gave him the illusion of being scrupulous and rational—a clear-headed scientist. What he liked about his yacht—after the money it cost and the prestige it bought—were the specifications. 'This boat has two General Motor diesels, each 600-horsepower. It is the only boat in the world with these engines. An engineer flew from Detroit to Monte Carlo to install them. We cruise at twenty-three knots! Top speed twenty-seven.' The boat, eighteen metres long and fifty tons in weight, had a rotation radar dish, echo-sounding apparatus, automatic pilot, a radio telephone system, full air-conditioning, automatic anchor winches—all in addition to the engines. 'They have turbo blowers, principally because my kids get bored at sea, so when we go somewhere, we have to get there fast.' There was also a bicycle on board, so that the fed-up passengers could whizz away inland.

Of course, the speedboat/fear of boredom business was a personal anxiety of the master's. Sellers' children didn't have disaffections of their own, not so far as he was concerned. That is why he so often trained cameras on them. To have, later, his children playing over his walls as home-movies was preferable to having them in the home, as real people. Home-movies kept them at a distance—he could turn their caperings into a story, and give random life a form, a narrative. I am not being fanciful. In July 1970 he contributed his advice on home-movie making to some magazine or other and he stressed the importance of devising 'a theme and movement, and everything else fits in.' Whilst magic lantern images danced on a sheet Sellers said: 'I think the main reason for this great nostalgia and excitement in home-movies, and why they have become so popular, is that you can watch your children growing. They themselves don't particularly enjoy the films now, but I wonder how they'll feel in years to come. It's like a short piece of cine-film I saw of my father the other day, from some time in the twenties. Before that I'd only seen old faded shots of him. Then, there he was on the film, a young man, larking about, alive and moving.'

Where is that fragment of Bill now? What happened to Sellers' own trove, which was apparently destined for Michael, Sarah, and Victoria when they grew up? Destroyed in one of his fits of pique? Thrown out by his widow's assigns, who can have had no interest in forgotten foreign holidays or baby-on-the-lawn stuff? (Who can deny Michael's words: 'When he was alive you'd think, God, when you're gone it will be different. That shadow won't be over me anymore. But even in his death he's denied me my right—not the money; but I should have been allowed to go to Switzerland and sift through everything that was his. Because he was my father. I should have been allowed to find out about things.')

Sellers had adored photography because it brought back a remembrance of things past; in his last months he hated it for the same reason. (Hence the bonfires at La Haute Grange.) Pictures were evidence of time's passage—no mystery there—but they also reminded him that his happy days were now very far off. During one of his final trips to London, he bade his chauffeur, Peter Greenwood, take him on a tour of his favourite shutterbug shops. The car was piled high with new cameras and cine equipment, thousands of pounds' worth. Just as he was being returned to the Dorchester, Sellers turned to his driver and said: 'You have it. Photograph your baby growing up.'

It was a generous gesture, yet there was weariness and bitterness in Sellers' tone. He was in a leave-taking mood. His preferred occupation was to sit alone in the dark. 'I don't mind being alone,' he claimed. 'I really don't mind. I'm quite happy to sit here and look out of the window.' He was always self-isolating. As Janette Scott testified, he would lock himself in bathrooms—and he had a fondness of rooms entirely made of mirrors, where his image could repeat itself and stretch away to the vanishing point forever. His Clarges Street apartment had curved, cracked, and mottled mirrors. With the curtains drawn and Sellers in dark glasses it resembled a crypt—'a general air of gloom used to hang over the meetings,' recalls Jocelyn Rickards, who met him there when she was to have designed the costumes for *The Magic Christian*.

Dressing-rooms have a triptych of mirrors, and Sellers liked to watch himself take shape as somebody new. 'I walk around, trying different accents, feeling my way to the character. I do this every time,' he once said of his methodology. 'I stare at my own image in the mirror every morning, waiting for the other fellow—

the man I'm going to play to emerge, and stare back at me. I am waiting for this stranger to come into my life. When it happens, I have this flush of happiness.' He waited for a double—a lost twin, or brother? The process certainly sounds supernatural. In a way, he was *never* alone, if these alien voices and detachable identities could pour forth at will.

'I never remember him living in a place that seemed lived-in,' says Joe McGrath. 'It was always as if he'd moved into a hotel room... When he'd moved into the Hampstead penthouse... he wanted to buy some paintings... In those days you could buy Bonnards or Raoul Dufys for less than three thousand pounds... He ended up buying some cheap prints. Years later, when they'd soared in price, he said he wished he'd bought those Impressionists—yet he'd never quibble about spending forty thousand on a Rolls-Royce.'

There was something about him that didn't like old things. Always it had to be the most up-to-date cameras, cars, and gadgets. Was he fearful of the intellectual/cultural aspects of art works? Or was it their rootedness—their antiquity—which unsettled him? Also, if you are only happy in a hotel, or somewhere that resembles a hotel, that says a great deal about your own impermanence. It is as if everywhere he stayed was a preliminary to that final scene in the Dorchester, enacted in the suite that is not there now, when he went blue and was stretchered to Intensive Care.

◆ ◆ ◆

If Sellers inhabited castles in the air, his characters, too, were provided with mysterious retreats. Old Sam has his eyrie, papered with music hall posters, which is reached by a vertiginous rusty outside staircase. 'Peter came up with a sight gag,' says Larry Pizer, 'when the character arrived home drunk and distressed after the death of his dog. He tries to walk up the iron steps. He staggers towards the steps, and makes it up three or four, and staggers back, his impetus unable to take him further. Wearing a huge coat with huge pockets and, like ballast, he occasionally reveals empty bottles and throws them away. With the reduction in weight, he makes it up some more steps, falls back again, and throws more ballast out from his pockets—eventually, having dispensed enough, he has a run, and makes it right to the top of the stairs. This shot went on forever! Wonderful to see—he suddenly just did it! We kept turning, turning, turning to take it all in.' It is not retained in the finished film, alas.

There was no need for solicitude in *What's New, Pussycat?*, another film where a Sellers character has a particular relationship with his surroundings. Dr Fassbender lives in an Art Nouveau funhouse—a folly of windows and mazy passageways. The film begins with the psychiatrist being chased around the balconies and turrets by his Brünnhilde of a bride. She is accusing him of having a mistress, and demands to know how pretty she is by comparison. 'Prettier than you?' screeches Fassbender. '*I* am prettier than you!' He also insists she shut up: 'Silence, when you are shouting at me!' (Sellers, ad-libbing, purloins the Lionel Jeffries line from *Two Way Stretch*.) The camera remains outside the building. We never know where the two warring figures will pop up next. (They are like puppets, Punch and Judy.) What we are certain of, however, is that the teetering, rambling edifice, all curlicues and battlements, is an image of the insides of Fassbender's head—Sellers', too, with the bric-à-brac, shadowy corners, flights of fancy; it is half-ruin, half-Xanadu. (Clare Quilty may have been a riotous resident at one time.)

Dr Strangelove and Rouquet have their bunkers; Dodger Lane his jail cell; John Lewis his library; Dr Pratt his cat-infested consulting room; and Clouseau his Cato-booby-trapped flat-cum-gymnasium. *The Party* might be said to be about Hrundi's dangerous liaison with a Hollywood mansion, its gadgetry and sliding walls; and *Hoffman* and *There's a Girl in My Soup* are about playhouses and bachelor pads—habitats which are so important to, and revealing of, their owners. *Being There*, I think, would be much less of a film, atmospherically, without that cathedral-sized ice palace of Biltmore; and *The Prisoner of Zenda*, *Murder By Death*, and *The Fiendish Plot of Dr Fu Manchu* unfold in ornate, encrusted, Ruritanian lodges, towers, or hideaways, which are all the more apt and beautiful, perhaps, because, like Mrs Wilberforce's villa in *The Ladykillers*, they are mere movie sets, built not to last.

Then there are the islands: Gaillardia and Huwyat, for example. Aldo Vanucci turns Ischia into a film set in *After the Fox* (he pretends to take a call from Sophia Loren: 'I'm sorry. There's no part for you in this picture ... She'll kill me, it'll be in all the Italian newspapers'); and then there is the Cyprus carry-on of *Ghost in the Noonday Sun*, which provides my favourite expanding and contracting perspective on Sellers the hopping hobgoblin: 'One day I was shooting with a helicopter,' says Medak. 'Peter had to be way below on this boat. I was giving him my direction by radio. This argument started between me and Peter, because I wanted him to go near Franciosa, and he didn't want to go near him ... I got so angry I said for the pilot to take us ten thousand feet up. We are sitting up there having a beer and I see ... Russian and American jets ... screaming across the sky. It was just before the Arab-Israeli War broke out. So war is about to break out up here, and there's that lunatic on a pirate ship below.'

◆ ◆ ◆

It had always been his ambition, when he had the lolly, to purchase his own desert island and live like Robinson Crusoe, all-powerful in his own little world. As early as 1954, he had said he was labouring towards and searching for an island—to get right away and live in a state of idyllic happiness, like a noble savage. He never did get his island, but he did buy that boat, *The Bobo*, later re-named *The Victoria Maria* ('which may have been the only public compliment he ever paid to one of us,' says Michael).

'My real home is on the boat,' he said, 'got all my bits in there ... I can run the boat myself. You're not stuck in one place. You get out to sea—and there's nobody there ... Vast expanses of blue ... If you said to me, what is the most material super-luxury you have in your life, I'd say my boat.'

Of course, yellow sands and wild waves soon lost their appeal. Though he kept saying 'It's the only place where I can relax. There is no one there but the water', the sea and being adrift—the dead calm—like the peace and the snows of his Alpine fastness—made him moody and reflective, his mind dwelling on imagined hurts and insults. He once went stir-crazy in the Adriatic and the gleaming white motor yacht, flying the Panamanian flag, had to return to Venice. They dropped anchor off the Piazza San Marco, and Sellers used a megaphone to give the vote-garnering speech of a British Conservative candidate: 'Let me, as a good politician, make my position quite clear...' Didn't anybody *ever* think to knock the mad bastard off?

Hattie Stevenson, who had the unenviable task of keeping abreast of her master's non-stop global criss-crossings, says that 'his answer to everything was hiring speedboats or yachts. Nuts about that. All through their lives, the main meeting point for his children was to get them on a boat. I don't know why, but I remember this.' I should think it would have registered with anybody who knew Sellers that boats and oceans were his symbol of escape—to vanish into the wilderness. As Louis MacNeice might have said, or Ralph Reader, when you are riding along on the crest of a wave, time is away and somewhere else. But Sellers was often somewhere else, too: his notorious non-appearance after he had invited Nanette Newman and Bryan Forbes; the occasions when his children arrived on board to find their father packing up and leaving. If ever he invited one of his wives on a cruise, she was soon his ex-wife. The engine's throb and the vastness of the dark green oceans filled him with nausea. Alan Clare's wife, Bloom, recalls receiving an urgent ship-to-shore telephone call from the Aegean: 'I am sailing around the Greek islands,' explained Sellers, 'and I'm bored to death.'

The beauty of natural scenery, the majesty of the Greek civilisation's sticks and stones, etc., reminded him of his own irrelevance; his puniness in the scheme of things. As Milligan said: 'When the boat was finished, he thought, "Well, there's the blue moon; there's the stars... So what happens now? I've seen the stars before; I've seen the ocean; I've heard the music; I know the tune—what else is there? Nothing else? Let's all go back to London." Like everything else in his life, faced with the reality, he had no choice but to run away. The yacht; his home: all a dream.'

Sellers didn't need semaphores to see the comparison between aimlessly voyaging aboard his boats and pleasure steamers and wandering London with Peg or touring the rackety music halls as a child. He was richer, but no happier. Within the adult Sellers, searching for distractions, was still the St Aloysius' Jew who had to keep on the move. Feeling a sense of entrapment, separated, he identified with the nothingness and mindlessness of his surroundings, which were closing in. Air, earth, fire, water. The monotony, too, the vibration of the waves and sea-swell, was rhythmic, like a drumming—a heart-beat, familiar and lulling. Sellers, in his entrails, knew that there was something about sailing ships and the sea which would explain him. The sea, Elias Canetti once said, is like a powerful crowd, a mob: it is 'multiple, it moves, and it is dense. Its multiplicity lies in its waves... it can soothe or threaten or break out in storms. Its sublimity is enhanced by the thought of what it contains, the multitudes of plants and animals hidden within it;

it is an image of stilled humanity; all life flows into it and it contains all life.' Gazing for hours out at the sea's flashing surface, freely floating, Sellers was seeing himself as a desert island, a desolate atoll. To try and know him, Milligan has said, was 'like going to a desert island. In the middle is a lake, and in the middle of that, another deserted island. He's that lonely. He's desperate to be happy, successful, wanted, happily married. He's desperate not to destroy his past. It's all desperation. He *is* desperation.'

Afterword

'Happy endings are only possible if you don't tell the rest of the story.'
Orson Welles

Did this book—i.e. did I—kill Lynne Frederick? She turned up her toes on April 27, 1994, the eve of my hardback publication day, and that's a very eerie coincidence. For some weeks previously the newspapers had been previewing my material—and given that she professed to idolize Sellers ('I am still in love with Peter, I hold his memory very dear,' she'd said after her divorce from Dr Barry Unger in 1991), how was she going to react to my portrait of her fatal marriage? To my account of Sellers as a sort of evil father figure? He was evil, and this book details what Charles Laughton called the *strain* of being evil, so it was quite likely that Lynne would object, yammering about 'an insult to his memory' and so on. She'd go into screaming orbit, unleash the dogs of war (i.e. expensive lawyers). Instead of which she choked on spaghetti and meatballs and ended up as cadaver no. 94-3840 in the Beverly Hills police department morgue.

In fact, if I (fancifully) contributed to her exit it was only because I'd written what she knew to be the truth; and how could she bear the truth? She'd married Sellers virtually in good faith—believing, like Dorothea of Casaubon in *Middlemarch*, that his 'odd habits would be a glorious piety to endure'—and yet he systematically destroyed her, preying upon her weakness and devotion. 'She'd hang on to his words,' Sarah Sellers told the *Daily Express* on May 4. 'If Dad said something unpleasant about someone in passing, she'd echo it six times more.' Lynne to appease him, grew to be like him. She became, a film executive told me, 'Iago whispering into Othello's ear'—compounding Sellers' megalomania and causing directors and crew to be sacked. Determined not to let him down, she was pulled towards the abyss at Sellers' core; and, unable to reconcile his genius as a performer with the intensities of his madness as a man—his shiftiness, his fluidity—she embarked upon what the Los Angeles coroner called 'a history of alcohol and seizures' and the route towards her under-attended funeral at the little Chapel of the Dawn in Santa Monica at the age of thirty-nine.

She'd wanted a consuming passion, and (as Wilde said of Salome) she was consumed by it. About this she never had illusions: 'I learned what it really meant to love another person. A total all-consuming love. It consumed every minute of my life,' she claimed with an irony that emerges only now. But was it love? Wasn't it, in its self-destructiveness and its total absence of happy memories, more akin to hate? She was immersed in Sellers; he held her attention for so long that her view of him was a delusion (as Sellers' was for Peg, whom he could find no fault with once she was dead). She forgot—and spent the fourteen years of her

widowhood sinking deeper down a drain of vodka and pills in order to forget—
the reality, the bitterness, the threats and counter-threats and legal commu-
niqués. Sellers, indeed, was set to divorce her—his lawyer was to return to the
Dorchester on the afternoon of July 22, 1980 with the papers for his signature.
As we know, Sellers croaked into his Dover sole. He was, as it happens, seriously
deceased—brain dead—long before he reached the Middlesex Hospital, attached
to wires and tubes. That was all a grisly farce for Lynne's benefit. She had to fly
from America and insisted on giving that weepin' an' wailin' act for the photographers; and if you've watched her in *Vampire Circus* or *Village of the Damned*,
you'll agree it was her best performance—one which sickened Sellers' real family and friends. Even before the funeral she was giving press interviews in the hotel suite; she went over the will avidly with a solicitor; she began speaking on the
phone to David Frost—whom she was to marry a few months later. It was her
finest hour.

I have yet to find anyone with a good word to say about Lynne: a hypocrite,
a nymphomaniac, a hysteric; she was impossible to do business with; she was
prone to screaming and crying. (To me, in a transcontinental phone call that went
on and on, she played the part of a coquettish little girl.) She was self-destructing.
Her lawyer told me back in 1989, 'She is not going to live very long. You just get
that feeling about her.' She carried with her a sense of morbidity, of shadows and
unrest. She'd failed to evolve. Despite two intervening marriages she was still Mrs
Peter Sellers on her credit cards; she still wore Peg's wedding ring. 'Lynne talked
about Peter constantly. You know ... what might have been,' the few people who
met her reported. She lived in the past and denied herself a future (she retained
no agent or publicist; she did not open her mail); but it was an invented past, as
she secretly knew. Nobody was allowed to mention the Dorchester heart attack;
she was suspicious and jealous of people who'd known Sellers before she'd come
along—the worthy Milligan was sent packing, for example, when he asked for the
return of some comedy material; Sellers' children were refused access to photos
their father had taken of them.

It was the actual past, the past detailed in this book, which ate her mind away.
As Michael Sellers remarked with grim satisfaction: 'As we understand it, she's not
a very happy person. A bloated, alcoholic drug addict.' Another enemy crowed,
'She was haunted by guilt which finally destroyed her.' It wasn't guilt—it was a
sense of waste. You don't only have to be partial to wrecks, ruins, and witches
(from Lucia di Lammermoor to Norma Desmond) to appreciate her tragedy that,
not allowing Sellers' life to end, Lynne's never began. She was virtually his last
victim. She'd get up late and start boozing on her own; she squandered her inheritance, £2,500 a week going on nose candy. (Sellers did nothing good with his
money when he lived, and nothing good was done with it when he died.) Her
slender figure ballooned to almost two hundred pounds. She pined and raged, and
perhaps in her rise and fall, her thinness and fatness, and the way that she was
melancholy and craven ('We can never forget how callous she was after our father
died,' says Michael), we have an encapsulation of Sellers' own personality. Lynne

was, in a way, his supernatural double or fellow lost soul; except that she acquired his insanities without the compensations of his genius.

♦ ♦ ♦

Currently there is a wrangle about the destination of Lynne's ashes. She'd wanted to be sprinkled under Sellers' rose bush at Golders Green—though might not that create an atomic explosion like the quicklime put down to rid Trafalgar Square of squawking birds in 'The Starlings' episode of 'The Goon Show'? The scheme is certainly repugnant to Sellers' children, and the intervening events have made me wonder if my Sellers file can ever be closed. I'm still being sent clippings; the *Newsletter* of the Goon Show Preservation Society continues to compile its notes and queries with the diligence of *Der Shakespeare Jahrbuch*; the man who pinched Sophia Loren's jewels when she was making *The Millionairess* was only arrested in March 1994—thirty-four years after the theft ('We hired a Rolls-Royce to blend in because it was a very rich area,' bragged Ray 'The Cat' Jones); and Peter Ackroyd has published a novel about Dan Leno, whom Sellers believed himself to be the reincarnation of ...

This is a long book—it could easily be longer, a *gesamtkunstwerk*, to use a word that once wafted around Wahnfried. Biography is an ever-widening sea: new facts, new names, the criss-cross of relationships; there is always more to add—and add to *that* the biographer's endless reconsiderations... What is the truth? What is the answer? It was my intention, by devising a non-circumspect all-inclusive style, consisting of interconnecting monologues and digressions, to get just this flux and reflux on to my pages—so that here we have a meditation on Sellers which is also, perhaps primarily, a book about somebody finding out about Sellers. For as that old joke about the Grail Knights—What would they do if they found it?—it is the quest which counts; what happens on the journey as I wrestle with and try to understand what Nabokov would call Sellers' 'inner attitude in regard to the outer world'.

To explore the issues involved when imposing order and finding patterns and directions in another person's life, I have put a fallible sleuth actually in the text, groping and swerving, following clues, meeting people, making mistakes, coming to conclusions (some of which were unpalatable to fans and reviewers)—and perhaps, in the process of reliving a life that is not his own, he loses his identity and takes on Sellers'? Though I remain fascinated with the relationship of the biographer to his work, thankfully this book can be read without ever dealing with that level if you don't want to; and though many critics have called this book definitive, it is not.

First, anecdotes previously unknown to me have come to light: Sellers taking a goat into the Dorchester lift, announcing that he was going to kill it and barbecue it in the bathroom (his protest against Arabs residing in his favorite hotel); Sellers, in late 1950, appearing at the Grimsby Fish Merchants' Annual Dinner Dance, at the Winter Gardens, Cleethorpes ('a little bit of last night's supper left in the teeth is very tasty on a cold morning'); Sellers participating in The Who's *Tommy* at the Royal Albert Hall in December 1972, playing (as a Nazi stormtrooper) the rôle of the Doctor: 'He seems to be completely unreceptive/The

tests I gave him show no sense at all/He hears but cannot answer to your call';
Sellers in a daze because he'd been thwacked over the noggin, so that a picture
frame was round his neck and glass covered his face: 'She hit me with me mum!'
he whimpered, which was indeed the truth, as Britt Ekland had brandished a cherished photograph of that appalling pterodactyl Peg in self-defense...

Then there are the people I failed to find and interview—for example, Mr
Walter Jokel, who knew Sellers from 1948 and attended the private funeral service and subsequent reception at the Dorchester. Jokel was Sellers' and Milligan's
personal manager in the early days, and introduced him to Bill Wills (who *is*
dead), his secretary, Sue Evans, and Patricia Hammond (a name which is new to
me), who took over when Miss Evans had a leave of absence. 'Even Britt Ekland
in her book *True Britt* writes about me,' chides Mr Jokel in a recent letter.

No joke at all was the fate of a lady, who wrote to me in May 1994:

> At the time that Ted Levy, architect, met Anne and Peter Sellers, I was his wife. We
> were living together in a house we had recently bought in...Hampstead. We had a
> son who was five. I cannot speak of the accuracy of the information given to you by
> Anne Sellers-Levy nor Michael Sellers in general. However, I can tell you [that] I
> was in my mid-twenties when my marriage broke up...Michael Sellers was old
> enough to remember coming to my son's fifth birthday party, yet he states [in *P.S. I
> Love You*] that when his mother met Ted, Ted was separated from his wife. Further
> on he states that 'Ted and myself were separated on the recommendation of a psy-
> chiatrist. Fact! I was pregnant when Ted left. He made me have an abortion. In those
> days a psychiatrist had to sanction it...Also, for the record, on the night when Peter
> Sellers and I went to look for Ted and Lynne at Golden Yard, it was Anne who was
> screaming, not me. I was quiet, overwhelmed by the screaming and theatricals I was
> witnessing. It was Anne who ran into the kitchen and came out with a bread knife,
> aiming it at Peter [who was] morose, hideously self-centered and nasty.

Well, it was a long time ago. But my point is that as Sellers had made life absolute hell for Anne, his first wife, and their children, he'd therefore prepared the
ground for her to seek the sanctuary of somebody else. That somebody else was
unfortunately my correspondent's first husband—and the knock-on effects were
additionally destructive and painful, evidently, to Ted's family. Adam, the five-
year-old, grew up to be severely mentally disturbed; he lived in terrible hostels for
the homeless and when Levy died (I was told):

> Anne turned her back on us and swooped her family into the service. The rabbi
> who officiated shook hands with Anne, Michael, Sarah, and Katie and Loretta
> Feldman. Adam was completely ignored. He looked awful, hunched and cold. I
> took him to the rabbi and said he was Ted's only son...

Nobody wants to be reminded of ancient injustice, old wives, castoff families—
that pile of debris, the past. Yet is there any link between this lad's psychiatric distress and the 'loss' of his father in the divorce? ('Yes, I do think that Ted's absence
had a profound effect on Adam's mental state.') How much blame for this can be assigned to Sellers—for was he not the first to disrupt people's harmony, like Alberich,
whose cavortings on the bank of the Rhine bring about, several music dramas later,
the end of the world? (Sellers embodied Original Sin.) If he was the initiator, years

ago, if my correspondent and her son were innocents dragged into his orbit, where and when can his actions and decisions be said to start ceasing to matter?

◆ ◆ ◆

Which brings us to Victoria, who told the *Daily Mail* in July 1994 that 'my dad was really nice and normal'. She's been in and out of the slammer so often I've given up keeping track. The latest news, which will be way out of date by the time you read this, is that she faces a possible two-year sentence on a charge of receiving stolen goods. Her lover, Oscar Lopez, and his friend, Anthony Zapata, have been arrested at her house and accused of murder and armed robbery.

Victoria once said, 'I want to be a comedy actress, a kind of female Peter Sellers,' and she is indeed a comedian in a certain sense. She is not only daughter to Sellers' blood—but to his manners. Victoria has come in for his sultry, long, thin face—the Portuguese-Jewish coloration—and his recklessness and amorality. Her alleged contempt for proprieties, for law, order, and the feelings of others, is a dreadful resurfacing of her father's mentality—of his way of looking dead behind the eyes. To try and expel him from her system she is undergoing $10,000 worth of plastic surgery: 'Ms Sellers said she wanted to be rid of creases around her mouth which make her look like her late father,' readers of the *Evening Standard* were told on September 27, 1994. Apparently she wants to start looking like Audrey Hepburn instead.

So much is easily said: that the innocent and cunning Victoria is the spawn of a shameful human being who, through his films and other repercussions, is still laughingly alive. Sellers had never allowed her mother to be maternal. The way he reasoned it, attention spent on the baby meant less time spent on him. A good mother was a disloyal wife. Victoria was raised in hotel suites by nannies, and Britt—in despair—claimed that not only did she never change any diapers, but also, 'I could dispense with the necessity of breast feeding, the thought of which was alien to my nature.' Victoria was never to be read bedtime stories, nor did anyone sit 'at the kitchen table with a tube of glue and make animal cardboard cutouts.' She was purposefully neglected and being outrageous became her way of registering that she existed. She has had involvement with cocaine-trafficking gangs, and after the modeling and hostessing at night-clubs it was inevitable that she would think that being a hooker was an up-market career path. (Her sole consolation is to gloat on Lynne's worse fate: 'The fact that she blew up as a big fat giant and was drinking vodka all day long, taking pills and doing coke—I don't know, but that makes me feel better.')

Britt, who must loathe and fear the side of Victoria that resembles Sellers, optimistically stated in 1992 that 'all Victoria's problems are in the past'. She meant over and done with. The real meaning is that it is in the dark intricacies of her past that Victoria's present problems have their roots. She has no conception of right and wrong; she is a naughty, naughty girl—and she appears to enjoy every minute of it.

R.L., Manitoba, January 1995

PETER SELLERS: FILMOGRAPHY

1950   *Black Rose**

1951   *London Entertains*
       Let's Go Crazy†
       Burlesque of Carmen†
       Penny Points To Paradise

1952   *Down Among The Z Men*

1953   *Beat The Devil**
       The Super Secret Service†

1954   *Orders Are Orders*
       *Our Girl Friday**
       *Malaga**

1955   *The Ladykillers*
       John and Julie

1956   *The Man Who Never Was**
       The Case of the Mukkinese Battle Horn†

1957   *Your Past Is Showing: The Naked Truth*
       The Smallest Show On Earth

1958   *Tom Thumb*
       Up The Creek
       I'm All Right Jack

1959   *Man In A Cocked Hat: Carlton Brown of the F.O.*
       The Mouse That Roared
       The Running, Jumping and Standing Still Film [also producer]†

1960   *Two Way Stretch*
       The Battle of the Sexes
       The Millionairess
       Never Let Go

1962   *The Road to Hong Kong* (Guest Star)
       Only Two Can Play
       The Dock Brief: Trial and Error
       I Like Money: Mr. Topaze— [also Director]
       Lolita
       Waltz of the Toreadors: Amorous General
       The Wrong Arm of the Law

1963   *Heavens Above!*

1964   *Dr. Strangelove, Or: How I Learned to Stop Worrying and Love the Bomb*
       The Guest: The Caretaker
       The Pink Panther
       A Shot In the Dark
       The World Of Henry Orient

1965   *What's New, Pussycat?*

1966   *After The Fox: Caccia Alla Vope*
       The Wrong Box

1967   *The Bobo*
       Casino Royale
       Woman Times Seven

1968   *I Love You, Alice B. Toklas*
       The Party

1969   *The Magic Christian*

1970   *Hoffman*
       There's A Girl In My Soup

1972   *Alice's Adventures In Wonderland*
       Where Does It Hurt?

*   Supplied post-production voices

†   Short

1973   *The Blockhouse*
        Ghost In the Noonday Sun
        The Optimists of Nine Elms
1974   *The Great McGonagall*
1975   *The Return of the Pink Panther*
        Undercover Hero: Soft Beds and
            Hard Battles
1976   *Murder By Death*
        The Pink Panther Strikes Again
1977   *To See Such Fun*[1]
1978   *Revenge Of the Pink Panther*
1979   *The Prisoner of Zenda*

Posthumous Releases

1980   *Being There*
        The Fiendish Plot of Dr. Fu
            Manchu [also took over as
            director]
1982   *Trail of the Pink Panther* (out-
            takes and unused footage
            from the previous
            Panthers)

Peter Sellers Recordings[°]

1953   *Jakka and the Flying Saucers*
        78:Parlophone R 3785
1955   *Dipso Calypso/Never Never Land*
        78:HMV B10724
1957   *Boiled Bananas and Carrots/Any*
            Old Iron
        78 &45: Parlophone R4337
1958   *I'm So Ashamed/A Drop of the*
            Hard Stuff
        78 &45: Parlophone R4491
1958   *The Best Of Sellers*
        LP (10"): Parlophone PMD
            1069
1959   *Puttin on the Smile/My Old*
            Dutch
        45: Parlophone R4605

1959   *Songs for Swingin' Sellers*
        LP: Parlophone PMC
            111/PCS 3003
1960   *Goodness Gracious Me/Grandpa's*
            Grave
        45: Parlophone R4702
1960   *Bangers and Mash/Zoo Be Zoo*
            Be Zoo
        45: Parlophone R4724
1960   *Peter and Sophia*
        LP: Parlophone PMC
            1131/PCS 3012
1965   *A Hard Day's Night/Help*
        45: Parlophone R5396
1979   *Sellers Market*
        LP: UA UAG 30266

[°] Excluding Goon shows—For full details about which, please contact The Goon Show Preservation Society, 7 Frances Gardens, Ramsgate, Kent, CT 11 8AF, England

1993 *A Celebration of Sellers*
  4 CD Boxed Set
  1993 EMI UK Sellers
  1 7243 8 27781 2 7

A Celebration of Sellers: Volume I
The Best of Sellers

1. The Trumpet Volunteer 7:28
2. Auntie Rotter 3:08
3. All the Things You Are 2:12
4. We Need the Money 5:49
5. I'm So Ashamed 3:03
6. Party Political Speech 3:03
7. Balham—Gateway to
  the South 6:04
8. Suddenly It's Folk Song 5:20
9. Any Old Iron 2:56
10. Boiled Bananas and Carrots
  (Boiled Beef and Carrots)2:21
11. Unchained Melody 2:55
12. Dance With Me, Henry 3:17
13. Dipso Calypso 2:58
  (produced by Walter Ridley)
14. Never Never Land 2:30
15. A Drop of the Hard Stuff 3:17
16. Jakka and the Flying Saucers
  (An Interplanetary Fairy Tale)6:46

Total length 63:15

A Celebration of Sellers: Volume II
Songs for Swingin' Sellers

1. You Keep Me Swingin' 2:56
2. So Little Time 6:38
3. Lord Badminton's Memoirs4:16
4. The Critics 6:35
5. My Old Dutch 2:52
6. Face to Face 2:14
7. In A Free State 2:02
8. Puttin' On the Smile 5:29
9. Common Entrance 5:06
10. I Haven't Told Her, She
  Hasn't Told Me 1:16

11. Shadows On the Grass 6:38
12. Wouldn't It Be Lovely 6:02
13. We'll Let You Know 3:37
14. Peter Sellers Sings
  George Gershwin 0:20
15. Fullest Earth 4:31
16. After the Fox 2:20
  (produced by AIR (London) Ltd.)
17. A Right Bird 1:51
18. The House On the
  Rue Sichel 4:49
  (produced by Derek Lawrence)

Total length 69:39

A Celebration of Sellers: Volume III
Peter and Sophia

1. Goodness Gracious Me! 3:02
2. 'Smith'-An Interview with
  Sir Eric Goodness 5:38
3. Zoo Be Zoo Be Zoo 2:22
4. Ukulele Lady 2:49
  (The Temperance Seven, with
  vocal refrain by Peter Sellers
5. Setting Fire to the
  Policeman 5:54
6. Bangers and Mash 2:35
7. Oh! Lady Be Good 3:46
8. To Keep My Love Alive 2:54
9. Why Worry? 2:28
10. Grandpa's Cave 3:20
11. I Fell In Love With an
  Englishman 4:30
12. Africa Today 3:53
13. Fare Thee Well 3:50
14. A Hard Day's Night 1:50
15. She Loves You (Chinless
  Wonder) 1:40
16. Can't Buy Me Love 1:30
17. She Loves You
  (Cockney version) 1:40
18. Yes It Is 1:23
19. She Loves You
  (Irish version) 1:38

20. Help!   2:25
21. Now Is The Winter
       Of Our Discontent   1:58

Total Length 61:04

A Celebration Of Sellers: Volume IV
Sellers Market—The Musical Scene

1. Night and Day   4:54
2. The All-England George
       Formby Finals   14:06
   The Chinese Laundry Blues
   My Grandad's Flannelette
       Nightshirt
   Guarding the Home of the Home
       Guard
   Hold Tight, Keep Your Seats
       Please
   They're Parking Camels Where
       Taxis Used To Be
3. Gefrunk   3:33
4. Singin' In The Rain   2:14
5. The Eaton Square Blues   5:30
6. Peter Sellers Sings
       Rudolph Friml   0:58
   (Featuring: Only A Rose)

Sellers Market—The Cultural Scene

1. Compleat Guide To Accents
       of the British Isles   16:00
   (Featuring: Don't Cry For
   Me Argentina)

2. The Whispering Giant   12:47
3. New York Girls   3:16
   (Steeleye Span with Peter Sellers
   on acoustic ukulele; Produced by
   Robin Black & SS)
4. Come To Me   4:40
   (Produced by Joe Resman)
5. Thank Heaven for
       Little Girls   2:33
6. We'll Meet Again   1:33

Total Length 72:11

Peter Sellers' Recordings for/with Others

1961   *Bridge on the River Wye*
        LP: Parlophone PMC
            1190/PCS 3036;
        Peter Sellers, Spike Milligan,
        Jonathan Miller and Peter
        Cook

1992   *Bridge on the River Wye/It's A
        Square World*
        Double Cassette: EMI
            0777 7 99836 4 3

Sources and Acknowledgments

Not that I quite know indeed what situations the seeking fabulist does 'find'; he seeks them enough assuredly, but his discoveries are, like those of the navigator, the chemist, the biologist, scarce more than alert recognitions. He comes upon the interesting thing as Columbus came upon the isle of San Salvador, because he had moved in the right direction for it...'

Preface to *The Aspern Papers*, by Henry James

I was Professor Humbert Humbert pursuing Quilty—or perhaps Clouseau chasing Sir Charles Phantom, the famous Litton (as he puts it). As long ago as August 1989 there was a reporter from the *Sunday Mirror* on my doorstep, wanting to know my intentions. GOON FURY AT A 'SLUR' ON SELLERS ran the subsequent headline. "The author would only have been eighteen when Peter died and could not have even met him,' Michael Bentine was quoted as saying. 'The two other books written about Peter are both rubbish—and this sounds exactly the same.' As I'd not yet written a word, this seemed a bit scathing—and, in fairness, when he discovered my work was still in progress, Mr Bentine did apologise to me and was amiableness itself. But word was out and the following year the tabloids had another go at scuppering the project. INSPECTOR CLOUSEAU'S SNORTIN' SEX SECRETS, bellowed the *Sunday Sport*, on July 2nd 1990. "Sex-crazed ex-Goon Peter Sellers died a gibbering LOONY after DESTROYING himself with mind-blowing BONKING drugs, we can reveal today... The zany star MASHED his brains in a bizarre bid to get a better STIFFY and in an EXPLOSIVE new book it is claimed the man who made millions laugh had a long history of mental problems...'

Again, I'd not yet started to scribble—but as an example of long—distance mind-reading it is pretty impressive. Not funny at all was the punishment I received over a two-year period from an eminent firm of British libel lawyers on behalf of a client who was once—hilariously but quite misleadingly—described by John Le Mesurier as 'the only man in London with a flat up Peter Sellers' arse'. People were starting to get jittery—fearful of my investigations. On April 18th 1991, my solicitor, Richard Sykes, received a summons for 'Notes and Transcripts of Mr Lewis' interviews with those that he saw in connection with his proposed book... and Correspondence between Mr Lewis and others concerning his proposed book—relevant to malice'. I instructed my lawyer to issue a Grade A Fuck Off (to use a legal term). He did so—but it took a Queen's Counsel and getting on for a six figure sum to despatch the opposition. It was all too complicated and Kafka-esque and eye-opening glimpse into the British concept of justice—its priggishness and its relish for vague concepts ('reputation' for one) which, as David Hare says in *Murmuring Judges*, cannot be proved. One thing was clear, however. The Velociraptors in *Jurassic Park*, all agile fangs and claws, never became extinct. They'd evolved into devotees of Peter Carter-Ruck's tip-top text books on defamation and slander.

As a result of the legal hair-pulling, I became the more resolved to carry on and root out the truth. Eventually I had accumulated a wide Sargasso Sea of documents and letters, statements from Sellers' acquaintances, papers, fragments, diary jottings, tape recordings and pictures. Like Boswell, I know exactly how it feels to have 'spared no pains in obtaining materials concerning [my subject], from every quarter where I could discover that they were to be found and have been favoured with the most liberal communications.' It therefore gives me much pleasure to acknowledge my indebtedness to the following authors, publishers, institutions and individuals out of whose words and works the present book has been created:

(a) Principal printed material cited and quoted

i. Books

ALLEN, Steve. *Funny People* (New York, 1981).

AMIS, [Sir] Kingsley. *That Uncertain Feeling* (London, 1955).
  I Want It Now (London, 1968).
  Girl, Twenty (London, 1971).
  The Old Devils (London, 1986).
  The Amis Collection (London, 1990).
  Memoirs (London, 1991).

ANON. *A Pictorial and Descriptive Guide to Ilfracombe*, Tenth Edition [no date— c. 1930s].

BACH, Steven. *Final Cut* (London, 1985).

BALCON, [Sir] Michael. *Michael Balcon Presents a Lifetime of Films* (London, 1969).

BARTHES. Roland. *Camera Lucida* (New York, 1981).

BEHAN, Dominic. *Milligan* (London, 1988).

BELL, Simon, et al. *Who's Had Who* (London, 1987).

BENDAZZI, G. *The Films of Woody Allen* (Milan, 1984).

BENTINE, Michael. *The Long Banana Skin* (London, 1975).
  The Best of Bentine (St Albans, 1983).
  The Reluctant Jester (London, 1992).

BERGAN, Ronald. *Beyond the Fringe ... And Beyond* (London, 1989).

BIRKIN, Andrew. *J.M. Barrie and the Lost Boys* (London, 1979)

BRODE, Douglas. *Woody Allen: His Films and Career* (New York, 1985).

BULL, Peter. *I Say, Look Here* (London, 1965).
  Life is a Cucumber (London, 1973).

BYGRAVES, Max. *I Wanna Tell You a Story* (London, 1976).
  Afterthoughts (London, 1988).

CHAPLIN, Charles. *My Autobiography* (London, 1964).

CHAPMAN, Graham. *A Liar's Autobiography* (London, 1980).

CIMENT, Michel. *Kubrick* (New York, 1982).

COLLINS, Doris. *Woman of Spirit* (London, 1983).

CREWE, Quentin. *Well, I Forget the Rest* (London, 1991).

DAHL, Tessa. *Working For Love* (London, 1988).

DAVIDSON, Gerald and John M. Neale. *Abnormal Psychology: An Experimental Clinical Approach* (Toronto, 1978).

DRAPER, Alfred. *The Story of the Goons* (London, 1976).

DUNN, Clive. *Permission to Speak* (London, 1986).

EKLAND, Britt. *True Britt* (London, 1980).
Sensual Beauty—and How to Achieve It (London, 1984).

EMETT, Rowland. *From Punch to Chitty Chitty Bang Bang ... and Beyond* [sale exhibition catalogue, Chris Beetles Ltd.] (London, 1988).

EVANS, Peter. *The Mask Behind the Mask* (London, 1968; updated edition, 1980).
Soft Beds, Hard Battles (London, 1974)

FIELD, Andrew. *The Life and Art of Vladimir Nabokov* (London, 1986).

FLASHNER, Graham. *Fun with Woody* (New York, 1987).

FLEISCHMAN, Sid. *The Ghost in the Noonday Sun* (Boston, 1965).

FORBES, Bryan. *Notes for a Life* (London, 1974).

FRANCIS, Anne. *Julian Wintle: A Memoir* (Brighton, 1984).

FRAYN, Michael. *The Book of Fub* (London, 1963).

FREEDLAND, Michael. *Liza With a Z* (London, 1988).

FUSSELL, Paul. *Wartime: Understanding and Behaviour in the Second World War* (New York, 1989).

GEBLER, Ernest. *Hoffman* (London, 1969).

GELDRAY, Max. *Goon with the Wind* (London, 1989).

GELMIS, Joseph. *The Film Director as Superstar* (New York, 1970).

GILLIAT, Penelope. *To Wit: In Celebration of Comedy* (London, 1990).

GIFFORD, Denis. *The Armchair Odeon* (n.p., n.d.).

GRADE, Lew. *Still Dancing* (London, 1987).

GRAHAM, Sheilah. 'Caesar Sellers', in *Scratch an Actor* (London, 1969).

GROBEL, Lawrence. *The Hustons* (London, 1990).

GUINNESS, [Sir] Alec. *Blessings in Disguise* (London, 1985).

GUNDEN, Kenneth Von. *Alec Guinness: The Films* (North Carolina, 1987).

HACKNEY, Alan. *I'm All Right, Jack* (London, 1958).

HAILL, Catherine. *Dear Peter Pan* [Foreward by Nanette Newman], (London, 1983).

HARWOOD, Ronald, ed. *Dear Alec: Guinness at Seventy-Five* (London, 1989).

HILL, Leonard. *Saucy Boy: The Life Story of Benny Hill* (London, 1990).

JULIAN, Desmond G. *Cardiology,* Fifth Edition (London, 1988).

KEMP, Philip. *Lethal Innocence: The Cinema of Alexander Mackendrick* (London, 1991).

KENNER, Hugh. *Paradox in Chesterton* (London, 1948).

KOSINSKI, Jerzy. *Being There* (New York, 1970).

KOTSILIBAS-DAVIS, James. *Myrna Loy: Being and Becoming* (London, 1987).

LAX, Eric. *Woody Allen: A Biography* (London, 1991).

LEAMING, Barbara. *Orson Welles* (London, 1985).

LEHMAN, Peter and Willaim Luhr, *Blake Edwards* (Ohio, 1981).

LE MESURIER, Joan. *Lady Don't Fall Backwards* (London, 1988)

LEWIS, Roger. *Stage People* (London, 1989).
     ed. *Confessions of a Justified Sinner* (London, 1992).

LODGE, David. *Up the Ladder to Obscurity* (Bognor Regis, 1986).

MacLAINE, Shirley. *Out On a Limb* (London, 1983).

McKERN, Leo. *Just Resting* (London, 1983).

MAGRIEL, Paul, ed. *Memoirs of the Life of Daniel Mendoza* (London, 1951).

MARTIN, George. *All You Need Is Ears* (London, 1979).

MASON, James. *Before I Forget* (London, 1981).

MILLIGAN, Spike. *The Goon Show Scripts* (London, 1972).
     More Goon Show Scripts (London, 1973).
     The Book of the Goons (London, 1974).
     The Great McGonagall Scrapbook (London, 1975).
     William McGonagall: The Truth at Last [illustrated by Sellers], (London, 1976).
     The Spike Milligan Letters (London, 1977).
     Indefinite Articles & Scunthorpe (London, 1981).
     More Spike Milligan Letters (London, 1984).
     Where Have All the Bullets Gone? (London, 1985).
     Goodbye Soldier (London, 1986).
     The Lost Goon Shows (London, 1987).
     Scunthorpe Revisited (London, 1989).

MINNEY, R.J. *Puffin Asquith* (London, 1973).

MORTIMER, John. *Clinging to the Wreckage* (London, 1982).

NABOKOV, Vladimir. *Lolita* (London, 1959).
     Lolita: A Screenplay (New York, 1974).
     Selected Letters: 1940-1977 (London, 1990).

NATHAN, David. *The Laughtermakers* (London, 1971).

OAKES, Phillip. *Tony Hancock* (London, 1975).

OWEN, Maureen. *The Crazy Gang* (London, 1986).

PARRISH, Robert. *Hollywood Doesn't Live Here Anymore* (Boston, 1988).

PERRY, George. *Forever Ealing* (London, 1981).

PETRUCELLI, Alan W. *Liza! Liza!* (Bromley, 1983).

PLOMLEY, Roy. *Plomley's Pick* (London, 1982).

POLANSKI, Roman. *Roman* (London, 1984).

POWELL, Michael. *Million Dollar Movie* (London, 1992).

RANDALL, Alan and Ray Seaton. *George Formby* (London, 1974).

RAPHAEL, Frederic. *Think of England* (London, 1986).

RAY, Satyajit. *The Chess Players* [includes *The Alien*] (London, 1989).

RAY, Ted. *Raising the Laughs* (London, 1952).
   My Turn Next (London, 1963).

READER, Ralph. *It's Been Terriffic* (London, 1953).
   Ralph Reader Remembers (London, 1974).

RICKARDS, Jocelyn. *The Painted Banquet* (London, 1987).

ROSS, Lilian and Helen. *The Player: A Profile of an Art* (New York, 1962).

ROSSO de, Diana. *James Mason: A Personal Biography* (London, 1989).

RUTHERFORD, Margaret. *An Autobiography* (London, 1972).

SCUDAMORE, Pauline. *Spike Milligan: A Biography* (London, 1985).
   ed. *Dear Robert, Dear Spike: The Graves-Milligan Correspondence* (Stroud, 1991).

SECOMBE, Sir Harry. *Arias and Raspberries* (London, 1989).

SELLERS, Michael. *P.S., I Love You* (London, 1981).

SHERRIN, Ned. *A Small Thing—Like an Earthquake* (London, 1983).

SHILLINGFORD, J.P. *Coronary Heart Disease* (London, 1981).

SIMMONS, Anthony. *The Optimists of Nine Elms* (London, 1964); [a 1974 edition contains stills from the film].

SINCLAIR, David. *Snowdon: A Man for Our Times* (London, 1982).

SONTAG, Susan. *On Photography* (New York, 1977).

STARK, Graham. *Remembering Peter Sellers* (London, 1990).

STARR, Michael. *Peter Sellers: A Film History* (London, 1992).

SYLVESTER, Derek. *Peter Sellers* (New York, 1981).

TAYLOR, John. *Love, Cricket, Peter Sellers* (Birmingham, 1988).

TAYLOR, John Russell. *Alec Guinness: A Celebration* (London, 1984).

TERRY-THOMAS. *Terry-Thomas Tells Tales* (London, 1990).

THURBER, James. 'The Catbird Seat', in *The Thurber Carnival* (London, 1945).

TODD, Richard. *In Camera* (London, 1989).

TOMLINSON, David. *Luckier than Most* (London, 1990).

TOOK, Barry. *Comedy Greats* (Northamptonshire, 1979).
　Laughter in the Air (London, 1976).
　A Point of View (London, 1990).

WALKER, Alexander. *Stanley Kubrick Directs* (New York, 1971).
　Peter Sellers: The Authorized Biography (London, 1981; reprinted with an After-
　　word, 1990).

WHICKER, Alan. *Within Whicker's World* (London, 1982).

WILMUT, Roger. *The Goon Show Companion* (London, 1976).
　Kindly Leave the Stage (London, 1985).

WINTERS, Shelley. *Best of Times, Worst of Times* (New York, 1990).

ZEC, Donald. *Sophia Loren* (London, 1975).

ZETTERLING, Mai. *All Those Tomorrows* (London, 1985).

ZOLOTOW, Maurice. *Billy Wilder in Hollywood* (London, 1977).

ii Periodicals and Newspapers

ANON. 'Being There'. *Listener*, July 31, 1980.
　'The Changing Face of Sellers', *Film Show Annual*, 1962.
　'Dan Mendoza', *Egan's Boxiana*, Vols I and III, 1818.
　'The Day Peter Sellers Died', *Headlines*, Number 53.
　'For TV Humour, A Goon Twist', *TV Mirror*, March 31, 1956.
　'Friends Mourn Sellers', *Sunday Telegraph*, July 27, 1980.
　'How to Get into Films', *Films and Filming*, May 1961.
　'It's Sellers for President', *Evening News*, April 3, 1979.
　'Life Lines of Peter Sellers' [obituary], *The Stage and Television Today*, July
　　31, 1980.
　'The Sellers Marriage Go Round', *TV Times*, March 15, 1986.
　Profile of Dennis Main Wilson, *Observer*, June 26, 1988.
　'Seven Characters in search of one voice—and the object is PETER SELL-
　　ERS', *Sound and Vision*, October 1950.
　'Should Sellers Have Said It?' *Sun*, January 16, 1969.
　'Spiked', *Listener*, September 30, 1982.
　St Aloysius' College: 1879-1979 [Centenary brochure].
　'String and Teeth: The Property of Spike Milligan, Esq.' [Lot 215 in a
　　Christie's auction catalogue, c. April 15, 1980.

AYRE, Leslie. 'Who Would Be a BBC Announcer?' *Radio Times*, March 21, 1958.

BARBER, Lynn 'The Unforgiving Goon', *Independent on Sunday*, September 9,
　1990.

BALL, Ian 'Plea Deal for Miss [Victoria] Sellers', *Daily Telegraph*, May 25, 1986.

BAUER, Ed. 'Our Marriage Won't Last [says Lynne]', *Titbits*, March 15, 1980.

BERMAN, Charles. 'No Lynne, No Me, Angry Peter Told the Palace', *Daily Mirror*, June 28, 1983.

BILLINGTON, Michael. 'Hancock's Laugh Hour', *Radio Times*, April 20, 1985.

BOULTING, Roy and John. "Sellers Market', *New Standard*, September 29, 1981. 'Notes from a director's thought-book', *Films and Filming*, Feb. and Mar. 1974.

CALLAN, Paul. 'Talks to Lynne Frederick', *Daily Mirror*, October 6, 1981. 'Turmoil of the star's daughter on drug charges', *Daily Mirror*, March 14, 1986.

CASTELL, David. 'Best Sellers', *Films Illustrated*, February 1976.

CHAMBERS, Peter. 'Sellers Buys His Second Cadillac', [source untraced].

CLAYTON, Freddy. 'Meet Peter Sellers', *The Musician* [c.1970.] 'Spike, Peter and Harry Who?' *Punch* [c. 1976.]

COWLEY, Elizabeth. 'The Best Sellers Buys', *Radio Times* [date untraced].

CRAWLEY, Tony. 'Kosinski, body and soul', *Films Illustrated*, September 1980.

DANGAARD, Colin. 'Loving—one day at a time', *Daily Express*, July 14, 1978.

DAVIES, Shan 'Bert Mortimer; the Man Who Knew Sellers Best', *Sunday People*, August 3, 1980.

DAVIS, Victor. 'Sellers, the mad genius, by Pink Panther Blake', *Daily Express*, December 14, 1982.

DONNELLY, Paul. 'Behind the Mask; The Secret World of Peter Sellers', *Idols*, No. 15, May 1989.

DUNCAN, Andrew. 'A Most Successful Ongoing Failure', *Radio Times* [c. July 1987].

EDWARDS, Blake and Julie Andrews. "Interview', *Playboy*, December 1982.

EDWARDS, Lewis. 'Daniel Mendoza', *Transactions of the Jewish Historical Society of England*, Vol. XV, 1938.

FAWCETT, Ian. 'I Want to Start Living Agian', *Photoplay*, April 1965.

FERGUSSON, Ken. 'Sellers', *Photoplay Film Monthly*, June 1971.

FORBES, Bryan. 'On the dark side of the Goon', *Independent*, July 21, 1990.

FOSTER, Edwin. 'Guess Who Is Playing Sellers' Sister—It's Britt!', *Showtime*, November 1966

FRANKLIN, Olga. 'In Search of Sellers', *Daily Mail*, June 21, 22, and 23, 1960.

FRATER, Alexander. 'Status Symbols Are a Lot of Bananas!', *Sunday Telegraph Magazine* [c.1968].

FROST, Tony, 'Sellers' Last Pledge', *Sunday Mirror*, July 27, 1980.

GRAHAM, Keith. 'Send for Sellers', *TV Mirror*, October 30, 1954.

GRANT, Steve. 'The Laugh Donor', *Time Out*, February 20, 1986.

GLAZER, Mitchell. 'The Strange World of Peter Sellers', *Rolling Stone*, April 17, 1980.

GRETTON, Charles. 'The Tragic Secret of Spike Milligan', *TV Mirror* February 1, 1958.

GRIFFITH, Kenneth. 'Looking for the best of Sellers', *The Times*, October 8, 1981.

HAIGH, Peter S. 'Peter Sellers: Star Interview', [source untraced, c. 1960].

HALL, Judith. 'Why Victoria Sellers' heart will always belong to Daddy', [source untraced, c. 1981].

HART, Melanie. 'Victoria Sellers', *Hello*, [late 1992].

HILL, Derek, 'Camera Magic', *Amateur Cine World*, February 1959.

HUTCHINS, Chris. 'Why I Worried about Lynne's Marriage—interview with Iris Frederick' [source untraced, c. 1978].

HUTCHINSON, Tom. 'Look Out—Here They Are', *Picturegoer*, Nov. 26, 1955.
'The Naked Truth', *Picturegoer*, July 20, 1957.
'The Search for Peter Sellers', *Picturegoer*, December 19, 1959.
'Sellers Outgrows the Goons', *Picturegoer*, [c. 1960].

JOSEPH, Joe. 'What's it all about, Michael [Caine]?' *The Times*, August 26, 1992.

KOFF, Sidney. 'I think I'm having a heart attack', *Modern Screen*, July 1964.

KRETZMER, Herbert. 'Goon in a Nightmare', *Daily Sketch*, February 28, 1958.
'Sellers: Now I Will Tear My Palace to Bits', *Daily Sketch*, March 9, 1963.
'A Wizard Running the Peter Sellers Empire', *Daily Sketch*, June 15, 1963.

LAWRENCE, Hamilton. 'Should You Tip Your Pilot?' *Mensan* (San Diego), February 1984.

LEACH, Robin. 'Death is not far away, said Peter', *News of the World*, July 27, 1980.

LEE, Carol. 'Lynne Makes a New Date with Sellers [via a spirit medium]', *News of the World*, August 10, 1980.

LEE-POTTER, Lynda. 'Yes, Dad was an idiot [says Michael]', *Daily Mail*, September 29, 1981.

LEWIN, David. 'Peter the Great', *Sunday Mirror*, August 3, 10, and 17, 1980.
'Exclusive! Lynne Frederick Sellers', *Woman's Own* [late 1980].

LINDEN, Livia. 'The Way They Were; Peter Sellers', *Rona Barrett's Hollywood*, July 1980.

MANN, Roderick. 'If he is happier without me, says Mrs Sellers', [Lynne responds to Sellers' desire for a divorce] *Sunday Express*, May 20, 1979.

MARLBOROUGH, Douglas. 'Sophia scares so-shy Sellers', *Daily Mail*, May 19, 1960.

McASH, Ian F. 'Said the March Hare', *Film Review*, (1972).
'The Changing Face of Peter Sellers', *Films Illustrated*, May 1974.

MIDWINTER, Janet. 'Sellers Dies', *Sun*, July 24, 1980.

MORRIS, Ronald. 'By Gad, Sir,' *Picturegoer*, September 20, 1958

MORTIMER, John. 'Second Opinion', *Films and Filming*, May 1963.
    Creative Force of a Meticulous Clown', *Sunday Times*, July 27, 1980.

O'DOWD, Brian. 'My Friend Peter Sellers', *Hollywood Studio Magazine* [c. 1980].

OUGHTON, Frederick. 'The Secret Life of Peter Sellers', *Picturegoer Film Annual*, 1959-60

OWEN, Jane. 'Britt—the Unwanted Mourner', *Sunday People*, July 27, 1980.

PACTER, Trudi. 'Tears and Tantrums Finished Us', *Sunday Mirror* [c. August 1980].

PEDRICK, Gale. 'Finkel's Cafe', *Radio Times*, June 29, 1956.

PETERSEN, Eric. 'Victoria Sellers', *Hello*, October 13, 1990.

POWELL, Dilys. 'Peter Sellers: A Recorded Dialogue', *Sunday Times*, January
    14 and 21, 1962.
'The delicate balance of Peter Sellers', *Sunday Times* July 27, 1980.

PURSER, Philip. 'Beyond Experience', *Sunday Telegraph Magazine* [c. November 1972].

READ, Piers Paul. 'Small Expectations: profile of Alec Guinness', *Independent
    Magazine*, October 1, 1988.

ROCHE, Ken. 'On the Trail of the Real Peter Sellers', *TV Times*, Christmas issue, 1983.

RUSSELL, Sue. 'Meet Mademoiselles Clouseau [i.e. Victoria],' *You Magazine*,
    November 15, 1992.

SALE, Jonathan. 'The Men in the Goons', *Punch*, September 26, 1979.

SALEWICZ, Chris. 'Comic View: Milligan on Sellers', *Sunday Times*, [c. 1980].

SAVAGE, Paul. 'Peter Sellers is a keen home movie maker', *Sunday Telegraph
    Magazine*, July 3, 1970.

SAXTY, Dick. 'Was Sophia the big love of Sellers?' [source untraced].

SCHICKEL, Richard. 'Sellers Strikes Again', *Time Magazine*, March 3, 1980.

SEDWARDS, Lisa. 'Victoria's Victory', *Daily Express*, October 1, 1992.

SELLERS, Peter. 'You Tell Me', *Picturegoer*, February 19, 1955.
    Star Turn Table', *TV Times*, July 20, 1956.
    'A Serious Look at Laughter', *Film and Filming*, March 1960.
    [Entry] *Current Biography 1960* (New York).
    'Candid Conversation', *Playboy*, October 1962.
    'Sellers Mimes the Movie Lovers', *Playboy*, April 1964.
    'New Books about Cars', *Sunday Times*, October 24, 1965.
    'My First Encounter with an Impressario', in *The Vogue Bedside Book*, ed.
        Josephine Ross (London, 1984).

SELLERS, Victoria. 'Best Sellers', *Playboy*, April 1986.

SHERIFF, Paul. 'Designing for an Heiress', *Films and Filming*, November 1960.

SIMONS, Judith, 'Inspired—by the NAAFI canteen', *Daily Express* [c. 1979].

SINEUX, Michel. 'Bye Bye Birdie-Num-Num', *Positif* (Paris), February 1981.

SMITH, Marjorie. 'He Was Just One of the Boys', *My Weekly*, June 7, 1980.

SPEED, F. Maurice. 'The Sellers Story', The Sellers Story', *Film Review* (1964).

STAMP, Gavin. 'Dreams and Nightmares of a Changing City', *Times*, November 3, 1990.

STARK, Graham. 'The Peter Sellers Only I Knew', *Woman's Realm*, July 3, 1983.

STOPPARD, Tom. 'The Constance Cummings Story', *Bristol Evening World*, May 12, 1960.

STUTTAFORD, Thomas. 'Portrait of a President', *Times*, February 7, 1991.

TAYLOR, Norman. 'Best Sellers', *Film Review*, March 1959.

THIRKELL, Arthur. 'Who Is This Man?' [source untraced, c. 1961].

TOMKIES, Mike. 'My Man Peter', *Photoplay*, September 1966.

WAGGONER, Walter. 'Arrival of Sellers', *New York Times Magazine*, March 27, 1960.

WALKER, Alexander. 'Alas, Some of them Die', *Evening Standard*, July 24, 1980. 'My Life with Peter Sellers [i.e. Lynne's]', *Evening Standard*, August 14, 1981.

WALKER, Derek. 'He Doesn't Want to be Funny', *Picturegoer*, July 21, 1956.

WALKER, John. 'A Role that Mirrors the Real Sellers?', *Now*, June 6, 1980.

WARGA, Wayne. 'Not Exactly Being There', *Los Angeles Times*, March 30, 1980.

WAUGH, Auberon. 'The Last Thoughts of Peter Sellers', *Sunday Telegraph*, July 27, 1980.

WELLS, Tony. 'The Waltz of the Corridors', *Today*, January 19, 1963.

WIGG, David. 'My Beloved Peter', *Daily Express*, July 31, 1981. 'Ohh, Dick [Emery] You Were Wonderful', *Daily Express*, January 3, 1983.

WILSON, Cecil. 'Mr Sellers Buys Car No. 53', *Daily Mail*, May 6, 1960.

ZASLOW, Esther. 'Why Peter Sellers is so afraid of real women', *Hollywood Screen Parade*, June 1969.

ZEC, Donald. 'Wham! 24 Hours from Meeting to Mating [with Liza Minnelli]', *Daily Mirror*, September 26, 1977.

(b) Institutions

I am grateful to the following curators, archivists and reference librarians, administrators, managers and editors: Bantam Press (Nina Martyn); BBC Enterprises Ltd.; BBC Written Archives Centre, Caversham Park (Jacqueline Kavanagh); Bloomsbury and Islington Health Authority; Bradford Cathedral (Barbara L.

Craven); Brothers of Our Lady of Mercy (Bro. F. Kean); Bodleian Library, Oxford (Miss M. Sheldon-Williams); Boston University, Special Collections (Mugar Memorial Library—curator: Howard B. Gotlieb); Chichester Festival Theatre (Paul Rogerson); EMI Music Archives (Sarah Hobbs); Entertainment Artistes' Benevolent Fund (Peter Elliott); Evergreen Communications Ltd. (Peter Morley); The Goon Show Preservation Society (Mark Cousins, Mike Coveney, Bill Nunn, Tony Reynolds and Keith Vincent); Hampshire County Council (J. Thorn, Divisional Librarian); Ilfracombe Museum (Joy Slocombe, Hon. Curator and Secretary); The Jewish Historical Society (Charles Tucker); Library and Museum of the United Grand Lodge of England, Freemasons' Hall (K.A. McQuillan); Library of Congres, Motion Picture, Broadcasting and Recorded Sound Division (Madeline F. Matz); the Library of St John's College, Oxford; the Library of Wolfson College, Oxford; the *Los Angeles Times*; the Middlesex Hospital (Jim Stapleton, Medical Records Manager); *The Nation* (Nicholas W. P. Clegg); National Film Archive/British Film Institute; National Film Information Service, Academy Foundation (Kristine Krueger); Omega Lighting (Keith Applin); Pan American Airways (Barbara Yager, Flight Services Headquarters); Parkfield Entertainment (Ken Hill); The Raymond Mander and and Joe Mitchenson Theatre Collection; Robson Books (Cheryll Roberts); Southbrook Group Ltd. (Sue J.Coombes); The Spanish and Portuguese Jews' Congregation (Miss Miriam Rodrigues-Pereira); Spike Milligan Productions Ltd. (Norma Farnes); St Aloysius' College (J.A. Mackersie, Headmaster); Stoll Moss Archives, Theatre Royal, Drury Lane (George Hoare); Strategic Marketing (EMI Records UK—David Hughes, and J. Nagle, Publicity Department); the *Sunday Times Magazine* (Susan Raven); Telstar Video Entertainment; Tessa Le Bars Management; Thames Television (Joanna Wood); Twentieth Century Fox (Paul Higginson); University of California, Los Angeles, Film and Television Archive (Charles Hopkins).

(c) Individuals

I wish to thank the following people, whom I had the joy of interviewing and/or corresponding with expressly for this book; Dave Allen; Sir Kingsley Amis; John Antrobus; the late Ben Arbeid; Steven Bach; the late Terence Baker; Ken Barnes; Michael Bentine; Dick Bentley; the late Peta Bentley; John Bird; Ron Bishop (son of Waldini); John Bluthal; Roy Boulting; Peter Boyle; Ronnie Bridges; Tony Britton; Mark Burns; Max Bygraves; Dave Callaghan; Ian Carmichael; the late Alan Clare; Bloom Clare; Doris Collins; Bryan Connon; Alan Cooper; the late Theo Cowan; Gerry Crampton; Quentin Crewe; Bernard Cribbins; Charles Critchton; Constance Cummings; Sinead Cusack; the late Roald Dahl; Monja Danischewsky; Clive Donner; Alfred Draper; Joe Dunne; Mathew Dunne; Shirley Eaton; Martin Esslin; Peter Evans; Bryan Forbes; Anthony Franciosa; Michael Frayn; Dennis Frazer; Liz Frazer; Iris Frederick; the late Lynne Frederick (Mrs Barry Unger); Ray Galton; Kathy Ganis Gardner; Lord Grade of Elstree; Mike Grady; Kenneth Griffith; the late Dimitri de Grunwald; Michael Gough; Val Guest; Sir Alec Guinness; Piers Haggard; John Hamilton; Hermione Harvey; Mary Harvey; Joseph Heller; John Heyman; the late Benny Hill; Al Hix; the late Jack Hobbs; Mr Justice

Hobhouse; Ken Hughes; the late Raymond Huntley; David Jacobs; Michael Jeffery; Dr A. P. Joseph; Alice Joyce; Miriam Karlin; Elliot Kastner; Jeremy Kemp; Philip Kemp; Deborah Kerr; Dennis King; the late Jerzy Kosinski; Herbert Kretzmer; Bert Kwouk; Col. Hamilton Lawrence; Rosemary Leach; Peter Lepino; Dick Lester; Anne Levy; Leslie Linder; Russell Lloyd; David Lodge; Herbert Lom; Shirley MacLaine; Wolf Mankowitz; Vera Marks; Joe McGrath; Peter Medak; Murray Melvin; Gerald Mendoza; Beatrix Miller; Jonathan Miller; Spike Milligan; Charlotte Mitchell; the late Joe Mitchenson; Angela Morley (Wally Scott); Sheridan Morley; Peggy Mount; Frank Muir; the late Stanley Myers; Margaretta Neilly (Paddy Black); Anthony Newley; Peter Noble; Tony Palmer (and his staff at Isolde Films); Michael Parkinson; Elaine Parsons; John Penrose; Tom Pevsner; Larry Pizer; Miranda Quarry; Alvin Rakoff; Frederic Raphael; Robin Ray; the late Satyajit Ray; the Marquess of Reading; Clive Rees; Elwood Rickless; the late Cardew Robinson; Norman Rossington; Colin Ross-Munro Q.C.; Sir Evelyn de Rothschild; Pierre Rouve; Lord Anthony Rufus-Isaacs; Jack Salt; Prunella Scales; Danny Schelmerdine; Victor Schlienger; Janette Scott; Anne Scott-James (Lady Lancaster); Ronald Searle; Michael Sellers; Sarah Sellers; Michael Selsman; John Sessions; Bryn Siddall; Anthony Simmons; Alan Simpson; Hattie Stevenson; J.E. Sumpton; John Taylor; Lady (Peggy) Tedder; the late Andrew Timothy; Richard Todd; David Tomlinson; Barry Took; Peter Vaughan; Hugo Vickers; Darren Vidler; Dick Vosburgh; Alexander Walker; Ray Walston; Auberon Waugh; John Wells; Gareth Wigan; Frank Wildish; Simon Williams; and Donald Zec.

(d) Photograph acknowledgements

The plates in this book emanate from the following sources, to whom the publishers gratefully offer acknowledgement: Author Collection (nos. 6, 7, 16 [National Screen Service Ltd.], 18 [photograph by Kiki Howell, © Allen Hutton Gallery, Whetstone], 29 [Warner-Pathe Distributors Ltd.], 31, 40, 41 [Universal City Studios Inc.], 43, 46); George Brown Collection (2 [Adelphi Films Ltd.], 3, 4, 5, [Group 3 Ltd.], 8 [Columbia Pictures Corp. Ltd.], 9, 11 [photograph by Harry Gillard], 12, 13, 19, 27, 30, 35 [Hemdale International Films], 44); Peter Evans and Bryan Connon (1); Michael Jeffery (42, 47); Peter Medak (37, 38); Satyajit Ray (28); Michael Sellers Collection (10, 14 [photograph by Norman Hargood], 15 [photograph by George Ward: Rank Productions Ltd.], 17, 20, 22 [photograph by Norman Hargood], 23, 26, 32, 33, 36 [Scotia-Barber Distributors], 9, 45; Hattie Stevenson (21, 24, 25). *n.b.* Dates in the captions refer to the year photographs were taken—which may not necessarily be the same as the year films were released.

(e) Special acknowledgements

To assemble my own archive of Sellers material, I acquired the collections of clippings and memorabilia which were formerly in the possession of Larry Turnbull, of Cardiff; J. Skinner gave me all the Sellers material which was on file at his Celebrity Information Bureau; and I am grateful to Tony Broughton, of West Sussex, for lending me dozens of videotapes of Sellers' out-of-the-way films. I have also made full use of the articles and reminiscences published over the years in the quarterly *Newsletter* of the Goon Show Preservation Society. The full set of the (defunct) *Goonews*, given to me by Bill Nunn, was also of much interest. Dr Bernard Richards, of Brasenose College, Oxford, and Francis Wheen, of *Private Eye*, sent me useful articles and provided general enlightenment, as did (as ever) Mark Rylance, John Bayley and Iris Murdoch. George Brown was virtually my acting (unpaid) research assistant. Hardly a fortnight went by without his sending letters and nuggets; this book would be impoverished without his discoveries. Al Hix performed a similar function for me from America. I am much indebted to such selfless vigilance.

Of the other people who helped me, it would be invidious to start singling them out and ranking them—but I want it to be recorded that Roy Boulting opened his address book and introduced me to, amongst others, the members of Sellers' family. Michael Sellers, his mother, Anne Levy, and his sister, Sarah Sellers, endured months of my cross-examinations. Peter Evans, who had mapped out Sellers *with* Sellers, also gave me hours of his time—as well as copies of letters and interview transcripts he had not, owing to the pressure of space, been able to include in his own book. Wolf Mankowitz let me loose in his extensive archives; Peter Medak succumbed to a long interview and loaned me the original battle-scarred copy of the *Ghost in the Noonday Sun* script, plus some marvellous photographs; Spike Milligan rose from his sickbed to give me a candid interview at this house near Rye; and Clive Rees screened *The Blockhouse*.

On a personal level, David Huw Harries, my old school pal, will be amused to see the results of my teenage Sellers fad. He'd always said that his auntie, Elaine Parsons, had taught Sellers to play the drums, and frankly I'd never believed him. But Sellers' origins—his end-of-the-pier beginnings which haunted him and were part of the sadness which followed him, were right there in Wales, where I grew up. Through Elaine Parsons I met other survivors of that music hall era, and I was off.

Leslie Gardner, my agent, and Mark Booth, my editor, have been models of patience and wise counsel—which I frequently and no doubt infuriatingly disregarded. This is, after all, my book—and all the research, classified above, was only a preliminary. Sellers still had to be conjured up in the writing—all by hand, non-stop over eleven months with a Waterman fountain pen—and for this reason I must emphasize that this is *my* version of Sellers, a Sellers ordered and shaped by my own imagination and judgements. I make no claims for objectivity or comprehensiveness. (Why ever should I? The concept of a definitive biography is a nonsense. The best you can hope for is a spirited and unsettling personal essay—and this [Poop! Poop!] is what you are now holding in your hands). The typing was done in a matter of weeks by Suzanne Anderson and Lesley Caldwell. My conscientious copy-editor and proof-reader was Kate Pleydell-Bouverie—a name the Goons would have savoured.

My flesh and blood—that's Anna, Tristan, Oscar and Sébastien—won't believe that this book is finished, and I can never adequately thank them for enduring the hardships and deprivations which its long genesis and frenzied composition imposed upon them. If it wasn't for the very practical assistance and alms yielded by my parents-in-law and my brother-in-law, the last chapters wouldn't have been written in France—they'd have been collected from the Marshalsea, whither we'd have had to go, like the Dorrits.

For midway through my research I decided I could no longer bear to remain in Oxford as a classroom technician (to use Gore Vidal's apt and contemptuous phrase). I moved the family to Normandy and metamorphosed from a quicksilvery don to a morose writer-in-exile—a non-smoking Anthony Burgess. This book, then, changed my life. Children of mine, not born when I began it, were able to tell their teacher, Mme. Claudine Chastang, that papa was not, like everybody else in the bocage, a peasant farmer, a woodcutter or an iron foundryman. His metier was 'Piter Seleux et tout le bataclan du tralala'.* I couldn't put it better myself.

Roger Lewis
Oxford, July 11, 1989
France, July 11, 1993.

---

*   Peter Sellers and all the rest of that rubbish.

Index